HANDBOOK OF PUBLIC MANAGEMENT IN AFRICA

Handbook of Public Management in Africa

Edited by

Gerrit van der Waldt

Research Professor of Public Governance, Department of Public Management and Governance, North-West University, South Africa

ELGAR HANDBOOKS IN PUBLIC ADMINISTRATION AND MANAGEMENT

Edward Elgar
PUBLISHING

Cheltenham, UK • Northampton, MA, USA

Published by
Edward Elgar Publishing Limited
The Lypiatts
15 Lansdown Road
Cheltenham
Glos GL50 2JA
UK

Edward Elgar Publishing, Inc.
William Pratt House
9 Dewey Court
Northampton
Massachusetts 01060
USA

A catalogue record for this book
is available from the British Library

Library of Congress Control Number: 2023946646

This book is available electronically in the **Elgar**online
Political Science and Public Policy subject collection
http://dx.doi.org/10.4337/9781803929392

Printed on elemental chlorine free (ECF)
recycled paper containing 30% Post-Consumer Waste

ISBN 978 1 80392 938 5 (cased)
ISBN 978 1 80392 939 2 (eBook)

Printed and bound in the USA

Contents

Figures

Tables

Editor

Gerrit van der Waldt holds a PhD from the University of Stellenbosch, South Africa (1992) and is currently Research Professor: Public Governance attached to North-West University, South Africa. Prior to his academic appointment, he was employed at the Bureau for Information and served in the Parliament of South Africa during CODESA.

His research output includes 52 academic textbooks and more than 150 scholarly journal articles. He is also the author of 94 internal handbooks for various tertiary institutions and to date supervised 39 Master and 27 PhD studies. According to the World Scientist and University Ranking (AD Scientific Index) 2023, he is ranked fourth on the African continent in the field of Public Management/Administration (https://www.adscientificindex.com/scientist/gerrit-van-der-waldt/98190). He serves on the advisory boards of several institutions and acts as editorial board member and deputy editor of several journals. He also partook in multiple contract research projects including the Office of the Presidency, the Joint Centre for Political and Economic Studies (USA), Price Waterhouse Cooper, Enterprises UP, the South African Local Government Association, and the National School of Government. He also served on the Audit and Risk Committee of Dr Kenneth Kaunda District Municipality.

Professor van der Waldt presented papers at various national and international conferences including at the World Economic Forum's (WEF) Africa Summit on the role of local and provincial government in the implementation of NEPAD. He is also a member of the global Associate Academic Federation attached to the WEF as well as rapporteur of the United Nations Humanitarian Affairs' University Scholars Leadership Programme.

He lectured and conducted research at the Vrije Universiteit, Amsterdam, the Netherlands, and was also appointed as global expert by the International Swedish Institute for Public Administration (SIPU) to partake in the design and development of a Master Programme in Local Government Studies for central African countries. He further serves on Poland's National Science Centre as governance expert assigned to the Norms and Governance panel and represented South Africa on the External Expert Committee of the African Union's Africa Peer Review Mechanism for the design of a Governance Index for the continent.

Contributors

Adedeji Adeniran, Director of Research, Centre for the Study of Economies of Africa (CSEA), Abuja, Nigeria.

Joseph R.A. Ayee, Department of Political Science, University of Ghana, Legon, Ghana.

Kunle Balogun, Centre for the Study of Economies of Africa (CSEA), Abuja, Nigeria.

Benon C. Basheka, Deputy Vice Chancellor-Academic Affairs, Kabale University-Uganda and Professor of Governance, Department of Governance, Faculty of Arts and Social Sciences, Kabale University.

Vincent Chakunda, Department of Governance and Public Management, Midlands State University, Zimbabwe.

Innocent Chirisa, Acting Vice Chancellor, Zimbabwe Ezekiel Guti University, Bindura, Zimbabwe; Research Fellow, Department of Urban and Regional Planning, University of the Free State, Bloemfontein, South Africa.

Mufaro Dzingirai, Department of Business Management, Midlands State University, Gweru, Zimbabwe.

Andrew Enaifoghe, Research Fellow, Public Administration, University of Zululand, South Africa.

Augustin K. Fosu, Institute of Statistical, Social and Economic Research (ISSER), University of Ghana, Legon, Ghana.

Dede W. Gafa, Department of Economics, Faculty of Economics and Management Sciences (FASEG), University of Lomé, Togo.

Chinyeaka J. Igbokwe-Ibeto, Department of Public Administration, Nnamdi Azikiwe University, Awka, Nigeria.

Ezra Ihezie, Centre for the Study of Economies of Africa (CSEA) Abuja, Nigeria.

Nokukhanya N. Jili, HOD Department of Public Administration, University of Zululand, Kwadlangezwa, South Africa.

Paul Kariuki, Executive Director: Democracy Development Programme, Durban, South Africa.

Muhiya T. Lukamba, Department of Public Management and Governance, North-West University, South Africa.

David Mhlanga, College of Business and Economics, University of Johannesburg, Johannesburg, South Africa.

Thekiso Molokwane, Department of Political and Administrative Studies, University of Botswana, Gaborone, Botswana.

Zebediah Muneta, Department of Urban and Regional Planning, University of Zimbabwe.

Alex Nduhura, School of Business and Management, Uganda Management Institute, Kampala, Uganda.

Danielle Nel-Sanders, School of Public Management, Governance and Public Policy, University of Johannesburg, Johannesburg, South Africa.

Eric B. Niyitunga, School of Public Management, Governance and Public Policy, University of Johannesburg, Johannesburg, South Africa.

Innocent Nuwagaba, Uganda Management Institute, Kampala, Uganda.

Nicholas D. Ogola, Uganda Management Institute, Kampala, Uganda.

Benson B. Okech, Uganda Technology and Management University (UTAMU), Kampala, Uganda.

John P. Settumba, Uganda Management Institute, Uganda.

Elvin Shava, School of Management, IT and Governance, University of KwaZulu Natal, South Africa.

Theophilus T. Tshukudu, Faculty of Business (HR), University of Botswana, Gabarone, Botswana.

Ivan K. Twinomuhwezi, Uganda Management Institute, Uganda.

Gideon Zhou, Department of Governance and Public Management, University of Zimbabwe, Harare, Zimbabwe.

Hardlife Zvoushe, Department of Governance and Public Management, University of Zimbabwe, Harare, Zimbabwe.

Preface

Public management is a highly dynamic and evolving study domain merging multidisciplinary perspectives. Mainly evolving from public administration, public affairs, public policy, and the political sciences, public management as a scholarly field has accumulated a matured corpus of knowledge aimed at the study of the complex nature of contemporary governance. As a professionalised practice-based field, public management mainly entails the operationalisation of public policy in the executive structures of the public sector.

Literature on governance on the African continent is often pervaded with examples where problems such as poor leadership, low managerial capacity and competency, limited and failing infrastructure, corruption, and malpractice, as well as political tension, are the centre of attention. In this volume we find examples of that as well, such as the exposition of conflict, systemic malpractice, and failed policy programmes. However, the dominant tone of the contributions in this volume is one of positive prospects for governance on the continent. Government administrations can learn valuable lessons from one another and leapfrog developed countries in the adoption and adaption of certain managerial models, techniques, and applications for government.

The *Handbook on Public Management in Africa* expands the corpus of knowledge related to good governance praxis. The general aim of this volume is to serve as a guide for scholars and practitioners in the field of public administration, public affairs, public management, and governance in domains such as the optimal implementation of public policy, an analysis of contemporary governance realities, the improvement of the efficacy and performance of public institutions, and the enhancement of good governance on the African continent. Best practice pertaining to public management and lessons learned by governments in the region are extracted and accentuated. It also covers the broad spectrum of government functions and operations and as such, it equips current and prospective public managers with essential skills and knowledge to successfully perform their obligations. The focus that is placed on ethical principles, normative guidelines, and good governance practices furthermore facilitates the inculcation of the required behaviour, conduct, and attitude of public managers to serve citizens. This is essential to promote the overall well-being, prosperity, and interest of society.

This handbook surveys core themes of the field within the broader context of good governance on the continent. As such, the book offers the following value propositions:

- Generic management information as well as country-specific applications per chapter.
- Contributions from eminent scholars from reputed universities and agencies on the continent.
- Perspectives from countries representative of the five main regions on the continent.
- Cases and examples from countries enabling comparative analyses, the discovery of management best practice, and the detection of lessons to be learned.

Written by 31 eminent scholars across the continent, this book is intended for adoption by universities across the continent to help capacitate scholars and students in the field. It offers novel insight into the current status of key managerial issues and the core themes of the scholarly discourse in the field. It also serves as a guide to offer best practice and lessons learned to contemporary public managers and provide concrete advice and examples (e.g. case studies) to navigate key issues. It also offers insight into future governance challenges and anticipates directions for Public Management as a study domain.

Acknowledgements

A publication of this extensive nature is simply not possible without the collective efforts of several actors.

I would like to thank all the contributors from across the African continent. Your insight and knowledge regarding public managerial challenges and applications in your respective countries enriched the publication enormously. Thank you also for your patience with my impatience in getting the respective chapters finalised. Each chapter is a testament to your knowledge, expertise, and dedication to the field. You generously shared your time making this book a comprehensive and authoritative resource for students, scholars, and practitioners alike. I am also grateful to the peer reviewers who provided feedback and constructive criticism on the chapters, helping to ensure that the book meets the highest standards of quality and rigour.

To the staff of Edward Elgar Publishing and in particular Daniel Mather who gave me this opportunity and assisted with professional language and technical editing of the manuscript. Thank you all for your hard work and dedication to this project. It has been an honour to work with each and every one of you.

To my wife Helah and daughter Elné, thank you for your patience, encouragement, and emotional support. I love you immensely.

Finally, I want to express my sincere gratitude to my Creator for giving me the ability to pursue my personal and career goals.

Abbreviations

4IR	Fourth Industrial Revolution
ACBF	Africa Capacity Building Foundation
AEC	African Economic Community
AfCFTA	African Continental Free Trade Area
Africa CDC	Africa Centre for Disease Control and Prevention
AFROSAI	African Organisation of Supreme Audit Institutions
AGA	African Governance Architecture
AGR	African Governance Report
AI	Artificial Intelligence
AII	African Integrity Indicators
APRM	African Peer Review Mechanism
APSA	African Peace and Security Architecture
AU	African Union
BBBEE	Broad-Based Black Economic Empowerment
BCCI	Bank of Credit and Commerce International
BOOT	Build Own Operate Transfer
BOT	Build Operate Transfer
BPR	Business Process Reengineering
BSC	Balance Score Card
BTO	Build Transfer Operate
CBP	Community-based planning
CBRD	Community-Based Rural Development Strategy
CCMT	Centre for Conflict Management and Transformation
CGU	Corporate Governance Unit
COMESA	Community of Eastern and Southern Africa
COVID-19	Coronavirus disease 2019 (SARS-CoV-2)
CSRP	Civil Service Reform Program
DBFO	Design Build Finance Operate
DBFOM	Design Build Finance Operate Maintain
DDC	District Development Committee
DEDH	Direct Effect of Debt Hypothesis
EAC	East African Community
EBP	Evidence-based policymaking
EC	Equity Capital
ECCAS	Economic Community of the Central African States
ECOWAS	Economic Community of West African States
EFA	Education for All
EGDI	E-Governance Development Index
ePPPs	Public Private Partnerships in Education
ESAP	Economic Structural Adjustment Programme

ESD	Education for Sustainable Development
FDI	Foreign Direct Investment
FOEI	Friends of the Earth International
FTLRP	Fast-Track Land Reform Programme
G2B	Government to Business
G2C	Government to Citizens
G2E	Government to Employees
G2G	Government to Government
GDP	Gross Domestic Product
GNP	Gross National Product
GPoA	Government's Programme of Action
HIPC	Heavily Indebted Poor Countries
HRD	Human Resource Development
HRM	Human Resource Management
ICPAU	Institute of Certified Public Accountants of Uganda
ICT	Information and Communication Technologies
IFIs	International Financial Institutions
IMF	International Monetary Fund
IMTT	Intermediated Money Transfer Tax
INTOSAI	Organisation of Supreme Audit Institutions
IoT	Internet of Things
IPCC	Intergovernmental Panel on Climate Change
IWA	International Water Association
JSE	Johannesburg Stock Exchange
LED	Local Economic Development
LGSC	Lagos State Service Commission
MDA	Ministries, Departments and Agencies
MDC	Movement for Democratic Change
MDR	Multilateral Debt Relief
MMDA	Metropolitan, Municipal and District Assemblies
MTEF	Medium-Term Expenditure Framework
MTP	Medium-Term Plan
MYIEE	Ministry of Youth, Indigenisation and Economic Empowerment
NDS	National Development Strategy
NEPIS	National Energy Policy Implementation Strategy
NGO	Non-governmental organisation
NPA	New Public Administration
NPG	New Public Governance
NPM	New Public Management
NPS	New Public Service
NSFAS	National Student Financial Aid Scheme
NSSA	National Social Security Authority
NSSF	National Social Security Fund
NYDA	National Youth Development Agency
OECD	Organisation for Economic Co-operation and Development
OFID	OPEC Fund for International Development

OPC	Office of the President and Cabinet
PAYE	Pay as You Earn
PAZ	Privatization Agency of Zimbabwe
PFM	Public Financial Management
PLAP	Parastatals and Loans Authorities Orientation Programme
PME	policy monitoring and evaluation
PMFA	Public Finance and Management Act
POSDCORB	planning, organising, staffing, directing, coordinating, reporting and budgeting
PPP	Public-private partnership
PSNP	Productive Safety Net Program
PTC	Postal and Telecommunications
RA	Resident's Association
RBM	Results-based management
RDC	Rural District Councils
RDDC	Rural District Development Committee
RE	Reinvested Earnings
REA	Rural Electrification Agency
REC	Regional Economic Community
ROT	Rehabilitate Operate Transfer
SADC	Southern African Development Community
SARS	South African Revenue Services
SDGs	Sustainable Development Goals
SERA	State Enterprise Restructuring Agency
SOE	State-owned enterprises
SONA	State of the Nation Address
SSA	sub-Saharan Africa
STERP	Short-Term Economic Recovery Programme
TSP	Transitional Stabilisation Programme
UCA	Urban Councils Act (Zimbabwe)
ULP	Youth Livelihood Programme
UN	United Nations
UNCTAD	United Nations Conference on Trade and Development
UNDESA	United Nations Department of Economic and Social Affairs
UNDP	United Nations Development Programme
UNSDGs	United Nations Sustainable Development Goals
UPE	Universal Primary Education
USEPA	US Environmental Protection Agency
UWEP	Women Entrepreneurship Programme
VAT	Value Added Tax
VIDCO	Village Development Committee
WADCO	Ward Development Committee
WEF	World Economic Forum
WGI	Worldwide Governance Indicators
WHO	World Health Organisation
WHT	Withholding Tax

WOP	Water Operator Partnerships
WSP	Water Safety Plan
ZACC	Zimbabwe Anti-Corruption Commission
ZANUPF	Zimbabwe African National Union – Patriotic Front
ZCTU	Zimbabwe Congress of Trade Unions
ZETC	Zimbabwe Electricity Transmission Company
ZIMCODE	Zimbabwe National Code in Corporate Governance
ZIMPREST	Zimbabwe Programme for Economic and Social Transformation
ZIMRA	Zimbabwe Revenue Authority
ZINWA	Zimbabwe National Water Authority

Introduction: public management from an African perspective
Gerrit van der Waldt

CONTEXT

Governments play a pivotal role in the sustainable growth, general well-being, and prosperity of countries. It is a well-established fact that the level of goodness of governments positively corresponds with the growth and development trajectory of states. The effective management of public institutions is thus essential to harness the collective capacities and abilities of government to render a broad range of services (e.g. education, health, transport, policing, and telecommunications) to citizens. Management of government institutions leads to the efficient and economical delivery of essential services to citizens, which can improve their standard of living and contribute to the overall prosperity of society. Through their conduct, attitude, and behaviour public managers generally also promote transparency, accountability, and the rule of law, which are essential for creating a favourable environment for political stability, economic growth, and social development. On the other hand, poor public management can lead to a breakdown in public trust, poor services, malpractice, and wastage of resources. Therefore, effective management of government institutions is key to promoting efficiency, effectiveness, and productivity towards a better future for all.

Since the late 1800s, public administration as a study domain has undergone a series of paradigm shifts and changes in its approach and focus. Initially, public administration was focused on the traditional politics-administration dichotomy, where politicians were responsible for policy formulation while administrators were responsible for implementing the policies. This model was used as the basis for the scientific management movement, which focused on increasing the efficiency and effectiveness of government operations. The New Public Management (NPM) approach is a management strategy that aims to improve public service delivery by introducing market-oriented reforms to the public sector. NPM originated in the 1990s, largely in response to criticisms of the traditional model of public administration, which was seen as bureaucratic, slow-moving, and inefficient. The NPM approach has been widely adopted in Africa, but its effectiveness in addressing governance issues is a matter of debate.

NPM gave rise to the notion of governance and also led to the rise of the New Public Service paradigm of governance. The latter refers to a modern approach to public administration that emphasizes improving the quality of services offered to citizens, increasing accountability and transparency, and promoting citizen engagement and participation. It stresses the importance of results-oriented governance, the use of technology, and the need to embrace innovation and change. This approach seeks to create a more efficient, responsive, and citizen-centred public service that delivers better outcomes for communities and individuals.

The main paradigms of the discipline have evolved and interacted over time to shape the discipline as it is today. Each paradigm has contributed important insights and ideas, and they continue to influence the field of public administration and management and inform the development of new theories and practices. For example, the emergence of managerialism in the government sphere has had far-reaching implications for the way governments operate. It has shifted the focus from the traditional top-down approach to a more collaborative approach, where the public and private sectors can work together to achieve their goals. It has also enabled governments to become more agile and responsive to the changing needs of their citizens.

Public managers are individuals who work in government institutions, entities, and agencies and are responsible for the effective and efficient delivery of public services. Public managers are responsible for implementing policies and programmes, managing resources, and delivering public services in a variety of settings. Some of the main responsibilities and functions of public managers include:

- Planning and policy development: Public managers are responsible for developing and implementing plans and policies that align with government goals and objectives.
- Policy implementation: Public managers are responsible for executing policies and programmes that have been developed by elected officials or higher-level administrators.
- Budgeting and resource allocation: Public managers are responsible for managing budgets and allocating resources to various programmes and initiatives.
- Programme and project management: Public managers oversee the implementation of programmes and projects, ensuring they are delivered on time, within budget, and to the expected standards of quality.
- Service delivery: Public managers are responsible for ensuring that public services are delivered effectively and efficiently to the communities they serve. They are responsible for delivering a wide range of public services, including healthcare, education, law enforcement, and other essential services, to the citizens they serve.
- Staff supervision: Public managers supervise and lead teams of government employees, providing guidance and direction to ensure the smooth and effective operation of government programmes and services.
- Stakeholder engagement: Public managers are responsible for engaging with stakeholders, including other government agencies, the private sector, and the general public, to build partnerships and ensure the effective delivery of public services. Public managers must build and maintain relationships with a wide range of stakeholders, including elected officials, community organizations, and the general public, to ensure that their needs are met and their concerns are addressed.
- Performance management: Public managers monitor and evaluate the performance of government programmes and services, making recommendations for improvement where necessary.
- Resource management: This includes managing budgets, personnel, and other resources to ensure that public services are delivered effectively and efficiently.
- Programme evaluation: Public managers are responsible for evaluating the effectiveness and efficiency of programmes and services, and making recommendations for improvement.
- Proactive and crisis management: Public managers should strategically plan for the future and pre-empt potential crises. However, should crises arise they are called upon to respond to emergencies, natural disasters, and other crises, and to coordinate the efforts of multiple agencies and organizations to ensure a prompt and effective response.

The responsibilities and functions of public managers are varied and complex, requiring a combination of technical, managerial, and interpersonal skills. Public managers play a crucial role in ensuring that public services are delivered effectively and efficiently, and in building trust and accountability in government. They play a crucial role in the effective and efficient delivery of public services. Their responsibilities and functions are diverse, encompassing everything from policy development to programme implementation and staff supervision.

With its 54 states, 11 dependent territories, an estimated 3000 distinct ethnic groups speaking over 2000 languages, and great disparities as far as socioeconomic conditions are concerned, Africa is arguably the most diverse continent in the world. As such, public management on the African continent displays an array of permutations influenced by the historical context, cultures, traditions, ideological perspectives, and geopolitical realities of individual countries. State architecture of countries therefore also displays divergences in design, composition, and function. However, despite variations in the way states are governed, the basic tenets of good governance and the universally accepted principles of effective public management remain the same. In other words, despite the contrasts in statehood, the theory and praxis of public management are generic in nature.

Public managerial traditions, conventions, and practices are largely the result of the political culture of a state. There are significant variations in political culture observable, reflecting the continent's rich cultural and historical heritage. It is thus difficult to identify a single dominant political ideology in Africa. However, there are mainly three dominant types of political ideologies discernible. The first is Pan-Africanism. This is a political and social movement that promotes the unity and solidarity of African people and nations. It seeks to address the challenges faced by Africa, such as poverty, conflict, and underdevelopment, through collective efforts. Authoritarianism is the second type and can be regarded as a political system in which power is held by a single individual or group, typically characterized by strict control over the political, social, and economic life of the country, limited political freedoms, and lack of accountability. Finally, liberal democracy that can be viewed as a system of government in which power is held by elected representatives who are accountable to the people. It is characterized by the protection of individual freedoms and the rule of law. These ideologies, among others, have influenced the way governments, and their managers, function in Africa. Again, it should be emphasized that the extent of their influence varies from country to country and region to region. For example, in some countries, authoritarianism is widespread, while in others, liberal democracy is gaining ground. Ultimately, the dominant political ideology in Africa depends on various factors, including the historical, cultural, and economic context of each country, as well as the distribution of power and resources within society.

In spite of variations, some common themes can be identified that distinguish African approaches to governance from those of the Western and Eastern worlds. One of the defining characteristics of African political culture is the emphasis on community and consensus-building, rather than the individual rights and freedoms emphasized in Western political cultures. This has led to a tradition of consultation and negotiation in government decision-making processes, with a focus on reaching consensus and maintaining social harmony. Another important aspect of African political culture is the emphasis on extended family relationships and the importance of loyalty and solidarity within social networks. This has often resulted in the development of patronage networks, where leaders distribute resources and favours to their supporters in exchange for political loyalty. The dynamic nature of political cultures and traditions means that they are continuously evolving, adapting to changing circumstances and influences.

In contrast, Eastern political cultures, particularly in East Asia, have been influenced by Confucianism and its emphasis on hierarchy, order, and respect for authority. This has resulted in highly centralized and hierarchical systems of governance, with a strong emphasis on the rule of law and the role of the state in maintaining order. It is worth noting that these generalizations are not absolute, and there is considerable diversity within each region. Moreover, the influence of globalization and modernization as well as the legacies of colonialism have had a profound impact on political cultures and governance traditions in Africa. As far as the latter is concerned, colonialism had a profound impact on the governance traditions and political culture of African countries. During the colonial period, European powers imposed their own systems of governance, administration, and laws on African societies, often disregarding local customs and traditions. This led to the development of a legacy of authoritarianism and centralized power, where decision-making was largely centred in the hands of a small elite, and little space was given to participation and representation. Post-independence, many African countries inherited these governance structures and political cultures, leading to a continuation of authoritarian rule, corruption, and limited accountability. The legacy of colonialism also contributed to the weak and fragmented nature of civil society, as well as the marginalization of certain ethnic and cultural groups.

However, some observers may argue that the influence of colonialism is not solely negative. Some African countries have drawn on their colonial histories to develop stable and democratic systems of governance, by incorporating democratic norms and practices into their political cultures. Nevertheless, the legacy of colonialism continues to shape the political landscape of many African countries and remains a significant factor in their ongoing growth and development. It should be noted that historical legacy is often cited as one of the primary reasons why some states in Africa have failed to develop effective governance systems and have regressed into so-called 'failed states'. Many African states have a legacy of colonial rule, which often left behind fragmented and artificially created borders, weak institutions, and little infrastructure. This has made it difficult for these states to develop stable and effective governance systems. Additionally, the arbitrary borders established by colonial powers often created ethnic and linguistic divisions that have made it difficult to build national unity.

Apart from historical legacies, some other reasons cited for African governance weaknesses include the following:

- Conflict and political instability: Often driven by competition for resources, ethnic tensions, or disputes over leadership, instability can disrupt governance and make it difficult for governments to effectively address the needs of their citizens. In many African countries, ethnic and tribal tensions have also undermined governance by creating competing power centres and hindering the development of national unity.
- Corruption: Corruption is a pervasive problem in many African countries, undermining the rule of law and eroding trust in public institutions. It can also undermine economic growth and deter investment. It also undermines the legitimacy of governance systems and public officials. Despite efforts of many African governments to improve good governance practices, corruption remains a major problem. In order to tackle this issue, it is important to build strong and independent institutions that are able to hold politicians

and public servants accountable for their actions. This can be done by strengthening the judiciary, the media, and civil society organizations.

- Weak public institutions: Institutions such as the judiciary, legislature, and civil service that are not adequately managed and politically governed make it difficult to enforce laws, deliver services, and hold leaders accountable.
- Lack of resources: Many African countries are poor, with limited resources to invest in building strong institutions and delivering essential services. Many African countries are also plagued by poverty and a lack of financial resources, which makes it difficult for them to invest in critical areas such as education, healthcare, and infrastructure.
- External factors and interference: External factors, such as conflicts and interventions by other countries, can also contribute to the failure of governance systems in Africa. African countries can also be impacted by interference from other countries or international organizations that may undermine the ability of national governments to make independent decisions and act in the best interests of their citizens.

It is important to note that while these factors can contribute to poor governance and failed states in Africa, there is also significant variation across the continent and many African countries have made significant progress in recent years. These factors are complex and interrelated and addressing them through effective management praxis will improve governance by promoting stability, development, and prosperity in Africa. There are already positive signs that these and other factors are successfully addressed. A few examples of service delivery excellence and good governance initiatives in Africa include the following:

- Ghana: The National Health Insurance Scheme was launched in 2003 to provide affordable health coverage to millions of Ghanaians. The Scheme has improved access to healthcare and has helped to reduce the financial burden on families.
- Kenya: The country's M-PESA mobile money platform was launched in 2007 and has revolutionized financial inclusion in Kenya by allowing users to access banking services through their mobile phones. It has been widely credited with improving the lives of millions of people in the country.
- Mauritius: Mauritius is widely recognized as one of the most stable and prosperous nations in Africa, with a strong tradition of good governance and a well-developed social welfare system. The government has implemented policies aimed at reducing poverty and promoting economic growth, and the country has a highly developed tourism industry, which is a major source of income. Mauritius' e-Government initiative has transformed the way the government of Mauritius delivers services to its citizens. The initiative has made it easier for citizens to access government services online and has improved the efficiency and transparency of the government.
- Morocco: Morocco has made significant investments in infrastructure and social services, resulting in improved access to clean water, electricity, and education for its citizens. The government has also implemented reforms aimed at reducing corruption and improving the business environment.
- Rwanda: Rwanda has made significant progress in terms of good governance and socio-economic development, with a focus on providing quality healthcare and education to its citizens. The country has implemented innovative healthcare initiatives, such as a national health insurance scheme, which provides access to medical care for a large

portion of the population. Rwanda's Vision 2020 was launched in 2000 with the goal of transforming Rwanda into a middle-income country by 2020. The government has focused on developing infrastructure, improving education and health systems, and attracting investment.

- Seychelles: Seychelles has made significant progress in terms of good governance and socioeconomic development, with a focus on sustainability and the protection of the environment. The government has implemented policies aimed at reducing poverty and promoting economic growth, and the country has a strong tradition of political stability and a well-developed tourism industry.

- South Africa: The Public and Community Works Programme was launched in 2004 to create job opportunities for unemployed people in rural areas. The Programme has provided work for hundreds of thousands of people to date and has helped to reduce poverty and inequality.

These are just a few examples, and there are many other countries in Africa that are making significant progress in terms of good governance and socioeconomic development. Some African countries, such as South Africa, Egypt, and Morocco, have relatively strong economies and are considered to be middle-income countries. Political stability also remains a concern in some African countries, with several ongoing conflicts and political crises. Compared to Western countries, many African countries have weaker political systems and less political stability.

The presence of malpractice and corruption in Africa undermines the effectiveness of governance and affects the lives of citizens negatively. To address this, there is a need for state capacity building and public managerial competence, as well as strong state institutions that can enforce the rule of law and prevent corruption. The performance of governments in Africa should also be closely monitored to ensure that they are meeting the needs of the citizens. The Mo Ibrahim Index is a useful tool for evaluating governance on the African continent, and highlights areas where improvement is needed. Governments should address the weaknesses highlighted in this regard and develop the capacity to collect and analyze data, design and implement policies, and monitor and evaluate the impact of their actions.

To promote good governance, African governments should focus on building strong state institutions and public managerial competence. To enhance public managerial competence, African governments should invest in the training and development of public sector workers and promote a culture of service delivery that focuses on meeting the needs of citizens. The need for state capacity building is vital to ensuring that governments have the resources, skills, and systems necessary to perform their functions effectively. This requires investment in areas such as education, infrastructure, and technology. As alluded to earlier, the government's typical responsibilities for delivering quality public services include providing essential services such as healthcare, education, public safety, and infrastructure, ensuring access to these services for all citizens, protecting citizens' rights, and managing public resources effectively. The role of public managers in this regard is to implement policies and programmes that support these responsibilities, as well as to manage the delivery of public services in an efficient, effective, and accountable manner. This often involves working with a diverse range of stakeholders, such as elected officials, community-based organizations, and other government agencies, to ensure that public services meet the needs of the community and are delivered in a cost-effective and sustainable manner.

Public managers are also responsible for ensuring that public resources are used appropriately and effectively, and for setting performance standards and goals for public service delivery. This includes understanding how to prioritize competing demands and make informed decisions about resource allocation that maximize public benefit. Moreover, training and development help to build a culture of continuous learning and improvement in the public sector. As new challenges and opportunities arise, public officials need to be able to adapt and evolve their knowledge, skills, and competencies to effectively respond to changing circumstances. With competent public managers, government institutions can make informed decisions, allocate resources effectively, and implement policies effectively to achieve their goals and serve the citizens. Additionally, possessing the necessary knowledge, skills, and capacity allows managers to respond to emerging challenges, innovate, and continuously improve the quality of services provided. Ultimately, strong government institutions with capable managers can lead to improved governance and development outcomes for African countries. Strong administrative leadership and competent public managers are important factors in promoting good governance because they can help to create and maintain a supportive environment for effective public service delivery.

There are several reasons why one should read about the world of governance in general. Some of these reasons include the following:

- Civic literacy: Understanding how government works and its role in society is an important part of being an informed and engaged citizenry. By studying government, one can develop a deeper understanding of the political system, its institutions, and processes, and how they affect one's daily life.
- Career opportunities: Knowledge of government and politics can be useful for pursuing careers in public service, law, journalism, diplomacy, and many other fields.
- Political activism: Studying government can equip individuals with the knowledge and skills they need to participate in political activism and advocacy efforts and to work towards positive change in their communities and the world at large.
- Improved critical thinking skills: Analyzing government policies and processes requires critical thinking and the ability to assess information objectively. Studying government can help develop these skills and encourage a lifelong interest in learning and self-improvement.
- Understanding of global issues: Governments play a crucial role in addressing global issues such as poverty, conflict, human rights, and environmental sustainability. Studying government provides a deeper understanding of the complex challenges facing the world and the role that governments play in addressing them.

It is evident that reading about government can broaden one's perspectives, deepen their understanding of the world, and equip them with the knowledge and skills they need to make a positive impact in their communities and beyond. Similarly, the study of public management can provide practitioners and scholars with the tools and knowledge needed to contribute to good governance as well as the general welfare and prosperity of society in several ways:

- Understanding of government processes and policies: Studying public management provides students with a comprehensive understanding of the government processes, systems, and policies that shape our communities and societies.

- Critical thinking and problem-solving skills: The curriculum helps students to develop critical thinking skills, which enable them to analyze complex societal concerns, formulate policies, and make decisions that positively impact their communities. Studying public management equips students with the skills needed to identify and address complex societal concerns, such as poverty, inequality, and environmental degradation. The study domain thus makes a significant contribution to the personal and professional growth of students.
- Knowledge of public service norms and values: Public management emphasizes the importance of public service norms and values such as transparency, participation, responsiveness, accountability, and integrity, which are essential for good governance. By learning these norms and values, students can become better citizens who hold government officials accountable and contribute to the overall well-being of their communities.
- Career opportunities: Graduates of public management programmes can pursue careers in various fields, including government, non-profit organizations, and international organizations, where they can use their skills and knowledge to improve the lives of people and communities. The study domain thus empowers students and opens a range of career opportunities. These careers allow graduates as public managers to make a difference and contribute to the general well-being and prosperity of society.
- Understanding complex societal concerns: Public management courses equip students with a comprehensive understanding of complex societal concerns, such as poverty, inequality, greener energy, sustainable development, and environmental degradation. This understanding allows them to formulate public policies to address these issues and make a positive impact on society. Ultimately, the goal of studying public management is to empower students to make a positive impact on society. Whether they choose to work in government, the private sector, or a non-profit organization, they will have the skills and knowledge needed to contribute to the well-being of society and promote a better future for all.

It is the primary objective of this publication to make a significant contribution in all of these respects by surveying multiple contours of the governance of public affairs and accentuating the role that public managers should play in addressing the complexities and challenges associated with societal dynamics. In the 21 chapters of this book, current trends and approaches to public management as discipline and public management as practice are explored. As such the handbook focuses on public management in Africa. Unfortunately, not all 54 states could be accommodated due to space limitations. The countries covered, however, do provide a snapshot of realities on the continent at large.

PART I

PUBLIC MANAGEMENT IN AN AFRICAN CONTEXT

1. The dynamic world of public management

Thekiso Molokwane

INTRODUCTION

This chapter explores the ever-changing world of public management. Like every particular focus within the broader discipline of public administration, the managerial dimensions of the executive structures of government have undergone a series of paradigmatic changes. These changes include a transition from conventional or traditional public administration to neoclassic public administration and contemporary public management. These changes were mainly brought about due to administrative reforms such as the New Public Management (NPM) that came into existence as cooperation between the public and private sector increased. The managerial focus of public administration also co-exists with other related study domains such as public financial management, public human resource management, and organizational studies. Public management can thus be regarded as an all-inclusive concept that incorporates all managerial aspects of governance, inclusive of managerial applications, approaches, skills, tools, and techniques associated with particular managerial foci.

The purpose of this introductory chapter is to lay a solid foundation for the study of Public Management and include clarification of the concept 'governance', a brief analysis of the changing nature of the world of governance, and an overview of public management applications for the successful management of executive structures of the public sector. The latter will be done by probing best practices in selected countries on the African continent.

THE WORLD OF PUBLIC GOVERNANCE

For centuries, governance has been part of human history (Lynn, 1998; Weiss, 2000), but notions of governance in the social, economic, and political spheres have gained increased prominence in scholarly literature since the beginning of the new millennium (Blatter, 2012, p. 2). Especially since the 1990s, public governance has gradually become a common denominator in the scholarly discourse regarding the best approaches to govern the modern public sector. According to analysts such as Fukuyama (2013) and Klausen (2022), this interest was mainly brought about because of efforts to more closely align public and private spheres as far as good corporate governance is concerned. Corporate governance has a much longer stance in laws, regulations, codes of conduct, and best practices and has been a global movement to adapt and adopt similar practices in the public sector. The primary aim was to prevent scandals, fraud, corruption, and criminal liability, while also being good for economic prosperity and growth (Klausen, 2022, p. 355).

Often, the concept of governance is easily construed to mean 'government' (Plumptre and Graham, 1999). However, governance (an act) is broader than government (an institution) contextually. The World Bank (1992) defines governance as 'the manner in which governments (i.e. public officials and state institutions) acquire and exercise authority to shape public policy and provide public goods and services'. For Fukuyama (2013, p. 3) governance means a government's ability to make and enforce rules, to engage society, and to deliver services. Fukuyama (2013, p. 2) further observes that governance should be regarded as the implementation of government decisions and include the normative dimensions (i.e. values, ethics, and norms) that government should comply with in fulfilling its mandate to govern in a democratic, participatory and inclusive way. Within this context the functioning of the executive branches of government and their bureaucracies (i.e. state departments) is primarily the study focus of Public Management. As a professionalized practice-based field, Public Management mainly entails the study of the operationalization of public policy in the executive structures of the public sector (Gruening, 2001; Pollitt, Van Thiel and Homburg, 2007).

According to Borders (2019), the evolution of public governance can be traced through the centuries by considering the particular nature of statehood. In a historical context he mentions clans, kingdoms, and empires. More contemporary forms of statehood include democracies, republics, and constitutional dispensations. Borders (2019) argues that the way states are governed is a direct result of the prevailing norms, values, and ideological perspectives of society. By taking a longer-term view, Borders (2019, p. 2) predicts new forms of statehood to emerge including 'Start-up Nations' and 'Cloud Governance'.

It should be evident that governance (actions of government institutions), public administration (executive structures of government), and public management (managerial dimensions of the public administration) have a symbiotic interrelationship. However, since the nature of statehood and the particular government dispensation (e.g. socialistic, democratic, autocratic, dictatorial, etc.) are subject to change, this interrelationship is also dynamic in nature. According to Pfiffner (2004, p. 2), an analysis of this vigorous interrelationship should commence by considering the tenets of the traditional model of public administration. This model was mainly founded on the articulations of Max Weber regarding the nature of bureaucracies. Weber emphasized control from top to bottom in the form of monocratic hierarchies, that is, a system of control in which policy is set at the top and carried out through a series of government offices, with each manager and worker reporting to one superior and held to account by that person. This bureaucratic system is based on a set of rules and regulations flowing from public law and rational and legal control systems. The role of the bureaucrat (i.e. public official) is strictly subordinate to the political superior (Motshegwa, 2017, p. 38).

Premised on the conventional principles of government bureaucracies, modern forms of governance emerged as a result of developments such as the Industrial Revolution, breakthroughs in technology, and economic growth (Pfiffner, 2004, p. 1). Especially after World War II, scholars and politicians reassessed and questioned the classical notions of public administration. One of the most rigorous critics in this regard was Herbert Simon, whose work set the tone and direction for neoclassic public administration. Simon argued that the principles of administration were not scientific, but rather, were inconsistent proverbs that were drawn from common sense (Simon, 1976). But at the end of the 20th century that classical model of public administration would again be challenged by what came to be known as New Public Management (NPM). The conventional wisdom holds that NPM has its origins in public-choice theory and managerialism (Gruening, 2001, p. 1; Lynn, 1998). Gruening (2001, p. 2) observes that it emerged in the late 1970s and early 1980s in the United Kingdom under former Prime Minister Margaret Thatcher. It also became embedded in the municipal governments in the U.S. (e.g. Sunnyvale, California) that had suffered from economic recession and tax reforms. The NPM movement also became popular in New Zealand and Australia.

NPM was mainly characterized by the adoption of private sector approaches, principles, and practices in the public sector with the aim of making government institutions more efficient, effective, productive, and economical.

EVOLUTION OF PUBLIC MANAGEMENT AS A DISCIPLINE AND PRACTICE

The practice of management is probably as old as humankind, but the formal corpus of management knowledge is relatively new (Wren, 2009, p. 3). This body of knowledge emerged as a result of the work of management pioneers such as Robert Owen, Charles Barbage, Andrew Ure, Charles Dupin, Henri Fayol, and Fredrick Taylor (Shafritz and Hyde, 2017; Wren, 2009). Since then, the study and practice of public management continue to experience constant change throughout the world. This is largely due to indigenous and exogenous factors impacting governments.

The origins of public management cannot be traced to any one particular era with certainty. The definitions of related concepts are context-sensitive. However, as argued by Vigoda (2002), the primary purpose of public management is generic in nature and entails the aim that governments and their public servants should work closely with society in implementing public policy and in rendering services in the most efficient, effective, and economical ways possible. Emphasis is thus placed on reducing cumbersome bureaucratic systems and procedures while maintaining public sector integrity and accountability. The current scholarly discourse is therefore shaped by a common concern to improve the overall performance of government institutions. Management applications, skills, tools, and techniques are universally accepted as the core activities to realize this ideal. The discourse is further directed by the application of the so-called POSDCORB (planning, organizing, staffing, directing, coordinating, reporting, and budgeting) principles. These principles confirm the prominence of private sector styles of management in the running of government institutions (Basheka, 2018, p. 3).

In the subsections below, the evolution of public management both as a discipline and practice is placed under the searchlight. The focus is on the trajectory of management from the period prior to industrialization to the present age.

Public Management before Industrialization

Before widespread industrialization, social organizations were primarily the household, tribe, church, military, and government. As groups of affiliations evolved from simple structures such as the family to the nation-state, issues regarding organizational obligations, authority, responsibility, and accountability became far more complex. The pre-industrial era was characterized by strong centralized authority vested in the patriarch or monarch and in chiefs and priests; the former claiming circular power and the latter heavenly dominion. From this struggle and this division of authority came the idea of a priest ruler or divine King. A King was not a King until ordained by a priest, a tradition that long endured (Wren, 2009, p. 13). In the Far East, the Han dynasty (206BC to AD 220) adopted a Confucian precept that government should be handled by men chosen, not by birth, but by virtue and its main aim was the happiness of the people (Hughes, 2019). Public management in this period was thus not legalized, institutionalized, or formalized. The selection of public officials on the basis of affiliation to tribes and allegiance to rulers did not always bring the best administrators to office.

In Africa, recognizable administrative systems existed in countries such as Egypt and Ethiopia. These systems were established mainly for agricultural purposes such as irrigation from the annual flood of rivers and the construction infrastructure. In particular, three aspects should be noted as far as the emergence of 'management' in the civil sphere of society is concerned. The first is that the creation of systems, structures, processes, and procedures of government institutions usually took place in conjunction with the legislative process. This means that a parliamentary act usually announced the creation of a government institution. There is great disparity on the continent as far as this aspect is concerned. The second aspect is the influence of the dominant political ideology in the country. This ideology will be evident in the way public institutions are formalized and managed. The third aspect is that the system of (Western) governance was often transplanted to various African countries mainly due to colonialization processes. This, in general, had a significant impact on traditional, tribal, and customary systems of governance and public 'management' in these countries. After independence, a 'hybrid' system of governance usually resulted where vested colonial systems merged with more traditional and conventional systems of public administration.

Public Management during the First, Second, and Third Industrial Revolutions

The notion of 'revolution' denotes abrupt and radical change. Revolutions have occurred throughout history when new technologies and novel ways of perceiving the world trigger a profound change in political and economic systems as well as social structures. Given that history is used as a frame of reference, the abruptness of these changes may take years to unfold. The First Industrial Revolution spanned from about 1760 to around 1840. It heralded a new age for civilization and the way public institutions were managed (Kohnová and Salajová, 2019; Wren, 2009). Triggered by the construction of railroads and the invention of the steam engine, it ushered in mechanical production (Schwab, 2016, p. 11).

The Second Industrial Revolution, or Industry 2.0, followed and continued into the 20th century. This period was mainly characterized by the electrification of production lines. During this period new means of production transformed into machinery such as the spinning jenny, agricultural tools, and puddling and rolling processes for making iron products (Kohnová and Salajová, 2019; Mohajan, 2019). It is commonly argued that this period ended at the beginning of World War I.

The Third Industrial Revolution commenced after World War I in 1947. It is usually called the computer or digital revolution because it was catalyzed by the development of semiconductors, mainframe computing (1960s), personal computing (1970s and 1980s), and the internet (1990s) (Schwab, 2016, p. 11). This revolution was mainly characterized by partial or full automation using memory-programmable controls and computers. These technologies made it possible to automate the production process without human assistance. This period thus created new socioeconomic and political conditions and was mainly characterized by the emergence of scientific management and the influence of behaviourism (e.g. Hawthorne Experiments) on the way in which organizational systems, structures, and people were managed.

Public Management during the Fourth Industrial Revolution

The Fourth Industrial Revolution (4IR) refers to the 'fusion of technologies that is blurring the lines between the physical, digital, and biological spheres' (Schwab, 2019, p. 13). The concept is an umbrella term to frame and examine the impact of emerging technologies on all aspects of society in the 21st century. Technologies that characterize this era include the following:

- artificial intelligence;
- augmented reality;
- blockchain;
- cloud computing;
- drones;
- fifth-generation mobile networks;
- genomics and biometrics;
- internet of things;
- robotics;
- three-dimensional (3D) printing;
- virtual reality.

These technologies are commonly included in the emerging technologies anticipated to provide human societies with the means to overcome global challenges like disease, poverty, and ignorance (PwC, 2017, pp. 3–25; Watson, 2020, p. 3). According to Watson (2020, p. 3), 4IR is distinct from prior revolutions in at least three ways. First, by building upon the legacy of digital networks from the Third Industrial Revolution, the speed, scope, and scale of technological advance and diffusion in 4IR is quite unlike the world has ever seen before. Second, it is about the dynamic fusion of digital, physical, and biological technologies, and third, many of the emerging technologies are personalized in nature that, while facilitating rapid societal integration, also create new normative challenges that require major changes in the foundations of existing technology governance institutions.

Schwab (2016, p. 12) observes that the 4IR is not only about 'smart' and 'connected' machines and systems. Its scope is much wider. Occurring simultaneously are 'waves of further breakthroughs' in areas ranging from gene sequencing to nanotechnology, from renewables to quantum computing (Schwab, 2016, p. 12). It is the fusion of these technologies and their interaction across the physical, digital, and biological domains that make this period fundamentally different from previous revolutions. These technologies have certainly revolutionized public management and governance. Studies have found that 4IR technologies can have a profound transformational impact on the ways in which organizations are managed. A 2019 report issued by Deloitte and the Global Enabling Sustainability Initiative identified and quantified how digital technologies can help governments, businesses, and philanthropic organizations accelerate their efforts to achieve each of the United Nations' 17 sustainable development goals (Deloitte Insights, 2020).

When assessing the impact of the 4IR on governments, the use of digital technologies to govern better is top of mind. More intense and innovative use of web technologies can help public administrations modernize their structures and functions to improve overall performance, from strengthening processes of e-governance to fostering greater transparency, accountability, and engagement between the government and its citizens (Schwab, 2016, p. 66). On the negative side, the challenges created by the 4IR appear to be mostly on the supply side – in the world of work and production.

THE CHANGING NATURE OF PUBLIC MANAGEMENT AND GOVERNANCE

The concept of governance can be found in both normative-programmatic contexts as a reform approach as well as in analytical-descriptive contexts as a category for describing and interpreting current transformation processes in politics and the state (Blatter, 2012, p. 5). Blatter (2012, pp. 9–20) presents varied perspectives on governance. One of these is a debate on governance as a normative and disciplinary alternative to government and management while the other speaks to governance as a transdisciplinary field of study bringing perspectives from a number of adjacent reference disciplines such as sociology, political science, economics, and business management (Van der Waldt, 2014a, p. 70; Van der Waldt, 2014b, p. 126). Governance usually constitutes a programmatic alternative to other paradigms for organizing and reforming the state and its public administration. For analytical purposes, the term governance is typically used to investigate change in statehood, politics, and the management of public institutions.

As stated earlier, governance has always been a changing phenomenon. Determinants of this change have varied over time and space. In some cases, for instance, the change is instigated by public sector reforms. In other situations, the change was due to domestic political and ideological turmoil. In this respect, Fukuyama (2013, p. 2) observes for instance, that there has been a significant corpus of scholarly literature on public sector reform coming out of institutional economics, public administration, and from the communities of practice surrounding development agencies seeking to improve the goodness of governance globally. For governance scholarship, the main methodological challenge is to demarcate the field and focus scholarly inquiry without losing sight of the multitude of variables that may influence governance structures, civil society, economics, and politics (Rigaud and Côté, 2011). Governance studies can, for example, be narrowed down in scope to a particular region, country or sphere of government; a normative principle; a particular managerial sector of intervention (e.g. urban governance, democratic governance, and educational governance); or particular public managerial domains (e.g. finance, strategies, programmes, policy, projects, human resources, etc.)

As alluded to in the introductory section of this publication, scholars typically utilize some kind of typology or classification system to make sense of the changing nature of Public Management as a field of study. One such typology is to differentiate between the different theoretical models (i.e. Classical Public Administration Theory, New Public Management Theory and Postmodern Public Administration Theory). Another system is to consider the evolutionary developments within the corpus of knowledge of the domain by considering its paradigms (i.e. politics-administration dichotomy, the principles of administration, public administration as political science, public administration as management, new public management, and governance). Much of the contemporary literature on public management is dominated by the new public management (NPM) paradigm as a reform that took centre stage in management in recent decades. It is far from simple to separate NPM from governance since policy documents, politicians, and managers draw freely from arguments that come from two different perspectives and both reinforce each other (Klijn, 2012; Rigaud, 2012). In this regard, the subsections below attempt to demonstrate the ever-changing nature of governance and its bearing on public management. Given this context, the subsections that follow explore the dynamism of governance illustrated through the lenses of reinventing government, network governance, and holistic governance approaches as a further classification system.

Changes Brought about by the Reinventing Government Movement

The reinventing government movement came about as a result of major administrative reforms in especially western countries and the pioneering work by David Osborne and Ted Gaebler titled *Reinventing Government: How the Entrepreneurial Spirit is Transforming the Public Sector* in 1992. Kearney and Hays (1998) argue that reinventing government reforms is mainly due to the constraining nature of conventional bureaucratic power. To this end, governments have been adopting new public sector reforms to correct problems associated with ineffectiveness, inefficiency, poor policy coherence, and lack of direction that resulted in poor management practices in the public sector (Molokwane, 2019). Governments thus have been restructuring and realigning public organizations with the view to make them operate in an efficient and effective manner (Mothusi, 2008). Gumede and Dipholo (2014) therefore opine that the traditional model of organization and delivery of public services based on the principles of bureaucratic hierarchy, planning, centralization, direct control, and self-sufficiency have been largely replaced by the reinventing approach, leading to the NPM paradigm. There was also an effort to reform public institutions with an emphasis on their financial and economic performance.

Changes Brought about by Network Forms of Governance

Network governance is a form of governance based on social controls, rather than bureaucratic structures and/or formal contractual relationships (Junki, 2006). According to Ouden (2015), it can be described as a form of alliance in which relevant policy actors are linked together as co-producers, where they are more likely to identify and share common interests. They develop a culture of trust; thus, the relationship is symbiotic and interdependent. This coordinated, mutual relationship tends to develop trust and reciprocity among actors. This is where network partners bring important and strategic assets that contribute to addressing common societal concerns. Dedeurwaerdere (2005) and Namara, Karyeija and Mubangizi (2015) argue that there is a growing interest in network governance as a method of organizing economic, political, and administrative activities through inter-agency and intersocietal coordination and cooperation.

The process of creating a meaningful and effective network in public administration is directly linked to the ability and willingness of the state to coordinate various activities while maintaining the structural or organizational integrity of the governing system. Ouden (2015) observes that governance networks provide new and distinctive mechanisms of governance on that which might be referred to as negotiation rationality. Moreover, public policy is shaped and reshaped through negotiations between interdependent actors, who have capacity and resource bases of their own.

In South Africa, Mothetho (2017) maintains that the Department of Social Development is one of the first government departments to have adopted the network governance model in ensuring that non-profit organizations become an extension of the Department by assisting in providing services that it cannot adequately provide due to capacity constraints. The strengthening of relations between civil society and the Department was enhanced and formalized by the promulgation of the Non-Profit Organisations Act 71 of 1997 (Wyngaard and Hendricks, 2010). This Act aims to strengthen the relationship between government and civil society organizations with the primary intention of improving services and ensuring good, inclusive governance.

In the local sphere of government, networks emerge to successfully reach all citizens in providing essential services. Municipalities in South Africa struggle to efficiently provide services for all residents, especially in deep rural areas. It is for this reason that the White Paper on Municipal Service Partnerships of 2000 acknowledges the inability of many municipalities to render services effectively to their communities, hence the introduction of service delivery agreements between municipalities and service providers. To formalize this, the Local Government: Municipal Systems Act 32 of 2000 stipulates that a municipality may provide its services through either internal or external agreements (partnerships) undertaken within the periphery of the municipal authority (Phago and Malan, 2004).

Changes Brought about by Holistic Governance and a Whole-of-government Approach

Holistic governance aims to move towards an integrated whole-of-government planning and coordination approach to overcome limitations brought about by silo-planning and fragmented bureaucratic responses. Holistic governance is about joining up at the top (i.e. political and strategic layers of government) but also joining up at the base (i.e. operational, managerial echelons) by engaging all tiers and spheres of government and various stakeholders outside the government (Li and Ding, 2020). Firmreite and Legreid (2005) and Gregory and Robert (2006) argue that NPM overlooked the problems of horizontal coordination and rather focused on performance management and structural devolution. In addition, Renwu and Guoqin (2012, p. 44) hold that NPM's 'blind pursuit of efficiency has weakened some core values of public administration such as fairness, justice, representativeness, and public participation'. In response, holistic governance emphasizes alignment, synergy, coordination, and integration between all actors involved. Mechanisms such as information and technology, interministerial coordinating committees, and senior management forums typically facilitate such a whole-of-government approach by integrating all functions of government. It also increasingly facilitates a process that moves traditional bureaucracies from 'decentralised to centralised, from parts to the whole, and from fragmentation to integration' (Yang, 2021, p. 45). Yang (2021) cautions, however, that establishing and maintaining a whole-of-government approach is rather time-consuming and requires the alignment of diverse capabilities, the reform of organizational culture, and building of mutual trust relationships.

Changes Brought about by the New Public Management Paradigm

New Public Management (NPM) is commonly regarded as one of the most influential meta-concepts in public management, especially between about 1980 and 2000 (Schedler, 2022, p. 16). The emergence of New Public Management can primarily be attributed to the financial difficulties in the (English-speaking) countries of origin, which in turn were a consequence of the change in the international economic system as well as increasing demands of the citizens in New Zealand (Schedler, 2022, p. 16). Others trace the genesis of NPM to the United Kingdom and the United States which were anti-public sector and pro-market coinciding with the market-oriented change emphasis and strategy by the World Bank and the International Monetary Fund (Dassah, 2018, p. 91). Among others, NPM has variously been described as a concept (Hope, 2001, p. 120; Gangte, 2012; Dassah, 2018, p. 91), a movement (Hope, 2001, p. 120), a paradigm (Vyas-Doorgapersad, 2011, p. 235), as well as a set of techniques and practices (Gangte, 2012, p. 46; Dassah, 2018, p. 91).

The model was strongly supported by market advocates, who argued that governments were engaged in inappropriate activities and needed to reduce their size; and, in effect, the role of government has to be scaled down through a number of reforms (Basheka, 2018, p. 4). A wide variety of NPM reforms were adopted in order to address policy problems faced by governments which in Robinson's (2015, p. 4) view have been increasingly complex, wicked, and global, rather than simple, linear, and national in focus. Various countries in sub-Saharan Africa experimented with specific NPM initiatives. For instance, the following have been documented: performance management in Cameroon; training, accountability, and transparency in the DRC; 'agentification', privatization, and decentralization in South Africa; restructuring and rationing of public sector administration in Tanzania; as well as a public enterprise, rationalization, and public-private partnerships in Zimbabwe (Molefhe and Molokwane, 2018).

Critics of NPM observe that since the beginning of the new millennium, the active dissemination of the NPM has largely levelled off. They argue that NPM also hinders delivery, due to its businesslike and corporate focus (Noordegraaf, 2022, p. 158). Further to this, they attest that in practice, the initial enthusiasm has given way to a certain disillusionment, as even the NPM did not prove to be a panacea for all diseases of governmental mismanagement. In this respect, the NPM can also be regarded as a 'management mode' that has been replaced by new more policy-oriented approaches and fashions.

Changes Brought about by the New Public Governance Movement

The New Public Governance (NPG) movement emanated mainly from the work by Osborne (2005, 2010). New conceptions of public governance address a different mix of features from those once prevalent. This set of ideas has been recognized for addressing the limitations of other models by emphasizing the range of actors outside government, horizontal relationships, and the centrality of networks (Osborne, 2010; Pollitt and Bouckaert, 2017). In contrast with the emphasis on bureaucracy hierarchy and administrative interest that are the defining features of the old public administration, managerial discretion, and the contractual mechanisms associated with NPM, the NPG approach places citizens rather than government at the centre of its frame of reference (Zhou and Zvoushe, 2018, p. 214). Molokwane and Lukamba (2018) conclude that, to assist the government in determining its mandate and correctly choosing what to do, citizens should be involved as they best know their needs.

PUBLIC MANAGEMENT APPLICATIONS, SKILLS, TOOLS, AND TECHNIQUES

The philosophical foundation of Public Management came about by, among other things, expecting public servants to focus on the outcome of their work by meeting their objectives (Tshombe, Molokwane and Nduhura, 2022, p. 55). Countries in the African continent have over the years utilized a multitude of public management applications, skills, tools, and techniques to improve among others, efficiency and performance in the public sector. In Botswana for instance, prior to 1999, one of the leading concerns for the government of Botswana in the public service was productivity. Reforms were centred on this phenomenon and these included Job Evaluation, Parallel Progression, Work Improvement Teams, Organization, and Performance-Based Rewards Systems and Methods (Kaunda, 2004; Republic of Botswana, 2002). The country would later on implement a number of NPM initiatives.

According to Van der Waldt (2023), typical public management applications, skills, tools, and techniques can be summarized as follows:

- *Applications*:
    - Human resource management.
    - Financial management.
    - Development management.
    - Policy analysis.
    - Strategic management.
    - Organizational development.
    - Project management.
    - Knowledge management.
    - Supply chain management.
- *Skills*:
    - Decision-making.
    - Communication and negotiation.
    - Interpersonal and labour relations.
    - Conflict management.
    - Change management.
    - Diversity management.
    - Networking and partnerships.
- *Tools*:
    - Computer technology (ICT, software, e-government, AI, digitalization).
    - Management information systems.
    - Work study.
    - Research.
    - Consultation.
- *Techniques*:
    - Decision support techniques.
    - Organization techniques.
    - Human resource techniques.
    - Control techniques.

It should be noted that this summary is not exhaustive and that the adoption and utilization of these applications, skills, tools, and techniques are dependent on the managerial level of officials, the particular circumstances, and the area of specialization. It does, however, illustrate the diverse and rather complex nature of the public management function in government.

More recent developments in the field include the adoption of results-based management (RBM) and integrated results-based management (IRBM). Results-based management is a management application by which all actors, contributing directly or indirectly to achieving a set of results, ensure that their processes, products, and services contribute to the desired results (outputs, outcomes, and higher-level goals or impact) and use information and evidence on actual results to inform decision-making on the design, resourcing, and delivery of programmes and activities as well as for accountability and reporting (United Nations Development Groups, 2011, p. 7). In Zimbabwe, the RBM systems linked results and expenditure targets. The system was expected to improve the performance of the public sector through the implementation of cost-effective measures as well as better monitoring and evaluation of activities and programmes. The Government adopted the IRBM systems in 2005 (Zhou and Zvoushe, p. 211).

A further field of application is e-government. E-government is an essential part of the 4IR. Many countries have adopted e-government programmes, laws, and policies that have created the legal, strategic, and organizational basis for widespread e-government applications (Yildiz, 2007). E-government has therefore become a tool for modernizing public administration internally and externally (Guenduez, 2022, p. 222). Countries that are implementing e-government practices are already addressing issues of internet security, providing certain services online, and operating generally through the internet. Those that are leaders in e-government conduct most of their business online and deal with issues such as integrated data management. Selfridge, Ferose and Kumar (2018) observe that while these are admirable outcomes of e-government and highlight how advanced technology enables civil service transformation, the key to its success has been to design appropriate applications with the end-users (citizens) in mind. In this sense, building an effective e-government model requires that its application in public management addresses both operational and policy governance matters.

MANAGING EXECUTIVE STRUCTURES OF THE PUBLIC SECTOR: EXPERIENCES FROM SUB-SAHARAN AFRICAN COUNTRIES

In Africa, the governance debate gained renewed prominence following a report by the World Bank in 1992 by accentuating the fundamental deficiencies in African governments to implement good government programmes despite financial assistance from development agencies. The expectation was that the continent would develop prudent governance structures during the postcolonial era thus leading to improved public management. This, and other donor and development agency reports, stressed the fact that the democratic content of governance in Africa remains a matter of serious domestic and international concern (Idowu, 2020, p. 3; Obasi and Lekorwe, 2014, p. 1).

To probe the management of executive structures in the public sector, three countries were selected as cases to illustrate the dynamic nature of public management and governance in sub-Saharan Africa, namely Lesotho, Ethiopia, and Ghana. In an attempt to obtain a more balanced perspective, a single country was selected from each of the three subregions namely East, South, and West Africa. The management of executive structures within the public sectors of these countries covers governance in pre-independence and post-independence eras. The latter half focuses particularly on the managerial influences of reinventing government, network governance, and holistic government movements.

Similar to other countries in southern Africa, the precolonial era form of governance in Lesotho was anchored on traditional authority (Du Plessis and Molefi, 2019). The Basotho people participated in making major decisions on diverse public issues through consultation

(Monyane, 2009). The British found an existing indigenous governance structure which was accountable to the people through public gatherings led by the Paramount Chief, King Moshoeshoe I. One of the first actions taken by the British colonial regime from 1871 to 1884 was to break down the existing indigenous governmental institutions and to introduce direct rule (Mofuoa, 2005).

The East African governance experience of Ethiopia goes back to the early periods of the twentieth century during the era of Meneliik II in 1889–1913. This is the era well-known for state formation, inclusive of the introduction of formal public administrative systems and structures, and the establishment of ministries (Adebabay, 2011, p. 10). During the period of Emperor Meneliik II, civil servants were appointed based on their political loyalty. Following Emperor Meneliik II's rule, Emperor Haile Selassie I introduced various reform measures modernizing the public administration. This era saw amongst others, the professionalization of public administration (Paulos, 2001, p. 79; Adebabay, 2011, p. 10). Administrative reforms were mainly aimed at clarifying and defining the powers and duties of ministries and establishing a central personnel agency so that it could maintain a standardized public service governed by uniform rules and regulations (Paulos, 2001, p. 82).

In West Africa, the British Governor, aided by the Executive Council and the Legislative Council took charge of Ghana during the 1850s. The Executive Council comprised a small group of European officials who served as an advisory body and who voted on legislation and taxes with the Governor's consent (Ayee, 2001). Members of the Executive Council and unofficial members initially selected from British business interests made up the Legislative Council (Ayee, 2001). Three chiefs and three other Africans joined the Legislative Council after the 1900s. These Chiefs were selected from the Europeanized Accra, Cape Coast, and Sekondi communities (Ayee, 2001). Almost solely village councils of Chiefs and elders were in charge of addressing local communities' urgent needs, including traditional law and order and the general welfare (Ayee, 2001).

Reinventing Government Management Experiences

During the postcolonial period, changes that swept through governments globally also did not leave countries on the African continent unaffected. Internationally, governments adopted new public sector reform programmes to correct problems of poor policy coherence and lack of strategic direction that resulted in poor management of the executive structures and systems of government (Molokwane, 2019). Restructuring and realigning public sector institutions became some of the major aims of these reforms. The overall goal was to improve efficiency in the public sector (Mothusi, 2008). In the case of the government of Lesotho, it has on many occasions instituted public sector reforms in a similar form as those characterizing the reinventing government movement. This emanated from the recognition that the country needed far-reaching reforms to ensure more stability and prosperity (Government of the Kingdom of Lesotho, 2019). Relative political stability was fostered through constitutional reviews and changes. On the administrative front some of the most notable reform programmes were launched in the public health sector. Through the 2016 National Health Policy, the government of Lesotho decentralized health services to achieve greater efficiency, effectiveness, and economy in healthcare delivery (Dick-Sagoe, Asare-Nuamah and Dick-Sagoe, 2021, p. 3; Ministry of Health, 2016). Healthcare service decentralization was meant to reverse the poor result that negatively affected the Lesotho government's ability to deliver healthcare services

(World Bank Group, 2017), characterized by dilapidated healthcare buildings, lack of healthcare equipment, and lack of adequate and inadequate healthcare staff in rural healthcare centres. Service users attested to the fact that health services have improved considerably due to these reforms. Some of the particular improvements included:

- better services and conditions of health facilities;
- improved access to health services and facilities;
- more affordable services;
- increased human resource capacity and skills to manage healthcare facilities;
- improved healthcare in rural communities;
- upgraded access to electricity supply.

To reinvent the government in Ethiopia, political leaders introduced a series of reforms beginning during the early 1990s. The reforms were a drastic response to the general lack of capacity, transparency, and accountability that had hindered the government from achieving economic and socioeconomic developments, including adequate service delivery, citizen empowerment, and good governance (Ministry of Capacity Building, 2014). In 1996 the Civil Service Reform Programme (CSRP) was introduced together with managerial efficiency and reform tools like Citizen Charters, Business Process Reengineering (BPR) initiatives, and the adoption of the Balance Score Card (BSC). The CSRP was mainly inspired by the reinventing government movement and the perceived benefits of NPM and the adoption of good governance principles (Mengesha and Common, 2006). The reforms were aimed to influence policy changes from a one-party to a multi-party system and transform the centralized economy into a market-based economy in Ethiopia. Reforms also sought to change the form of government from unitary to federal and institute regional and local governments by decentralizing power, tasks, and authority to the new subnational entities (Debela, 2020). On the economic side, CSRP sought to denationalize and de-regularize public enterprises that were run by the state (Mengesha and Common, 2006). Mengesha and Common (2006) indicated that CSRP was introduced to build a fair, transparent, efficient, ethical public sector basically by forming enabling legislature, developing operational systems, and training staff in key departments like human resource management, service delivery, top management, and ethics.

In Ghana, the period prior to the introduction of NPM-led reforms witnessed a number of major managerial and administrative challenges in the public sector such as financial and project mismanagement, lack of transparency and accountability, public funds embezzlement due to widespread corruption among both politicians and civil servants, inefficiency and ineffectiveness in the delivery of public services among others (Fobih, 2020, p. 126). These challenges existed across all levels and structures of government. Ghana's public sector has improved tremendously since the 1990s; however, it still requires a sustained and coordinated effort aimed at maximizing its benefits to the citizenry. In 2010, the government of Ghana came up with a new approach to public sector reforms. Previously, Government and policymakers blamed the failure of various attempts at reforms on poor institutional capacity, inadequate support from central agencies, and poor coordination between sectors (David and Derrick, 2018). NPM reforms focused on promoting efficiency and effectiveness in the Ministries, Departments, and Agencies (MDAs) and Metropolitan, Municipal, and District Assemblies (MMDAs) (Fobih, 2020, p. 126). The new reforms as such, focused on delivering public service through a new delivery model. This model is premised on a problem-solving approach that tasks various units under the municipals and district assemblies to devise performance improvement strategies that will improve service delivery (David and Derrick, 2018).

Network Governance Management Experiences

Some of the contemporary policy problems have been resolved through the application of network governance. The Lesotho experience illustrates that the country has been one of those in network governance. This is attributed to international partner agencies who had helped the country address governance issues (African Development Bank, 2006). Some of these partner agencies include the European Union, the United Kingdom's Department for International Development, and German Technical Assistance and their role is to enhance and improve the effectiveness and efficiency of public service delivery to spur economic growth and reduce poverty (African Development Bank, 2006). There are also notable developments, where NGOs and research organizations have gone into partnership with the government in a bid to initiate policies beneficial to the citizens. This displays the concept of network governance where different players contribute to the running of the country. The government of Lesotho has on many occasions instituted public sector reforms in a form of reinventing government. This sprung from the appreciation that the country requires extensive reforms to guarantee stability and prosperity (Government of the Kingdom of Lesotho, 2019).

Ethiopia made initiatives to introduce and pave the way for network governance in their public administration as it came up with decentralization waves which occurred in 1991–1995 and 2001 (Afesha, 2015). Despite the statutory gap in network governance, different informal network governance forums were formed after the enactment of the constitution. The government ministries utilized direct communication such as letters and telephone conversations between the federal government and regional government. That also strengthened the link between the federal government and the Bureau of Regional Government (Afesha, 2015). The close link and interdependence were critical in executing their responsibilities in a coordinated way. To illustrate this point, the Ministry of Health had close links with the Regional Health Bureau and this facilitated the implementation of prevention and control policies. It also assisted in making health services accessible to the communities. Ministry of Health and Health Bureau signed a memorandum of understanding to reinforce their integration and collaboration. To further strengthen network governance the Ethiopian government introduced e-governance programmes. One such programme was *WoredaNet* which is primarily a public network to connect citizens with federal and regional administrations, foster participation, enhance decision-making, improve service delivery, and foster accountability (Belachew, 2010).

Holistic Government Management Experiences

Literature on the whole-of-government or holistic government approach in Lesotho remains elusive. Fortunately, the mid-term report by the Kingdom of Lesotho, titled *Global Compact of Migration* (2022) reflects that the country has been implementing a whole-of-society and whole-of-government approach. This was spearheaded by the implementation of a new management system for migration. In this regard, the National Consultative Committee on Migration (NCC) was established which is based on a holistic government approach by ensuring synergy and alignment across administrative clusters of government and the work of different UN agencies NCC, 2022, p. 4). Further to this is another report entitled *The Lesotho We Want: Dialogue and Reforms for National Transformation* that identifies coordination gaps between Ministries and executive structures. A close analysis of the report indicates that the government seeks to reform its administration by introducing a whole-of-government approach by introducing one-stop service centres. The intention among others is to reduce waste and minimize duplication (Government of the Kingdom of Lesotho, 2019).

In 2003, the Ethiopian government embarked on a holistic governance approach to design, implement, and monitor its food security programme. In partnership with development agencies and NGOs, the government formulated and proceeded with the implementation of its food security programme which included the Productive Safety Net Program (PSNP). The Ministry of Agriculture was the frontrunner to lead the PSNP by coordinating activities regarding food security and job creation schemes. In addition, the PSNP distributed food to poor households in exchange for labour. NGOs play a vital role in the successful implementation of the PSNP by ensuring that there is better coordination in efforts (Li and Ding, 2020). The NGOs facilitate information and knowledge sharing among all actors and address many of the typical implementation challenges associated with initiatives of this nature. NGOs are also successful in communicating real-life community situations with relevant government institutions.

As far as Ghana is concerned, a study by Mukhtar (2014) indicated that the holistic government approach is a relatively new reform initiative to more successfully manage executive structures. This approach was adopted based on recommendations made by the Commonwealth Secretariat in an attempt to facilitate better achievement of national development goals for Commonwealth African countries. This recommendation is premised on the realization that better interstate coordination and alignment will improve managerial praxis and the overall goodness of government. It will also alleviate the problems associated with management in silos.

CONCLUSION

Public management remains in a state of flux as it continues to experience change. Experience has shown that no management agenda remains static. This explains the continuing efforts by governments to reinvent themselves. In terms of network governance, it is evident that it can contribute significantly to assisting African governments in attaining their various socioeconomic and developmental goals. It is also clear that governments should prioritize a more citizen-centred managerial approach in the managing of the executive structures of government.

The whole-of-government approach is yet another managerial reform initiative that African countries adopted. As an externally proposed initiative, the approach is likely to see different levels of success and possibly resistance in some counties on the continent. The success of the reform will be highly dependent on various governance factors such as political and administrative leadership, resource allocation and utilization, coordination mechanism, partnership strategies, transparency, and accountability as well overall commitment of the government of the day. Further to this, it is always important that counties in the developing world consider their context prior to implementing externally proposed reforms as adopting the wholesale only sets the reform and the countries to failure. Robinson (2015, p. 4) confirms that public sector reform efforts in developing countries need to embrace changes selectively and draw on a range of public management models that are appropriate to different contexts while putting the needs and interests of citizens at the heart of public sector reform efforts.

REFERENCES

Adebabay, A. (2011), 'Promoting and Strengthening Professionalism in the Civil Service: The Ethiopian Case', Paper Presented at the Capacity Building Workshop on Promoting Professionalism in the Public Service, 14–18 March 2011, Addis Ababa, Ethiopia.

Afesha, N. (2015), 'The Federal-state Intergovernmental Relationship in Ethiopia: Institutional Framework and its Implication on State Autonomy', *Mizan Law Review*, **9** (2), 342–366, doi.org/10.4314/mlr.v9i2.4.

African Development Bank (2006), 'Lesotho – Country Governance Profile', accessed 15 August 2023 at https://www.afdb.org/en/documents/document/2006-lesotho-country-governance-profile-13276.

Ayee, J.R.A. (2001), 'Civil Service Reform in Ghana: A Case Study of Contemporary Reform Problems in Africa', *African Journal of Political Science*, **6** (1), 1–41.

Basheka, B. (2018), *Public Sector Management: An Introduction, New Public Management Issues in Africa: Emerging Issues and Challenges*, London: Routledge.

Belachew, M. (2010), 'e-Government Initiatives in Ethiopia', Proceedings of the 4th International Conference on Theory and Practice of Electronic Governance, Beijing, China, October 25–28, 2010, doi.org/10.1145/1930321.1930332.

Blatter, J. (2012), 'Forms of Political Governance: Theoretical Foundations and Ideal Types', Working Paper Series, Global Governance and Democracy, Lucerne: University of Lucerne Press.

Borders, M. (2019), 'The Evolution of Governance in 9 Stages', accessed 12 November 2022 at https://fee.org/articles/the-evolution-of-governance-in-9-stages/.

Dassah, M.O. (2018), 'New Public Management Issues in Ghana', in Tshombe, M.T. and B.C. Basheka (eds.), *New Public Management in Africa*, New York, NY: Routledge, Taylor & Francis Group.

David, A. and S.A.A.D.O. Derrick (2018), 'Improving Public Sector Service Delivery in Ghana: The Application of Innovation and ICT', *Public Policy and Administration Research*, **8** (7), 1–9.

Debela, B.K. (2018), 'The COVID-19 Pandemic and the Ethiopian Public Administration: Responses and Challenges', in Joyce, P., F. Maron and S. Reddy (eds.), *Good Public Governance in a Global Pandemic*, IIAS Public Governance Series, Brussels: IIAS, pp. 113–124.

Dedeurwaerdere, T. (2005), 'The Contribution of Network Governance to Sustainable Development', *Chaire Développement Durable Ecole Polytechnique*, accessed 17 January 2023 at https://www.iddri.org/sites/default/files/import/publications/id_0504_dedeurwaerdere.pdf.

Dick-Sagoe, C., P. Asare-Nuamah and A.D. Dick-Sagoe (2021), 'Public Choice and Decentralised Healthcare Service Delivery in Lesotho: Assessing Improvement and Efficiency in Service Delivery', *Cogent Social Sciences*, **7** (1), 2–16, doi.org/10.1080/23311886.2021.1969737.

Du Plessis, A. and M. Molefi (2019), 'The Evolution of Lesotho's Political-Administrative Interface through its Different Regime Types: A Case Study of the Ministry of Home Affairs', *Administratio Publica*, **27** (3), 227–235.

Firmreite, A. and P. Leagreid (2005), *The Regulatory State and Executing Municipality*, Stein: Rokkan Centre for Social Studies.

Fobih, N. (2020), 'NPM Reforms in Ghana's Public Sector Management & Administration: Changing Trends in MDAs & MMDAs Functions', *Journal of Public Administration and Governance*, **10** (4), 126–139, doi.org/10.5296/jpag.v10i4.17955.

Fukuyama, F. (2013), 'What is Governance', Working Paper 314, Washington, DC: Center for Global Development, accessed 11 October 2022 at https://www.cgdev.org/sites/default/files/1426906_file_Fukuyama_What_Is_Governance.pdf.

Gangte, M. (2012), 'The Boom and Bust in New Public Management', *Global and Business Economics Research Journal*, **1** (1), 45–56.

Government of the Kingdom of Lesotho. (2019), *The Lesotho We Want: Dialogue and Reforms for National Transformation: Vision, Overview and Roadmap*, Maseru, accessed 6 December

2022 at https://www.gov.ls/wp-content/uploads/2019/07/Lesotho-Reforms-Framework-and-Road-Map-Final-Draft-1-30-November-2017.pdf.

Gregory, R. and S. Robert (2006), *Theoretical Faith and Practical in the New Zealand*, Cheltenham, UK and Northampton, MA, USA: Edward Elgar Publishing.

Gruening, G. (2001), 'Origin and Theoretical Basis of New Public Management', *International Public Management Journal*, **4** (1), 1–25, doi.org/10.1016/S1096-7494(01)00041-1.

Guenduez, A.A. (2022), 'Digital Government', in Kuno, S. (ed.), *Elgar Encyclopaedia of Public Management*, Cheltenham, UK and Northampton, MA, USA: Edward Elgar Publishing, pp. 222–228.

Gumede, N. and K.B. Dipholo (2014), 'Governance, Restructuring and the New Public Management Reform: South African Perspectives', *Journal of Educational and Social Research*, **4** (6), a43, doi.org/10.5901/jesr.2014.v4n6p43.

Hope, K.R. (2001), 'The New Public Management: Context and Practice in Africa', *International Public Management Journal*, **4** (2), 119–134.

Hughes, O. (2019), *Public Management and Administration*, London: Red Globe Press.

Idowu, H.A. (2020), 'Understanding Governance Challenges in Africa', in Farazmand, A. (ed.), *Global Encyclopaedia of Public Administration, Public Policy, and Governance*, Cham: Springer International Publishing, accessed 25 October 2022 at https://doi.org/10.1007/978-3-319-31816-5_4013.

Junki, K. (2006), 'Network Governance and Networked Networks', *International Review of Public Administration*, **11** (1), 19–34, doi.org/10.1080/12294659.2006.10805075.

Kaunda, J.M. (2004), *Public Sector Reforms*, Gaborone: BIDPA Briefing.

Kearney, C.R and S.W. Hays (1998), 'Reinventing Government, The New Public Management and Civil Service Systems in International Perspective: The Danger of Throwing the Baby Out with the Bathwater', *Review of Public Personnel Administration*, **18** (4), 38–54, doi.org/10.1177/0734371X9801800404.

Kingdom of Lesotho. (2022), 'The Kingdom of Lesotho Global Compact of Migration (GCM) Mid-term Report', accessed 5 December 2022 at https://migrationnetwork.un.org/sites/g/files/tmzbdl416/files/docs/gs_report_on_gcm_progress_lesotho_final_002.pdf.

Klausen, K.K. (2022), 'Public Governance and Public Management', in Kuno, S. (ed.), *Elgar Encyclopedia of Public Management*, Cheltenham, UK and Northampton, MA, USA: Edward Elgar Publishing, pp. 355–359.

Klijn, E.H. (2012), 'Public Management and Governance: A Comparison of Two Paradigms to Deal with Modern Complex Problems', in Levi Faur, D. (ed.), *The Oxford Handbook of Governance*, Oxford: Oxford University Press, pp. 201–214.

Kohnová, L. and N. Salajová (2019), 'Industrial Revolutions and their Impact on Managerial Practice: Learning from the Past', *Problems and Perspectives in Management*, **17** (2), 462–478, doi.org/10.21511/ppm.17(2).2019.36.

Li, X. and Y. Ding (2020), 'Holistic Government for Sustainable Service: Reshaping Government–Enterprise Relationships in China's Digital Government Context', *International Journal for Environmental Research and Public Health*, **17** (5), 117–178, doi.org/10.3390/ijerph17051778.

Lynn, L.E. (1998), 'The New Public Management: How to Transform a Theme into a Legacy', *Public Administration Review*, **58** (3), 231–237.

Mengesha, G.H. and R.K. Common (2006), 'Civil Service Reform in Ethiopia: Success in Two Ministries', Research Memorandum 59, accessed 15 August 2023 at https://www.researchgate.net/publication/237523633_Civil_Service_Reform_in_Ethiopia_Success_in_two_ministries.

Mofuoa, K.V. (2005), *Local Governance in Lesotho: In Search of an Appropriate Format*, EISA Occasional Paper Number 33, June 2005, accessed 6 December 2022 at https://www.semanticscholar.org/paper/Local-Governance-in-Lesotho%3A-In-Search-of-an-Format-Mofuoa/8480909e54265506ef7a4eecd71f6dd12bec05f2.

Mohajane, H.K. (2019), 'The First Industrial Revolution: Creation of a New Global Human Era', *Journal of Social Sciences and Humanities*, **5** (4), 377–387.

Molefhe, K. and T. Molokwane (2018), *New Public Management in Botswana – New Public Management in Africa*, London: Routledge, Taylor & Francis Group.

Molokwane, T. (2019), 'New Public Management in Botswana: Contemporary Issues and Lessons', *African Journal of Public Affairs*, **11** (1), 48–63.

Monyane, C. (2009), *The Kingdom of Lesotho: An Assessment of Problems in Democratic Consolidation*, unpublished PhD Thesis, University of Stellenbosch, accessed 1 November 2022 at https://core.ac.uk/download/pdf/37319062.pdf.

Mothetho, C.D. (2017), 'Network Governance In The Tshwane Metropolitan Municipality', unpublished Master dissertation, Wits School of Governance, Faculty of Commerce, Law and Management, Johannesburg.

Mothusi, B. (2008), 'Public Sector Reforms and Managing Change in Botswana: The Case of Performance Management System (PMS)', Doctoral dissertation, Cleveland State University. OhioLINK Electronic Theses and Dissertations Center. Available at http://rave.ohiolink.edu/etdc/view?acc_num=csu1213282797.

Motshegwa, B. (2017), 'An Assessment of the Evolution of the Public Sector in Botswana', *Botswana Journal of Business*, **10** (1), 38–52.

Mukhtar, M.I. (2014), 'Whole of Government Approach to Achieving National Development Goals: The Reform Managerial Roles and Processes in Ghana', *Review of Public Administration and Management*, **2** (1), 2–9, doi.org/10.4172/2315-7844.1000141.

Namara, R.B., G.K. Karyeija and B.C. Mubangizi (2015), 'View of Network Governance and Capacity of Local Governments to Deliver LED in Uganda', *Commonwealth Journal of Local Governance*, **18**, 82–103, doi.org/10.5130/cjlg.v0i18.4844.

Noordegraaf, M. (2022), 'Professionalism in Public Management', in Kuno, S. (ed.), *Elgar Encyclopedia of Public Management*, Cheltenham, UK and Northampton, MA, USA: Edward Elgar Publishing, pp. 158–172.

Obasi, I.N. and M.H. Lekorwe (2014), 'Citizen Engagement in Public Policymaking Process in Africa: The Case of Botswana', *Public Policy and Administration Research*, **3** (4), 1–11.

Osborne, S. (2010), 'The (New) Public Governance: A Suitable Case for Treatment?', in Osborne, S. (ed.), *The New Public Governance: Emerging Perspectives on the Theory and Practice of Public Governance*, Abingdon: Routledge, pp. 1–16.

Osborne, S.P. (2005), 'Introducing the (New) Public Governance: A suitable case for treatment?', in Pierre, J. and B.G. Peters (eds.), *The New Public Governance? Governing Complex Societies: Trajectories and Scenarios*, New York, NY: Palgrave McMillan, pp. 17–32.

Ouden, T.D. (2015), 'A Contribution to the Understanding and Strengthening of Network Governance: A Theoretical and Empirical Exploration of Governance Capabilities', Master of Science thesis, Wageningen University, The Netherlands, accessed 17 January 2023 at https://edepot.wur.nl/347962.

Paulos, C. (2001), 'The Challenges of Civil Service Reform in Ethiopia: Initial Observations', *The Eastern Africa Social Science Review*, **17** (1), 79–102.

Pfiffner, J.P. (2004), 'Traditional Public Administration versus the New Public Management: Accountability versus Efficiency', in Benz, A., H. Siedentopf and K.P. Sommermann (eds.), *Institutionenbildung in Regierung und Verwaltung*, Berlin: Festschrift fur Klaus Konig, pp. 1–2.

Phago, K.G. and L.P. Malan (2004), 'Public Private Partnerships (PPPs) and their Role in Extending Access to Local Governance', *Journal of Public Administration*, **39** (1), 481–491.

Plumptre, T. and J. Graham (1999), *Governance and Good Governance: International and Aboriginal Perspectives*, accessed 7 December 2022 at https://www.files.ethz.ch/isn/122184/govgoodgov.pdf.

Pollitt, C. and G. Bouckaert (2017), *Public Management Reform. A Comparative Analysis – into the Age of Austerity*, 4th ed., Oxford: Oxford University Press.

Pollitt, C., S. van Thiel and V. Homburg (2007), *New Public Management in Europe*, Basingstoke: Palgrave.

PwC. (2017), 'Fourth Industrial Revolution for the Earth: Harnessing the 4th Industrial Revolution for Sustainable Emerging Cities', accessed 17 January 2023 at https://www.pwc.com/gx/en/sustainability/assets/4ir-for-the-earth.pdf.

Renwu, T. and Z. Guoqin (2012), 'The Structural Logic of the Holistic Governance and its Response to Political Fragmentation', *Crisis Management in the Time of Changing World*, **33** (1), 1–7.

Republic of Botswana. (2002), *Botswana Public Service: Implementation of Performance Management System (PMS): The PMS Philosophy Document*, Gaborone: Government Printer.

Rigaud, B. (2012), 'Public Governance', in Côté, L. and J.-F. Savard (eds.), *Encyclopedic Dictionary of Public Administration*, accessed 7 December at https://dictionnaire.enap.ca/dictionnaire/docs/definitions/definitions_anglais/public_governance.pdf.

Rigaud, B. and L. Côté (2011), 'Comparer l'État québécois: pertinence et faisabilité', *Politique et sociétés*, **30** (1), 19–41, doi.org/10.7202/1006057ar.

Robinson, M. (2015), *From Old Public Administration to the New Public Service, Implications for Public Sector Reform in Developing Countries*, New York, NY: United Nations Development Fund.

Shafritz, J.M. and A.C. Hyde (2017), *Classics of Public Administration*, 8th ed., New York, NY: Cengage Learning.

Schedler, K. (2022), 'New Public Management', in Kuno, S. (ed.), *Elgar Encyclopedia of Public Management*, Cheltenham, UK and Northampton, MA, USA: Edward Elgar Publishing, pp. 16–18.

Schwab, K. (2016), *The Fourth Industrial Revolution*, World Economic Forum, Switzerland, accessed 16 January 2023 at https://www.weforum.org/about/the-fourth-industrial-revolution-by-klaus-schwab.

Schwab, D. (2019), 'How Artificial Intelligence is Redefining the Role of the Manager', Davos World Economic Forum, accessed 17 January 2023 at https://www.weforum.org/agenda/2019/11/how-artificial-intelligence-is-redefining-the-roleof-manager/.

Selfridge, P., V.R. Ferose and A. Kumar (2018), 'From Digital Government to Intelligent Government', accessed 15 October 2022 at https://www.digitalistmag.com/digital-economy/2018/10/24/from-digital-government-to-intelligent-government-06191223.

Simon, H.A. (1976), *Administrative Behavior: A Study of Decision-Making in Administrative Organisation*, 3rd ed., New York, NY: The Free Press.

Tshombe, L.M., T. Molokwane and A. Nduhura (2022), 'Africa – Public Management Concepts and Developments', in Kuno, S. (ed.), *Elgar Encyclopedia of Public Management*, Cheltenham, UK and Northampton, MA, USA: Edward Elgar Publishing, pp. 55–71.

United Nations Development Group. (2011), *Results-Based Management Handbook: Harmonizing RBM Concepts and Approaches for Improved Development Results at Country Level*, New York, NY: United Nations.

Van der Waldt, G. (2014a), 'Towards the Construction of Knowledge in Public Governance as Field of Scientific Enquiry', *International Journal of Humanities and Social Sciences (IJHSS)*, **4** (3), 67–80.

Van der Waldt, G. (2014b), 'Public Administration and Transdisciplinarity: A Modalistic Approach toward Knowledge Co-Construction', *International Journal of Humanities and Social Science*, **4** (6), 120–134.

Van der Waldt, G. (2023), *Managing for Excellence in the Public Sector*, 4th ed., Cape Town: Juta.

Vigoda, E. (2002), 'From Responsiveness to Collaboration: Governance, Citizens, and the Next Generation of Public Administration', *Public Administration Review*, **62** (5), 527–540.

Vyas-Doorgapersad, S. (2011), 'Paradigm Shift from the New Public Administration to New Public Management: Theory and Practice in Africa', *The Journal of Transdisciplinary Research in Southern Africa*, **7** (2), a240, doi.org/10.4102/td.v7i2.240.

Watson, V.B. (2020), 'The Fourth Industrial Revolution and its Discontents: Governance, Big Tech, and the Digitization of Geopolitics', in Vuving, A.L. (ed.), *Hindsight, Insight, Foresight: Thinking About Security in the Indo-Pacific*, Honolulu: Daniel K. Inouye Asia-Pacific Center for Security Studies, pp. 3–11.

Weiss, T.G. (2000), 'Governance, Good Governance and Global Governance: Conceptual and Actual Challenges', *Third World Quarterly*, **21** (5), 795–814, doi.org/10.1080/713701075.

World Bank Group. (2017), 'Lesotho: Public Health Sector Expenditure Review', Washington, DC: World Bank Group and UNICEF.

World Bank. (1992), *Governance and Development*, accessed 2 December 2022 at https://elibrary.worldbank.org/doi/abs/10.1596/0-8213-2094-7.

Wren, D.A. (2009), *The Evolution of Management Thought*, Campbell, CA: George Hoffman.

Wyngaard, R. and P. Hendricks (2010), 'South Africa's King III: Highlighting the Need for a Separate Non-Profit Governance Code', *International Journal of Civil Society Law*, **8** (2), 1–13.

Yang, H. (2021), 'Holistic Governance: Explanatory Framework', in Yang, H. (ed.), *Urban Governance in Transition*, London: Springer, pp. 57–95.

Yildiz, M. (2007), 'E-government Research: Reviewing the Literature, Limitations, and Ways Forward', *Government Information Quarterly*, **24** (3), 646–665, doi.org/10.1016/j.giq.2007.01.002.

Zhou, G. and H. Zvoushe (2018), 'New Public Management Issues in Zimbabwe', in Tshombe, M.T. and B.C. Basheka (eds.), *New Public Management in Africa*, New York, NY: Routledge, Taylor & Francis Group, pp. 211–221.

2. Public management in Africa

Benon C. Basheka

INTRODUCTION

Africa, through its 54 member states, is a diverse continent whose systems for managing public affairs reveal some peculiarities. However, due to almost similar colonial history, there are some fundamental resemblances. Moreover, governments have a similar goal, that of promoting the general welfare and prosperity of society through service delivery. The variations in Africa's public management systems emerged mainly due to variations in the administrative systems, approaches, and organizational arrangements in implementing public policies. Africa is also intimately part of the world's economic and political system and subject to influences from other countries. The global system also has undisputed influence on the continent's public management systems and structures. Despite these influences, there are some features that make public management in Africa quite unique. Most public management discourses tend to ignore this reality and often get obsessed with Western-style philosophies and approaches to public management thereby overshadowing indigenous, homegrown governance solutions.

This chapter attempts to craft a general framework for probing public management praxis as differentiated from conventional business management, notwithstanding the fact that business management has since the 1980s provided fundamental best practice for the management of public affairs in Africa. The chapter further reveals some common features that shape public management systems in Africa, outlines the typical pitfalls of these systems, and highlights some interventions required to address existing deficiencies in Africa's systems of governance.

TOWARDS A CONCEPTUAL FRAMEWORK FOR UNDERSTANDING PUBLIC MANAGEMENT

Curious analysts would find that history reminds us that human civilizations require key institutions to render certain services and perform essential functions. The church, the state (Government), the family, and businesses have proved to be some of these key institutions and have always been important players in the public management domain. Other institutions such as civil society organizations, professional associations, the media, policy think-tanks, and private sector enterprises also jointly and individually play a significant role in the general management of public affairs. Government as a key societal institution was called upon to promote both public interest and the common good through appropriate policies, structures, systems, processes, and procedures. The efficient and effective management of these functions is the responsibility of senior public officials. These officials are typically categorized as top, middle, and operational managers tasked with directing all activities and functions of civil servants.

The scholarly field charged with the analysis of government's role in society as well as the managerial processes and functions of senior officials is public management (PM). An effort to craft a conceptual framework for the analysis of public management in Africa presents its own difficulties. The first difficulty is the unique context in which public management as a practice in Africa finds itself where balance between the western ideologies and indigenous values unique to Africa has to be put into sharp focus. Secondly, the expansive scope of public management presents a challenge since any sharp delineation of the subject domain and any effort to ringfence its corpus of knowledge may lead to reductionism (Van der Waldt, 2019). To circumvent these conceptual complexities, it makes sense to differentiate between the private (business) and the public sectors as well as between state and non-state actors. These sectors and actors complement each other in society but have different objectives.

The basic objective of private sector enterprises is to make a profit for shareholders and investors. Businesses aim at growth and sustainability as the other two primary goals in addition to profitability (Gildenhuys and Knipe, 2000, p. 123). The management approaches and philosophies in the private sector strive to balance competing interests but at no time can businesses compromise profitability, growth, and sustainability (Shaw, 2008). Business management is the discipline broadly concerned with probing the processes and systems of these enterprises. In contrast, the primary motive of the public sector is service delivery. PM as the study of the public sector is thus concerned with the scrutiny of roles, responsibilities, processes, and functions of public managers. Broadly speaking, PM is generally regarded as an integrative discipline and a field whose understanding and description requires knowledge from various other references of adjacent disciplines (Van der Waldt, 2014b). Scholars often allude to this field being multidisciplinary, interdisciplinary, and transdisciplinary (MIT). Transdisciplinarity of PM is important because the real complex nature of managing public affairs demands this multiple framework and given its political nature the field of public management has to rely on multiple disciplines (Van der Waldt, 2014a, p. 122). It is undisputed that PM needs to borrow from several disciplines to exercise its broad mandate. Within the many disciplines, law is one such discipline which intimately offers us a vital context in which public management is undertaken. The earliest philosophers like Socrates, Aristotle, and Plato, in their ideological philosophies, pointed out the value of law in managing society. Almost all public administration functions like public finance, personnel management, budget management, public procurement, and international affairs are conducted based on law (Hughes, 2003) and law facilitates public managers in executing their mandates and resolving disputes among administrative units. Law in its broad sense can be classified as public and private law or civil and criminal law. Law can also be substantive law or procedural law. Some countries have written laws while others have unwritten laws for managing public affairs. Civil law is that branch of law that deals with disputes between individuals, organizations, or between the two, in which compensation is awarded to the victim, while criminal law deals with crimes and the legal punishment of criminal offences. Law is not necessarily what is written in statutes and law books. Customs and decisions of judicial officers constitute law. Administrative circulars and practices may equally constitute rules and guidelines for undertaking certain functions. Customary practices constitute an important legal structure for managing public affairs in both domestic and international spectrums. Within individual countries in Africa, a custom which prohibits marriage of blood relatives is an important known principle for managing that field of public management. A custom on how the dead should be handled in most African countries is in existence and the rights of the dead are enforced by public managers.

Such customs are integrated with modern public management practices. Marriage, birth, and death certificates are key public management documents which help in the execution of critical public management functions (Mugambi, 2016).

PM is commonly regarded as both an art and a science. The scientific nature of PM was a key ideological school of thought in the early stages of the paradigmatic development of the field of study. Mainly due to the emergence of postmodernism, behaviourism, and interpretivism as research traditions, PM evolved to also incorporate 'art' dimensions into conventional scientific traditions. The artistic dimensions concern issues such as insight, intuition, creativity, innovation, vision, and inspiration of public officials.

The complexities associated with the demarcation of PM are further challenged by the fact that it is both a field of practice and an academic discipline. This makes the field so expansive that covering its full scope is an uphill task. The scope of public management as practice, whether in Africa or otherwise, covers every aspect of human life. From birth through human growth and life events and up to the death of human beings, public management is inescapable (Shepherd, 2006). In every country there must be a good public management system for records of birth, citizenships, marriage, businesses, and death, among others. A well-developed and functioning civil registration system ensures the registration of all vital events and issuance of relevant certificates as proof of such registration prompt efficient government planning, effective use of resources and aid, and more accurate monitoring of progress towards achieving the planned interventions. Public management as a practice also conveys the intentions of government in society and its presence is felt before birth, during the actual birth, growth, death, and even after death. Public management thus provides the machinery in which governments govern and manage state affairs. The chain and hierarchy of public managers in the government machinery concerned with maintaining law and order and the provision of other government services provide an avenue through which public management is exercisable. PM as a study domain scrutinizes this machinery of the state and suggests new approaches, models, methods, and techniques for the continuous improvement of government systems, structures, and processes. PM is thus located within the province of the public sector but due to the changing context in which governments operate, it serves a directing and regulatory role to the private sector. Similarly, business enterprises may be engaged in the delivery of goods and services conventionally residing under the auspices of the public sector. Through network forms of governance, public-private partnerships and compliance with corporate social responsibilities businesses may transcend the traditional 'private' domain to play a role in the public arena. Just like businesses, civil society organizations, community-based organizations, and non-governmental organizations can be categorized as non-state actors, although they increasingly play a significant role in governance.

It is evident that the scope of activities and range of demands placed on contemporary public managers have expanded beyond their traditional nature (Vyas-Doorgapersad, Tshombe and Ababio, 2017). The entry of new actors in the public sphere including the private sector, civil society organizations, religious institutions, international agencies, the media, and other actors has expanded the governance domain and associated management praxis. The actors who used to be previously regarded as 'outsiders' in public service delivery have found their way inside the apparatus for managing public affairs (Ayee, 2012). These new entrants into the traditional domain of government have placed more regulatory responsibilities on public managers thereby expanding the scope of the field. The effects of globalization processes and the automation of most service delivery processes have brought new unimagined dimensions that would hardly be considered as part of what constitutes the scope of PM. E-(electronic) service delivery systems and technological advancement have also created new managerial applications and tools.

Designing a conceptual framework is furthermore complicated by the fact that PM goes beyond the nature and scope of individual states. It is rather interwoven within the geopolitical and economic international system (Hague and Harrop, 2010, p. 14). Public management practices in one continent or state may thus be strongly influenced by trends and events in others. To accommodate this reality several emergent approaches and governance norms have birthed a more detailed analysis of concepts like statehood, sovereignty, state interventionism, territorial integrity, self-determination, and the use of legitimate force (MacFarlane and Sabanadze, 2013, p. 609). For example, legitimate force in states concerns matters such as individual and collective conflict, the use of the police and military in political unrest, safety and security concerns, and self-defence. As far as the latter is concerned, Martyn (2002) argues that self-defence is generally required to conform to three elements: (a) Was the state's response necessary? (b) Was the state's response proportionate? and (c) Was the state's response immediate; in other words, did the imminence of a threatening situation warrant such rapid response? These elements are commonly debated in modern public international law.

To summarize this part of the exposition of PM, dimensions of a conceptual framework for PM should at least incorporate the following:

- Dynamics between public and private sector actors.
- The interrelationship between public management as a practice and Public Management as a study domain.
- The inter-, multi-, and transdisciplinary nature of the field of study.
- The nature and scope of the network of state and non-state actors in government affairs.
- The artistic and scientific dimensions of the discipline.
- Narrow state dimensions as well as global, international arena settings.
- The nature and scope of PM functions, skills, and applications.
- Complexities brought about by issues such as globalization, technological advancement, and environmental concerns.

Key Features of Public Management

The meaning, nature, scope, functions, and concept of PM cannot be understood without considering notions of the state and government. Both concepts have not been static and scholars and policymakers have deliberated on their exact meaning and application (Cheshire, Higgins and Lawrence, 2007, p. 1). The central feature of the distinction between the state and government relates to how power and authority are exercised. The concept of 'state' refers to a politically organized society with defined territorial boundaries and a government that exercises control over its citizens and territory. It is the concept of a sovereign entity with a centralized authority, a permanent population, and defined territories. The concept of 'government' refers to the group of people or institutions that hold authority and make decisions for a state. It refers to the means by which a state is controlled, maintained, and regulated. It is the institutional apparatus through which the state carries out its policies and makes decisions that affect society and its citizens. The state is thus the entity, and the government is the means by which the state is governed.

Public management in its broad usage implies the systems, structures, processes, and actors involved and accountable for managing public affairs. As a practice, it has developed as part of the evolving field of public administration. The managerial dimensions of public administration gained significant prominence during the 1980s and relate to process and implementation arrangements for managing the public value, i.e. what benefits society (Gildenhuys and Knipe, 2000, p. 133). Public managers should be aware that they occupy their offices to serve the people in constructive and positive ways and thereby upholding values such as:

- Integrity: upholding ethical and moral standards in decision-making and behaviour.
- Responsibility: being accountable to the public for decisions and actions and for policy programme effectiveness.
- Impartiality: making decisions objectively and without political or personal bias.
- Transparency: ensuring open and accessible government processes.
- Efficiency: maximizing resources and minimizing waste in delivering services.
- Effectiveness: delivering services that meet the needs and expectations of the public.
- Representativeness: reflecting the diversity of the community in decision-making and service delivery.
- Responsiveness: being attentive to the needs and concerns of the public.
- Development: promoting economic and social progress for the community.
- Collaboration: working with other organizations and the public to achieve common goals.
- Public participation: engage and collaborate with citizens as partners in decision-making.

The demands placed on the adherence to these values make government institutions different from business organizations and, indeed, there should be some activities purely to be performed by the public sector and those to be performed solely by the private sector. Unlike business management driven by profiteering, public management is driven by the common good, social well-being, and service delivery excellence. Public value has been used to measure the total impact of government activities to create value for its citizens (Kelly et al., 2002) and it is helpful for governments to develop good relationships with citizens by connecting the activities and decisions of government to the needs of the people. Public value is a philosophy of public management in which public managers should think and act strategically to create public value, and success is drawn from initiating and reshaping public sector enterprises in ways that increase their value to the public (Staples, 2010).

PM as a discipline concerns scrutiny of the successful management of departments, entities, and agencies of government for the benefit of society. It also entails studying managerial functions employed during the design and implementation of public policies and programmes. Especially since the 1980s, governments have increasingly applied a more business-like style for the management of their affairs. This new style is commonly referred to as New Public Management (NPM) (Rubakula, 2014). This demands special skills and the adaption of conventional PM theories and approaches. It also entails the adoption and application of sound governance principles (Gildenhuys and Knipe, 2000, p. 124).

Several PM scholars have defined and dissected the key features of public management. Guta (2012), for example, asserts that public management represents the set of processes and management relations, well defined, which exist between the components of the administrative system by which the laws are put into force and/or the activities in the delivery of services satisfying the public interest are planned, organized, coordinated, managed, and supervised.

From his definition, public management is seen to relate to the orderliness of the systems of government intended to serve citizens. The definition also speaks of a need to have a coordinated power centre for driving the activities of a public management structure. On this same subject, Pollitt (2016, p. xi) makes a distinction between public management and public administration. The author characterizes the importance of public management to society. In this endeavour, Pollitt (2016, p. xi) connects the importance of public management to its scope by stating as follows:

> If you want to specifically deal with matters of pressing international, national and local concern, then study public management. If you would like to do field research that involves dedicated, highly skilled professionals working for a fairer, less hazardous and more caring society, then study public management. If you are interested in where all the taxpayer's money goes and how people are held accountable for its spending or not, then study public management. If you are interested in the causes and effects of government corruption, and wondering why some countries are evidently more prone to this cancer than others, then study public management. If you want to know more about the largest and most powerful organisations that have existed for the last 100 years, then study Public Management.

Some important observations emerge from the above description on the nature, function, purpose, and functioning of public management. The description also speaks to the ideological orientation of public management in as far as its financing is concerned. The above describes what constitutes the scope and parameters of public management. This one-sided view, however, helps us draw some important lessons:

- Scope of public management: the scope of public management is wide and touches every corner of human existence.
- Societal order: public management exists for the betterment of society and good public management creates social order where every member of society can feel valued. Public management in this sense holds society together.
- Resilience of public management: public management has existed in the past, is present today, and will continue to exist. Depending on the historical and modern situations, only the format and actors engaged may change.
- Evils (misdeeds) of public management: whereas public management is well-intentioned, evils like corruption emerge which, if uncontrolled, dilute its societal benefits.
- Institutions of the state: public management facilitates the establishment and nurturing of strong state institutions.
- Duality of public management: public management is both a theory (field of academic study) and a field of practice. Their dual nature means they go hand in hand, and changes in practices and academic study influence one another.
- Skills and competences: public managers require multiple skills and a set of competences for them to discharge their duty to the public. Whereas some of these can be acquired through training in schools of public managers, others emerge from practical work.
- Integrative nature: the definition and description by the author speaks of a broad spectrum of disciplines which constitute the province of public management.

From these deliberations, it is evident that several key features of public management both as a practice and as an academic field are evident. Figure 2.1 portrays some of these key features.

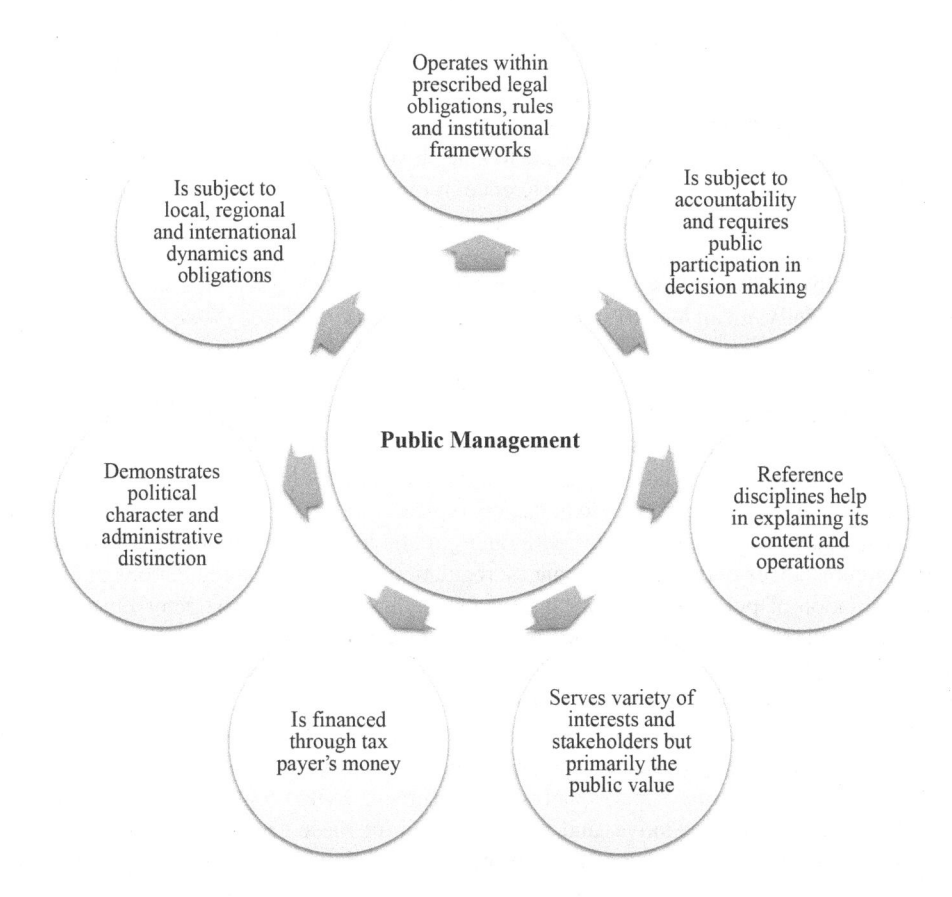

Source: Author's own construction.

Figure 2.1   Key features of public management

An analysis of these key features and the application of public management values reveals that public management does not always portray a positive picture. There are unfortunately misdeeds of public managers that erode public trust in government. In this regard, Ayee (2012, p. 86) remarks that,

> even though the public sector in African countries was expected to spearhead socioeconomic development to reduce poverty, it has proved largely ineffective in performing this task. Some of the reasons for this ineffectiveness are excessive politicization, lack of accountability and representation, inability to promote the public interest and authoritarian tendencies.

In addition, Pollitt (2016) confirms that this ineffectiveness of public management has led to the call for a redefinition of the role of the public sector in society.

There are several reasons why the public perception of public managers may be negative, including:

- Corruption and unethical behaviour: reports of corruption and unethical behaviour by public managers can damage their reputation and lead to negative public perception.
- Lack of accountability and transparency: public managers may be perceived as lacking accountability and transparency, leading to mistrust and a negative image.
- Inefficient bureaucracy: a bureaucratic and inefficient public sector can lead to dissatisfaction among citizens and contribute to a negative image of public managers.
- Political interference: political interference in the workings of the public sector can lead to a negative perception of public managers, who may be seen as serving the interests of politicians rather than the public.
- Poor delivery of services: if public managers fail to deliver essential services effectively and efficiently, it can lead to a negative public perception.

These are some of the reasons why public managers may have a negative image, but it is important to note that there are also many dedicated and hard-working public managers who are making a positive impact in their communities.

It is at this stage appropriate to pay some attention to the 'who' and 'what' dimensions of managers in the public sector. Public managers typically do what Guta (2012, p. 96) describes as 'the act of adopting normative acts with inner juristic force, the adoption of laws or according to circumstances of decrees, ordinances, regulations, organisation regulations or effective implementation of public services'. Public management used to be characterized under the traditional wide field of public administration, but now focuses mainly on managerial skills, functions, applications, tools, and methods. It also considers the different managerial echelons such as top (senior), middle, and operational (supervisors) managers who, depending on their level of seniority perform strategic, tactical, and operational roles in the machinery of the state. Furthermore, government has numerous institutions in central (national), regional (provincial), and local (municipal) spheres of government. It also comprises three main arms, namely the executive, legislative, and judiciary. Each of these arms consists of institutions that are managed by skilled and competent officials. Good public managers ought to be men and women with the skills and competencies to plan, organize, motivate, communicate, lead, staff, control, and report on how public resources allocated for a public purpose are mobilized and expended. Irrespective of their position, all public managers are called upon to serve the public and uphold the values and tenets of good governance.

PECULIARITY OF PUBLIC MANAGEMENT IN AFRICA

The peculiarity of PM in Africa should be considered in terms of the unique features of public management as practised in governments on the continent. While there may be resemblance of some of the features to public management to those beyond Africa, this section is concerned with what can be described as indigenous managerial systems of government. Western public management systems have tended to be biased against African values and practices and this has led to a neglect of what was the foundation of African public management systems. Undisputedly, African public management systems have historically been a target of foreign exploitation (Rutanga, 2011). Scholars such as Grillo, Klinken and Ndzovu (2019) argue that it was only in the late 19th century that Africans themselves, especially led by intellectuals in the diaspora, began to appropriate the ideas of what came to be known as Pan-Africanism.

Pan-Africanism can be regarded as a political and social movement that seeks to unify and empower people of African descent around the world, with the goal of promoting their common interests and issues. It generally aims to build solidarity and cooperation among African nations and people and to promote the cultural, social, and economic development of Africa. Pan-Africanism also seeks to address the legacy of colonialism, slavery, and discrimination against people of African descent, and to work towards greater autonomy and independence for Africa and its diaspora.

The African diaspora has had a significant influence on public management in Africa. On this subject, Rutanga (2011, p. 30) holds that had it not been for the intellectual efforts of the African diaspora to salvage Africa from western ideologies through pan-African projects, not much would have been known about Africa's governance, cultural, and social systems. The pan-Africanists have made efforts in probing backwards into the origins and development of humankind with the view of historically locating its origins and the systems which existed for public affairs. Through the dominant Western narrative, managerialism was believed to offer a more efficient and more direct approach to public sector management. This belief was mainly due to the opinion that it would address inefficiencies and ineffectiveness which had come to characterize the traditional bureaucratic model for public administration. Countries across the globe were encouraged to adopt the principles of managerialism in government; African countries were not left out of this movement, and some governments have adopted the principles of the New Public Management (NPM) paradigm. It is hence crucial that the perceived successes and failures of NPM in Africa be assessed. It should be noted that the Western narrative has generally ignored the unique features of African governance systems in general and public management in particular.

Public management in Africa has unique features which ought to inform any assessment of indigenous governance systems. Some of the unique features which require scholarly attention include the following:

- Diversity: African countries are diverse with multiple tribal groupings and societies divided by ethnicity, religion, and other social characteristics. These make public management not only a complex undertaking but a challenging one.
- Openness and integrity: honesty, sincerity, truthfulness, compassion, empathy, dignity, and respect for others have been key values in the African public sphere (Ncube, 2010). African Chiefs (commonly perceived as public managers) have long been expected to be honest and dignified leaders of society, ruling with compassion and empathy for the betterment of their people in primitive times. These were key qualities people looked for in their leaders in indigenous Africa.
- Unity and togetherness: these concepts accentuate brotherhood, togetherness, a harmonious community, peacefulness, synonymous, mutually reinforcing, complementary community, and as a picture of an ideal society. The Ubuntu belief system in indigenous public administration reflects how the African culture and way of life have been crafted around the principles of mutuality, unity, and kinship.
- Protection of human rights: traditionally, Africa's systems of managing public affairs have valued the rights of people. This is a subjection assertion as the continent itself has had situations of abuse of people's rights. Generally, an African Chief had to ensure that all members of society were treated with respect, integrity and had their rights to self-determination. Africans have long cherished a desire to live on as different racial and

ethnic groups with their own cultures, languages, values, and ways of life, many of them still endure grave difficulties and daily human rights violations.

- Role of elders in society: African systems have cherished the role of elders in the management of public affairs. A solid foundation for a strong self-image and a healthy identity was provided by traditional teachings and knowledge and elders were the educators of the time. Elders in the current structure of African public management represent an essential connection with the past. They are keepers of community knowledge and supporters of its collective spirit. Elders serve as role models for fostering a good sense of cultural identity and connections to indigenous customs, values, and practices such as truthfulness, compassion, empathy, dignity, and respect.
- Unwritten norms: probably the most basic description of culture is that it entails the unwritten norms values and behaviour that direct societies. It may be argued that unwritten norms are behavioural restraints imposed in indigenous African communities but are not expressed or officially recorded. They typically exist in an unheard and unwritten manner. These social norms are the unspoken guidelines for what is proper or acceptable in specific groups or cultures. They frequently involve things people 'just know' to be true or appropriate, and they are frequently upheld by others through rewards or penalties, such as social exclusion. In African traditional events, for instance, one should wait for elderly people to select seats rather than squabbling for them.

To further probe the peculiarity of PM in Africa, it is helpful to consider trends and shifts prior to, during, and after the colonial era. These considerations receive attention in the next subsections.

Public Management in Precolonial Africa

Whereas most literature on African public administration and management systems tends to highlight the colonial setting and overlook this precolonial Africa, this period also presented some features which characterize how public affairs were handled. In fact, Gennaioli and Rainer (2007) suggest that the period had some stronger political institutions than those that follow during colonialism. This is mainly due to the 'foreign' nature of these institutions and the implementation of Western modernization programmes in government. The key feature of precolonial public management was that it was coordinated by dominant ethnic groups through local chiefs.

Indigenous systems refer to systems which are original and intrinsic to a place (Grillo et al., 2019, p. 17). It also means what is local as opposed to what is imported or transplanted, foreign or alien. Indigenous public management in the African context relates to the systems that existed before colonialism. Zeleza (2006, p. 197) argues that notions of 'indigenous' are often construed as 'primitive, crude, rudimentary, undeveloped or unsophisticated', as suggested in some Western literature. Public management in precolonial Africa was strongly based on indigenous values, practices, systems, and knowledge of the respective communities. This period was also characterized by disruptions in sound public management. For example, there was a tendency for warlord rulers and their allies to disrupt existing authority. Such rulers ignored the significance of sound governance practices and obstructed state power by controlling markets and other resources for their expansionist power agenda (Reno, 1998).

A further characteristic of precolonial public management was that governance systems were largely based on community participation, consensus-building, and people-centred decision-making. Consultation was (and still largely is) a key element of public management. The management of public affairs was also connected to the religious beliefs of particular communities. Public managers took decisions with due cognisance of local traditions, customs, and indigenous knowledge and belief systems. Decisions were seen as the collective contributions and shared commitment of citizens and public institutions (Basheka and Auriacombe, 2019).

The role of government bureaucracies in these early kingdoms was mainly to facilitate the transfer of resources from different geographical areas to the king's or chief's court. This typically entailed the administration of irrigation systems and agricultural output. More recently, it also included the administration of construction work and wealth transfers (i.e. taxes). It should also be noted that before the colonial enterprise, indigenous healers had intimate botanical knowledge of the environment including of plants and their healing properties. Indigenous farmers were also thoroughly acquainted with the vegetation, soil, and climatic conditions of a place. Indigenous hunters had extensive knowledge of the life cycle of certain animals including the kinds of foods they ate, and natural habitat. These indigenous knowledge systems were largely disrupted and replaced due to scientific and technological advancements brought to the African shores by colonial powers.

Public Management during the Colonial Period

The colonial conquest of Africa had a significant influence on indigenous public management systems. Knowledge production and dissemination of information in government as well as consumption patterns have all tended to reflect a strong Western hegemony (Zeleza, 2006, p. 196). This negatively deflated what Africans knew and could do to govern their societies (Basheka and Auriacombe, 2019). Ayee (2005) probed the impact of the colonial period on African public management and argues that the colonial legacy on indigenous administrative and governance systems gave rise to the following:

- The replacement of competitive politics by one or no-party systems ostensibly dedicated to national unity.
- Reliance upon unified bureaucratic structures exclusively accountable to the central government to define, organize, and manage the production of public goods and services along lines determined at all levels by a 'national plan'.
- No legitimate significant role was allowed for local government, including traditional, ethnic groups as well as modern institutions of governance.
- Executive authority was maximized at the expense of other institutions such as the legislature, judiciary, regional governments, and press and private organizations.
- The national budget was regarded as the primary source of funding for the development agenda and was mainly compiled based on income generated from the largest economic sectors.

The colonial legacy is summarized by Rodney (1982, p. 240) as follows:

> The main purpose of the colonial school system was to train Africans to help man the local administration at the lowest ranks and to staff capitalist firms owned by Europeans ... It was not an educational system designed to give young people confidence and pride as members of African societies, but one which sought to instil a sense of deference towards all that was European and capitalist.

In response to the observation that Western scholars typically portray African traditional governance systems as irrelevant and not worthy of scholarship, Basheka and Auriacombe (2019) argue that African scholars should document indigenous knowledge practices and, in the case of public administration, develop suitable theories of public administration based on indigenous knowledge systems and practices. Furthermore, Basheka and Auriacombe (2019) maintain that African societies had religious beliefs, norms, and practices which connected their existence to God. Societies had strong systems of health, mainly by using indigenous medicinal plants. African societies also had mechanisms of commerce and trade, similar to economics and market systems practised elsewhere. Barter was the main medium of commerce and trust played a fundamental role in trade and commerce. In addition, traditional societies had systems of governance which were aligned with democratic principles such as checks and balances as well as demanding responsiveness and accountability from public leadership. It could thus be argued that the Africans of the time had systems for running the governments of the times.

The colonial inheritance created basic problems for the establishment of effective governments during the post-independence period. African leaders faced manifold difficulties in gathering stable governing coalitions, fostering durable institutions, and extending substantial control over the masses of their populations. The emergent governing formulas typically blended traditional modes of authority with institutional forms inherited from the colonial regime (Uzo, Shittu and Meru, 2018). These strategies often stabilized nascent political elites, yet they were less effective in building sound governing structures (Ayee, 2012). At the same time, as Tapscott (2021) intimates, given its enduring legacy, it is essential to reference the history when analyzing the current trajectory of public policy and governance on the continent.

Public Management in Postcolonial Africa

The postcolonial public management systems in Africa were largely shaped by some key internal and external factors. Internal factors had to do with the pressures from citizens for improved service delivery and fulfilment of political promises leaders had made at independence. External factors mainly include the following:

- The colonial legacy: most governments inherited systems of managing public affairs which were implanted by the colonial regimes. The judicial systems, for example, and structure of African public service remained significant features during the colonial era.
- Leaders' education levels: when colonial governments left the stage, most government systems remained in the hands of less educated Africans who did not have experience and skills of running complex public management systems. The virtual absence of bureaucratic state institutions or state collapse meant that outsiders took a wider range of political roles conventionally reserved for state institutions (Reno, 1998, p. 1). There were also postcolonial demands upon African leaders to realize the promises they had made to citizens during their agitation for independence.
- Changing nature of the role of the state: the changing nature and role of the state immediately after independence was an important factor which shaped postcolonial systems.
- Lending conditions: the dictates of the multilateral agencies and lending institutions gave prescriptions on the nature of public management systems in Africa as a condition for development assistance.

- Pressures of globalization: the effects of globalization, such as the 'brain drain', the emergence of new actors involved in governance, as well as new role-players such as development and donor agencies on the international scene are highly influential in African countries.

One of the first problems African countries tend to contend with came with the granting of independence. The colonial 'law and order' administrative structures were no longer adequate. The public services had to be made more responsive to the public demands which would accompany statehood. They had to be geared to dealing with the problems of nation-building and associated new functions. The implementation of Africanization policies also necessitated reforms since one consequence of this policy was the lowering of standards within the public services which adversely affected efficiency as well as morale. Conditions of service, salaries, codes of practices, and operations had to be modified. The increase in the number of employees caused by the more expansive role played by governments necessitated further reforms (King, 1987).

Public management in the postcolonial era is furthermore characterized by conflict and political instability in many countries. Francis (2006, p. 34), for example, blames the majority of the conflicts and security problems on the continent on the failure of the postcolonial state. The argument is that African countries inherited a colonial legacy which was predicated on Westapharian sovereign state which divided Africa into nation states that divided the African peoples. The postcolonial period was characterized by democratization projects. Donor countries and development agencies recommended reforms to developing countries in the form of Structural Adjustment Programmes which included a wide range of economic, political, and administrative reforms. Economic reforms emphasized the need for liberalization of the economy by reducing controls, denationalization, privatization, private sector orientation, and reliance on market forces. Political reforms, which included democratization, decentralization, increased people's participation, and public accountability, had to accompany economic reforms (Dzimbiri, 2008).

One of the noticeable thrusts of administrative reforms was to reduce the direct involvement of the state in economic activities, enhance the role of the private sector, create an enabling environment for the growth of the private sector, and develop public–private sector partnership (Sharma, 2006). The New Public Management paradigm staunchly advocates a basic change in the role of the state in society and economy. It emphasizes the vital role of the 'market' as against the 'state' as the key regulator of society and economy. Thus, it involves a shift from the direct provision of services by government to indirect methods like policymaking, facilitating, contracting, providing information, and coordinating other actors (Philip and Daganda, 2013).

Following the changed role of the state and growing demands for good governance globally, the New Public Management paradigm emerged to implant a new approach into traditional public administration. It was geared toward enhancing efficiency, productivity, improved service delivery and accountability (Hughes, 2003), and emphasized result-orientation as opposed to the process-orientation of traditional public administration. It called for a reduction in the exclusive reliance on public bureaucracy for service delivery and instead advocated the increased use of the private sector and non-governmental organizations as alternative mechanisms of service delivery (Dzimbiri, 2008).

TYPICAL PITFALLS AND PREREQUISITES FOR EFFECTIVE PUBLIC MANAGEMENT IN AFRICA

Africa is a continent where those in charge of managing public affairs have generally demonstrated a sharp drift away from the expectations, wishes, and aspirations of the general public. In many countries, access to quality public services is limited and where they are offered it falls below societal expectations. Corruption, nepotism, bribery, greed, and all forms of manipulative traits generally stand in the way of an efficient public management system (Mhone, 2003). Observers such as Iheriohanma and Oguoma (2010) and Moti (2019) confirm that political and administrative leaders were no longer acting for and on behalf of broader citizenry interests but rather pursuing their own personal agenda. This and other realities created a number of pitfalls for PM in Africa. Among several such pitfalls, the following have tended to characterize Africa:

- The get-rich mental fixation: public management has been bedevilled by the appetite to acquire quick finances and assets with their primary occupation of getting rich but not executing entrusted public responsibility of service. 'An African would for example appear to be happy stealing from one side of his pocket and transfers the "loot" to the other side of his pocket and congratulate himself for a job well done' (Iheriohanma and Oguoma, 2010, p. 411). Public managers in most African jurisdictions appear to be turning into businessmen and women as opposed to civil servants. The political leadership on the continent has not been saved from this pitfall (Moti, 2019). Leaders accumulate and convert wealth into political resources to use 'to buy the royalty of some rivals and the remaining chunk of this wealth is used to buy weapons' (Reno, 1998, p. 1). Africa remains a continent rich in natural resources like oil, gas, diamonds, and other extractive resources, but made poor by human errors that are fed by greed (Coleman, 2011).
- Loyalty buy-offs: loyalty buy-offs involve securing the allegiance of the army top-brass by providing material incentives and thus ensuring that they have a vested interest in the maintenance of the status quo (regime survival) (Florea, 2018). Some military officers are entrenched in public management systems as a way of promoting this scheme. Military interference in governmental affairs was more a political than a military problem, an observation that remains particularly relevant for most African countries.
- Ethnic divisions: in Africa, sound public management has been undermined by ethnicity and other divisive elements. By appointing loyal co-ethnics, autocrats address two key principal-agent issues: monitoring and defection (McLauchlin, 2010). This strategy has been fairly common in societies where communal identities are salient and form the basis of political mobilization (Harkness, 2016). Co-ethnics appointed at higher echelons of power tend to be 'more loyal due to trust developed over years of repeated interactions, embeddedness within the same social networks that facilitates information exchange and makes plotting more difficult, and stronger in-group norms of reciprocity' (Harkness, 2016, p. 589).
- Declining corporate governance practices: Iguisi (2014) acknowledges that African values are to a large extent lacking in corporate management practices in the continent with most organizations practising Western management models. The author argues that the application of Western management models in human management practices in Africa has created several challenges for managers in motivating their workers.

- Presence of multiple power groups: in most African countries, there are several actors involved in the legitimate domain of public managers and this has been common in certain sectors like the oil and mineral sector (Moti, 2019). All actors exert a certain degree of power and multiple interests and where power is concentrated in ruling families, the legal system and other institutions, especially economic ones, have been either weak or marginalized (Abbas, 2009).
- Inefficient spending and borrowing: resource-rich governments tend to overspend on government salaries, inefficient fuel subsidies, and large monuments and to underspend on health, education, and other social services (Moti, 2019). The amount that governments collect in resource revenues can change drastically from year to year because of changes in commodity prices and production. Several studies have shown that it is very difficult to effectively spend fluctuating and unpredictable revenues. Governments often get trapped in boom-bust cycles where they spend on legacy projects, such as airports and monuments, when revenues are rising and then must make painful cuts when revenues decline.
- Government's failure to perform regulatory roles: since the 1980s, the New Public Management (NPM) was entrenched in theory and practice across the world. Many governments and several international organizations embraced the NPM as the framework or paradigm through which governments are modernized and the public sector re-engineered to 'strengthen the connections between government and the mechanisms' (Hope, 2001). Unfortunately, its expectation of a strong regulatory function has not been fully realized in the African context (Mhone, 2003).

What needs to be done to address these pitfalls? How can good and effective public management in Africa be fostered? Answers to these questions vary due to the diverse nature of the disciplines that shape our understanding of public sector management. Public sector management borrows from several disciplines. The wish of many governments to have a functional public sector management is precipitated by the fact that an efficient public administration based on a worthy leadership is required to implement policies needed for the development of a country (Bodolica and Spraggon, 2021). The prescriptions on what needs to be done to improve public sector management in Africa still take these disciplinary orientations. The economics-oriented analysts are likely to prescribe a checklist based on economic-related variables, while the legal experts are likely to centre their arguments on laws and institutions. Management scholars would call on behavioural changes, while historians would suggest we look at the past with a view to making sense of what happens today.

All good governments require a capable public administrative and management system (Evans, 2010). Karyeija (2012) reported how African countries have undergone some government reforms in an attempt to align them with global good governance principles and standards and how these reform programmes have mainly been driven by development institutions and donor agencies. The reforms were generally aimed at correcting colonial distortions still bedevilling the public sector. Some of the prerequisites for effective PM in Africa include the following:

- The establishment of policies, rules, and regulations based on African values and norms: as alluded to earlier, the foundation of good public management, the establishment of sound rules and regulations for executing public policy. An effective public management system needs to have predictable policies, rules, and regulations that control behaviour of the political leaders and administrative officials. There should be a meritocratic recruitment system in the public sector to support bureaucratic effectiveness. Political patronage and public sector recruitments based on the wishes of those in the ruling class simply cannot ensure an efficient public sector. African scholars need to have transformative models of policy formulation and governance which more accurately reflect African contexts (Uzo, Shittu and Meru, 2018).

- Role of elites and political classes: the political-administrative dichotomy debate anticipated a separation of powers between the political and administrative class. The elites play a central coordination role. They help in synthesizing the problems and crafting a strategy that is critical. Their involvement and cooperation build the government's success and avoid the patrimonial trap which has been accused of leading to crony capitalism (Ricz, 2021). Powerful political and administrative leadership should have the capacity to enforce policies, rules, and regulations and should be able to withstand undue influences by the elites.
- Institutional arrangements: strong legal and political institutions play an important role in the development of any country. Government functions well through its machinery. The respective tiers and spheres of government should function independently but in support of each other.
- Competent and skilled public servants: an efficient public sector management system in Africa will need public servants with the right skills, competencies, and attitudes to serve. Public servants need to be motivated and availed of the necessary tools to perform their functions. Public servants need to be continuously capacitated through suitable training and development initiatives to keep pace with the changing governance environment and the adoption of new technology and service delivery approaches. They should be constantly equipped with strong competencies and values to serve the broader public interest.
- Stable non-state actors: unlike in the past when public sector processes were dominated by the state, attention has increasingly turned to non-state actors. Actors such as the business sector, the church, the media, civil society organizations, and the international community generally need to play a stabilizing role in building oversight structures for a well-functioning public management system.
- Institutional leadership: leadership implies directing management activities in utilising public resources. Institutional leadership is usually regarded as vital to the overall development of Africa. An efficient public management infrastructure will be established if the leadership deficit is bridged (Moti, 2019).
- Values and beliefs: African countries have generally performed below expectations in their reform and transformation agenda due to the absence of values and beliefs. It has previously been suggested, and more correctly so, that the failure by the promoters of PSR to take into consideration the ethical and communal values and peculiar situations in various African countries dealt a devastating blow to the reform agenda. The challenges arose as a result of the failure to change people from their long-established ways of doing things as well as their ingrained cultural beliefs (Omoyefa, 2010). To formulate a good public sector management system, therefore, there is a need to integrate values, customs, and beliefs which are identifiable with the people.
- Indigenous knowledge: there is a need to exploit indigenous knowledge systems to support administrative and managerial activities and reform programmes in the public sector. International development institutions and donor agencies typically rely on their own

foreign technical expertise and public management practices. The importation of foreign practices and approaches hampers a homegrown public management approach in the African public sector (Omoyefa, 2010).

- Public service values: there is a need to revisit and educate public managers on core values for a sound public service. These values include integrity, competence, a merit system, sensitivity, and respect for societal needs as well as low tolerance for laxity, corruption, and crime. Other values include recognition of neutrality of civil servants and sensitivity to cross-cultural values.

This concludes a brief exposition of the typical prerequisites to address some of the pitfalls associated with public management on the continent. This exposition is not complete and additional research is necessary to share best practice and lessons learned on the continent.

CONCLUSION

Public Management is an expansive field of study and its corpus of knowledge is expanding due to the sharing of approaches, theories, and models from other disciplines. Public management is not a single discipline but can rather be regarded as an interdiscipline since it is shaped by the viewpoints of several disciplines. The field is also rapidly growing within the African context, mainly due to the diversity of the continent's governance and policy systems. The chapter has offered a conceptual framework to broaden understanding of public sector management. This conceptual framework is mainly characterized by the dynamics between public and private sector actors, the interrelationship between public management as practice and public management as a study domain, the inter-, multi- and transdisciplinary nature of the field of study, as well as the nature and scope of the network of state and non-state actors in government affairs. Furthermore, scholars of PM should consider both the artistic and scientific dimensions of the discipline, narrow state dimensions as well as global, international arena settings, as well as the broad nature and scope of PM functions, skills, and applications. Complexities brought about by issues such as globalization, technological advancement, and environmental concerns all influence the study of PM in Africa and beyond.

There are several pitfalls of public management in Africa and the concern for both scholars and practitioners should be to revive a culture of working towards reversing potential harmful effects and negative trends. Strong political and administrative leadership is critical to reform the public sector and to harness the collective indigenous knowledge systems on the continent. Public management as a practice should be founded on homegrown governance values and be operationalized by competent and skilled public servants with a zeal to serve.

REFERENCES

Abbas, A.J. (2009), *Business and Management Environment in Saudi Arabia: Challenges and Opportunities for Multinational Corporations*, New York, NY: Routledge.

Ayee, J.R.A. (2005), 'Public Sector Management in Africa'. Economic Research Working Paper Series No 82. Tunis Belvedere: African Development Bank. Available at https://www.afdb.org/fileadmin/uploads/afdb/Documents/Publications/00457499-EN-ERWP-82.PDF.

Ayee, J.R.A. (2012), 'Improving the Effectiveness of the Public Sector in Africa through the Quality of Public Administration', in Hanson, K.T. (ed.), *Rethinking Development Challenges for Public Policy*, London: Palgrave Macmillan, pp. 83–116.

Basheka, B. and C.J. Auriacombe (2019), 'Abusive Constitutionalism in Africa – A Threat to Efficient and Effective Public Administration Systems?', *African Journal of Public Affairs*, **11** (2), 103–127.

Bodolica, V. and M. Spraggon (2021), 'Leadership in Times of Organisational Decline: A Literature Review of Antecedents, Consequences, and Moderators', *International Journal of Organisational Analysis*, **29** (2), 415–435, doi.org/10.1108/IJOA-04-2020-2123.

Cheshire, L., V. Higgins and G. Lawrence (2007), 'Introduction: Governing the Rural', in Cheshire, L., V. Higgins and G. Lawrence (eds.), *Rural Governance: International Perspectives*, New York, NY: Taylor and Francis Group.

Coleman, K. (2011), 'Africa's Natural Resources: Blessing or Curse?', in Mabikke, S.B. (ed.), *Africa's Wealth of Resources, Blessing or Curse*, accessed 12 January 2023 at https://www.academia.edu /54411474/Africa_s_Wealth_of_Resources_Blessing_or_Curse.

Dzimbiri, L.B. (2008), 'Experiences in New Public Management in Africa: The Case of Performance Management Systems in Botswana', *Africa Development*, **33** (4), 43–58, doi.org/ 10.4314/ ad.v33i4.57339.

Evans, P. (2010), 'The Challenge of 21st Century Developmental State', in Edigheji, O. (ed.), *Constructing a Democratic Developmental State in South Africa: Potentials and Challenges*, Pretoria: HSRC Press, pp. 72–84.

Florea, A. (2018), 'Spatial Rivalry and Coups against Dictators', *Security Studies*, **27** (1), 1–26, doi.org /10.1080/09636412.2017.1360072.

Gennaioli, N. and I. Rainer (2007), 'The Modern Impact of Precolonial Centralization in Africa', *Journal of Economic Growth*, **12** (3), 185–234.

Gildenhuys, J.S.H. and A. Knipe (2000), *The Organisation of Government: An Introduction*, Pretoria: Van Schaik.

Grillo, S.L., V.A. Klinken and H.L. Ndzovu (2019), *Religion in Contemporary Africa: An Introduction*, London: Taylor and Francis.

Guta, A.J. (2012), 'Characteristics of Public Sector Management, Annals of the University of Petroşani', *Economics*, **12** (4), 95–102.

Hague, R. and M. Harrop (2010), *Comparative Governments and Politics: An Introduction*, 10th ed., London: Macmillan.

Harkness, K.A. (2016), 'The Ethnic Army and the State: Explaining Coup Traps and the Difficulties of Democratization in Africa', *Journal of Conflict Resolution*, **60** (4), 587–616.

Hope, R.K. (2001), 'The New Public Management: Context and Practice in Africa', *International Public Management Journal*, **4**, 119–134.

Hughes, O. (2003), *Public Management and Administration*, 3rd ed., London: Palgrave Macmillan.

Iguisi, O. (2014), 'African Values for the Practice of Human Resource Management', *Beykent University Journal of Social Sciences*, **7** (1), 56–77.

Iheriohanma, E.B.J. and O. Oguoma (2010), 'Governance, Leadership Crisis and Underdevelopment in Africa: An Explorative Discourse', *European Journal of Social Sciences*, **12** (3), 409–416.

Karyeija, G.K. (2012), 'Public Sector Reforms in Africa: What Lessons have We Learnt?', *Forum for Development Studies*, **39** (1), 105–124.

Kelly, G., G. Mulgan and S. Muers (2002), *Creating Public Value: An Analytical Framework for Public Service Reform*, London: Strategy Unit, Cabinet Office.

King, V.E. (1987), 'The African Public Services: Problems and Challenges', *Social and Economic Studies*, **36** (2), 207–215.

MacFarlane, N. and N. Sabanadze (2013), 'Sovereignty and Self-Determination: Where Are We?', *International Journal: Canada's Journal of Global Policy Analysis*, **68** (4), 609–627, doi.org/10 .1177/00207020135111.

Martyn, A. (2002), 'The Right of Self-Defence under International Law—the Response to the Terrorist Attacks of 11 September', Department of the Parliamentary Library, Current Issues Brief No. 8 2001–02, accessed 8 January 2023 at https://www.ojp.gov/ncjrs/virtual-library/abstracts/right-self -defence-under-international-law-response-terrorist.

McLauchlin, T. (2010), 'Loyalty Strategies and Military Defection in Rebellion', *Comparative Politics*, **42** (3), 333–350.

Mhone, G. (2003), 'The Challenges of Governance, Public Sector Reforms and Public Administration in Africa: Some Research Issues', *IDMN Bulletin*, **X** (1), 1–18.

Moti, U.G. (2019), 'Africa's Natural Resource Wealth: A Paradox of Plenty and Poverty', *Advances in Social Sciences Research Journal*, **6** (7), 483–504, doi.org/10.14738/assrj.67.6814.

Mugambi, P. (2016), *The Basics of Law: Questions and Answers*, Dar-es-salaam: Law Africa.

Ncube, L.B. (2010), 'Ubuntu: A Transformative Leadership Philosophy', *Journal of Leadership Studies*, **4** (3), 77–82, doi.org/10.1002/jls.20182.

Omoyefa, P. (2010), 'Public Sector Reforms In Africa: A Philosophical Re-Thinking', *Africa Development*, **33** (4), 15–30, doi.org/10.4314/ad.v33i4.57332.

Philip, D.D. and A.T. Daganda (2013), 'New Public Management (NPM) and Public Sector Administration in Nigeria', *International Affairs and Global Strategy*, **14** (1), 9–15.

Pollitt, C. (2016), 'Advanced Introduction to Public Management and Administration', *Public Administration Review*, **78** (2), 321–323, doi.org/10.1111/puar.12928.

Reno, W. (1998), *Warlord Politics and African States*, London: Lynne Reiner Publishers.

Rice, J. (2021), 'The Anatomy of the Newly Emerging Illiberal Model of State Capitalism: A Developmental Dead End?', *International Journal of Public Administration*, **44** (14), 1253–1263.

Rodney, W. (1982), *How Europe Underdeveloped Africa*, Washington, DC: Howard University Press.

Rubakula, G. (2014), 'The New Public Management and Its Challenges in Africa', *Public Policy and Administration Research*, **4** (4), 85–96.

Rutanga, M. (2011), *Politics, Religion and Power in the Great Lakes Region*, Kampala: Fountain Publishers.

Sharma, K. (2006), 'Public Sector Management Reforms in Botswana', University of Botswana (unpublished book proposal).

Shaw, M.N. (2008), *International Law*, 6th ed., Cambridge: Cambridge University Press.

Shepherd, E. (2006), 'Why are Records in the Public Sector Organisational Assets?', *Records Management Journal*, **16** (1), 6–12.

Staples, W. (2010), 'Public Value in Public Sector Infrastructure Procurement', thesis submitted in fulfilment of the requirements for the degree of Doctor of Philosophy from the Royal Melbourne Institute of Technology, accessed 2 January 2023 at https://www.researchgate.net/publication/228894634.

Tapscott, C. (2021), 'Overcoming the Past and Shaping the Future: The Quest for Relevance in Teaching and Researching Public Administration in Africa', *Global Public Policy and Governance*, **1**, 468–484, doi.org/10.1007/s43508-021-00030-x.

Uzo, U., O. Shittu and A.K. Meru (2018), 'Introduction: Indigenous Management Practices in Africa', *Indigenous Management Practices in Africa*, **20**, 1–7, doi.org/10.1108/S1877-636120180000020001.

Van der Waldt, G. (2014a), 'Public Administration and Transdisciplinarity: A Modalistic Approach toward Knowledge Co-Construction', *International Journal of Humanities and Social Science*, **4** (6), 120–134.

Van der Waldt, G. (2014b), 'Towards the Construction of Knowledge in Public Governance as Field of Scientific Enquiry', *International Journal of Humanities and Social Sciences (IJHSS)*, **4** (3), 67–80.

Van der Waldt, G. (2019), 'Constructing Conceptual Frameworks in Social Science Research', *TD: The Journal for Transdisciplinary Research in Southern Africa*, **16** (1), 1–9, doi.org/10.4102/td.v16i1.758.

Vyas-Doorgapersad, S., L.-M. Tshombe and E. Ababio (2017), *Public Administration in Africa: Performance and Challenges*, New York, NY: Routledge, doi.org/10.4324/9781315089324.

Zeleza, P.T. (2006), 'The Inventions of African Identities and Languages: The Discursive and Developmental Implications', Selected Proceedings of the 36th Annual Conference on African Linguistics, Somerville, MA: Cascadilla Proceedings, pp. 14–26, accessed 18 January 2023 at https://www.lingref.com/cpp/acal/36/paper1402.pdf.

3. Systems of government: a comparative analysis of selected African countries

Gerrit van der Waldt

INTRODUCTION

From the content of Chapters 1 and 2 it is evident that public management applications are significantly influenced by the way in which a society or nation is organized and governed. The architecture of the tiers (i.e. executive, judiciary, and legislative authorities) and spheres of government (e.g. national/central, provincial/regional, and local/county) are ultimately dependent on the system of government. The origins of a system of government can vary depending on the specific system in question. In many cases, the origins of a system of government can be traced back to the historical, cultural, and social contexts in which it emerged. Some systems of government, such as monarchy, have origins that date back to ancient times, while others, such as democracy, emerged more recently in response to specific political, economic, or social circumstances. The system of government is ultimately absorbed in the constitution of the country. The constitution also mandates the respective tiers and spheres of government to execute certain responsibilities and to exercise prescribed powers.

The design and development of a system of government are influenced by a range of factors, including historical legacies, economic and technological developments, social and cultural values, political ideology, and power relations. The rise of liberal ideas and values, the development of modern communication technologies, the establishment of a network of actors involved in governance, and the growth of urbanization and industrialization all influence the system of government. These factors contribute to the emergence of new forms of political organization, such as political parties, the media, and civil society organizations, which in turn help to shape the development of modern systems of government.

There are various types of systems of government, ranging from democracies and dictatorships to theocracies and monarchies. Each system of government has its own unique features and characteristics, which can shape the political, economic, and social landscape of a country. Comprehension of the various systems of government and their strengths and weaknesses is crucial for anyone interested in public management, politics, and governance. It encompasses the political, legal, economic, and social institutions that work together to maintain order and regulate interaction between individuals and groups within a society. This knowledge can help scholars, practitioners, and policymakers better understand and navigate the complexities of modern governance and develop strategies for creating more effective and equitable systems of government. With this perspective in mind, the purpose of this chapter is to outline the typical systems of government by contrasting and comparing selected countries on the African continent. The chapter commences with a brief exposition of a conceptual clarification of 'systems' and contextual perspectives pertaining to its application. Thereafter, the respective types of systems of government are probed by providing examples thereof on the African continent. The chapter concludes with a comparative analysis of the systems of government of selected countries.

SYSTEMS OF GOVERNMENT: A CONCEPTUAL AND CONTEXTUAL EXPOSITION

A system of government can be regarded as the way in which power and authority are organized in a society. This sets the framework and parameters for the establishment of policies, rules, and procedures for decision-making and general governance (Edelenbos, van Schie and Gerrits, 2009, p. 75). It usually determines how government power is distributed and exercised among different individuals and institutions, and how laws and policies are formulated and implemented (Fagerholm, 2016).

Scholars such as Claassen and Magalhães (2021), Harrison and Boyd (2018) and Martin (2012) illustrate how political ideologies such as nationalism, conservatism, liberalism, socialism, and fascism influence systems of government. Political ideologies can be regarded as a set of beliefs about how society should be organized, including the role of government, the distribution of power, and the allocation of resources (Fagerholm, 2016, p. 138). These ideologies influence the way that governments are structured and function, shaping the political and economic systems that are implemented. For example, a government that is based on a socialist ideology would prioritize the collective ownership of resources and the redistribution of wealth to create a more equal society. In contrast, a government that is based on a capitalist ideology would prioritize individual ownership of resources and the free market to drive economic growth.

Political ideologies can also influence the structure of government institutions, such as the separation of powers, the role of the judiciary, and the relationship between the central government and regional or local authorities. For example, a government based on a liberal ideology may prioritize individual rights and freedoms and would therefore establish a system of checks and balances to limit the power of the state. Similarly, a government based on a conservative ideology may prioritize traditional values and social stability and would therefore establish strong institutions to maintain order and stability. In some cases, political ideologies can also lead to the establishment of authoritarian regimes, where power is concentrated in the hands of a single ruler or ruling party. It is thus evident that political ideologies play a significant role in shaping the systems of government, influencing the way that power is distributed, resources are allocated, and society (and government) is organized.

An analysis of the systems of government should always be contextualized, meaning that every country's history, development trajectory, dominant political ideology, and demographical realities will uniquely shape its particular system. In the case of countries on the African continent colonial systems of government were established by foreign powers during the late 19th and early 20th centuries through the process of colonization. These systems were designed to serve the interests of the colonial powers and were imposed on African societies without much regard for their existing political structures and institutions. The new systems of government often stood in stark contrast to traditional native systems of government that were developed over centuries. These traditional systems were predominantly based on the principles of consensus, community, and communal ownership (Megisteab, 2019). These systems varied widely depending on the specific culture and geography of the region, but they generally emphasized the importance of social harmony and the collective good (Mengisteab and Hagg, 2017).

In comparison, the colonial systems of government in Africa were typically characterized by centralized authority, a hierarchical bureaucracy, and a reliance on formal legal institutions. Power was concentrated in the hands of European administrators and a small group of African elites who were trained and selected by the colonial authorities (Vaughan, 2003). These systems were often marked by corruption, oppression, and a lack of accountability to the people (Asimeng-Boahene, 2017; Martin, 2012). Traditional systems of government in Africa, on the other hand, were more decentralized and participatory. They typically relied on informal dispute resolution mechanisms, such as village elders or clan leaders, rather than formal courts of law. Decision-making was often based on consensus, with an emphasis on consultation and dialogue between different stakeholders (Graham, 2019).

While colonial systems of government in Africa were generally intended to be temporary, they had a lasting impact on the continent's political landscape. The legacy of colonialism is still evident in many African countries' systems of government today, with centralized, top-down systems of government that often fail to represent the interests of ordinary citizens (Asimeng-Boahene, 2017). Nonetheless, traditional systems of government continue to play an important role in many African societies, particularly at the local level. The origins of a system of government are often complex and multifaceted, reflecting a range of historical, social, economic, and political factors. Comprehension of these factors is essential for understanding how different systems of government operate and evolve over time.

TYPES OF SYSTEMS OF GOVERNMENT

The literature reveals that there are several types of systems of government evident. Five of the main types are briefly outlined below. It should be noted that a particular system of government may be characterized by characteristics and principles of several systems.

Anarchy

The origins of anarchism can be traced back to the Enlightenment era and the writings of philosophers such as Jean-Jacques Rousseau, who believed in the natural goodness of human beings and the need for individual freedom and autonomy (Fiala, 2017).

Anarchism is a political theory that favours a society with no centralized power or government.

Pierre-Joseph Proudhon, who thought that such a system would be more democratic and equitable than conventional institutions, originally used the term in the middle of the 19th century. A society based on voluntary collaboration, mutual aid, and individual freedom would be established under anarchy, a political ideology that calls for the elimination of all kinds of government and authority. Because there is no organized government or authority in this style of administration, people are free to govern themselves. Although anarchy is frequently perceived as a radical, perilous, or revolutionary philosophy, it has actually been applied in a number of historical contexts.

Government, capitalism, and all social hierarchies are condemned by the political theory of anarchism. Its fundamental tenets include the notion that everyone has the right to make their own judgments and that society should be built on voluntary cooperation and consensus rather than hierarchy or force. Anarchism has existed throughout history, with various groups and communities sprouting up in various locations. All kinds of authority and government should be abolished, according to anarchists, who think that society should be free to rule itself and make choices collectively without the need for a centralized power. Also, they support complete individual freedom and autonomy, which they consider as the cornerstone of human ingenuity, invention, and social collaboration.

Anarchists support decentralized systems of self-governance that are founded on the ideas of direct democracy and consensus decision-making because they feel that these concepts are essential to the development of a free and just society. They consider that there should be no hierarchy or dominance within a community and that all members should have an equal say in all decisions.

A society without a government, according to anarchists, would be chaotic and lack the structure, discipline, order, and organization required to meet the demands of a contemporary civilization. Yet, proponents of anarchism contend that it offers a workable alternative to the repressive and hierarchical forms of governance that are now in place and that it is the ultimate manifestation of individual freedom and autonomy (Prichard, 2022).

Critics of this system of government argue that an anarchist society would be chaotic and lack the necessary structure, discipline, order, and organization to meet the complex needs of a modern society. Proponents, however, argue that anarchism represents the ultimate expression of individual freedom and autonomy and that it provides a viable alternative to the oppressive and hierarchical systems of government that exist today.

As far as the application of anarchism on the African continent is concerned, there have been instances of anarchist movements and groups, although they have been relatively rare and have not gained widespread popularity or influence. One example of an anarchist movement in Africa was the Makhnovist movement, which advocated for the creation of a decentralized, self-governing society based on principles of mutual aid and voluntary cooperation. The movement inspired similar anarchist groups in other countries, including in Egypt, where the Egyptian anarchist movement emerged in the early 20th century and advocated for the abolition of all forms of government and the establishment of self-governing communities based on principles of mutual aid and voluntary cooperation.

Anarchist activism has occasionally surfaced in Africa in recent years, notably in the context of anti-globalization and anti-capitalist movements. These movements haven't, however, had much of an impact on the continent's political climate because they have a tendency to be small and isolated. It is also important to note that anarchism has not gained much traction as a political theory in many African societies, which have a tendency to have more communal and collectivist ideals and traditions and frequently turn to state-based solutions to solve their social and economic problems.

Democracy

A democratic system of government can be regarded as a system where power is held by the people, either directly or through elected representatives. The origins of democracy as a system of government can be traced back to ancient Greece, where citizens participated in direct democratic decision-making through assemblies and councils (Fleck and Hanssen, 2006, p. 116). According to Claassen and Magalhães (2021), the principles and main tenets of democracy include equal representation, freedom of expression, and the right to vote.

People have the right to hold their leaders accountable in a democracy and to take part in decision-making. Human rights and civil freedoms are crucial components of democracy. Democracy depends on free and fair elections as well as the division of powers among various government branches.

There are several types of democracy evident. These include:

- Direct democracy: In a direct democracy, citizens participate directly in decision-making through assemblies and councils.
- Representative democracy: In a representative democracy, citizens elect representatives to make decisions on their behalf.
- Presidential democracy: In a presidential democracy, the president is directly elected by the people and holds significant executive power.
- Parliamentary democracy: In a parliamentary democracy, the executive branch is made up of a prime minister and cabinet, who are accountable to the legislature.
- Constitutional democracy: In a constitutional democracy, the powers of government are limited by a constitution, which outlines the rights and freedoms of citizens and establishes the framework for government decision-making.

Each type of democracy has its own strengths and weaknesses, and different countries and societies have adopted different forms of democratic governance depending on their historical, cultural, and political contexts.

There are several examples of democracies on the African continent. In fact, since the 1990s, there has been a significant wave of democratization across the continent, with many countries transitioning from authoritarian or one-party rule to multi-party democracy (Khodaverdian, 2022). Some examples of democratic countries in Africa include:

- Botswana: Botswana is a parliamentary democracy with a president and a unicameral legislature. The country has a strong record of political stability and economic growth and has held several free and fair elections since gaining independence from Britain in 1966.
- Ghana: Ghana is a parliamentary democracy with a president and a unicameral legislature. The country has a strong tradition of democracy and has held several peaceful transitions of power through democratic elections.
- Senegal: Senegal is a semi-presidential democracy with a president and a bicameral legislature. The country has a vibrant civil society and media and has held several peaceful transitions of power through democratic elections.
- South Africa: South Africa is a constitutional democracy with a president and a bicameral parliament. The country has held several free and fair elections since the end of apartheid in 1994.
- Tunisia: Tunisia is a parliamentary democracy with a president and a unicameral legislature. The country has made significant strides in democratization since the 2011 Arab Spring protests, including the adoption of a new constitution and several free and fair elections.

The quality and stability of democracy in these countries and others on the continent vary significantly. Furthermore, there are still many challenges to democratic governance in Africa, including issues such as corruption, weak public institutions, and political instability.

Dictatorship

A dictatorship is a system of government in which one person or a small group of people hold absolute power and authority (Lidén, 2014, p. 51). Dictatorships have been present in human history for thousands of years. In modern times, dictatorships have often emerged in the context of political instability, economic crises, or social upheaval.

Often, tyrants impose their will on people rather than gain power democratically (Lidén, 2014). While in power, tyrants frequently work to quell dissent and criticism, and they may resort to violence, censorship, or propaganda to keep the populace under control. Such a society is characterized by the repression of individual liberties and rights, the lack of political transparency and accountability, and the absence of mechanisms for limiting the authority of the ruling class (Wahman, Teorell and Hadenius, 2013).

There are several types of dictatorships, including:

- Military dictatorship: A military dictatorship is a form of dictatorship in which a country is ruled by the military, often following a coup or other violent overthrow of the previous government.
- Personal dictatorship: A personal dictatorship is a form of dictatorship in which power is held by one person, who exercises near-absolute control over the government and society.
- Communist dictatorship: A communist dictatorship is a form of dictatorship in which the ruling elite espouse communist ideology and seek to create a classless society through central planning and government control of the economy.
- Fascist dictatorship: A fascist dictatorship is a form of dictatorship in which the ruling elite espouse nationalist and authoritarian ideology and seek to maintain strict control over the population through propaganda, censorship, and repression.
- Monarchical dictatorship: A monarchical dictatorship is a form of dictatorship in which power is held by a monarch or royal family, who exercise near-absolute control over the government and society.

In all types of dictatorship, power is concentrated in the hands of a small group of people, often at the expense of individual rights and freedoms and democratic governance.

There have been several examples of dictatorship on the African continent, although many countries have transitioned to more democratic forms of governance in recent years. Some examples of dictatorships in Africa include:

- Equatorial Guinea: Under the rule of Teodoro Obiang Nguema, who has been in power since 1979, Equatorial Guinea has been characterized by political repression, corruption, and limited political freedom.
- Eritrea: Under the rule of Isaias Afwerki, who has been in power since 1993, Eritrea is considered one of the most repressive and closed countries in the world, with limited political freedom, censorship, and widespread human rights abuses.
- Libya: Under the rule of Muammar Gaddafi, who came to power in a coup in 1969 and ruled until he was overthrown in 2011, Libya was a repressive dictatorship with limited political freedom and widespread human rights abuses.
- Sudan: Under the rule of Omar al-Bashir, who came to power in a coup in 1989 and ruled until he was ousted in a popular uprising in 2019, Sudan was characterized by political repression, censorship, and human rights abuses.

- Zimbabwe: Under the rule of Robert Mugabe, who came to power in 1980 and ruled until he was ousted in a coup in 2017, Zimbabwe was characterized by political repression, corruption, and economic mismanagement.

It should be noted that the term 'dictator' is in the eyes of the beholder; for some the 'dictator' may be regarded as a liberator or a freedom fighter holding legitimate power; for others the dictator is just that – a dictator. It is also worth noting that many African countries have made significant strides towards democratic governance in recent years, with many holding free and fair elections and adopting more transparent and accountable political systems.

Monarchy

A system of government where power is held by a single individual, usually a king or queen, who inherits the position. A monarchy is a system of government in which a monarch (usually a king or queen) serves as the head of state for life or until abdication (Anchar, 2021).

Tridimas (2021) asserts that monarchies have existed throughout human history for thousands of years, with the ancient Egyptian, Chinese, and Roman empires serving as some of the earliest instances. The Middle East, Europe, Asia, and other parts of the world have all had monarchies at one time or another. The fundamental tenet of a monarchy is that the king, frequently with the assistance of advisors or a governing elite, holds supreme authority and power over the state and society. The authority of the monarch is frequently inherited, which means that it is transferred down the royal family line from one generation to the next.

There are several types of monarchies evident, including:

- Absolute monarchy: An absolute monarchy is a form of monarchy in which the monarch holds supreme authority and power over the government and society, with no checks or balances on their power.
- Constitutional monarchy: A constitutional monarchy is a form of monarchy in which the monarch's power is limited by a constitution or other legal framework. In many cases, the monarch serves as a figurehead or symbolic representative of the state, with actual governing power held by elected officials or a parliament.
- Elective monarchy: An elective monarchy is a form of monarchy in which the monarch is chosen by a group of electors or other ruling elite, rather than inheriting the position through birthright.
- Federal monarchy: A federal monarchy is a form of monarchy in which the monarch serves as the head of state for multiple semi-autonomous or federated regions, each of which has its own government and governing system.

In all types of monarchy, the monarch holds supreme authority and power over the government and society, often with the help of advisors or a ruling elite. However, the extent of the monarch's power and authority may vary depending on the type of monarchy and the legal framework in place. There are examples of monarchies on the African continent, including Eswatini (formerly known as Swaziland). Eswatini is a small landlocked country located in southern Africa, bordered by South Africa to the west and Mozambique to the east. Eswatini is an absolute monarchy, which means that the king holds supreme authority and power over the government and society, with no checks or balances on his power. The current king of Eswatini is Mswati III, who has been in power since 1986.

There are also other examples of traditional monarchies or chieftaincies in various African countries, where traditional rulers hold significant influence and authority over their communities. These traditional rulers may play an important role in local governance and may have significant cultural and ceremonial roles in their societies. However, their powers and authority may be limited by the national government or by the legal system in place. Examples of traditional monarchies or chieftaincies in Africa include the Ashanti kingdom in Ghana, the Buganda kingdom in Uganda, and the Zulu kingdom in South Africa.

Oligarchy

A governing system known as an oligarchy is one in which a small number of individuals, frequently belonging to a particular social, economic, or political elite, have all the power (Bulaong, Mendoza and Mendoza, 2022). The fundamental tenet of oligarchy is that power is concentrated in the hands of a small number of individuals who have disproportionate control over society and the government. Oligarchies can be founded on things like wealth, kinship connections, or political influence and can be organized around economic, social, or political elites.

The two basic principles of oligarchy are the idea of privilege and the idea of exclusivity. The idea of privilege says that the ruling elite has a superior rank or social standing than the rest of the population. The notion of exclusivity suggests that membership in the ruling elite is limited and exclusive to a select few.

There are several types of oligarchies, including:

- Aristocracy: An aristocracy is a form of oligarchy in which power is held by a hereditary class of nobility or aristocrats, who often possess significant wealth, social status, or political influence.
- Plutocracy: A plutocracy is a form of oligarchy in which power is held by a small group of wealthy individuals or families who control the economy and exert significant influence over government and society.
- Military oligarchy: A military oligarchy is a form of oligarchy in which power is held by a small group of military leaders or officers, who often seize power through a coup or other form of forceful takeover.
- Technocracy: A technocracy is a form of oligarchy in which power is held by a small group of experts or professionals, who possess specialized knowledge or skills in a particular field and are appointed to positions of power and influence based on their expertise.

A few examples of oligarchy in Africa can be found in Egypt and Zaire. Egypt under the rule of the pharaohs was an oligarchy, where a small group of elite families held power and controlled the wealth of the nation. In the 20th century, Mobutu Sese Seko's regime in Zaire (now the Democratic Republic of Congo) was an oligarchy, where a small group of loyalists held power and enriched themselves while suppressing dissent and opposition.

Theocracy

A religious institution or group that exercises political power is known as a theocracy. Theocracy's founding ideas and beginnings can be found in prehistoric communities, particularly those where religion was a major influence on political and social life. The fundamental principles of theocracy include the notion that religious leaders are best fitted to rule in accordance with divine intent and that political authority is divinely ordained (Prinz and Sander, 2020).

There are several types of theocracy:

- Monarchical Theocracy: This is a form of theocracy in which the ruler is considered to be both a political and religious leader. Examples include ancient Egypt and the historical Papal States.
- Hierocratic Theocracy: This is a form of theocracy in which religious leaders hold political power. Examples include Iran's Islamic Republic and the former Taliban regime in Afghanistan.
- Ecclesiocracy: This is a form of theocracy in which religious leaders or institutions hold all political power. Examples include the Vatican City and the former Calvinist Republic of Geneva.
- Caliphate: This is a form of theocracy in which the leader, known as the caliph, is considered to be both a political and religious leader. Historically, the caliphate has been associated with Islam.

The people are generally subject to severe religious laws and moral and ethical norms under theocratic administrations. They might even try to impose their religion on neighbouring nations or regions. Theocratic opponents claim that it can be tyrannical and restrict personal freedoms, while proponents claim that it offers moral direction and guarantees that the government is in accordance with the will of God. It is important to note that many African nations currently do not have theocratic forms of administration but rather secular ones.

From the brief overview it is evident that each system of government has its own strengths and weaknesses and can have different influences on the way societies are governed. Often combinations of these systems of government are evident.

SYSTEMS OF GOVERNMENT IN SELECTED AFRICAN COUNTRIES

For illustrative and comparative purposes, five countries in Africa were selected, namely South Africa, Ethiopia, Tanzania, Uganda, and Ghana. In this comparative analysis, we will examine the key features of each system of government and highlight some similarities and differences.

South Africa

South Africa has a parliamentary system of government with a constitutional democracy. The President is both the head of state and head of government and is elected by the National Assembly. The National Assembly is the lower house of Parliament, and members are elected through proportional representation. The upper house is the National Council of Provinces, which represents the nine provinces of the country. Local government comprises 257 metropolitan, district, and local municipalities. This number comprises eight metropolitan, 44 districts, and 205 local municipalities. They are mandated by the Constitution of the

Republic of South Africa, 1996 to facilitate local economic growth and provide infrastructure and essential services.

South Africa also has a strong judiciary, with the Constitutional Court as the highest court in the land. The system of government is known as 'cooperative governance' meaning that the respective spheres of government, namely national, provincial, and local, are interdependent but autonomous in nature. The system of cooperative governance is maintained by intergovernmental relations, decentralization of powers, and fiscal arrangements. It thus has both unitary and federal elements in its form of government.

Ethiopia

Ethiopia is a federal parliamentary republic, which means that it is a country with a federal system of government, where power is divided between a central government and regional governments. The country is divided into nine regions, each of which has its own government and parliament, as well as two administrative cities.

The federal government is led by the Prime Minister, who is the head of government, and the President, who is the head of state. The Prime Minister is appointed by the party or coalition of parties that holds a majority in the House of People's Representatives, which is the lower house of parliament. The President is elected by the joint session of both houses of parliament for a six-year term.

The House of People's Representatives has 547 members who are elected for a term of five years. Members are elected through a mixed electoral system, which combines first-past-the-post and proportional representation. The House of Federation is the upper house of parliament and is responsible for protecting the rights of the regions and ensuring that federal laws do not infringe on the rights of the regions. Ethiopia also has a unique system of ethnic federalism, where regions are based on ethnic groups.

Tanzania

Tanzania is a unitary presidential republic, which means that it is a country with a centralized system of government, where power is concentrated in the hands of the central government led by the President. The President of Tanzania is both the head of state and head of government and is elected through a direct popular vote for a term of five years. The President is also the Commander-in-Chief of the armed forces and has the power to appoint and dismiss members of the government.

Tanzania's unicameral parliament is called the National Assembly and has 393 members. Of these, 264 members are directly elected by the people, while 113 are women nominated by political parties based on their representation in the National Assembly. An additional ten members are appointed by the President, bringing the total number of members to 393. The National Assembly is the unicameral parliament, and members are elected through a mixed electoral system. It is responsible for making laws, approving the national budget, and overseeing the work of the government. The Prime Minister, who is appointed by the President, leads the government and is responsible for implementing national policies and programmes.

Tanzania's unitary presidential republic system of government is designed to ensure that power is centralized in the hands of the President and the national government, with the

National Assembly playing a key role in law-making and oversight. Tanzania also has a strong judiciary, with the Court of Appeal as the highest court in the land.

Uganda

Uganda is a presidential representative democratic republic, which means that it is a country with a system of government in which the President is both the head of state and head of government, and there is a representative democracy in place where citizens vote for representatives to govern on their behalf. The President of Uganda is elected through a direct popular vote for a term of five years and is both the head of state and head of government. The President has significant executive powers, including the power to appoint and dismiss government officials, dissolve parliament, and veto legislation.

Uganda's parliament is composed of the National Assembly and the indirectly elected House of Representatives. The National Assembly has 426 members, who are directly elected through a first-past-the-post system for a term of five years. The House of Representatives is composed of 112 members, who are indirectly elected by special interest groups such as workers, youth, and persons with disabilities.

Uganda's judiciary is independent and composed of the Supreme Court, the Court of Appeal, the High Court, and other subordinate courts. The judiciary has the power to interpret the law and provide checks and balances on the executive and legislative branches of government. The judiciary is also intended to ensure that the rule of law is maintained.

The system of government is designed to ensure that citizens have the opportunity to participate in representative democracy by electing their leaders, while also granting significant powers to the President to govern the country.

Ghana

Ghana has a unitary presidential constitutional republic system of government, which means that it is a country with a centralized system of government, where power is concentrated in the hands of the central government led by the President. The President of Ghana is both the head of state and head of government. The President is elected through a direct popular vote for a term of four years. The President is also the Commander-in-Chief of the armed forces and has the power to appoint and dismiss members of the government.

The Parliament of Ghana is a unicameral body composed of 275 members, directly elected by the people through a first-past-the-post system for a term of four years. Parliament is responsible for making laws, approving the national budget, and overseeing the work of the government.

Ghana's judiciary is independent and composed of the Supreme Court, the Court of Appeal, the High Court, and other subordinate courts. The judiciary has the power to interpret the law and provide checks and balances on the executive and legislative branches of government.

In terms of similarities, all five selected countries have a President as the head of state and head of government, and all have unicameral parliaments. In terms of differences, Ethiopia has a unique system of ethnic federalism, while South Africa has a strong judiciary and a separate upper house. Tanzania has a two-round system for electing the President, while Uganda and Ghana have a mixed electoral system.

The systems of government in South Africa, Ethiopia, Tanzania, Uganda, and Ghana are diverse, with different strengths and weaknesses. However, all five countries have made progress in establishing democratic systems of government and promoting good governance.

CONCLUSION

The purpose of this chapter was to probe the systems of government with particular reference to countries on the African continent. It is evident that the continent is home to a diverse array of systems of government, ranging from federal parliamentary republics to unitary presidential constitutional republics. While each country has its own unique system of government, there are some common themes across the continent, such as a focus on centralization of power, the importance of the executive branch, and the role of the judiciary in providing checks and balances on the other branches of government.

Despite these similarities, it is important to note that each country's system of government is shaped by its own unique history, culture, and political circumstances. As such, it is difficult to make broad generalizations about the state of governance across Africa. Nonetheless, the continent continues to make progress towards strengthening democratic institutions and ensuring that all citizens have a voice in their government.

REFERENCES

Anckar, C. (2021), 'Constitutional Monarchies and Semi-Constitutional Monarchies: A Global Historical Study, 1800–2017', *Contemporary Politics*, **27** (1), 23–40, doi.org/10.1080/13569775.2020.1824360.

Asimeng-Boahene, L. (2017), 'Issues and Prospects of African Indigenous Systems of Governance: Relevance and Implications for Global Understanding', in McKinley, E.A. and L.T. Smith (eds.), *Handbook of Indigenous Education*, Singapore, Springer, pp. 1–20, doi.org/10.1007/978-981-10-1839-8.

Bulaong, O., G.A.S. Mendoza and R.U. Mendoza (2022), 'Cronyism, Oligarchy and Governance in the Philippines: 1970s vs. 2020s', *Public Integrity*, a19, doi.org/10.1080/10999922.2022.2139656.

Claassen, C. and P.C. Magalhães (2021), 'Effective Government and Evaluations of Democracy', *Comparative Political Studies*, **55** (5), 869–894, doi.org/10.1177/00104140211036042.

Edelenbos, J., N. van Schie and L. Gerrits (2009), 'Organizing Interfaces between Government Institutions and Interactive Governance', *Policy Science*, (2010), 73–94, doi.org/10.1007/s11077-009-9086-2.

Fagerholm, A. (2016), 'Ideology: A Proposal for a Conceptual Typology', *Social Science Information*, **55** (2), 137–160, doi.org/10.1177/0539018416629229.

Fiala, A. (2017), 'Anarchism', *Stanford Encyclopedia of Philosophy*, accessed 12 March 2023 at https://plato.stanford.edu/entries/anarchism/.

Fleck, R.K. and F.A. Hanssen (2006), 'The Origins of Democracy: A Model with Application to Ancient Greece', *The Journal of Law and Economics*, **49** (1), 115–146.

Graham, M. (2019), *Contemporary Africa*, London: Red Globe Press.

Harrison, K. and T. Boyd (2018), *Understanding Political Ideas and Movements*, Manchester: Manchester University Press, doi.org/10.7765/9781526137951.

Khodaverdian, S. (2022), 'The African Tragedy: The Effect of Democracy on Economic Growth', *Empirical Economics*, **62** (2022), 1147–1175, doi.org/10.1007/s00181-021-02049-9.

Lidén, G. (2014), 'Theories of Dictatorships: Sub-Types and Explanations', *Studies of Transition States and Societies*, **6** (1), 50–67.

Martin, G. (2012), 'The Political Ideology of Indigenous African Political Systems and Institutions from Antiquity to the Nineteenth Century', in Martin, G. (ed.), *African Political Thought*, New York, NY: Palgrave Macmillan, pp. 11–19, doi.org/10.1057/9781137062055_2.

Mengisteab, K. (2019), 'Traditional Institutions of Governance in Africa', *Oxford Research Encyclopedia of Politics*, accessed 14 March 2023, at https://oxfordre.com/politics/view/10.1093/acrefore/9780190228637.001.0001/acrefore-9780190228637-e-1347.

Mengisteab, K. and G. Hagg (eds.) (2017), *Traditional Institutions in Contemporary African Governance*, London: Routledge.

Prichard, A. (2022), *Anarchism: A Very Short Introduction*, 2nd ed., Oxford: Oxford University Press, doi.org/10.1093/actrade/9780198815617.003.0001.

Prinz, A.L. and C.J. Sander (2020), 'Political Leadership and the Quality of Public Goods and Services: Does Religion Matter?', *Economics of Governance*, **21**, 299–334, doi.org/10.1007/s10101-020-00242-7.

Tridimas, G. (2021), 'Constitutional Monarchy as Power Sharing', *Constitutional Political Economy*, **32**, 431–461, doi.org/10.1007/s10602-021-09336-8.

Vaughan, O. (ed.), (2003), *Indigenous Political Structures and Governance in Africa*, Ibadan: Sefer.

Wahman, M., J. Teorell and A. Hadenius (2013), 'Authoritarian Regime Types Revisited: Updated Data in Comparative Perspective', *Contemporary Politics*, **19** (1), 19–34, doi.org/10.1080/13569775.2013.773200.

4. Good governance in Africa in the era of the Fourth Industrial Revolution

David Mhlanga and Mufaro Dzingirai

INTRODUCTION

The world of governance has been significantly impacted by the exponential development of the digital world. These innovations have simplified information acquisition, expedited communication, and improved service delivery modalities. The effective delivery of public goods like education, health care, social security, and transportation, among other things, as well as the prohibition of corrupt practices, are just a few of the many ways that the use of new technology has the potential to improve government efficiency. The adoption of technological advancements has the possibility of making the government more effective, transparent, responsive, and efficient. According to Williamson and Piattoeva (2019), emerging data-driven technologies will usher in a new era in which public policy and governance operations will be more evidence-based, accurate, efficient, and objective. However, governments are often hesitant to adopt such new innovations, especially in Africa (Bush, 2019).

Scholars such as Castellanos (2020), León and Rosen (2020), and Woo (2018), maintain that technological advancement will reduce the need for cumbersome regulatory prescripts, make civil servants more responsive and efficient, and improve ineffective government systems and processes. In this regard, Balcerzak et al. (2022) and Bush (2019) contend that technology has significant potential to improve the overall 'goodness' of governments. Internet-based and wireless technologies have, for example, significantly improved the ways in which government interacts with society. The speed of communication has furthermore resulted in knowledge reaching out to target populations virtually seamlessly and ensuring that policy decisions made can be disseminated across the depth and breadth of the country. In addition to this, it fosters transparency and accountability, as well as a prompt and efficient response from the government to issues and recommendations raised by its constituents.

The purpose of this chapter is to explore the potential of technology in enhancing the standard (i.e. 'goodness') of governance in Africa within the context of the Fourth Industrial Revolution. In its most simple form, good governance refers to the extent to which governments and a collaborative network of actors succeed in complying with constitutional obligations and adhering to good governance principles such as accountability, responsiveness, transparency, responsibility, rule of law, and participation. It also refers to decision-making processes that are fair, equitable, and just – placing the interests of society first.

GOOD GOVERNANCE: A CONCEPTUAL AND CONTEXTUAL ORIENTATION

Notions of good governance can be traced to the early 1990s when large-scale public sector reforms characterised governments across the globe (Chien and Thanh, 2022). To become 'good' requires that governments follow an incremental process in their adherence to certain norms and principles. Chien and Thahn (2022) therefore maintain that good governance is generally hailed as an 'ideal' state – a foundation upon which socioeconomic prosperity and sustainable development strategies are built. In this sense, good governance is an ideal state characterised by sound public management and harmony between the growth and sustainable development of a country (Giao, 2021). At a national level, good governance concerns the effective management of political, economic, and administrative processes when running national affairs across all spheres of society (World Bank, 2006).

Good governance is a multidimensional and complex concept that has been conceptualised from diverse fields such as economics, management, public administration, and law. From a Public Management perspective, Chien and Thanh (2022) and Nanda (2006) define good governance as multistakeholder engagement between multiple actors such as the government, the private sector, non-governmental organisations, civil society organisations, development agencies, and multinationals to address societal needs and concerns. This collaborative engagement should be characterised by accountability, transparency, the rule of law, dedication to quality, and effective management. To this, Dayanandan (2013) and Islam (2017) add that good governance encompasses the well-functioning capability of both public and private sectors as well as the rules and institutions that develop the network frameworks relating to corporations, countries, companies, and partnerships. The World Bank (2006) holds that good governance includes best practices related to the functioning of political structures of governments and the effective and efficient management of their administrations. These perspectives indicate the complex nature of good governance and that permutations thereof are visible in different countries. Scholars such as Chien and Thanh (2022) and Nanda (2006) confirm that adherence to the universally accepted principles and characteristics of good governance are difficult in developing countries. Developing countries on the African continent, for example, are unfortunately characterised by complex societal concerns such as systemic government corruption, inequality, chronic poverty, and insufficient and ineffective government systems and structures. As such, good governance is commonly regarded as a prerequisite for a country's prosperity, socioeconomic development, and growth.

GOOD GOVERNANCE IN AFRICA

There has been a long-standing scholarly discourse regarding the underlying reasons why Africa as a continent remains largely underdeveloped. Observers contemplate why Africa is still characterised by chronic poverty whilst it is the wealthiest continent in the world in terms of natural resources. Africa has approximately eight per cent of the world's natural gas reserves, 45 per cent of the globe's oil reserves, 47 per cent of its diamonds, 49 per cent of its manganese, and 57 per cent of the world's cobalt reserves (Yaro, Hanka and Engbers, 2019, p. 57). Answers to this question have been proposed from different disciplines such as economics, law, development studies, and psychology. From a good governance perspective, scholars such as Wani (2014), Asefa and Huang (2015), and Yaro, Hanka and Engbers, 2019) insist that the continent is lagging behind mainly due to poor governance, leading to broadbased underdevelopment. It is not encouraging to observe that many African leaders have been implicated in some sort of misgovernance and corruption scandals as they did not work in the best interests of their countries and people. It is also disturbing to observe that political independence from former colonial powers has been followed by a series of governance crises and shenanigans that hindered progress on the continent. This is why Africans still lament extreme poverty and income inequality (Yaro, Hanka and Engbers, 2019). This situation is exacerbated by political turmoil and conflict. Tension between tribes and between governments and militia groupings seriously hamper social cohesion and sustainable development. Moreover, the lack of rule of law, and an increase in corrupt practices are hampering good governance initiatives (Newiak, Wane and Segura-Ubiego, 2022). Against this backdrop, international development agencies and institutions such as the International Money Fund, the United Nations Development Programme (UNDP), and the World Bank designed some governance intervention strategies with the purpose to ensure greater stability and general prosperity on the continent.

Interrogation of the status of good governance in Africa deserves serious attention by scholars, policymakers, and public managers. In an attempt to investigate governance in Africa, issues emanating from the economy, politics, and education should be scrutinised.

From an economic perspective, reforms have been suggested to utilise models, approaches, and technological know-how of developed countries. It is argued that their utilisation will significantly improve the overall effectiveness and efficiency of governments and the way raw materials are exploited. Bretton Wood institutions therefore compel African governments to adopt neoliberal reform programmes (Yaro, Hanka and Engbers, 2019). These reform programmes emphasise privatisation and accelerated job creation initiatives. Johnson (2016) argues, however, that the adoption of neoliberal economic models and approaches are largely hindered by bureaucratic inertia, governance traditions, and issues such as corruption and incompetence. Economic observers thus maintain that poor governance hinders the success of economic reforms in Africa. They advocate for the formation of regional economic blocks such as the Economic Community of West African States (ECOWAS), the Economic Community of the Central African States (ECCAS), the Community of Eastern and Southern Africa (COMESA), the Southern African Development Community (SADC), and the East African Community (EAC) to act as catalysts and drivers for economic prosperity and good corporate governance (Johnson, 2016).

From a political vantage point, scholars explore good governance on the continent by considering issues of political reform and transformation. Although African countries regained their political independence, it is discouraging to observe that 'the interests of the colonial masters are being cherished by the African leaders' (Yaro, Hanka and Engbers, 2019, p. 59). Former colonial powers left behind certain government traditions, systems, and processes and it is difficult to overturn this in a relatively short period of time. A further issue that African governments inherited is the fact that colonial powers unilaterally divided countries and established borders that do not correspond with geographical, tribal, and ethnic realities. This state of affairs has created a deeply divided Africa. As such, it limits socioeconomic development. A further issue that deserves attention is the issue of youth participation in African politics. The youth is a demographic dividend in Africa given its demographics (Yaro, Hanka and Engbers, 2019), and is generally neglected in the upper echelons of politics. To promote good governance it is thus argued that the youth should be afforded more opportunities to become involved in government decision-making processes.

Regarding educational concerns, some scholars maintain that good governance should be supported by suitable educational reforms. The continent is in dire need for an adequately skilled and competent work force to drive government programmes and utilise natural resources (Yaro, Hanka and Engbers, 2019). Educational programmes should promote the principles of good governance, human rights, good citizenship, and generally empower communities to hold governments accountable. There is also a need to invest in educational technology, science, innovation, and research.

Despite the challenges associated with good governance, there are some positive signs. African countries like Botswana, Ghana, Mauritius, and Senegal are increasingly complying with the principles of good governance by adopting government reform programmes and suitable technology to improve the way services are rendered. Scholars such as Asefa and Huang (2015) and Yaro, Hanka and Engbers (2019) argue that there is increasing evidence of pockets of governance excellence on the continent visible and that some countries are making great strides towards service delivery excellence.

GOOD GOVERNANCE IN THE ERA OF THE FOURTH INDUSTRIAL REVOLUTION

Governance in a knowledge-based society cannot be effectively structured without capturing the role of information technology. Technological tools like the web and the Internet of Things can facilitate the nurturing of demographic culture in a country (Thomas et al., 2009). In this sense, technology tools open the platforms for interaction between government and citizens. Government institutions can provide information to citizens using online platforms and citizens can respond in real time (Mohanty, 2005). In the same vein, Kalsi, Kiran, and Vaidya (2008) contend that technology can significantly enhance the goodness of governance by improving decision-making and utilising technological tools in government operations.

The arrival of the COVID-19 crisis exposed the need to embrace technology in the governance discourse. Private companies, non-governmental organisations, and public entities were forced to incorporate various technologies into their day-to-day activities in line with pandemic restrictions and regulations across the world (Dzingirai, 2021; Dzingirai, Sikomwe and Tshuma, 2022). Moreover, disruptive technologies provide a powerful advantage in terms of increased performance, reduced costs, high-quality-density storage, video, and voice, fibre optics and transparency as well as disclosure (Otiko and Inuwa, 2021). More interestingly, the adoption of emerging digital technologies can lead to the low cost of providing public services such as education and health care. The adoption of wireless technologies like satellite receivers, radio paging, cellular telephony, and communication exchange technology is necessary when promoting and cultivating good governance.

The implementation of advanced technology can stimulate good governance in the sense that it increases transparency, accountability, and information sharing; facilitates accurate and real-time decision-making, and public involvement; and augments the delivery of public services and goods (African Governance Architecture, 2019). This implies that access to information is key in promoting good governance since the rights and privileges of the members of the society can be easily disseminated to the government and civil society organisations. Governments can reduce costs by creating databases and updating information systems. At a global level, the technology drive is dominated by numerous communication channels that open international collaboration in a global knowledge economy (Dzingirai and Ndava, 2022). This means collaboration among countries is facilitated given that hindrances to engagement are significantly reduced (Otiko and Inuwa, 2021). Therefore, advanced technology plays a catalyst role in promoting good governance.

Revolution in technology is transforming every facet of society. As such, governance is no exception. Information technology has been regarded as the engine that is driving rapid advancement in policymaking, service delivery modalities, production, and operations. With this in mind, the Fourth Industrial Revolution (4IR) is a powerful catalyst in instituting good governance in every county, especially in developing contexts like Africa (Otiko and Inuwa, 2021).

There is no unequivocal definition of the 4IR in the current body of knowledge. The term was proposed by Klaus Schwab who described it as 'a world in which people move between digital platforms and offline reality with the adoption of advanced and connected technology to manage and enable their respective lives' (Xu, David and Kim, 2018, p. 90). The 4IR generally refers to the postmodern world of rapid technological growth which is changing the way society lives and is governed (Mhlanga, 2020; Pitsikalis et al., 2022). Deloitte (2020) regards the 4IR as the interface between physical assets and more advanced digital technologies such as robots, the Internet of Things, drones, artificial intelligence, cloud computing, autonomous vehicles, and nanotechnology. From this conception it is evident that there are various types of technologies that are at the disposal of governments to enhance its capacity to deliver services, engage citizens, improve its performance, and design evidence-based public policy.

Balcerzak et al. (2022) argue that blockchain technology can help governments to become 'smarter' by utilising coded augmentation systems, computer algorithms, transactional data, and business intelligence analytics. Blockchain generally refers to a system in which transactions made in Bitcoin or another cryptocurrency are recorded on a network of computers. Blockchain or distributed ledger technology also enables transactions between wireless devices. It is thus generally accepted that the technologies that underpin blockchain transactions have the potential to design smart and intelligent government systems. These technologies include biometrics, digital assets and the predictive maintenance thereof, edge computing, simulation modelling, spatial computing, and machine vision algorithms (Balcerzak et al., 2022, p. 4). In addition, Woo (2018) argues that government policymakers should leverage technology solutions like data analytics to address new and progressively complicated societal challenges. In the case of Singapore, the adoption of technological solutions has culminated in the government's 'Smart Nation' programme as an endeavour to digitise governance transactions and all policymaking processes. Woo (2018) maintains that this programme has resulted in organisational restructuring, administrative reorganisation, and enhanced citizen interaction with the government.

According to Steenmans, Taylor, and Steenmans (2021), emerging technical breakthroughs that characterise the 4IR are increasingly analysed as potential tools to support public management. These tools are particularly aimed at the more economical, effective, and efficient utilisation of government resources for successful service delivery. It includes the use of wireless sensor networks to enhance the on-site management of water, electricity, transport and waste. As far as waste management is concerned, Steenmans, Taylor and Steenmans (2021) contend that especially blockchain technology positively influences waste management methods. Particular domains in this regard include the use of smart contracts, the monitoring and tracking of waste, payments for recycling and reuse, and recycling and reuse rewards.

In the current knowledge-based society, it is no surprise that 4IR technologies can enhance efficiency, effectiveness, and productivity in government. These technologies appear to add

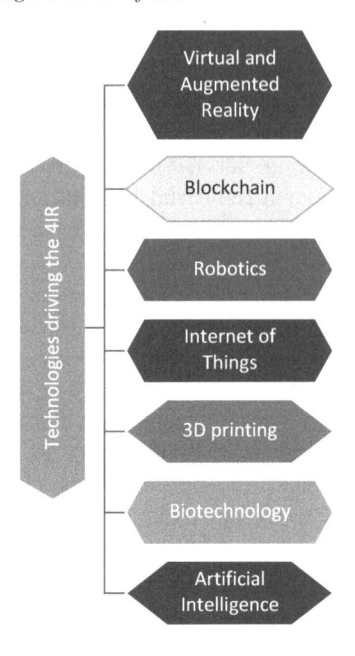

Source: Authors' own.

Figure 4.1   4IR technologies driving good governance

value to the good governance discourse, especially from the perspective of African countries. Figure 4.I outlines the typical 4IR technologies that act as catalysts for good governance.

Increasingly, these technologies alter the conventional ways governments operate and render services. It ultimately enhances the level of goodness of governance. It is argued that governments on the African continent should not be left behind in the global race towards more streamlined transactions, operations, and engagements. They should therefore be more flexible to adopt new technology and adjust their systems, processes, and functioning accordingly.

OPPORTUNITIES PROVIDED BY TECHNOLOGY TOWARDS GOOD GOVERNANCE

A growing number of countries are looking into cloud computing because of the many benefits it offers to government and public institutions, including cost savings and more mobility. With the help of these programs and apps, locals, visitors, and companies have easier access to government services, leading to higher levels of participation and satisfaction. By connecting and automating tasks, we can increase productivity without sacrificing quality. The fundamental 'blocks' of digital transformation have been implemented by government and public sector organisations. Benefits to African governments in terms of governance can be realised through the application of technology in the framework of the Fourth Industrial Revolution, as shown in Figure 4.2.

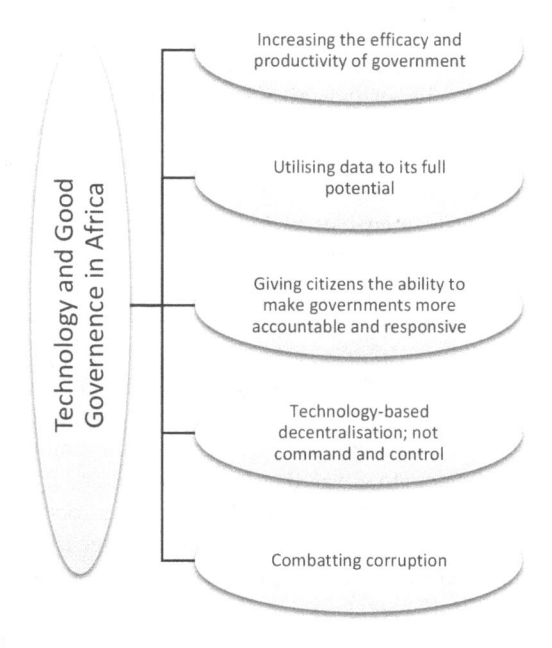

Source: Authors' own.

Figure 4.2   *Technology for Africa towards good governance*

Figure 4.2 illustrates how technological advancements can pave the path for more efficient government administrations. The efficient provision of public goods including education, health care, social security, and transportation are just a few examples of how new technologies have the potential to increase government efficiency. Similarly, technology can aid in boosting governmental output by optimising data use, empowering individuals to keep an analytical eye on their government, and facilitating decentralised, technology-driven reform rather than top-down management.

Increasing the Efficacy and Productivity of Government

One facet of emerging technologies that receives significant attention is the ways in which it can improve the efficacy and productivity of government. Government efficacy broadly encompasses the effective, efficient, and economical provision of services such as those provided by education, health, safety, and transport departments (De Zúñiga, Diehl and Ardévol-Abreu, 2017). From a normative perspective it also refers to compliance with good governance principles, administrative excellence, and the prevention of corruption. Improved efficacy naturally leads to higher productivity of government institutions.

Examples of technological applications for increased efficacy and productivity in government include the use of big data for urban service delivery, the use of smart systems for citizen identification, the use of surveillance systems for improved traffic flow and security, and tax enforcement and compliance systems. Bush (2019) reasons that the use of mobile apps for parking efficiency, for example, eliminates the need for traditional parking meters while also warning attendants of spaces that are about to become unavailable. Parking guidance and information systems use cameras or inductive loops, which are more commonly known as the mechanism by which smart streetlights detect waiting cars. These loops and cameras can detect exactly which parking spots are occupied and which spots are not, enabling drivers to be given precise directions to an open parking spot. These intelligent parking systems also allow for dynamic pricing, which enables parking places to be distributed more effectively during times of high demand (Bush, 2019).

Utilising Data to Its Full Potential

One of the many benefits of integrating technology into government operations is that it will make it much simpler for officials to utilise data at their disposal in the most effective ways. Using data to its fullest extent entails giving the government the ability to respond to the continuing needs of the stakeholders in a way that is methodical and dynamic to drive choices, and more crucially, in a way that is repeatable and removes errors and inefficiencies in the process. Governments can, for example, dispatch safety and security agencies to crime hotspots, proactively construct schools and clinics in growth areas, and construct roads and other infrastructure in congested traffic areas.

The use of data in government has the potential to offer the general public services that are more reliable, effective, and efficient. There is practically no end to this potential. Governments should identify and adopt a data governance model that establishes the necessary framework for a data-driven public sector. A data-driven public sector can better meet the requirements of the general population by evidence-based and objective decision-making. Figure 4.3 breaks down the benefits of complete data utilisation by governments into various categories.

The benefits of full data utilisation include increased openness, public confidence, responsibility-encouraged innovation, and even promoting community participation.

Empowering Citizens to Make Governments More Accountable, Responsible and Responsive

As stated, technology has the potential to simplify and streamline interactions between citizens and government institutions. Good governance will not naturally follow unless citizens demand government officials to be accountable for their actions and to be responsive towards the needs and aspirations of citizens. The interaction between governments and citizens is commonly referred to as a social contract. Kendall-Taylor, Frantz and Wright (2020), however, lament the fact that such a social contract has proven to be a persistent obstacle for Africa in the post-independence period. To foster this social contract, MacLachlan et al. (2018) argue that citizens need to have access to government-related information as well as some understanding of policies and instruments that allow them to hold those in power accountable. This will increase government responsiveness and improve overall accountability and transparency arrangements.

Internet World Stats (2022) cites data from the International Telecommunications Union that estimates that around 28.6% of Africa's population of 1.1 billion people can currently

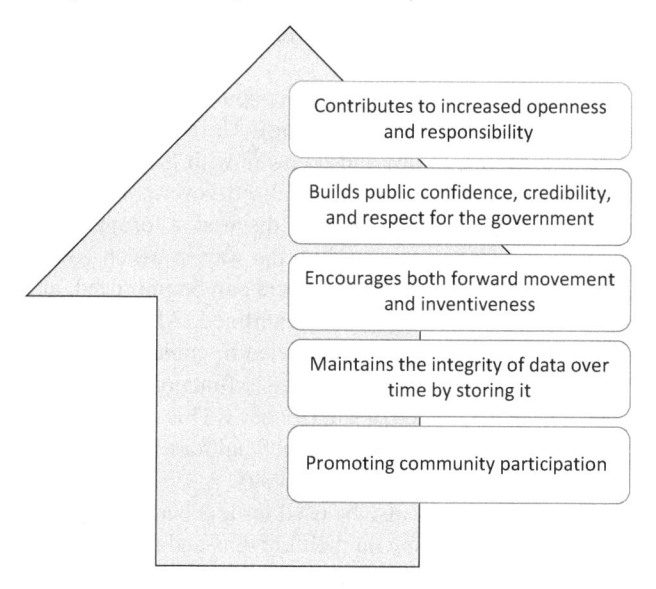

Contributes to increased openness and responsibility

Builds public confidence, credibility, and respect for the government

Encourages both forward movement and inventiveness

Maintains the integrity of data over time by storing it

Promoting community participation

Source: Authors' own.

Figure 4.3   *Summary of data utilisation*

access the internet using their mobile phones or personal computers (see https://www.internetworldstats.com/stats.htm). Postal and telephone services, which were notoriously unreliable and expensive, are gradually becoming relics of a bygone era. It is now increasingly possible to report an issue or make a complaint to a government department over the internet, either through a website, social media, or an app. The use of social media platforms has skyrocketed in popularity, particularly among younger generations. The enthusiasm of this demographic to adopt it for political and social activism has been demonstrated in Tunisia, Libya, and Egypt during the so-called Arab Spring, as well as recent protests at higher education institutions in South Africa (e.g. '#RhodesMustFall' and '#FeesMustFall' campaigns).

An increasing number of young Kenyans have taken to social media to bring attention to important concerns in the realm of government, such as the misappropriation of government funds and allegations of corruption levelled against members of the government. Consumer technology that is not only affordable but also easily accessible, such as mobile phones and other gadgets, makes it possible for eyewitness testimonies of governance malpractices to be recorded. For example, the cameras on mobile phones have been used to record election results that have been put outside counting locations in Zimbabwe. This has significantly reduced the likelihood of electoral fraud being committed by election and oversight authorities. Citizen activism in Kenya has also been created around more complicated, locally designed systems. During the political unrest that occurred in Kenya in 2008 and 2009, the open-source software system known as *Ushahidi*, which was powered by Google Maps, enabled users to report instances of voting irregularities and political violence by using geo-tagging to identify where they were located geographically. *Ushahidi* was able to spot outbreaks of violence more swiftly than traditional media.

Technological Empowerment Instead of Central Control

To engage with and empower their constituent populations, some African governments have started to utilise various forms of technology. Utilising cutting-edge technology has the potential to address localised issues and do away with the need for central government control. Technology thus enables a more decentralised governance model. The government of Morocco, for example, has established online discussion forums where members of the general public can express their views regarding the way in which government services are provided, make input on how administrative matters can be improved, and offer suggestions for how administrative procedures might be streamlined. Also Kenya's government developed the *Kipokezi* online chatting and email service in conjunction with the mobile phone service provider Safaricom. *Kipokezi* was developed to function on mobile devices that are not dependent on the most recent generation of smartphones. This makes it simpler for individuals and authorities to connect, which is especially beneficial for those living in rural regions who may not have access to the most up-to-date technology.

On the other hand, technology may also be used for less beneficial purposes. Authoritarian governments may use technology to spy on their citizens and unduly control democratic processes. Citizens too, may utilise technology to promote their ideas. For example, activists in Ethiopia used so-called 'radical blogging' on Facebook posts to disseminate extremists' points of view. The proposed Online Regulation Policy in South Africa, which is an amendment of the Films and Publications Act 2019, has the potential to make it easy to restrict online content in comprehensive ways should it be passed into law. Voices of strong opposition have already been heard citing infringements on the constitutional right to freedom of expression. The proposed policy also stands in contrast to legislation that promotes information sharing such as the Promotion of Access to Information Act 2 of 2000 and the Administrative Justice Act 3 of 2000.

Combatting Corruption in Government

When it comes to providing services, governments are frequently forced to make trade-offs between efficiency and fairness. Unfortunately, picking one efficiency or fairness above the other typically increases the chance of corruption (Van Niekerk, 2021). When a system is efficient, the public is generally willing to function within the boundaries the system establishes. When a system is inefficient, however, people may exploit loopholes and resort to illegal activities.

As stated earlier, technology brings the possibility of making government operations more efficient, transparent, and equitable. Blockchain technology is one example of such possibility by exercising adequate monitoring and control over public procurement processes. There are different reasons why public procurement is so susceptible to corruption. The number of financial transactions, the close engagement between public officials and businesses (e.g. tender processes), and the relative ease with which corrupt actions of willing parties can be concealed all play a role in inducing corrupt conduct. Blockchain technology possesses the ability to guard against these vulnerabilities. Recent studies conducted by Transparency International in India, for example, confirmed that blockchain technology can significantly reduce the number of malpractices in government procurement (Abiad and Khatiwada, 2018; Van Niekerk, 2021). A wider range of stakeholders may be encouraged to engage in and monitor procurement cycles using blockchain technology. Currently, monitoring and oversight agencies, end-users, the media, and ordinary citizens are all deterred from taking part in the procurement process because information on the process is either difficult to get, unreliable, subject to change, or delayed. A blockchain platform that offers real-time information, is tamper-proof, and easy to access can significantly reduce these obstacles and contribute to combatting corrupt practices.

CONCLUSION

Within the framework of the 4IR the purpose of this chapter was to investigate the potential of technology to promote good governance in Africa. It was established that technological advancement can make governments more effective and governance more 'good'. It may further be deduced that the level of goodness of governance on the African continent is in its infancy stages and that much more needs to be done to improve the levels of efficacy of government administrations. Despite the lightning-fast pace at which change has occurred in the domain of technology, governments have been slow to adapt it. In particular, technologies associated with 4IR can significantly enhance the level of good governance on the continent.

The application of new technologies holds a great deal of potential for enhancing the efficiency of government, among other things, the suppression of corrupt practices, and the effective provision of public goods such as education, health, social security, and transportation. It was also pointed out that technology can help in increasing the productivity of the government, can also allow the government to utilise data to its full potential, can give citizens the ability to keep a critical eye on their government, and that technology-based decentralisation, as opposed to command and control, can become a reality. As a result, governments in Africa must become serious about investigating the technologies that can genuinely assist them in improving governance in the context of the 4IR.

REFERENCES

Abiad, A. and S. Khatiwada (2018), 'Five Ways Technology is Improving Governance', Public Service Delivery in Developing Asia, accessed 30 June 2022 at https://blogs.adb.org/blog/5-ways-technology -improving-governance-public-service-delivery-developing-asia.

African Governance Architecture. (2019), 'The African Governance Report', accessed 12 August 2022 at https://au.int/sites/default/files/documents/36843-doc-final_draft_-_the_africa_governance _report_-_21_january_2019_1.pdf.

Asefa, S. and W.-C. Huang (2015), 'The Challenges of Good Governance and Leadership in Developing Countries: Cases from Africa and China', in S. Asefa and W.-C. Huang (eds), *The Political Economy of Good Governance*, Kalamazoo, MI: W.E. Upjohn Institute for Employment Research, pp. 131–153.

Balcerzak, A.P., E. Nica, E. Rogalska, M. Poliak, T. Klieštik and O.M. Sabie (2022), 'Blockchain Technology and Smart Contracts in Decentralized Governance Systems', *Administrative Sciences*, **12** (3), 96–112, doi.org/10.3390/admsci12030096.

Bush, J. (2019), 'Unlocking the Power of Technology for Better Governance', accessed 2 Oct 2022 at https://www.hoover.org/research/unlocking-power-technology-better-governance.

Castellanos, W.S. (2020), 'Impact of the Information Technology (IT) Governance on Business-IT Alignment' (Doctoral dissertation), Pontificia Universidad Catolica del Peru-CENTRUM Catolica, Peru.

Chien, N.B. and N.N. Thanh (2022), 'The Impact of Good Governance on the People's Satisfaction with Public Administrative Services in Vietnam', *Administrative Sciences*, **12** (1), 35–47, doi.org/10.3390 /admsci12010035.

Dayanandan, R. (2013), 'Good Governance Practice for Better Performance of Community Organisations-Myths and Realities', *Journal of Power, Politics and Governance*, **1** (1), 10–26.

Deloitte (2020), 'The Fourth Industrial Revolution: At the Intersection of Readiness and Responsibility', Deloitte Insights, accessed 10 August 2022 at https://www2.deloitte.com/content/dam/Deloitte/de/Documents/human-capital/Deloitte_Review_26_Fourth_Industrial_Revolution.pdf.

De Zúñiga, G.H., T. Diehl and A. Ardévol-Abreu (2017), 'Internal, External, and Government Political Efficacy: Effects on News Use, Discussion, and Political Participation', *Journal of Broadcasting and Electronic Media*, **61** (3), 574–596, doi.org/10.1080/08838151.2017.1344672.

Dzingirai, M. (2021), 'Managerial Challenges under FinTech: Evidence from Zimbabwean Commercial Banks', in Sghari, A. and K. Mezghani (eds.), *Influence of FinTech on Management Transformation*, Hershey, PA: IGI Global, pp. 141–166, doi.org/10.4018/978-1-7998-7110-1.ch007.

Dzingirai, M. and R. Ndava (2022), 'Global Institutional Role to Promote Achievement of the Sustainable Development Goals in Zimbabwe', in N. Baporikar (ed.), *Handbook of Research on Global Institutional Roles for Inclusive Development*, Hershey, PA: IGI Global, pp. 99–117.

Dzingirai, M., S. Sikomwe and N. Tshuma (2022), 'Corporate Governance Challenges for Small and Medium Enterprises in the Constrained Zimbabwean Economy', *International Journal of Applied Management Sciences and Engineering*, **9** (1), 1–14.

Giao, C.V. (2021), 'Good Governance and Problems for State Management in Vietnam', *State Organisation Journal*, **2**, 48–58.

Islam, M.S. (2017), 'Governance and Development', in A. Farazmand (ed.), *Global Encyclopedia of Public Administration, Public Policy, and Governance*, Cham: Springer, pp. 2771–2779.

Johnson, O.E.G. (2016), *Economic Diversification and Growth in Africa: Critical Policymaking Issues*, Cham: Palgrave Macmillan.

Kalsi, N.S., R. Kiran and S.C. Vaidya (2008), 'ICT and Good Governance: A Study of Indian Environment', *E-Governance in Practice*, 11–25, accessed 8 August 2022 at https://www.eldis.org/document/A59563.

Kendall-Taylor, A., E. Frantz and J. Wright (2020), 'The Digital Dictators: How Technology Strengthens Autocracy', *Foreign Affairs*, **99**, 103, accessed 22 July 2022 at https://www.foreignaffairs.com/articles/china/2020-02-06/digital-dictators.

León, L.F.A. and J. Rosen (2020), 'Technology as Ideology in Urban Governance', *Annals of the American Association of Geographers*, **110** (2), 497–506, doi.org/10.1080/24694452.2019.1660139.

MacLachlan, M., D. Banes, D. Bell, J. Borg, B. Donnelly, M. Fembek and H. Hooks (2018), 'Assistive Technology Policy: A Position Paper from the First Global Research, Innovation, and Education on Assistive Technology (GREAT) Summit', *Disability and Rehabilitation: Assistive Technology*, **13** (5), 454–466, doi.org/10.1080/17483107.2018.1468496.

Mhlanga, D. (2020), 'Industry 4.0: The Challenges Associated with the Digital Transformation of Education in South Africa', *The Impacts of Digital Transformation*, **13**, 12–25.

Mohanty, P.K. (2005), 'Using e-tools for Good Governance and Administrative Reforms. IAS Centre for Good Governance', accessed 8 August 2022 at https://www.academia.edu/7703670/Using_e_Tools_for_Good_Governance_and_Administrative_Reforms.

Nanda, V.P. (2006), 'The "Good Governance" Concept Revisited', *The Annals of the American Academy of Political and Social Science*, **603** (1), 269–283.

Newiak, M., A.A. Wane and A. Segura-Ubiergo (2022), 'Good Governance in Sub-Saharan Africa: Opportunities and Lessons', *International Monetary Fund*, doi.org/10.5089/9781513584058.071.

Otiko, A.O. and M.M. Inuwa (2021), 'The Role of Information Technology in Good Governance and Economic Development of Nigeria', *United International Journal for Research and Technology*, **3** (1), 95–99.

Pitsikalis, S., I. Lasica, A. Kostas and C. Vitsilaki (2022), 'Preparing Teachers for the 21st Century: A Mixed-Methods Evaluation of TPD Programs Under the Lens of Emerging Technologies in STE(A)M Education', in S. Xefteris (ed.), *Handbook of Research on Integrating ICTs in STEAM Education*, Hershey, PA: IGI Global, pp. 153–175, doi.org/10.4018/978-1-6684-3861-9.ch008.

Steenmans, K., P. Taylor and I. Steenmans (2021), 'Blockchain Technology for Governance of Plastic Waste Management: Where Are We?', *Social Sciences*, **10** (11), 434–458, doi.org/10.3390/socsci101 1043.

Thomas, C.A., V.W. Mbarika, R. Nwogu, P.F. Musa and P. Meso (2009), 'Facilitating Better Governance through E-Government Initiatives: Successful Case in Sub-Saharan Africa', accessed 21 September 2022 at https://repository.upenn.edu/cgi/viewcontent.cgi?article=1016&context=ictafrica.

Van Niekerk, M. (2021), 'How Blockchain Can Help Dismantle Corruption in Government Services', accessed 18 September 2022 at https://www.weforum.org/agenda/2021/07/blockchain-for-government-systems-anti-corruption/.

Wani, H.A. (2014), 'Constraints and Impediments of Good Governance in Africa: Prospects', *Afro-Asian Journal of Social Sciences*, **5** (1), 1–21.

Williamson, B. and N. Piattoeva (2019), 'Objectivity as Standardization in Data-Scientific Education Policy, Technology and Governance', *Learning, Media and Technology*, **44** (1), 64–76.

Woo, J.J. (2018), 'Technology and Governance in Singapore's Smart Nation Initiative', Ash Center Policy Briefs Series, accessed 18 August 2022 at https://dash.harvard.edu/handle/1/42372461.

World Bank. (2006), 'Making PRSP Inclusive', accessed 7 September 2022 at http://siteresources.worldbank.org/DISABILITY/Resources/280658-117.

Xu, M., J.M. David and S.H. Kim (2018), 'The Fourth Industrial Revolution: Opportunities and Challenges', *International Journal of Financial Research*, **9** (2), 90–95, doi.org/10.5430/ijfr.v9n2.

Yaro, I.F., M. Hanka and T. Engbers (2019), 'Good Governance in Africa: Necessary Reforms for the Development of the Continent', *International Journal of Multidisciplinary Thought*, **8** (1), 55–64.

5. Good corporate governance in state-owned entities: the case of Zimbabwe
Gideon Zhou

INTRODUCTION

A corporate governance-compliant state-owned sector is the bedrock of national development. Across African nations and indeed the world over, state-owned entities (SOEs) account for significant shares of gross domestic product (GDP) and are also involved in strategic, large-scale, capital-intensive projects in the areas of energy, transport, and communication (OECD, 2016). They serve as the main vehicles through which core basic services relating to information, health, water, transport, electricity, education, waste management, defence, and security are provided to the public. In post-independence Africa, SOEs have also served as a means of encouraging new African states to be the main investors and producers in their economies – indeed potent means – of indigenising economies, promoting regionally balanced development, and local entrepreneurship. An expanded SOE therefore symbolises state ownership and economic sovereignty. Thus, as argued by Eddie Cross, a local economics expert and former Minister of Education in Zimbabwe during the Inclusive Government of 2009 to 2013, 'when state-managed institutions fail, everyone suffers the consequence' (Cross, 2022b, p. 1). Indications suggest that SOE sectors have continued to expand in both the developed and the developing countries despite rollback reforms, with China in the lead with around 51 000 SOEs and most African countries having portfolios generally not less than 100 (OECD, 2021). Zimbabwe has over 103 SOEs, a figure that is generally consistent with Ghana and South Africa numbers of 132 SOEs and 300, respectively. These SOEs reflect varied ownership models that take the forms of wholly state-owned and managed, and those in which governments hold a majority of the share capital. Ginting and Naqvi (2020, p. 1) provide useful insights on the definitional discourses of SOE:

> Any commercial entity in which the government has significant control through direct and indirect ownership. An enterprise that is 100% government-owned is obviously categorized as an SOE. But other enterprises may also qualify as SOEs, such as those in which the government has a majority equity stake; and those in which the government owns a minority stake, but the government retains a controlling vote in major financial and management decisions.

These introductory remarks strongly suggest that SOEs, if effectively managed, are strategically placed to spearhead the development agendas of nations. In the context of Zimbabwe's current development agenda, SOEs should serve as hubs through which the national vision for a middle-income status by 2030 can be realised. Yet, reviews of SOE contribution to the process of socioeconomic development of nations across the global divide suggest that SOEs have not lived up to national expectations (Clarke, 2017; Moyo, 2022; Nhema, 2015; OECD, 2021; Wright, 2004; Zhou, 2017). SOEs that were expected to generate an investible surplus to the treasury have in many instances required massive subsidisation, imposing a fiscal burden on economies. Literature generally points to pervasive cultures of opaque corporate practices (Chigudu, 2020; Chifaka, Foya and Ncube, 2022). In South Africa, formerly leading SOEs such as the Eskom, South African Airways, and Transnet were by 2022 facing deep-seated service delivery and governance challenges. Zimbabwe's SOE contribution to GDP has continued to decline so by 2022 it had dropped to levels of five per cent (Cross, 2022b) from the 40 per cent level in the 1980s and the 12 per cent level in the 1990s (Government of Zimbabwe, 1991). In the case of the Cotton Company of Zimbabwe (COTTCO), corruption, as argued by Cross (2022b, p. 1), cost the cotton sector around US$50 million. These challenges were vividly echoed in remarks made by the President of Zimbabwe, Emmerson Mnangagwa when he addressed a seminar for cabinet ministers held in Harare on 3 March 2022:

> The time has come for parastatals to propel the growth of the economy by meaningfully contribut-ing to the country's GDP, fiscus and job creation. After all, State-controlled entities are obligated by section 195 of our National Constitution to be profitable and viable. They were created for growing our economy, providing quality goods, as well as reliable and affordable services to industry and the public at large. Under the Second Republic's whole of Government approach, State-owned enter-prises must stand on their own feet as opposed to being a perpetual burden to the fiscus. The non-pay-ment of rates, fines and other statutory obligations should now be a thing of the past. The culture of flimsy excuses for breaching statutory requirements with regards the disclosure of financial and non-financial information must stop forthwith. Inefficiencies in the operations of State-owned enterprises as well as malfeasance such as nepotism and opaque personnel management practices must be a thing of the past. Hence, the onus is on the boards and management to guarantee adherence to mechanisms that have been put in place to prevent these practices. (Munangagwa cited in The Herald, 2022, p. 1)

The Zimbabwe Minister of Finance and Economic Development, Mthuli Ncube, also expressed similar concerns when he remarked that public entities which were supposed to realise a profit close to USD200 million in 2017 ended up incurring losses of USD340 million (Ncube, 2020, p. 1). Consultancy and government reports have over decades routinely referred to cases of entities operating without Boards for long periods; failure to hold meetings regu-larly in accordance with their enabling Acts; weak internal controls leading to cases of pay-ments with no proof of authorisation; failure to honour statutory obligations to the National Social Security Authority (NSSA), Zimbabwe Revenue Authority (ZIMRA), pension funds and Medical Aid Societies; failure to pay dividends to government; unauthorised increase of board fees and salaries, benefits and allowances for executives; weak due diligence in procure-ment processes; failure to submit annual financial statements to the Auditor-General office; failure to comply with issues raised in Auditor-General reports (International Transparency, 2015; Zhou and Zinyama, 2016; Foya and Changunda, 2019; Mpedzisi, 2021; ZIMCODD, 2022). As depicted in one local media outlet, 'the reports on government finances always read like a roll call of most corrupt, extravagant and poorly managed entities' (Editorial Comment, 2020). This is also captured by Cross (2022a, p. 1) as follows:

> Our State-owned power utility is generating half of what we consumed in power 20 years ago. Cities are receiving less than half the water that they require for normal use. Our railways which used to handle the great majority of our freight, now handles less than 10 per cent; if that. Air Zimbabwe, once the African airline that had never had an accident, is no more and barely functioning with a couple of small aircraft. Our road infrastructure, once one of the best in Africa is in a terrible condi-tion in rural and urban areas and our national roads need rehabilitation and repair. At one stage we advocated privatisation. But even that has had little impact and, in many cases, has actually made the situation worse with private sector interests exploiting their monopoly rights and not doing their job. Levels of corruption have sometimes been made worse by incorporating private interests.

However, it is important to appreciate from the outset that SOE governance is inherently intractable because it entails a delicate balance between the 'public' and 'enterprise' dimensions of an entity's concerns that embody the generational contestations between 'state' and 'market' as alternative forms of governance. The 'public' dimension underlines the inevitability of political intrusions in the governance of public entities or as put by Nellis (2001, p. 15), 'unintended governance failures' arising from the vulnerability of SOEs to 'political and patronage considerations'. SOE corporate governance brings into question broader issues relating to the nature of state politics and leadership. The search for good SOE corporate governance thus goes beyond technical concerns relating to the existence of appropriate frameworks and principles to issues of political will.

Against this background, this chapter takes a holistic review of SOE corporate governance in Zimbabwe in a bid to find out how it can be sustainably improved in line with emerging regional and global best practices. To this end, the concepts of corporate governance and state-owned enterprise are explored; regional and global codes of corporate governance critically reviewed; and SOE corporate governance scenarios in Zimbabwe examined to create a basis for evidence-informed recommendations. These substantive concerns animated the formulation of the questions of the chapter: What is corporate governance? What fundamental principles underpin corporate governance? What are state-owned entities (SOEs)? Why is good corporate governance critical in state-owned entities in general and in Zimbabwe in particular? What initiatives have been adopted to improve corporate governance in SOEs in Zimbabwe over the years? To what extent do these initiatives comply with regional and global codes of corporate governance? How can good corporate governance be strengthened in SOE in Zimbabwe? The study methodology is thus largely documentary and content analysis anchored.

GLOBAL CONTEXTS OF CORPORATE GOVERNANCE

Although the term 'corporate governance' came into vogue at the onset of the second millennium, its generic precepts can be traced as far back as the writings of the ancient Greek philosophers. Plato's *Republic* and Aristotle's *Politics* were principally concerned with finding values and ethics essential for moulding a 'good citizen' and 'just state' (Rodee et al., 1983, p. 7). These normative concerns revolved around understanding what is justice, what makes political power and its exercise legitimate, and how property and other forms of material possession should be distributed among citizens. These normative questions resonate with the King IV notion of corporate governance in which 'those tasked with governance duties lead ethically and effectively' while corporates are expected to view themselves as 'integral parts of society and accountable to both present and future generations' (King, 2016).

Viewed this way, corporate governance fundamentally entails checks and balances in the conduct of corporate affairs through proper delineation of the roles and responsibilities of boards of directors and executive management to make them accountable to shareholders and stakeholders (Paces, 2015; Wen, 2015). These concerns inform Cadbury's (1992) definition of corporate governance as systems of directing and controlling companies; the OECD (2015) depiction of corporate governance as structures of relationships among corporate management, board, shareholders, and stakeholders; and the King Committee (2016) view of corporate governance as 'governing bodies' exercising ethical and effective leadership. The emphasis on ethical and effective leadership is deliberately used to project corporate governance as a long-range, holistic, and integrative process concerned with promoting governance outcomes that resonate with those of communities. Good corporate governance is not a strait-jacket process but one that is shaped by concerns in the social settings of entities.

In terms of impetus, the impression is that global concerns for corporate governance were triggered by outbreaks of corporate scandals in countries that include Britain, the United States, and Australia, among others. In Britain, financial scandals that rocked formerly glob- ally reputed companies such as the Bank of Credit and Commerce International (BCCI) in the mid-1990s jolted the Government to set up the Cadbury Committee whose findings resulted in the release of the Cadbury Report on Principles of Good Corporate Governance in 1992. The Report, among other issues, called for the separation of the roles of board chairman and CEO, a minimum of three non-executive directors, strengthening of internal controls, creation of audit committees, and strengthening oversight on financial reporting. In the United States, the sudden collapse of Enron, a globally reputed company which had just been audited and its accounts cleared by an equally highly reputable audit firm – Arthur Anderson – triggered the setting up of the Committee of Sponsoring Organisations in 1991 whose findings guided the Congress to introduce far-reaching regulations on auditing and financial reporting in public entities under the Sebanes-Oxley Act of 2003. The regula- tions called for corporate code of ethics, oversight on the accounting processes of public entities, whistle-blower protection, internal and external audit reports, creation of independ- ent Audit committees, and empowering chief executive offices and financial directors to verify and endorse company accounts, among others. The collapse of One Tel and Tyco in Australia led to the release of a series of the Organisation for Economic Co-operation and Development (OECD) Principles for Good Corporate Governance starting in 1999. These Principles and later versions, among other issues, advocate for clear delineation of the responsibilities of the board and the rights of shareholders, equal treatment of all share- holders, the enhanced role of stakeholders, protection of whistle-blowers, and disclosures, among others (OECD, 2003, 2015, 2021).

In the southern African region, South Africa led the pace by setting up the King Committee whose findings led to the release of a series of The King Report on Good Corporate Governance beginning with the 1994 version. The Code prioritised regulating the conduct of boards of companies that were listed on the Johannesburg Stock Exchange (JSE), banks, and listed SOEs. It can thus be argued that the King approach to corporate governance was ini- tially not all-sector-focused. It had a financial and banking sector bias. In the second edition, King (2002) provided broadened guidance on sustainability reporting, stakeholder interest, remuneration, checks and balances, audit committees, risks in management, role of directors, and financial committees. The third version reflects emerging notions of networked corporate governance-hence reference to 'ecosystems of players guided by sustainability concerns of the environment, society and economy' (King, 2009).

Within this evolving notion of corporate governance, entities are expected to conduct their business operations in ways that are fair to both present and future generations. These emerg- ing views of corporate governance should be appreciated within the context of twenty-first- century precepts informed by the Sustainable Development Goals (SDGs) and New Public Governance. These precepts enjoin public entities to operate in partnerships with private play- ers for quality outcomes. Communities are not just viewed as consumers of corporate services but active participants in the processes of design and production of those services (Basu, 2017;

Denhardt and Denhardt, 2000; Howlett, Anka and Ora-orn, 2017; Osborne, 2010; Osborne, Zoe and Kirsty, 2016; Torfing, Sorensen and Roiseland, 2016).

The visibility of the 'apply and explain' principle in King (2016) highlights the shift from 'all-size-fit-all' approaches that were dominant under managerialism to context-specific governance models in which the application of a principle is contingent on the obtaining contexts of entities. This emphasis is very important because a success story best practice in one setting may not necessarily be successful in another setting. Corporate governance should be pragmatic, flexible, and context-conscious. Equally visible in the King IV version is the emphasis on the role of the 'governing body' as the 'focal point and custodian' for value creation and outcomes-focused corporate governance (Harduth and Alexander, 2021, p. 4).

Clearly emerging from the foregoing discussion is that good corporate governance entails social responsibility. A good corporate entity is one that is socially responsible. The basis of this thinking is that corporate entities operate in communities and therefore derive their social existence and logic from those communities. This social existence obliges corporate entities to be sensitive to their communities – that is, the environment, economy, and society. For example, extractive corporate entities should demonstrate responsibility by developing the communities in which they are operating, by refraining from polluting the environment, by adopting internal codes of conduct, adopting anti-corruption measures, respecting basic human rights, protecting whistle-blowers, and considering the interests of both current and future workers. Good corporate social responsibility thus denotes intergenerational positive thinking and practices. These notions of corporate social responsibility are also echoed in the OECD (2015, 2021) reports in which corporate governance is conceptualised as 'a platform for building an environment of trust, transparency and accountability necessary for fostering long-term investment, financial stability and business integrity, and more inclusive societies'. Responsible corporate governance is thus ethical, protective, responsive, accountable, transparent, accountable, intergenerational, and socially legitimate.

CORPORATE GOVERNANCE IN SOES IN ZIMBABWE

This section situates the discussion of corporate governance within SOEs in Zimbabwe. Its main concern is to trace the origin and evolution of corporate governance as an issue of national concern. In Zimbabwe, corporate governance emerged as a public domain issue in the early 2000s following a series of unanticipated cases of company bankruptcies in the financial and banking sectors (Zhou, 2007; Maune, 2015). In 2004, the CFX Bank Ltd collapsed hardly a year after its establishment, raising fundamental questions in the public domain on the adequacy of internal checks and balances. There were claims that top bank management executives had fraudulently misrepresented the bank's financial conditions by overstating interest income and understating interest expenses. Subsequent collapses of other financial and banking entities such as the United Merchant Bank, the First National Building Society, and the ENG Asset Management Company further rattled the banking and financial sectors as they occurred at a time when Zimbabwe was experiencing deep-seated economic challenges in the form of continued decline of the value of local currency, cash hoarding and shortages, and externalisation of foreign currency, among others.

Reserve Bank Regulations-led Corporate Governance

Corporate governance interventions in Zimbabwe initially had a banking and financial sector focus, with the Reserve Bank of Zimbabwe as the key enforcing agent. In the non-banking and financial sectors, corporate governance was initially enforced mainly through suasion or exhortations. Regulatory instruments utilised in the banking and financial sectors included the Companies Act (Chapter 24:03) which covered corporate governance matters relating to registration, incorporation, conduct of business by private and public companies, and roles and responsibilities of directors and shareholders; the Zimbabwe Stock Exchange Act which provided registration requirements, conduct of business on the stock exchange, and prevention of insider trading; the Reserve Bank of Zimbabwe Act (Chapter 22:15) which outlined expected corporate best practices within banking institutions in the areas of shareholding, capitalisation, structure of boards, board committees, and senior management as well as roles of auditors.

The Reserve Bank interventions were also through directives. These included the 2004 directive which required banks to have independent non-directors in the majority in boards in line with regional and global best practices espoused in King (2002) and Cadbury (1992). Another directive of 2005 compelled bank compliance with international rating standards. Shareholders with ten per cent or above were also not allowed to serve either at the level of management or as board chairmen. It is clear that corporate governance in Zimbabwe was drifting from traditional owner-managed company models of having chief executive officers in the majority of shareholding.

Exhortative Governance Instruments

Corporate governance ideals of integrity, accountability, and transparency were also enforced through yearly fiscal and monetary policy instruments. For instance, the Government of Zimbabwe (2003, 2005) presented corporate governance as a vehicle for fighting corruption, advocated an all-sector-focused corporate governance approach, introduced a code of ethics for both the private and public sectors, and also the setting up of a financial intelligence centre that was housed in the Reserve Bank (Zhou, 2007). The call for an 'all-sector-focused' approach to corporate governance signalled a shift in approach to corporate governance in Zimbabwe. Corporate governance ceased to be narrowly viewed as a banking and financial sector concern but an issue for both public and private entities. This saw the broadening of corporate governance interventions to SOEs and local authorities through the Parastatals and Loans Authorities Orientation Programme (PLAP) Guidelines of 2005 which outlined corporate governance requirements to be complied with by public entities accessing funding under PLAP (Government of Zimbabwe, 2005). These requirements included establishment of substantive boards, board committees, management structure, academic and professional qualifications for committee members, and audited statements. These exhortations echoed best practices outlined in regional global codes such as the Cadbury (1992) and King (1994, 2002) reports.

Other supportive instruments included the Anti-Corruption Commission Act (Chapter 9:22) of 2004 which provided a legal basis for the establishment of an independent anti-corruption body – the Zimbabwe Anti-Corruption Commission (ZACC) – in 2005 with specific mandates to investigate and expose corruption, abuse of power, and theft in both public and private entities. Although the operational effectiveness of ZACC has been constrained by a lack of resources and prosecuting powers, the creation of ZACC was in line with global anti-corruption initiatives as stipulated by the OECD (2015). The setting up of a Department of State Enterprises in 2006, the creation of the Zimbabwe Republic Police's Economic Crimes Unit, the National Economic Conduct Inspectorate, and the Economic Crime Court provided additional frameworks for enforcing corporate governance, notwithstanding challenges relating to delineation of roles and responsibilities.

Unbundling of SOE Monopolies

Equally notable in the pursuit of good governance in SOEs was the decision to demerge SOE monopolies into smaller business-oriented units – a process that saw the rebranding of the Privatization Agency of Zimbabwe (PAZ) as State Enterprise Restructuring Agency (SERA); the breaking of Postal and Telecommunications (PTC) into ZIMPOST, Net-One, and Tel-One; the restructuring of the Zimbabwe Broadcasting Corporation (ZBC) into nine subsidiary companies – National Television, NEWSNET, Radio Zimbabwe, Power FM, SFM, and National FM with Zimbabwe Broadcasting Holdings as the new holding company; and also the splitting of ZESA into five smaller units – the Zimbabwe Power Company (ZPC), the Zimbabwe Electricity Transmission Company (ZETC), the Zimbabwe Electricity Distribution Company (ZEDC0, the ZESA Enterprises, and the Power Tel) operating under the ZESA Holdings Ltd as the new holding company. However, the adopted top-heavy executive structures in the wake of demerging compromised the expected cost savings. Corporate checks and balances were dented by perceived tendencies to operate for years without well-constituted boards; political interference into 'matters of appointment of board members and selection of strategic partners' (Zhou, 2012). Those in executive positions had propensities to award themselves huge perks even at times when these entities were failing to pay employees and even services to the public (Zhou, 2017).

THE CONSTITUTIONAL BASIS OF SOE CORPORATE GOVERNANCE

The year 2013 is absolutely crucial in Zimbabwe's history as it saw the replacement of the Lancaster House Constitution of 1979 by the Constitution of Zimbabwe Amendment (No. 20) Act of 2013. Unlike the old Constitution, the new one has specific sections that relate to corporate governance and in this way lent a constitutional basis to corporate governance. Section 195 of the new Constitution defines and stipulates the responsibilities, explicitly emphasising the need to 'conduct their operations so as to maintain commercial viability and abide by generally accepted standards of good corporate governance … establishment of transparent, open and competitive procurement systems' (Government of Zimbabwe, 2013). Sections 194 to 196 of Chapter 9 reinforce this corporate governance stance by stipulating the fundamental values and principles that should guide their operations. According to Section 194 Subsection 1 of the 2013 Zimbabwe Constitution, all tiers of government (state institutions and other public enterprises) should be governed by the following values and principles:

(a) a high standard of professional ethics must be promoted and maintained;
(b) efficient and economical use of resources must be promoted;

(c) public administration must be development-oriented;
(d) services must be provided impartially, fairly, equitably and without bias;
(e) people's needs must be responded to within a reasonable time, and the public must be encouraged to participate in policy-making;
(f) public administration must be accountable to Parliament and to the people;
(g) institutions and agencies of government at all levels must co-operate with each other;
(h) transparency must be fostered by providing the public with timely, accessible and accurate information;
(i) good human-resource management and career-development practices, to maximise human potential, must be cultivated;
(j) public administration must be broadly representative of the diverse communities of Zimbabwe;
(k) employment, training and advancement practices must be based on merit, ability, objectivity, fairness, equality of men and women and the inclusion of persons with disabilities; and the State must take measures, including legislative measures, to promote these values and principles.

The Zimbabwe National Code on Corporate Governance (ZIMCODE)

A positive development was the launch of the Zimbabwe National Code in Corporate Governance (ZIMCODE) in 2015, a framework that was developed along the lines of the Cadbury and third versions of the King Codes. Drawing from the 2013 Constitution of Zimbabwe, the ZIMCODE explicitly emphasised corporate transparency, accountability, and efficiency; fair distribution of power among corporate players; clearly defined roles boards, stakeholders, and parent ministries. In this way, the ZIMCODE sets parameters for corporate governance and ethical leadership in SOEs.

The Public Entities Corporate Governance Act (Chapter 10:31) of 2018

The adoption of this Act provides legal authority to the ZIMCODE. Among other things, the Act calls for a corporate governance framework that is guided by Chapter 9 of the Constitution, establishment of the Unit in the Office of the President and Cabinet, and how the Corporate Governance Unit (CGU) relates to line ministers, appointments, and conditions of service of CEOs and Boards. The Unit is headed by a person of the grade of a permanent secretary. The functions of the Unit as outlined in the Act include:

- providing the advisory support mechanism for line Ministries in enforcing compliance by all public entities in line with the Act;
- advising line ministries with regard to the regular evaluation of the performance of public entities, boards, and employees;
- providing advice relating to designing performance contracts between line ministries and the boards; and those between boards, CEOs, and senior managers;
- overseeing how line ministries discharge the duties of monitoring boards, CEOs, and management compliance with the performance contracts;
- creating an up-to-date detailed directory or database that helps line ministries and boards to identify suitably qualified candidates for appointment to boards of public entities; and
- providing advice to line ministries on professional development, induction and training programmes for board members and senior staff members. (Government of Zimbabwe, 2018)

Within the stipulated governance framework, ministers, through the Office of the Chief Secretary to the President and Cabinet, provide policy direction, guided by national concerns. Reporting procedures entail submission of yearly Annual reports by entities 'not later than the 1st of October to the responsible Minister, through the Office of the Chief Secretary to the President and Cabinet. After receiving the report, the Minister is expected to present a copy of the report before the National Assembly 'one of the thirty days on which the Assembly next sits'. As stated, the report, 'with the leave of the minister', may be availed in electronic form for inspection by members of the public on the website of the Corporate Governance Unit.

SOE CORPORATE GOVERNANCE IN ZIMBABWE

This section explores factors at both the levels of framework and practice that are either strengthening or weakening SOE corporate governance in Zimbabwe. To this end, the section kicks off with a review of the legal frameworks, primarily focusing on the Zimbabwe National Constitution of 2013 and the Public Entities Corporate Governance Act of 2018.

The following provisions in the national Constitution, if mindfully applied, have the potential to strengthen SOE corporate governance:

- The national Constitution has specific provisions that call for good corporate governance in SOEs. Chapter 9 (Sections 194, 195, and 196) outlines the fundamental values and principles of governing public administration and leadership in SOEs. Underscored by these constitutional provisions is that promotion of good corporate governance in SOEs should be treated as an issue of national concern. In practice, policy enforcement is easier when it has the full backing of the primary law of the country – the national Constitution.
- The national Constitution explicitly acknowledges the roles of Parliament and the Auditor-General in strengthening good corporate governance in SOEs. Chapter 17 (Sections 298, 299, and 300) outlines the oversight roles of Parliament in SOEs. These provisions are very significant because worldwide, Supreme Audit Institutions serve as the bedrock of enforcing corporate accountability.
- Chapter 13 of the national Constitution also clearly delineates the 'institutions to combat corruption and crime' as the Zimbabwe Anti-Corruption Commission, and the National Prosecuting Authority as well as outlining their specific roles and responsibilities. These provisions are highly critical because the pursuit of good corporate governance inescapably entails anti-corruption initiatives.
- The national Constitution also provides a governance framework based on the separation of powers and checks and balances among the executive, judiciary, and legislature.
- The national Constitution also provides for the Presidential Question Time – a framework in which as clearly outlined in Section 140(3) of the national Constitution, 'The President may attend Parliament to answer questions on any issue as may be provided in Standing Orders'. In the old national Constitution, the Lancaster House Constitution of 1979, only Government ministers were obliged to attend the Question and Answer Sessions and respond to questions from backbenchers. The provision for the Presidential Question Time, if fully utilised, as is the case in South Africa and the United Kingdom, carries the seeds of good corporate governance in SOEs. The more the President is forced to directly answer questions relating to SOE governance, the more prone he or she is likely to keep

abreast with fundamental issues facing the SOE sector – a sector that holds huge potential to contribute to the national fiscus.

- Sections 309, 310, 311, 312, 313, and 314 of the national Constitution read with Section 10(1) of the Audit Office Act [Chapter 22: 18] oblige the Auditor-General Office to ensure accountability, transparency, and value-for-money audits by examining, enquiring into, and auditing accounts of all Accounting Officers; carrying out value-for-money audits in both Central Government and designated bodies; preparing and submitting reports; and safeguarding public money and state property, among others. These provisions, if dutifully complied with, are poised to enhance good governance in SOEs.

There are also notable provisions in the Public Entities Corporate Governance Act, which, if mindfully applied in conjunction with the constitutional provisions highlighted above, are poised to strengthen good governance practices in public entities. These include provisions that:

- line ministries should make board appointments in accordance with provisions of the enabling Act;
- appointments to the board can only be renewed for one further term;
- members of the board should not be reappointed to a board after having served for one or more periods totalling eight years;
- those in government full-employment may be appointed to the board of an SOE on condition that do not constitute 'a majority' in the board;
- permanent secretaries of line or other ministries should not be appointed as board members;
- appointments should be on the basis of relevant administrative or management knowledge or experience; and
- ministers should ensure gender equality and regional representation when making appointments to the boards.

There are, however, some gaps in the Public Entities Corporate Governance Act that have the potential to weaken good governance practices. It should be noted that as much as the provision for the establishment of a Corporate Governance Unit (CGU) in the Public Entities Corporate Governance Act of Zimbabwe is in line with King (2016) calls for 'governing bodies' that serve as central institutions for coordinating and enforcing corporate governance, the net operational effectiveness of the Unit may be compromised by several factors. The housing of the Corporate Governance Unit (CGU) in the Office of the President and Cabinet (OPC) may compromise the operational independence of the Unit. The Act reposes too much control on the Secretary to OPC. For instance, SOE annual reports are submitted to the responsible Minister via the Office of the Secretary to the OPC. This centralised set-up carries the risk of not only overshadowing the roles of the CGU and SOE boards but also the oversight roles of Parliament and Auditor-General. The housing of the CGU in the OPC also runs counter to regional and global best practices which call for reasonable distance between the 'regulating' and 'regulated' bodies to allow space for operational autonomy (King, 2016; OECD, 2015). Twenty-first-century governance models informed by the New Public Governance and Sustainable Development Goals (SDGs) envisage open, networked public sectors that utilise expertise from industries and universities. The heavy bureaucracy also carries the risk of relegating SOE boards superfluous. Similar reservations on the role of the OPC as the central institutional framework for SOE governance in Zimbabwe were also expressed by Honourable Member of Parliament Tendai Biti and former Minister of Finance during the Inclusive Government of Zimbabwe 2009 to 2013, thus,

> The OPC is an errant ministry, an errant vote, and so you can't expect a mosquito to cure malaria, it doesn't happen. There is no political will. Remember they are the perpetrators so they cannot have the political will to extinguish corruption. We need to impose a penalty on non-compliance. (ZIMCODD, 2022)

The Public Entities Corporate Governance Act also creates a very dense governance architecture comprising the OPC, line ministries, responsible ministries, minister of finance, among others. In practice, bureaucratic set-ups of this nature tend to fuel bureaucratic politics, corruption, duplication, coordination problems, and delays in the processing of investment proposals. Bureaucratic red tape not only runs counter to the 'easy of doing business' and 'Zimbabwe is open to business' policy mantras of the government of Zimbabwe but also carries the risk of stifling prospects for attracting professionals with highly sought corporate skills and leadership attributes. Commenting on the provisions in The Public Entities Corporate Governance Act, Tafataona Mahoso, the sitting Chief Executive Officer of the Zimbabwe Media Commission (ZMC) observed:

> The danger of relying on controls by a small number of bureaucrats in the state structure is obvious. A small number of state bureaucrats cannot provide the corporate leadership needed to make parastatals productive and efficient in a fully integrated economy. The sophistication and specialisation should come from industry, from polytechnics and universities at home and abroad. Government officials should exercise oversight, mainly to regulate how to reward performance measured by results. They should develop strategies for attracting the best corporate leaders into public enterprises so that the latter can compete locally and globally. The Act seems to be trying to enforce a culture of discipline through bureaucratic control to the extent of making the results-based planning also subject to bureaucratic prescription. (Mahoso cited in *The Patriot* 2018, p. 1)

Malpractices Governance Practices in SOEs

The Auditor-General has over the years released reports pointing to embedded mal-governance practices in public entities (Government of Zimbabwe, 2015, 2017, 2019, 2021). Among others, they relate to:

- SOEs operating without Boards of Directors; boards that were not fully constituted; and permanent secretaries serving the role of the board. Cited cases included the Zimbabwe Revenue Authority, the Grain Marketing Board, the Securities and Exchange Commission of Zimbabwe, and Marange Resources.
- SOE boards that were not meeting regularly as stipulated in their enabling Acts and regional and global best practices. Cited cases included the Zimbabwe Schools Examination Council, the National Social Security Authority, and the National Biotechnology Authority.
- SOES that did not comply with 'declaration of interest' requirement as per regional and global best corporate governance practices. Those cited included the Civil Aviation of Zimbabwe and the Petrotrade.
- Weak internal controls that resulted in payments that were not supported by authorised payment vouchers, entities that were operating without books of accounts and using personal

accounts of executive management. Cited cases include the Parliament of Zimbabwe, the Zimbabwe National Road Authority, the Zimbabwe Minerals Development Corporation, the Parirenyatwa Group of Hospitals, the National Aids Council, and the Anti-Corruption Commission of Zimbabwe.

- Failure to honour statutory obligations to the National Social Scheme Authority, the Zimbabwe Revenue Authority, the pension funds and Medical Aid Societies. Institutions associated with these malpractices included the Zimbabwe National Roads Authority, the Agricultural Marketing Authority, the Civil Aviation Authority of Zimbabwe, and the Zimbabwe Minerals Development Corporation.
- Revision of board fees and management salaries and benefits without authorisation from parent ministries. Institutions associated with these governance malpractices included the Environmental Management Agency, the Zimbabwe National Road Authority, the National Aids Council, the Zimbabwe Minerals Development Corporation, the Health Services Board, the Post Office Savings Bank.
- Opaque procurement processes characterised by lack of due diligence and non-compliance with regulations Cited cases included the Zimbabwe National Road Authority, Parirenyatwa Group of Hospitals.
- Dual regulatory roles. According to Transparency International (2015), SOEs such as the National Railways of Zimbabwe, Zimbabwe Broadcasting Corporation, and the Civil Aviation Authority of Zimbabwe have dual roles of being both regulators and the regulated. Closely related to this is that they have duplicate functions, that is, regulating the same functions. Cited cases include the Broadcasting Authority of Zimbabwe and the Postal and Telecommunications Regulatory Authority of Zimbabwe, the Ministry of Mines and Mining Development, and the Minerals Marketing Corporation of Zimbabwe which both regulate the functions of the sale of minerals. Regional and global best practices call for the separation of functions.
- Regulatory agencies that are housed by parent ministries. This includes the Zimbabwe Regulatory Authority. Best practices emphasise some degree of space between the parent ministry and the regulated board to allow independence.
- Absence of standalone whistle-blower legislation and a whistle-blower agency. This is in contrast to regional and global practices as espoused in King (2016) and OECD (2015) which call for legislation that protects both public and private whistle-blowers.

Patronage-based appointments

Claims of patronage-based appointments have been recurring issues in academic and consultancy publications on SOE governance in Zimbabwe (Chifaka and Foya, 2022; Chigudu, 2020; Chimbari, 2017; Moyo, 2016; Transparency International, 2015; Zhou, 2007; ZIMCODD, 2022). The parent-SOE governance frameworks in which ministries give policy direction to boards have been abused to serve as avenues for patronage-based appointments. Cases in which entire SOE boards were dismissed following the appointment of a new minister suggest that more than merit considerations could have been at play in the appointments of board members. This risk is very high in highly politically polarised countries where the zero-sum or win-win nature of politics inclines ruling political parties to use the ministerial power framework to reward political connections. These scenarios incline board members to concede to the invisible hands of politics as ways of protecting contracts. This is aptly captured by Cross (2022a, p. 1) as follows:

We need to accept that the main mistake we have made since independence is that we have appointed Boards of Directors of these major State-Owned Enterprises (SOE's) and management on a political patronage basis. Ministers, representing the shareholders, viewed these enterprises as cash cows. If they needed something not provided for in their budgets, they called the Chairman or the CEO. Often this led to manipulation of the accounts or the audit at the year end. It was not long before the rot set in and the whole management structure, built up over many years, collapsed and the SOE with it.

Muted political will and seeming tolerance for corruption

Cases of corruption highlighted over the years in Auditor-General Reports (Government of Zimbabwe, 2015, 2017, 2019, 2021) have not been receiving visible follow-up action. Although Chapter 13 of the Constitution of Zimbabwe obliges the ZAAC and the National Prosecuting Authority to 'combat corruption and crime', cases in which those arrested face imprisonment has been very low note. These sentiments were also echoed in Cross (2022a, p. 1):

> In Africa, by and large, such malpractices are not only tolerated, but they are also accepted as a 'normal' part of life. The spectacle of a manager driving a top of the range luxury vehicle out of the gate of a derelict state-owned plant is not queried. We build a state-of-the-art glass factory near a mountain of the raw material, see it opened by the State President, stop operating a week later and never reopened, and no one asks why? We watch 300 kilometres of electric cable stolen from the railway line between Gweru and Harare, costing over US$100 million, in broad daylight. No outcry, not a single person arrested and the case closed – millions of dollars' worth of railway infrastructure destroyed and equipment rendered idle.

Weak parliamentary oversight

Across the globe, parliamentary oversight serves as the linchpin of good governance in public institutions. While the roles of the bicameral legislature of Zimbabwe are clearly outlined in the national Constitution as discussed in earlier sections of the chapter, robust oversight has over the years been compromised by myriad factors that include (Zhou, 2016; Zhou, 2022):

- lack of resources;
- weak legislature versus the executive arm;
- lacking of knowledge and skills need to scrutinise policies and bills;
- lacking of good understanding of parliamentary procedures and law-making processes;
- bunking of sessions by cabinet ministers;
- limited time accorded to the review of submitted by ministers to the Public Accounts Committee of Parliament;
- partisan parliamentary debates and preoccupation with retaining seats at the expense of holding the Executive accountable;
- failure to utilise the Presidential Question which is provided for in the Zimbabwe Constitution Amendment (No. 20) Act of 2013.

ENTRY POINTS FOR STRENGTHENING SOE CORPORATE GOVERNANCE

Given these highlighted gaps, what then should be the entry points for improving governance in Zimbabwe's public entities? Reviewed experiences in China, South Africa, and Singapore suggest that in cases where appropriate governance practices were followed, SOE contributions to national development have been notable (Transparency International, 2015). Below are some of the entry points for strengthening corporate governance frameworks and practices in SOEs in Zimbabwe.

Office of the Auditor-General

Although the Office of the Auditor-General is a critical player in the enforcement of good governance in public entities, the Office does not have the power to force state entities to submit their reports for audit. It also has no powers to enforce SOE compliance with its recommendations. Confirming these circumstances, the Auditor-General, Mildred Chiri was quoted on 6 October 2022 saying, 'We do not have that mandate; we wait for them to submit. What we can do is to recommend, and the authorities above them should enforce and give them guidance or penalties' (ZIMCODD, 2022, p. 1). Against this background, the following actions may be taken to empower the Office of the Auditor-General:

- Parliament should be consulted in the appointment of the Auditor-General. The Organisation of Supreme Audit Institutions (INTOSAI) and the African Organisation of Supreme Audit Institutions (AFROSAI) require that Supreme Audit Institutions should be independent of the Executive and also that Parliament should be consulted in the appointment of the Auditor-General.
- The Auditor-General should report directly to Parliament. The current reporting framework in which the Auditor-General reports to Parliament through the parent ministry may compromise accountability in the event of an adverse report on the parent ministry. Reporting frameworks like those obtained in South Africa, the United Kingdom, New Zealand, and the United States of America where the Auditor-General reports directly to the House of Assembly or Congress may provide valuable lessons for Zimbabwe.
- There is need to consider giving sanction powers to the Auditor-General so that the Office can force public entities to comply with the requirements of submitting returns. There are no provisions for sanction powers in both the Constitution of Zimbabwe of 2013 and the Audit Office Act. Under these circumstances, Audit reports that have been issued over the years have not been taken seriously by both Treasury and the Accounting Officers. Absence of remedial action renders audit reports symbolic.

Parliamentary Oversight

Parliamentary oversight is integral to good governance in public entities. The Constitution of Zimbabwe, Chapter 17 (Sections 298–300) explicitly provides for parliamentary oversight. To address the oversight gaps highlighted in the earlier sections of the chapter, Parliament, among other things, should set minimum educational qualifications for one to qualify for selection as a legislator. The legislators are expected to execute high-level responsibilities that demand certain levels of knowledge appreciation and analytical skills. Zhou and Zinyama (2016) noted that the Parliament of Zimbabwe has no clearly defined criteria for the selection of Members of Parliament and Senators and that the national Constitution is also silent on this matter – only stating that aspiring Members of Parliament should be registered voters and that they should be over 21 years of age. This silence effectively places the responsibility of the setting the criteria in political parties. Consequently, Members of Parliament with very low educational qualifications have been appointed to the detriment of quality and research informed debates that are critical for enhancing good governance in SOEs. Parliamentary debates should also be issue-focused rather than party-focused. National interests should prevail over partisan interests. Parliament should adopt a policy that obliges appointment to portfolio clusters to be skills and relevant experience based. Claims of committees that lack the competency to verify reports made by the Auditor-General continue to the detriment of the quality of the work which committees produce.

Whistle-blower protection legislation

Zimbabwe is yet to have either specific legislation on whistle-blowing or a whistle-blower institution. There are no specific legislations to protect witnesses. Entity employees who choose to report corruption are also not protected. Specific legislation on whistle-blowing will not only reduce the coordination challenges confronting extant frameworks but also place Zimbabwe in the league of countries such as South Africa, Namibia, Uganda, Ghana, Netherlands, South Korea, Japan, the United States of America, New Zealand, Australia, and the United Kingdom which have specific legislations on whistle-blowing (OECD, 2021). In Africa, countries such as Kenya, South Africa, and Botswana have since adopted Witness Protection legislation. The 2003 United Nations Convention Against Corruption (UNCAC) exhorts countries to adopt comprehensive whistle-blower protection legislations.

Disclosure requirements

Disclosure of information, assets, and remuneration packages reduces risks arising from conflict of interest. Disclosures also avert insider-trading, a major issue in cases of public procurement and employee recruitment. The issue of public disclosure is particularly pertinent because where conflict of interests emerges, corporate interests are often sacrificed at the expense of personal gain. Ensuring that board members and senior management disclose their ownership status at the time of appointment and subsequently periodically will go a long way in building trust. Submission of entity annual financial reports also enhances public scrutiny of SOE activities.

State Procurement Board

Procurement processes are highly prone to political intrusions, state capture, and insider trading. Cases in which tenders were allegedly awarded to losing bidders have been extensively documented relating to local authorities and SOEs (Transparency, 2015). There is a need to reflect on how best the issue of independence can be enhanced without sacrificing the transparency and accountability of the SPB. OECD (2016) calls for some level of distance between the regulator and the regulated. In line with sustainability concerns, bid assessments should also go beyond traditional concerns with value for money to include green procurement issues. This is particularly pertinent in view of the evolving thinking on corporate social responsibility.

Appointments to SOE boards

The parent-SOE governance frameworks in which ministries give policy direction to boards are seemingly abused to serve as avenues for patronage-based appointments. Cases in which entire SOE boards are dismissed following the appointment of a new minister suggest that more than merit considerations could be at play in the appointments of board members.

CONCLUSION

State-owned entities (SOEs) dominate national economies and as such are expected to be economic hubs of national development. They account for significant shares of GDP and are also involved in strategic, capital-intensive projects in the areas of energy and communications. An ailing SOE sector translates into an ailing nation. Therein lies the case for sound SOE governance. This chapter seeks to expose the corporate governance experiences in Zimbabwe, highlighting strengths and weaknesses at both the levels of framework and practice. Regional and global corporate governance best practices are reviewed in order to uncover valuable lessons for strengthening future corporate governance in Zimbabwe. The chapter revealed that while the frameworks of SOE corporate governance are in some areas lagging regional and global practices, lack of political will and a culture of tolerance of corruption largely account for the observed scenarios in which frameworks were more visible in breach than observance.

An analysis of corporate governance in state-owned entities invariably brings into focus broader issues relating to national politics and leadership. The intractability of SOE corporate governance largely arises from their ownership structure which automatically requires policy direction by parent ministries. This policy direction requirement is frequently used as an avenue for political and patronage-based appointments of board members. In this way, the problem of SOE governance in Zimbabwe is not one of inadequate frameworks but largely one of political will to enforce extant frameworks. A culture of tolerating corruption accounts for the cases highlighted scenarios in which principles and legislations were largely more visible in breach than observance. Though lagging behind regional and global best practices in some areas, elements of both the South Africa King (2016) and OECD (2015) codes are visible in the Public Entities Corporate Governance Act (Chapter 10.31). Corporate governance is thus a hybrid of regional and global codes. In the context of increasing threats from climate change, SOE corporate governance is strategically played to rally the campaign for just and sustainable climate change action in various sectors of the economy.

REFERENCES

Basu, R. (2017), 'Rethinking Public Administration in the 21st Century: Today's Research and Tomorrow's Agenda', *Public Administration Review*, **18** (1), 1–12.

Cadbury, A. (1992), *Report of the Committee on the Financial Aspects of Corporate Governance*, London: GEE.

Chifaka, G., D. Foya and N. Ncube (2022), 'Challenges of Corporate Governance in Zimbabwe: What is the Problem? A View from Selected Managers in Harare', *Global Economy Journal*, **10** (8), 33–49, doi.org/10.11216/gsj.2022.08.73921.

Chigudu, D. (2020), 'Public Sector Corporate Governance: Zimbabwe's Challenges of Strategic Management in the Wake of Sustainable Development', *Academy of Strategic Management Journal*, **19** (1), 1–13.

Chimbari, P. (2017), 'Public Sector Corporate Governance in Zimbabwe: The Nexus between the ZIMCODE and State-Owned Enterprises', *International Journal of Economics, Commerce and Management*, **5** (7), 212–221.

Clarke, T. (2017), *Institutional Corporate Governance: A Comparative Approach*, London: Routledge, Taylor and Francis.

Cross, E. (2022a), 'When State Managed Institutions Fail, Everyone Suffers the Consequence', accessed 16 July 2022 at https://newsreport.co.zw/news/2022/09/22/when-state-managed-institutions-fail -everyone-suffers-the-consequences.

Cross, E. (2022b), 'Corruption in Cottco Cost the Industry in 2021 Nearly US$50 million', accessed 8 September 2022 at https://nehandaradio.com/2022/09/13/corruption-in-cottco-cost-the-industry-in-2021-nearly-us50-million/.

Denhardt, R.B. and J.V. Denhardt (2000), 'The New Public Service: Serving Rather than Steering', *Public Administration Review*, **60** (6), 549–559, doi.org/10.1111/0033-3352.00117.

Editorial Comment. (2020), 'Corruption: A National Security Threat', *The Sunday Mail*, 19 January 2020, accessed 21 July 2022 at https://www.sundaymail.co.zw/corruption-a-national-security-threat.

Foya, D. and G. Changunda (2019), 'An Investigation of Corporate Governance Challenges Facing Indigenous Banks in Zimbabwe', *International Journal of Research and Innovation in Social Science*, **3** (10), 100–115.

Ginting, E. and K. Naqv (eds.) (2020), *Reforms, Opportunities, and Challenges for State-Owned Enterprises*, Mandaluyong City: Asian Development Bank.

Government of Zimbabwe. (1991), *Zimbabwe: A Framework for Economic Reforms, 1991–95*, Harare: Government Printer.

Government of Zimbabwe. (2005), *Parastatals and Local Authorities Orientation Programme Guidelines*, Harare: Government Printer.

Government of Zimbabwe. (2009), *Ministry of Parastatals and State Enterprises*, Harare: Government Printer.

Government of Zimbabwe. (2013), *Constitution of Zimbabwe Amendment (No.20) Act 2013*, Harare: Government Printer.

Government of Zimbabwe. (2015), *The Report of the Auditor-General for the Financial Year Ended December 31, 2014 on State Enterprises and Parastatals*, Harare: Government Printer.

Government of Zimbabwe. (2017), *The Auditor General Report on State Enterprises and Parastatals*, Harare: Government Printer.

Government of Zimbabwe. (2018), *Public Entities Corporate Governance Act* [Chapter 10.31], Harare: Government Printer.

Government of Zimbabwe. (2019), *Auditor-General's Report on Financial Year Ended December, 2019 on State Enterprises and Parastatals*, Harare: Government Printer.

Government of Zimbabwe. (2021), *The Auditor General Report on State Enterprises and Parastatals*, Harare: Government Printer.

Harduth, N. and L. Alexander (2021), *A Review of the King IV Report on Corporate Governance*, Johannesburg: Werksmans Attorneys.

Howlett, M., K. Anka and P. Ora-orn (2017), 'Understanding Co-Production as a Policy Tool: Integrating New Public Governance and Comparative Policy Theory', *Journal of Comparative Policy Analysis: Research and Practice*, **19**, 487–501, doi.org/10.1080/13876988.2017.1287445.

King Committee. (1994), *King I Report on Corporate Governance*, Sandton: Institute of Directors in Southern Africa (IoDSA).

King Committee. (2002), *King II Report on Corporate Governance*, Sandton: Institute of Directors in Southern Africa (IoDSA).

King Committee. (2009), *King III Report on Corporate Governance*, Sandton: Institute of Directors in Southern Africa (IoDSA).

King Committee. (2016), *King IV Report on Corporate Governance*, Sandton: Institute of Directors in Southern Africa (IoDSA).

Mahoso, T. (2018), 'Critique of Public Entities Corporate Governance Act of 2018', *The Patriot*, accessed 7 June 2022 at https://www.thepatriot.co.zw/oldposts/critique-of-public-corporate-governance-act-of 2018/06/11.gif.

Maune, A. (2015), 'Corporate Governance in Zimbabwe: An Overview of its Current State', *Asian Economic and Financial Review*, **5** (1), 167–178, doi.org/10.18488/journal.aefr/2015.5.1/102.1.167.178.

Moyo, N.J. (2016), *Corporate Governance: A Critical Analysis of the Effectiveness of Board of Directors in Public Entities in Zimbabwe*, Pretoria: University of South Africa, accessed 22 August 2022 at http://hdl.handle.net/10500/21719.

Moyo, N.J. (2022), *Corporate Governance in Zimbabwe's Public Entities: Comparisons with South Africa and Australia*, London: Routledge, Taylor and Francis.

Mpedzizi, P. (2021), 'Corporate Governance: The Case of Parastatals', Presentation at APRM Submission Validation Workshop, 8 July 2021. Harare, accessed 15 August 2023 at https://saiia.org.za/wp-content/uploads/2021/07/08_Corporate-Governance-in-Zimbabwe_PMpedzisi.pdf.

Ncube, M. (2020), 'Zimbabwe Reviewing Ownership Model for SOEs to Improve Efficiency', *XINHUANET*, 14 October 2020, accessed 28 July 2022 at www.xinhuanet.com.

Nellis, J. (2007), 'Back to the Future for African Infrastructure? Why State-Ownership is No More Promising the Second Time Around', *Working Paper Number 84*, February 2007, doi.org/10.2139/ssrn.983201.

Nhema, A.G. (2015), 'Relevance of Classical Management Theories to Modern Public Administration: A Review', *Journal of Public Administration and Governance*, **5** (3), 165–179, doi.org/10.5296/JPAG.V5I3.8337.

OECD. (1999), *Principles of Corporate Governance*, Paris: OECD.

OECD. (2003), *G20/OECD Principles of Corporate Governance*, Paris: OECD.

OECD. (2015a), *Committing to Effective Whistleblower Protection*, Paris: OECD.

OECD. (2015b), *G20/OECD Principles of Corporate Governance*, Paris: OECD, accessed 15 September 2022 at http://dx.doi.org/10.1787/9789264236882-en.

OECD. (2021), *Ownership and Governance of State-Owned Enterprises A Compendium of National Practices*, Paris: OECD, accessed 14 September 2022 at https://www.oecd.org/corporate/ownership-and-governance-of-state-owned-enterprises-a-compendiumof-national-practices.htm.

Osborne, S.P. (2010), *The New Public Governance: Emerging Perspectives on the Theory and Practice of Public Governance*, New York, NY: Taylor and Francis.

Osborne, S.P., R. Zoe and S. Kirsty (2016), 'Co-Production and the Co-Creation of Value in Public Services: A Suitable Case for Treatment?', *Public Management Review*, **18**, 639–653, doi.org/10.1080/14719037.2015.1111927.

Rodee, C.A., C.Q. Christol, T.J. Anderson and T.H. Greene (1983), *Introduction to Political Science*, London: McGraw-Hill.

The Herald. (2022), *President Dares Public Enterprises*, 3 March 2022, accessed 10 March 2023 at https://www.herald.co.zw/president-dares-public-enterprises/.

Torfing, J., E. Sørensen and A. Røiseland (2016), 'Transforming the Public Sector into an Arena for Co-Creation: Barriers, Drivers, Benefits, and Ways Forward', paper presented at the EGPA 2016, Utrecht, The Netherlands, April 24–26.

Transparency International. (2015), *Annual State of Corruption Report: Focus on State-Owned Enterprises*, Harare: Transparency International.

Wright, R. (2004), *The History of Corporate Governance* (Vol. 3), London: Routledge, Taylor and Francis.

Zhou, G. (2007), 'The Corporate Governance Question in Zimbabwe: Experiences from the Corporate Sector', *ZAMBEZIA*, **34** (i/ii 2007), 1–20.

Zhou, G. (2012), *Rolling Back State Ownership in Public Enterprises in Zimbabwe: The Question of Broad-Based Participation*, Berlin: Lambert Academic Publishing.

Zhou, G. (2017), *Four Decades of Public Sector Management Reforms in Zimbabwe*, Harare: University of Zimbabwe Publications.

Zhou, G. (2022), 'The Public Policy Question', in Zhou, G. and H. Zvoushe (eds.), *The Public Policy Question in Zimbabwe's Evolving National Agenda: Policy and the Hub of National Development*, Johannesburg: SAAPAM.

Zhou, G. and T. Zinyama (2016), *Strengthening Institutional Capacity for Policy Analysis, Management and Governance in Zimbabwe*, Harare: University of Zimbabwe Publications.

ZIMCODD. (2022), 'Government is Sleeping on the Wheel', accessed 15 September 2022 at https//www.newsday.co.zw/local-news/article/200001431/govt-sleeping-on-the-wheel-zimcodd.

6. Monitoring and evaluation in government: the case of South African municipalities

Nokukhanya N. Jili and Andrew Enaifoghe

INTRODUCTION

Monitoring and evaluation (M&E) as government functions are becoming increasingly important for public institutions, entities, and agencies that design and oversee policy programmes and service delivery projects, inclusive of the local sphere of government. In the South African system of government, this sphere comprises of metropolitan, district, and local municipalities. Though a comprehensive M&E system for gauging a programme and project's effectiveness is commonly regarded as an essential prerequisite for adequate political oversight and managerial control, establishing such a system may be highly challenging (Khawula, 2016). Insufficient stakeholder buy-in, the absence of political will, unsuitable methodology, technological and resource limitations, as well as unreliable and inaccurate management information are but some examples of such challenges. For a local government to flourish, an M&E system is essential to constantly gauge the overall performance of municipal systems and operations. The design and implementation of such a system also helps to inculcate a performance culture and directs a municipality towards adhering to its constitutional mandate and statutory obligations. In addition, M&E is increasingly seen as instrumental to foster a responsive, transparent, and accountable municipal council, one that complies with the aspirations, wishes, and reasonable demands of communities.

To advance local democracy in South Africa it is essential that communities are afforded the opportunity to participate in local affairs and keep decision-makers responsive to their needs. Upholding the tenets of local democracy also implies that municipalities ensure that all residents have access to basic services (Durokifa and Enaifoghe, 2022). Both these dimensions call for a comprehensive performance management system (PMS) in municipalities that enables ongoing M&E of the performance of municipal structures to make sure they are accountable for their actions. Furthermore, to guarantee that performance targets are achieved, the PMS of a municipality should be fully aligned with the country's National Development Plan (NDP), the Provincial Growth and Development Strategy (PGDS), the integrated development plan (IDP), local economic development (LED) strategies, as well as the budget of the municipality (Jordaan and Fourie, 2013). In other words, the PMS should be seen as the main mechanism through which the performance monitoring and evaluation of all municipal functions and operations is enabled. It can also be regarded as the instrument that guarantees that the social contract between government and its constituents is upheld.

It should be noted that notions of performance and M&E are relevant to the institutional performance of government structures such as municipalities (i.e. its policies, strategies, structures, systems, operations, procedures, and methods) as well as the performance of individuals working in municipalities (i.e. councillors, managers and officials). The success of an organization is dependent on employees' level of performance (i.e. skills, competencies, productivity, motivation, efficiency, and effectiveness).

This chapter surveys the significance of M&E in governance settings by also outlining the typical challenges associated with its application in South African municipalities. These challenges are generally related to larger systemic issues and municipal-specific challenges. It also includes cultural and operational issues.

MONITORING AND EVALUATION IN PERSPECTIVE

Post-apartheid South Africa confronts significant obstacles in ensuring that it delivers sustainable, high-quality services that live up to residents' expectations. The general populace expects municipalities to be attentive to their needs and aspirations and to offer 'optimal and professional services' in all sectors (Meyiwa et al., 2014, p. 4). Therefore, it is the government's duty to create and operationalize a framework for broad-based socioeconomic development. Municipalities are urged to come up with proactive solutions to help residents escape underdevelopment and chronic poverty (Govender, 2011, p. 113). One such solution is the design and implementation of comprehensive performance management systems to gauge the performance of all municipal functions and operations. A PMS also enables M&E of these functions and operations.

According to Bussin (2017), since democratization in 1994 the government has embarked on a programme to foster democracy in the country by informing the populace about human rights, the stipulations of Constitution, and other obligations they have to participate in the affairs of government. It was hoped that civic education would foster transparency, openness and empowerment of people to hold government decision-makers responsible for their actions while also enabling them to demand better, higher-quality services (Naidu, 2012, p. 279). Unfortunately, as the country has grown over the past decades, the provision of essential services has been declining, as witnessed by persistent citizen demonstrations and service delivery protests in several municipalities. The main reasons for subpar service delivery, according to Govender (2011, p. 6), include a lack of coordinated organizational structures, political meddling, bad financial management, and a poor performance culture in many cities and towns.

To address these inconsistencies, the government created a service delivery framework in 1997 through the White Paper on Transforming Public Service Delivery, commonly known as the 'Batho Pele' (Sesotho words meaning 'people first') White Paper. This policy instrument's main goal was to motivate public employees to strive and maintain excellence in the delivery of essential services. The framework also attempted to change how basic services are delivered in terms of access, civility, information, transparency, and openness. It may be argued that these guidelines help gauge local government's commitment to delivering results accurately that are sustainable and of higher quality.

To further promote performance oversight and transparency in government, the former President of the country Thabo Mbeki instructed Parliament in 2005 to design a comprehensive Government-wide Monitoring and Evaluation System (GWM&ES). This system can be regarded as an overarching M&E framework designed to improve the performance and accountability of government programmes and initiatives. It aims to provide an accurate and comprehensive understanding of the impact of government policies and interventions on citizens, and to ensure that government resources are used effectively and efficiently to achieve desired outcomes. The system includes a set of policies, systems, and processes that support the collection and analysis of data, the development of evaluation plans, and the integration of monitoring and evaluation into decision-making processes at all levels of government. It also supports the sharing of information and learning across government, and the development of capacity within government to design and implement effective M&E systems. The GWM&ES is intended to promote evidence-based decision-making, enhance the transparency and accountability of government, and support the improvement of government performance and the achievement of national priorities. The main instrument through which this is done in municipalities is the design and implementation of performance management systems.

According to Mpisi (2013), key stakeholders in the implementation of the GWM&ES include the Department for Performance Monitoring and Evaluation, Statistics South Africa, the Public Service Commission, the Auditor General, and the National School of Government. These institutions must make sure that the appropriate line departments carry out certain tasks aligned with monitoring and evaluation. Systems of monitoring and evaluation are also created in the provincial sphere to make sure that the goals for provincial development are achieved. This entails managing the delivery of fundamental services as well as coordinating interdepartmental activities in terms of policy formation, review, and planning (Govender, 2011, p. 106). Nevertheless, difficulties have been encountered in establishing M&E systems in provinces. These include complicated reporting procedures, a lack of alignment and coordination between national, provincial, and municipal priorities, and the lack of M&E competencies and skills. Should these challenges not be addressed, provincial M&E structures will struggle to perform a successful oversight role regarding the functioning of municipalities located in the province.

Performance management systems in local government in South Africa aim to improve the performance and accountability of municipalities by using a range of performance-related tools and metrics. These systems help local governments to assess the effectiveness of their programmes and initiatives, identify areas for improvement, and make informed decisions about how to allocate resources to achieve their goals. Performance audits are a key component of a PMS. These audits provide an independent assessment of a municipality's performance and are used to identify areas where improvements can be made. Performance audits often examine the processes and systems used by local governments to deliver services, as well as the outcomes that these services achieve.

In addition to performance audits, municipalities in South Africa also use performance reports, performance indicators, and key performance areas to assess their performance. Performance reports provide regular updates on the progress of local government initiatives, while performance indicators help to measure and track progress against specific goals. Key performance areas identify the most important areas of a municipality's performance that need to be monitored and evaluated. Thus, in general, the use of a PMS is intended to improve the effectiveness and efficiency of government programmes, promote evidence-based decision-making, and enhance the accountability of local government to its citizens. It also promotes political oversight of municipal programmes and projects using several M&E mechanisms.

An M&E system is necessary to improve good corporate governance in municipal councils (Enaifoghe, 2022; Hargreaves, 2010). Good corporate governance in municipalities refers to the effective and efficient management of a local government's resources, and the accountability of local government officials to the public. It is based on principles of transparency, accountability, and the responsible use of public resources. In practice, good corporate governance in municipalities involves a range of processes and systems designed to ensure that local government is run effectively and efficiently. This includes:

- Clear roles and responsibilities: Defining the roles and responsibilities of local government officials and ensuring that these are carried out effectively.
- Effective decision-making: Implementing processes that ensure that decisions are made in a timely, transparent, and accountable manner and that they are based on reliable information.
- Financial management: Ensuring that public resources are managed effectively and efficiently and that the use of these resources is accounted for in a transparent and accountable manner.
- Stakeholder engagement: Encouraging active engagement with stakeholders, including citizens, community organizations, and other local government officials, to ensure that local government is responsive to the needs and interests of the community.
- Monitoring and evaluation: Regularly monitoring and evaluating the performance of local government to identify areas for improvement, and to ensure that public resources are being used effectively and efficiently.

By promoting good corporate governance in municipalities, the local sphere of government can increase its effectiveness, efficiency, and accountability, and build trust with the public. This, in turn, can support the development of sustainable communities and improve the quality of life for citizens.

Some of the key M&E mechanisms and structures in South African municipalities include:

- Performance management systems: These systems are designed to track and assess the performance of local government, and to identify areas for improvement. They often include performance audits, performance reports, performance indicators, and key performance areas.
- Oversight bodies: These bodies are responsible for overseeing the performance of local government and ensuring that it is accountable to the public. Examples of oversight bodies include the Auditor-General, the Public Protector, and the National and Provincial Treasuries. Within municipalities, standing or portfolio committees of council play an important role as oversight mechanisms. These committees are responsible for overseeing the performance of local government, and for ensuring that it is accountable to the public. They are permanent committees that are established by the local government to deal with specific functions, such as finance, public safety, and human settlements. Each standing committee has a specific area of responsibility, and its members are elected by the local government council. The role of the standing committees is to provide oversight and scrutiny of the work of the local government and to make recommendations for improvement. Portfolio committees, on the other hand, are temporary committees that are established to consider specific policy issues or projects. Portfolio committees are usually established for a limited period and are tasked with carrying out a specific investigation or review. Both standing and portfolio committees play a critical role in ensuring that local government is transparent, accountable, and effective. They provide

a mechanism for public oversight and help to ensure that council remain responsive to the needs of communities by providing a forum for community engagement and collaboration. Other oversight mechanisms include internal audit and the municipal public accounts committee.

- Stakeholder engagement: Municipalities engage with several stakeholders, including citizens, local businesses, community-based organizations, and other government officials, to gather feedback and to ensure that local government is responsive to the needs and interests of the community.
- Data collection and analysis: Municipalities collect and analyze data to better understand the impact of their programmes and initiatives, and to inform decision-making.
- Training and capacity building: Municipalities invest in training and capacity building to develop the skills and knowledge required to design and implement effective monitoring and evaluation systems.

These mechanisms and structures help to ensure that local government in South Africa is accountable, effective, and efficient.

OPERATIVE MONITORING AND EVALUATION CLARIFIED

Performance monitoring is an important tool for organizations to ensure that they are achieving their goals and objectives, and to make informed decisions about how to allocate resources. By regularly monitoring performance, organisations can identify areas for improvement, track progress over time, and make course corrections as needed to improve results.

Monitoring, according to Engela and Ajam (2010, p. 11), is a continuous process that evaluates whether projects and their everyday operations provide the desired results. Performance is followed by data collection and evaluations. This definition is broadened by Uys (2010, p. 12), who points out that monitoring is a regular internal organizational activity to ensure that initiatives provide the desired results. Performance monitoring thus refers to the ongoing process of collecting, analyzing, and reporting on data to assess the performance of an organization, programme, or initiative. The purpose of performance monitoring is to track progress towards goals and objectives, identify areas for improvement, and make evidence-based decisions. It typically involves tracking key performance indicators (KPIs) that are aligned with the goals and objectives of the organization, programme, or initiative. This can include metrics such as output, outcome, impact, and efficiency indicators. The data collected through performance monitoring is analyzed to understand trends and patterns and to identify areas for improvement.

Performance monitoring is often integrated into a broader performance management system, which includes a range of processes and tools designed to improve the performance and accountability of organizations. These can include performance audits, performance reports, and stakeholder engagement, among others.

Operative monitoring can be described as an ongoing function that uses the systematic collection of data on predetermined indicators to inform management and the primary stakeholders of an ongoing development intervention about the level of progress and achievement of goals as well as the progress being made in the use of allocated resources (Public Service Commission [PSC], 2008, p. 11).

Evaluation, in turn, can be defined as 'the systematic use of social research methodologies for analysing the conception, design, execution, and utility of social intervention programmes' (Rossi, Lipsey and Freeman, 2004, p. 16). To assess issues like relevance, performance (efficiency and effectiveness), value for money, impact, and sustainability and to make recommendations for the future, the Department of Planning, Monitoring, and Evaluation ([DPME], 2012, p. vii) defines evaluation as the systematic collection and objective analysis of the evidence on public policies, programmes, projects, and functions. In this view, evaluation is a time-bound activity carried out across specified timeframes that contrasts intended and achieved performance (Govender, 2011, p. 75). Applied to a performance context, evaluation refers to the process of systematically assessing the achievements of an organization, programme, or initiative to determine its effectiveness, efficiency, and impact. Its main purpose is to determine whether an organization is achieving its goals and objectives and to identify areas for improvement.

Performance evaluation typically involves collecting and analyzing data, comparing results to established performance standards, and making recommendations for improvement. This process can involve a range of techniques and tools, such as performance audits, performance reports, benchmarking, and KPI analysis, among others. The results of performance evaluations are often used to inform decision-making and to guide the allocation of resources. They can also be used to support continuous improvement, by identifying areas for improvement and making recommendations for change.

Performance evaluation is an important component of a broader performance management system, and is typically integrated with performance monitoring, which is the ongoing process of collecting and analysing data to assess performance. Performance evaluation and monitoring are key tools for municipalities to ensure that they are achieving their goals and objectives and to make informed decisions about how to allocate resources for effective service delivery.

M&E APPLICATIONS IN THE SOUTH AFRICAN LOCAL GOVERNMENT SPHERE

From the conceptualization of monitoring and evaluation above, it is evident that both entail complementary activities (Mpisi, 2013). In general, if M&E operations are carried out properly and the findings are appropriately understood, both of these activities offer certain benefits to municipalities. M&E in local government aid in the formulation of policies, ensure sound fiscal management and enables municipal officials to coordinate their efforts with those of the national government (National Treasury, 2010, p. 5). M&E systems are used to give information that supports the development of good governance and accountability in government (Engela and Ajam, 2010, p. 11).

It is crucial to examine the application and institutionalization of M&E in South African local government to summarize the potential advantages and challenges associated therewith. The Republic of South Africa's Constitution, 1996, charges the local government with the duty of providing equitable public services as the branch of government that is closest to residents (Koma, 2010, p. 113). This constitutional mandate's main goal is to reverse the ills of socioeconomic underdevelopment. In this sense, the national government envisions a local government that is capable of collaborating with residents in their area to address their challenges and provide collaborative, sustainable solutions.

According to Davids (2011, p. 3573), many municipalities in the country are finding it difficult to carry out its Constitutional and other statutory obligations, particularly in light of the shift from an inward-looking approach—that is, an approach that focuses primarily on municipal internal processes—to an outward-looking approach, meaning an approach that focuses on the improvement of the general well-being and prosperity of communities. Unfortunately, the majority of people continue to live in extreme, ongoing poverty, while inequality and unemployment are rapidly increasing. Phillips et al. (2014) indicate that it is up to municipalities to address these issues.

M&E give the required impetus to improve the delivery of essential services (Schurink and Schurink, 2010, p. 16). Although the provision of basic services has been a persistent difficulty for local government in South Africa, a greater appreciation of the need for M&E among public employees may transform this situation (Olumuyiwa, 2015). There is rising recognition that the results and impact of government initiatives are related to the provision of fundamental services; as a result, municipalities that are not providing high-quality services are failing in their constitutional mandate (Olumuyiwa, 2015).

To precisely gauge each employee's productivity, the national government has implemented performance contracts for all public employees. This practice is also instituted in municipalities but unfortunately only for those officials in senior managerial positions. Performance contracts are agreements between councils and municipal officials, which set out specific performance targets and objectives that must be achieved. The purpose of performance contracts is to provide clear, measurable goals and expectations for municipal employees, and to link performance to rewards and incentives. Performance contracts are designed to encourage employee accountability and to promote a culture of performance, by linking performance to remuneration and career advancement. These contracts typically include a range of performance targets and objectives, such as service delivery targets, financial management targets, and employee development targets, among others. The performance targets are usually aligned with the strategic goals and objectives of the municipality and are reviewed on a regular basis to assess progress and to identify areas for improvement. Performance contracts help to promote accountability and transparency in South African municipalities, by linking performance to rewards and incentives. They also serve as foundations for performance appraisals and assessments to assist officials to advance in their careers.

Govender (2011, p. 88) contends that municipal leadership must recognize the significance and importance of M&E as a performance management tool. The rise in service delivery protests and boycotts makes it evident that communities are increasingly getting impatient with the sluggish delivery of essential services. Uys (2010, p. 4) argues that especially the absence of competent technical professionals with adequate M&E experience hampers the institutionalization of performance-based practices in municipalities. Although substantial funds have been spent on enhancing the skills of public employees, mainly through learnership programmes offered by the Local Government Sector Education and Training Authority (LGSETA), audit reports continuously reveal that most municipalities still experience serious competency and capacity gaps (State of Municipal Capacity Report [SMCR], 2012, p. 8).

Rural communities serviced by low-capacity local municipalities often experience more significant service delivery deficits than high-capacity metropolitan municipalities (Ajam, 2012, p. 4). The provision of essential services in deep rural areas is severely constrained by poor municipal infrastructure (e.g. roads, markets, and distribution chains), a low tax income base, limited skills, and critical staff shortages. In addition, rural municipalities find it difficult to align their integrated development plans with the growth and development targets of provinces. This results in a mismatch in priorities between municipalities and respective premiers' offices in the provinces. Therefore, the performance targets that rural towns establish for themselves are frequently not realized, further tarnishing community trust.

CHALLENGES AFFECTING M&E APPLICATIONS IN LOCAL GOVERNMENT

As alluded to, the South African Constitution requires local government to implement development programmes to enhance the welfare and well-being of the citizens in their area of jurisdiction. However, metropolitan, district and local municipalities experience significant challenges in fulfilling their obligations. These challenges can be categorized into broad-based systemic challenges as well as municipal-specific challenges.

As far as systemic challenges are concerned, municipalities in South Africa face a range of issues that impact their ability to deliver effective and efficient services to their communities. Some of the main challenges include:

- Financial viability and sustainability: Many municipalities in South Africa face significant financial challenges, including revenue collection issues, limited budgets, and high levels of debt. This limits their ability to invest in infrastructure, provide basic services, and address the needs of their communities.
- Capacity constraints: Many municipalities in South Africa lack the technical and managerial capacity to effectively manage their operations and deliver services. This often results in poor service delivery, inefficiencies, and a lack of accountability.
- Corruption and maladministration: Corruption and maladministration are significant challenges in many South African municipalities. This undermines public trust in government, discourages local business investment, and limits the effectiveness of service delivery.
- Inadequate infrastructure: Municipalities in South Africa struggle to provide adequate infrastructure to their communities, including basic services such as water, sanitation, and electricity. This impacts the quality of life for residents and limits economic growth and social development.
- Political instability: Political instability, including changes in political leadership, factionalism, and disputes between political parties, impact the effectiveness and stability of municipal councils. This usually results in delays in decision-making, a lack of continuity in service delivery, and a lack of accountability.
- Community involvement: Limited community involvement and engagement in local government processes hamper the effectiveness of service delivery and result in limited oversight and a lack of public trust in government.

To address these challenges, municipalities in South Africa are working, with limited success, to improve their financial sustainability, build institutional capacity, address corruption, invest in infrastructure, promote political stability, and engage with their communities.

Concerning municipal-specific challenges, scholars such as Lawal and Onohaebi (2010) argue that internal institutional issues hamper the successful application of M&E practices in local government. According to Enaifoghe and Adetiba (2019a), the biggest problem in most municipalities is the lack of officials with the expertise, knowledge, abilities, and competence required to execute performance-based activities linked to the monitoring and evaluation of municipal programmes and projects. Municipal political representatives (i.e. councillors) are generally speaking incapable of comprehending the significance of M&E and to successfully utilize oversight mechanisms (Mthethwa and Jili, 2016, p. 109). Consequently, they have been unable to create an institutional M&E system, inclusive of suitable M&E plans, indicators, and tools. It is evident that although the majority of South Africans have access to essential services, considerable work still has to be done in terms of M&E training, capacity building, and skills development. In particular, rural, low-capacity municipalities find it difficult to retain and attract skilled and talented employees. The 'brain-drain' seriously hampers the ability of municipalities to successfully institutionalize M&E practices and procedures. According to the M&E guide issued by the Presidency (2008), titled 'The Role of Premiers' Offices in Government-Wide Monitoring and Evaluation Practice Guide: A Good Practice Guide', effective M&E is seriously constrained by employees' general lack of knowledge of municipal systems and procedures. To add value to the organization, municipalities should make sure that the right people with the right skills are in the right place at the right time to carry out their duties successfully (Enaifoghe and Adetiba, 2018).

A further challenge highlighted by Mthethwa and Jili (2016, p. 109) is the general absence of consequence management practices. Those that transgress municipal policies and prescribed procedures and do not comply with their performance contracts should experience appropriate consequences for their actions – or lack thereof. Especially officials that are so-called 'politically connected' are often protected by councillors from any consequences. Senior managers thus find it difficult to institute prescribed disciplinary procedures against wrongdoers. Coupled with this challenge is the absence of signed performance contracts between lower-level officials and municipal councils. There is thus no legal, mutually agreed instrument to hold people accountable for their actions. Successful M&E are thus constrained by the lack of a performance orientation and M&E culture often leading to improper financial management, malpractice, and corruption. This situation is regularly reflected in the audit outcomes of the Auditor General accentuating fruitless and wasteful expenditure.

The general absence of adequate political will to drive the institutionalization of M&E in municipalities can be regarded as a further key challenge. Political representatives usually have a short-term perspective, meaning that they only focus on issues during their term of office. These issues thus fall within the election cycle of local government. Longer-term issues such as inculcating a performance orientation and an M&E culture in the municipality are usually not adequately 'visible' to get them re-elected. As a result, they simply do not place it high on their political agenda. Performance and evidence-based governance as well as M&E institutional arrangements are generally not prioritized and as a result, limited resources are allocated to it. Instead, highly visible projects such as clinics, water supply, electrification, and housing are prioritized (Mpisi, 2013).

A further challenge is the general absence of reliable, accurate, and up-to-date municipal performance data and statistics. The Presidency (2008, p. 4) holds that municipalities, as a result of 'a lack of precise M&E data, limits producing meaningful, evidence-based decision-making'. Because they are unable to effectively monitor progress made in decreasing basic services backlogs, many cities and towns will continue to fall behind in the delivery of these services.

Govender and Reddy (2014) accentuate the absence of an M&E culture and adequate organisational buy-in as further challenges. Institutionalizing M&E in municipalities has been hampered by both council and employees' limited awareness of the value of performance monitoring and evaluation. There is seemingly 'an unwillingness to shift mindsets' about how performance should be improved (Govender and Reddy, 2014, p. 70). This mentality typically rejects any innovation or adjustment that threatens the status quo. Institutionalizing monitoring and evaluation in local government will remain a distant reality without acceptance among municipal personnel and senior management.

This concludes a brief exposition of some of the main challenges associated with the implementation of M&E arrangements in municipalities. The next section accentuates potential interventions required to address these and other challenges.

INTERVENTIONS REQUIRED TO INSTITUTIONALIZE M&E IN LOCAL GOVERNMENT

Municipalities frequently run into difficulties when attempting to institutionalize M&E (Enaifoghe and Adetiba, 2019). To mitigate the challenges associated with the institutionalization of M&E in local government, it is crucial to remember that every challenge presents opportunities for councils to improve the overall performance of the institution and to design innovative interventions. Such interventions should address typical challenges experienced in the operationalization of performance targets and ultimately lead to improved service delivery. The typical interventions required to successfully institutionalize M&E in local government are highlighted in the sections below.

Strengthening Accountability

Municipalities are relatively complex organizations with a wide range of stakeholders and role-players interacting in general governance affairs. The network of collaborators and multiple interconnections are largely a result of the complexity of the statutory obligations and mandates of local government. Municipalities simply do not have the required capacity to address these obligations in isolation. Multiple actors make it difficult to pinpoint responsibility and ultimately hold single actors accountable for certain actions (Motingoe, 2012). This problem is compounded by the delineation of geographical areas and demarcation of municipal territories. According to Kroukamp and Lues (2008, p. 111), the complex demarcation of municipal boundaries has further complicated accountability arrangements.

The general decrease in the revenue base through rates and taxes makes it difficult for municipalities to comply with citizens' service delivery expectations. This requires decisive action to address systemic issues like the misappropriation of scarce resources and the mismanagement of municipal departments and entities. Strong accountability arrangements are thus essential.

A further challenge hampering the institutionalization of M&E in local government is the highly politized nature of municipal governance. The Department of Co-operative Governance and Traditional Affairs (COGTA, 2010) holds that municipal councils will always struggle with intra- and inter-party disputes as political parties compete to further their interests. The overall result of such political meddling is polarization within municipalities, which negatively influences accountability arrangements. In addition, Enaifoghe and Adetiba (2019) argue that the political nature of municipal governance often leads to irrational decisions in council. Rather than focusing on equitable service delivery, dominant political parties further their own interests. Strengthening accountability within councils and holding political leadership responsible for their decisions are vital in this regard. Municipal oversight structures should use M&E as an accountability instrument management tool aimed at promoting the successful delivery of public services in a responsive way that fits residents' demands and expectations.

As far as particular accountability arrangements are concerned, the following should be accentuated:

- Improved transparency and openness: Making council meetings, records, and decisions more accessible to the public can increase accountability by allowing constituents to see what their elected officials are doing on their behalf. This can be achieved through livestreaming or recording of council meetings, and publishing meeting minutes, budgets, and other important documents online.
- Fostering public participation: Encouraging and enabling greater public participation in council meetings, such as through public comment periods or town hall meetings, can give constituents a voice and increase accountability by allowing them to hold their elected officials accountable for their actions.
- Strengthening independent municipal oversight: Establishing independent oversight mechanisms, such as regular audits and performance reports can help to monitor the actions of municipal councils and hold them accountable to the public.
- Improved communication: Building better communication channels between council members, constituents, and other stakeholders can help to increase transparency and accountability, by allowing for regular feedback and updates on the work of the council.
- Stricter ethical standards: Establishing and enforcing ethical standards for council members, such as codes of conduct, conflict of interest rules, and financial disclosure requirements, can increase accountability by reducing the potential for unethical behaviour.
- Regular local elections: Holding regular elections and promoting a competitive political environment can increase accountability by giving voters an opportunity to hold elected officials accountable through the ballot box.
- Effective complaint and grievance mechanisms: Establishing effective complaint and grievance mechanisms, such as a citizens' hotline or a formal process for raising concerns, can help to address problems and hold council members accountable for their actions.

Implementing these measures can help to increase accountability in municipal councils and improve the quality of governance in the local sphere of government.

Staff Competencies and Skills Development

A second typical intervention required to successfully institutionalize M&E in local government is to address the skills and competency deficit in municipalities. High staff turnover and a serious lack of skills, particularly in essential technical fields like information technology and engineering, are arguably some of the biggest problems facing municipal councils (Govender, 2011, p. 123). The same applies to particular competencies in M&E applications.

Innovative recruitment, selection, appointment, and skills development arrangements are necessary to attract and retain competent, talented employees. This should include incentives to partake in training and skills development opportunities.

Municipal Oversight and Support

The oversight obligations of provincial and national governments to support municipalities are outlined in the Constitution and it is intimately part of the system of cooperative governance and intergovernmental relations in the country. Some common obligations of national and provincial governments with respect to municipalities include:

- Funding: National and provincial governments often provide funding to municipalities to support infrastructure projects, social services, and other programmes.
- Policy guidance: National and provincial governments may provide policy guidance and directives to municipalities on issues such as land use planning, environmental protection, and economic development.
- Regulation: National and provincial governments may regulate certain aspects of municipal operations, such as procurement processes, financial management, and transparency.
- Technical assistance: National and provincial governments may provide technical assistance to municipalities, such as training and capacity-building programmes, to help them improve their services and operations.
- Emergency support: In the case of natural disasters or other emergencies, national and provincial governments may provide financial and other forms of support to municipalities.

Some examples of support programmes for municipalities in South Africa include the following:

- The Integrated National Electrification Programme: This is a programme run by the national government that provides financial and technical support to municipalities for the development of electrification infrastructure.
- The Municipal Infrastructure Grant: This is a grant provided by the national government to municipalities to support the development of basic infrastructure such as water, sanitation, and roads.
- The Municipal Capacity Building and Support Programme: This programme is run by the national government and provides training, mentoring, and support to municipalities to help them improve their service delivery and financial management.
- The Metropolitan Governance Support Programme: This programme provides support to metropolitan municipalities in South Africa to help them improve their governance and service delivery.
- The Municipal Institutional Strengthening Programme: This programme provides support to municipalities to help them improve their institutional capacity and governance.

The exact support provided to each municipality depends on its specific needs and circumstances. It should be noted that there is currently no clear national programme aimed at improving M&E applications in the country.

Financial Viability of Municipalities

The financial viability of municipalities in South Africa is a complex and ongoing concern. Many municipalities in South Africa face significant financial challenges, including:

- Limited revenue-generating capacity: Many municipalities in South Africa have limited revenue-generating capacity and depend heavily on transfers (i.e. grants) from national and provincial governments.
- High operational costs: Municipalities in South Africa face high operational costs, such as salaries, utilities, and maintenance costs, which can put pressure on their budgets.
- Poor financial management: Some municipalities in South Africa have a history of poor financial management, including mismanagement of funds, corruption, and lack of accountability.
- Ageing infrastructure: Many municipalities in South Africa are facing the challenge of maintaining ageing infrastructure, which requires significant financial investment.
- Growing demand for services: As populations grow, the demand for services such as housing, water, and sanitation is increasing, putting pressure on municipal budgets.

Despite these challenges, there have been efforts by the national government and other stakeholders to improve the financial viability of municipalities in South Africa. For example, the Municipal Finance Management Act was introduced in 2003 to improve the financial management and accountability of municipalities. Additionally, the national government has launched various programmes to provide financial and technical support to municipalities, including the Municipal Infrastructure Grant and the Municipal Capacity Building and Support Programme. It is further important to note that the financial viability of municipalities varies widely between different municipalities, depending on factors such as geographical location, the size of the municipality, the level of economic activity, and the quality of governance and financial management.

The financial viability of municipalities significantly influences the ability of municipalities to implement innovative institutional arrangements and mechanisms to institutionalize M&E. Priority is rather given to short-term service delivery projects to address immediate reasons cited for service delivery protests and boycotts. As a result, inadequate time, resources, and finances are devoted and allocated to address M&E matters.

CONCLUSION

For the local sphere of government in South Africa to adhere to its statutory and regulatory obligations, they must develop a comprehensive M&E system. Such a system must enable officials in municipalities to measure the performance of the total municipality (i.e. input, management, output, and outcomes) to identify weaknesses in this value chain. M&E thus becomes a way of considering all programmes and projects undertaken by a municipality. This should be done in alignment with a municipality's IDPs and service delivery outcomes, as well as operational plans for implementing the budget. It requires looking at environmental constraints, capacity and resource management, working conditions, and numerous other aspects which could have either a positive or a negative impact on institutional performance.

The development of such a comprehensive system is, however, not without challenges, and municipalities should consider innovative measures to institutionalize M&E in all its functions and operations.

Of particular importance is the political nature of municipal decisions. Political representatives (i.e. councillors) should have the necessary political will to inculcate a performance culture and drive M&E applications. M&E can largely contribute to more rational and objective decision-making and promote the overall responsiveness and accountability of councils. The chapter shows that M&E can be regarded as a powerful management tool that can assist local government to improve the manner in which tasks are undertaken to achieve a country's development goals.

REFERENCES

Ajam, T. (2012), 'Proposals on Municipal Capacity Building: Doing Things Differently or Re-packaging the Past Initiatives', *Local Government Bulletin*, pp. 1–16, Community Law Centre, Cape Town.

Bussin, M. (2017), *Performance Management Reboot*, Randburg: KR Publishing.

Davids, G.J. (2011), 'Local Government Capacity Challenges in Post-Apartheid South Africa: Lessons Learnt', *African Journal of Business Management*, **5** (7), 3570–3576, doi.org/10.5897/AJBM10.1503.

COGTA (Department of Co-operative Governance & Traditional Affairs. (2010), *KwaZulu-Natal Provincial Government, Toolkit: Performance Management Made Simple*, Pretoria: COGTA.

Department of Planning, Monitoring and Evaluation (DPME). (2012), *Evaluation Competency Framework for Government*, Pretoria: The Presidency, DPME.

Durokifa, A.A and A.O. Enaifoghe (2022), 'Politics of Public Administration: Creating a Balance for Effective Service Delivery in Selected African Countries', *African Journal of Development Studies*, **12** (1), 333–353, doi.org/10.31920/2634-3649/2022/v12n1a17.

Enaifoghe, A.O. (2022), 'Challenges of Municipal Service Delivery and Instruments for Enhancing South African Local Government Administration', *African Journal of Development Studies*, **12** (3), 105–124.

Enaifoghe, A.O. and T.C. Adetiba (2018), 'Implication of Community Engagement in the Decision-Making Process in South African Local Municipalities', *Administration Acta Universitatis Danubius* (AUDA), **10** (1), 17–38.

Enaifoghe, A.O. and T.C. Adetiba (2019), 'Decentralization Problem with Citizenry Participatory Democracy in Local Municipal Development in South Africa', *AFRIKA: Journal of Politics, Economics and Society*, **9** (1), 91–116, doi.org/10.31920/2075-6534/2019/9n1a5.

Engela, R. and T. Ajam (2010), *Implementing a Government-Wide Monitoring and Evaluation System in South Africa*, ECD Working Paper Series, No. 21, Washington, DC: The World Bank.

Govender, I. (2011), 'Monitoring and Evaluation Systems Enhancing Corporate Governance in Local Government: A Case Study of KwaZulu-Natal', unpublished doctoral thesis, Public Administration, School of Public Administration and Development Management, Faculty of Management Studies, University of KwaZulu-Natal.

Govender, I. and P.S. Reddy (2014), 'Monitoring and Evaluation in Local Municipalities: A Case Study of KwaZulu-Natal Province', *Administratio Publica*, **160** (22), 4–15.

Hargreaves, M.B. (2010), *Evaluating Systems Change: A Planning Guide*, Princeton, NJ: Mathematica Policy Research Inc.

Jordaan, J. and D. Fourie (2013), 'Towards Best Practice Financial Performance Management: A Platform Design for Stewardship in Public Administration', *African Journal of Public Affairs*, **6** (1), 19–40.

Khawula, B. (2016), 'An Evaluation of Community Participation in the Integrated Development Planning (IDP) Process: A Case Study of Umzumbe Municipality in the Province of Kwazulu-Natal in South AFRICA', unpublished master's thesis, Public Management, Faculty of Public Management and Economics, Durban University of Technology.

Koma, S.B. (2010), 'The State of Local Government in South Africa: Issues, Trends and Options', *Journal of Public Administration*, **45** (1.1), 111–120.

Kroukamp, H. and L. Lues (2008), 'Improving Local Management', in De Vries, M.S., P.S. Reddy and M. Haque (eds.), *Improving Local Government: Outcomes of Comparative Research*, London: Oxford University Press, pp. 111–123.

Lawal, T. and S.O. Onohaebi (2010), 'Project Management: A Panacea for Reducing the Incidence of Failed Projects in Nigeria', *International Journal of Academic Research*, **2** (5), 292–295.

Meyiwa, T., M. Nkondo, M. Chitiga-Mabugu, M. Sithole and F. Nyamnjoh (2014), *State of the Nation 2014. South Africa 1994–2014: A Twenty-Year Review*, Cape Town: HSRC Press.

Motingoe, R.S. (2012), 'Monitoring and Evaluation System Utilisation for Municipal Support', unpublished doctoral thesis, Degree of Public Management and Governance, Potchefstroom campus, North-West University.

Mpisi, M. (2013), *The Model of Inter-Governmental Relations: Presentation in the Technical Premier's Co-ordinating Forum on 29 November 2014 in Durban*, KwaZulu Natal Premiers Office, Durban.

Mthethwa, R.M. and N.N. Jili (2016), 'Challenges in Implementing Monitoring and Evaluation (M&E) The Case of the Mfolozi Municipality', *African Journal of Public Affairs*, **9** (4), 103–113.

Naidu, R. (2012), 'Subduing Local Voice-Public Participation and Ward Committees', in S. Booysen (ed.), *Local Elections in South Africa: Parties, People, Politics*, Bloemfontein: SUN MeDIA, pp. 279–293.

National Treasury. (2010), *Framework for Strategic Plans and Annual Performance Plans*. Pretoria: National Treasury.

Olumuyiwa, A. (2015), 'Bureaucratic Politics and Policy Development: Issues and Challenges', *African Journal of Political Science and International Relations*, **10** (2), 16–24, doi.org/10.5897/AJPSIR2015.0787.

Phillips, S., I. Goldman, N. Gasa, I. Akhalwaya and B. Leon (2014), 'A Focus on M&E of Results: An Example from the Presidency, South Africa', *Journal of Development Effectiveness*, **6** (4), 392–406.

Public Service Commission (PSC). (2008), *Basic Concepts in Monitoring and Evaluation*, Pretoria: PSC.

Rossi, P., M. Lipsey and H. Freeman (2004), *Evaluation: A Systematic Approach*, 7th ed., Thousand Oaks, CA: SAGE.

Schurink, W. and E. Schurink (2010), 'Outcomes-Based Evaluation within a Systems Perspective: Moving Beyond a Theory of Change to System Change Reform in Public Governance', *Administration Publica*, **18** (2), 13–38.

State of Municipal Capacity Report (SMCR). (2012), *State of Municipal Capacity Report (SMCR) for the 2010/11 Financial Year*, accessed 6 September 2014 at www.dplg.gov.za.

The Presidency (2008), *The Role of Premiers' Offices in Government-Wide Monitoring and Evaluation Practice Guide: A Good Practice Guide*, Pretoria: The Presidency.

Uys, F.M. (2010), 'Improving Performance in the Public Sector', *Administration Publica*, **18** (2), 54–73.

PART II

PUBLIC MANAGEMENT FUNCTIONS AND APPLICATIONS

7. Public policymaking in Africa: experiences of Zimbabwe

Hardlife Zvoushe

INTRODUCTION

Generally, public policies constitute a critical instrument in governmental efforts to address distressful socioeconomic conditions ranging from complex and far-reaching wicked and super-wicked problems, to social concerns of varying magnitudes. This follows from the understanding that a public policy is 'a purposive course of action … in dealing with a problem or matter of concern' (Anderson, 1984, p. 3). Dealing with troublesome public issues of the day is part of governmental responsibility, and in the present era, delivering on this function is becoming challenging by reason of the increasing numbers and complexity of issues that governments have to address. By and large, public policymaking sits at the heart of the governance discourse, and policies often serve as indicators of the quality of governance in any given territory. Policies are further perceived as expressions of state formation, and on this note, the existing repertoire on the formation of the post-independence African state carries an excessive imagery of governance morass, tragedies of policymaking, and failed instrumentalisation of public policy in driving national development (Chazan et al., 1999; Herbst and Mills, 2012; Sandbrook, 1985). Claims of failure to apply policy as a governance resource have sometimes been linked with arguments portraying the state in Africa as a purely Western creation inherited from colonial governments and superimposed on Africa's indigenous traditional systems (Aihie, 2014). Holding this position further pushes a sub-narrative which sees processes of state formation in postcolonial Africa as having rested in the hands of novices who lacked both experience and technical capacities to get the best out of policymaking. For Hyden (2022), these experiences are part of the colonial legacy in the African region. In cases such as Zimbabwe, the inherited policymaking practices and models were originally designed to serve white minority interests, and yet the postcolonial reality is a whole new world completely divorced from any exigencies of the colonial world. The transition from the colonial to the postcolonial eras therefore practically underscores the need for innovating 'the institutional pathways to effective and legitimate forms of public policymaking' (Hyden, 2022, p. 46). It then begs the question: 'How much has been done by the postcolonial African governments to attune the policymaking architecture for the present realities and national imperatives?' Responding to this question should bring out an evaluation of the efforts, and an assessment of the effectiveness of the same. In the post-2010 period, a few positive depictions have tampered with the predominant Afro-pessimism by projecting a positive outlook read from narratives of 'Africa rising' (Frankema and Van Waijenburg, 2018) and from portrayals of economic progress in selected countries which is viewed as signifying the 'arrival of African lions' (Kelsall, 2013). Objective evaluations to ascertain the veracity of both pessimism and optimism may only be expected from sustained, comprehensive, and dedicated scholarship on the subject of public policy development in the region. For now, it appears there is a concurrence that academically, attention to the study of policymaking in Africa is still minimal, and for the few major works done to date, the efforts were externally driven with the effect that the analytical framing of the discourses is conditioned by internationally determined constructs (Onyango, 2022). External influences on policy studies in Africa are particularly linked to donor hegemony (Hyden, 2022) which explains the reliance on international indices and foreign models that, in many instances, are not necessarily fit for the African purpose.

This chapter presents some of the practical experiences of African policymaking by drawing mainly from the experiences of Zimbabwe. The discussion is largely predicated on a combination of theoretical and practical aspects of policymaking to bring out an evaluative effect in the narrative. Efforts are mainly directed towards understanding the practical process of policymaking, the dynamics involved, the challenges experienced, and the general developments in the practice of policymaking in Zimbabwe and Africa at large. The chapter is organised as follows: it starts by briefly presenting a general overview of the policymaking experiences of Zimbabwe across the four decades of its independence (1980–). This is meant to provide both a cursory review of the nation's policymaking trajectory and a foundational context to the subsequent discussions in other sections. The chapter then proceeds to delve into the theoretical and practical processes of policymaking. The final sections of the chapter are reserved for the other critical aspects of policymaking such as evidence-based policymaking, policy instruments and policy implementation, and the challenges commonly faced at the implementation stage. The discussion ends with a look at some of the critical skills relevant for capacitating actors involved in policy management and execution.

A GENERAL OVERVIEW OF ZIMBABWE'S POLICYMAKING TRAJECTORY

Zimbabwe has recently entered its fifth decade of independence which started in 2020 and is currently under the Second Republic which began in July 2018. From a policymaking perspective, each of the four-and-a-half decades has tended to follow an observable trend of policymaking paradigms which can actually serve as a basis for distinguishing between policy experiences of the different decades (Chipika and Malaba, 2017; Zhou and Zvoushe, 2012; Zhou and Zvoushe, 2017). Each decade appears to reflect some distinctiveness in terms of the overarching policy thrust and focus. Policymaking experiences in the decades also reveal the dominant roles of contextual dynamics, ideas of policy actors, and institutional influences in driving the policymaking agenda in the country. Contextual dynamics in Zimbabwe are explained by the fact that there has always been an 'intimate link between public policies and their ecological contexts', and that 'public policies in terms of content and practice usually carry the imprint of their environment' (Zhou and Zvoushe, 2012, p. 213). Most of the public policies formulated since independence have been intricately connected to the socioeconomic and political developments obtained at different periods in the country. Generally, post-independence policymaking in Zimbabwe has been viewed as having taken a 'partocratic' (Zwizwai et al., 2004, p. 237) approach, which speaks of the domineering role of the ruling ZANU-PF party in policy matters over the years. Taken from that perspective, post-independence policymaking became predominantly top-down and exclusionary. It was therefore not surprising that the entire policymaking process was practically shrouded in secrecy and remained a preserve of bureaucrats and other official state actors. All the documentation on policies was classified, implying that the general public only had access to such when Cabinet had already approved the policies.

1980–1989: State-centric Policymaking

18 April 1980 marked the end of colonial white minority rule and the installation of a new black majority government. Policies of the colonial government typically addressed socioeconomic and political issues along racial lines. They practically initiated and perpetuated racial inequalities in social and economic sectors through a carefully crafted and systematically maintained separatist system. The marginalisation of the African population was systematic and widespread. With this background, a transition to majority rule had wide implications for policymaking. State policy became guided by a discernible fixation on the objective of radically reversing the debilitating legacies of colonial policies across all sectors of the economy. In the pursuit of this objective, the state's preference for an interventionist approach at policy level was noticeable. The idea was to distribute state largesse to the previously marginalised population by way of subsidisation of public services, redistribution of land, professional advancement of blacks through Africanisation of the public service, indigenisation of the economy, and other policy initiatives. Most of the policy initiatives were made possible by the state's expansionary, pro-poor, and welfare-centric fiscal policies of the first decade (Zhou, Mukonza and Zvoushe, 2016). The pursuit of welfarism was in keeping with the state's socialist ideological leaning and egalitarian ideals.

1990–1999: Policymaking under Neoliberalism

Towards the end of the first decade (around 1988), the economy showed signs of stress and stagnation, with the effect that the subsidisation of public services and the distributive policies that the state had initiated at the beginning of independence became difficult to maintain going forward. There was a need for a solution to stimulate economic growth and revive economic performance. The government approached the IMF and World Bank for assistance, and the organisations recommended a radical shift from expansionary policies to contractionary policies by way of cutting government spending, removal of subsidies, downsizing the civil service, and many other cost-saving initiatives. The full package of policy prescriptions from IMF and World Bank was contained in the Economic Structural Adjustment Programme (ESAP), which the government implemented between 1991 and 1995 (Mlambo, 1997). Key highlights from the package included a minimalist role for the state by 'rolling back its frontiers' in the economy. This was to involve liberalisation of trade and allowing unhindered play of market forces. The pursuit of these policies meant that policymaking in the second decade was mainly defined by economic reforms.

After the ESAP (1991–1995), the government launched the Zimbabwe Programme for Economic and Social Transformation (ZIMPREST) (1996–2000). Both ESAP and ZIMPREST reform programmes failed to deliver the expected outcomes for various reasons. An evaluation of ESAP, on the one hand, revealed a mismatch between policy prescriptions and the socioeconomic problems they sought to address (Mlambo, 1997). On the other, ZIMPREST was an over-ambitious programme that was further affected by lack of sufficient financial resources to support its implementation (Zhou, Mukonza and Zvoushe, 2016). With worsening poverty levels, underperforming economy, high inflation, and increasing unemployment, the state found itself facing an increasingly restive population led by civil society organisations, labour unions, and war veterans who were voicing varied demands from the state.

2000–2009: Policymaking under Authoritarianism

The persisting socioeconomic challenges of the second decade inspired the leadership of the Zimbabwe Congress of Trade Unions (ZCTU) to search for a political solution by forming a political party, the Movement for Democratic Change (MDC) in 1999 under the leadership of the late Morgan Tsvangirai. This arguably marked the beginning of formidable opposition politics, considering that in the general elections of 2000, the opposition won 57 out of 120 parliamentary seats. For the ruling ZANU-PF party, this marked the arrival of a political opponent with the potential to take over state power. With these issues and more, the government practically faced multiple problems of a socioeconomic and political nature. It is in the state's responses to these threats that some commentators saw the birth of authoritarianism and predatory tendencies of the state (Raftopoulos, 2003). The evidence of it was the array of regulatory policies and draconian legislation that, combined, served the sole purpose of containing opposition politics and subsequently ring-fence the ruling party's political ground (Sachikonye, 2012). The unprecedented economic crisis of the decade—which led some to label the period the 'lost decade' (Bratton, 2014, p. 74) and 'crisis decade' (Bratton and Masunungure, 2011, p.iv)—seemed to justify the state's embrace of radical economic nationalism which came in the form of mainly two controversial redistributive policies: the Fast-Track Land Reform Programme (FTLRP) and the indigenisation and economic empowerment policy. The multi-dimensional crisis the country faced mainly between 2002 and 2008, eventually subsided with the formation of the coalition government (2009–2013).

2010–2019: Policymaking under Stabilisation and Change

The beginning of the third decade (2010–2013) was marked by macro-economic stability and recuperation of the capacities of public institutions following dollarisation of the economy in 2009. This was achieved under the Short-Term Economic Recovery Programme (STERP 1, March to December 2009), STERP 2 (2010–2012), and the Medium-Term Plan (MTP 2011–2015). The policymaking arena was characterised by ideational rivalry and political bickering of the two major parties in the coalition government, the MDC and ZANU-PF. Often, inter-party rivalry resulted in gridlocks and 'immobilism' (Le Van, 2011) which in turn caused policy implementation inertia. One of the notable cases is that of the indigenisation and economic empowerment policy whose implementation often suffered the effects of contradictory statements between policy pronouncements of the then Prime Minister Morgan Tsvangirai and the then Minister of Indigenisation, Saviour Kasukuwere. The end of the coalition government in 2013 saw ZANU-PF recording landslide victory in elections and regaining total control of state structures. With this development, policies that were associated, or originated with, the opposition MDC ministers were abruptly discontinued. The Medium-Term Plan (2011–2015), for example, was abruptly dropped and replaced with ZANU-PF's five-year blueprint, the Zimbabwe Agenda for Sustainable Socio-Economic Transformation (ZIM-ASSET 2013–2018). In November 2017, Mugabe was removed from power, and his former deputy, Emmerson Mnangagwa took over. One distinguishing feature of the policy regime under President Mnangagwa is its movement away from Mugabe's radicalism. One of the defining flagship policies under Mugabe's radical economic nationalism—the indigenisation and economic empowerment policy—for example, was discontinued in 2018 in favour of economic reforms focusing on increasing foreign direct investment inflows. After the ZIM-ASSET, the government introduced the Transitional Stabilisation Programme (October 2018–December 2020) which sought to achieve economic stabilisation, stimulation of economic growth, and employment creation (MoF, 2018).

2020–2022: Policymaking under Resurgent Crises and Continuing Authoritarianism

From the beginning of the Second Republic in July 2018, the government embraced a new vision, the Vision 2030, which seeks to make the country an industrialising upper-middle-income economy by 2030. To pursue this vision, the government crafted a first five-year blueprint, the National Development Strategy 1 (NDS 1, 2021–2025) which will be succeeded by the National Development Strategy 2 (NDS 2, 2026–2030) at the end of 2025. Evaluations of economic performance so far, however, paint a less positive outlook. For instance, investment is at the time of writing only 10% of GDP, and this was considered one of the lowest in the world (Mangudhla, 2022). The combined effects of increasing rates of unemployment, company closures, inflation upsurge, increasing informality, and impacts of the coronavirus pandemic have only worsened levels of poverty. These negative developments have triggered unrest in the labour sector. The government has not only ducked the critical questions on livelihoods and citizen welfare, but it has revived its authoritarian tendencies by enacting controversial pieces of legislation with an inhibiting effect on the enjoyment of freedoms by citizens. These include the Maintenance of Peace and Order Act (No. 9 of 2019), Freedom of Information Act (No. 1 of 2020), the Patriotic Act (No. 10 of 2023), and one bill, the Private Voluntary Organisation Bill).

POLICYMAKING IN THEORY AND PRACTICE

There are several models and theories that have been developed to give a theoretical portrayal of the policymaking practice, and so far, what appears to be the most popular conceptualisation of the policy process is the policy cycle model which breaks the process into distinct stages of activities, actors, and sub-processes. Drawing from insights of the model, many have gone on to apply it in analysing practical policymaking in different countries and diverse policy sectors. Others have broken down the stages of the process by analysing them individually to test and evaluate assumptions of the model. One of the most important strengths of the policy cycle framework is its explanatory quality that simplifies the otherwise complex practical process of policymaking (Lindquist and Wellstead, 2021). The model generally retains simulative abilities that enable it to serve as a means for mentally organising policymaking activities and processes as well as policy actors and their disparate roles. These qualities have made the model a popular tool for teaching public policy and public administration. Following Howlett, Ramesh and Perl (2009, p. 12), the stages of the policy cycle are as follows:

* *Agenda-setting*, which is a process whereby public problems come to the attention of governmental authorities.
* *Policy formulation*, which covers the process of identifying and selecting courses of action to address public problems on the governmental agenda.

- *Decision-making*, where governmental authorities make the choice either to implement a certain course of action, or not to implement.
- *Policy implementation*, which involves putting government decisions on policy problems into action.
- *Policy evaluation*, which is about assessing the consequences of policies to establish whether or not objectives have been achieved.

The policy cycle model projects a picture of policymaking as a linear, systematic, and rational process with distinct stages. It has fared well as an analytical framework for appreciating the roles of actors, institutions, and ideas. Some of the often-highlighted weaknesses of the model include its failure to 'illuminate the nuances and complexities of public policymaking within each stage or over the cycle as a whole' (Howlett, Ramesh and Perl, 2009, p. 14). This points to the dynamics within each of the stages of policymaking, which the model fails to capture. Further, realities of policymaking point to a complex process that is neither linear nor rational owing to the trade-offs between forces in policy sectors. Using the model, it is impossible to tell the motivations, personal interests, and ideological leaning of policy actors as they go through the policymaking process.

POLICYMAKING IN ZIMBABWE: ACTORS, ROLES, FRAMEWORKS, PROCESSES

The starting point in appreciating the practical process of policymaking in Zimbabwe is to identify the various political and administrative structures as well as legal frameworks that together enable the process to take place the way it does.

- *Constitution of Zimbabwe Amendment (No. 20) Act 2013*: As the supreme law of the land, the national constitution provides the basis for the practice of policymaking by government. It provides for the creation of specific structures of governance and spells out their roles in policy formulation and implementation.
- *Office of the President and Cabinet (OPC)*: This is the topmost executive structure which is critical in the development, approval, and implementation of public policies. Through its own structures, the OPC also gives policy direction and further performs coordination, monitoring, supervisory and evaluation roles in the implementation of policies.
- *Parliament*: This structure is involved in the initiation, preparation, consideration, and sometimes rejection of legislation in the country. Parliament further scrutinises policies and holds the executive arm of government to account for all their activities and use of public resources.
- *Attorney-General*: This office acts as the legal advisor of government, and in the process of policymaking, its main responsibility is to draft legislation on behalf of government. When a ministry has brought a policy proposal which gets approved by cabinet, it proceeds to give the office of the auditor-general instructions to draft a bill to give effect to the proposed policy.
- *Permanent Secretaries*: These are the chief administrators of government ministries, and their roles range from day-to-day supervision of administrative staff to the management of operations in their respective ministries. As the face of the administrative dimension

of ministries, they act as secondary policymakers involved in spearheading and giving direction to the implementation of policies within their ministries.

*   *Commissions of Inquiry*: These are ad-hoc structures created by government from time to time to investigate any matter of public concern that government may consider acting on. They are also sometimes tasked with evaluating the performance of policies and generate recommendations. As the discussion below will show, commissions of inquiry have been a frequent feature in policymaking, with demonstrable impact on public policies across sectors.
*   *Societal actors*: These may include individual citizens, citizens' groups, civil society organisations, and any other forms of grassroots representative organisations. The official structures of policymaking are obligated by the national constitution to consult the public on policy and legal matters that may affect them. This provision has seen government ministries conducting stakeholder consultations as the entry point to policy development. Parliamentary committees also undertake public hearings and open consultations of members of the public on proposed laws. Citizen input in the development of laws and policies gives legitimacy, ensures acceptance, and reduces the chances of resistance at the implementation stage.

A simplified policymaking process in Zimbabwe shows that the impetus for the process to start comes from two possible sources: first, from the policy environment, as stakeholders and societal groups press demands for governmental action on specific policy issues, very much in the Eastonian sense of placing demands onto the political system. This way, policy decisions will be public need driven, and the 'policy environment is perceived as providing the trigger that turns on the policy process' (Zhou and Zvoushe, 2012, p. 220). Second, the state may, in some instances, craft policies but not necessarily in response to known societal demands. Such are typical cases of 'policy makers originating a policy for the environment' (Zhou and Zvoushe, 2012, p. 220).

In the bottom-up mode of policymaking depicted in the first scenario, everything starts with public demands for governmental action on some matters of concern. In response to this pressure (which normally comes from citizen representative organisations in specific policy sectors), the respective sectoral ministries would undertake broad-based consultations with the societal groups lobbying for policy action on specific problems. The essence of consultations—which are normally not a one-day event—is to establish what the problem is from the affected communities' perspective, and to solicit public input into the policy development process. Holding consultations has a further advantage of securing citizen buy-in for policies that will be developed. Civil society organisations are normally active in these processes as they discharge their citizen mobilisation and interest articulation roles. The consultations stage of the policy process, however, is often affected by citizen apathy and disinterest. A study conducted in Zimbabwe in 2020 found that 60.18% of the survey participants had never been involved in the processes of policy formulation in the country (Murisa, Kushata and Rwapunga, 2020, p. 13). In addition, in many instances, government officials were accused of coming for consultations when in actual fact they had already finalised drafting policy documents, thereby reducing the whole process to a mere procedural ritual devoid of citizen input, which should—in the first place—be the most critical ingredient of that process (Murisa et al., 2020). These experiences expose the government's appetite for an elite-driven, top-down policymaking process which, as Masunungure and Zvoushe (2023) argue, stems from the state's long-standing *modus operandi* of centralism and unilateralism in policymaking.

Assuming public consultations are done as they should, a ministry may proceed to prepare a draft policy document that will be submitted to the relevant Cabinet Inter-Ministerial Committee (known as the working party of permanent secretaries) for consideration. Upon receiving the draft policy document, the Committee discusses and where necessary, makes recommendations for improvement to the ministry. Once the ministry fully complies with the instructions of the Committee, normally by effecting changes and improvements as may have been recommended, the draft document is then submitted for consideration by select ministers represented in the working party. If the select ministers reject the draft document, it will be sent back to the working party for revision. After successfully improving the draft document, the select ministers will proceed to approve the draft document which will then be forwarded to the full Cabinet for consideration and approval. If the full Cabinet does not approve the draft policy document, it will be sent back to the select ministers for revision in line with comments that the full Cabinet may have made. Conversely, if the Cabinet is satisfied with the policy draft, it will be launched as government policy. What follows thereafter is the policy implementation process. It is instructive to note that as the draft policy document goes through all the stages above, an 'implementation matrix' would have been prepared already. This is a plan giving an outline of how the implementation processes will happen. It also specifies the actors and implementing agencies involved, their relationships, timeframes where necessary, and inter-agency arrangements, if necessary. The matrix may also capture any other information relevant to the implementation process.

Experiences from the past have shown that not all policies will be successfully implemented on the basis of moral suasion, implying that in some cases there is a need for an enabling or supporting legislation (an Act of Parliament). Where legislation has to be developed, it is the ministry proposing the policy that will put down principles of the draft legislation which will be sent to Cabinet for consideration. When the Cabinet agrees to the need for a law, it will approve the principles, and the ministry will then give instructions to the Attorney-General's Office to draft the bill. Once the draft bill is prepared, it will be sent to the Cabinet Committee on Legislation for consideration. The Committee will debate the bill after which it will make its recommendations to the Cabinet. When Cabinet approves the bill, it will be sent to Parliament where it will go through stages of first, second, and third reading in the lower house (Zimbabwe has a bicameral parliament). Thereafter, it will be sent to the upper house for debating and approval. Once approved at parliamentary level, the bill will be sent to the President for assent. Once the President signs the bill, it becomes law. If the bill fails to secure presidential assent, it will be sent back to parliament which will be instructed to attend to specific issues concerning the bill before assent can be given.

EVIDENCE-BASED POLICYMAKING PRACTICES

Globally, there have been calls to a practice of policymaking informed by systematically gathered policy-relevant evidence. The assumption is that policies formulated on the bases of systematic evidence have high chances of recording better outcomes. Evidence-based policymaking (EBP) as explained by Davies (2004, p. 3), is an approach that 'helps people make well-informed decisions about policies, programmes, and projects by putting the best available evidence from research at the heart of policy development and implementation'. To some, it signifies a shift from 'ideologically driven politics' and 'opinion-based policy' to 'rational

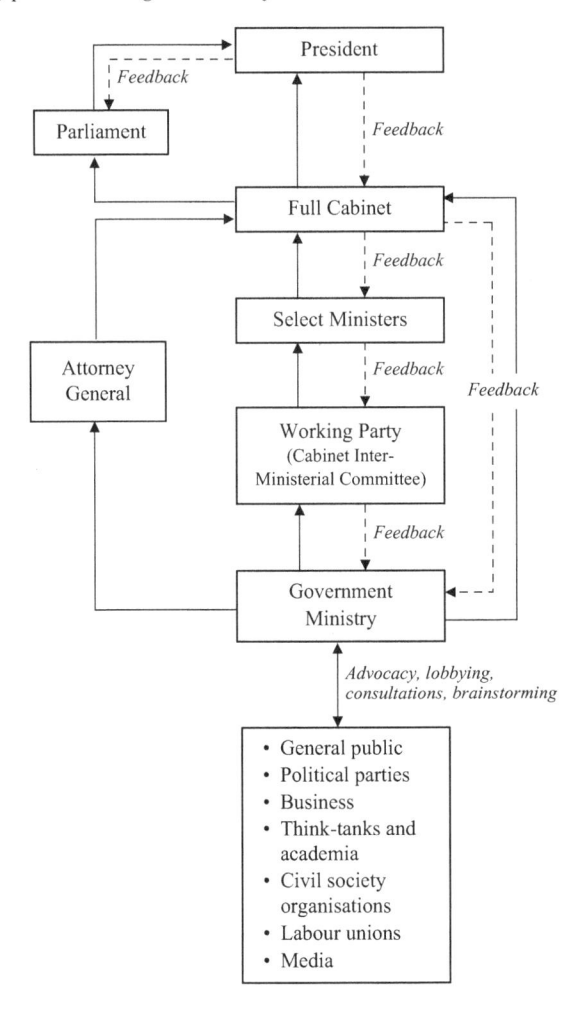

Source: Author's own construction.

Figure 7.1   The policymaking process in Zimbabwe

decision making' (Sutcliffe and Court, 2005, p. ii). Usually, the institutions involved in the production of evidence for policy include universities, think-tanks, policy innovation labs, policy research institutes, parliamentary committees, commissions of inquiry, and internal research structures of government. EBP has widely been embraced in policymaking by many countries, mostly in the developed world. Developing countries in regions such as Africa are slowly catching up and adopting the practice. In Tanzania, for example, a survey was once conducted on household diseases, and the results provided evidence that informed health service reforms later implemented by government. Results of the reforms showed a reduction of infant mortality rates by 40% in two districts between 2000 and 2003 (Sutcliffe and Court, 2005, p. iii). In Malawi, the government created the Knowledge Translation Platform which brings together researchers and government officials in policy development. While researchers, from time to time, send policy-relevant findings to government officials, the partnership arrangement between the two parties permits government officials to ask for evidence on specific policy issues. So far, research evidence submitted to government is showing the impact on policymaking. For example, the government's introduction of voluntary medical male circumcision meant to lower HIV infections was informed by evidence from research teams (International Initiative for Impact Evaluation, 2022).

In Zimbabwe, multiple institutions are involved in the generation of evidence for policy, from parliamentary portfolio committees, research organs of government, universities, think-tanks, through to commissions of inquiry and special ad-hoc committees of government. Among these, what appears as one of the most popular and long-standing instruments of evidence-based policymaking are the commissions of inquiry. These are a common feature of evidence gathering in the policymaking history of the government, and most of these have produced findings and recommendations that contributed to government policy in both the colonial and postcolonial periods. The colonial government used reports produced by commissions of inquiry to influence policy and 'to enhance its power to control' (Mungazi, 1989, p. 267) specific sectors of the economy as well as the broader society. Reliance on commissions of inquiry to generate policy-relevant evidence continued into the post-independence period. Table 7.1 presents a sample of some of the commissions established in that period. Globally, commissions of inquiry are historically appreciated as ad-hoc advisory structures established by government to investigate specific matters of concern or social problems in a country at a given time. In the United Kingdom, for example, Rowe and McAllister (2006, p. 99) noted that the Royal Commissions contributed to policymaking by systematically introducing 'expertise, research and statistical evidence to the policymaking process'. In addition, Clokie and Robinson (1937, p. 123) explained that one of the major roles of the Royal Commissions was to offer 'expert advice in areas where the government [had] no policy'.

Despite the cases of ad-hoc commissions highlighted in the table above which illustrate an observable influence on policies, there is generally a lack of consistent application of policy-relevant evidence produced by various institutions, including parliament. While the government itself occasionally commissions research on specific policy issues or public problems, what is not obvious are the explanatory factors behind the uptake, or lack thereof, of evidence into policymaking. In other cases, government receives findings and recommendations, but indefinitely defers implementing them. In the case of the findings of the Nziramasanga Commission of Inquiry of 1999, the government implemented recommendations on curriculum adjustment sixteen years later in 2015, when the Ministry of Primary and Secondary Education crafted the new education curriculum (2015–2022) for primary and secondary schools.

One of the discernible factors that has affected uptake of evidence by government has been the mistrust and suspicion that has often characterised the relationship between government and academicians in local universities (Zhou and Zinyama, 2016). The state's suspicion of academics appears to be rooted in the embedded polarities of Zimbabwean politics that have divided academics into two schools of intellectuals: first, the 'regime intellectuals' who are uncritically supportive of government and its policies, and second, the 'anti-establishment intellectuals' who are critical of government. The state's mistrust of the latter is exemplified in the articulations of one of the former ministers and ZANU-PF long-serving member, Obert Mpofu (2020, p. 101), who sneered at the intellectuals as constituting 'a neoliberal captured academia … focused on anti-establishment manoeuvres'. These dismissive opinions

Table 7.1   Sample of commissions of inquiry and their influence on policy

Name of commission	Focus of investigation	Key findings	Resultant policies
• Smith Commission of Inquiry (2017)	• Conversion of insurance and pension values from the Zimbabwe Dollar to the United States dollar	• Prejudicial conversion of value from the Zimbabwe Dollar to the United States dollar • Laxity in the regulation of the insurance and pension sector by government	• Pensions and Provident Funds Act (Chapter 24:09) • Regulations governing the compensation of insurance policy holders
• Nziramasanga Commission of Inquiry (1999)	• Education and training	• Education curriculum was not accommodative to children with natural talents that would ideally require vocational education • The curriculum did not equip students with practical and entrepreneurial skills • Lack of standardisation of early childhood education centres	• National Early Learning Policy (in preparation) • National Non-Formal Education Policy (2015) • Curriculum Framework for Primary and Secondary Education (2015–2022) • National Early Childhood Development Policy (2004) • Two-pathway education policy of 2006
• Riddell Commission of Inquiry (1981)	• Incomes, prices and conditions of service	• Provided statistical data on the extent of landlessness, and the link between agriculture and livelihoods • Highlighted the need for legislation to promote increased worker participation in industrial relations	• Land policy • Resettlement schemes programme • Labour Relations Act of 1985

Source: Author's own compilation.

are reminiscent of historical experiences in the state-academics relationship in some African countries, especially in the opening decades of independence. In Ghana, for example, Kwame Nkrumah once characterised the university college as 'a veritable breeding ground of unpatriotic and anti-government elements' (cited in Mkandawire, 1998, p. 97). These experiences are reflective of unprogressive polarities under which a disconnect between *producers* and *consumers* of evidence is likely to be born.

The demonisation of anti-establishment academics has conversely served to create participation space for the politically correct, that is, the 'intellectuals … [that are] provided space in state papers such as *The Herald, Chronicle* and *The Sunday Mail* and on state radio and television [and are] mostly state-aligned' (Sachikonye, 2012, p. 175). Most of them cannot easily be absolved of partisan policy analysis. Their standing with the state guarantees them frequent engagement to give policy commentary and spearhead policy conversations on public media. One direct effect of relying on partisan advisory input is the questionable objectivity of opinions, given the likelihood of cherry-picking knowledge in support of established political interests and ideological positions. This is closely related to what Parkhurst (2017, p. 73) calls 'issue bias', which occurs when actors select evidence for policy on the basis of their own values.

Sometimes, use of evidence may be competing with established policymaking practices. Such practices come close to what has been termed 'national policy styles', which are usually born out of the interplay of 'constitutional arrangements, party systems, electoral devices, and political cultures' (Freeman, 1985, p. 467). The peculiarity of the structure and organisation of politics in a country is believed to produce 'distinctive public policies' that bear the hallmarks of the established national policy styles (Freeman, 1985, p. 467). Hence, evidence-based policymaking at times has to contend with enduring traditional decision-making structures that are unlikely to be accommodative to policy inputs originating from external sources outside government. This also speaks to the inclination of prevailing organisational cultures and their levels of receptivity to new ideas and evidence-generating practices such as policy monitoring and evaluation (PME) which by nature, generates evidence useful for assessing the progress of policies and programmes. In other cases, consumption of evidence-for-policy may be inhibited by the influence of powerful lobby groups who may be pushing propositions that are neither based on empirical facts nor scientific data.

INSTRUMENTS OF GOVERNMENT AND POLICY IMPLEMENTATION

Policy instruments, or 'policy tools', are 'the set of techniques by which governmental authorities wield their power in attempting to ensure support and effect or prevent social change' (Vedung, 1998, p. 21). They serve to provide a bridge to the attainment of policy goals of government. This way, they become means to an end. The appreciation of policy instruments proceeds from the premise that every government has at its disposal policy tools, or 'governance resources', which can be used in responding to problematic or distressful situations that warrant governmental intervention. The primary aim in the application of policy tools is to influence behaviour change in society according to predetermined pathways set by government. Change in behaviour implies that policy tools exploit the authority of government to impose the force of official decisions on society, with the result that those caught on the wrong side of a policy directive face negative consequences and sanctions. Each policy, therefore, impliedly points to 'do's' and 'don'ts' within its confines.

Whether a policy succeeds in achieving its goals or not depends so much on the government's ability and capacity to apply an optimal combination of tools against the target situation. This calls for a thorough appreciation of not only the 'behaviours' of policy tools in different situations, but also whether the tools are being applied in isolation or in combination with others. This is despite the fact that some scholars have long acknowledged the fact that tool selection is not a straightforward and easy exercise mostly because of the potential ambiguities in selecting tools in different policy cases (Capano and Lippi, 2016). In addition, Linder and Peters (1989) also argue that instrument selection mostly depends on consideration of macro and micro variables including the national policy style, institutional setting, problem situation, and cognitive aspects. It is precisely because of the existence of a host of determinants that tool selection becomes cumbersome and dependent on trade-offs in a particular policy situation.

Several authors have made contributions to the current taxonomy of policy instruments, but making an exhaustive discussion of each and every model is beyond the scope of this chapter. Our discussion shall therefore be limited to the insights from frameworks developed by Christopher Hood (1986) and Evert Vedung (1998). Hood (1986) created four broad categories of policy instruments: (a) nodality, where governments use of information-based policy responses; (b) authority, where governmental policy responses take the form of regulations, laws, rules, prohibitions, executive orders, permits, etc; (c) treasure, where governmental responses involve use of financial resources; and (d) organisation, which involves using established public sector organisational structures in rolling out governmental policy responses. Another notable framework which largely complements and agrees with Hood's was created by Evert Vedung (1998). It puts policy instruments into three categories: 'the stick' (use of regulation), 'the carrot' (application of economic means), and 'the sermon' (use of information/exhortation).

To demonstrate the application of policy instruments in practice, this section applies the taxonomies by Christopher Hood (1986) and Evert Vedung (1998) in the context of the Government of Zimbabwe's responses to the Covid-19 pandemic since the year 2020. This is one public problem that has been addressed across the African continent and the world at large in an almost uniform manner, mainly because most response actions were derived from guidelines given by the World Health Organisation (WHO). Zimbabwean experiences further show that contrary to the typical policy process discussed above, there were no wide public consultations by government because of the nature of the problem. The situation was an emergency which called for rapid responses from the government. Another notable issue in the case is the influence of international actors such as the WHO, in guiding courses of action by governments. This is not unusual in policymaking, as international players form part of policy communities in policy sectors across countries. Some of the most common international actors that sometimes influence domestic policymaking include intergovernmental organisations such as the United Nations agencies, regional blocs, and International Financial Institutions (IFIs). As states become members of these organisations, they will likely be signatories to treaties made at those platforms. They cannot avoid policy influences originating from international platforms where they are participants and signatories.

In responding to the Covid-19 pandemic, the government of Zimbabwe generally relied on four classes of tools: information-based tools, authority-based tools, treasure-based tools and organisation-based tools. Operationalisation of these tools was a joint effort of a host of actors and agencies who were expected to cooperate and collaborate in their activities. The Ministry of Health played a lead role in coordinating the activities of many other organisations including the Ministry of Finance, Ministry of Defence, Department of Social Welfare, Ministry of Home Affairs, Department of Immigration, local authorities, Zimbabwe Revenue Authority (ZIMRA), and the Zimbabwe Republic Police. Non-state organisations involved in implementing some of the measures included churches, NGOs, and donors who provided food and other material assistance to poor and low-income households.

Information-based Tools

The government relied on its ability to educate the public about the disease. By providing free information, it sought to encourage responsible conduct and to provide precautionary measures against the pandemic. Various platforms were used in reaching out to the public: the local press, national broadcast, government websites, Twitter spaces, and short message services (SMSs). Telecoms service providers such as Econet Wireless also came on board to help spread educative messages about Covid-19 and to give daily updates on death toll. The Covid-19 information disseminated was meant to help the public understand what the pandemic is all about; its symptoms; its medium of spreading; how to report cases; and the precautionary and preventive measures that could be taken by members of the public. To effectively reach a wider audience, the government translated information into vernacular languages. Provision of Covid-19 information to the public had the effect of dispelling myths about Covid-19 and undoing the stigmatising social perceptions which projected the pandemic as a disease of the rich (Smith and Crone, 2020). The government's internal efforts were further complemented by those found at the international level. For example, since the beginning of the year 2020, the Southern African Development Community (SADC) was periodically publishing reports and bulletins on the situation as well as the impact of the pandemic in the subregion. The information tool generally served to inform, and even more importantly, to counter the effects of the often-misleading 'infodemic' that was coming through social media. Effects of the infodemic manifested in public resistance of the vaccination programme rolled out by government in 2020.

Authority-based Tools

The government also put in place several statutory instruments to regulate public behaviour, institute curfews and lockdowns, close non-essential businesses, and implement mandatory quarantining of returning citizens. From time to time, ministerial and presidential pronouncements were made to complement the statutory instruments. Non-compliance to the regulations attracted significant sanctions which have mostly constituted fines, penalties, and imprisonment. As a way of quickening the importation of essential goods, the procurement regulations were in some cases reviewed to rid them of any cumbersome provisions that could lengthen the times of importing essential Covid-19 medical supplies. Government also banned local inter-city travelling, public gatherings, entertainment, and recreational activities. Country-level regulations and laws were further complemented by international suspension of flights and banning of cross-border human traffic.

Treasure-based Tools

In terms of financial resources, the government came up with various initiatives ranging from tax relief, duty waivers on Covid-19-related imports, financial support to critical industries, and social protection to the vulnerable citizens. The government initially set aside finances to the tune of ZWL$100 million meant to support national efforts to combat Covid-19. Proceeds from the 2% Intermediated Money Transfer Tax (IMTT) were also channelled towards Covid-19 mitigatory expenditures (Ministry of Finance, 2020). Treasury further availed US$2 million towards the acquisition of health-related imports. Moreover, the Ministry of Finance drafted a raft of measures to financially support the productive sector, and these included giving value-added tax (VAT) refunds, extending periods for paying corporate taxes, and giving tax incentives for the production and importation of Covid-19 essential goods. Collaboration between government and private sector players saw government receiving financial and logistical support from private companies under the initiative 'Business Fighting Covid-19'.

Further support in cash and in kind was received from the government's development partners which included countries (the USA, UK, and China), regional blocs (EU), and international organisations (World Bank, Global Fund, Chinese Foundation). The government implemented a social protection and cash transfer programme which was meant to cushion and sustain vulnerable social groups especially during lockdown periods. About ZWL$200 million was being disbursed monthly to indigent families.

Organisation-based Tools

At the continental level, the World Health Organisation and Africa Centre for Disease Control and Prevention (Africa CDC) played an instrumental role in training health officials from various countries on Covid-19 case management and infection prevention and control. At the national level, the government established dedicated isolation centres and rapid response teams tasked with handling the control and prevention of the Covid-19 pandemic. These organisational structures were actively involved in implementing national Covid-19 preparedness and response plans. The government also received in-kind and financial support from businesses, churches, charities, and NGOs.

Common Implementation Challenges

Policy implementation has been one of the most problematic stages of policymaking, often cited as a stage where even the most promising policies sometimes get stalled, maimed, revised, or even killed by the implementers. The publication of Pressman and Wildavsky's (1973) book, *Implementation* which exposed implementation challenges in the pro-poor social welfare programmes of the 1960s and 1970s in the USA drew so much scholarly attention to the implementation challenge in policymaking. The book's subtitle, *How Great Expectations in Washington are Dashed in Oakland*, actually captured the disconnect between the intents of policymakers and the implementation activities of bureaucrats. Numerous studies conducted on the critical variables of policymaking point to the recurrence of factors such as political support, bureaucratic politics, resources, incentives, institutional factors, competence, communication, coordination, commitment, policy design and inter-organisational relations as some of the key determinants of policy success (Edwards, 1980; Mazmanian and Sabatier, 1983). Most of these variables can also be clustered in a universal analytical framework known as the 5C protocol which is made up of: (a) policy content, (b) policy context, (c) commitment to policy implementation, (d) capacity to implement policy, and (e) clients and coalitions involved in a particular policy. Depending on the dynamics in a given policy, variables in the 5C protocol combine in complex ways to create challenges and opportunities for policies.

Capacity Issues

Literature is replete with cases of implementation failure stemming from capacity-related challenges in the African context. For purposes of clarity and avoiding the controversies around the multiple dimensions and categories associated with the term 'capacity', what we refer to here is the state's administrative capacity which is often portrayed as 'the implementation power of the state' (Cingolani, 2013, p. 22) or the ability to 'execute implementation

Table 7.2   *Summary of policy instruments adopted by Zimbabwe in responding to the Covid-19 pandemic*

Nodality	Authority	Treasure	Organisation
• Educative awareness campaigns on multiple media platforms	• Mandatory testing and quarantining of returning citizens	• Financial resource mobilisation towards preventive efforts	• Creating national testing centres, rapid response teams and Covid-19 national taskforces
• Promotion of use of indigenous knowledge systems	• Social distancing	• Customs duty waivers on Covid-19 medical supplies	• Clinical trials, vaccine development/ importation and treatment
• Periodic reports, briefs and updates	• Mandatory wearing of masks	• Creation of Covid-19 National Funds	• National laboratories and hospitals
• Notifications and moral suasion	• Curfews and lockdowns	• Economic stimulus packages	• Investigation, surveillance, case management
• Benchmarking and performance indicators	• Designating and prioritising of essential services	• External financial assistance/ development partners' support	• Resource planning
	• Closure of schools; restriction/banning of social gatherings	• Relaxed taxation terms	• Infection prevention and control
	• Cancellation of local and international flights	• Unfreezing health sector posts and hiring of additional medical staff	• Participation of churches and charities
	• Closure of borders	• Social protection and cash transfers	• Participation of private companies
	• Restriction of travelling	• Economic support/relief to productive sectors	

Source: Author's own compilation.

actions' (Pires and Gomide, 2014, p. 6). When available, that capacity enables the state to achieve effectiveness in policy decisions and operationalisation of policy goals. As argued by El-Taliawi and Van Der Wal (2019, p. 244), 'Capacity to effectively implement policy plans and programmes is crucial to the success of nations. Indeed, having a capable public sector that is able to optimally align resources with actions and actually implement designed policies, is widely considered to be a crucial factor in any state's quality of government'. Weak implementation capacities usually explain the states' failure to effectively police their territories, extract taxes, and meaningfully deliver public goods and services on a sustainable basis.

Capacity challenges affecting policy implementation in many African states mostly relate to the quality, autonomy, and professionalism in the bureaucratic machinery of the state. There is an apparent yet persisting pervasion of the Weberian bureaucratic standard and principles. In the Zimbabwean context, bureaucratic practice has long occurred in a neopratrimonial context with an embedded culture of political patronage and clientelism. This has seen all key and critical appointments in government being made through a political process and along party lines such that individuals of unquestionable allegiance to the ruling ZANU-PF party are prioritised. This has become an entrenched practice which, unfortunately, has not particularly led to successes in bureaucratic operations. Actually, following the numerous challenges that the Zimbabwean bureaucracy has been facing over time, Naing (2012, p. 222) notes that patronage politics have resulted in the 'freedom-fighter curse' phenomenon or the 'liberator syndrome', meaning the problems caused by yesteryear heroes who defeated colonial rule but went on to ruin the country through tendencies of dictatorship and poor governance. Patronage politics have also been used to explain the failure of civil service reforms to produce a strict adherence to the principle of meritocracy on hiring and promotions in the civil service (Naing, 2012). Some of the bureaucratic challenges attached to patronage politics include rampant corruption stemming from failure of accountability at the top levels of the professional bureaucracy.

Resource support is another aspect of capacity that is usually problematic. Policy implementation sometimes suffers lack of sufficient numbers of human resources to man organisations tasked with implementation activities. Further, implementers of policy may not have the required levels of skills demanded by implementation activities. This becomes a big issue in cases where implementation of policy involves executing mega-sized complex construction projects that would require diverse and specialised skills ranging from architects, engineers, surveyors, project managers, to bricklayers and many others. Implementers of policy are sometimes starved of information necessary to guide their actions in implementing policy. Information may not smoothly flow where implementers are operating from different organisational units with different organisation cultures and different standard operating procedures (Wu et al., 2018). Challenges relating to information sharing will be closely connected to complexities of joint action associated with inter-agency sharing of implementation responsibilities. Another critical resource that is usually a challenge is the bestowing of authority on actors involved in policy implementation. That authority relates to the permission to apply financial and other resources, and to make decisions in the course of implementation activities. Equally worrying is the fact that policy implementation may not get the required financial support from government. On this, two explanations may be made: first, it may be the usual cases of poor planning, or second, the government may have set over-ambitious policy goals whose costs outweigh governmental capacity to finance the activities. Shortage or lack of finances means that supplies, equipment, and other materials required for implementation activities may not be procured.

Design Failures

One of the effects of administrative incapacity in a state is poor policy design, and in some cases, even complete failure of design. By nature, policy design is a technocratic exercise which calls for a certain level of skill and technical competence from those involved. It is necessary to distinguish between cases of poor policy design and cases of lack of policy design. In the former case, designers of policy would have failed to find an effective fit between the nature and dynamics of a policy problem, and the structure of the proposed solution. This may include instances of wrong choices of policy instruments which would effectively produce a mismatch between the problem and the policy tool. In the case of lack of policy design, normally there will only be policy pronouncements which are nothing more than political utterances unsupported by a technically crafted governmental response to a policy problem. In Zimbabwe, one of the policies that has existed at the level of pronouncements and sloganeering is the Look East Policy (Moyo, 2011). That policy was introduced against the background of the Mugabe administration's fall-out with Western countries. Hence Mugabe would frequently declare at gatherings: 'Look east, I say, because that is where the sun rises and where the people are awake. We should wake up with them' (cited in Centre for Peace Initiatives in Africa, 2005, p. 76). These pronouncements were not immediately followed up with the required policy design to give structure and guide to implementation activities in the pursuit of goals of that policy.

Coordination Challenges

Sometimes, implementation of policy may be a task shared among several agencies (also known as fragmentation), which then calls for inter-agency cooperation, without which policy implementation will be affected by coordination problems. Evidence of coordination challenges includes duplication of activities, role conflicts, and communication breakdown. These challenges normally thrive under conditions of organisational siloes where agencies involved in a joint implementation effort consider their own core objectives without giving much regard to the responsibilities they have to share with other entities. In the course of implementing the indigenisation and economic empowerment policy in Zimbabwe, for example, the government decentralised implementation activities from the Ministry of Youth, Indigenisation and Economic Empowerment (MYIEE) to all line ministries. Implementation activities were then supposed to take a sector-based approach, with the MYIEE retaining the overall coordinating role. The lack of harmonisation of implementation efforts resulted in inter-ministerial clashes, lack of consensus, and policy discord. These were a result of the emergence of two ideationally and ideologically opposed camps. On the one hand, there were 'policy radicals' who took extremist positions in implementing policy, and on the other, there were 'policy moderates' who took a more cautious and sober approach to policy implementation (Zvoushe, Uwizeyimana and Auriacombe, 2018). Radicals and moderates clashed on the basis of their rather divergent approaches to implementing the policy, and this lack of a shared understanding saw different ministers crafting conflicting regulations meant to guide implementation activities in the different sectors.

Policy Management Culture

The success of policy implementation activities is closely tied to the established policy management culture in an implementing agency. Over time, implementing agencies come to be associated with certain values and manners of handling government business. The Zimbabwean public service in the first decade of independence, for example, became infamous for rigidly sticking to rules and regulations to such an extent that even in cases of emergency where discretion should have been applied, they could not. Out of this religious regard to rules is often born an unprogressive managerial culture that distances itself from flexibility and is generally unaccommodating to change. Policy implementation does sometimes require a certain amount of flexibility and allowance for changes in order to open a way for the smooth flow of implementation activities. The managerial culture in an agency, however, cannot be too far removed from the interests of the influential actors within it. In fact, organisational culture is likely to be attuned to protect and advance interests of the key actors. Actor interests further influence their attitude or dispositions towards a policy, which will in turn determine whether or not there will be the desire to implement policy. Where negative dispositions towards a policy prevail, implementers may abuse their discretionary power to shirk and sabotage policies.

BUILDING ADMINISTRATIVE CAPACITY AND COMPETENCE FOR POLICYMAKING

Reviews of policymaking experiences often show the discrepancy between policy intentions and the end results after implementation. Wu et al. (2018, p. 19) note trends of 'chronic policy underperformance, spectacular policy failure, or "window dressing" activities that simply perpetuate the status quo'. Most of such end results can be explained by the lack of requisite managerial expertise among the actors tasked with actioning policies. The persisting practical deficits of policy management skills and administrative capacity challenges in much of sub-Saharan Africa call for 'capacity construction' at institutional levels. One way of doing it is to professionalise the bureaucracy (Haque et al., 2021). This entails training of the technocratic cadre to equip them with necessary policy management skills particularly because of the link between administrative capacity and effectiveness of implementation activities. Practical experiences so far show that some efforts are being made by governments and non-state actors to equip public officials with skills and knowledge to help them manage the policies and programmes of their governments. Specialist organisations such as the Africa Capacity Building Foundation (ACBF), whose work mainly revolves around implementing policy-related capacity building programmes in African countries, have shown dedicated commitment to assist African governments in reducing capacity gaps in the public sector. Initially, they do capacity needs assessments on a country-by-country basis, and these help designers of capacity-building programmes in crafting more accurate and relevant training packages.

Taking a broad view of the activities and stages of the policy cycle (agenda-setting, formulation, decision-making, implementation, and evaluation), public managers particularly need administrative capabilities summed up by Wu et al. (2018, p. 20) as 'political acumen', 'analytical skills' and 'managerial expertise'.

- *Political acumen*: Refers to the knowledge and experience gained by public managers over a period of time through their involvement in the policy process. That involvement practically affords managers a window to appreciate the interests of key actors, their preferred strategies, and the resources at their disposal. If all this information is combined with knowledge of what goes on in specific policy sectors of other countries, public managers should then be able to make a judgement on what is likely to work and what will not in specific circumstances and context (Wu et al., 2018).

- *Analytical skills*: Mainly encompass the ability of public managers to diagnose public problems and designing the most appropriate solutions for addressing them. Public managers are expected to be well-versed in the application of relevant scientific and analytical tools to help them ascertain the most worthwhile policy alternatives in a given situation.
- *Managerial expertise*: This relates to the performance of major functions of management in the course of managing policy activities. These include planning, organising, staffing, directing, coordinating, controlling, budgeting, and monitoring. A good performance of these functions should lead to a smooth handling of a host of actors involved in the policy process. It should also translate to prudent financial management, good handling of the scope of activities, and economical application of material resources throughout the process.

CONCLUSION

Public policymaking is a critical function of governing authorities in a country. It is such an important mandate for governments to the extent that it is one of the often-cited factors used in explaining variations in levels of national development and economic growth across the world. This chapter uses the case of Zimbabwe to discuss the experiences of policymaking in sub-Saharan Africa. The chapter observed that the policymaking enterprise is conditioned by contextual variables that include a nation's history, colonial legacy, ideological orientation of the ruling class, nature of the ruling regime, nature of the politics, and the broader political culture in a country. In addition, while some challenges experienced in policymaking are peculiar to the African context, some resonate well with international experiences reported in literature.

The chapter focused on presenting the experiences of policymaking from Zimbabwe. It traced the historical trajectory of policymaking, revealing the major policymaking highlights across the country's four decades of independence. The chapter also discussed the theoretical and practical processes of policymaking, and in the process revealed the emerging differences between the two. What also came out from the discussion of the Zimbabwean experiences is that what lends uniqueness to the policymaking practice are the contextual dynamics and determinants peculiar to a particular polity. For example, Zimbabwe's colonial history has cast a long shadow on policymaking activities in the country by inspiring the preparation of policies meant to address historical colonial imbalances and continuing inequalities. The inherited structural setup is also partly conditioning the practice of policymaking in the country.

REFERENCES

Aihie, J. (2014), 'Africa at Fifty: The Paradox of the Postcolonial State', Conference Paper prepared for the 23rd World Congress of the International Political Science Association, Montreal, Canada, 19–24 July.

Anderson, J.E. (1984), *Public Policy-Making: An Introduction*, Boston, MA: Houghton Mifflin.

Bratton, M. (2014), *Power Politics in Zimbabwe*, London: Lynne Rienner.

Bratton, M. and E. Masunungure (2011), 'The Anatomy of Political Predation: Leaders, Elites and Coalitions in Zimbabwe, 1980–2010', accessed 4 May 2022 at https://www.dlprog.org/publications/research-papers/the-anatomy-of-political-predation-leaders-elites-and-coalitions-in-zimbabwe-1980-2010.

Capano, G. and A. Lippi (2016), 'How Policy Instruments are Chosen: Patterns of Decision Makers' Choices', *Policy Science*, **50** (2017), 269–293, doi.org/10.1007/s11077-016-9267-8.

Centre for Peace Initiatives in Africa (CPIA) (2005), *Zimbabwe: The Next 25 Years*, Harare: Benaby.

Chazan, N.P., R. Lewis, R.K. Mortimer, D. Rothchild and S.J. Stedman (1999), *Politics and Society in Contemporary Africa*, Boulder, CO: Lynne Rienner.

Chipika, J.T. and J.A. Malaba (2017), 'Towards a Transformative Democratic Developmental State in Zimbabwe – The Complex Journey', in Kanyenze, G., H. Jauch, A. Kanengoni, M. Madzwamuse and D. Muchena (eds.), *Towards Democratic Developmental States in Southern Africa*, Harare: Weaver Press, pp. 200–256.

Cingolani, L. (2013), 'The State of State Capacity: A Review of Concepts, Evidence and Measures', UNUMerit Working Paper Series on Institutions and Economic Growth (IPD WP13), Working Papers No. 053.

Clokie, H. and J. Robinson (1937), *Royal Commissions of Inquiry: The Significance of Investigations in British Politics*, Stanford: Stanford University Press.

Edwards, G.C. (1980), *Implementing Public Policy*, Washington, DC: Congressional Quarterly Inc.

El-Taliawi, O.G. and Z. van der Wal (2019), 'Developing Administrative Capacity: An Agenda for Research and Practice', *Policy Design and Practice*, **2** (3), 243–257, doi.org/10.1080/25741292.2019.1595916.

Frankema, E. and M. van Waijenburg (2018), 'Africa Rising? A Historical Perspective', *African Affairs*, **117** (469), 543–568, doi.org/10.1093/afraf/ady022.

Freeman, G.P. (1985), 'National Styles and Policy Sectors: Explaining Structured Variation', *Journal of Public Policy*, **5** (4), 467–495.

Haque, M.S., M. Ramesh, J.A.P. de Oliveira and A.A. Gomide (2021), 'Building Administrative Capacity for Development: Limits and Prospects', *International Review of Administrative Sciences*, **87** (2), 211–219, doi.org/10.1177/0020852320943656.

Herbst, J. and G. Mills (2012), *Africa's Third Liberation: The New Search for Prosperity and Jobs*, New York, NY: Penguin Books.

Hood, C. (1986), *The Tools of Government*, Chatham: Chatham House.

Howlett, M., M. Ramesh and A. Perl (2009), *Studying Public Policy: Policy Cycles and Policy Subsystems*, Oxford: Oxford University Press.

Hyden, G. (2022), 'Theorising Public Policy in Africa', in Onyango, G. (ed.), *Routledge Handbook of Public Policy in Africa*, London: Routledge, pp. 46–56.

International Initiative for Impact Evaluation (2022), 'Policymakers Call for More Research Evidence', accessed 23 June 2022 at https://www.3ieimpact.org/media-room/features/evidence-informed-policy-Africa.

Kelsall, T. (2013), *Business, Politics and the State in Africa: Challenging the Orthodoxies on Growth and Transformation*, London: Zed Books.

Le Van, C.A. (2011), 'Power Sharing and Inclusive Politics in Africa's Uncertain Democracies', *Governance: An International Journal of Policy, Administration, and Institutions*, **24** (1), 31–53, doi.org/10.1111/j.1468-0491.2010.01514.x.

Linder, S.H. and B.G. Peters (1989), 'Instruments of Government: Perceptions and Context', *Journal of Public Policy*, **9** (1), 35–58, doi.org/10.1017/S0143814X00007960.

Lindquist, E.A. and A. Wellstead (2021), 'The Policy Cycle: From Heuristic to a Theory-Informed Research and Advice', in Hildreth, B., G. Miller and E. Lindquist (eds.), *Handbook of Public Administration*, London: Routledge, pp. 303–322.

Mangudhla, T. (2022), 'Poor Policies, Informal Sector Hamstring Zim Growth: WB', *The Standard*, accessed 23 July 2022 at https://www.newsday.co.zw/thestandard/local-news/article/200001898/poor-policies-informal-sector-hamstring-zim-growth-wb.

Masunungure, E. and H. Zvoushe (2023), 'An Analysis of the Existing Form of Politics and Proposals for a New Kind of Policymaking', *African Journal of Inclusive Societies*, **2**, 14–30, doi.org/10.59186.

Mazmanian, D.A. and P.A. Sabatier (1983), *Implementation and Public Policy*, Glenview, III: Scott & Foresman.

Mkandawire, T. (1998), 'The Social Sciences in Africa: Breaking Local Barriers and Negotiating International Presence', in Arnfred, S. and H.S. Marcussen (eds.), *Concepts and Metaphors: Ideologies, Narratives and Myths in Development Discourse*, Roskilde: International Development Studies, pp. 92–119.

Mlambo, A.S. (1997), *The Economic Structural Adjustment Programme: The Case of Zimbabwe, 1990–1995*, Harare: University of Zimbabwe Press.

MoF. (2018), *Transitional Stabilisation Programme*, Harare: Government of Zimbabwe.

MoF. (2020), *Press Statement on Economic Mitigatory Measures to Contain the Impact of Coronavirus 2019 (Covid-19)*, Harare: Government of Zimbabwe.

Moyo, J.N. (2011), 'Challenges of Public Administration in Zimbabwe Today', Public Lecture Delivered at the University of Zimbabwe on 21 October, accessed 14 October 2022 at https://bulawayo24.com /index-id-opinion-sc-blogs-byo-8792-article-challenges+of+public+administration+in+zimbabwe +today.html.

Mpofu, O. (2020), *On the Shoulders of Struggle: Memoirs of a Political Insider*, Bulawayo: LAN Readers.

Mungazi, D.A. (1989), 'A Strategy for Power: Commissions of Inquiry into Education and Government Control in Colonial Zimbabwe', *The International Journal of African Historical Studies*, **22** (2), 267–285, doi.org/10.2307/220034.

Murisa, T., J.N.T. Kushata and T. Rwapunga (2020), *Dancing on the Same Spot: Survey Report on Citizen's Perceptions and Expectations*, Harare: Sivio Institute.

Naing, M. (2012), 'Upgrading Zimbabwe's Bureaucratic Quality', in Masunungure, E. and J. Shumba (eds.), *Zimbabwe: Mired in Transition*, Harare: Weaver Press, pp. 205–229.

Onyango, G. (ed.), (2022), *Routledge Handbook of Public Policy in Africa*, London: Routledge.

Parkhurst, J. (2017), *The Politics of Evidence: From Evidence-Based Policy to the Good Governance of Evidence*, New York, NY: Routledge.

Pires, R.R.C. and A.D.A. Gomide (2014), 'A "New Democratic-Developmental State" in Brazil? A Comparative Analysis of Governance Arrangements, State Capacities and Policy Results', Paper prepared for delivery at RC37.283, the 23rd International Political Science Association World Congress, Montreal, July 19–24.

Pressman, J. and A. Wildavsky (1973), *Implementation: How Great Expectations in Washington are Dashed in Oakland*, Berkeley, CA: University of California Press.

Raftopoulos, B. (2003), 'The State in Crisis: Authoritarian Nationalism, Selective Citizenship and Distortions of Democracy', in Hammar, A., B. Raftopoulos and S. Jensen (eds.), *Zimbabwe's Unfinished Business: Rethinking Land, State and Nation in the Context of Crisis*, Harare: Weaver Press, pp. 217–241.

Rowe, M. and L. McAllister (2006), 'The Roles of Commissions of Inquiry in the Policy Process', *Public Policy and Administration*, **21** (4), 99–115, doi.org/10.1177/095207670602100408.

Sandbrook, R. (1985), *The Politics of Africa's Economic Stagnation*, Cambridge: Cambridge University Press.

Smith, E. and D. Crone (2020), 'Insights from Africa's Covid-19 Response', accessed 28 August 2022 at https://institute.global/advisory/insights-africas-covid-19-response.

Sutcliffe, S. and J. Court (2005), *Evidence-Based Policymaking: What is it? How Does it Work? What Relevance for Developing Countries?*, London: Overseas Development Institute.

Vedung, E. (1998), 'Policy Instruments: Typologies and Theories', in Bemelmans-Videc, M-L., R. Rist and E. Vedung (eds.), *Carrots, Sticks, and Sermons: Policy Instruments and Their Evaluation*, London: Transaction Publishers, pp. 21–58.

Wu, X., M. Ramesh, M. Howlett and S.A. Fritzen (2018), *The Public Policy Primer: Managing the Policy Process*, London: Routledge.

Zhou, G., R.M. Mukonza and H. Zvoushe (2016), 'Public Budgeting in Zimbabwe: Trends, Processes, and Practices', in Haruna, P.F. and S. Vyas-Doorgapersad (eds.), *Public Budgeting in African Nations: Fiscal Analysis in Development Management*, New York, NY: Routledge, pp. 234–268.

Zhou, G. and T. Zinyama (2016), *Strengthening Institutional Capacity for Policy Analysis, Management and Governance in Zimbabwe*, Harare: University of Zimbabwe Press.

Zhou, G. and H. Zvoushe (2012), 'Public Policymaking in Zimbabwe: A Three-Decade Perspective', *International of Humanities and Social Science*, **2** (8), 212–222.

Zhou, G. and H. Zvoushe (2017), 'The Evolving Policy Discourse and Practices in Zimbabwe', in Zhou, G. and A. Nhema (eds.), *Evolving Issues in Public Administration and Governance in Zimbabwe*, Harare: University of Zimbabwe Press, pp. 187–199.

Zvoushe, H., D. Uwizeyimana and C. Auriacombe (2018), 'Radicals, Moderates and Policy Change in Zimbabwe's Indigenisation and Economic Empowerment Policy', *Administratio Publica*, **26** (1), 306–332.

Zwizwai, B., A. Kambudzi and B. Mauwa (2004), 'Zimbabwe: Economic Policy-making and Implementation: A Study of Strategic Trade and Selective Industrial Policies', in Soludo, C., O. Ogbu and H.-J. Chang (eds.), *The Politics of Trade and Industrial Policy in Africa: Forced Consensus?*, New Jersey: Africa World Press, pp. 225–252.

8.   Public financial management in Africa

Benson B. Okech and Nicholas D. Ogola

INTRODUCTION

The Public Financial Management (PFM) system all over Africa consists of a set of rules and institutions, policies, and processes that govern the use of public funds across government ministries, departments, and agencies. It includes revenue collection, budgeting, appropriation, and the monitoring of public expenditure. Public financial management policies vary from country to country and cover specific areas such as tax laws, budget preparation and management, debt management, the finances of state-owned enterprises, and matters pertaining to foreign direct investment. It is therefore important to point out that a well-established and functioning public financial management system is critical to ensure good and full accountability and efficiency in the use of public financial resources. Cases in Africa where there is evidence of weak PFM systems usually result in significant wastage of public funds. A strong PFM system is therefore essential to facilitate good corporate governance and to address typical finance-related challenges such as corruption, abuse of power, disinvestment, maladministration, and high inflation.

Based on the above background, the purpose of this chapter is to highlight some of the core issues related to the management of public finances from an African perspective. Particular reference is made to the Government of Uganda, a country situated in East Africa.

PUBLIC FINANCIAL MANAGEMENT IN AFRICA

Recent publications by the Afrobarometer (2020) and the International Monetary Fund (IMF, 2022) as well as research conducted by Opalo (2021) show that weak PFM systems are a significant impediment to economic growth and prosperity in African countries. As far as revenue collection is concerned, the majority of African countries underperform, especially in the area of tax collection. The average tax collection as a share of gross domestic production in Africa currently stands at 16.5% with Nigeria at the lowest (6.3%) and the Seychelles the highest (32.4%). Governments increasingly resort to borrowing to supplement weak revenue collection. Debt repayment therefore remains to be a significant challenge. Also on the government spending side, weak political oversight often results in low levels of transparency and accountability as well as wasteful and fruitless expenditure.

Generally, in Africa in general and Uganda in particular, there are several challenges the public sector faces in the effective and efficient management of public finances. Scholars such as Baubion (2013), Munyambonera et al. (2015), and Tkachenko (2020) accentuate the following key challenges:

- Lack of proper and adequate financial planning and budgeting, inclusive of inadequate statistics on expenditure and revenue collection trends.

- Misappropriation of public funds by public officials. A case in point is the misappropriation of money in the Office of the Prime Minister and the Pensioner Fund in Uganda.
- Significant delays in the disbursement of funds, particularly from the Ministry of Finance to government ministries, departments, and agencies which seriously affects service delivery across the public service.
- Low levels of spending of allocated funds by some government ministries, departments, and agencies. As a result, most institutions return large sums of money back to the treasury with unfilled or incomplete services delivered to citizens. In addition, the Ministry of Finance fails to account for balances of funds returned from previous financial years by the different budget votes.
- Limited capacity of the central government as well as political oversight structures to supervise and monitor government expenditure programmes. This challenge is exacerbated by the decentralisation of certain powers and functions to the local sphere of government as well as the high level of privatisation of conventional government services and products. Privatisation disburses accountability and responsibility to the private sector, causing oversight to be fragmented and expenditure trends complex to track.
- The emerging network form of governance brought new actors with different agendas and approaches to the governance arena. International agencies, the business sector, non-governmental organisations, and civil society organisations increasingly become involved in traditional government functions making coordination and a common socioeconomic development agenda difficult.
- Higher demands and expectations from the citizens for the government to fulfil its policy and service delivery mandate with limited financial resources. Failure to deliver on this mandate often left citizens disgruntled leading to protest and the loss of legitimacy of government institutions.
- Insufficient budgeting processes, inclusive of inadequate budget consultations, poor allocations, and limited approvals. In the case of Uganda, the Ministry responsible for Finance often does not take views from opposition parties or civil society into consideration. There is thus a growing call for broader public financial reforms in government, inclusive of broader consultation in budgeting processes.
- Inadequate implementation of Auditor General's audit findings and recommendations. Every financial year, the Auditor General conducts statutory as well as value-for-money audits and puts forth several recommendations to government institutions. Some of these recommendations require the recovery of money misappropriated and wasted by public officials. However, the implementation of these recommendations remains a significant challenge due to the lack of political will, the general absence of consequence management, and the selective application of financial rules and regulations.

These and related challenges neatly summarise the major dimensions and aspects of the PFM system in African countries. One should, of course, be careful not to generalise since there are countries with excellent financial systems and policies in place. A detailed analysis of the PFM system is country-specific and should consider matters such as the particular constitutional dispensation, the growth trajectory of the economy, the status of infrastructure and natural resources, the level of investment confidence, demographics of the population, and the maturity of political oversight structures. To address these challenges, change and reform to financial systems are required. Such changes and reform should especially focus on the technical capacity of states to manage financial affairs, the development of infrastructure, the improvement of political oversight, the prioritisation of government of spending, and the adjustment of financial policies.

REVENUE BASES IN THE PUBLIC SECTOR

The revenue base in the public sector is composed of tax revenue, non-tax revenue, loans and external debt from foreign countries, as well as grants from developed countries among others. In the case of Uganda, revenue collected from the oil industry can also be added. In this section, we provide details of each revenue base by differentiating between tax revenue and non-tax revenue.

Tax Revenue

In many countries, taxes are the single most critical source of government revenue. Individual income tax forms a significant part of the revenue bases of a country. Tax revenue can be regarded as revenue collected from the payment of taxes such as profits, personal income, social security, and the delivery of goods and services (OECD, 2022). Taxes are a compulsory payment by the citizens and business entities operating in a country without any direct *quid pro quo* (mutual benefit). This means that citizens expect to pay taxes but should not expect benefits in return. Benefits are rather indirect in the form of infrastructure development, educational and health systems, and public safety. Other taxes like corporation tax, value-added tax, land tax, and consumption tax among others also contribute to the revenue base. Categories of tax revenue include the following:

- *Individual income tax*: This type of tax in Uganda is commonly referred to as Pay as You Earn (PAYE). This tax is levied on the gross income of individuals and is deducted at source by the employer and remitted to Uganda Revenue Authority. The rates range between 10% and 40%, based on the individual's income bracket. For income tax purposes, an individual is referred to as a tax resident if that individual is a permanent resident in Uganda, the individual has spent a minimum of 183 days or more in any 12-month period in Uganda, and the individual has been present in Uganda for an average of 122 days or more during any three consecutive tax years. These incomes are subject to tax and are derived after deducting all allowable eligible expenses for the applicable periods.

Table 8.1   PAYE rates

Monthly Taxable Pay (UGX)	Annual Taxable Pay (UGX)	Rate of Tax (%)
0–235,000	2,820,000	0
235,001–335,000	2,820,001–4,020,000	10
335,001–410,000	4,020,001–4,920,000	20
410,001–10,000,000	4,920,001–120,000,000	30
10,000,000+	120,000,001+	40

Source: Uganda Revenue Authority (2021).

- *Corporation tax*: Corporation tax is a tax which is levied on the net profits of business entities at a rate of 30% of income. This tax applies not only to resident entities but also to non-resident business entities. A business entity is resident in Uganda for tax purposes if the entity is incorporated under the Ugandan laws, if its management as well as control is exercised in Uganda. Resident entities are taxed on all their worldwide sources of income while for non-residents, they are taxed on the income derived from Uganda only. For non-resident entities, besides payment of corporation tax at a 30% rate, a withholding tax of 15% is further levied on a domestic branch of a foreign entity on any business profits repatriated from Uganda to their head offices.
- *National Social Security Fund contributions*: In Uganda, contribution to the National Social Security Fund (NSSF) is compulsory. This is payment to a government body that confers entitlement to a Ugandan or non-Ugandan to receive a social benefit in the future after retirement. This contribution is levied on employees at 5% while at 10% for employers, making a total of 15% monthly. The Government body mandated to manage this social security contribution is called the National Social Security Fund under the oversight of both Ministries of Finance and Gender.
- *Withholding tax*: In Uganda, Withholding Tax (WHT) is a type of tax on income which is withheld at source by the withholding agent upon payment to a third party and remitted to the Uganda Revenue Authority in advance by the withholding agent. The Income Tax Act of Uganda stipulates who is required to withhold this tax as well as the people from whom the tax should be withheld. This tax of course is dependent on the nature of the transaction. For residents, it is taxed at 6% while for non-residents, it is taxed at 15% (Uganda Revenue Authority, 2021).
- *Rental income tax*: This is tax on income derived from properties. The rate of tax is directly related to the value of rent of a property. The tax may take the form of land and buildings owned by government which are leased out. Business entities, therefore, are required to disclose the rental incomes derived for the period separately from the other main business income. The taxable rental income is computed from the net business income after certainly allowing for any expenditures or losses. In Uganda, as per the Income Tax Act, both the individual and business entities taxpayers are allowed a standard deduction of 75% of their gross rental business income and the rate is 30%.
- *Casino tax*: Because of the evolving nature and expansion of businesses in Uganda and globally, the government according to statutory instrument, specifically supplement Number Two, from Government of Uganda, all promoters of gaming and pools within the Ugandan jurisdiction including principal agents of promoters of gaming and pools who are outside Uganda are required pay taxes at a rate of 15% of the total value of money that has been received or of the total value of all betting (The Uganda Gazette, 2010).
- *Value added tax (VAT)*: This tax is governed and administered through the VAT Act at a rate of 18% on any supply of goods and services in the ordinary course of business within Uganda. While some goods and services including exports outside Uganda have zero rate of tax and others are exempt, the standard VAT rate, however, for Uganda is 18% of the gross value paid (Value Added Tax Act Cap 349). Exempted items include livestock and its products, all unprocessed foods as well as all agricultural products and financial services (details are in the Second Schedule of the VAT Act). Examples of zero-rated goods and services include drugs, medicines including all medical services exported from Uganda (see details in the Third Schedule of the VAT Act). Under the East African

Community Customs Management Act, some of the imports are also exempt from customs duty (Fifth Schedule of EAC-CMA).

Non-tax Revenue

Non-tax revenue is duties, levies, or fees charged by governments for the provision of services including the penalties charged on certain offences committed by citizens and non-citizens. It also includes grants and donations. Categories of non-tax revenue include the following:

- *Grants*: Grants are financial transfers to government Ministries, Departments, and Agencies from either international organisations or similar bodies without the receiving government unit paying anything in return. Grants by their nature are received in cash but could also be payments in kind. The term grants does not in any way refer to transfers to or from civil society organisations like NGOs and strictly excludes any transfers between governmental bodies. It's important to stress that the remission of resources that are collected by a government on behalf of another in the capacity of an agency should not be reflected as a grant by the beneficiary government body but instead as a direct receipt of revenues.
- *Property tax*: This is recurrent as well as non-recurrent taxes which are levied on ownership or use or on the transfer of property between two parties. It also includes tax on some immovable properties even on change of ownership of a property by way of inheritance. It further includes taxes on capital as well as financial transactions.
- *Sale of goods and services tax*: Revenues that are generated through the sale of goods and services are key as a source of non-tax. For example, connections to electricity, water, and postal services, among others. Revenues that come under this type are always reported on a gross basis and not net basis. They are reported on a gross basis because their costs can be significant in proportion to the revenues.
- *Fines and penalties*: These are compulsory cash transfers that are imposed by Ugandan courts of law for any violations of laws and administrative procedures. Forfeits are monetary amounts which are deposited by the offender with a competent government authority pending determination of the case which subsequently is transferred to the unit upon resolution of the legal case. For instance, traffic fines and penalties for not filling revenue returns timely. Fines and penalties that are charged on overdue taxes including the penalties that are imposed for tax evasion are recorded as fines or penalties. However, it is important to appreciate that in some cases it may not be possible to differentiate the amounts paid as tax from that paid as fine. In such a case, the whole amount should be treated under the tax to which the fine relates.
- *User fees*: These are incomes that the Government of Uganda receives for the various services it offers. These services include among other services in public schools, public health units, and insurance services. User fees are paid for receiving services or privileges from a government unit. For example, one pays a fee for the government to issue a building permit, pays fees for getting a driving permit, entry visa fees passport fees, and work permits for foreigners among others.
- *Royalties tax*: Rent is revenue that is generated from natural resources like land and mining resources of a country particularly if the government authority gives these to the private sector or non-residents. Any payments for the exploration rights are regarded as

rent derived from using a government facility or resource. This rent shouldn't be mixed up with other payments that government could receive in relation to the exploitation of subsoil and related assets like severance taxes and business licenses. But the general rule and principle is that royalty incomes are taxed as part of business income at 30% and subject to WHT at 15%.

- *Dividends tax*: The general rule on this is that income from dividends is taxed as part of the whole business income at 30%. It is also subject to 15% withholding tax. Withholding tax which is paid as a result of dividend income is also creditable if income is subject to the 30% corporation tax. As such, withholding tax on the dividend paid to resident individuals at 15%. However, for dividends paid by business entities that are on the stock exchange to individuals, the tax is at 10%. Importantly, any dividend income is exempted from tax if the recipient business entity directly or indirectly means to control the paying entity by ownership of more than 25% of the voting rights of the paying entity.
- *Oil revenue*: The 2008 National Oil and Gas Policy for Uganda required a framework to be in place to aid the sustainable management of oil and gas revenues. In its February 2012 Oil and Gas Revenue Management Policy paper, the Ugandan Ministry of Finance, Planning, and Economic Development committed to policy decisions for oil revenue management given the technical advice based on some lessons that were learned. In Chapter 7 of the Public Finance Bill of Uganda, provision has been made for the creation of a Petroleum Fund to receive all revenues from the oil sector. Therefore, any spending of oil revenue would be through the Medium-Term Expenditure Framework which the Parliament of Uganda would give approval to the expenditures every year. Confirmed oil and gas reserves available in Uganda are roughly estimated to be 3.5 billion barrels, (Ministry of Energy and Mineral Development, 2020) while the confirmed recoverable reserves of 1.2 billion barrels and a recovery factor of 35%. However, a benchmark of Tullow's estimate stands at 1.7 billion barrels within Lake Albert areas. Looking at international prices of oil today, the average cost is $100 US$ per barrel but are subject to fluctuations. The estimate is based on the IMF World Economic Outlook forecasts and the future international benchmark oil price (2019 and after) at US$75 US$ in real terms and Uganda's oil is presently valued with a discount of 5% accounting for its lower quality. Therefore, with the benchmark estimates, oil revenues could rise to US$3.3 billion per year by 2025/2026, stay on a plateau for about a decade and then decrease in current US$ terms, along with production, to end in the 2050s.

Uses and Appropriation of Revenue

As already seen above, taxation is the primary source of most revenues to governments. Therefore, the governments collect revenues for two main purposes, namely to finance the goods and services provided to citizens and businesses (e.g. public roads to ease transportation, financing public services notably in public schools and health centres), and to fulfil the redistributive role of public service.

An appropriation is a legal authorisation given to a government entity by an appropriate legislative body like Parliament for the relevant entity to make specified approved expenditures for specified purposes. This also means that a separate set of accounts with funding codes is set up for this purpose. Appropriations may be created through legislative provisions and other statutory, including using constitutional, provisions as provided for under the legal framework of Uganda.

The legal framework for Uganda's debt Policy and Cash Management is set out in the 2005 Constitution as well as in the Public Finance and Management Act (PFMA), Treasury Bill Act 1969, Treasury Instructions 2017, and the Bank of Uganda Act 2000, among others. Every financial year, the Minister of Finance, Planning, and Economic Development of the Republic of Uganda is mandated to prepare and provide a report on the management of Public Debt, Guarantees, Financial Liabilities, and Grants. Reports on this indicated that public debt increased from US$ 15.34 billion, in 2020, to US$ 19.54 billion by the end of June 2021. Public debt levels further increased to US$ 20.74 billion by the end of December 2021.

BUDGETING PROCESSES IN GOVERNMENT: THE CASE OF UGANDA

In Uganda, budgeting process is centred around budget preparation, approval, and management as outlined in the Public Finance Management Act 2015 (as amended). The budget process begins with the review and update of the Medium-Term Expenditure framework (MTEF) and the country portfolio performance review between July and August every year. The budget cycle is undertaken at four key levels involving institutions such as the Ministry of Finance, Planning, and Economic Development; sector working groups; line ministries and local governments; and Cabinet and Parliament.

In Uganda, the budget process is premised on four critical pillars, namely:

• Good governance, involving issues of accountability of the actions of public officers.
• Transparency, relating to access to relevant information.
• Predictability, involving clarity of laws and regulations.
• Participation, involving general consensus among stakeholders and the continuous dissemination of relevant information to all parties involved.

The budgeting process starts in October of every year and has distinct phases. These phases are briefly outlined below.

Budget Preparation

Preparation of the budget commences with the establishment of the macro-economic framework for the country. This stage is led by the Ministry of Finance, Planning, and Economic Development that is responsible for determining the resource envelope in consultation with the Uganda Revenue Authority and Bank of Uganda. The resource enveloped is derived from the projected domestic revenues and external financing.

The second step involves the setting of national priorities and sector expenditure ceilings. This process starts after the resource envelope has been determined and includes broad allocations of government resources between sectors based on priorities that have a direct bearing on poverty and growth, party manifesto, and constraints faced during budget implementation. The indicative budget figures are given to sectors in September under a budget call circular.

An important third step entails budget consultations. The consultations involve the following stages and processes:

- *Cabinet retreat*: This starts with a retreat in September. The retreat provides an opportunity for the Minister of Finance to present the budget strategy paper that spells out the major economic developments and government priorities that need to be addressed.
- *First budget call circular*: This involves communication of the Medium-Term Expenditure Framework to sectors in September asking them to prepare and submit their Budget Framework paper.
- *Local government workshops*: This is held in October or November to launch the preparation of the Local Government Budgets framework papers and guided by the long-term local government development plans.
- *First budget consultative workshop*: This is held in November to officially launch the budget preparation. This offers an opportunity to communicate the economic outlook for the country and the challenges in budget execution and discuss the budget strategy and priorities.
- *Sector working group consultations*: These take place in October or November.
- *Inter-ministerial consultative meetings*: This is held around February between sector Ministers and that of Finance to discuss sector budget priorities and allocation at a political level to resolve any policy issues.
- *Mid-term expenditure framework*: This is held in February to discuss the half-year budget performance report, identify areas that need corrective actions, and agree on the way forward.

The final step involves the preparation of budget estimates. This starts with the preparation of the National Budget Framework Paper by the Ministry of Finance, background to the budget and Budget Speech as per the requirements of the Public Finance Management Act, 2015.

Budget Approval

The approval of the National budget involves the following key stages:

- *Cabinet approval of National Budget Framework Paper*: This is done in December by the Minister of Finance to Cabinet on government strategy for the financial year for approval before it is submitted to Parliament.
- *Parliamentary approval of National Budget Framework Paper*: The National Budget Framework Paper is submitted to Parliament by December 31 and discussed by Seasonal committees of Parliament which submits their report to the Parliamentary budget committee for consideration by the President.
- *Ministerial policy statements*: Each Ministry is required to prepare and submit its policy statement with detailed information on planned expenditures and outputs for the next year to Parliament by March 15.
- *Approval of budget estimates*: After Parliament has concluded its review of the budget and the concerns addressed, the Minister of Finance seeks appropriation and approval of the budget estimates through the appropriation bill. The bill must be passed into law in accordance with the Public Finance Management Act, 2015.
- *Presentation of budget speech*: This is made by the Minister of Finance by 5 June in a seating of Parliament. The budgets of the Member Countries of East African Community are read at the same time. The speech highlights fiscal and economic performance and outlook for the financial year, and emerging trends, among others.

Budget Management and Execution

Budget execution is the process of monitoring and adjusting including reporting on the current year's budget. This process starts in July and ends in June when the financial year ends and includes the following stages:

- *Commitment of approved budget*: The Secretary to the Treasury issues the annual cash flow plan of the government based on the procurement plans, work plans, and HR plans approved by Parliament. The Accountant General uses the annual cash flow plan to release funds to Accounting Officers.
- *Budget execution by Accounting Officers*: Accounting Officers plan and manage their activities in the policy statement of their votes in accordance with the annual cash flow plan.
- *Grants of credit from the consolidated fund*: The Public Finance Management Act, 2015 requires the Minster on the advice of the Accountant General to request the Auditor General to issue a grant of credit on the consolidated fund and should be for statutory expenditure, services to be rendered during the financial year.
- *Withdrawals from the consolidated fund*: This is upon the authority of a warrant issued by the Minister of Finance to the Accountant General. A warrant is only issued by the Auditor General and for authorised expenditure, statutory expenditure, repaying money received in error, etc.
- *Virements*: The Public Finance Management Act, 2015 allows the Minister of Finance within the prescribed limits to vary within a vote, the amount of money allocated to it upon request by the Accounting Officer.
- *Supplementary budgets*: The Minister through a supplementary appropriation bill is permitted to lay a supplementary estimate before Parliament showing the amount required in respect of any financial year where it is found that the amount appropriated is insufficient.
- *Report on expenditure commitments*: Accounting Officers are required to prepare and submit to the Secretary of Treasury an expenditure commitment report indicating the actual and forecast commitments of the cash position of the vote every three months. The Secretary to Treasury then consolidates the report and submits it to the Minister within 30 days after the end of three months.

Budget Oversight

Budget oversight is highly significant to ensure checks and balances in government expenditure. Oversight is mainly institutionalised in the Office of Workings of Parliament and the Office of the Auditor General. Parliament does this through oversight committees and the Parliamentary Budget Office. The Auditor General does this through external audits and other reports to Parliament. In government departments, oversight is mainly the responsibility of political heads (e.g. Ministers, councillors, etc.), financial auditing, accounting, and reporting processes.

AUDITING AND ACCOUNTING STANDARDS: THE CASE OF UGANDA

Auditing Standards refer to the criteria against which the quality of audit results is evaluated. The auditors in Uganda are regulated by the Institute of Certified Public Accountants of

Uganda (ICPAU). This is in sync with the Accountants Act of 2013. As such, audits should therefore, be done by only members of the institute who have practising certificates.

Under Uganda's Companies Act 2012, all public sector entities are required to have their financial statements audited by the office of the Auditor General. ICPAU was established as the main and statutory auditing standard regulator under the Accountants Act 2013. This includes the mandate to the use of the International Standard on Auditing which has been issued by the IAASB for the performance of all financial statement audits.

The institute is responsible for the following:

- Setting as well as maintaining auditing standards.
- Issuing practicing certificates and maintaining a register of practitioners.
- Setting initial professional development and continuing professional development requirements and regulating practical training.
- Establishing ethical requirements.
- Monitoring the conduct and performance of its members, including quality assurance reviews.
- Investigating and disciplining members for misconduct and breach of professional standards.

Accounting standards refer to authoritative statements approved by the Accountant General of Uganda and indicate how some transactions including other events are reflected in the financial statements of a given vote. The Uganda's Companies Act of 2012 and the Accountants Act of 2013 do provide clear specifications related to the accounting as well as auditing. The Act stipulates that all entities both private and public are required to prepare financial statements in compliance with the Act.

The Accountants Act 2013 empowers the Institute to not just set the accounting standards but also adopt International Financial Reporting Standards which are issued by the International Accounting Standard Board.

THE SIGNIFICANCE OF FOREIGN DIRECT INVESTMENT IN THE FINANCIAL SYSTEM OF GOVERNMENT

Foreign Direct Investment (FDI) can be regarded as the acquisition of an interest in an entity by an investor who is located in another country. In its simplest form, FDI is the term generally used to describe an investor's business decision to acquire a substantial stake in a foreign business or for an investor to outrightly buy an investment. The primary reason for this acquisition or purchase is mainly to expand its market share as well as business operations to a new geographical area. However, FDI is said to refer to the net inflows of investment to acquire a lasting management interest (10% or more of voting stock) in an enterprise operating in an economy other than that of the investor. Similarly, the United Nations Conference on Trade and Development (UNCTAD) defines FDI as an investment reflecting a lasting interest and control by a foreign direct investor, resident in one economy, and an enterprise resident in another economy (UNCTAD, 2018). As such, it has significant bearing on the economic growth trajectory and financial sustainability of a country.

It ought to be recognised that globally, the top ten economies for FDI inflows in 2021 were the following: the United States of America, the People's Republic of China, Hong Kong, Singapore, Canada, Brazil, India, South Africa, Russia, and Mexico. However, it's interesting as well to note that the top ten included India which witnessed a decline in inflows. Out of the top ten, the following were the top recipients of FDI: the United States of America with US$ 367 billion; the People's Republic of China with US$ 181 billion; and Hong Kong with US$ 141 billion (UNCTAD, 2022).

FDI flows to the African continent in 2021 reached US$ 83 billion from US$ 39 billion in 2020, representing 5.2% of global FDI. The total for Africa was inflated by intra-firm transactions in South Africa in 2021. Without this from South Africa, the increase is still quite significant although comparable with the others. For example, East Africa, Southern Africa, and West Africa saw their flows rise; while Central Africa remained flat and North Africa declined (UNCTAD, 2022). Despite this flow of FDI, the overall greenfield remained low, at U$$ 39 billion, clearly indicating just a moderate recovery from US$ 32 billion in 2020. However, international project finances which target Africa indicated an increase of 26% in the form of numbers while a resurgence in value to US$ 121 billion from US$ 36 billion in 2020. As is seen, this rise was focused more on power which was US$ 56 billion as well as on renewable energy with a total of US$ 26 billion.

In Uganda, FDI increased from US$ 874 million in 2020 to US$ 1,142 billion in 2021 recording an increase of US$ 268 million representing an increase of 31.64%. The reason for the increase is the relaxation of the restrictions imposed by the government of Uganda in an effort to contain COVID-19 infection. A five- (5) year flow of FDI to Uganda from 2017 through to 2021 in millions of dollars is shown in Table 8.2.

From the table, it can be seen that in 2017, the FDI value was US$ 803 million while in 2018 it increased to US$ 1,055 billion by US$ 252 thousand, the equivalent of 31%. Further, in 2019, the FDI flows reached their highest value at US$ 1,274 billion increasing by US$ 219 or 21%. Between 2020 and 2021, the flow was US$ 874 million and US$ 1,142 billion respectively. However, it is worth noting that in 2020, there was a significant drop by US$ 400 million or −31%. This represents the highest record of the drop both in value and percentage. The core reasons for the drop are obvious, the COVID-19 pandemic which hit every economy hard including both developed and developing economies. Overall, the cumulative total FDI flow from 2017 through to 2021 was US$ 5,148 billion and the overall percentage change was 42%.

Table 8.2   *FDI flows to Uganda*

Year	Value (million US$)	Change in FDI (US$)	Change (%)
2017	803.00		
2018	1,055.00	252.00	31
2019	1,274.00	219.00	21
2020	874.00	(400.00)	−31
2021	1,142.00	268.00	31
Total	**5,148.00**		**42**

Source: Researchers' own computation based on UNCTAD (2022) datasets.

Benefits of FDI for Public Financial Management

The first and foremost benefit is that it boosts international trade. FDI promotes international trade between and among nations because it facilitates the production to flow to other parts of the world which provides cheap costs. For example, Coca-Cola was able to set up its production facilities in Uganda to assist with the manufacturing of its products even if it's a US-based entity. The same applies to MTN Uganda, Airtel Uganda, and many other entities which have set up their businesses in Uganda even when they are not originally registered in Uganda.

A second benefit is the reduction in regional and global tensions. Normally a supply chain is created between and among the nations involved. For example, Uganda currently hosts several Kenyan Banks like KCB, Equity Bank, Fina Bank, and the Commercial Bank of Africa all operating under the regulatory frameworks of the Ugandan Government. Therefore, it is in the best interest of all parties to ensure the stability of its trading partners. As a result, FDI creates some level of dependency between nations, which ultimately creates peace. To use a well-known idiom, don't bite the hand that feeds. In other words, if nations are reliant on each other for their income, then the likelihood of war is also reduced.

A third advantage is that FDI typically facilitates transfer of technology, culture, and knowledge between and among countries. For example, when an entity from Uganda invests in another entity from South Sudan, because of the shareholding rights, the entity will have a say in how the entity in South Sudan is managed. What then happens is that very useful techniques are transferred from Uganda to South Sudan. Furthermore, personnel working for the entities will benefit from having direct access to any new technology being used.

A further benefit is that FDI reduces enterprise risks through diversification. By making investments in other countries, it spreads the company's risk exposures. This allows entities to reduce any domestic exposures. For example, if a Ugandan-based business entity invests in Rwanda, the level of enterprise risks is kind of reduced because the entity is not reliant on one market in Uganda alone, but also the market in Rwanda. Also, in case there is a decline in demand from one country, there may be growth in demand from the other country.

Increased efficiency and lower costs are further benefits. FDI derives some benefit from lower labour costs. In most cases, business entities will leave production to countries abroad that may offer cheaper labour costs in comparison to the home costs. Whereas it appears that labour costs are lower, consideration of productivity is very important. Take, for example, one personnel in Uganda may seem cheaper by producing one unit for U$$ 1 for one hour. However, another personnel in Rwanda may be producing 20 units for U$$ 10 for one hour. Therefore, whereas the Ugandan personnel is seen as cheaper, the personnel only make one unit per U$$ 1, in comparison to two units per U$$ 1 in Rwanda.

A final benefit is that FDI leads to innovative tax incentives. Reduced levels of corporate tax payable can save business entities millions of dollars each year. Nations that have lower tax brackets usually are more favoured than those with high taxes. Uganda particularly has high taxes within East Africa Community compared to Somalia and South Sudan with very low tax regimes (Business Insider Africa, 2022).

Disadvantages of Foreign Direct Investment

Some of the major disadvantages of FDI include the following:

- *Foreign control*: One of the serious concerns especially among developing countries is that FDI brings in control by foreign powers. As such, labour and land including capital are somehow cheap in some nations like Uganda and South Sudan. Therefore, developed nations like the United States of America and the United Kingdom could come in with large sums of cash and buy up land within the nations where land is cheap. It is because of this that some nations place very strict restrictions on FDI acquisitions in developing nations.
- *Loss of domestic jobs*: When an entity significantly transfers large sums of money from its home investment to another foreign investment, it is important to appreciate that the investment would have been used in the home market. As such, the FDI will therefore, boost employment in foreign countries and not the home country. So instead of the funds available to be invested locally to create more jobs, it is invested overseas rather.
- *Risk of political change*: When taking the decision to invest abroad, there is usually a big risk associated with it. For example, there may be serious political uncertainties including interstate wars. This could include a new government in another country where the investment is made which is somehow not favourable to foreign investors. Therefore, this brings in an element of significant political risk. For example, the South Sudan conflicts, Somalia, and the Democratic Republic of Congo among others.

Types and Components of FDI

FDI has four basic types:

- *Horizontal FDI*: In this type of FDI, a business entity expands its domestic business model of operations to a foreign country. In this type, a business enterprise conducts the same type of activities but in a foreign country. For example, the opening of restaurants in several other countries by McDonald's is considered a horizontal FDI.
- *Vertical FDI*: In this type of FDI, a business entity expands into a foreign country by moving to a different level of the supply chain. Simply put it implies that a business enterprise conducts different activities in another country although the activities are still related to the main business of the entity. Taking the McDonald's example above, and for ease of understanding, we could therefore say that acquisition of a large farm by McDonalds in Uganda to produce meat for their several restaurants is a classic example of a vertical FDI.
- *Platform FDI*: In this type of FDI, a business entity expands into a foreign country but the output from the foreign branch of its operations is exported to a third country. This type of FDI is sometimes called export-platform FDI. This type of FDI is very common in low-cost locations inside free-trade areas. For example, if Spear Motors purchased some manufacturing plants in Tanzania with the primary purpose of exporting cars to other countries in the East African Community (EAC) member states.
- *Conglomerate FDI*: In this type of FDI, a business enterprise acquires an unrelated business in a foreign country. This type of FDI is still evolving and is also uncommon. This is not uncommon for two critical reasons. First, the barriers of entry into a foreign country and secondly, barriers of entry into a new industry as well as new market. An example of this type of FDI would be if NBS TV, which is based in Uganda, acquired a transportation business in Central African Republic.

FDI comprises three key components namely Equity Capital, Reinvested earnings, and Intra-company loans. The Equity Capital (EC) component of the FDI is said to be the foreign direct investor's purchase of shares of an enterprise in a country other than its own (UNCTAD, 2022). The Reinvested Earnings (RE) component of FDI comprise the direct investor's share (in proportion to direct equity participation) of earnings not distributed as dividends by affiliates, or earnings not remitted to the direct investor. Such retained profits by affiliates are reinvested. (UNCTAD, 2022). Finally, the Intra-Company Loans component of FDI comprises transactions between the parent and the subsidiary on matters related to both short- as well as long-term borrowings and/or lending of finances (UNCTAD, 2022).

Methods of FDI

Investors can make a foreign direct investment in other jurisdictions by expanding an entity's business in a foreign country. Kampala International University opening branches in most parts of the East African Countries of Kenya, Rwanda, and South Sudan are examples of this.

- *Acquiring voting rights/stock*: Voting rights are those that give the shareholder the right to vote on critical issues affecting the entity. There are different classes of shares; for example, preference shares which in most cases do not allow those holding them to vote. It should be appreciated that the holders of voting rights also do have the ability to weigh in on decisions about a company's strategic direction. For example, if an entity is deciding to acquire another entity, the holders of voting rights would, therefore, be able to cast their vote on the matter.
- *Mergers and acquisitions*: These describe the consolidation of entities as well as assets through various types of financial transactions. These can include mergers, acquisitions, consolidations, tender offers, purchase of assets, and management acquisitions. Generally, the terms 'mergers' and 'acquisitions' are often used interchangeably, but the two differ in meaning. Whereas in acquisition, one entity acquires another entity outright, a merger on the other hand is the combination of two or more entities with the objective of forming a new legal entity altogether under the auspice of one entity. Whereas in a merger, the board which could be of Directors or the Trustee of the two entities provides their approval of the combination with another entity and seek approval from the shareholders; in an acquisition, the entity acquiring the other entity obtains the majority stake in the acquired company, which does not change its name. In Uganda in 2019, Absa Bank PLC acquired Barclays Bank PLC. Meanwhile, Barclays Bank PLC acquired Nile Bank way back in 2008.
- *Joint ventures*: This occurs when two business entities based in two or more jurisdictions form a partnership. An entity that wants to pursue international trade without the need to take on full responsibilities of cross-border business transactions has this option of joint venture. Joint venture facilitates entities to form strategic alliances, which allow them to gain competitive advantage through access to a partner's resources, including markets, technologies, capital, and people. Generally, joint ventures are seen as a means through which there is a transfer from one entity to another. There are many factors that lead to the establishment of a joint venture including risk sharing, economies of scale, market access, geographical reasons, funding constraints, and acquisition.

- *Starting a subsidiary of a local entity in a foreign nation*: A foreign subsidiary is an entity which is majority owned and is also controlled by an entity based in another country. In some jurisdictions, subsidiaries are called 'daughter companies', while the entities which own the subsidiaries are called 'parent companies'. Where a parent entity does not have any other business except hold shares in a subsidiary entity, it is then called a 'holding company'. Therefore, collectively, all these related entities are called a 'corporate group'.

What Governments Can Do to Attract FDI

The following are some of the strategies that governments can pursue to attract FDI:

- Institute low corporation tax for business entities and fix individual income tax rates.
- Allow tax holidays given to entities that produce products that are not easily available.
- Consider other types of tax concessions as determined by the relevant countries.
- Establish special economic zones to stimulate growth and development.
- Create export processing zones.
- Establish bounded warehouses for classified imports and exports.
- Set up investment financial subsidies provided to business entities by government.
- Provide free land or land subsidies provided to foreign investors.
- Consider relocation and expatriation.
- Establish adequate economic infrastructure such as roads and industrial zones.
- Provide subsidies granted by government.
- Provide sufficient research and development support to businesses.
- Ensure that cheap energy (i.e. electricity) is available for production and conversion of materials into finished products.

THE SIGNIFICANCE OF PRIVATE SECTOR INVESTMENT AND PARTNERSHIPS IN THE FINANCIAL SYSTEM OF GOVERNMENT

Due to the network form of governance, partnerships between government entities and private sector enterprises are growing exponentially. Governments simply do not have the financial capacity and competency to address the scope of societal challenges and concerns. The distinction between 'public' and 'private' is rapidly blurring but in general the private sector is defined by the OECD (2016) as any organisation that engages in any profit-seeking activities and has a majority private ownership. The terminology 'organisation' includes both financial institutions as well as intermediaries including the multinational corporations, MSME, co-operative societies, sole traders, and many others. As such, the terminology, therefore, excludes all the actors seeking a non-profit focus like private foundations and civil society entities (Di Bella et al., 2013).

Private Sector Investment refers to 'an activity that aims to engage the private sector for development results, involving active participation of the private sector' (OECD, 2016, p. 17). Further, OECD defines private sector partnership to mean a set of the private sector engagement and partnerships and is characterised by formal relationships between the parties involved and generally include but are not limited to higher levels of structures (Commonwealth of Australia, 2015). However, the other part of the economy which is not the private sector is the public sector. The public sector is the part of the economy which is controlled and managed solely by the government. Public sector services include the provision of public goods and services such as education, law enforcement, health facilities, public infrastructures like roads, among other services. Therefore, when we refer to private sector investment and partnership, we specifically refer to the partnership between the private sector and the public sector. This partnership is commonly referred to as Public Private Partnership abbreviated as (PPP). So, based on the above background, Public Private Partnerships (PPPs) are a common mechanism for governments to procure and implement public infrastructures including public services using resources and expertise of the private sector. So, the private sector partners with the public sector to provide necessary services and goods to the people in partnership in creating value for money to the citizens.

According to the Government of Uganda major source of publication of policies for awareness and approval (Uganda Gazette, 2011), the following are the key principles in undertaking private sector partnership with the public sector.

- *Value for money*: Value for money consideration is important in the PPP because the outcome is usually the most critical consideration in all phases of a PPP project. The concept of value for money is a considerable aspect which is a combination of the outcome of the service delivered by the private sector partner to the populace including the degree of risks which have been transferred with all the associated financial implications for the public sector.
- *Public interests*: Consideration of the interests of the general public is important and requires ensuring that the project provides high-quality projects including reliable services that meet the needs as well as the expectations of the communities and promote social inclusion. The PPP should also ensure that there is fair treatment of all personnel employed in the public service who are to a great extent affected by the partnership between the government and private sector.
- *Risk allocation*: In a PPP arrangement, risk is always allocated to a party best suited to handle and mitigate it well while considering the interest of the public in consideration. In most instances, inherent risks are transferred by the public sector to the private sector, who are seen as best suited to handle. The mitigation of risks could be done through insurance, treatment, or avoidance completely.
- *Output orientation*: Public Private Partnership projects always give focus to the specification of the possible services that can be executed and delivered through the private sector rather than focusing on the ways in which the projects should be completed. Specific but also measurable (SMART) performance indicators are set up and agreed between the two parties (private and public sectors) to ensure that all the required services requested are delivered as well as executed in accordance with the agreed output specifications as provided in the scope of works and/or services.
- *Transparency*: In a complex project like in PPP, transparency as well as openness are critical aspects of any partnership. Use of PPP should be taken with extreme caution so that it does not diminish any available information on use of public sector resources to different stakeholders including the public at large. More emphasis needs to be put not just on transparency but on the disclosure of information and more importantly, the protection of confidential details in commercial transaction wherever appropriate.

- *Accountability*: The use of a PPP approach in delivery of services to the population does not in any way absolve government Ministries, Departments, and Agencies (MDAs) from the responsibility of providing public services. Delivery of all infrastructure projects is the responsibility of government and it is worth noting that public institutions cannot in any circumstances transfer this serious accountability to the private sector.

Types of PPPs

According to the World Bank (2022), various types of PPPs generally exist and are also used in Uganda on some projects funded by the World Bank. The following are some of the most common types of PPPs:

- *Design Build Finance Operate Maintain (DBFOM); Design Build Finance Operate (DBFO); Design Construct Manage Finance (DCMF)*: Under this type of partnership, the range of PPP contracts are described by functions which are transferred from the public sector to the private sector organisations. The function may as well be omitted from the description so that as opposed to it being called DBFOM, it becomes DBFO only, but with the responsibility for maintenance just implied to mean a part of the operations of the facility.
- *Build Operate Transfer (BOT); Build Own Operate Transfer (BOOT); Build Transfer Operate (BTO)*: in this type of approach to the partnership, new assets provide the capturing of the legal ownership as well as the control of all assets of the projects. With the BOT arrangement, the private entity owns the project assets up until they are transferred to the public sector when the contract ends. As Yescombe (2007) holds, it is important to note that BOOT is often used interchangeably with BOT. In contrast, in BTO, project asset ownership can only be transferred from the private sector to the public sector once construction is completed (Delmon, 2015).
- *Rehabilitate Operate Transfer (ROT) type*: In this PPP approach, rehabilitation of the facility may also sometimes take the place of Build. This applies particularly when the private entity has a responsibility toward the rehabilitation of the facility, upgrade of the facility and/or extending the existing assets for the project.
- *Concession PPP*: Under the Concession type of PPP approach as described by Delmon (2010), it may mean in some countries very specific types of contracts meanwhile in other jurisdictions, the same type of contract is used more widely than in some context. In a PPP arrangement, concession is used mostly to refer to when users pay for PPP. Take for instance, in a country like Brazil, Concession Law applies only to any user-paid contracts, meaning that the PPP Law makes provision for contracts which require some kind of payment from the public sector.
- *The Private Financing Initiative (PFI)*: In this PPP approach, it's important to recognise that the United Kingdom (UK) was the first country to come up with the PPP idea under this category. This type is mainly used to provide ways in which a project to finance, but also build and manage any new infrastructure projects.
- *Affermage type*: An Affermage PPP approach is somewhat similar to a concession PPP type. In this arrangement, the public sector remains solely responsible for any capital expenditures on the project. An Affermage as such may have a specific meaning in

countries. For example, the World Bank's explanatory notes on water regulation. Groom et al. (2006) describe lease contracts including concessions.

- *Franchise PPP*: The Franchise approach is used to mean an arrangement which is similar to a concession (Yescombe, 2007).

Legal and Institutional Frameworks for PPP in Uganda

In Uganda, the government adopted formally the (PPP) Framework Policy in 2010 when Uganda had several ongoing PPP projects (Government of Uganda, 2015). The Government's main goal in setting up the PPP Policy including improved utilisation and allocation of government funds; efficiency in delivery of public infrastructures; quality public services provision to the citizens; increased economic growth including value for money consideration, consideration related to public interest; enterprises risks allocation; output orientation consideration; transparency; as well as accountability considerations. Therefore, the PPP Policy informed the formulation of the PPP Act in 2015 (Government of Uganda, 2015).

The Government of Uganda therefore, enacted the Public Private Partnerships Act of 2015 on 5 August 2015. This Act is the supreme law regulating developments and the implementation of PPPs arrangements in Uganda. The Act establishes the PPP Committee that directly manages all PPP projects with the PPP Unit serving as the secretariat of the Committee providing all technical support.

Development of the Regulations related to the PPP gives effect to the Act and provides more details in the Act. The Regulations provide among others the management of PPP projects, the procedures for projects inception as well as all feasibility studies, bidding methods under PPP, negotiation procedures with the private sector entity, restricted bidding process and procedures, direct procurement procedures, and levies and tariffs which the contracting unit of government may levy.

Benefits and Challenges Associated with the Formation of PPPs

According to Catsi (2018), the following benefits can typically be attributed to PPP arrangements:

- Efficient delivery of the project on time and on budget.
- Cost certainty as the PPP project follows the costed plan.
- Accountability of the resources committed to the PPP project by both public as well as private sectors.
- Greater innovations by the private and public sectors during the design and implementation of the PPP project.
- Lifecycle maintenance of the facilities.
- Accelerated delivery of the project within the projected timeframe.
- Public ownership and control of the facilities.
- Effective risk transfer to the party best suited to manage.
- Job creation for the population hence economic development.

According to Batjargal and Zhang (2021), the following are the critical challenges facing public sector investment and partnerships:

- Different organisational cultures and goals between the partners involved.
- Poor institutional support by government towards the PPP arrangement.
- Weak political as well as legal institutional frameworks.
- Unreliable procedures for sharing risks and responsibilities.
- Inadequate and unclear procedures for selection of PPP partners.
- Inconsistency in application of resource inputs and quality in the project.
- Inadequate monitoring, evaluation, and supervision of the PPP processes.
- Lack of transparency and accountability of the parties involved in a PPP project.

CONCLUSION

In this chapter the most critical aspects of public financial management from an African perspective were highlighted. Specific focus was placed on the Government of Uganda as a case study. This chapter provided practical and current examples, analysis and synthesis related to public financial management in Africa generally with specific focus on Uganda, revenue base (tax and none tax) in the public sector, budgeting process in government with special focus on Uganda and highlighted (budget preparation, approval, management and execution and oversight), Auditing and Accounting Standards, Foreign Direct Investment (benefits, disadvantages, types, methods and attraction of FDI) and concluded with private sector investment and partnerships with clear emphasis on the types of PPP, legal and institutional frameworks for PPP, and their benefits and challenges. While the entire content of this chapter covers very topical issues of public management, the reader should pay special attention to the coverage related to the revenue base, budgeting process, and private sector investment and partnerships as they are subject to changes based on the 'interest' of the government in place at the time. The chapter also explored challenges of public financial management, aspects of foreign direct investment, private sector investment and partnerships, revenue and budgeting process in the public sector, as well as accounting and auditing standards. It is evident that countries on the African continent should fully exploit revenue collection methods to improve their revenue base and promote public-private partnerships and foreign direct investment as instruments to enhance the efficacy of public financial management systems and processes on the continent.

REFERENCES

Afrobarometer (2020), 'Keeping an Eye on Government', Data Round 8, accessed 5 October 2022 at http://www.afrobarometer.org.
Batjargal, T. and M. Zhang (2021), 'Review of Key Challenges in Public-Private Partnership Implementation', *Journal of Infrastructure, Policy and Development*, **5** (2), 1378, doi.org/10.24294/jipd.v5i2.1378.
Baubion, C. (2013), 'OECD Risk Management: Strategic Crisis Management', OECD Working Papers on Public Governance, No. 23, Paris: OECD Publishing, accessed 7 October 2022 at http://dx.doi.org/10.17 87/5k41rbd1lzr7-en.
Business Insider Africa (2022), 'Top 10 African Countries with the Highest Corporate Tax Rates', accessed 18 September 2022 at https://africa.businessinsider.com/local/markets/top-10-african-countries-with-the-highest-corporate-tax-rates/y7jp05h.
Catsi, M. (2018), 'Public-private Partnerships: Delivering Civic Infrastructure through P3s', *Economic Development Journal*, **7** (3), 12–20, doi.org/10.24294/jipd.v5i2.1378.

Commonwealth of Australia (2015), 'Creating Shared Value Through Partnership: Ministerial Statement on Engaging the Private Sector in Aid and Development', Department of Foreign Affairs and Trade, Canberra, accessed 12 August 2022 at http://dfat.gov.au/about-us/publications/aid/Pages/creating-shared-value-through-partnership.aspx.

Delmon, J. (2010), 'Understanding Options for Public-Private Partnerships in Infrastructure: Sorting Out the Forest from the Trees', Policy Research Working Paper No. 5173, New York, NY: The World Bank Finance Economics and Urban Department Finance and Guarantees Unit.

Delmon, J. (2015), *Private Sector Investment in Infrastructure: Project Finance, PPP Projects and PPP Frameworks*, 3rd ed., Alphen aan den Rijn: Wolters Kluwer.

Di Bella, J., A. Grant, S. Kindornay and S. Tissot (2013), 'Mapping Private Sector Engagements in Development Cooperation', Ottawa: The North-South Institute, accessed 7 August 2022 at www.nsi-ins.ca/publications/mapping-private-sector-engagements-in-development-cooperation.

Government of Uganda (2000), *Value Added Tax Act, Chapter 349*, Kampala: The Law Reform Commission of Uganda.

Government of Uganda (2010), *Statutory Instruments Supplement No. 2*, Entebbe: UPPC.

Government of Uganda (2011), *Ministry of Finance, Planning and Economic Development Public-Private Partnership Framework Policy*, Entebbe: UPPC.

Government of Uganda (2015a), *The Public-Private Partnership Act 2015*, Entebbe: UPPC.

Government of Uganda (2015b), *The Public Finance Management Act*, Gazette No. 11 Volume CVIII, Entebbe: UPPC.

Government of Uganda (2020), *Annual Revenue Performance Report FY 2019/2020*, Entebbe: Revenue Authority.

Government of Uganda (2021), *A Simplified Guide on Withholding Tax*, Vol. 1 Issue 4 FY 2021-22, Entebbe: Revenue Authority.

Government of Uganda (2022), *Ministry of Finance, Planning and Economic Development. Report on Public Debt, Grants, Guarantees and other Financial Liabilities for Financial Year 2021/2022*, March 2022, Entebbe: UPPC.

Groom, E., J. Halpern and D. Ehrhardt (2006), 'Explanatory Notes on Key Topics in the Regulation of Water and Sanitation Services', Water Supply and Sanitation Sector Board Discussion Paper Series Paper No. 6, New York, NY: The World Bank Group.

International Monetary Fund (IMF) (2022), *Africa at a Crossroads: Learning from the Past and Looking to the Future*, Finance and Development (Report), New York, NY: IMF.

Munyambonera, E. and M.M. Lwanga (2015), *A Review of Uganda's Public Finance Management Reforms: 2012 to 2014*, Research Series No. 121, Entebbe: Economic Policy Research Centre.

OECD (2016), *Private Sector Peer Learning Peer Inventory 1: Private Sector Engagement Terminology and Typology. Understanding Key Terms and Modalities for Private Sector Engagement in Development Co-operation*, Paris: OECD.

OECD (2022), 'Tax on Personal Income (Indicator)', accessed 4 September 2022 at doi.org/10.1787/94af18d7-en.

Opalo, K. (2021), 'It's Time to Democratize Public Financial Management Systems in African States', New York, NY: IMF, accessed 6 August 2022 at https://www.imf.org/en/Publications/fandd/issues/2021/12/Africa-Democratize-Public-Finance-Management-Systems.

South Africa (Republic). (2015), 'Public Finance and Management Act (PFMA), Finance Act 19 of 2015, accessed 15 August 2023 at https://www.treasury.gov.za/legislation/acts/2015/Act%2019%20of%202015%20-%20Finance%20Act.pdf.

Tkachenko, L. (2020), 'Public Finance Management: Challenges and Opportunities', *Athens Journal of Business & Economics*, **6** (1), 73–98, doi.org/10.30958/ajbe.6-1-4.

United Nations Conference on Trade and Development (UNCTAD) (2018), UNCTAD Annual Report 2018, New York, NY: UNCTAD.

United Nations Conference on Trade and Development (UNCTAD) (2022), 'World Investment Report 2022. International Tax Reforms and Sustainable Investment', New York, NY: UNCTAD, accessed 21 August 2022 at https://unctad.org/news/global-foreign-direct-investment-rebounded-strongly-2021-recovery-highly-uneven.

World Bank (2022), 'The World Bank's PPP in Legal Resource Center', accessed 8 August 2022 at https://ppp.worldbank.org/public-private-partnership/ppp-contract-types-and-terminology.

Yescombe, E.R. (2007), *Public-Private Partnerships: Principles of Policy and Finance*, Oxford: Butterworth-Heinemann.

9. Governance and debt accumulation in Africa

Augustin K. Fosu and Dede W. Gafa

INTRODUCTION

Sovereign borrowing in developing countries is often used to bridge the domestic saving-investment gap for the purpose of economic growth and development. Investments financed through such loans are expected to yield socioeconomic benefits, as well as sufficient resources for debt repayment and servicing. Such expectations may not be realized, however, resulting in significant debt accumulation, particularly in a context of weak governance.

Over the last decade, sovereign debt has increased rapidly in the emerging and developing world including sub-Saharan Africa (SSA). In many countries this increase in debt has been exacerbated by the Covid-19 pandemic. Amidst the already high debt vulnerabilities, the required response to limit the spread and effects of the pandemic drove borrowing upward as public revenue shrank and the demand for government expenditure rose. Although many initiatives led by the International Financial Institutions (IFIs) and G20 creditors provided financial buffers for poor countries facing financial distress, such assistance was mostly short-lived. As of November 2022, 22 low- and middle-income countries in SSA were identified as being at high risk of debt distress or in debt distress (International Monetary Fund (IMF), 2022a). Consequently, debt reprofiling or restructuring has emerged as an inevitable recourse. Yet, many low-income countries' debts were written off in the 2000s through the Heavily Indebted Poor Countries (HIPC) and Multilateral Debt Relief (MDR) initiatives. Critics of these initiatives argued that debt forgiveness in a context of institutional bottlenecks and weak governance would inhibit the implementation of adequate tax reforms and create incentives for excessive debt accumulation in beneficiary countries (Brown and Martinez-Vazquez, 2019; Coulibaly et al., 2019; Easterly, 2002).

The aim of this chapter is to first provide an overview of Africa's debt situation within the global context. Second, it probes the literature linking sovereign debt to economic development and highlights the role of governance and institutional quality in debt accumulation in African countries. The third section of the chapter analyzes the trends and composition of debt in Africa in the global context and furthermore scrutinizes the theoretical and empirical relationship between sovereign debt and economic development, while also providing insights into the importance of governance in debt accumulation in the region. The last section of the chapter summarizes and concludes the chapter.

AFRICA'S DEBT IN THE GLOBAL CONTEXT: TRENDS AND COMPOSITION

The sovereign debt-to-GDP ratio fell globally since the turn of the century, that is, until the late 2000s. Between 2001 and 2007, global public debt (relative to GDP) fell by 10%, mainly driven by the trend in developing countries, particularly in the wake of the debt relief programs of the late 1990s and 2000s (IMF, 2023a). Since the 2007–08 financial crisis, however, the government debt-to-GDP ratio has increased across the globe, albeit for different reasons (Table 9.1; Koh et al., 2020). While advanced countries borrowed heavily to rebound from the recession, in low- and lower-middle-income economies, debt accumulation was mostly intended to bridge investment gaps in infrastructure, urbanization, and economic development

Table 9.1   Trends in gross general government debt (% of GDP) across regions and income groups, 1995–2021

Region	1995–99	2000–04	2005–09	2010–14	2015–19	2020	2021
Weighted Averages							
East Asia and Pacific (EAP)	30.7	32.8	31.7	36.0	48.0	63.6	67.0
Europe and Central Asia (ECA)	69.4	47.0	20.5	20.0	23.4	29.7	28.0
Latin America and Caribbean (LAC)	35.2	53.3	50.1	51.0	66.1	80.5	74.4
Middle East and North Africa (MENA)	69.4	54.6	46.8	38.0	59.7	61.8	55.7
South Asia (SA)	67.1	78.1	69.1	63.0	65.7	81.8	78.6
Sub-Saharan Africa (SSA)	46.4	56.8	29.2	30.9	47.1	61.7	59.3
High income	75.6	76.2	76.0	98.8	100.7	120.4	114.9
Low income	126.3	106.5	50.2	40.7	57.9	70.8	66.0
Lower middle income	56.6	61.9	47.6	43.7	53.7	64.2	62.0
Upper middle income	33.3	40.6	35.5	37.3	49.2	63.7	64.8
Simple Averages							
East Asia and Pacific (EAP)	36.8	47.6	35.6	33.4	37.3	43.1	45.7
Europe and Central Asia (ECA)	61.9	51.4	26.2	31.0	39.1	46.0	42.4
Latin America and Caribbean (LAC)	38.9	57.6	47.5	48.3	59.3	84.0	76.3
Middle East and North Africa (MENA)	89.9	78.5	65.0	51.0	68.7	78.8	68.0
South Asia (SA)	59.1	74.7	55.8	49.7	56.6	79.2	85.8
Sub-Saharan Africa (SSA)	72.0	94.9	59.7	39.0	56.5	72.1	68.5
High income	56.6	53.0	48.5	62.9	63.4	75.6	73.2
Low income	109.7	124.3	72.9	40.3	58.8	73.0	72.9
Lower middle income	49.7	65.6	44.4	38.7	50.9	62.0	58.8
Upper middle income	47.8	49.7	39.2	40.3	47.8	62.4	58.7

Notes: Gross debt refers to the sum of all liabilities that require future payment of interest and/or principal by the debtor (general government) to the creditor. Due to paucity of data for several countries, the averages reported for the period 1995 to 1999 may not be representative and comparable with the other periods.
Source: Authors' computation using data from IMF Fiscal Monitor database (IMF, 2023b).

by taking advantage of the improved global conditions and fiscal space created by the debt cancellation (Kose et al., 2021).

From the turn of the century until 2008, Africa – coming out of the economic turmoil of the 1980s and 1990s with high and unmanageable debt burden – witnessed the greatest fall in outstanding public debt (relative to GDP): 44.4%, followed by East Asia and Pacific (EAP) by 37.4% each (Figure 9.1). This decline in SSA's debt was mainly due to the debt relief under the HIPC and MDR initiatives led by the IFIs and other multilateral and bilateral creditors. Overall, 33 SSA countries (out of the 40 potential HIPCs globally) were eligible to participate in the HIPC program (IMF, 2023b). To date, 30 out of the 33 countries in the region have reached the completion point and have received debt cancellation under the initiative. Over half of these beneficiaries had met the HIPC-defined criteria before 2008; and by 2011, the ratio had increased to 88 per cent, leading to considerable debt reductions (IMF, 2019). Furthermore, in most countries including non-HIPCs, high commodity prices as well as the growth revival following the adjustment reforms led to declines in current account and fiscal deficits, with positive implications for debt-to-GDP ratios (World Bank, 2023a, b).

In the years following the 2007–08 financial crisis, however, the increase in the public debt-to-GDP ratio was larger in SSA compared with other developing regions, except EAP (Figure 9.1). The rise in public borrowing in SSA is explained by governments' thirst for accelerated development and optimism about the global outlook. Increasing indebtedness was also encouraged by the favourable liquidity conditions, low interest rates on the international market, and market confidence following the near-decadal high growth rates and improved macroeconomic performance in many African countries. Between 2008 and 2014, government debt increased by 8.7% of GDP in SSA, compared with 5.3% in Europe and Central Asia (EAC), 5.2% in Latin America and Caribbean (LAC), 4.5% in the Middle East and North Africa (MENA), and a decline of 4.4% in South Asia (SA) – supported by relatively stable and high growth rates. As global conditions changed with the 2014–16 oil price shock, SSA, LAC, MENA, and EAP all experienced accelerations of sovereign debt relative to GDP (Figure 9.1 and Table 9.2). However, when global conditions changed from the mid-2010s – with a series

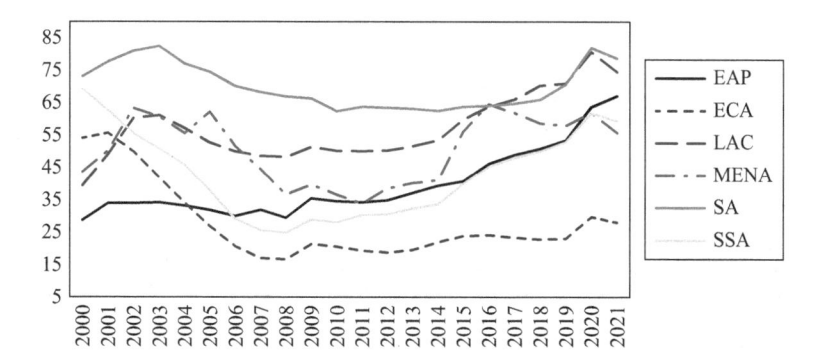

Notes: EAP = East Asia and Pacific; ECA = Europe and Central Asia; LAC = Latin America and Caribbean; MENA = Middle East and North Africa; SA = South Asia; SSA = sub-Saharan Africa. For each region, the data excludes high-income countries. The values reported are weighted averages computed by the authors.
Source: Authors' computation using data from IMF Fiscal Monitor database (IMF, 2023b).

Figure 9.1   *Trends in public debt across regions, weighted averages, 2000–2021*

Table 9.2   *Public debt (% of GDP) by SSA countries, five-year averages (1995–2021)*

Country	Subregion	1995–99	2000–04	2005–09	2010–14	2015–19	2020	2021
Angola	CA		73.2	32.2	33.3	81.7	136.5	86.4
Benin	WA		30.6	17.3	20.6	37.7	46.1	49.9
Botswana	SA		8.6	9.4	20.2	16.3	19.7	20.2
Burkina Faso	WA		40.2	26.2	24.4	35.6	46.4	52.4
Burundi	CA		157.8	105.0	41.4	49.2	66.0	66.6
Cabo Verde	WA	76.1	82.0	71.0	92.1	122.2	145.1	142.3
Cameroon	CA	68.4	59.6	19.7	16.4	36.0	44.9	45.5
CAR	CA	84.7	98.4	50.7	37.0	52.2	43.4	47.6
Chad	CA		51.2	25.7	31.6	48.4	54.2	56.0
Comoros	EA	71.7	49.8	35.8	21.1	17.4	24.0	26.0
Congo, Dem. Rep.	CA		143.5	93.7	22.6	17.2	16.5	16.1
Congo, Rep.	CA	0.0	159.3	88.3	36.9	84.3	114.0	103.6
Côte d'Ivoire	WA	76.6	64.2	53.4	34.3	33.6	47.6	52.1
Equatorial Guinea	WA	78.8	18.6	1.9	8.2	38.7	48.4	42.8
Eritrea	EA		234.8	214.4	167.5	184.7	179.7	176.2
Eswatini	SA	13.8	17.9	13.9	14.5	29.3	42.1	45.8
Ethiopia	EA	105.8	101.0	49.5	42.2	54.2	53.7	52.9
Gabon	WA	71.1	73.0	34.8	25.9	58.5	78.3	65.8
Gambia	WA		85.5	57.3	54.2	80.8	85.9	83.8
Ghana	WA	48.4	58.8	25.3	38.8	58.3	79.1	82.1
Guinea	WA	74.1	86.6	74.7	44.6	41.4	47.5	42.5
Guinea-Bissau	WA	109.5	200.9	171.0	52.1	57.0	76.5	78.5
Kenya	EA	38.4	42.2	35.8	38.2	53.1	68.0	67.8
Lesotho	SA	71.8	74.3	47.9	38.6	45.2	54.2	53.5

Liberia	WA		541.6	352.8	22.7	34.2	58.7	53.2
Madagascar	EA	99.4	85.4	40.1	33.4	41.6	50.8	53.1
Malawi	SA		79.7	31.0	27.4	40.4	54.8	63.9
Mali	WA		51.7	25.1	25.6	36.2	47.3	51.9
Mauritania	WA		107.9	52.3	42.1	56.7	55.8	51.7
Mauritius	EA		65.7	56.8	58.5	69.0	100.6	99.1
Mozambique	SA		78.0	42.1	45.2	104.7	120.0	106.4
Namibia	SA	19.2	24.8	21.5	24.4	48.3	66.6	72.0
Niger	WA	64.3	68.2	23.1	17.9	35.7	45.0	51.2
Nigeria	WA	34.1	46.3	10.5	16.0	25.2	34.5	36.6
Rwanda	CA	76.0	84.5	28.1	22.2	41.0	65.6	66.6
São Tomé and Príncipe	CA		345.1	160.0	75.8	86.5	81.4	72.4
Senegal	WA	33.9	48.7	24.3	36.2	55.7	69.2	73.2
Seychelles	EA	148.8	182.7	144.3	76.7	60.4	84.8	72.9
Sierra Leone	WA		156.9	75.6	38.2	63.8	76.3	79.3
South Africa	SA		33.0	26.6	37.4	49.8	69.0	69.0
South Sudan	EA				21.4	59.7	36.4	64.7
Sudan	EA	193.5	121.1	63.9	92.1	148.0	263.4	182.0
Tanzania	EA		45.4	30.0	31.0	39.9	40.5	40.7
Togo	WA			67.5	38.8	55.9	60.3	63.7
Uganda	EA	46.4	51.7	23.5	20.5	33.1	46.3	51.8
Zambia	SA		170.0	32.5	25.7	74.8	140.2	119.1
Zimbabwe	SA			51.0	41.6	63.0	102.5	66.9

Table 9.2   *(continued)*

Country	Subregion	1995–99	2000–04	2005–09	2010–14	2015–19	2020	2021
Share of countries with debt-to-GDP ratio less than 40 %		25.0	13.6	50.0	70.2	31.9	10.6	8.5
Share of countries with debt-to-GDP ratio greater or equal to 40% and less than 60%		8.3	25.0	21.7	19.1	40.4	40.4	38.3
Share of countries with debt-to-GDP ratio greater or equal to 60% and less 90%		45.8	29.5	13.0	4.3	19.1	29.8	38.3
Share of countries with debt-to-GDP ratio greater or equal to 90%		20.8	31.8	15.2	6.4	8.5	19.1	14.9
Min.		0.0	8.6	1.9	8.2	16.3	16.5	16.1
		Congo	Botswana	Equatorial Guinea	Equatorial Guinea	Botswana	Congo	Congo
Max.		193.5	541.6	352.8	167.5	184.7	263.4	182.0
		Sudan	Liberia	Liberia	Eritrea	Eritrea	Sudan	Sudan

Source: Authors' own computation using data on interest payment (% of revenue) from the World Development Indicators database (World Bank, 2023b) and the International Debt Statistics (IDS).

of negative financial and commodity price shocks – many African countries could not scale back spending, and thus resorted to borrowing to finance fiscal deficits, bolster foreign currency reserves, and limit currency risks (IMF, 2018). The share of SSA countries with an outstanding debt-to-GDP ratio exceeding 60% increased from 10.7% in 2010–14 to 27.6% in 2015–19 (Table 9.2).

When the Covid-19 pandemic hit the world in 2019–20, Africa – but also the developing world as a whole – was already struggling with high debt levels. In 2019, the public debt-to-GDP ratio exceeded 100% in Angola, Cape Verde, Eritrea, and Sudan and 90% in Mozambique, Zambia, and Zimbabwe (Table 9.2).

In many African countries, fiscal positions were typically weak from the consecutive years of fiscal deficits and poor external positions, reserve buffers were low, and debt servicing obligations rose. The increasing pressure on government coffers amidst the pandemic further worsened the situation. On average, sovereign debt in SSA rose 9% of GDP between 2019 and end of 2020 – the highest annual increase over the past two decades – with over 30% of the countries recording increases of more than 10%, attributable mostly to the Covid-19 pandemic (IMF, 2023a). Debt services on external debt reached 20% of exports of goods and services and primary income in 2020 (compared with 4.6% in 2010) (Figure 9.2; World Bank, 2023a).

Debt service on external debt refers to the sum of principal repayments and interest actually paid in currency, goods, or services on long-term debt, interest paid on short-term debt, and repayments (repurchases and charges) to the IMF. Interest payments on external debt include interest paid on long-term debt, IMF charges, and interest paid on short-term debt.

Africa's debt situation improved, however, in 2021, thanks largely to growth recovery and the IMF's SDR allocations. The IMF's new Special Drawing Rights (SDRs) general allocation

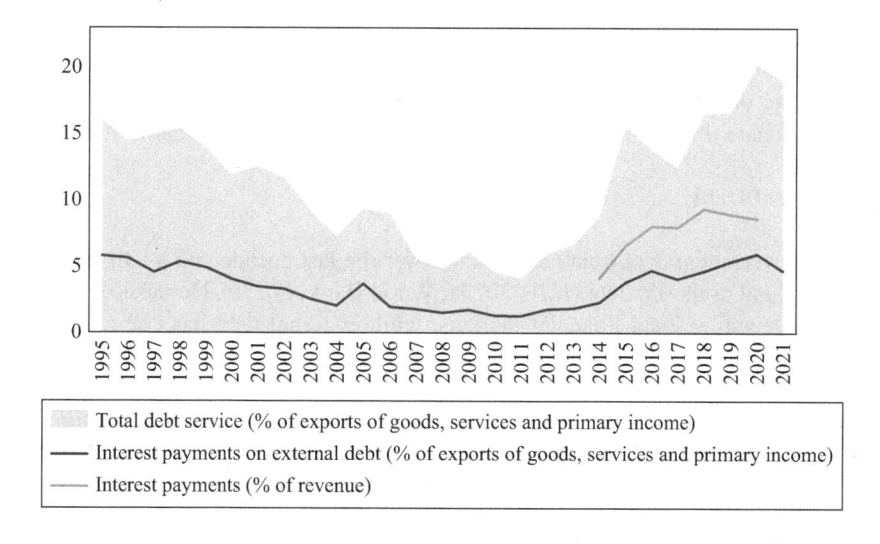

Total debt service (% of exports of goods, services and primary income)

Interest payments on external debt (% of exports of goods, services and primary income)

Interest payments (% of revenue)

Note: The values reported are weighted averages, excluding high-income countries.
Source: Authors' own computation using data on interest payment (% of revenue) from the World Development Indicators database (World Bank 2023b) and the International Debt Statistics (IDS) database.

Figure 9.2   Trends in debt servicing and interest payment, SSA (1995–2021)

of SDR 456.5 billion (US$ 650.2 billion) in August 2021 supported recovery in the developing world. Furthermore, 2021 marked the return of economic growth in many SSA countries, with the region recording per capita GDP growth that averaged 6% higher than in the previous year (IMF, 2022a; World Bank, 2023a). Out of a general allocation of SDR 456.5 billion (US$ 650.2 billion) in August 2021, SSA received nearly SDR 17 billion (i.e., 3.7% of the total allocation). These allocations enabled countries in the region to buffer their reserves, finance pandemic-related expenditures, reduce their fiscal deficits, and repay outstanding obligations (IMF, 2022b). Higher oil and commodity prices in 2021 relative to the preceding year also led to significant improvements in government revenues in resource-intensive countries (IMF, 2021a). In oil-exporting countries (excluding Nigeria), debt-to-GDP ratio declined by 19% between 2020 and 2021 (IMF, 2022c). Angola, for instance, registered a 37% reduction in sovereign debt (relative to GDP) in 2021 from its level of 136.5% in 2020, mainly due to an improvement in the macroeconomic outlook and higher fuel prices (Table 9.2).

Yet, debt vulnerabilities remain high in SSA (Tables 9.1 and 9.2; Figure 9.1). Amidst the current global uncertainties fuelled by the Russia-Ukraine war, sovereign debt is expected to rise and there are growing concerns that debt levels in Africa are nearing the pre-HIPC levels (IMF, 2022b). Several governments are taking steps towards fiscal consolidation and debt restructuring. Countries such as Chad, Ethiopia, Zambia, and Ghana are at varying stages of debt restructuring within the G20 Common Framework. To support countries beyond 2020, the Debt Service Suspension Initiative (DSSI) deferred debt service payments for most vulnerable countries, and the G20 official bilateral creditors together with the Paris Club have agreed to adopt a Common Framework which aims to ease debt restructuring by facilitating coordination among creditors of highly indebted low-income countries. The Framework benefits from the support of the IMF and the World Bank. Debt restructuring under the Common Framework is initiated upon a sovereign's request, and debt treatment is made on a case-by-case basis, accompanied with reforms aimed at restoring the country's debt sustainability (IMF, 2021b). For these and other SSA countries with elevated solvency risks, access to private lending on international sovereign bond markets has been disrupted and financing options to navigate the current crises and build long-term resilience remain limited.

Composition of Debt

The rise in government debt (relative to GDP) over the last decade and a half was driven by both external and domestic debt (IMF, 2023a; World Bank, 2023b). Domestic debt increased because of deepening local financial markets, while external debt has risen mainly due to increases in the long-term public and publicly guaranteed (PPG) debt (Bua et al., 2014; World Bank, 2023b).

Contrary to the pre-HIPC period, countries have relied more on private loans from international financial markets and non-Paris Club lenders rather than concessional borrowings from official creditors that are often disbursed with conditionalities attached. Additionally, new debt commitments have generally been contracted with lower average maturity, leading to an increase in roll-over risks (IMF, 2023a).

Since the mid-2000s, 18 SSA countries – including 11 HIPC beneficiaries – have been active borrowers on the international bond market (Bloomberg, 2022). These countries are South Africa (which has been an active participant in the private international bonds market since the 1990s), the Seychelles, Ghana, the Republic of Congo, Gabon (joined in the second half of the 2000s), Côte d'Ivoire, Namibia, Nigeria, Senegal, Zambia, Rwanda, Tanzania, Ethiopia, and Kenya (joined in the early 2010s), Angola, Mozambique, Benin, and Cameroon. In 2021, SSA's debt from bondholders accounted for 30.8% of the region's PPG debt (World Bank, 2023b). Furthermore, China has become the third largest lender to African countries. China accounts for nearly 16.8% of SSA's total PPG debt, following bondholders (30.8 per cent) and World Bank-IDA (17.8%) (World Bank, 2023b). Chinese investors held nearly 17% of SSA's PPG external debt in 2021, mostly on non-concessional terms. There also seems to be a growing reliance of resource-rich SSA countries on resource-backed and collateralized loans from China (Mihalyi et al., 2021). These countries include the Democratic Republic of Congo, Angola, and Sudan. This shift in SSA's debt from traditional creditors and concessional loans to multiple private lenders and non-conventional forms of borrowing has introduced new complexities in the debt structure and in the ongoing debt resolution and restructuring initiatives in the region.

A BRIEF REVIEW OF PUBLIC DEBT LITERATURE: SOVEREIGN DEBT AND ECONOMIC DEVELOPMENT

A wide theoretical literature exists on the link between sovereign debt and economic growth and development. It mainly suggests that at an early stage of development, debt provides important public funds to address existing resource gaps to kick-start the process of development. Since expected returns to investments tend to be relatively high in low-income countries with little physical capital, public borrowing is anticipated to yield benefits for both the debtor and its creditor(s). However, as debt obligations accumulate over time, countries could fall into a 'liquidity trap' or experience a 'debt overhang'. A liquidity trap occurs when countries face severe liquidity constraints due to high debt burden and repayment obligations such that public consumption is at its lowest level and public investments to support growth and development are limited or nonexistant (Claessens and Diwan, 1989). A 'debt overhang' is traditionally defined as a situation in which the burden of existing debt hampers countries' ability to generate sufficient future financial flows to repay and service their debt obligations (Krugman, 1988; Sachs, 1989). The literature describes an inverted-U relationship between the outstanding debt and expected debt repayment. This relationship which is often represented by the 'debt Laffer curve' suggests that at the initial stage, the probability of debt repayment increases with debt accumulation. However, beyond a certain threshold, the country's repayment ability begins to fall with any additional borrowing (Claessens and Diwan, 1989; Elbadawi et al., 1997).

Debt overhang adversely affects growth and development through the expected tax liabilities faced by investors, thus constraining the level of investment (Krugman, 1988; Greene, 1989; Sachs, 1989; Cohen, 1993; Servén, 1997). In a context of debt overhang, private investors also expect governments to implement ineffective reforms leading to potential economic instabilities in the medium- and long-term. Such uncertainties about the business environment cause a reduction in investment levels by discouraging new investments or encouraging capital flights (Elbadawi et al., 1997; Servén, 1997). Similarly, liquidity constraints would limit public investment levels. Debt servicing by governments tends to constrain fiscal space and may lead to less public investment, particularly in the infrastructure required for private investment. Furthermore, high debt-servicing obligations distort governments' incentive to implement credible reforms and adjustment policies. The disincentive effect emanates from policymakers' sociopolitical considerations as they anticipate that any financial gains generated from difficult and costly adjustment policies would largely accrue to creditors through repayment and servicing of debt to the detriment of citizens (Borensztein, 1990; Krugman, 1988). Thus, the traditional channels of debt, whether overhang or liquidity constraint, have been via saving and investment levels. However, as argued in Fosu (1996, 1999), even in the absence of investment curtailment, the efficiency and productivity of investment may be adversely affected: the 'Direct Effect of Debt Hypothesis' (DEDH). Governments and private investors, to limit risks, are more inclined to sacrifice productivity and efficiency by undertaking short-term investments to generate quick returns rather than long-term irreversible capital investments. Under DEDH, therefore, debt would enter directly into the production function, that is, in addition to labour and capital (Fosu, 1999).

In the context of Africa, Elbadawi et al. (1997) showed that in the 1980s and 1990s, African countries experienced debt overhang, which negatively affected investment levels, prevented development-oriented expenditures and reforms, and hampered growth on the continent. However, consistent with DEDH, Fosu (1996, 1999) found that the effect of external debt on growth in African economies has been primarily through the diminution in productivity of investment rather than reductions in investment levels per se. A high external debt burden may also alter the allocation of public expenditure against the social sector, namely education and health (Fosu, 2007, 2008a, 2010). Thus, transforming economic growth into human development may be limited by a binding debt constraint.

THE ROLE OF GOVERNANCE IN PUBLIC DEBT ACCUMULATION

In several developing countries, the current debt challenges present an opportunity to tackle the structural as well as institutional causes of recurring unsustainable debt accumulation. 'Good' governance and strong institutions are said to reduce public debt directly through sound fiscal management (Cooray et al., 2017; Fosu, 2022) and indirectly via economic and development performances (Bates et al., 2013; Tarek and Ahmed, 2017). For instance, democratic governance may raise productivity and economic growth, increase public revenue, and reduce debt accumulation (Bates et al., 2013). It enables countries to better translate sovereign debt into economic growth by promoting a more efficient use of debt for investment and growth-enhancing projects (Rajkumar and Swaroop, 2008; Kim et al., 2017). The positive outcomes would in turn generate sufficient resources for debt servicing and growth sustainability. Similarly, political and economic governance matter in building efficiency in the management of public funds, public resources generation, government expenditure, and fiscal allocation (Cooray et al., 2017; Fosu, 2022; Mauro, 1998). It also affects the cost and sustainability of sovereign borrowing (Block and Vaaler, 2004; Presbitero et al., 2016; Subramaniam, 2021).

In the literature, the effects of political governance and institutions on debt accumulation are ambiguous. Cukierman and Meltzer (1989), for example, show that in democratic political systems, under majority rule, the level of public deficit and debt would be determined by the choice of the decisive voter, which in turn is influenced by several factors including his/her position in wealth distribution and the characteristics of the economy. Other studies also find that the alternation of civilian governments in democracies may lead to higher deficit and public debt levels than the socially optimal level (Alesina and Tabellini, 1990). Such a situation may arise when in highly polarized systems political disagreements on policy priorities distort the incumbent governments' incentives to fully internalize the cost of outstanding debt that would be inherited by its successor. Hence, there is a tendency for debt accumulation, and borrowing is used as a means to influence policy options and choices of the next government (Alesina and Tabellini, 1990; Debortolli and Nunes, 2008). Furthermore, the effects of democratic institutions on the efficiency of fiscal spending and debt management depend on the characteristics of the prevailing political system. In democracies, electoral competitiveness gives politicians in power an incentive for more efficient governance leading to socioeconomic gains (Doucouliagos and Ulubaşoğlu, 2008; Vergne, 2009). However, as argued by Acemoglu et al. (2011), while competitive civilian elections confer de jure power to the electorate, under some democratic systems the elites – through lobbying – may distort regulations and legislations and maintain weak institutions in their interest with implications for debt accumulation. In the context of Africa, Fosu (2008b, 2011, 2013) showed that economic gains are only achieved and sustained in 'advanced-level' democracies, characterised by high levels of electoral competitiveness, accountability, and restraint on the executive branch of government. Meanwhile, 'intermediate-level democracy' – with low levels of electoral competitiveness and weak mechanisms for accountability – tends to promote political disorder which is growth-inhibiting (Fosu, 2008b, 2011).

Other forms of governance such as economic governance, control of corruption, rule of law, political stability, and absence of violence, voice and accountability may either encourage or impair debt accumulation. For instance, Presbitero et al. (2016) found that well-performing developing countries with better fiscal position and governance are more likely to issue bonds on the international capital market, and also tend to benefit from lower-bond spread as credit ratings are relatively favourable. The risk premium on private lending is largely influenced by the market's perceptions of governments' capacity to maintain political stability and implement good domestic policies which would guarantee repayment of debt obligations (Block and Vaaler, 2004; Presbitero et al., 2016; Subramaniam, 2021). Meanwhile, poorly governed and unstable countries tend to pay higher premiums on loans, thus attenuating their incentive to borrow on private financial markets (Block and Vaaler, 2004; Subramaniam, 2021). In recent years, regular sovereign Eurobonds issuances in SSA mostly occurred among the fastest growing, relatively more stable, and well-governed economies. In addition, improvements in governance through institutional reforms have been found to ease access to concessional lending as well as debt relief in low-income countries in the late 1990s and early 2000s (Asiedu, 2003).

Another strand of the literature suggests that corruption and poor rule of law weaken the penalty for tax evasion and jeopardize tax revenue collection, thus leading to over-reliance on debt for deficit financing and rapid debt accumulation (Friedman et al., 2000). The prevalence of illicit financial flows is mostly explained by the weakness of the legal systems and the lack of constraints on executives, corruption, and little transparency in fiscal systems (Nkurunziza, 2012), with symptoms such as embezzlement of funds, theft of public assets, among others. Due to such outflows of public resources, poorly governed countries are unable to implement growth-enhancing investment and generate sufficient resources to service debt obligations, creating an unhealthy cycle of over-borrowing and low debt effectiveness (Thiao, 2021). The lack of transparency in debt management also encourages the incidence of phenomena such as 'underreported' and 'hidden' debts, which have been recently reported in different contexts in the developing world. Furthermore, weak institutions distort the functionality of the public sector (e.g., through nepotism in the appointment of public servants leading to poor performance and low capacity), and adversely influence the size, composition, and efficacy of the public spending (Lambsdorff, 2003; Rajkumar and Swaroop, 2008).

Mauro (1998) and Wei and Zeckhauser (1999), for example, show that highly corrupt governments have higher levels of public expenditure, which are likely to be more biased towards the least transparent budgetary items (e.g., military and defence), to the detriment of productivity-enhancing investment (e.g., social expenditures in health and education). In addition, corruption and inefficiencies in fiscal allocations generate greater demand for public funds (e.g., undertaking 'white-elephant projects'), which leads to faster debt accumulation and over-investment (Cooray et al., 2017; Tanzi and Davoodi, 1998).

TRENDS IN GOVERNANCE AND IMPLICATIONS FOR DEBT ACCUMULATION IN AFRICA

Since the early-mid 1990s, Africa has witnessed a significant improvement in political as well as economic governance (Bates, 2006; Fosu, 2022). On the economic front, there has been a change in the economic policy framework on the continent from import-substitution to a more liberal economic governance. The economic freedom index – which captures the extent to which the business environment and macroeconomic policies are market friendly – has followed an upward trend globally since the early 1990s (Figure 9.3; Gwartney et al., 2021). Economic governance, as measured by the economic freedom index, has been positively associated with economic growth (de Haan and Sturm, 2000). In SSA, the improvement in economic freedom seems to have coincided with the period of growth reversal from the dismal performance of the 1980s and early 1990s (Fosu and Gafa, 2021; Fosu, 2022; World Bank, 2023a). Such an improvement should help yield the resources required for debt management.

Political reforms in many African countries have led to a transition from single-party autocratic/military regimes to multiparty democracy with competitive civilian governments,

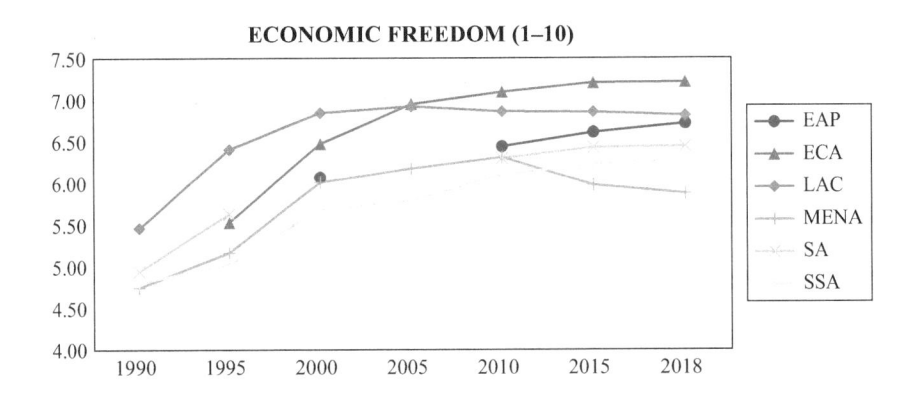

ECONOMIC FREEDOM (1–10)

Notes: The Economic Freedom index ranges from 1 (low freedom) to 10 (high freedom).
Source: The data is obtained from Fraser Institute (2020).

Figure 9.3   Trend in Economic Freedom index, SSA vs other regions (1990–2018)

which enhanced electoral competitiveness and reduced the prevalence of 'opportunistic' governance (Bates, 2008). As shown in Figure 9.4, there has been a notable shift in the developing world towards more democratic political systems since the mid-1980s. Over the period, SSA experienced the greatest progress on democratisation, with a steady rise in the Polity2 score. The Polity2 score captures different aspects of the political system, namely, the openness and competitiveness of the electoral process, and constraints on executives. The measure ranges from −10 (strongly autocratic) to 10 (strongly democratic) (Polity5 Project, 2020). Institutionalised constraint on the executive branch of government which limits their decision-making power with mechanisms of accountability, measured by XCONST, has also improved over the period (Polity5 Project, 2020). The values of XCONST range from 0 to 7. Zero represents 'a state of disorder or perfect incoherence', 1 represents 'no institutionalized constraints on government chief executives' and 7 represents 'restrictions on the decision-making powers of chief executives and limited authority'. For details see Polity5 Project (2020). However, in many African countries, democratisation of the political system has not fostered improvements in 'developmental' governance and institutions, mainly because the democratization process usually involving electoral competitiveness has not entailed significant government effectiveness, which often requires meaningful constraint on the executive branch of government (Fosu, 2022).

The World Governance Indicators (WGI) make provision for six indicator categories: control of corruption, government effectiveness, rule of law, regulatory quality, voice and accountability and political stability and absence of violence. The WGI are a set of subjective measures of governance capturing key aspects of governance and institutional quality. The indicators range from −2.5 to 2.5, and zero (0) represents the world average. In a diverse context, these indicators have been associated with economic growth and social welfare (Tebaldi and Mohan, 2010; Fayissa and Nsiah, 2013). Africa's performance on all the WGI indicators

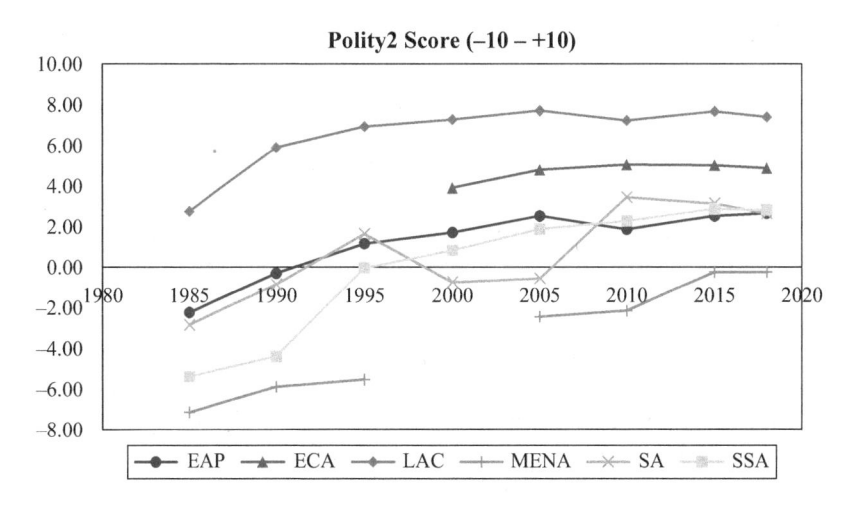

Figure 9.4   *Trend in Polity2 score, SSA vs other regions (1985–2018)*

has declined, particularly since the early-mid-2000s, except for voice and accountability. As argued by Fosu (2022, p. 44),

> Under the current democratic framework adopted by many African countries, democratically elected governments are unlikely to undertake certain growth-enhancing policies that may be unpopular with the electorate and would show a propensity to spend more and tax less, resulting in unsustainable fiscal deficits.

This political dispensation results in a 'politico-economic disequilibrium', which would likely promote chronic debt accumulation in the region (Fosu, 2018a, 2021).

To provide further insights into the importance of governance in sovereign debt accumulation in Africa, Table 9.3 reports the zero-order correlation coefficients between governance and institutional quality indicators and public debt-to-GDP ratios for the period 1995–2018 and for the more recent period 2010–2018. Governance and institutions are measured by the Economic Freedom Index, World Bank WGI (control of corruption, government effectiveness, rule of law, regulatory quality, voice and accountability, and political stability and absence of violence), the Polity2 score, and XCONST. Overall, 'good' governance and strong institutions are associated with low levels of public debt (relative to GDP) in SSA countries. This association seems respectively stronger for 1995–2018 than for the more recent 2010–2018 period, probably because debt forgiveness involving the HIPC and MDRI rewarded governance quality. Thus, perhaps the evidence for the latter period may be more telling in terms of the effect of governance since these programs had petered out by 2010. In this regard, the strongest governance effects are apparent for Government Effectiveness, Regulatory Quality, Voice and Accountability, Polity2, and XCONST.

CONCLUSION

Over the decade and a half following the HIPC initiative, sovereign debt levels have rapidly risen in SSA countries, and the structure of public debt has shifted towards less concessional loans with the multiplicity of creditors and the adoption of non-conventional financing models (such as resource-backed or collateralized loans). The emergence of new lenders and the relatively more expensive and sometimes complex forms of loans have not only exposed countries to higher debt burdens, increasing risks of debt overhang, but has also complicated recent debt resolution initiatives.

Although the G20 official bilateral creditors together with the Paris Club have adopted a Common Framework to facilitate debt restructuring in a coordinated manner for highly indebted low-income countries, debt restructuring under the Framework has been delayed, adversely affecting economic recovery in countries that have initiated the process (IMF, 2020). Yet, a strong recovery remains essential for mitigating debt vulnerability, lowering countries' borrowing costs on the international market, and building resilience in this increasingly uncertain global context. As suggested by theory, a high and unmanageable debt burden is detrimental to economic growth and development through 'debt overhang' or 'liquidity constraints'.

The chapter has shown that the nature of governance and institutional quality has played an important role in countries' debt accumulation in Africa. Countries with greater government

Table 9.3   *Zero-order correlation coefficients: public external and total debt (% of GDP) vs. Economic Freedom index, World Governance Indicators (WGI), Polity2 and XCONST*

	1995–2018	2010–18
	Gross government debt (% of GDP)	Gross government debt (% of GDP)
Economic Freedom Index	−0.263***	−0.047
	(−6.88)	(−0.88)
Control of Corruption	−0.090**	−0.02
	(−2.51)	(−0.39)
Government Effectiveness	−0.199***	−0.105**
	(−5.64)	(−2.07)
Political Stability and Absence of Violence	−0.125***	0.025
	(−3.50)	(0.49)
Regulatory Quality	−0.339***	−0.313***
	(−10.02)	(−6.46)
Rule of Law	−0.192***	−0.097*
	(−5.45)	(−1.91)
Voice and Accountability	−0.166***	−0.183***
	(−4.68)	(−3.66)
Polity2	−0.119***	−0.181***
	(−3.47)	(−3.57)
XCONST	−0.171***	−0.153***
	(−5.05)	(−2.99)

Notes: t-statistics are in parentheses. *** $p < 0.01$, ** $p < 0.05$ and * $p < 0.1$. The correlation coefficients are calculated using data from 44 SSA countries. However, the sample size varies based on data availability. Polity2 captures different aspects of the political system, namely, the openness and competitiveness of the electoral process, and constraints on executives. It ranges from −10 (strongly autocratic) to 10 (strongly democratic). The World Bank governance indicators range from −2.5 to 2.5, and zero (0) represents the world average. The Economic Freedom index (EF) comprises five dimensions corresponding to five subcomponents, namely, (1) size of government, (2) legal system and property rights, (3) sound money, (4) freedom to trade internationally, and (5) regulations. The variable ranges from 1 to 10, with 1 representing the lowest performance and 10 the highest. XCONST measures the level of constraint on the executive branch of government. It ranges from 0 to 7, with 0 representing 'a state of disorder or perfect incoherence', 1 representing 'no institutionalized constraints on government chief executives' and 7 representing 'restrictions on the decision-making powers of chief executives and limited authority'.
Source: Authors' own computation based on data on Polity2 score and XCONST obtained from the Polity5 Project (2020) and EF is from the Fraser Institute (2021).

effectiveness, regulatory quality, voice and accountability, Polity2, and constraint on the executive branch of government, inter alia, are apparently associated with lower debt levels. Furthermore, debt accumulation is likely to be higher in democratic systems that fail to address the 'politico-economic disequilibrium' problem, which tends to encourage recurrent over-indebtedness amongst African governments (Fosu, 2018a, 2021, 2022).

REFERENCES

Acemoglu, D., D. Ticchi and A. Vindigni (2011), 'Emergence and Persistence of Inefficient States', *Journal of the European Economic Association*, **9** (2), 177–208, doi.org/10.111/j.1542-4774.2010.01008.x.

Alesina, A. and G. Tabellini (1990), 'A Positive Theory of Fiscal Deficits and Government Debt, *The Review of Economic Studies*, **57** (3), 403–414, doi.org/10.2307/2298021.

Asiedu, E. (2003), 'Debt Relief and Institutional Reform: A Focus on Heavily Indebted Poor Countries', *The Quarterly Review of Economics and Finance*, **43** (4), 614–626.

Bates, R. (2006), 'Institutions and Development', *Journal of African Economies*, **15** (1), 10–61, doi.org/10.1016/S1062-9769(03)00038-3.

Bates, R.H. (2008), 'Political Reform', in Ndulu, B.J., S.A. O'Connell, R.H. Bates, P. Collier and C.C. Soludo (eds.), *The Political Economy of Economic Growth in Africa, 1960–2000*, Volume 1, Cambridge: Cambridge University Press, pp. 348–391.

Bates, R.H., S.A. Block, G. Fayad and A. Hoeffler (2013), 'The New Institutionalism and Africa', *Journal of African Economies*, **22** (4), 499–522.

Block, S.A. and P.M. Vaaler (2004), 'The Price of Democracy: Sovereign Risk Ratings, Bond Spreads and Political Business Cycles in Developing Countries', *Journal of International Money and Finance*, **23** (6), 917–946, doi.org/10.1016/j.jimonfin.2004.05.001.

Bloomberg (2022), 'Bloomberg Database', accessed 21 February 2022 at https://www.bloomberg.com/graphics/2022-in-graphics/#xj4y7vzkg.

Borensztein, E. (1990), 'Debt Overhang, Credit Rationing and Investment', *Journal of Development Economics*, **32** (2), 315–335, doi.org/10.1016/0304-3878(90)90041-9.

Brown, L.A. and J. Martinez-Vazquez (2019), 'Addiction to Debt Forgiveness in Developing Countries: Consequences and Who Gets Picked?', *Review of Development Economics*, **23** (2), 902–921.

Bua, G., J. Pradelli and A.F. Presbitero (2014), 'Domestic Public Debt in Low-income Countries: Trends and Structure', *Review of Development Finance*, **4** (2014), 1–19, doi.org/10.1016/j.rdf.2014.02.002.

Claessens, S. and I. Diwan (1989), 'Liquidity, Debt, and Conditionality', in Hussain, I. and I. Diwan (eds.), *Dealing with the Debt Crisis*, Washington, DC: World Bank, pp. 76–93.

Cohen, D. (1993), 'Low Investment and Large LDC Debt in the 1980's', *The American Economic Review*, **83** (3), 437–449.

Cooray, A., R. Dzhumashev and F. Schneider (2017), 'How does Corruption affect Public Debt? An Empirical Analysis', *World Development*, **90** (C), 115–127, doi.org/10.1016/j.worlddev.2016.08.020.

Coulibaly, B.S., D. Gandhi and L.W. Senbet (2019), 'Is Sub-Saharan Africa Facing Another Systemic Sovereign Debt Crisis?', *Policy Brief*, Brookings Africa Growth Initiative.

Cukierman, A. and A.H. Meltzer (1989), 'A Political Theory of Government Debt and Deficits in a Neo-Ricardian Framework', *The American Economic Review*, **79** (4), 713–732.

Debortolli, D. and R.C. Nunes (2008), 'Political Disagreement, Lack of Commitment and the Level of Debt', FRB International Finance Discussion Paper No. 938, accessed 7 March 2023 from https://www.federalreserve.gov/pubs/ifdp/2008/938/ifdp938.htm.

De Haan, J. and J.E. Sturm (2000), 'On the Relationship between Economic Freedom and Economic Growth', *European Journal of Political Economy*, **16** (2), 215–241.

Doucouliagos, H. and M.A. Ulubaşoğlu (2008), 'Democracy and Economic Growth: A Meta-Analysis', *American Journal of Political Science*, **52** (1), 61–83, doi.org/10.1111/j.1540-5907.2007.00299.x.

Easterly, W. (2002), 'How did Heavily Indebted Poor Countries become Heavily Indebted? Reviewing Two Decades of Debt Relief', *World Development*, **30** (10), 1677–1696, doi.org/10.1016/S0305-750X(02)00073-6.

Elbadawi, I.A. (1997), 'Debt Overhang and Economic Growth in Sub-Saharan Africa', in Iqbal, Z. and R. Kanbur (eds.), *External Finance for Low-income Countries*, Washington, DC: International Monetary Fund, pp. 49–76.

Greene, J. (1989), 'The External Debt Problem of Sub-Saharan Africa', *IMF Economic Review*, **36**, 836–874, doi.org/10.2307/3867242.

Fayissa, B. and C. Nsiah (2013), 'The Impact of Governance on Economic Growth in Africa', *The Journal of Developing Areas*, **47** (1), 91–108, doi.org/10.1353/jda.2013.0009.

Fosu, A.K. (1996), 'The Impact of External Debt on Economic Growth in Sub-Saharan Africa', *Journal of Economic Development*, **21** (1), 93–118.

Fosu, A.K. (1999), 'The External Debt Burden and Economic Growth in the 1980s: Evidence from Sub-Saharan Africa', *Canadian Journal of Development Studies*, **20** (2), 307–318.

Fosu, A.K. (2007), 'Fiscal Allocation for Education in Sub-Saharan Africa: Implications of the External Debt Service Constraint', *World Development*, **35** (4), 702–713.

Fosu, A.K. (2008a), 'Implications of External Debt-Servicing Constraint for Public Health Expenditure in Sub-Saharan Africa', *Oxford Development Studies*, **36** (4), 363–377.

Fosu, A.K. (2008b), 'Democracy and Growth in Africa: Implications of Increasing Electoral Competitiveness', *Economics Letters*, **100** (1), 442–444, doi.org/10.1016/j.econlet.2008.03.016.

Fosu, A.K. (2010), 'The External Debt-servicing Constraint and Public-expenditure Composition in Sub-Saharan Africa', *African Development Review*, **22** (3), 378–393.

Fosu, A.K. (2011), 'Democracy and Growth in Africa: Evidence on the Impact of Political and Civil Rights', *Empirical Economics Letters*, **11** (1), 19–25.

Fosu, A.K. (2013), 'Growth of African Economies: Productivity, Policy Syndromes and the Importance of Institutions', *Journal of African Economies*, **22** (4), 523–551.

Fosu, A.K. (2018a), 'Rethinking Governance and Development', in Oloruntoba, S. and T. Falola (eds.), *The Palgrave Handbook of African Politics, Governance and Development*, New York, NY: Palgrave/Macmillan, pp. 883–898, doi.org/10.1080/02589346.2020.1848757.

Fosu, A.K. (2021), 'Democracy and Development in Africa', in Crawford, G. and A.-G. Abdulai (eds.), *Research Handbook on Democracy and Development*, Cheltenham, UK and Northampton, MA, USA: Edward Elgar Publishing, pp. 174–193.

Fosu, A.K. (2022), 'Governance, Politics, and Economic Development: Some African Perspectives', *Governance and Politics*, **1** (1), 29–49.

Fosu, A.K. and D.W. Gafa (2021). 'Economic Neoliberalism and African Development', in Tribe, M. (ed.), *Economic Neoliberalism and International Development*, Abingdon: Routledge (Chapter 7).

Friedman, E., S. Johnson, D. Kaufmann and P. Zoido-Lobaton (2000), 'Dodging the Grabbing Hand: The Determinants of Unofficial Activity in 69 Countries', *Journal of Public Economics*, **76** (3), 459–493.

Gwartney, J.D., J.C. Hall and R. Lawson (2021), 'Economic Freedom of the World: 2021 Annual Report', Vancouver, BC: The Fraser Institute.

IMF (2018), 'The Debt Challenge to African Growth', Washington, DC: International Monetary Fund.

IMF (2019), 'IMF Policy Paper: Heavily Indebted Poor Countries (HIPC) Initiative and Multilateral Debt Relief Initiative (MDRI) – Statistical Update', Washington, DC: International Monetary Fund.

IMF (2020), 'The International Architecture for Resolving Sovereign Debt Involving Private-Sector Creditors—Recent Developments, Challenges, and Reform Options', Washington, DC: International Monetary Fund.

IMF (2021a), 'Regional Economic Outlook: Sub-Saharan Africa; One Planet, Two Worlds, Three Stories, October 2021', Washington, DC: International Monetary Fund.

IMF (2021b), 'The Common Framework: Utilizing its Flexibility to Support Developing Countries' Recovery. Strategy, Policy and Review: Special Series on Covid-19', Washington, DC: International Monetary Fund, June 2021.

IMF (2022a), 'List of LIC DSAs for PRGT-Eligible Countries as of November 30, 2022', Washington, DC: International Monetary Fund.

IMF (2022b), 'Tracker on the Use of Allocated SDRs: Promoting Transparency and Accountability in the Use of the 2021 SDR Allocation', accessed 23 January 2023 at https://www.imf.org/en/Topics/special-drawing-right/SDR-Tracker.

IMF (2022c), 'Regional Economic Outlook. Sub-Saharan Africa: Living on the Edge, October 2022', Washington, DC: International Monetary Fund.

IMF (2023a), 'Fiscal Monitor', Washington, DC: International Monetary Fund.

IMF (2023b), 'Debt Relief Under the Heavily Indebted Poor Countries (HIPC) Initiative', Washington, DC: International Monetary Fund, accessed on 30 January 2023 https://www.imf.org/en/About/Factsheets/Sheets/2023/Debt-relief-under-the-heavily-indebted-poor-countries-initiative-HIPC.

Kim, E., Y. Ha and S. Kim (2017), 'Public Debt, Corruption, and Sustainable Economic Growth', *Sustainability*, **9** (3), 433, doi.org/10.3390/su9030433.

Koh, W.C., M.A. Kose, P.S.O. Nagle, F. Ohnsorge and N. Sugawara (2020), 'Debt and Financial Crises', Policy Research Working Paper 9116, Washington DC: World Bank.

Kose, M.A., P. Nagle, F. Ohnsorge and N. Sugawara (2021), 'Global Waves of Debt: Causes and Consequences', Washington DC: World Bank.

Krugman, P. (1988), 'Financing vs. Forgiving a Debt Overhang', *Journal of Development Economics*, **29** (3), 253–268, doi.org/10.1016/0304-3878(88)90044-2.

Lambsdorff, J.G. (2003), 'How Corruption affects Productivity', *Kyklos*, **56** (4), 457–474, doi.org/10.1046/j.0023-5962.2003.00233.x.

Mauro, P. (1998), 'Corruption and the Composition of Government Expenditure', *Journal of Public Economics*, **69** (2), 263–279, doi.org/10.1016/S0047-2727(98)00025-5.

Mihalyi, D., J. Hwang, D. Rivetti and J. Cust (2021), 'Resource-Backed Loans in Sub-Saharan Africa', Washington DC: World Bank.

Nkurunziza, J.D. (2012), 'Illicit Financial Flows: A Constraint on Poverty Reduction in Africa', *Association of Concerned Africa Scholars Bulletin*, **87**, 15–21.

Polity5 Project (2020), 'Political Regime Characteristics and Transitions', accessed 23 July 2022 at http://www.systemicpeace.org/polity/polity4.htm.

Presbitero, A.F., D. Ghura, O.S. Adedeji and L. Njie (2016), 'Sovereign Bonds in Developing Countries: Drivers of Issuance and Spreads', *Review of Development Finance*, **6** (1), 1–15.

Rajkumar, A.S. and V. Swaroop (2008), 'Public Spending and Outcomes: Does Governance Matter?', *Journal of Development Economics*, **86** (1), 96–111, doi.org/10.1016/j.jdeveco.2007.08.003.

Sachs, J.D. (1989), *Developing Country Debt and Economic Performance, Volume 1: The International Financial System*, Chicago, IL: University of Chicago Press.

Servén, L. (1997), 'Uncertainty, Instability, and Irreversible Investment: Theory, Evidence, and Lessons for Africa', World Bank Policy Research Working Paper No. 1722, Washington, DC: World Bank.

Subramaniam, S. (2021), 'Geopolitical Uncertainty and Sovereign Bond Yields of BRICS Economies', *Studies in Economics and Finance*, **39** (2), 311–330.

Tanzi, V. and H. Davoodi (1998), 'Corruption, Public Investment, and Growth', in Sturm, J.E., J. de Haan and G.H. Kuper (eds.), *The Welfare State, Public Investment, and Growth: Selected Papers from the 53rd Congress of the International Institute of Public Finance*, Tokyo: Springer, pp. 41–60.

Tarek, B.A. and Z. Ahmed (2017), 'Governance and Public Debt Accumulation: Quantitative Analysis in MENA Countries', *Economic Analysis and Policy*, **56**, 1–13, doi.org/10.1016/j.eap.2017.06.004.

Tebaldi, E. and R. Mohan (2010), 'Institutions and Poverty', *The Journal of Development Studies*, **46** (6), 1047–1066, doi.org/10.1080/00220380903012730.

Thiao, A. (2021), 'The Effect of Illicit Financial Flows on Government Revenues in the West African Economic and Monetary Union countries', *Cogent Social Sciences*, **7** (1), a1972558, doi.org/10.1080/23311886.2021.1972558.

Vergne, C. (2009), 'Democracy, Elections and Allocation of Public Expenditures in Developing Countries', *European Journal of Political Economy*, **25** (1), 63–77.

Wei, S.J. and R. Zeckhauser (1999), 'Dark Deals and Dampened Destinies: Corruption and Economic Performance', *Japan and the World Economy*, **11** (3), 443–454.

World Bank (2023a), 'World Development Indicators', Washington, DC: World Bank, accessed 10 January 2023 at https://databank.worldbank.org/source/world-development-indicators.

World Bank (2023b), 'International Debt Statistics', Washington DC: World Bank, accessed 10 January 2023 at https://databank.worldbank.org/source/international-debt-statistics.

10. Government planning in Africa

Innocent Chirisa and Zebediah Muneta

INTRODUCTION

Planning as a management function has always been a focal point in public sector studies and community development initiatives. It also receives increasing scholarly attention to analyse the successes and failures of governments' sector plans (Loh, 2012). Such studies reveal that a lack of managerial planning capacity can significantly reduce governments' ability to successfully operationalise government policies and programmes and thereby compromise a government's responsibilities such as the protection of the environment, facilitation of economic growth, and the fostering of social development. Planning capacity generally refers to the competencies of public managers, the amount of professional and budgetary resources that are available for planning endeavours, the availability of accurate statistics, and the degree of sophistication with which the planning process is carried out. The planning process in government is further complicated by the expectation of close engagement and the involvement of multiple stakeholders in the planning processes. These stakeholders may have competing interests and expectations. The absence of such involvement usually leads to illegitimate plans and the lack of buy-in and political support to participate in the execution of government plans (Schulze, 2016).

In the context of African governance, government planning processes are characterised by political interferences, factionalism, and potential conflict between different groups in society. Government planners should thus be sensitive to these dynamics and carefully navigate the design and implementation of policy and sector plans.

This chapter seeks to explore the ways in which government planning is done in different sectors of African governments. Not much scholarly attention has been devoted to analysing the nature, impact, and implications of government planning capacity. This chapter synthesises the literature concerning capacity in planning and related fields and proposes criteria that future definitions and measures of planning capacity should include. Emphasis is placed on government plans in different sectors.

CONCEPTUALISING GOVERNMENT PLANNING

Planning in government is highly significant since it allows policymakers to identify and prioritise socioeconomic development goals, allocate resources efficiently, and anticipate and mitigate potential risks and hazards. It helps to ensure that government actions and policies are aligned with the needs of citizens and are effective in achieving desired outcomes. Planning can also promote transparency, accountability, and collaboration among different stakeholders, leading to more effective and sustainable solutions to complex problems.

Government planning can be conceptualised by considering different time horizons. Here is a brief overview of short-, medium-, and longer-term strategic planning in government:

- Short-term planning: Short-term planning typically covers a period of up to one year and focuses on immediate actions and operational activities that need to be taken to achieve specific objectives. Short-term planning is useful for addressing pressing issues that require quick action and for ensuring that day-to-day operations in government departments, entities, and agencies run smoothly.
- Medium-term planning: Medium-term planning typically covers a period of one to five years and involves setting priorities and developing strategies that align with the government's overall vision and goals. This planning horizon is useful for addressing issues that require a longer-term perspective, such as infrastructure development, economic growth, and social development.
- Longer-term strategic planning: Longer-term strategic planning typically covers a period of five to 20 years or more and involves developing a comprehensive vision of the future and identifying the major strategic priorities required to achieve that vision. This planning horizon is useful for addressing complex, long-term issues that require a holistic and integrated approach, such as climate change, demographic shifts, and technological disruption. Longer-term planning requires the involvement of a wide range of stakeholders, including experts, citizens, and businesses, and often involves significant public consultation and engagement.

Government planning can be defined as:

- A linear or iterative process and associated dynamics.
- An outcome (i.e. a particular result of the implementation of a plan).
- Managerial competencies and capacities to plan.
- The application of planning tools and techniques.
- Specific sectoral plans.

Linear planning can be regarded as a sequential approach to planning where each step must be completed before moving on to the next. This model is often used in situations where the steps involved in the planning process are well-defined and the objectives are clear. This approach is common in large, complex government programmes and projects that require a high degree of precision and control, such as infrastructure development or military operations. Iterative planning, on the other hand, is a far more flexible and adaptive approach that allows for continuous improvement and iteration throughout the planning process. This approach is often used in situations where the objectives are not well defined or the project is subject to change. This model is more common in complex, dynamic environments where the outcome is uncertain and the process is ongoing, such as in urban planning, disaster response, or policymaking.

The outcomes of government plans are, of course, dependent on the original intentions of the plans and the particular sector for which it was designed. Some common outcomes of government plans include:

- Improved public services: Government plans can lead to better quality and more accessible public services, such as education, healthcare, and transportation.

- Economic growth: Government plans can stimulate economic growth by creating jobs, attracting investment, and promoting entrepreneurship.
- Social development: Government plans can promote social development by addressing issues such as poverty, inequality, and homelessness.
- Infrastructure improvement: Government plans can result in the construction of new infrastructure or the upgrade of existing infrastructure, such as roads, bridges, and public buildings.
- Environmental protection: Government plans can promote environmental sustainability by addressing issues such as climate change, air and water pollution, and waste management.
- Public safety: Government plans can enhance public safety by providing better emergency services, improving crime prevention and control, and reducing the risk of natural disasters.
- Political stability: Government plans can contribute to political stability by addressing issues such as corruption, conflict, and social unrest.

As far as managerial competencies and capacities to plan are concerned, literature typically emphasises the following competencies:

- Strategic thinking: The ability to analyse complex information, identify trends and patterns, and develop innovative solutions.
- Problem-solving: The ability to identify problems, analyse data and information, and develop and implement effective solutions.
- Communication: The ability to clearly and effectively communicate plans, ideas, and decisions to stakeholders.
- Leadership: The ability to inspire, motivate, and guide others towards achieving common goals.
- Collaboration: The ability to work effectively with others, build strong relationships, and resolve conflicts in a constructive manner.
- Project management: The ability to effectively manage resources, schedules, and budgets to achieve project goals.
- Adaptability: The ability to respond quickly and effectively to changing circumstances, and to make decisions under uncertainty.
- Financial management: The ability to analyse financial information, create budgets, and make informed financial decisions.
- Analytical skills: The ability to collect, analyse, and interpret data to inform decision-making.
- Attention to detail: The ability to identify potential problems and pay close attention to details that can impact the success of the plan.

There is a variety of managerial tools, techniques, and instruments to plan. These include scenario planning, PERT and Gantt charts, decision trees, contingency planning, SWOT analyses, brainstorming, and the Delphi technique. Big data and ICT-based tools are also increasingly utilised to improve the quality of government plans. Managers should be aware of the benefits associated with each and also know which tool or technique is more suitable for particular circumstances.

As far as sector plans are concerned, Loh (2012) argues that it is aimed at addressing issues with a specific focus such as energy, housing, transportation, and water. These plans are far more complex than the ordinary functional and operational planning that managers undertake to operationalise institutional objectives. It should, for example, consider systemic issues such as the availability of resources, human capital, socioeconomic and political realities, and spatial contexts. Sector plans should also follow a more whole-of-government approach by considering the coordination and alignment of plans in the different spheres of government as well as intergovernmental arrangements. It should thus attempt to coordinate the efforts of other sectors of government into a cogent strategy to enhance the standard of living for citizens.

CONTINENTAL, REGIONAL, NATIONAL, AND INSTITUTIONAL FRAMEWORKS FOR GOVERNMENT PLANNING IN AFRICA

In Africa, there are several frameworks that guide government planning at various levels, including continental, regional, national, and institutional frameworks.

As far as the continental framework is concerned, the African Union (AU) serves as the primary coordinating body to direct government planning on the continent. The AU's Agenda 2063 is a long-term vision for the future of Africa, outlining aspirations for economic growth, social development, and political stability. Agenda 2063 can thus be regarded as a blueprint or master plan for transforming Africa into a future global powerhouse. It also serves as the continent's strategic framework that aims to deliver on its goal for inclusive and sustainable development as well as unity, self-determination, freedom, progress, and collective prosperity pursued under the ideas of Pan-Africanism and the African Renaissance. The genesis of Agenda 2063 was the realisation by African leaders that there was a need to refocus and reprioritise Africa's agenda from the struggle against exclusion and the attainment of economic and political independence.

Regional planning frameworks on the continent refer to the concerns of geographical areas. There are several regional economic communities in Africa, including the East African Community, the Economic Community of West African States, and the Southern African Development Community. These communities provide a planning framework for regional cooperation and integration, and support government planning by promoting cross-border trade, investment, infrastructure development (e.g. electricity, water supply, roads, and railways), and economic integration.

National planning frameworks refer to the design of national development plans and broad-based strategies to realise socioeconomic growth, prosperity, and the improvement of the general living standards of citizens of a country. National development plans typically outline the development priorities and goals of the government. It generally focuses on addressing pressing or 'apex' priorities such as poverty alleviation, inequality, unemployment, and infrastructure development. In the case of South Africa, for example, the National Development Plan: Vision 2030 outlines focus areas such as economic growth and job creation, education and skills development, health, rural development, fighting corruption and improving good governance, as well as reducing social inequality.

As far as institutional planning frameworks are concerned, it generally refers to organisational arrangements, systems, and structures to facilitate planning in government. This includes the establishment of government ministries, departments, and agencies to coordinate government's planning efforts. Institutional frameworks should also accommodate the involvement of civil society organisations, private sector enterprises, non-governmental organisations, and academic institutions. These organisations typically provide expertise, support, and oversight for government planning and help to ensure that plans are effectively implemented. Overall, these frameworks provide a structure and support system for government planning in Africa, helping to ensure that plans are aligned with broader regional and continental goals and that they effectively address the challenges facing the continent. However, the effectiveness of these frameworks can be limited by factors such as lack of resources, political instability, and weak governance. As far as the latter is concerned, the African Development Bank (2022) holds that good governance is the single most significant factor influencing the planning competency and capacity of African countries. Good governance should be based on stable states, an active and mobilised civil society, and a prosperous private sector. Values and norms such as accountability, openness, combatting corruption, public engagement, and an enabling judicial framework are commonly regarded as crucial parts of good government. In response to this realisation, many African countries have now implemented institutional reforms that have dramatically altered their governance architecture. Ghana, for example, has rigorously pursued governance reforms since the early 1990s, including the creation and ratification of a new democratic constitution that emphasises the separation of powers with checks and balances to improve its governance arrangements. Also, countries such as Kenya, Morocco, and Côte d'Ivoire instituted several reform programmes aimed at improving the overall performance of their governments (African Development Bank, 2022).

INTEGRATED GOVERNMENT PLANNING IN AFRICA

Integrated government planning in Africa typically refers to the process of aligning and coordinating different sectors and departments within a government to achieve a common set of goals and objectives. It involves the development of a comprehensive and integrated plan that takes into account the interconnections and interdependencies between different sectors and areas of government responsibility (Watson et al., 2019).

The nature of integrated government planning is to ensure that government resources are used in a strategic and coordinated manner, with a view to achieving greater impact and outcomes. The scope of integrated government planning can vary depending on the country and the specific objectives but typically covers a range of sectors such as economic development, social welfare, education, health, and the environment.

The aims of integrated government planning in Africa typically include the following:

- Promoting sustainable development: By aligning different sectors and government departments, integrated government planning aims to support national sustainable development, taking into account the interconnections and interdependencies between different areas of government responsibility.
- Improving efficiency and effectiveness: By coordinating and aligning resources, integrated government planning aims to ensure that government activities are carried out in the most efficient and effective way possible.

- Fostering collaboration and coordination: Integrated government planning encourages collaboration and coordination between different sectors and departments, helping to break down silos and promote a more integrated and coordinated approach to government activities.

Examples of integrated government plans in Africa include Kenya's Vision 2030, which is a long-term development plan that outlines the country's vision and goals for 2030, and the Integrated National Development Plan of Namibia. This plan is a comprehensive plan that outlines the country's vision and goals for sustainable development. It is an integrated plan that covers a range of sectors, including economic development, education, health, and the environment.

An integrated analysis also provides information on the trade-offs and synergies that exist across different policies and can help planners to make decisions on how to manage them i.e., investing in policies for which the positive synergies with other policies are the greatest and therefore the impact higher. These are known as SDG accelerators. Integrated planning provides the means to choose a future trajectory that is not a repetition of the past. The Guide for Integrated Planning in Africa aims to help countries recover and build resilience through integrated development planning, leveraging on the SDGs, Africa's Agenda 2063, and the NDCs. As such, it intends to facilitate recovery pathways crafted by national governments, based on their own priorities. Integrated planning provides the means to choose a future trajectory that is not a repetition of the past.

Overall, integrated government planning in Africa aims to support sustainable development by aligning and coordinating government activities across different sectors and departments. By improving efficiency and effectiveness and fostering collaboration and coordination, integrated government planning helps to ensure that government resources are used in a strategic and impactful way.

Whole-of-government Planning

Closely related to notions of integrated government planning is whole-of-government planning which generally refers to an approach to policy and resource allocation that involves all relevant departments and agencies within a government working together towards a common set of goals and objectives. The goal of whole-of-government planning is to ensure that government activities are coordinated and aligned and that resources are used in the most efficient and effective way possible. It typically involves the development of a comprehensive and integrated plan that covers all relevant sectors and areas of government responsibility. This plan outlines the government's vision and goals and sets out the policies, programmes, and initiatives that will be implemented to achieve these goals. The main benefits of whole-of-government planning include:

- Improved efficiency and effectiveness: By ensuring that government activities are coordinated and aligned, whole-of-government planning helps to reduce duplication, minimise waste, and improve the efficiency and effectiveness of government activities.
- Better policy outcomes: By taking into account the interconnections and interdependencies between different areas of government responsibility, whole-of-government planning helps to ensure that policies and programmes are designed to achieve the best possible outcomes.

- Enhanced collaboration and coordination: Whole-of-government planning promotes collaboration and coordination between different departments and agencies, helping to break down silos and improve the overall effectiveness of government.

Overall, whole-of-government planning is a key element of effective governance and a critical component of government reform efforts. By ensuring that government activities are better coordinated and aligned, whole-of-government planning helps to support sustainable development and improve the living conditions of citizens.

OPERATIONAL GOVERNMENT PLANNING IN AFRICA

Operational planning in government refers to the processes and activities involved in planning and coordinating the day-to-day operations of a government department, entity, or agency. It is a crucial aspect of government management and is concerned with the effective and efficient delivery of services to citizens and the achievement of government objectives.

The nature of operational planning in government involves the development of detailed plans and procedures for the implementation of policy programmes and projects. This typically involves the identification of activities and tasks, the allocation of resources, and the setting of performance targets.

The scope of operational planning in government covers a wide range of activities and functions, mainly revolving around service delivery. This includes the planning and coordination of the delivery of government services to citizens, including the provision of health care, education, housing, and social services. The focal areas of operational planning in government can vary depending on the specific context and needs of each department or agency but typically include resource allocation, management controls, performance reviews, and internal audits. Overall, operational planning in government is a critical component of effective governance and public management. By ensuring that government activities and operations are well-planned and effectively coordinated, operational planning helps to improve the efficiency and effectiveness of government and support the achievement of government objectives.

African countries have taken different approaches to operational planning, influenced by ideological choices and governance traditions. However, unlike in more affluent nations, where planning strives to fine-tune the economy, planning in developing and crisis-affected countries is burdened with a more transformational function. This is mainly due to widespread institutional weaknesses and market failures (Rockström, Karlberg and Falkenmark, 2020). Abrupt, usually unexpected, and significant change in the political and economic landscape of nations on the continent furthermore have come to characterise government planning. Especially political instability is a key aspect influencing operational planning. Remembering that governments rarely stick to the medium- or long-term development plans of their predecessors helps one understand the impact these changes have on operational planning. Additionally, even if a government's senior officials remain unchanged, political instability may make the execution of such plans difficult or impossible (Watson et al., 2019). This was true, for instance, in countries like Nigeria where public unrest reached levels that interfere with the smooth operation of government. In addition, excessive economic uncertainty also hinders the creation and implementation of development initiatives. It becomes difficult for some countries to stick to medium-term plans and targets when short-term issues are the main sources of uncertainty.

A further issue that hampers successful operational planning in governments on the continent is the incapability of public administrations to design and implement it successfully. This includes the lack of effective planning systems and tools as well as the absence of managerial planning skills and experience (Falkenmark, 2018). It is thus evident that governments should improve operational planning by promoting a capable state.

It should be noted that both integrated and operational planning should occur within the respective functional domains or sectors of government. A sector of government refers to specific areas or focal domains of responsibility. Related ministries, organisations, or industries are usually clusters or grouped per sector. A sector may also be used to describe specific areas of the economy, such as the energy sector, the financial sector, or the agricultural sector, among others. Sectoral planning in Africa receives attention in the next section.

SECTORAL PLANNING IN AFRICA

Sectoral government planning is a critical tool for governments to address specific social, economic, and environmental challenges in a comprehensive and coordinated manner, and to ensure that public resources are used in the most effective and efficient manner possible. Sectoral government planning generally refers to the systematic and comprehensive approach that government departments, entities, and agencies use to develop and implement plans to address specific social, economic, and environmental issues in specific sectors of the economy. The scope of these plans involves the identification of specific problems and challenges within a particular sector, the development of strategies and policies to address these issues, and the allocation of resources to implement associated plans. This type of planning involves a range of stakeholders, including government agencies, private sector entities, and civil society organisations, who work together to achieve common goals.

The general purpose of sectoral government planning is to enhance the effectiveness and efficiency of government programmes and services, to promote economic growth and development, and to improve the quality of life for citizens. This type of planning is intended to align the policies and programmes of various government agencies with the broader goals of the national development plan and to ensure that public resources are used in the most effective and efficient manner possible.

It should be noted that the design and implementation of projects in a sector can also influence or be related to projects in other sectors such as the completion of complementary projects in the transport or energy sector. This implies strong alignment and coordination between the different sectors to prioritise projects and to determine which projects are multisectoral in nature. This requires the establishment of a combination of mechanisms to align sectoral plans and ensure that they are aligned with the broader national development goals. This includes integrated development planning structures, inter-ministerial committees, the use of performance management and evaluation systems, and the alignment of the budget process. These mechanisms help to ensure that public resources are used in the most effective and efficient manner possible to achieve the country's broader development goals. Some examples of sectoral planning are provided in the subsections below.

Energy Sector Planning

Energy is fundamental to human and economic development. The recent Intergovernmental Panel on Climate Change (IPCC) report, published in multiple parts from 2021 to 2022, provides government planners with the information they need to make informed decisions about how to mitigate and adapt to the impacts of climate change. The IPCC is an intergovernmental body established by the United Nations to provide the world with scientific information on climate change and its impacts.

In response to these realities, Friends of the Earth International (FOEI) published its 'A Just Recovery Renewable Energy Plan for Africa' (FOEI, 2021). This publication shows that it is not only urgent, but entirely possible, to reduce emissions, transform the energy system, and support a just recovery on the continent. The Energy Plan outlines how the continent can dismantle existing so-called 'dirty' energy systems to leapfrog Africa to 100% renewable energy by 2050.

In sub-Saharan Africa, population growth is outstripping growth in electricity access. The percentage of people in the region with access to electricity is further expected to decline. This has serious economic implications. In Nigeria, for example, homes and businesses spend a significant portion of their income on fuel for small backup and full-time generators because the power grid is not meeting their needs. In addition, electricity that is generated must be transmitted to centres of demand via a transmission and distribution system. Such systems are not adequately maintained. Similarly, a coal power plant may provide little to no useful electricity if it is separated from demand by a congested transmission line or if it is operating in a system where the real limiting factor is distribution network capacity.

Effective energy planning and associated plan-based investments require intensive collaboration across governments, utilities, investors, development partners, and project developers. A positive development in this regard is that Power Africa, an energy and power company based in South Africa, entered into partnership agreements with governments across East and West African countries to supply energy. With a combined population of approximately 750 million, these nations represent approximately 73% of sub-Saharan Africa's population (World Bank, 2021). Providing access to electricity has far-reaching positive outcomes for these nations, including improving educational services and access to health care.

Water Sector Planning

Water is a pivotal factor in sustainable development and requires serious consideration for government planners. In water-scarce parts of Africa, water planning is an essential government function because it involves the development and implementation of policies, programmes, and projects that ensure the sustainable and efficient management of water resources. It plays a crucial role in addressing water-related challenges such as water scarcity, water pollution, floods, droughts, and other environmental problems. Ineffective water planning may lead to water insecurity concerns. Effective water planning helps ensure the availability and reliability of water supplies for various purposes, including domestic, agricultural, industrial, and environmental uses. Water planning furthermore helps to preserve and restore the ecological health of watersheds, rivers, lakes, and groundwater aquifers, which are critical components of the natural environment.

Most African countries have extensive water safety plans (WSPs) as the most effective way to consistently manage drinking water supplies and to safeguard public health. The International Water Association (IWA) is supporting water service providers in several African countries, with support from the US Environmental Protection Agency (USEPA) and the OPEC Fund for International Development (OFID), to develop, implement, and monitor the successful design and implementation of WSPs. The IWA also assists countries with training programmes and tools to facilitate water operator partnerships (WOPs) (Falkenmark, 2018, 2020).

Housing Sector Planning

The provision of adequate housing for citizens increasingly receives prominence due to rapid urbanisation in African cities. Government planners have to carefully consider current urbanisation trends and embark on spatial planning initiatives to prepare government institutions for the influx of people and associated demands placed on infrastructure development and service delivery.

Innovative schemes are necessary to address the housing backlogs. Fortunately, there are some positive developments in this regard as government planners devise creative strategies to address shortages. These include:

- Government partnerships with the private sector.
- Administrative and policy instruments to streamline housing delivery.
- Site and service programmes.
- Financial investment support.
- Urban renewal programmes.
- Squatter or slum upgrading.
- Self-help construction schemes.

Falkenmark (2020) accentuates the significance of housing planning to promote general local economic and social development. In developed economies housing is one of the most important tangible assets, and in Africa it has the potential to make a substantial and prolonged contribution to socioeconomic development. Falkenmark (2020) furthermore reasons that insufficient housing planning may have important political consequences. Slums may become incubators for political instability. On the other hand, home ownership promotes responsibility and stable social life.

Large-scale investment in the housing sector is not yet evident on the continent. Such investment requires a series of supporting conditions such as affordable construction material, good and stable governance, the effective administration of legal titles, and financial support for mortgages. Infrastructure must be planned and provided in advance of settlements, and residential services must follow construction. Each of these issues can be addressed by appropriate government planning. Addressing only one or two areas of housing usually has little payoff if the others remain unresolved.

Transport Sector Planning

Transport is not an end in itself but rather a means allowing people to access what they need: jobs markets and goods, social interaction, education, and a full range of other services contributing to healthy and fulfilled lives. A move towards a more sustainable transport system is therefore imperative and really is our only option for the future. Transport infrastructure encompasses every mode of transportation such as bicycles, bus rapid transit, railways, roads, ports, and airports. Transport planning in government is a complex and multidisciplinary field that plays a critical role in ensuring the development of efficient, safe, and sustainable transport systems. Transportation planning is one of the overarching drivers of sustainability and applying it successfully can benefit the residents of a community, the travellers passing through it, and the environment.

Positive developments on the continent regarding government transport planning include:

- Transport infrastructure development projects to construct roads, bridges, ports, and airports.
- Support for more sustainable transport including the use of greener energy for rapid bus transit in cities.
- The use of public transport instead of private vehicles.
- The use of natural gas for public transport.
- The improvement of freight transport systems to remove heavy trucks from roads.
- Cycle network improvements in urban areas.

Government planners increasingly follow a more sustainable mobility approach in transport sector plans. Sustainable transportation can be regarded as the capacity to support the mobility needs of a society in a manner that is the least damageable to the environment and does not impair the mobility needs of future generations. It also includes cognisance of the interdependent relationship between transport and other sectors such as health, education, housing, and the protection of the environment.

Public Health Sector Planning

The status of public health in Africa varies widely from country to country. While some countries have made significant progress in improving health outcomes, others continue to struggle with high levels of disease and mortality.

One of the major challenges facing the public health system in Africa is a lack of access to basic health services. Many communities lack access to essential medicines, vaccines, and other health technologies, and there is a shortage of trained health workers in many areas. This can lead to high levels of preventable diseases and conditions, such as malaria, tuberculosis, and maternal and child mortality.

Public health care planning is critical in addressing these challenges. A well-designed and implemented public health care plan can help ensure that health services are available to everyone who needs them, regardless of where they live or their socioeconomic status. This can involve a range of activities, such as strengthening health systems, improving access to health services, and increasing the availability of essential medicines and vaccines. It is also important for public health care plans to take into account the unique cultural, social, and economic context of each country (Falkenmark, 2020). This can involve working with local communities to identify their specific health needs, as well as addressing any barriers that may prevent people from accessing health services. Overall, public health care planning plays a crucial role in improving the health of populations in Africa. By addressing the underlying causes of poor health outcomes and ensuring that essential health services are available to all, public health care plans can help to build healthier and more equitable communities.

Due to the significance of health care planning for socioeconomic prosperity, it is not surprising that the African Union's Agenda 2063 stresses the need to focus on sound health and social well-being. This aspiration recognises the significance of health care planning, inclusive of related aspects such as clean drinking water, the quality of food systems, and the reduction in noise, air, and soil pollution.

The next sections aim to survey government sectoral planning by making use of a particular country as a case, namely Zimbabwe.

GOVERNMENT SECTORAL PLANNING: THE CASE OF ZIMBABWE

As alluded to earlier, national planning frameworks serve as overarching architecture to direct the planning activities of each sector. Similarly, the Government of Zimbabwe launched its national planning framework, titled Vision 2030 in 2016 to outline a transformative and inclusive development agenda for the country. This Vision was further supplemented by the National Development Strategy 1: 2021–2025 to transition towards achieving an upper-middle-income society by 2030. The NDS1 is also aimed at addressing the Sustainable Development Goals (SDGs) and the Africa Union's Agenda 2063. The Government furthermore developed the Transitional Stabilisation Programme (TSP) in 2018 to guide reform initiatives in different sectors of the economy.

The Government's national planning framework continues, however, to be challenged with socioeconomic issues such as severe fuel shortages, electricity load-shedding, public service strikes, civil society protests, and a fragile health care system. This makes sectoral planning even more essential to address the country's challenges.

Energy Sector Planning

Zimbabwe's electrical grid is in dire need of maintenance and upgrades to address the disparity between the supply and demand of electricity. While the total demand for electricity is 2029 MW, the supply is only around 1200 MW. This incongruency is also created by the outdated status of electrical power plants. Zimbabwe's electrical power is generated by two methods: coal and hydropower. None of the coal-powered plants (i.e. Hwange, Bulawayo, Harare, Munyati) meet their advertised power output. The Hwange plant boasts an installed capacity of 920 MW (megawatts), yet it only produces between 400 and 500 MW. Even worse, the rest of the coal plants rarely generate electricity. Coal production is further complicated by the fact that Zimbabwe only has 502 tons of coal reserves left as of the end of 2017. This amount does not suffice to keep providing the energy necessary for its plants and burgeoning population. While coal production went up by 8.7% in 2017, the increase in production will be pointless if reserves are not adequately managed. Hydropower is nearly the same story, except that the Kariba South Bank station is well-maintained and efficient. As a result of the unreliability of national energy production, many citizens have turned to more independent means of energy production: solar power and wood fuel.

The renewable energy potential of Zimbabwe is revolving around three main aspects: hydropower, solar power, and biogas. The majority of Zimbabwe's hope for hydropower lies along the Zambezi River. The country currently meets 80% of its hydropower demands from the Kariba South Bank power station on the Zambezi River, and the potential hydropower that can be derived from the Zambezi River is estimated to be around 18600 GWh per annum. The main obstacles to stable hydropower production are the underdeveloped electrical grid of the country, lack of funding to build and maintain more stations, and volatile weather conditions from climate change. Solar power in Zimbabwe is mostly found within individual homes, but there is potential for larger private or public ventures. Solar radiation averages 16 MJ square metres during the winter to around 22 MJ square metres in midsummer. Much like hydropower, large-scale solar power is limited by a lack of capital to build plants. Zimbabwe has multiple municipal sewage plants that create biogas from both human and animal waste, but most of it is flared into the open air. In the future, plants could be adapted to better handle biogas storage and usage. Zimbabwe's current energy policy, the National Energy Policy, is focused on rural electrification, promoting small, decentralised initiatives to transition to clean energy, and diversifying national energy supply options.

The Ministry of Energy and Power Development in Zimbabwe has the proliferation of renewables and electric power to rural areas for practical purposes such as land irrigation and small cottage industries. On a very large scale, the National Energy Policy Implementation Strategy (NEPIS) sought to create an agency to oversee the development of rural parts of Zimbabwe. In 2002, Parliament passed the Rural Electrification Fund Act, which mandated the complete electrification of rural Zimbabwe via government stipends and electrification levies. Consequently, this act led to the birth of the Rural Electrification Agency (REA). The REA has put forth the Rural Energy Master Plan, a blueprint for the development of environmentally and economically viable electric grid and renewable energy development which was launched in 2017. A new National Renewable Energy Policy was promulgated in 2019 to exploit the country's renewable energy resources like solar, hydro, biomass, and to a limited extent, wind and geothermal, which to date have largely remained unexploited. These policies direct planning in the sector.

Zimbabwe's main challenges in the future will be moving away from wood fuel for households to more sustainable energy alternatives. A more suitable environment for foreign direct investments should also be established and individual independent energy producers should be allowed to add energy to the power grid (Rockström, Karlberg and Falkenmark, 2020). These aspects will remain the dominant themes of planning in the sector.

Water Sector Planning

The Zimbabwe National Water Authority (ZINWA) was established in 2000 as a parastatal agency responsible for water resources planning, development, and management. Its functions include the provision of bulk water supply from state dams as well as potable water to about 500 local authorities and government institutions (MWRDM, 2012). All city and town councils and other water service providers operate under the Urban Councils Act (UCA), Chapter 15:29, which is legislation complementing the Zimbabwe National Water Act of 1998 (Marumahoko et al., 2020). The UCA relates to the provision of water supply services in urban areas and informs the planning and management of urban water supply. However, analysis of the UCA indicates that it lacks adequate regulations for the management of urban water supply services (Hove and Tirimboi, 2011; Marumahoko et al., 2020).

The UCA does not spell out procedures of setting water tariffs, roles, and responsibilities of institutions, or the regulation of the water management systems in urban areas, which are very important policy instruments for the effective delivery of water services (Watson et al., 2019). Chigonda (2010) holds that the Zimbabwe National Water Act of 1998 was simply an organisation-focused policy which only provided guidelines about water catchment management and did not address urban water management concerns. Consequently, the lack of clearly stated roles for the ZINWA with regard to urban water management was of major concern (Nhapi, 2009). Hove and Tirimboi (2011) indicated that while ZINWA manages urban water services, there is no other organisation that regulates ZINWA's operations, which ultimately creates a conflict of interest. Given these challenges, the Government of Zimbabwe decided to formulate a national water policy.

The Zimbabwe National Water Policy was promulgated in 2012 with the aim of addressing the deterioration of water services and infrastructure decay. As far as water planning is concerned, the policy encourages engagement with key stakeholders in the economy to jointly plan and implement the recovery of water services (Chirenda et al., 2015).

Transport Sector Planning

Transport planning and spatial modelling are two key aspects of sustainable development that involve complex management methodologies, efficiency matters, technological implementations, consistency, and environmental concerns.

The Ministry responsible for public transport reviewed the status of transport planning during 2018 and identified two main problems: the first problem concerns the inefficiency and ineffectiveness of policy makers and technical planning factors which have led to continuous reconfigurations and replications of the transport system. The second problem relates to the fact that transport planning is characterised by uneven growth of different transport modes. This leads to imbalanced urban growth and economic development in the country. Additionally, transport planning is severely hampered by the lack of clear and reliable transport data. These challenges still seriously constrain transport planning in the country.

Land-use (Spatial) Sector Planning

Land-use planning should be analysed within the context of political and economic dynamics associated with land reform in the country. Experts in the sector, such as Rukuni (2012), concur that planning is essential to give direction and establish stability in this sector. Managing land is generally highly politicised, despite the proclamations of the state that science should prevail (Newman, 2012).

Currently, planning regarding land use is largely dominated by the agricultural sector and large-scale commercial farming. Planning is complicated by the perception that indigenous systems for soil and water conservation are not considered and that agricultural solutions derived from elsewhere are simply imposed on traditional farmers. In addition, optimal land uses are mainly defined according to 'suitability' and 'capability' maps (e.g. soil, rainfall, and vegetation patterns) and not on people's social-cultural and economic needs. The World Bank is reportedly contemplating a major planning exercise to address these concerns. Some areas need to be protected from encroachment, such as agricultural land near urban areas, and therefore some form of regulated zoning is required. A land administration system that enables registration and the issuance of leases should be designed with a deeper understanding of how land is being used.

Public Health Sector Planning

Public health sector planning should be seen against the backdrop of significant health challenges in the country. The provisioning of adequate health care services and clinical services in deep rural areas remains a major concern. Positive developments in this sector include the fact that the Ministry of Health and Child Care works closely with the Global Fund's Country Coordinating Mechanism to ensure the alignment and coordination of health programmes. In addition, the Ministry of Health and Child Care has kick-started the process of developing the National Health Strategy 2021–2025 which would outline the roadmap towards turning around and restoring stability in the country's health system. The Ministry furthermore commenced with the launch of the Integrated Results-Based Management System. This System reiterates Government's commitment to improving the quality of the country's health care delivery system (Rockström, Karlberg and Falkenmark, 2020). Ten strategic focus areas were identified by the Ministry as priority areas for the health sector. These strategic focus areas are characterised by the attainment of key outcomes enunciated in the National Development Strategy, namely:

- Improve access to essential medicines and commodities.
- Increase access to water, sanitation, and healthy environment.
- Improve health infrastructure and medical equipment for Health Service Delivery.
- Improve governance of the Health Service.
- Improve health sector human resources performance.
- Increase domestic funding for health.
- Reduce morbidity and mortality due to communicable and non-communicable diseases.
- Improve reproductive, maternal, newborn child, and adolescent health and nutrition.
- Improve public health surveillance, and disaster preparedness and response.
- Improve primary, secondary, tertiary, quaternary, and quandary care.

GOVERNMENT PLANNING CHALLENGES ON THE CONTINENT

Planners cannot limit themselves by only indicating what is to be achieved without showing how, when, and by whom it is to be done. Unless they give attention to the means for reaching macroeconomic goals, there is little reason to expect that planned development will be more successful in the future than it has been in the past (Falkenmark, 2020).

Government planners in developing countries on the continent typically experience unique and peculiar challenges that planners in highly developed nations do not have. It is thus useful to pinpoint some of these challenges and to share best planning practices in addressing them. Probably the most significant challenge that planners in developing countries face is the absence of reliable, accurate, and suitable planning information, inclusive of baseline statistics per sector. To be more specific, government planners are constrained by the following:

- Incomplete or outdated data: Often, data in developing countries may be incomplete or outdated due to limited resources and capacity for data collection and management.

- Inaccurate data: In some cases, data may be inaccurate due to poor data collection methods or intentional misreporting.
- Limited capacity for data analysis: Even when data is available, there may be a limited capacity to analyse it, interpret it, and use it to inform policy decisions.
- Lack of coordination and standardisation: Data collection efforts may be fragmented across different sectors, agencies, and levels of government, and there may be a lack of standardisation in data collection methods and definitions.
- Limited access to technology: Access to technology and digital infrastructure, such as internet connectivity and computer systems, may be limited in some areas.

To address these challenges, developing countries can invest in building capacity for data collection, analysis, and management, and prioritise efforts to improve coordination and standardisation of data collection efforts. They can also invest in digital infrastructure and technology to improve access to data and facilitate data management and analysis. In addition, efforts to promote transparency and accountability can help to reduce intentional misreporting and increase the accuracy of data.

A further challenge is the lack of political will to support evidence-based solutions to governance challenges and to allocate sufficient resources to direct government planning efforts. Often political agendas overshadow rational decision-making. It is thus necessary to sensitise political decision-makers regarding the need for scientific-based planning. Planning in a political milieu is further complicated by matters such as corruption, inadequate stakeholder, and public participation in planning endeavours, and political instability. Political representatives come and go as per election cycle, leading to new policy directives and planning priorities. There is thus limited continuity in existing medium- to longer-term government plans. Existing plans may be disrupted by the agendas and priorities of newly appointed political heads.

Another challenge is the general lack of technical planning skills and expertise. Technical skills and expertise are crucial in government planning because they enable planners to make informed decisions based on current data and trends analysis. This is especially important in areas such as infrastructure development, economic policy, and public health, where technical knowledge is necessary to understand complex systems and anticipate potential outcomes. Without technical expertise, government planning may be less effective and may fail to achieve desired outcomes.

Considering the typical challenges experienced by government planners, Tramberend et al. (2021) reflect that governments should move away from conventional planning modalities which see the future as simply a continuation of the past. Government planners should rather pursue a more contingency and strategic approach to planning which entails a careful analysis of the context, circumstances, and environment. Government planners should thus assess the development needs of society and seek to optimally exploit growth and development opportunities, given the political, economic, and social realities of the country.

Lessons that can typically be learned from pockets of government planning excellence on the continent include the importance of building strong state institutions staffed with qualified and experienced staff, where human capital and talent management is recognised. A further lesson is to foster government planning responsiveness to emerging issues and accountability arrangements for such planning responses. Additionally, governments should promote transparency in government planning by engaging key stakeholders, inclusive of civil society, in all planning efforts. Finally, countries should share best practices and learn from successful planning experiences in other countries. However, it is important to tailor government plans to local contexts and circumstances and to align government plans with the long-term development vision of the country.

CONCLUSION

This chapter scrutinised and differentiated between the respective continental, regional, national, and institutional frameworks for government planning in Africa. It furthermore investigated the scope and significance of integrated government planning in Africa and clarified notions of 'whole-of-government' planning. In addition, the chapter outlined the nature and significance of operational government planning. Finally, the chapter surveyed the ways in which government planning is done in different sectors of African governments. In this regard Zimbabwe as a case study was used to reveal the practical manifestations of sector planning.

It is evident that government planning is designed and executed by public managers in different echelons of management. The lack of managerial planning capacity can significantly reduce governments' ability to successfully operationalise government policies and programmes and thereby compromise the government responsibilities such as the protection of the environment, facilitating economic growth, and fostering social development. In the context of African governance, government planning processes are typified by political dynamics, low technical capacity, and the absence of accurate and reliable planning statistics and data.

REFERENCES

African Development Bank. (2022), 'Africa's Economic Performance and Outlook', accessed 14 February 2023 at https://www.afdb.org/sites/default/files/2022/05/25/aeo22_chapter1_eng.pdf.

Chigonda, T. (2010), 'Water supply and Sanitation in the New Residential Areas in Zimbabwean Towns: The Case of Maridale High-Density Suburb in Norton', *Journal of Sustainable Development in Africa*, **12** (3), 349–360.

Chirenda, T.G., S.C. Srinivas and R. Tandlich (2015), 'Microbial Water Quality of Treated Water and Raw Water Sources in the Harare Area, Zimbabwe', *Water SA*, **41** (5), 691–697, doi.org/10.4314/wsa .v41i5.12.

Falkenmark, M. (2020), 'Water Resilience and Human Life Support-Global Outlook for the Next Half Century', *International Journal of Water Resources Development*, **36** (1), 377–396, doi.org/10.1080 /07900627.2019.1693983.

Friends of the Earth International (FOEI). (2021), *A Just Recovery Renewable Energy Plan for Africa*, accessed 13 February 2023 at https://www.foei.org/publication/a-just-recovery-renewable-energy -plan-for-africa/.

Hove, M. and A. Tirimboi (2011), 'Assessment of Harare Water Service Delivery', *Journal of Sustainable Development in Africa*, **13** (4), 61–84.

Loh, C.G. (2012), 'Four Potential Disconnects in the Community Planning Process', *Journal of Planning Education and Research*, **31** (1), 33–47, doi.org/I:10.1177/0739456X11424161.

Marumahoko, S., O.S Afolabi, Y. Sadie and N.T. Nhede (2020), 'Governance and Urban Service Delivery in Zimbabwe', *Strategic Review for Southern Africa*, **42** (1), 41–68, doi.org/10.35293/srsa .v42i1.194.

Ministry of Water Resources Development and Management (MWRDM). (2012), *The Zimbabwe National Water Policy*, Harare, Zimbabwe.

Newman, K. (2012), 'Benchmarking the Supply of Planning Graduates Against International Practice: Its Implications for Nigeria', *Development*, **54** (1), 71–94.

Nhapi, I. (2009), 'The Water Situation in Harare, Zimbabwe: A Policy and Management Problem', *Water Policy*, **11** (2), 221–235, doi.org/10.2166/wp.2009.018.

Rockström, J., L. Karlberg and M. Falkenmark (2020), 'Global Food Production in a Water-Constrained World: Exploring "Green" and "Blue" Challenges and Solutions', in Grafton, R.Q. and K. Hussey (eds.), *Water Resources Planning and Management*, Cambridge: Cambridge University Press, pp. 131–151.

Rukuni, M. (2012), 'Why Zimbabwe Needs to Maintain a Multi-Form Land Tenure System', Reliefweb, OCHA Services, accessed 23 November 2022 at https://reliefweb.int/report/zimbabwe/why-zimbabwe-needs-maintain-multi-form-land-tenure-system.

Schulze, R.E. (2016), 'Some Foci of Integrated Water Resources Management in the South Which Are Often Forgotten by the North: A Perspective from Southern Africa', in Craswell, E., M. Bonnell, D. Bossio, S. Demuth and N. van de Giesen, *Integrated Assessment of Water Resources and Global Change*, New York: Springer, pp. 269–294.

Tramberend, S., R. Burtscher, P. Burek, T. Kahil, G. Fischer, J. Mochizuki and Y. Wada (2021), 'Co-development of East African Regional Water Scenarios for 2050', *One Earth*, **4** (3), 434–447, doi.org/10.1016/j.oneear.2021.02.012.

Watson, R., I. Baste, A. Larigauderie, P. Leadley, U. Pascual, B. Baptiste and H. Mooney (2019), 'Summary for Policymakers of the Global Assessment Report on Biodiversity and Ecosystem Services of the Intergovernmental Science-Policy Platform on Biodiversity and Ecosystem Services', Bonn: IPBES Secretariat, pp. 22–47.

World Bank. (2021), 'Report: Universal Access to Sustainable Energy Will Remain Elusive Without Addressing Inequalities', Press Release, accessed 23 March 2023 at https://www.worldbank.org/en/news/press-release/2021/06/07/report-universal-access-to-sustainable-energy-will-remain-elusive-without-addressing-inequalities.

11. Rural and urban governance in Africa: the case of Zimbabwe

Vincent Chakunda

INTRODUCTION

Rural and urban governments in all parts of the world play an important role in the democratization of governance and the delivery of essential services. However, most rural and urban governance institutions in developing countries on the African continent are facing increasingly bigger challenges as a result of issues such as rapid urbanization, low economic growth, ailing infrastructure, and climate change (Muchadenyika and Williams, 2016; Zinyama, 2021). In the case of Zimbabwe, this is exacerbated by the widening gap between the availability of financial resources and local governments' spending needs. The increasing fiscal gap is explained by the rapid growth of urban populations which creates an ever-increasing demand for public services and new public infrastructure (Chakunda et al., 2021). In the same context, Mudau and Nyane (2022) added that centralization of government powers and authority has entrenched strong control systems that suffocate the capacity of rural and urban governments to spearhead socioeconomic and political transformation in their areas of jurisdiction. This reality, conjoined with a low revenue base due to limited property taxation and service charges, has depreciated the capacity of rural and urban governments to comply with their constitutional mandates. In this regard Chigwata (2019) submits that the more lucrative sources of revenue suitable for financing rural and urban services, such as income taxes, sales, and business taxes continue to be controlled by central governments. Where councils are able to derive revenues from property taxes and service charges, meaningful tax increases are sometimes refused or delayed by central government for fear of eroding political support from the population; or even rejected by the local institutions themselves for fear of political backlash from local taxpayers.

From these multiple perspectives this chapter seeks to examine the context and dynamics of rural and urban governance in Africa with specific reference to Zimbabwe. Issues such as policy and governance structures, service delivery frameworks, and challenges encountering local governments will receive attention.

UNPACKING THE CONCEPTS OF RURAL AND URBAN GOVERNANCE

Governance as a generic concept has multiple meanings. It can be used to represent a concept and analytical approach that opens up new ways of thinking about processes of government, politics, democracy, accountability, and transparency. To others, governance is a more descriptive term that focuses attention on concrete institutions and their financing, roles, and responsibilities (Kurebwa, 2014; Muchadenyika and Williams, 2016). Governance thus focuses on those interests that wield decision-making power about policies in urban and rural areas and the operations of decision-making mechanisms. The effectiveness of policymaking processes is dependent on how systems of governance are organized and structured. In a nutshell, governance centres around the political, technical, and bureaucratic organization of governments. It includes the processes and structures that shape and constitute broader relations of power, domination, and authority.

Rural and urban governance is defined by Muchadenyika and Williams (2016) as the systems and processes by which government is organized and delivered in urban and rural environments and the relationships between these agencies, civil society, and other organized actors. Other scholars such as Jonga (2014) and Zinyama (2021) refer to rural and urban governance as the ways by which a local government and stakeholders plan, finance, and manage urban and rural affairs. This involves continuous processes of actor-network formation, negotiation, and contestations over the allocation of resources and political power. It is thus intensely political, influenced by the creation and operation of political institutions, government capacity to make and implement decisions, and the extent to which these decisions recognize and respond to the interests of local communities. It furthermore encompasses a host of economic and social forces, institutions, and network relationships.

The significant developmental role that rural and urban governance should play is affirmed by the UN Sustainable Development Goals (SDGs). The SDGs are a universal call to action to end poverty, protect the planet, and ensure that all people enjoy peace and prosperity. While the SDGs are global in nature, their realization requires action at the local level. It confirms that local governments play a critical role in achieving the SDGs by implementing policies, plans, and projects that promote sustainable development in their communities. Local governments should set their own targets for the SDGs based on their specific needs and resources. This involves developing a local agenda that aligns with the global SDGs and prioritizing actions that are most relevant to the community. They should also mobilize financial resources from multiple sources, including local taxes, grants, and international aid, to finance SDG projects and programmes. They can also leverage public-private partnerships and other innovative financing mechanisms to attract investment. A further significant role of local government is to engage communities and stakeholders in the SDG implementation process, ensuring that local perspectives are reflected in decision-making and that communities are aware of and supportive of SDG efforts. Local governments can also promote sustainable development by incorporating SDG principles into their policies and plans, such as promoting renewable energy, reducing waste and emissions, and encouraging sustainable transport. They should furthermore monitor progress towards achieving the SDGs, using indicators and data to track progress and identify areas for improvement. This involves setting up monitoring and evaluation systems to assess the impact of SDG initiatives and adjust strategies accordingly.

In Zimbabwe there are four types of urban governance bodies, namely cities, municipalities, towns, and local boards. The mandate of these bodies to govern local affairs is primarily vested in Rural District Councils (RDCs). Scholars such as Muchadenyika and Williams (2016, p. 256) have noted that whereas rural governance is key to realising citizen rights, 'leaving no-one behind' rural development policies and achieving sustainability of rural development programmes, it has not yet received the necessary attention from the Government of Zimbabwe.

HISTORY OF RURAL AND URBAN GOVERNANCE IN ZIMBABWE

The advent of colonialism in Rhodesia (now Zimbabwe) in 1890 dismantled and attenuated African political and governmental systems and replaced them with colonial forms of governance. A dualistic model of local government was introduced with separate government structures for Europeans and Africans. The dualistic governance model applied in Southern Rhodesia, Mills (2012) argues, was the equivalence of the British policy of differentiation in South Africa. The policy of differentiation, as was with dualism, implied that there were separate governance systems for whites and blacks. Other scholars used different terms to refer to dualism with Muchadenyika and Williams (2016, p. 257) calling it the 'binary system' while Chigwata (2019, p. 12) refers to it as 'the system of separatist development of races'. In the case of institutional development and governance, colonial rule created what Matyszak (2008, p. 1) calls a 'bifurcated state' that distinguished between 'citizens' and 'subjects'. Citizenship was largely limited to the urban and European areas and enjoyed human rights, whereas subjects languished under the despotism of colonial subjugation.

It is evident that the local government system of Zimbabwe has a complex history which can broadly be categorized into two distinct phases; that is, the colonial phase and the post-independence phase. The colonial local government system was governed by a system of harsh ordinances which sought to distinguish local government for whites and blacks. According to Jonga (2014), the major forms of local government in the African areas were the Native Councils established in 1923 and the African Councils of 1957. These were preceded by native reserves created at conquest, particularly the Gwaai and Shangaani which were established through the 1895 Matebeleland Order in Council.

Adjacent to the native areas, the colonial system established Road Councils which later became Rural Councils for the white commercial farming areas in 1920. Chigwata (2019) submits that the thrust of the Road Councils was the single function of building and maintaining infrastructure in white commercial farming areas. In 1969, the Rural Councils assumed broadened responsibilities across a number of areas spanning health, social amnesties, housing, etc. As distinct white-run entities, the Rural Councils were substantially autonomous from the rest of the government apparatus and were better capitalized to provide services on a sustainable basis.

In major urban centres such as Salisbury, a number of local town management boards were created and local government legislative and policy changes were more pronounced in African than in European areas. Chatiza (2008) notes that the presence of Africans in urban areas was purely a basis for the availability of African labour for the Europeans. Resultantly, local government institutions in African areas lacked autonomy and did not pursue local interests, lacking local legitimacy and resources compared to those in European areas. There were distinct places of residence for whites and blacks; and in Salisbury (the colonial name for Harare) popular low-density areas such as Hatfield and Avondale were areas for whites whereas blacks lived in African townships such as Highfields and Mbare. Machivenyika (2014) argues that in cities, African housing was tightly controlled and restricted to those formally employed. This form of rural-urban migration control was a way of trying to manage the urban African population and the under-provision of services in African areas. Jonga (2014) further avers that both rural and urban areas were administered to the advantage of the whites while blacks were relegated to third-class citizens.

The collapse of colonialism ushered in a new dispensation in the rural and urban governance discourse. The advent of independence saw a single local government Ministry being created, the amalgamation of Rural Councils and District Councils to establish Rural District Councils through the Rural District Councils Act [Chapter 29.13], and the passing of the Urban Councils Act [Chapter 29.13]. Jonga (2014) submits that since 1980, the Rural District Councils and Urban Councils Act were amended several times to initiate efficiency and effectiveness in local governance. Key foci of the changes were varied, among them including removing racial discrimination, abolishing dual systems of development emphasizing white and black areas, deepening democracy and good governance, and aligning local government politics and policies in a way to support national strategies and visions for development.

DECENTRALIZATION AND THE CHANGING CONTEXT OF RURAL AND URBAN GOVERNANCE IN ZIMBABWE (1980–2013)

The rural and urban governance system of Zimbabwe is a product of the process of decentralization and the demands for more representative subnational governments as opposed to centralization. There is abundant literature supporting the commitment of the government of Zimbabwe to decentralization through legislative and institutional reforms. Decentralization started in 1980 with the purpose of redressing inherited colonial inequities; to improve people participation in governance and transfer powers and functions from central government to subnational levels (Chigwata, 2019; Kurebwa, 2014; Mudau and Nyane, 2022). At the same time, the government sought to reform the dualized colonial local government system. These reforms ranged from the removal of race-based restrictions, the creating of a new electoral system, and the redistribution of resources. Tanyanyiwa (2015) justifies decentralization in Zimbabwe as a reaction to the dysfunctional national government which was bureaucratic and the need for a growing commitment to a more socially just and equitable subnational government at independence.

According to Conyers (2003), the objectives and nature of decentralization in Zimbabwe have changed over time. In the 1980s, the thrust was to streamline and coordinate various agencies to accelerate local development, and hence decentralization of functions to provincial, district, and local development committees comprised of elected and appointed officials. In the early 1990s, decentralization was largely viewed as a vehicle for deepening democracy and rationalizing the public sector (Conyers, 2003; Muchadenyika and Williams, 2016). However, it is important to note that there is a gap between rhetoric and reality as little effective power was decentralized in practice for a myriad of reasons, among them lack of political will (Conyers, 2003). The situation was further compounded by the post-2000 political tensions, which resulted in a new wave of (re)centralization. The declining economic situation weakened central government's fiscal commitments to rural and urban councils leading to several unfunded mandates. An example is the national government's failure to disburse the health and education grant since 1997 to rural and urban councils.

In the facet of institutional development, the advent of independence in 1980 heralded the creation of a single local government Ministry and the amalgamation of African Councils into District Councils. At the same time the Prime Minister's Directive on Decentralization of 1984 captured the new political dispensation by establishing subdistrict organizational structures to implement decentralization. This saw the birth of Village Development Committees (VIDCOs) and Ward Development Committees (WADCOs) through which rural communities were networked into the district local governance system. Muchadenyika and Williams (2016) viewed VIDCOs and WADCOs as conduits for grassroots participation in governance which laid the basis for the coordination of government institutions and public participation in rural development. In 1985, the Provincial Councils and Administration Act Chapter 29:11 was enacted. The Act provided for the establishment of a Provincial Council (PC) for every province to spearhead and coordinate the planning and development of provinces. Adjunct to the PC was the Provincial Development Committee (PDC) to provide technical expertise to the latter. At the district level, the Rural District Development Committee (RDDC) was established to coordinate the development of the district.

The above institutional framework was supported by the 13 principles of decentralization gazetted in 1996. This created a clear intergovernmental network from the local level to the provincial level for promoting development within provinces. Nyikadzino and Nhema (2015), however, concluded that this institutional did not completely restrict central government interference and meddling with the affairs of local government as the Urban Councils Act (Chapter 29:15) and RDC Act (Chapter 29:13) subjected councils to too many central government strictures through unfettered ministerial discretion in local affairs. Chigwata (2019) concurs with this view and remarked that there is simply too much 'shall' concept in the above Acts citing over 250 instances in the RDC Act where the Minister responsible for local government can exercise control over councils. Equally, Nyikadzino and Nhema (2015) note that the relations are highly centralized and the balance of power is largely tilted in favour of the Ministry responsible for Local Government. Chigwata (2019) concludes that centralization is not peculiar to Zimbabwe alone but is operational in most African countries as central government politicians are sceptical of decentralization fearing that it represents a zero-sum game especially considering the level of political party incongruence in Zimbabwe.

Devolution and the Reconfiguration of Rural and Urban Governance

The Global Political Agreement of 2009 culminated in the promulgation of the Constitution of Zimbabwe Amendment Number 20 of 2013. The Constitution contains provisions for the devolution of power and the enshrinement of Local Government as a tier of government. Jonga (2014) submits that whereas devolution is not a new phenomenon in Zimbabwe's political organization, its incorporation in the constitution has far-reaching implications for intergovernmental reconfiguration and reorganization.

The provisions of devolution in terms of the Constitution are a culmination of struggles for governance contestations dating back to the pre-independence era and anchored on rich traditions and experiences that sought good local and national governance structures and institutions (Zinyama, 2021). This is premised on the notion that sustainable national development is necessitated by the presence of viable subnational governance institutions framed on such rich traditions and experiences. The constitutional provisions on devolution strategically derive from wider African governance goals of devolution as a governance framework. These are espoused in Articles 3 and 4 of the AU Constitutive Act of 2002, the 2005 Yaoundé Declaration, and the AU vision 2063. In particular, agenda 2063 pronounces a vision of 'an integrated and peaceful Africa driven by its citizens' lucidly anchoring continental operationalization of devolution.

Pro-devolutionist arguments both during and after the constitution-making process were that devolution promotes policy robustness and improves the overall responses of government to the needs of the people (Muchadenyika and Williams, 2016; Nyikadzino, 2015). Chigwata

(2019, p. 8) also justifies devolved subnational governments as 'laboratories for local decision-making and experimentation'. However, anti-devolution sentiments mainly streaming from the ruling Zimbabwe African National Union – Patriotic Front (ZANUPF) were that devolution will create complex governmental frameworks that are costly and fraught with duplication of services. Moyo and Ncube (2014) add that ZANUPF politicians sustained the view that devolved rural and urban governments may act as conduits of anti-state and terrorist sabotage and banditry and hence a catalyst in promoting constitutional instability. Masuku and Macheka (2020) argue that the major issues raised against devolution are that it limits the national government's oversight role over subnational government in intergovernmental relations terms and increases interregional conflict in areas such as resource allocation hence promoting separatism. Despite all the strong criticism and descending perspectives, the fact is that devolution in Zimbabwe has since 2013 become an integral part of the country's constitutional milieu.

Moyo and Ncube (2014) use deontological and consequentialist perspectives to support devolution of power to rural and urban governments in Zimbabwe. They argue that the currency and desirability for devolution are premised on consequentialist and deontological paradigms that see it as a democratic system of government which advances citizen participation in human development. These paradigms see devolved governance as a key for local democratization in Zimbabwe since it brings locally responsive governments. Despite criticism from the ruling ZANUPF that devolution may promote secessionism and separatism, a favourable opinion of devolution, as viewed by Chigwata (2019), Muchadenyika and Williams (2016) and Moyo and Ncube (2014), insists that devolution should never be confused with secessionism but is a solution to the challenges of asymmetric development usually perpetuated by centralism. From this perspective, devolution is seen as a means of delivering territorial justice. Districts that supported devolution include Chiredzi, Beitbridge, and Mangwe. Evidence shows that Chiredzi and Nyanga districts have the country's biggest and most profitable sugar estates, commercial logging forests, and huge alluvial diamond deposits but there is no diamond or sugar profit-driven socioeconomic development or public infrastructure investment in that province (Jonga, 2014; Muchadenyika and Williams, 2016).

POLITICS AND SERVICE DELIVERY DYNAMICS IN RURAL LOCAL GOVERNMENTS

As opposed to urban governance, rural local governance in Zimbabwe is yet to receive comparative research and intellectual analysis. This is despite two key factors: firstly, over 60% of the population of the country resides in rural areas and secondly most decentralization reforms in post-independence were aimed principally at transforming rural local governments where presumably the harshest forms of colonial injustices are visible. The major changes to rural local government were ushered by the policy on decentralization and development. The policy outlines decentralized planning and development structures through which the subdistrict level is connected to the district local governance framework. As such, it guides the development of grassroots participation structures such as VIDCOs and WADCOs and provides a framework for the coordination of government institutions and participation in rural development.

Kurebwa (2014) argues that the philosophy underpinning the new wave of decentralization was that it brings an essential aspect of good governance, accountability, and transparency. Both scholars and policymakers converged on the view that decentralization facilitates coordination among government agencies, in a manner that is difficult in centralized political systems where agencies operate independently, resulting in fragmented development (Chigwata, 2019; Conyers, 2003; Muchadenyika and Williams, 2016). However, the Centre for Conflict Management and Transformation (CCMT) (2014) views that decentralization of power to rural local governments is convoluted by the influence of political party affiliations. The decentralized planning and development structures were modelled on ZANUPF's local cell structures. This view is shared by Makumbe (1998) who submits that VIDCO and WADCO members were selected from among the party's local leadership. Thus, instead of being structures for robust development planning, they served a dual purpose, firstly as decentralized development organs and secondly as political mobilization for ZANUPF. Whereas during the first two decades of independence, these two roles were hardly in conflict under a one-party state, the advent of MDC ushered strong opposition to the ruling ZANUPF heightening competition for the rural vote. This led to the politicization of rural local government structures making them centres of conflict and in the process weakening their role in participatory development planning.

CCMT (2014) views rural district development committees (RDDC) as the most significant and influential among the decentralized planning and development structures in rural local governance. It is chaired by a district development coordinator (DDC) and constituted by the chairperson of committees, the chief executive officer, other council officers determined by council, senior members of the security forces, and heads of government ministries and departments in the district. The purpose of the RDDC is to prepare and implement the district development plan, which represents a consolidation of the plans of various council committees. Kurebwa (2014) analyzes the challenges of the RDDC and notes that principally, councillors as elected leaders of council hardly agree with the idea of the DDC (a civil servant) chairing a committee where political leaders are members. In the same context, empirical evidence shows that the RDDC is captured by the ruling ZANUPF and hence acts as an organ of protecting the interests of the party as opposed to promoting development with equity (Conyers, 2003; Masuku and Macheka, 2020). CCMT (2014) submits that whereas it is the responsibility of the council to approve the plan and monitor its implementation, the influence of the council in revising a plan it rejects remains unclear.

One of the major challenges in rural local governance is the existence of parallel structures with overlapping and conflicting roles, i.e. elected and traditional leadership structures (Conyers, 2003; Mudau and Nyane, 2022; Zinyama, 2021). This has resulted in wide-ranging conflicts that have stunted development in rural Zimbabwe (CCMT, 2014). The parallels and overlapping responsibilities are exacerbated by ambiguity in the legislation, which assigns the same powers and responsibilities to traditional and elected leaders' structures, hence promoting conflict between them. This makes the legislative alignment process crucial in defining the roles and responsibilities of various local governance structures.

The ambiguities in the definition of roles and responsibilities are evident in the legal assignment of land allocation authority. The Constitution provides that 'Except as provided in an Act of Parliament, traditional leaders have authority, jurisdiction and control over the Communal Land or other areas for which they have been appointed, and over persons within those Communal Lands or areas'. CCMT (2014) argues that this is a broad granting of power to traditional leaders which must be read together with other pieces of legislation. The Communal Land Act gives power for occupation and use of communal land to the RDC, though this consent should, 'where appropriate, have regard to customary law', and follow from consultation and cooperation with chiefs. In contrast, the Traditional Leaders Act, however, allocate the responsibility for allocation of communal land in accordance with the requirements of the Communal Land Act to the chiefs, and reiterates (somewhat redundantly) that land may not be allocated except in accordance with that Act.

Intergovernmental transfers are the cornerstone of subnational government financing in most developing and transitional economies. The existence of differences in resource endowment, revenue mobilization capacity, and expenditure needs among rural and urban governments leads to horizontal fiscal imbalances. Chakunda et al. (2021) submit that fiscal transfers resolve vertical fiscal imbalances, influence horizontal efficiency, and address inequality between local government units. However, the criterion for the distribution of fiscal powers and tax revenues from the central government to subnational levels is a source of severe conflict in Zimbabwe. The common centre of contestation is a methodological challenge of developing an equitable and transparent framework for a sustainable intergovernmental transfer system that will promote intergovernmental fiscal equalization. In Zimbabwe, this has been worsened by the conflicting objectives of devolution and low fiscal capacities at subnational government levels. Rural and urban governments in Zimbabwe are severely affected by a wave of recentralization wherein key sources of finance such as vehicle licensing are centralized. The expected disbursements from the Road Fund are hampered by the absence of a clear framework of allocating them leaving political elites with the discretion of determining allocations on the basis of political interests. In the same context, the intergovernmental grant in terms of section 301 is equally affected by the absence of a model to underpin the allocation, leaving it to the discretion of national political elites. The health and education grants are inconsistently disbursed leading to challenges in the provision of the service by rural local governments.

In relation to unfunded mandates, Conyers (2003) points out that the ability of RDCs to develop their districts has also been hampered by a severe reduction in their authority to collect revenue through encroachment by central government. Chigwata (2019) cites water and sewerage reticulation as examples. Before 2000, water provision was the responsibility of RDCCs and a key source of revenue. This was changed in 2001 when the government shifted that mandate to Zimbabwe National Water Authority (ZINWA) to manage water in urban and rural local authorities. Muchadenyika and Williams (2016) note that ZINWA lacked the technical resources for this new responsibility leading to the collapse of water provision in most council areas. In the same context, this deprived council of revenue. In 2009, the national government restored water to councils though local authorities are yet to gain full control. CCMT (2014) submits that conflicts over fiscal powers and revenue collection also exist in the areas of liquor licensing, collection of fines for environmental infractions, and vehicle license fees.

RAPID URBANIZATION AND SERVICE DELIVERY IN URBAN COUNCILS

Rapid urbanization represents a major demographic transformation in Africa with the continent projected to have the fastest-growing cities in the world over the next 40 years. Research and empirical evidence estimate that by 2050 Africa's urban centres will be host to over 1.5 billion people which represents 60% of the continent's projected population (Muchadenyika and Williams, 2016; OECD/SWAC, 2020). Much of this growth is occurring in small to medium-sized towns (OECD/SWAC, 2020). The urban transition in Africa offers great opportunities while equally posing significant challenges. OECD/SWAC (2020) submits that most often, urban agglomerations are developing without supportive policies and investments to meet these challenges. This makes urban planning and management key development issues. Understanding urbanization in the Zimbabwean context, its drivers, dynamics, and impact are therefore critical in the designing of targeted, inclusive, and forward-looking policies at local and national levels.

Urban governments in Zimbabwe play an important role in the delivery of fundamental public services in the context of the aforementioned global development trajectory. However, the political and socioeconomic environment presents insurmountable challenges emanating from rapid and chaotic urbanization versus the impact and frequency of natural disasters due to climate change. Zimbabwe's urban centres have experienced rapid urban sprawl into peri-urban state land and agriculture designated land. This urban sprawl is not supported by corresponding growth in urban infrastructure, such as water and sewage reticulation systems, health and education infrastructure to cater to the growing population. Rather, this has increased the risk of chronic health challenges such as cholera and typhoid outbreaks. In the same context the urban sprawl has taken up productive peri-urban agriculture land as demand for urban housing is growing.

The economic downturn, post-2000, broadly characterized by high rates of unemployment and hyper-inflation, coupled in some cases with increased service demands has contributed to a growing fiscal crisis in Zimbabwe's local government entities (Chigwata, 2019; Muchadenyika, 2017). An economic status survey conducted by the Confederation of Zimbabwe Industries (2012) revealed that at least 80% of industries in Gweru city (as an example) have closed due to acute viability challenges and an estimated 11% of those functional are operating at below 35% capacity utilization. This has affected the council in terms of both property and other taxes and has seen a number of employees being retrenched and hence compromising their ability to meet council tax obligations (Mudau and Nyane, 2022). At the same time, it has led to a surge in illegal street vending following the loss of formal jobs and livelihoods. Njaya (2016) estimates about 100 000 street vendors are operating in the CBD of Harare daily. While these statistics highlight general fiscal stress across urban councils, notable symptoms have been a decrease in revenues, increased service demands, and general budgetary constraints (Nyikadzino, 2015). Income from service charges and property taxes has decreased significantly in many cases due in part to the increase in unemployment, the informalization of the economy, and the decrease in consumer purchasing power.

Additionally, increased numbers of foreclosures contributed to a decrease in the assessed value of properties, which has significantly reduced property tax collections. Coupled together, these factors have forced urban councils to increase taxes, decrease expenditures, or in some cases both increase taxes and decrease spending (Muchadenyika and Williams, 2016; OECD/SWAC, 2020). With limited revenue options and the inability to deficit spend, this crisis has significantly impacted and crippled council operations. These fiscal constraints, exacerbated by the decreases in state funding and primary revenue sources (property tax and services charges), and increases in operational costs in particular labour costs and service expenditures, have created enormous challenges for urban councils. UNHABITAT (2015) concurs with the above argument and added that currently, many local governments in developing countries face the near-impossible task of funding the infrastructure and services required to meet the basic needs of growing urban populations, while forward-looking capital investments are not possible for financial reasons.

In addition to the above, the budgets of urban councils in Zimbabwe are directly and indirectly affected by fiscal issues at the central government level. More specifically, as budget cuts have occurred in critical areas such as the health grant and health expenditures for local government, the authority to review health fees in line with prevailing economic trends is censored by the national government. This funding stream has historically provided support for affordable health services and hence the general sustenance of health service delivery in the absence of the health grant is under threat of complete collapse. This is a classic case of an unfunded mandate.

In both rural and urban local governments, local financial management frequently suffers from lacking technological infrastructure and capacity, and opportunities for revenue generation are often restricted by inadequate regulatory frameworks and disadvantageous political structures (Chigwata, 2019). For example, due to chaotic and unregulated peri-urban housing development, over two-thirds of the new settlements in Chitungwiza are consuming council services while they are not on the billing list (Muchadenyika and Williams, 2016). Lagging public-sector spending takes a toll on urban efficiency and local economic activity, creating a vicious cycle of budgetary shortfalls, choking urban conditions, and economic stagnation. However, strategic governance and financing systems including e-government can provide hope for the struggling councils. Masuku and Macheka (2020) stress that there are opportunities for matching local needs with institutional frameworks and revenue-generation tools. Appropriate financial management can tap into strategies that improve efficiency of revenue collection, win public support, capitalize on urban economies of scale, curb land speculation and sprawl, incentivize economic activity, and improve urban affordability for the poor. The resulting budgetary improvements can allow councils to make strategic investments, stimulating a virtuous cycle of growth, revenue generation, and prosperity.

While the municipal financial discourse is fundamental to local government service delivery in Zimbabwe, it is also vital to examine the political economy issues of subnational governments. These issues are critical to understanding the consistent refusal of the central government to decentralize significant tax revenues, as well as the common refusal of local authorities to adequately use the tax revenue authority they are granted (Chigwata, 2019; Jonga, 2014). Local authorities need the capacity and political will to implement reforms. Additionally, they should generate political support among urban constituents to introduce the necessary legal and institutional changes with the aim of generating increased revenue through greater tax rates, improved tax collection, and reduced tax evasion. Moreover, central governments should offer municipal authorities more financial autonomy to restructure their tax bases and greater jurisdiction over revenue collection.

PUBLIC PARTICIPATION IN RURAL AND URBAN GOVERNANCE PROCESSES

The movement for public participation towards greater transparency, accountability, equity, and inclusivity in public service delivery in general and local governance in particular has been gaining traction in recent years. International financial institutions, credit rating agencies, regional economic blocs, and civil society organizations have all taken up the cause on strengthening the case for public participation as a key governance issue and intrinsic public good (Nyama and Mukwada, 2022). For ZIMCODD (2019), participatory governance is emerging as an innovative local governance practice with a high proclivity of unlocking citizen potential to contribute meaningfully to governance issues as well as promote principles of good governance. Citizen participation in local governance is thus largely viewed as a hallmark of democracy and good governance.

Fundamentally, the promulgation of the Constitution of Zimbabwe of 2013 and the inclusion of devolution ushered in a new dispensation that enshrined citizen participation as both a constitutional principle and a yardstick of democratic governance. From a constitutional standpoint, the concept of participation is related to the rights of citizenship and to democratic governance. Through devolution, the Constitution has, in principle, handed down executive powers to rural and urban governments, thereby bringing decision-making processes to the doorstep of the grassroots people. In practice, however, Zimbabwe has continued the trajectory of centralization. Whereas the Constitution of Zimbabwe entrenches public participation, studies conducted by Chikerema (2013) and Mapfumo (2019) show that public participation in the local government process has contextual, demographic, political, and administrative underpinnings. Factors such as cultural norms, class, gender, and education levels influence levels of public participation. Muchadenyika and Williams (2016) submit that linking citizen participation to the state at the local or grassroots level raises fundamental and normative questions about the nature of democracy and about the skills and strategies for achieving it.

Legal and Institutional Frameworks for Citizen Participation in Rural and Urban Governance

Contestations over the utility of legislative frameworks in public participation are a dominating subject in governance and public management discourses. Over the past three decades, countries have developed legislation and policies that entrench opportunities for citizen participation in governance. Much of this has taken the form of constitution-making and decentralization processes, often against a backdrop of transition from authoritarian to democratic governance regimes. An argument advanced by Muchadenyika and Williams (2016) indicates that effective legal frameworks contribute to promoting public participation in local governance, though they are an insufficient condition to ensure effective participation. This depends on contextual factors and the extent to which the legal framework attempts to enhance representative democracy with participatory measures.

The right to participate at local level is guaranteed in the Constitution of Zimbabwe. The Constitution expresses the people's commitment to building a just, democratic, and prosperous nation founded on the values and principles of constitutional supremacy, the rule of law, fundamental human rights and freedoms, equality, and good governance. The power to govern by any tier of government is derived from the people of Zimbabwe, an indication that they should be active participants in governance and development issues in their jurisdiction (Muchadenyika and Williams, 2016; Nyama and Mukwada, 2022). The Bill of Rights contained in Chapter 4 guarantees a number of justiciable rights. Madzivanyika (2014) argues that citizens have inalienable rights (freedom of expression, access to information, and right to be heard among others) which only a well-defined citizen participation agenda can satisfy.

More specifically, the supreme law of the land confers powers to the citizens of Zimbabwe, for which citizen participation is the only conduit to enjoying such powers.

As earlier mentioned, Chapter 14 of the Constitution contains provisions for the devolution of power to subnational government bodies. Two key objectives of devolution of governmental powers as stated in the constitution are: to give powers of local governance to the people and enhance their participation in the exercise of the powers of the state and in making decisions affecting them; to promote democratic, accountable, and transparent government. Madzivanyika (2014) argues that the realization of these objectives of devolution is hinged on effective public participation in the design and implementation of local government policies. For such participation to be effective, there is a need for unhindered public access to relevant information which is required in the interest of public accountability including any information held by local government institutions (Nyama and Mukwada, 2022). Madzivanyika (2014) states that if local government bodies decline to provide requested information, citizens have the right to demand such information through litigation. This, to Chikerema (2013) and Nyikadzino (2015), entails that where local government derogates from its obligation to provide information on request, any such person whose legitimate right and/or expectations are adversely affected by such derogation has the right to be given promptly and in writing the reasons for the conduct and can also approach the courts for redress. This is designed to impose a mandatory function on public bodies (including local government authorities) to afford citizens the right to information under their care.

From a service demand viewpoint, accountability and transparency issues are major drivers of stakeholders' involvement. Disappointingly though, the functionality of local government institutions has been hampered by citizens who lack a keen interest in matters of local development. The 2021 Zimbabwe Open Budget Survey by ZIMCODD for instance shows weak public participation in local government budgeting processes. The survey results for the budgeting year 2021 show that out of the 3500 survey respondents drawn from 10 councils, 31.73% (18.1% male and 13.63% female) participated in the local government budgeting respectively while 68.27% (35% female and 33.27%) did not participate. Many residents have tended to withhold payment for consumed council services, making it difficult for the latter to offer meaningful services. The absence of critical and elaborate interface platforms between citizens and their local authorities has also forced this rethink on remodelling the design of the approach to citizen participation. Where some local authorities have pioneered platforms for engagement in different media, it would also appear that usage is still low, presumably as a result of non-participation of citizens in their development.

Platforms and Mechanisms for Public Participation in Local Governance in Zimbabwe

Studies have shown that there are several platforms and mechanisms to facilitate public participation in local governance in Zimbabwe. These range from WADCO meetings, budget consultation and strategic planning forums, community feedback meetings, and policy dialogue platforms (Chikerema, 2013; Munyede and Machengete, 2020). Despite the existence of these platforms, the biggest challenge identified by Munyede and Machengete (2020) is the absence of a standard framework for citizen participation. This is left to the innovative capability of individual councils. In addition, there are no standard indicators which can be used to track how citizen participation would have performed. It is also important to note that most of the platforms are not in the legislation and hence ad hoc leaving local authorities with the discretion to convene them or not. For the purposes of this chapter VIDCOs and WADCOs and budget consultation forums are discussed.

VIDCOs and WADCOs

The lowest formal local government structures in Zimbabwe are VIDCOs and WADCOs. They are most defined in rural local governance and are established through the RDC Act. However, given their utility as platforms of engagement with citizens, they are now present in urban areas though not provided for in the Urban Councils Act. In terms of section 59 of the RDC Act, the WADCO shall consist of the councillor for the ward, who shall be the chairman of the committee; and the chairman and secretary of every VIDCO and neighbourhood development committee (NDCO) in the ward. A WADCO shall, on or before the 31st of March in each year, prepare and submit a ward development plan to the RDDC of the council area. As viewed by Muchadenyika and Williams (2016), VIDCOs and WADCOs are structures for decentralized planning and development and they play a significant role in coming up with development plans. However, practice has shown less robustness in the processes of VIDCOs and WADCOs as the structures are captured by political parties and hence acting as centres for party activism as opposed to community-wide development planning (Mudau and Nyane, 2022; Zinyama, 2021). Manhokwe (2010) gave a salutary remark pointing out that in practice WADCO plans are seldom a true reflection of the views of the communities. Very often they are dominated by other sources of planning information and in this case, central government field departments. The circumstances above necessitate looking at the general limits of decentralization to find ways to curb them and promote genuine public participation.

Chikerema (2013) concurs with the above view and adds that WADCOs in urban areas are extensions of political party activism as opposed to platforms for robust policy engagement with residents. Madzivanyika (2014) argues that, as a structure, the WADCO is an indispensable tool for citizen participation which, in terms of practice, has been crippled by several constraints and reduced to a redundant platform. Resultantly they abandon their functions and act as the nucleus for political activism. As advanced by Makumbe (1998), VIDCOs and WADCOs in rural areas were modelled along ZANUPF lines and thus could not perform their roles in terms of the Act. In their analysis, Munyede and Machengete (2020) argue that VIDCOs and WADCOs are an effective way of removing development deadlock caused by bureaucratic and top-down development practices as well as strengthening democratic social responsibility by giving voice to the poor and improving the relationship between a council and communities to build a responsible and accountable government. It should be involved in matters such as the council performance management, the annual budget, council projects, and other key activities. Moreover, it can support the councillor in dispute resolution and can identify and initiate projects to improve the lives of people in the ward. This chapter submits that, if properly modelled, VIDCOs and WADCOs present the only meaningful and viable opportunity for organized citizen participation in devolution. Not only do they facilitate participation but they promote inclusion. This is because of the multiplicity of social groups and sectors represented in the committee.

Budget consultations and strategic planning platforms

Local government budgeting and strategic planning processes are governed by a plethora of legislation which includes the Constitution, the Urban Councils Act, the Rural District Councils Act, the Public Finance Management Act and the Regional, Town, and Country

Planning Act. Local government budgets are fundamental macroeconomic and fiscal tools which require active and productive participation of citizens whose political, social, and economic lives are determined by the budget. Governance decisions on how resources are mobilized and utilized affect each and every citizen including their livelihoods. Therefore, public participation empowers citizens to contribute actively to public decisions and there is a need for authorities to elicit genuine public engagement to ensure that budgets are implemented in line with the aspirations of citizens. However, despite the existence of progressive legal frameworks which set out the basic budget processes which need to be followed, citizen participation in local budget processes is relatively low.

Muchadenyika and Williams (2016) submit that participation in strategic planning and budget consultation is much weaker in rural areas as compared to urban areas. This emanates from a multiplicity of factors which include low literacy levels and weak transport and communication networks, and low resources for RDCs to conduct robust consultations in the wards. Results from ZIMCODD (2021) surveys show that of the 3500 participants in the survey 31.73% (18.1% male and 13.63% female) participated in the 2021 local government budget consultation meetings while 68.27% (35% female and 33.27%) did not participate in the budget-making process. There are many reasons for non-participation. The survey identified lack of sufficient notice of the meetings, use of a very technical budget and financial language and the failure by authorities to produce citizen versions of the budget documents, use of venues that are not disability-friendly, limited opportunities to make contributions, and political interference as the major challenges.

According to ZIMCODD (2019), budgeting is a very complex process which is beyond the comprehension of the majority of citizens such that the bulk of the budgeting process remains a preserve of the few at the expense of the people who bear the brunt of those decisions. For Munyede and Machengete (2020) apathy in citizen participation in budget processes is driven by a number of factors ranging from lack of interest and confidence in the public finance management system for both national and local government, a belief that consultation does not proffer genuine engagement to influence the budget, inconvenient times and venues to allow for the participation of people living with disabilities.

ROLE OF CIVIL SOCIETY AND OTHER NON-STATE ACTORS IN RURAL AND URBAN GOVERNANCE IN ZIMBABWE

Masunungure (2014) argues that historically, and in contemporary development discourse, sustainable democracy can hardly be developed or crafted organically without a vibrant civil society. It is hardly disputable that civil society has emerged as a widely discussed facet of democracy in contemporary development. It is also celebrated as the 'missing middle' in democratic consolidation and transformation processes. Rifkin and Edwards (1998, p. 2) refer to civil society as 'our last, best hope'. It is indeed an essential though not sufficient condition for democratic transition and consolidation. However, Walzer (1992, p. 92) talks of the 'paradox of the civil society' given the contestation on the role of civil society from the views of the state on one end and the citizens on the other end. This contestation prompted Masunungure (2004) to argue that the Zimbabwe government is still mired in a distorted but politically convenient view of non-governmental organizations as 'anti-governmental organizations'. This explains the current Private and Voluntary Organisations bill which is largely viewed as a way of clamping the role of civil society organisations as a watchdog against state excess.

Muchadenyika and Williams (2016) maintain that the role of civic society organizations in engendering social accountability, transparency, and integrity in Zimbabwe is well documented and appreciated. As public watchdogs on good governance, their interaction with rural and urban councils has left landmarks and permanent footprints and has led to increased demand for accountability especially relating to budgetary oversight by both sets of institutions and that such interaction will forever strengthen a country's governance framework and the effectiveness and efficiency of its anti-poverty programmes. Related studies (Mapfumo, 2019; Nyama and Mukwada, 2022) have shown that most civil society organizations have demonstrated their ability to foster people-centred development through promoting ownership, inclusivity, and participation. Chigwata (2019) added that these organizations are engaged in a wide range of sector analysis and policy dialogue, independent research, and share valuable information on sustainable governance and economic development. For Muchadenyika and Williams (2016), civil society organisations involved in advocacy for economic and social justice have mobilized citizens in championing the cause for good and accountable governance. Social movements such as ZIMCODD and others have attempted to mobilize citizens to claim their rights and pressure for accountability and social justice in rural and urban councils. Mapfumo (2019) also identified a number of roles of CS in promoting citizen participation and sustainable local governance and these include advocacy and lobbying for enhancing public accountability and transparency and research as the basis for evidence-based advocacy.

An analysis of the findings of the 2019 survey by ZIMCODD (2019) shows that civil society has a role in improving the accountability of public service providers. However, the study shows that about 35% of civil society organizations, in particular resident's associations (RAs) are not institutionalized due to limited financial resources. As such their efforts to hold the duty bearers accountable remain minimal as they do not have significant contribution to the local authority governance processes. Whilst RAs have the potential to be a viable voice of the voiceless of the urban citizenry, the survey results indicated that there is often a discord in the policy direction of RAs in areas where there is more than one RA due to competition for donor funding. ZIMCODD (2019) reveals that there is less policy process integration among the wider civil society spectrum and competition among these institutions is often rife. This weakens their capacity to leverage on collective potential in advocating for a better local government system.

Adjunct to the aforementioned views, a consolidation of studies on public participation in local government budgeting and financial management involving ten major urban areas by Kademaunga and Saki (2020), Muchadenyika (2017), and ZIMCODD (2019) shows that the available spaces for public participation in budgeting do not give local citizens a genuine opportunity to productively input to the budget. The budget participation meetings are simply meant to legitimize the budget while disguised as a participatory process yet councils would have already drafted the budget. We Pay You Deliver Consortium (2018) argues that participation in the local budget process is also dependent on the citizens' knowledge of their ability to influence the process. Citizens who believe that their views would be taken into account are more likely to participate compared to those that do not. Results of the 2019 OBS presented by ZIMCODD (2019) show that of the 3500 respondents, the majority of the respondents (66.1%) do not believe that their contributions during the pre-budget consultations sessions will be adopted by the local government in the consolidation of the final budget and hence making public consultations an exercise in futility. The same survey shows that about 71% of young females aged between 18 to 35 years of age don't believe that their views matter in the budget-making process.

THE CONTEXT, DYNAMICS, AND INFLUENCE OF IGR ON RURAL AND URBAN GOVERNANCE

Intergovernmental relations (IGR) are indispensable to all political systems with a multilevel form of government. This arises from 'the necessity of governmental interaction to address the disputes, interdependencies and spill-over effects resulting from constitutional mandate overlaps', as well as the 'need to confront policy problems that defy competence divisions' (McEwen, 2015, p. 323). Nyikadzino (2015) submits that effective IGR is motivated by a variety of factors ranging from constitutional ambiguities, fiscal limitations, spillovers in public policy implementation, infrastructure management, and the sharing of other scarce resources. Added to this, Muchadenyika and Williams (2016) observe that partisan competition for political power and control and competing perspectives on approaches to achieve national and regional goals affect the modalities of interaction between intergovernmental partners. Intergovernmental collaboration gives public institutions the latitude to build relationships that help influence administrative policies. A viable IGR system has a competitive advantage in easing the tensions and complexities related to the execution of governmental activities.

Contrary to the above views, Zimbabwe faces a plethora of IGR problems with far-reaching implications on the policy and administrative processes of rural and urban councils. These range from political parties' incongruence, unfunded mandates, the problem of concurrency, and overlapping authority among others (Machivenyika, 2014; Moyo and Ncube, 2014). These problems have often weighed heavily on the capacity of local government institutions to deliver on their mandates. Thus, rural and urban governments, in fulfilling their communities' desire for voice and autonomy, have found themselves in confrontation with central government. The latter is often ambivalent as to whether the former present an opportunity or threat.

Chakunda et al. (2021) seem to concur with the above argument and added that functionally, the central government should provide a facilitative framework for subnational government to operate. In practice, however, the centre has played manipulative, controlling, and directive roles especially after the advent of the Movement for Democratic Change (MDC). According to Muchadenyika and Williams (2016), from 2000 the MDC, a powerful opposition political party to ZANUPF, dominated urban councils in elections and gained seats in RDCs as well. In 2008, MDC won almost half of the RDCs. Moyo and Ncube (2014) point out that the MDC's local government electoral dominance, especially in the major urban councils, gave rise to the operative intergovernmental political dynamics in Zimbabwe. As the ruling party, ZANUPF controls the Ministry of Local Government and levers of local power at the national level while MDC controls most of the councils. This level of political party incongruence has culminated into massive political conflict, including controversial suspension and dismissal of MDC mayors by the Minister of Local Government, claiming to be acting in the interest of effective administration.

Codification of IGR by Way of Legislation

The majority of modern Constitutions contain provisions governing IGR. Additionally, there are legislative instruments detailing the nature of this relationship such, as the

Intergovernmental Relations Framework Act (No 13 of 2005) and the Division of Revenue Act (No 3 of 2016). On the contrary, while the Constitution of Zimbabwe section 265 (3) provides for legal mechanisms and procedures to facilitate coordination between central government and subnational governments, it appears there is a lack of political will to create such legislation since the promulgation of the Constitution (Chigwata, 2019). This has compromised cooperative governance as central government seems to dominate subnational governance and hence negatively compromising rural and urban governance. Chakunda et al. (2021) argue that the absence of an Act of parliament to regulate IGR has created a legislative vacuum in synchronizing government and promoting cooperation among the three tiers of government. Thus, the constitutional and legislative guarantees for IGR in Zimbabwe are weak, leaving subnational policymaking susceptible to shifts in the allocation of power as it gives central government too much discretionary power over subnational government's policymaking domain. Machivenyika (2014) argues that due to the concurrency in functions, there tends to be considerable overlapping of roles and responsibilities of various levels of government which create a fertile terrain for IGR contestation and disputes. Codification of IGR therefore provides a systemic framework for how governance is managed in a decentralized system. Zinyama (2021) sees the failure to codify IGR as a strategy by the national government to promote ad hoc processes that limits the power of local governments in intergovernmental bargaining while strengthening the national political elites to influence their interests in local government institutions.

Fiscal IGR

Fiscal IGR is at the heart of the success of decentralized activities and this has seriously hampered the decentralization efforts of Zimbabwe through unfunded mandates. The tendency has been to decentralize functions to rural and urban councils without decentralizing requisite financial powers or resources to finance the functions. For example, development planning was decentralized in the 1980s, but the allocation of development funds remained centralized. Consequently, the main impact of decentralization is frustration at a subnational level. At the same time, while there are notable problems in relation to the consistent disbursement of fiscal resources from the central government, a study conducted by Conyers (2003) in Binga RDC concluded that certain fundamental problems within the councils compromised the capacity for proper utilization of the resources and these include, lack of planning and management skills, political conflicts among councillors and officials, and alleged abuses of power. Section 301 of the Constitution provides for 5% of all revenues collected by the national treasury to be decentralized to rural and urban governments. However, an Act of Parliament for the implementation of this clause as required by the Constitution is yet to be created. Resultantly, national government has retained discretion over the allocation. The allocation of the 5% is thus influenced by political interests with those rural and urban councils aligned to the ruling ZANUPF being allocated more funds.

Political Parties' Incongruence and IGR

One notable problem of IGR in Zimbabwe is political parties' incongruence. This chapter submits that in the context of different political parties in power at different levels of government in Zimbabwe, there is likely to be pressure on the constitutional, institutional, and financial arrangements for devolution to subnational tiers. Whereas the political system of Zimbabwe from 1980 was largely congruent, the advent of MDC has generated a serious margin of incongruence. In successive elections since 2000, ZANUPF has retained control of the national government with MDC gaining seats and controlling local governments. Muchadenyika and Williams (2016) argue that political parties' incongruence has worsened programmatic differences between levels of government leading to complications in the intergovernmental coordination of legislative and policy outcomes necessitated by overlapping competencies and spillover effects.

LOCAL GOVERNANCE: QUO VADIS?

What is the future of local governance on the African continent? To answer this question is no easy feat since the spectrum of change and the multitude of variables that should be considered are rather overwhelming. Based on trend extrapolation it is, however, possible to pinpoint key trends that will shape municipal priorities and strategies in the near future. Some of these trends include:

- SMART cities: The rise of technology is transforming the way cities are designed and managed. SMART cities are cities that use technology and data to improve the quality of life for their citizens, enhance sustainability, and increase efficiency in urban services. They leverage innovative technologies such as the Internet of Things (IoT), big data analytics, artificial intelligence (AI), and machine learning to gather and analyze vast amounts of information from various sources, such as sensors, social media, and mobile devices. SMART cities aim to improve the management of transportation, energy, water, waste, public safety, and other critical urban services, making them more responsive and effective.
- Digital governance: Closely related to the movement towards smarter cities is the increasing use of digital platforms and tools, local governments must be able to provide reliable and secure digital services to their citizens. This includes developing robust cybersecurity strategies, protecting citizens' privacy, and ensuring accessibility for all citizens. African cities should use technology to reduce traffic congestion, optimize energy consumption, provide better public transportation, enhance public safety and security, and promote citizen engagement and participation.
- Rapid urbanization: The world is becoming more urbanized, and local governments must respond to this trend by developing sustainable urban planning strategies. This includes investing in more sustainable public service delivery systems such as transport, energy, housing, water provisioning, and access to green spaces.
- Climate change: Local government plays a crucial role in addressing climate change, as cities and municipalities are responsible for a significant share of greenhouse gas emissions. At the same time, they are also on the front lines of climate impacts, such as sea-level rise, extreme weather events, and heatwaves. Therefore, local governments must take action to reduce emissions and build resilience to the impacts of climate change. Local governments can build resilience to the impacts of climate change, such as by developing emergency response plans, investing in infrastructure that can withstand extreme weather events, and protecting vulnerable populations from heatwaves and other impacts.

- Service delivery capacity: As the demand for city services grows, local governments must find ways to improve service delivery capacity. This may involve investing in new technologies, hiring more staff, or partnering with other organizations to provide services more efficiently.
- Housing: The affordable housing crisis is a major challenge for local governments. They must find ways to increase the supply of affordable housing, while also addressing issues such as gentrification, homelessness, and displacement.
- Cleaner and more sustainable energy: Climate change is a major concern, and local governments must play a role in reducing greenhouse gas emissions. This includes promoting the use of renewable energy, investing in energy-efficient buildings, and encouraging sustainable transportation options.
- Local economic development: Cities should serve as economic growth hubs and promote the local economy through investment, business development, and the facilitation of entrepreneurship. Local economic development refers to the efforts made by local government, businesses, and community organizations to improve the economic well-being of a particular geographic area. The goal of local economic development is to create jobs, increase economic opportunities, and promote economic growth while enhancing the overall quality of life in the community.

To respond to these trends, local governments must take a proactive approach that involves collaborating with stakeholders, investing in technology and infrastructure, and engaging with citizens to ensure their needs are being met. This may involve developing new policies and regulations, creating partnerships with other organizations, and engaging in community outreach and education. Ultimately, local governments must be agile and adaptable in order to meet the challenges and opportunities of the future. This requires overall resilience. Urban resilience is becoming increasingly important for local governments to adapt to the changing trends they face. Resilience is the ability of a city to withstand and recover from shocks and stresses, whether they are natural disasters, economic downturns, or social upheavals. To build resilience, local governments can take a number of actions, such as:

- Developing comprehensive resilience strategies: This involves identifying the key risks and vulnerabilities of cities and developing intervention plans to address them. This may involve investing in infrastructure, improving emergency response capabilities, and promoting social cohesion.
- Building partnerships and networks: Resilience requires collaboration and partnership-building across government agencies, the private sector, and community-based organizations. Local governments can build relationships with these stakeholders to share information, resources, and expertise.
- Investing in technology and innovation: Innovative technologies can help local governments to identify and respond to risks and to improve the efficiency and effectiveness of city services. For example, data analytics can help to identify areas of high risk for natural disasters, while smart technologies can improve energy efficiency and reduce greenhouse gas emissions.
- Prioritising social equity: Resilience planning should also prioritize social equity, ensuring that vulnerable populations are not left behind. This may involve investing in affordable housing, improving access to healthcare and social services, and promoting community engagement.

Building urban resilience requires a long-term, integrated approach that involves multiple stakeholders and considers a range of factors, such as the environment, the economy, and social equity. By prioritizing resilience, local governments can create more sustainable, equitable, and liveable cities that can adapt to changing trends and challenges.

CONCLUSION

The chapter explored the context and dynamics of rural and urban governance in Zimbabwe and concludes that while local-level governments are supported by constitutional principles of devolution, there is extensive evidence of centralization. Central government dominance is manifested in various forms including interfering with rural and urban governance structures and making policy directives that weaken the policy and administrative capacity of local-level institutions. This is exacerbated by the failure of central government to grant local governments sufficient taxing powers to generate revenue and deliver services on a sustainable basis. In addition, key governance institutions and structures are captured by political parties and hence compromising their capacity for robust participatory planning and development. Compressed local economies culminating in weak local fiscal capacity weaken local institutions' ability to deliver services and the symptoms are evident in uncollected refuse, water delivery constraints, poor road networks, and street lighting among others.

Key issues explored include the transformation of rural and urban governance, decentralization in post-independence Zimbabwe, legal and institutional frameworks for local governance, intergovernmental relations, and public participation in governance processes. Fundamentally, post-independence Zimbabwe introduced a myriad of policy reforms to transform the system of rural and urban governance. However, despite this plethora of reforms widely meant to dismantle historical colonial injustices, the post-independent government did not depose its excessive control on subnational government structures. The chapter advances the argument that sustainable rural and urban governance is measured and benchmarked by the capacity of local government structures to provide an integrated development approach to social and economic development issues and to supply essential services congruent with the needs and desires of the local communities.

REFERENCES

Centre for Conflict Management and Transformation (CCMT). (2014), 'Roles and Responsibilities in Rural Local Governance in Zimbabwe: Parallels, Overlaps and Conflict', accessed 15 February 2023 at http://www.ccmt.co.zw/publications.
Chakunda, V., C. Dzingirai and A.F. Chikerema (2021), 'Modelling Intergovernmental Fiscal Equalisation in Zimbabwe: Towards Resolving Vertical and Horizontal Fiscal Imbalances', *Public Finance Quarterly*, **66** (4), 535–550.
Chatiza, K. (2008), *Opportunities and Challenges in Institutionalizing Participatory Development: The Case of Rural Zimbabwe*, Swansea: Swansea University Press.
Chigwata, C. (2019), *Devolution demystified: Emerging debates and prospects for devolution in Zimbabwe: A discussion paper*, accessed 12 December 2022 at https://zimlii.org/.
Chikerema, A.F (2013), 'Citizen Participation and Local Democracy in Zimbabwean Local Government System', *IOSR Journal of Humanities and Social Science*, **13** (2), 87–90, doi.org/10.9790/0837-13 28790.

Conyers, D. (2003), 'Decentralisation in Zimbabwe: A Local Perspective', *Public Administration and Development*, 23 (2003), 115–124, doi.org/10.1002/pad.265.

Jonga, W. (2014), 'Local Government System in Zimbabwe and Associated Challenges: Synthesis and Antithesis', *Archives of Business Research*, **2** (1), 75–98, doi.org/10.14738/abr.21.89.

Kademaunga, M. and O. Saki (2020), 'Reclaiming Civil Society Legitimacy in Zimbabwe', in Youngs, R. (ed.), *Coronavirus as a Catalyst for Global Civil Society*, Washington, DC: Carnegie Endowment for International Peace, pp. 53–58.

Kurebwa, J. (2014), 'A Review of Rural Local Government System in Zimbabwe from 1980–2014', *IOSR Journal of Humanities and Social Science*, **20** (2), 94–108, doi.org/10.9790/0837-202594108.

Machivenyika, D. (2014), 'The Inevitable: Devolution in Zimbabwe – From Constitution-Making to the Future', in De Visser, J.S. (ed.), *Constitution-Building in Africa*, Cape Town: Nomos and Community Law Centre, pp. 104–134.

Madzivanyika, L. (2014), 'Local Government, Participatory Processes and Citizen Engagement', GIZ Paper, accessed 4 September 2023 at https://www.academia.edu/11043641/Local_gov ernment_Participatory_Processes_and_Citizen_Engagement.

Makumbe, J. (1998), *Democracy and Development in Zimbabwe: Constraints of Decentralisation*, Harare: SAPES Books.

Manhokwe, L. (2010), 'Top Down or Bottom Up? District Development Planning in Mudzi District, Zimbabwe', *Local and Regional Development*, accessed 15 August 2023 at http://hdl.handle.net /2105/11138.

Mapfumo, L. (2019), *Public Participation and Collaborative Governance in Zimbabwean Flea Markets: A Case Study of the City of Harare*. A thesis submitted in fulfilment of the requirements for the Degree of Doctor in Administration, University of Kwazulu-Natal, accessed 30 August 2022 from https://ukzn-dspace.ukzn.ac.za/.

Masuku, S. and T. Macheka (2020), 'Policymaking and Governance Structures in Zimbabwe: Examining their Efficacy as a Conduit to Equitable Participation (Inclusion) and Social Justice for Rural Youths', *Cogent Social Sciences*, **7** (1), a1855742, doi.org/10.1080/23311886.2020.1855742.

Masunungure, V.E. (2014), *The Changing Role of Civil Society in Zimbabwe's Democratic Processes: 2014 and Beyond*, accessed 11 January 2023 from https://www.afrobarometer.org/.

McEwen, N.P. (2015), *Intergovernmental and Parliamentary Scrutiny: A Comparative Overview*. Report prepared for the Devolution (Further Powers) Committee, Harare: Centre on Constitutiuonal Change.

Mills, G. (2012), 'Backwards to Beit Bridge? A Strategy to Revive Zimbabwe's Industry', Discussion Paper 7/2012, Johannesburg: Brenthurst Foundation.

Moyo, P. and C. Ncube (2014), 'Devolution of Power in Zimbabwe's New Constitutional Order: Opportunities and Potential Constraints', *Law, Democracy and Development*, **18**, 289–304. doi.org /10.4314/ldd.v18i1.14.

Muchadenyika, D. and J.J. Williams (2016), 'Social Change: Urban Governance and Urbanisation in Zimbabwe', *Urban Forum*, 27, 253–274, doi.org./10.1007/s12132-016-9278-8.

Mudau, P. and H.A. Nyane (2022), 'A Critical Analysis of Zimbabwe's Non-implementation of Constitutional Injunctions on Devolution', *Southern African Public Law*, 2022, doi.org/10.25159 /2522-6800/9584.

Munyede, P. and V.P. Machengete (2020), 'Rethinking Citizen Participation and Local Governance in Post Corona Virus Pandemic Era in Zimbabwe', *Transatlantic Journal of Multidisciplinary Research*, **2** (1), 1–16, doi.org/10.5281/zenodo.3934888.

Njaya, T. (2016), 'An Evaluation of Income Disparities between Male and Female Street Vendors of Harare in Zimbabwe', *Journal of Studies in Social Sciences and Humanities*, **2** (3) 106–114.

Nyama, V. and G. Mukwada (2022), 'Factors Affecting Citizen Participation in Local Development Planning in Murewa District, Zimbabwe', *Journal of Asian and African Studies*, 2022, doi.org/10 .1177/00219096211069643.

Nyikadzino, T.A. (2015), 'The Implications of Centre-local Relations on Service Delivery in Local Authorities in Zimbabwe: The Case of Chitungwiza', *Journal of Public Administration and Governance*, **5** (2), 149–168, doi.org/10.5296/ jpag.v5i2.7751.

Nyikadzino, T. and A.G. Nhema (2015), 'The Implications of Centre-local Relations on Service Delivery in Local Authorities in Zimbabwe: The Case of Chitungwiza', *Journal of Public Administration and Governance*, **5** (2), 149–168, doi.org/10.5296/jpag.v5i2.7751.

OECD/SWAC. (2020), 'Africa's Urbanisation Dynamics 2020: Africapolis, Mapping a New Urban Geography', in *West African Studies*, Paris: OECD Publishing.

Republic of Zimbabwe. (2012), *Constitution of the Republic of Zimbabwe*, Amendment Number 20, Harare: Government Printers.

UN-HABITAT (2015), 'Urbanization in Zimbabwe', accessed 15 August 2023 at https://unhabitat.org /zimbabwe.

Walzer, M. (1992), 'The Civil Society Argument', in Mouffe, C. (ed.), *Dimensions of Radical Democracy: Pluralism, Citizenship, Community*, London: Verso, pp. 89–107.

Zimbabwe Coalition on Debt and Development (ZIMCODD) (2019), 'ZIMCODD's 2019 National Budget Analysis', accessed 15 August 2023 at https://zimcodd.org/sdm_downloads/zimcodds-2019 -national-budget-analysis/.

Zimbabwe Coalition on Debt and Development (ZIMCODD) (2021), '2021 National Budget Analysis', accessed 15 August 2023 at https://www.facebook.com/zimcodd/videos/2021-national-budget -analysis/234226754710082/.

Zinyama, T. (2021), 'Local Government, Decentralisation, Devolution, and Service Delivery in Zimbabwe', in Khosrow-Pour, M. (ed.), *Encyclopaedia of Information Science and Technology*, 5th ed., London: IGI Global, pp. 1597–1611, doi.org/10.4018/978-1-7998-3479-3.ch109.

12. Ethical governance in Africa: the case of Nigeria

Chinyeaka J. Igbokwe-Ibeto

INTRODUCTION

It is generally accepted that unethical governance is an evil wind that affects everyone and retards societal progress and national development (Igbokwe-Ibeto and Okoye, 2014). The issue of ethical governance in Africa has been a high-priority subject for governance researchers and practitioners alike. Unethical governance has arrested national development in Africa. Indeed, unethical governance has become a crime that has made victims of everyone. While unethical governance is not a recent phenomenon, in contemporary Africa it has grown out of proportion to the extent that it has hampered socioeconomic and political development on the continent (Igbokwe-Ibeto and Okoye, 2014; Igbokwe-Ibeto and Osakede, 2019). It is therefore understandable why in recent times this social scourge has received so much attention from intellectual quarters, domestic and international observers, governments, and civil society organizations. After a critical analysis of the rate of unethical governance in Africa, Achebe (1983) posits that anybody who can say that unethical governance in Africa has not become alarming is either a fool, a crook, or else does not live in Africa. Unethical governance in Africa has passed the alarming and entered the fatal stage; and Africa will die if we keep pretending that she is only slightly indisposed (Achebe, 1983; Igbokwe-Ibeto and Osakede, 2019).

Civil bureaucracy is established to serve as the engine room of government, to use its repository of creative knowledge to advise government, and faithfully implement policies and programmes made by the political executive. Its creative talents help to articulate and aggregate the demands and expectations of the members of society. Distributive justice becomes one of the core goals of the bureaucracy particularly in social formations where there are deep currents of ethno-religious and sectional sentiments. It is strongly believed that the efficient and effective service delivery that it spawns will help assuage these sentiments. But after many years of independence, these mandates given to civil bureaucracy appear not to be realized.

Some areas where these defects have been pronounced are in the security, growth, and development of the economy. The feeling is palpable that if the country has not transited from an entity of multiple nationalities to a nation-state where everyone has a sense of belonging, feelings of pride and nationalism, it is perhaps because the civil bureaucracy has not been able to stand up to its responsibilities of good governance and a repository of the collective interest of the people (Akhakpe, 2019).

Several reasons can be adduced for this state of affairs in the policy think-tank of the country. Some scholars have argued that this could be as a result of the incongruence between an imposed public intuition and the environment where it operates (Akhakpe, 2019). Others have suggested the inadequacy of human capital and the expanded scope and responsibility of the growing state bureaucracy (Igbokwe-Ibeto, 2019). Yet, not a few points to the operational techniques of the bureaucracy which seem to be very rudimentary in an era where cutting-edge technology drives public sector institutions.

Unethical governance remains the widely held view of why the bureaucracy has failed to loyally serve the government in power and the communities and individuals it serves. This factor has been fingered as the most attritional and pernicious in the post-independence years. This is in spite of the realization of this challenge to curb this menace in the civil bureaucracy. What accounts for the spate of unethical governance and what nature has it taken in modern times? How can it be eliminated or attenuated? These and other issues germane to this subject will be addressed in the chapter.

To address the issues central to this chapter, this chapter is divided into seven sections. Aside from the introduction, the first part explores conceptual and theoretical epistemology. The second examines the prevalence of unethical governance and corruption in Africa. The third analyzes the nexus between ethical conduct and good governance. The fourth section explores the potential causes and consequences of unethical governance. The fifth discusses notions of ethical governance by focusing on Nigeria as a case study, whilst the sixth part suggests recommendations for resolving the identified challenges.

ETHICAL GOVERNANCE: A CONCEPTUAL AND THEORETICAL EXPOSITION

It is customary to begin an academic investigation by examining the conceptual and theoretical contours of the subject matter of analysis by analysing the views of various scholars and authors.

Ethics

Morality, ethics, and corruption are words commonly used in both private and public organizations. But these issues have become more worrisome in public sector discourse because of the burden they pose on the functionality or otherwise of government at all levels. Ethics may be referred to as rules and regulations guiding the conduct of official duties of public officers (Akhakpe, 2019). In public official circles, one can easily point to a deluge of ethical codes or codes of ethics put together by government at all levels. But articulating a code of ethics for public officials appears not to be the challenge, but rather how to ensure that public employees practice them. In most developing countries of Africa, Asia, and Latin America, it would seem, issues of ethics, morality, and integrity are yet to mediate the actions and activities of public employees. Some scholars attribute this to why these continents have some of the poorest countries in the world. This takes us directly to the issue of morality and values.

Morality and Values

Every society is governed by certain moral codes. These are activities and actions which society over time considers or regards as right or wrong. While these may not be codified, they remain in the realm of convention, traditions, and myths. Thus, morality and values are that conduct considered by society as either right or wrong and either of them is rewarded accordingly by society. As a system of morals and values, Asobie (2011) argues that ethics is connected with the rules of behaviour. It deals with standards that constitute unethical conduct, immorality, and/or corruption. How then do we conceptualize corruption?

Corruption

Corruption in the perspective of Ogbunwegeh (in Akhakpe, 2019, p. 45) is the 'organisation of fraudulence, the brazen celebration of impunity which pollutes the ethical hygiene of society'. One can deduce from this view that corruption is an organized crime that is unethical to the wellbeing of persons and society. Corruption can also be seen as the usurpation of resources of the public for private gains or uses. Lipset and Lenz (2000) exemplify this view by contending that corruption is 'efforts to secure wealth or power through illegal means; private gain at public expenses'. Corruption has become a much-discussed phenomenon, a social vice that has eaten and continues to eat up the body polity. It is not restricted to a particular sphere of societal or political life of a country and organisation. Also, its impact or effect has often been looked at more from its negative angles as hindering socioeconomic development, creating wrong values, and destroying those values that hold society together in peace and harmony. That is why Scott (in Ekiyor, 2019, p. 76) avers that corruption 'must be understood as a regular, repetitive and integral part of the operation of most political system[s]'.

Governance and Good Governance

The concepts of governance and good governance are used interchangeably in development discourse. The term 'governance' is not new in public administration literature. It is as old as human civilization. Governance can be defined as the process of decision-making as well as the process by which decisions are implemented. Governance can be categorized as national governance, local governance, international governance, and corporate governance. According to Smith (in Rahim, 2019), good governance can be regarded as an opening policy for establishing strong determination, where decision-makers are to create points of view after a period of consensus gaining.

Good governance has eight major characteristics which include: participation, consensus oriented, accountability, transparency, responsiveness, effectiveness and efficiency, equity and inclusiveness, and the rule of law. Good governance ensures that the views of minorities are taken into account while the voices of the most vulnerable in society are heard in decision-making. Good governance minimizes corruption; it is also responsive to the present and future needs of society.

Theory of the 'Two Publics'

Several perspectives have been put forward by scholars such as Ekeh (1975), Dudley (1987), and Joseph (1987) to explain the phenomenon of corruption in the public realm. The colonial legacies on the postcolonial state present a very insightful framework to situate these practices in the amoral-value system in the polity. The major thrust of Dudley's perspective is the importance placed on wealth by members of various communities. This factor among many others helps to explain the prevalence and ambivalence of unethical governance and corruption in Africa in general and Nigeria in particular. Ekeh (1975) drawing from Weberian theme of patrimonialism came up with the theory of the 'two publics' in Africa, where he argues persuasively that the imposed nature of the colonial state in Nigerian society forcedly created a moral attitude as the dominant code of political cum administrative behaviour in the public realm (Ekeh, 1975). This became the case because the public realm in Africa unlike its homologues in Europe and America developed as two publics instead of one. These are the 'civic public' which corresponds with citizenry and 'primordial publics' that are made up of ethnic and primordial associations. The latter is governed by the values, norms, and morals of the indigenous society (Ekeh, 1975). Beyond this structural dichotomy, there are also value differences between the two realms. While the civic public operates in an amoral environment, the primordial public retains and abiding morality which emphasizes the obligations of individuals to their extended family and community. Problems of unethical governance, corruption, or venality are attributed to the fact that the same individual operates in the two publics working at cross-purposes (Ekeh, 1975). Cross-purpose may refer to the class of morality on the one hand and amorality on the other hand.

The character of the state has also been put forward to explain the crisis of morality in public service. As one of the subsets of this genre avers, the postcolonial state not unlike its predecessor, the colonial one, is essentially a law-and-order state and continues to maintain its major characteristics, even as it struggles to legitimize its rule through some populist strategies like welfarist and socialist schemes. The preoccupation with law and order can only be maintained through the use of force, just as it was with the colonial state. The state has gone ahead to use its regularity and extractive power to centralize the production and distribution of federally collected resources which in effect encourages the view of the state as a vehicle for primitive accumulation and patron-client relations both in the political and administrative realms.

Consequent to this development, particularly the disjuncture between the state and society, a by-product of the imposed nature of the postcolonial state, there has arisen a negative attitude to government and its operators. The majority of Nigerians, just as in the days of colonial rule, still see postcolonial Nigeria state as an 'alien' force that must be resisted. In the words of Osaghae (2012, p. 87):

> The perception became ingrained in the popular consciousness (of Nigerians) with the result that society at large refused to develop any serious stake or interest in the States 'well-being and sustenance such would have emphasized accountability, transparency, responsiveness and other aspects of a moral ethos. Rather, the state and the government which animated it were approached as alien institutions which belonged to the Oyibo (whiteman), … not deserving of the citizen's obligations or duties, could be plundered to feather private nests, and whose survival only the few who benefited directly from it were prepared to fight for.

The popular feeling among Nigerians that government business is no man's business has robbed public service of the moral ethos that brings about national development. Consequently, the people have no propriety rights over the state because they felt it is imposed on them. Therefore, pillaging the state resources for personal and group gains is perceived as an honourable task, provided such persons remember to use part of such stolen funds to develop their communities. This practice has been ingrained in the cultural and behavioural norms of the people, so much so that they are gradually neglecting using such monies for their communities, leading to the spate of political instability all over the country.

All over the country, the majority of those holding public offices are inclined to abuse their positions to satisfy personal or group interests. Joseph (in Akhakpe, 2019, p. 73) describes this behaviour as 'prebendalism'. It entails the ruinous use of government position and resources for personal gains through the instrumentality of patron-client relations. Although this perspective was used to describe the reasons for the failed attempt at civilian rule in Nigeria, it has continued to find relevance in subsequent Republics in the country. Having said this, it should be remembered that no single perspective can adequately capture the essence or ramifications of either administrative or political corruption in Africa as each perspective carries its own pitfalls. Perhaps a combination of theories might do justice to this subject matter of investigation.

THE PREVALENCE OF UNETHICAL GOVERNANCE AND CORRUPTION IN AFRICA

This section of the chapter will examine the prevalence of unethical governance and corruption in Africa. Issues such as global integrity, the significance of the AfroBarometer and the Corruption Perceptions Index, as well as efforts toward curbing unethical governance in Africa will be examined closely.

African Integrity Indicators (AII) 2022

African Integrity Indicators (AII) is a research project with its main focus on African governance in practice with the aim of examining how government policies are implemented to support governments, citizens, and civil society. It also interrogates the different aspects of accountability, transparency and social developments across specific indicators that are collected annually. The data generated by AII is used by the researchers, concerned citizens, journalists, etc. interested in African public sector governance. Also, institutions like the Mo Ibrahim Index of African Governance and the World Bank's Worldwide Governance Indicators (WGI) integrate AII data into their research (AII, 2022).

The AII 2022 indicator on press freedom and government censorship indicates an increase in government censorship, lack of press freedom and freedom of speech by citizens. Only 14 African countries have met the 33 per cent threshold for women's representation in cabinet while only ten countries have met the threshold for women's representation in the legislature. Twenty-one African countries have met this threshold in the national-level courts. However, in Nigeria, the number of women in governance is on the decline. As regards the Covid-19 pandemic response in Africa, the AII 2022 indicator shows an improvement in the campaigns and responses to the epidemic.

African Governance Architecture (AGA)

The trends and dynamics of governance in some African Union (AU) member states call for a reflection on the underlying challenges in weak governance systems in Africa and the need for restoring and maintaining resilient governance in Africa. According to the African Governance Report (AU, 2019), African Governance Architecture (AGA) members have acknowledged significant improvements in the governance trend in Africa. However, a number of issues still remain subjects of concern for the AU. For example, some members of the African Peer Review Mechanism (APRM) expressed concerns over the protest taking place in some African countries as a result of the governance crisis. African leaders need to show serious commitment in dealing with the issues of governance. The deteriorating trend in governance in Africa should be an issue of priority to APRM and AGA in addressing the challenges.

The AGR assists in AU efforts in encouraging member states to enhance the performance of governance in Africa. The AGR is premised on the need to measure progress in African governance, which requires tracking, analyzing changes, and providing recommendations for the way forward. The AGR report prioritizes five key governance assessment areas as its baseline. These thematic indicators are constitutionalism and the rule of law; transformative leadership; peace, security, and governance; the role of RECs in governance; and the nexus between development and governance. Recognizing the centrality of democratic governance in the management of structural causes of conflict, crises, and unconstitutional changes of government in Africa, AGA complements the efforts of the African Peace and Security Architecture (APSA) as an affirmation of the interface between democracy, peace, and security.

Country Performance in Africa

The five top performing countries in Africa in 2021, in order, were South Africa, Seychelles, Mauritius, Tunisia, and Namibia (Ibrahim Index Report, 2022). While Tunisia remains among the top countries in the AGA index in terms of cumulative scores across all indicators, it has fallen from third to fourth, and has experienced one of the largest declines this round as compared to the previous round Eritrea, Equatorial Guinea, and Somalia remain the three worst-performing countries according to the Ibrahim Index in 2021, though Somalia has gained some ground overall.

Compared to the year 2020, a number of countries have improved their performance across several indicators. According to the Ibrahim Index Report (2022), the sharpest increases in cumulative scores compared to the previous round came from Mali (+275 points), Malawi (+225 points), and Morocco (+200 points). Morocco, in particular, has consistently improved its overall performance since the start of the project, while Mali and Malawi seem to be reversing their declining performance over the years. Mali's results are interesting because, despite a widely condemned *coup d'état*, the country improved in its performance on indicators such as transparency, freedom of assembly, and women's representation.

AfroBarometer Survey on Nigeria (2022)

Afrobarometer, a non-profit organization with its headquarters located in Ghana, is a pan-African, nonpartisan survey research network that provides reliable data on Africans' experiences and evaluations of democracy, governance, and quality of life. The surveys have been conducted in 39 countries since 1999 to date. Below is the round nine survey summary of results for Nigeria completed in 2022. Because of space, this chapter will analyze results of questions posed on corruption and citizens' experiences with public services.

As regards whether the president and officials in his office are involved in corruption, 37.7 per cent of the respondents said most of them; 35.4 per cent agreed some of them, while 20.8 per cent answered all of them are corrupt, totalling 93.9 per cent. Thus, the study concludes that the president and officials in his office are all corrupt. On the members of the National Assembly, 37.5 per cent of the respondents agreed that most of them are corrupt; 30.9 per cent said some of them are involved in corruption, while 26.3 per cent agreed that all members of the National Assembly are corrupt, totalling 94.7 per cent. With the preponderance of 94.7 per cent who answered in the affirmative, the study concludes that the members of the National Assembly are all corrupt. On whether civil servants are corrupt, 47.7 per cent agreed that some are corrupt; 32.1 per cent agreed that most are corrupt, while 12.1 per cent agreed that all are corrupt totalling 92.1 per cent.

Respondents were also asked to rate their local government councillors. Forty-one per cent agreed that some of their local government councillors are corrupt; 34.2 per cent said most of them. The study went further to probe the level of Nigerian police involvement in corrupt practices; 22.9 per cent said some of them and 42.1 per cent said most of them are corrupt, while 31.3 per cent of the respondents perceived that all members of Nigerian police are corrupt. On the involvement of Nigerian judges and magistrates in corrupt practices, 45.2 per cent and 33.2 per cent agreed that some of them and most of them are involved in corruption while 13.9 per cent agreed that all of the judges and magistrates in Nigeria are corrupt totalling 92.3 per cent. On whether tax officials such as officials of Federal Inland Revenue Service (FIRS) are involved in corruption, 41.2 per cent agreed that some of them are corrupt; 35.6 per cent agreed that most of them are corrupt, while 15.5 per cent agreed that all of them are corrupt totalling 92.3 per cent.

Regarding the question of whether traditional leaders are also involved in corruption, 52.4 per cent said 'yes', that some of them are involved, while 22.2 per cent said most of them. However, 14.8 per cent disagreed with the proposition. On whether religious leaders are involved in corruption, 51.8 per cent said 'yes', that some of them are corrupt, while 18.9 per cent said most of them are corrupt. However, 19.3 per cent disagreed with the proposition. As regards business executives and corruption in Nigeria, the survey recorded 49.5 per cent who agreed that some of them are corrupt; 32.5 per cent agreed that most business executives in Nigeria are corrupt, totalling 82 per cent. On the level of involvement of the non-governmental organizations in corrupt conduct, 50.5 and 27.5 per cent respectively agreed that some of them and most of them are involved in corrupt practices. In addition, 77.5 per cent agreed that the level of corruption has increased, while 86.4 per cent claimed that they stand the risk of retaliation or negative consequences if they speak out on the corruption going on in their organizations.

The summary of the Afrobarometer report indicates that the public perceptions of governance in Africa have declined. For example, between 2010 and 2019, Afrobarometer surveyed 39 African countries at least once, providing a sample of public perceptions for the equivalent of 86.8 per cent of Africa's total population. Of the 36 countries with multiple data points over the ten-year period, in more than half (23) citizens are less satisfied with their country's governance performance than ten years ago (Afrobarometer Report, 2022).

Ibrahim Index of African Governance (IIAG)

The Mo Ibrahim Foundation conceptualize governance as the provision of political, social, economic, and environmental public goods and services that every citizen has the right to expect from their government, and that a government has the responsibility to deliver to its citizens. According to the year 2020 IIAG report on security and the rule of law which consists of security and safety, rule of law and justice, accountability and transparency, and anti-corruption, of the 54 African countries surveyed, Nigeria is in the 34th position with 44.3 per cent. On citizens' participation, human rights, inclusion, and equity as well as gender, Nigeria is in the 32nd position with 43.6 per cent. In the area of human development which consists of health, education, social protection, and sustainable environment, Nigeria is in the 37th position with 46.5 per cent. With respect to foundations for economic opportunity, which consist of public administration, business environment, infrastructure, and the rural sector, of the 54 African countries surveyed, Nigeria is in the 28th position with 47.8 per cent. The African average score for Public Perception of Overall Governance (48.8) is the lowest registered over the decade (2010–2019). The pace of deterioration has nearly doubled within the last five years (2015–2019), with an annual average trend of –0.43 between 2015 and 2019 compared to –0.22 over the ten-year period (IIAG 2020).

THE NEXUS BETWEEN ETHICAL CONDUCT AND GOOD GOVERNANCE

In Africa, there were certain forms of conduct which were accepted prior to the coming of the European administrators, such as the giving and receiving of gifts and other forms of gratifications. Following the institutionalization of the Weberian bureaucratic model that requires rationality, objectivity, and impersonality in the discharge of official responsibilities, these acts became objectionable by government and the greater part of society. Yet, views are rife on the question of whether or not unethical conduct can help facilitate the achievement of the much sought-after efficiency and effectiveness in public service to the people. In the context of ravaging poverty and its accompanying greed by persons occupying public offices, there are cases of under-the-table and on-the-table transactions that are papered over by ethics watchdogs in the sector that have become rampant. This made federal, state, and local government ethics regulations complex and confusing.

In the public service, some of the ethical practices cover: gifts, conflicts of financial interests, impartiality, misuse of office seeking outside jobs, and outside work activities (Henry, 2015). Beyond coming up with the ethical standards registers for public administrators, putting them to practice presents the greatest challenges to creating an ethical climate in the public service. African public servants have fallen short in this aspect of ethical regime in government. How do we explain this deficit in public life?

Analyses of the state of ethical practices in the public sector may not be sufficient for one to have a good grasp of the entire gamut and intricacies of venality or its absence in the public service. Bureaucratic operations have expanded into many areas of societal life and with this has arisen the tendencies of breaches of the ethical codes and outright corrupt practices by public officers. Indeed, public service does not exist in isolation from the rest of society. The dominant societal values of materialism and amoralism permeate the public service. In essence, unethical conduct that is rampant in the political realm has found a fertile distinction between what constitutes unethical practices, corruption, and amoralism in the public sector. Therefore, we shall subsequently be using the generic term 'corruption' to refer to all practices which deviate from the moral codes in the public service.

The Nature of Ethical Governance and Social Justice

It is perhaps difficult to sketch the contour of ethical conduct and good governance in the public service. This is because as we have argued, ethical conduct and good governance are two sides of a coin that cannot be separated. Because the activities of bureaucrats have dovetailed into areas traditionally the purview of the executive politicians, they may as well be involved in unethical conduct. Therefore, it will be expedient to use the generic term 'corruption' to describe the gamut of unethical conduct in public service.

Bureaucracy is part and parcel of the larger Nigerian society. Therefore, it cannot be separated from values and happenings associated with it. In spite of attempts by political engineers to construct a political structure isolated from vices in civil society, they have managed to creep into the administrative system. Weberians had wanted to put in place institutions immune from irrationality, indiscipline, waste, mismanagement, infectiveness, and abuse of authority, among others. But these prescriptions, as pious as they may seem, have not been successfully ingrained into the consciousness of public servants whose varieties of reasons seek to lower its moral code as they deem necessary to achieve their personal and corporate interests. Their actions and activities in this regard take different forms. Chijioke (in Gboyega, 2005) gives an ideal of some of them: 'red-tapeism', favouritism and nepotism, rudeness, truancy, excessive use of authority, and secrecy, among others. Dike (in Aluko, 2009, p. 45) argues that unethical conduct occurs 'when one obtains a business from the public sector through inappropriate procedure'. Cases of import duty scams, fertilizer racketeering, over- and under-invoicing, inflation of contract costs, inflation of the costs of procuring government equipment, diversion of government funds, and misapplication of same for personal gains, also fall under the categories of unethical conduct.

Operationally or procedurally, Ake (1993, p. 71) gives a succinct description of venalities or unethical conduct by public servants thus:

> They (public servants) do not believe they are serving anybody else but themselves and exploit their position for personal gain. They generally arrive work late and leave early. They take extra-long lunch recesses. They steal public property. They accept bribe for performance of duties that are contractually part of their responsibilities. When they work, they work very slowly ... they stymie the public by losing their files through excessive review of the issue at hand, or by simple pretending that they have not heard of the matter before. For all of these, they acknowledge no wrong doing, for they do not believe that they are doing is wrong.

This arrogant display of uncontrolled power has become the bane of development and political stability in the Nigerian state in particular and Africa in general. They could do all these because as Ruth (in Akhakpe, 2019) first argues that bureaucracy is one of three political parties in Africa, the other two being executive politicians and the military. There is hardly any financial fraud in the public realm without the footprint of top public servants. Faroukgate, Oduahgate, Milnergate, Idrisgate, and the stealing of crude oil are but a few of the many financial frauds perpetuated in the public realm that could not have been carried out without the active connivance of top public servants. But unlike their political counterparts, they hide behind the veil of anonymity while the ministers, commissioners as the case may be, take the blame for any such act of unethical conduct carried out in the various departments and agencies.

By reason of their technical expertise and access to information, public servants have the where-with-all to resist, conceal, or thwart any move by the government in power to investigate, prosecute, and punish its members. Through their actions, they have prop-up governments, sustaining them or ensuring their collapse. Former president of Nigeria, Obasanjo (Madueaugum, 2008) observes that:

Public officers are the shopping floors of government business. Regrettably, Nigerians have for too long been feeling short-changed by the quality of public service delivery by which decisions are not made without undue outside influence, and files do not [make] move without being pushed with documents. Our public officers have for too long been showcase[d] for the combined evils of inef-, ficiency and corruption, whilst being impediments to effective implementation of government policies, Nigeria deserve better.

The parameter drawn by the above submission may not be exhaustive of the unethical practices in the public service, but it hinted at the role of outside influences in the operations of the public service and public servants. It suggests that civil bureaucrats or officers are being used as 'prebend' to satisfy personal interests and oil the wheel of the patron-client network. Weber (in Akhakpe, 2019, p. 102) description of this system is apt here:

We wish to speak of prebends and of a prebendal organisation of office, wherever the card assigns to the official rent payments for life, payments which are somehow fixed to objects or which are essentially economic usufruct [from] land or other sources. They must be compensations for the fulfilment of actual fictitious office duties, they are goods permanently set aside for the economic assurance of the office.

The past and present economic and political conditions in the country reinforce this form of political institution and the attitudes of public servants regarding their offices. They dwell on abnormality in the sense that 'impersonal norms determining the form of the state organisation, such legal-rational features largely serve to camouflage extensive prebendal practices' (Akhakpe, 2019, p. 103). This practice is further reinforced by the patron-client relationship which means that both complement each other in the pursuit of material goods. From all indications, this system has become rooted in the sociocultural and political economy of the polity. Having identified the nature of phenomenon of unethical conduct and social justice, how then can we rationalize its occurrence in the public service? How is it reinforced in the Nigerian condition? These questions shall be examined in the section that follows.

THE CAUSES AND CONSEQUENCES OF UNETHICAL GOVERNANCE

Several predisposing and actual factors could lead to unethical governance. This section will identify and analyze them with a view to laying bare their potential and actual strength in violating government policies and programmes. Before adumbrating further, the following statement suffices. Office holders who fail to comply with unethical practices are viewed as selfish rather than honourable. Those who refuse to be corrupted and are poor are called fools, so what use is it to be righteous? (Diamond in Akhakpe, 2019).

The pursuit of material gains still defines the quest for public office in Africa. It can be argued that it is the fundamental expectation of members of society. The country-wide perception of public offices as a means of accumulating wealth remains forceful and has not changed after many attempts at democratic rule. While scholars such as Akhakpe (2019) and Joseph (1987) have traced these practices to premodern societies in Africa, the traditional patron-client relationship has also been pursued to achieve material gains in public service.

The fear of material insecurity predisposes public servants to want to save for a rainy day by exploiting every means available to them to enrich themselves. The Nigerian economy is one of the most volatile, unstable, and unpredictable in the world (Akhakpe, 2019). Runaway inflation is the trend and no one can safely say that what he/she saves through legal means can fetch him/her a good lifestyle after retirement from public service. In the developed world, there is no such provision. Therefore, the pressure to steal public funds is more in Africa than in Europe.

Closely related to the above points is the perception of the state and its agency government as imposters, alien forces that have nothing to offer and cannot represent the interest of all in society. This perception of the state was the rallying point of the nationalist struggle against colonial rule. Yet, in the post-independence era it has continued to inform state-society relations. Government business is popularly regarded as nobody's business and should be put on the shoulder rather than on the head. In the colonial days, stealing from the public purse was celebrated and seen as a way of punishing the colonial government. This political culture of public finance has remained in the postcolonial era to date. Indeed, the nature of the political culture in the country would have been different if democratic rule had been allowed to progress uninterrupted by the military. Military authoritarian rule dominated the immediate post-independence years. By virtue of its organizational structure, it is only accountable to itself with little interest in civil governance. Therefore, its years in power were characterized by unbridled waste, mismanagement, and corruption. Also, under the military junta they found an ally in higher civil servants who gladly came in to fill the lacuna created by the usual sack of civilian politicians after a successful *coup d'état*. This situation has far-reaching implications for the public service. In the first place, the professional ethic of the civil service was breached by allowing civil servants to become politically visible. Under the military, they attended meetings of the Supreme Military Council (SMC) during the General Gowan era. Secondly, it increased the political clout of higher civil servants to the extent that today, they have become difficult to tame. Scholars have started referring to them as the fourth arm of government (Meier, 2007). They are also referred to as alternative government because of the enormous power they wield vis-à-vis other social groups in society (Amuwo, 1997). The implication of these developments is that unethical conduct-related issues in the public service are hardly persecuted with the thoroughness and doggedness they deserve.

The reward system in Nigeria would appear to be unsupportive of a dedicated and honest system of public service. The unrealistic wages and salary structure in the public service cannot promote and sustain rectitude in public service. Surprisingly, successive governments in the country appear not to be bothered about this aspect of motivating the public workforce. What public servants take home as salaries cannot in any way sustain them in a month. Ironically, it is made to be the living wage. For example, Nigerian public university lecturers have been on strike since 14 February 2022 to date over poor remuneration and working environment. In these circumstances, it is difficult to preach ethical standards and rectitude in public service. Most honest and dedicated men and women have left the public sector for green pastures in the private sector or outside the country. The now famous phenomenon of brain drain is not unconnected with the failure of government to retain its professional and experts in various fields of human endeavour due to its poor remuneration packages. Those who could not change jobs or travel out of the country explore all avenues to eke out a living or survive in an unstable socioeconomic environment.

Indeed, every Constitution the country has had since independence has reiterated that the ideology of the state primarily is to pursue and realize the welfare and well-being of the people under it. Yet, many years after independence, the same state has failed to realize this goal substantially as is evident in the decline in virtually all areas of societal life. All these it would seem came to the fore as a result of bad governance. Thus, in the absence of a national society governed by common moral, cultural, and behavioural norms, public officers are inclined to plunder state resources to feather their own nests! Furthermore, the failure of the state through its agencies and institutions to ensure distributive justice by making sure that resources from oil which since the 1970s has become the major source of revenue for the state accounting for between 85 and 90 per cent of its foreign earnings has alienated a lot of individuals, groups, and communities. Because the state through its agency government is unable to provide for the people in the areas of job creation, infrastructural development, health, education, and housing services to mention but a few, any opportunity to hold public office is seen by the citizens as an avenue to appropriate its resources to meet the needs of kin, ethnic nationalities, and other sectional tendencies. As Osaghae (2012) argues, those who had the opportunity to be in government were expected to use the power and resources at their disposal to advance private and communal interests. Without doubt, these unethical governance or conduct have far-reaching effects on the public service in particular and the polity in general. But the specific ways they could occur need to be interrogated to lay bare their nature for possible remedy. The persistence of unethical conduct has negated whatever potential may have existed to effect changes in the political (administrative) cultures(s) especially as regards the ethics of and motives for public service (Diamod in Akhakpe, 2019).

The above views aptly capture the complexities and multidimensional nature of unethical governance in Nigeria's public service. No single phenomenon has threatened the potential development of the entity called Nigeria than bureaucratic and political corruption. Here we shall explore the consequences of unethical governance in Nigeria and Africa in general. Unethical governance stifles the implementation of policies and programmes of government. Every government relies on its civil service to implement policies and programmes passed into law. It is important to have good policies but more important is to implement them efficiently and effectively. A corruption ridden civil service can be weighed down by the spectre of administrative corruption. Corrupt administrators may hinder good policies and programmes of government if not properly checked. Even institutional checks have presently been circumvented, making it difficult to identify and persecute corruption public officers. If Nigeria has not made much progress as an entity since independence, it is not unrelated to the problem of corruption in the execution of public policies and programmes of successive government.

Bureaucratic corruption has affected the nation-building agenda of successive governments in the country. Bureaucrats are principal instruments for nation-building. They bring the people together irrespective of their ethno-regional and sectional interests. Where proper advice is provided and bureaucrats respond to suggestions for effective policy implementation, the country generally experiences growth and development. This with time gives confidence to the people that they are in one country and not many nations forged into a tenuous unity. Corruption has been fingered as the cause of the present weak pursuit of nation-building in the country. Not at any time in the country's history have the people been drawn apart as it is today under President Buhari APC-led federal government. Many Nigerians are moving more into their ethnic cocoon than being integrated into a corporate entity. It has destroyed whatever common values the people had during the colonial nationalist struggle though this would appear tokenistic and self-serving in retrospect.

The situation in Nigeria is that of a paradox, despite the fact that the country is the largest producer of oil in Africa and the tenth among world oil-rich nations, it is currently the poverty capital of the world (Uzoho, 2021). So many Nigerians die of preventable diseases due to the absence of basic drugs in hospitals that have turned into mere consulting clinics (Igbokwe-Ibeto and Okoye, 2014; Igbokwe-Ibeto and Osakede, 2019). Basic infrastructural facilities such as schools, accessible and motorable roads, hospitals, clean water, and electricity supply are at various stages of dilapidation thereby increasing the sufferings and stress the ordinary citizens are going through.

Unethical governance in Nigeria has resulted in a financial haemorrhage in government by some public officers mostly on conspicuous consumption and extravagance lifestyle. These are monies that could have been used to provide the poor masses with basic infrastructures and necessities of life but are diverted into private accounts, thereby robbing society of much-needed funds for development (Igbokwe-Ibeto and Okoye, 2014).

Unethical governance has exacerbated the leadership crisis in the country. As the ruling elite concentrates on the pursuit of primitive accumulation of wealth and crass materialism, they neglect the people's welfare and well-being. Psychological and social distance between the people and bureaucrats has increased and with this has come an increasing pauperization of the people in all dimensions of human life. The declining standard of living of the people in Africa in general and Nigeria in particular is an eloquent testimony of this trend that poverty has been on the increase with majority living below the poverty line of less than one dollar per day. Indeed, the 2021 World Bank Report declared Nigeria the poverty capital of the world (Uzoho, 2021)

Unethical governance has also eroded values that promote development in Nigeria. It has made it possible for only those who steal to govern because in Nigeria politics is money and money is politics. In this context, stealing virtues of nationhood have been compromised by administrative and political corruption. Unethical governance at whatever levels have made Nigeria a blathering entity where privileged individuals and groups scramble for irregular personal and group enrichment, and this has become the bane of every Nigerian government (Diamond, 1991). The persistence of this phenomenon has led to an incremental depreciation of national and community values and norms that should be revered by all.

Development administration that is supposed to be the major preoccupation of civil servants appears to be progressing in error as made manifest by the decay in social infrastructures like electricity, water supply, health facilities, roads, education, transportation, and housing, among many others. Public service delivery has indeed been at its lowest ebb, not even government propaganda and palliative measures such as the subsidy reinvestment programmes (SURE-P), social security investment programmes such as N-Power, Conditional Cash Transfer (CCT), Home Grown School Feeding (HGCFP), Government Enterprises Entrepreneurship Programme (GEEP) etc. have been able to ameliorate the sufferings of the majority who increasingly come under the weight of disjointed and poor service delivery by public servants, fuelled by the pervasiveness of bureaucratic corruption. This has been worsened by the rate of insecurity in the country.

Unethical governance has furthermore diminished the governance essence of leadership and compromised the role of transparency, probity, and accountability as the hallmark of a civilized and modern government. Rather than unite the different nationalities for a concerted pursuit of the Nigerian project, it has progressed through divide-and-rule tactics putting one ethnic and religious group against the other. What appears to be the dominant philosophy or principle of government today is turn by turn Nigeria limited or everyone for himself, God for all. Little wonder therefore, that the country has been under siege by disenchanted youths who have taken to terrorism, banditry, kidnapping, militancy, religious insurgency, and secessionist agitations as coping strategies in the face of government neglect of their welfare and well-being.

GOVERNMENT EFFORTS AT COMBATING UNETHICAL GOVERNANCE

Unethical governance would seem to predate the modern Nigerian state. Formal bureaucracy preceded the Nigerian state as British administrators had a structure of administration before the present state form emerged. While one cannot deny the fact that unethical conduct was embedded in the colonial administrative set-up, for the system of colonialism was cast and weaned in unethical governance, its level was minimal and punishment for it was swift and drastic. According to Gboyega (2005), although the colonial administration was small and compact, it was efficient and effective.

In the postcolonial dispensation, the public service has been riddled with unbridled corruption. Successive governments realized this state of affairs and made several efforts to either attenuate or eliminate the debilitating scourge. For example, General Obasanjo, as military head of state in 1976, declared Operation Feed the Nation (OFN), the Shagari administration in the Second Republic brought the ethical revolution, and anti-corruption, patriotism-discipline, and self-reliance mobilizing programmes were launched by military regimes in the 1980s and 1990s. The War Against Indiscipline (WAI) was introduced by the Buhari administration. Under General Babangida's administration, there was equally Mass Mobilization for Economic Recovery, Self-Reliance, and Social Justice (MAMSER) and the War Against Indiscipline and Corruption was inaugurated under General Abacha's administration. With the return to civilian rule in 1999, the Chief Obasanjo civilian administration put the searchlight on the war against corruption with the inauguration of two strong anti-graft bodies (Agbiboa, 2011), namely the Independent Corruption Practice Commission (ICPC) and Economic and Financial Crimes Commission (EFCC). This coincided with the period Nigeria became the number one most corrupt country in the world based on the corruption perception index of Transparency International (IT) (Bazuaye and Oriakhogba, 2016). Although Nigeria has since climbed down the ladder a bit, the fact remains that the country is very much weighed down by bureaucratic and political corruption. While we acknowledge efforts made by successive governments to tackle the virus, such efforts have tended to be more admonitory in nature, making these organizations something close to toothless bulldogs. This becomes the case because the big corrupt and big corrupters usually find ways of avoiding the long hands of the law either because they are powerful people in the corridor of power and or they have stolen enough money to buy justice. In essence, the war against corruption in Nigeria does not apply to all equally, there are some sacred cows that cannot be touched or punished by extant laws of the land (Igbokwe-Ibeto and Okoye, 2014; Igbokwe-Ibeto and Osakede, 2019). A drastic problem surely requires a drastic cure.

In some developing countries desirous of development, corrupt practices by government officers attract the death penalty. In Nigeria, instead of tightening the punishment for corruption, it is being weakened by the so-called 'plea-bargain'. Some of the governors who were found guilty of stealing state resources were given 'soft' sentences which enable them to walk away after a few months in prison to enjoy their massive loot. Again, their punishment for stealing was not commensurate with what they stole. This has a way of encouraging others to attempt such acts, having at the back of their minds that they will be given very light punishment. Such a mindset can only increase rather than reduce unethical conduct in public sector management.

Unethical governance under President Buhari APC-led government has become so pervasive that young men and women in Nigeria do not see the essence of going to school to learn because they see daily how those who did not go to school or the half-baked educated ones control billions of naira while those who are studying to acquire knowledge are looked at with scorn. As has been argued, 'the gentlemen in power' indulge in an unrestrained provoking and enraging display of unsubstantiated means while the vast majority of Nigerians are asked to tighten their belts. Nigerians have all come to recognize the ruinous effect of unethical governance on the socioeconomic and political future of the country. Having discovered the effect of unethical governance, what are the ways out?

ETHICAL GOVERNANCE: THE WAY FORWARD

There is no problem without a solution. A problem identified is a problem half-solved. Luckily, the course, causes, and consequences of unethical governance have been identified and they are in the public domain. Whether or not they will be addressed and resolved will depend on the doggedness and sincerity virus. This section will attempt a modest but holistic discourse on how this phenomenon can be tackled and possibly eliminated from public sector management in Africa.

Several developments in Nigeria have lowered the morale and beliefs of the people in society. More than ever before, the country is a geographical expression that many think is not worth dying for. The ruling elite has to win the hearts and minds of the people to put the Nigerian project back on track. Nigerians have to be assured and reassured that their interests are the ultimate goal of government. This must not be done at the level of precepts alone, but also be matched by examples. Exemplary, missionary, and visionary leadership must be brought to the front burner in the life of the country. As it is said, 'when a righteous king is on the throne, the people rejoice'. The joy of the people is in the upliftment of their material conditions. What the country dearly need is a critical mass of men with integrity, imbued with moral tension. The moral imperative should be prioritized in the quest for leaders in public sector. In the words of Senghor former President of Senegal,

> We lack a moral tension … a true commitment to the service of our country. It is that I consider the most difficult task among all those I have undertaken (as president). To instil in my people that taste from work which nothing lasting can be accomplished. (Osaghae, 1994, p. 23)

Instilling this zeal and enthusiasm in the people requires leadership that is visionary and missionary, selfless, and dedicated to the common good. But this has to be carried within the appropriate democratic political culture that is conducive for administrative effectiveness, in order for bureaucratic corruption and other unethical practices to be reduced in the public and private sectors. Fortunately, some of the infractions that characterized the public sector under authoritarian rule can now be removed with the consolidation of democratic practices in the continent of Africa.

One element of political culture that is glaring in its absence in the polity is constitutionalism. There is enough in the country's statute books to check unethical governance. But they are not followed to mediate the actions or conduct of public office holders. The whistle-blower in public sector management should be activated at all times to play its watchdog role. It will bring officials' wrongdoings constantly to the fore in the public sector (Adenuga, 2011). Where laws are not respected, venality in public sector management becomes the order of the day. Yet, it is not enough to have laws documented and put in the hands of public servants; they should be seen as enforceable to all irrespective of their status in life. Public accountability should also be the driving force of public sector management in Africa. This pointed is made pointedly by Dwivadi (in Akhakpe, 2019, p. 97) as follows:

> If officials know that when caught engaging in something illegal, they have good prospect of avoiding punishment, they are bound to have [a] relaxed approach to the issue of morality in government. Any slowness of the administrative machinery and of the judicial process coupled with chance of 'winning' the witness to their side, contribute to the continuation of 'corrupt' environments.

The law against unethical conduct should therefore be drastic and dramatic to instil fear in would-be perpetrators of the crime. Punishment prescribed against unethical conduct should be commensurate with the crime committed even higher as the case may be, to serve as a deterrent to others. A situation where a public servant that stole billions of naira from the public purse is given two years imprisonment with the option of a few thousand naira fine is not healthy for the fight against unethical conduct.

Of all the development challenges that confront the country, the most pervasive and debilitating is poverty. Poverty is one of the fundamental causes of corruption (unethical conduct) in developing countries. A poor man hardly understands the language of morality. For him, what is moral is anything that can put food on his table. Therefore, to this category of people, if unethical practices will bring food to their table, so be it. Laski (in Isumanah, 1994) states his mind on the issue by contending that, a state divided into a small number of rich and a large number of poor will always develop a government by the rich to protect the amenities represented by their property. Protecting their properties will involve stealing more public funds to the detriment of the poor. Poverty has to be reduced and drastically too for unethical conduct to decline in the public sector in Africa.

The Nigerian state remains largely contested. There is need to renegotiate its contract in a no holds barred manner. The first contract in 1979 was done under duress. The people should be given the opportunity to negotiate the basis of their co-existence. Most of the issues being contested by ethnic nationalities can be fruitfully discussed in a cordial atmosphere with little politics involve. Former President Jonathan convened a National Conference in 2014 to discuss the country's challenges but could not win the 2015 presidential election to enable him to implement the 2014 conference report. President Buhari who took over from Jonathan jettisoned the confab report. It is hoped that the next president of the country will implement the 2014 national conference report so that it will not be another talk show that results in more words than deeds. There is a need for wide-ranging decentralization of power and resources and participation of autonomy for social formations that make up the Nigerian state. All these will impact positively on social values that are heavily tinted towards materialism. This would reflect in the character of politics that has become heavily monetized. If there is a change of values, the people will lay their treasure on things that endure not on those that are transient, like armoured cars, houses, aircraft, ships, etc. In developed countries, people invest in space technology and human development rather than esoteric things. When this change occurs, it will reduce politics of impunity and attract men and women of integrity and other sterling qualities into politics. The possible product will be a reduction in venality in public sector management in Nigeria in particular and Africa in general.

CONCLUSION

The concept of ethical governance as captured by scholars and social commentators has been espoused with an attempt at clarifying the intellectual cobweb surrounding the issue of ethical conduct and governance in Africa with specific reference to Nigeria. To scientifically undertake the purpose of this chapter, this chapter traversed theoretical frameworks, conceptualizations, and discussed dominant issues in ethical governance in Africa in general and Nigeria in particular. To this end, the theory of the two publics has been examined as postulated by scholars. An attempt has also been made to establish the nexus between unethical conduct and good governance.

In sum, the chapter has argued that unethical governance, be it bureaucratic or political, is a malignant phenomenon with devastating effects on national development. Over the years, it has grown to become a systemic problem that has to be traced to and uprooted from its base for it to be reduced or eliminated from society. Several possible measures have been suggested which could be taken to stem the growing tide of this plague. The issue of the Nigerian state has to be resolved to provide a solid base for the peoples' co-existence, leaders at all levels should win the hearts and minds of the people through good governance and winning the anti-graft war. There should be zero tolerance for unethical conduct by punishing adequately the big war against poverty in the land. This is where positive leadership is required more than ever before in the public sector management in particular and society in general.

REFERENCES

Achebe, C. (1983), *The trouble with Nigeria*, Enugu: Fourth Dimension Publishers.
Adenuga, A.O. (2011), 'Venality Inn Public Service: The Need for a Whistle Blower Law', in Olejede, I. and B. Fajonyomi (eds.), *Ethics and Public Accountability in Nigeria*, Lagos: A Triad Associate Publishers, pp. 145–162.
African Peer Review Mechanism (APRM) (2019), *The African Governance Report: Promoting African Union Shared Values*, prepared by the APRM and AGA, Addis Ababa, Ethiopia, accessed 16 August 2023 at https://au.int/sites/default/files/documents/36418-doc-eng-_the_africa_governance_report_2019_final-1.pdf.
African Union (2019), *The African Governance Report: Promoting African Union Shared Values*, Prepared by the APRM and AGA, Addis Ababa, Ethiopia, accessed 16 August 2023 at https://au.int/sites/default/files/documents/36418-doc-eng-_the_africa_governance_report_2019_final-1.pdf.
Afrobarometer. (2022), 'Round 9 Survey on Nigeria', accessed 22 July 2022 at https://www.afrobarometer.org/ publication/ nigeria-round-9-summary-of-results/.
African Governance Architecture (AGA). (2022), 'AGA Platform Raises Concerns Over Weak Governance Trends', accessed 18 July 2022 at https://au.int/en/pressreleases/20190604/aga-platform-raises-concerns-over-weak-governance-trends.
Agbiboa, D.E. (2011), 'Between Corruption and Development: The Political Economy of State Robbery in Nigeria', *Journal of Business Ethics*, **6** (2), 11–20, doi.org/10.1007/s10551-011-1093-5.
Ake, C. (1993), 'Deeper into Originals Sins: The Context of Ethical Crisis in Africa's Public Service', in Olowo, D. (ed.), *Ethics and Accountability in African Public Service*, New York: United Nations Economic Commission for Africa and Africa Association for Public Administration and Management, pp. 71–89.

Akhakpe, I.B. (2019), *Bureaucracy and Good Governance*, Lagos: Pumark Nig.

Aluko, A.Y. (2009), 'Corruption in Nigeria: Concept and Dimension', in Enweremadu, D.U. and E.E. Okafor (eds.), *Anti-Corruption Reforms in Nigeria: Issues, Challenges and the Way Forward*, Lagos: IFRA, pp. 45–61.

Amuwo, K. (1997), 'Critical Perspective on the Structure, Nature and Role of the Public Bureaucracy in Nigeria', *The Quarterly Journal of Administration*, **29** (1–2), 42–53.

Asobie, A. (2011), 'Nature and Ethics of University Administration', in Olojede, I. and B. Fajonyomi (eds.), *Ethics and Public Accountability in Nigeria*, Lagos: A-Triad Associates Publishers. pp. 84–99.

Bazuaye, B. and D. Oriakhogba (2016), 'Combating Corruption and the Role of the Judiciary in Nigeria: Beyond Rhetoric and Crassness', *Commonwealth Law Bulletin*, **42** (1), 125–147, doi.org/10.1080/03050718.2016.1157504.

Diamond, L. (1991), 'Political Corruption: Nigeria's Perennial Struggle', *Journal of Democracy*, **2** (4), 34–42.

Dudley, B. (1987), *An Introduction to Nigeria Government and Politics*, London: Macmillan.

Dwivadi, D. (ed.) (1996), *Readings in Contemporary Nigeria Politics*, Lagos: GoldHawk and Associate.

Ekeh, P.P.A. (1975), 'Colonialism and the Two Publics in Africa: A Theoretical Statement', *Comparative Studies in Societies and History*, **17** (1), 91–112.

Ekiyor, A. (2019), 'Corruption in Local Government Administration: A Historical Summary', in Odion-Akhaina, S. (ed.), *Local Government Administration in Nigeria: Old and New Visions*, Abuja: Panaf Press, pp. 123–139.

Gboyega, A. (2005), 'Civil Service Reforms in Nigeria and the Quest for Efficiency, Responsiveness and Accountability: A Critique', *Journal of Nigeria Public Administration Management*, **2** (2), 46–58.

Global Integrity. (2022), 'Africa Integrity Indicators: GI's Last Round of Data and Passing the Touch', accessed 18 July 2022 at https://www.globalintegrity.org/2022/04/12/africa-integrity-indicators-gis-lastround-of-data-and-passing-the-torch/.

Henry, N. (2015), *Public Administration and Public Affairs*, New Delhi: Prentice-Hall of India.

Ibrahim Index of African Governance (IIAG) Report. (2020), accessed 18 July 2022 at https://mo.ibrahim.foundation/sites/default/files/2020-11/2020-index-report.pdf.

Ibrahim Index of African Governance (IIAG) Index Report. (2022), accessed 16 August 2023 at https://mo.ibrahim.foundation/sites/default/files/2023-01/2022-index-report.pdf.

Igbokwe-Ibeto, C.J. (2019), 'African Bureaucracy and Public Administration: Analysing the Normative Impediments and Prospects', *Africa's Public Service Delivery and Performance Review*, **7** (1), 1–11, doi.org/10.4102/apsdpr.v7i1.323.

Igbokwe-Ibeto, C.J. and J.C. Okoye (2014), 'Anti-Corruption Crusade in Nigeria: More Words than Deeds', *International Journal of Public Policy and Administration Research*, **1** (2), 47–63.

Igbokwe-Ibeto, C.J and K.O. Osakede (2019), 'Corruption and Its Social Implication in Nigeria', in Namadi, M.M. and M.O. Haruna (eds.), *Sociological Insights on the Contemporary Social Problems in Nigeria*, Kashere: Federal University of Kashere Press, pp. 221–236.

Isumanah, V. (1994), *Grassroots Democracy in the Context of Democratization in Africa: Africa Perspective*, Abuja: Centre for Democratic Studies.

Joseph, R. (1987), *Democracy and Perbendal Politics in Nigeria: The Rise and Fall of the Second Republic*, New York: Cambridge University Press.

Lipset, S.M. and G.S. Lenz (2000), 'Corruption, Culture and Markets', in Huntington, S.P. and E.H. Lawrence (eds.), *Culture Matters*, New York: Basic Books, pp. 76–89.

Maduabum, C. (2008), *The Mechanics of Public Administration in Nigeria*, Lagos: Concept Publications.

Meier, K. (2007), *Politics and the Bureaucracy: Policymaking in the Fourth Branch of Government*, Belmont, MA: Thomson Wadsworth.

Osaghae, E.E. (1994), 'Sustaining Democratic Stability in Africa: The Moral Imperative', in Omoniyi, O. (ed.), *Democratization in Africa: Africa Perspectives*, Abuja: Centre for Democratic Studies. pp. 223–239.

Osaghae, E.E. (2012), *Crippled Giants: Nigeria since Independence*, Ibadan: John Archers Publishers.

Rahim, A. (2019), 'Governance and Good Governance – A Conceptual Perspective', *Journal of Public Administration and Governance*, **9** (3), 133–142, doi.org/10.5296/jpag.v9i3.15417.

Uzoho, P. (2021), 'Nigeria Still Poverty Capital of the World', accessed 21 July 2022 at https://www.thisdaylive.com/index.php/2021/09/06/report-nigeria-still-poverty-capital-of-the-world/.

13. Managing human resources in government: the case of Botswana

Theophilus T. Tshukudu

INTRODUCTION

Governments that want to maintain their competitive edge require public officials that are well-versed in the latest governance approaches, methods, and technology to deal with challenges associated with a global economy (Nasir, 2014). Ensuring that the right officials with the right attitude, skills, experience, and qualifications are appointed in the right position and the right time requires a strong strategic orientation for human resource management (HRM) in government. It also requires a strong people developmental approach to retain talent in the public service characterized by the establishment of a conducive work environment, compliance with a comprehensive policy framework, as well as good labour relations and supervisory practices.

Public institutions face a staggering number of normative, legal, and procedural obligations as far as the management of human resources is concerned. It includes changing working conditions, the retention of competent staff and their scarce skills, rapid technological advancements, new organizational partnerships with multiple governance actors, changing organizational arrangements, and demographic shifts. The demands placed on managers of human resources are significant because of these and related challenges. The HRM function has a crucial role to play in assisting with and navigating these dynamics. HRM must therefore boost both its strategic and operational value for the effective management of public sector institutions.

The purpose of this chapter is to probe the role of HRM in government by highlighting particular functions, applications, and challenges. HRM practices and realities in the Government of Botswana will be used as a case study to elucidate these and related aspects.

THE ROLE OF HUMAN RESOURCE MANAGEMENT IN GOVERNMENT

According to Schultz (2021), a 'role' can be perceived as influencing patterns of behaviour or actions. For the purposes of this chapter, a role can be regarded as the collection of functions, obligations, and procedures that HR practitioners are required to perform in order for government institutions to operationalize their constitutional mandates. To boost the efficiency of government operations, the HRM function should coordinate integrated governance processes inclusive of innovations and administrative reforms (Schultz, 2021).

The duties of HRM managers are changing from merely resolving personal matters to planning and implementing complex government policies through institutional plans, arrangements, and functions. Human resource (HR) managers are tasked with the responsibility of assisting line managers with the establishment of working conditions conducive to the retention of talent, to fulfil the demands of a multicultural workforce, and to costs associated with HR. Scholars such as Mondy and Moe (2005) accentuate the fact that the performance of public institutions is completely dependent on the employees' abilities, skills, and expertise in order to accomplish government goals. Similar to this, Modisane (2015) and Tzafrir et al. (2004) argue that the HR department must devote serious attention to the needs and aspirations of employees since they are crucial to the growth and success of any institution.

During the early 1970s the HRM function was known simply as 'Personnel'. This perspective accentuated the administrative duties of personnel staff such as recruitment, selection, appointment and placement procedures, payroll administration, and training needs identification. Due to paradigmatic developments in the field, the prominence of the managerial dimensions of this function began to gain prominence, hence the preferred new notion of 'Personnel Management'. Human Resource Management eventually took the place of 'People Management' and is regarded as an umbrella term for complex managerial and administrative functions associated with the management of human resources (Aslam et al., 2013; Beardwell, Holden and Claydon, 2004). Aslam et al. (2013) further explain that HRM should be regarded as a collection of integrated functions, obligations, and procedures that direct employees' performance, attitude, and behaviour at work. Some of these functions include managing employee relationships, employee remuneration, offering health and safety benefits, and providing employees with training and development opportunities. Applied to government contexts, HRM has the following characteristics:

- It includes both administrative and managerial dimensions.
- It also takes place in the public sector and therefore has a 'public' dimension.
- It utilizes certain resources to optimally direct and guide HR functions.
- It involves a number of actors that are assigned specific responsibilities such as political oversight (e.g. ministers), strategic and managerial obligations (e.g. line managers and HR managers), and administrative tasks (e.g. HRM department staff).
- It is directed by values and norms and codes of conduct to professionalize the function.
- All activities are aimed at enhancing organizational and human resource performance.

It should be noted that the HRM function can only be successfully executed if there is close cooperation between HRM staff and line managers. Often line managers regard certain responsibilities as those of HRM staff and therefore certain functions are not successfully performed. It is thus essential that there is clarification of the roles and responsibilities of the respective staff compliments. The typical responsibilities of line managers regarding the HRM function include the following:

- Adherence to all HRM policies, procedures, and guidelines.
- Close supervision and the establishment of a healthy work environment.
- The monitoring and appraisal of the performance of employees.
- The identification of training and development needs.
- Compile job specifications in the case of vacancies to aid recruitment and selection.
- Selecting and orienting new appointees to make them rapidly productive.
- Safeguarding employees from unsafe and unhealthy work conditions.
- Conflict management and disciplinary actions.

This list is not exhaustive but merely serves to illustrate the nature of the HRM function in government.

Human resource departments are confronted with the particular challenge to become more strategic by migrating the workforce from task- and skills-based employment to a more value- and purpose-based type of employment (Van der Westhuizen, 2005). This implies that senior HR managers assist top managers of public institutions to analyze the labour market, to assess institutional needs, and to align employee capacities with the strategic objectives of public institutions. This new role even further extends the role of HRM.

Trends in Public Sector HRM

Observers such as Decenzo and Robbins (2013) and Hashim and Hameed (2012) reason that recent shifts in the way society is governed have also far-reaching consequences for the HRM function in government. Trends such as technological advancement, e-commerce, workforce diversity, the establishment of global networks, and ethical considerations all influence contemporary HRM policies and practices such as recruitment, training, development, and job performance. Hashim and Hameed (2012) further accentuate the fact that the Fourth Industrial Revolution (4IR) will place new demands on HR practitioners but will also lead to new opportunities. Hybrid work environments where automation and more conventional HR practices align as well as the application of new technologies in government planning and policy implementation all place new demands on practitioners. One such demand is the retention of talented employees as well as the contracting of skills from outside of the public sector in cases of the absence of certain competencies. Additionally, human resource departments will need to help public officials adapt to and remain relevant in the modern workplace. They should also take advantage of any possibilities to enhance HR capabilities, service offerings, and performance (Schultz, 2021).

Agencies such as the International Labour Organization and the World Economic Forum anticipate that an increasing number of jobs will be lost due to automation, worsening economic conditions, and other governance-related concerns (Schultz, 2021). In addition, the Manpower Group (2017) warns that the skill deficit in government is worsening and that institutions struggle to fill vacant or new positions. It is evident that the labour market will be characterized by an oversupply of low-skilled employees and a shortage of talent, people with scarce and specialized competencies. In this regard, Dlamini and Zogli (2021) argue that the 4IR has divided experts in HRM. One group of experts applauds the new opportunities and contributions brought about by 4IR to increase productivity, efficiency, and improved quality of life for people around the world. On the other hand, the other group emphasizes that the labour market will be divided into low-skill/low-pay workers and high-skill/high-pay workers, which could lead to social tensions (Dlamini and Zogli, 2021). The talents that organizations will require will be hard to find, keep, and engage. To address these issues, it would be necessary for HRM practitioners to adapt training, development, and education practices to fit current global governance trends and implement human resources strategies that boost employees' existing competencies. Reducing the skills gap would enable workers to be redeployed rather than lost to unemployment by adjusting training and development interventions (Dlamini and Zogli, 2021).

HUMAN RESOURCE MANAGEMENT IN THE GOVERNMENT OF BOTSWANA

After 80 years as a British Protectorate, Botswana became independent on 30 September 1966 (NDP, 2009). When the nation gained its independence, its only two industrial facilities were a cattle slaughterhouse in Lobatse and a few businesses in Francistown (Modisane, 2015). Subsistence farming was the main source of income for most at the time. A sizable portion of the labour force was employed as migrant labour in South African mines. In addition to the mining of diamonds, the cattle sector made an important economic contribution (Modisane, 2015). The Government of Botswana spends a sizable portion of revenue collected from diamond sales on social services and infrastructure development in the domains of agriculture, health, and education. This generally aids economic growth and citizens' quality of life (Modisane, 2015).

As far as HRM is concerned, it is evident that the Government of Botswana is faced with a couple of challenges associated with economic diversification and the necessary skills and competencies of public employees to address them. It implies that public sector employees need to upskill to make them more resilient and employable during more turbulent times (Daft, 2013). The government continues to have a severe shortage of skilled labour despite years of efforts to improve the country's skills base (Modisane, 2015). In addition, the absence of adequate HRM qualifications and programmes at the University of Botswana, the nation's top educational and research institution, implies that little scholarly attention is paid to current challenges. It also implies that government institutions experience a shortage of adequately qualified HRM professionals. A positive trend in this regard, however, is that several private colleges provide undergraduate full-time HRM programmes.

All HRM practices and functions are regulated by the Botswana Employment Act (1982), as amended. This Act makes provision for a myriad of functions and applications and includes the following parts:

- Part II – General administration.
- Part III – Contracts of employment.
- Part IV – Special contracts in relation to recruitment.
- Part V – Recruitment.
- Part VI – Forced labour.
- Part VII – Protection of wages.
- Part VIII – Rest periods, hours of work holidays, and other conditions of work.
- Part IX – Contractors and contracting.
- Part X – Employees in special categories.
- Part XI – Employment of children and young persons.
- Part XII – Employment of females.
- Part XIII – Employment of the infirm and handicapped.
- Part XIV – Labour health areas (these include housing, feeding of employees, supply of water, provision of medicine and medical treatment, care of employees on journeys, return of employees to place of origin or engagement, and the power of the Minister to make regulations in relation to labour health areas).
- Part XV – Labour clauses in public contracts.
- Part XVI – Determination of minimum wages.

- Part XVII – Labour Advisory Board.
- Part XVIII – Remedies, jurisdiction, procedure, and penalties.

In addition to these legislative stipulations, each public institution has certain HR policies and procedures controlling its particular operations (Modisane, 2015).

According to the research done by Thornton (2020) in Botswana, deeper insight is becoming increasingly common as a result of HRM data analysis, which increases the value, commercial challenge, and degree of insight available to the public and private sectors. A recent positive development as far as HRM is concerned is the training and development initiatives carried out by Government. These initiatives make provision for tailor-made corporate workplace training and development programmes. Since significant money and resources are allocated to these programmes, their successes and weaknesses are continuously assessed. The outcomes of these programmes on making government more productive are also analyzed. Furthermore, as more organizations realize the importance of training, new training institutions are established. The Human Resource Development Council, for example, is playing a major role in planning and funding of public official training and education as well as in advising the Government on all matters related to human capital development.

It should be emphasized that the HRM function in the Government of Botswana is still in its infancy stages. Limited studies, official reports, and publications in the field thus characterize this domain. It should also be noted that there is no institution dedicated to conducting HRM research. Much can be learned from other African countries in establishing a more comprehensive statutory and regulatory framework for HRM, forming dedicated institutions, agencies, and entities to support the HRM function, and creating the necessary organizational arrangements and practices to further enhance the role that HRM could play in making government more productive, efficient, and effective.

CHALLENGES FACING HRM IN GOVERNMENT

As alluded to earlier, there are several challenges that contemporary HRM practitioners have to contend with. These challenges include the changing context or environment in which public institutions operate, cultural and legal concerns, dynamics associated with globalisation, economic and political instability, employers' and employees' concerns, and technological innovations. A more complete and detailed exposition of these challenges is not possible given the confinements of this chapter. However, to accentuate the typical skills and competencies HRM practitioners need to possess, some of the most pertinent challenges are briefly highlighted below.

Technological Advancement and a Changing Work Environment

The information age has fundamentally altered the world of work. Modern technology has transformed, and is still transforming, conventional HRM practices, processes, and procedures. Due to the accelerated rate and amount of information flow, information and communication technology (ICT) promotes change in work conditions (Hashim and Hameed, 2012). Remote or telework, the establishment of virtual teams, and web-based recruitment practices are some examples in this regard. The quality of work and life, employee perception and attitudes, and organizational effectiveness all alter to varying degrees when a person works remotely.

Technology has furthermore aided the shift from more conventional HRM practices to more contemporary dynamic and flexible operations. These dynamic and flexible HRM operations are, according to Nasir (2014) and Ritter (2016), characterized by a less formalized and hierarchical relationship between employees and managers within public institutions. Emphasis is more placed on teamwork, network formation, and professionalization. According to IHRIM (2003), HRM data analytics further characterizes HR decisions and applications. Issues such as staff retention statistics, database- and spreadsheet-based analyses, data mining, algorithms, customer satisfaction indexes, and cost-benefit analyses typically improve rational decision-making, ultimately enhancing HRM functions (Hashim and Hameed, 2012). They typically examine employee behaviour, productivity, and causes for turnover before developing a targeted recruitment plan that may include partnering with a university, launching an employee referral programme, reorganizing functions, and instituting job rotation between functions. Using historical data, data mining can anticipate an employee's performance, which could be utilized to advance them in their careers (Hashim and Hameed, 2012). In addition, Naorem (2020, p. 1) maintains that cloud technologies, robotic process automation, and HR analytics, all influence 'human-machine collaboration'. This allows public institutions to engage employees and customers in new, innovative, and improved ways (Strohmeier and Piazza, 2015).

It is evident that HRM has yet to fully grasp the use and significance of technological advancements and to navigate changing work environments. Too much attention is generally paid to straightforward reporting and metrics like staff turnover or engagement, but there is a lack of understanding of how to apply and incorporate these indicators to determine how they affect broader governance outcomes (Strohmeier and Piazza, 2015). In addition, HR specialists still lack advanced analytical abilities (IHRIM, 2003). The amount of data that can be analyzed is growing, which helps with management choices and organizational intelligence (Schultz, 2021). To create, acquire, and reuse the data required for HRM processes, it is crucial to design and use a comprehensive, formal HRM data strategy (Shukla, Wilson and Lavieri, 2017).

Workforce Diversity

The diversification of the workforce is another typical HRM challenge. To efficiently manage a workforce with diverse backgrounds in terms of locations, cultures, races, and genders requires formal workforce diversification (Shukla, Wilson and Lavieri, 2017). Institutions have to establish and make policies and practices in accordance with the culture and environment in which they function in order to manage such diversity successfully (Tzafrir et al., 2004).

According to Daft (2013), the issue of workforce diversity is complicated by related matters such as labour mobility, political pressures, and demographic realities. Therefore, Schultz (2021) argues that HRM should ensure that public institutions have the right staff with the necessary sociopolitical sensitivities, cultural knowledge, and skills that promote unity in diversity. It should be noted that employees thrive in stable and positive work environments, driven by core values. HRM functions such as recruitment, training, development, and organizational communication are all activities that may have a significant impact in this regard. HR managers in conjunction with other senior managers should create a positive and strong organizational culture to support teamwork and positive interpersonal relationships (Hashim and Hameed, 2012).

Changing Employee Expectations and Aspirations

There have been significant changes in the employees' career orientation (Naorem, 2020). This has led to changes in the way employees develop certain expectations and career aspirations. This is especially evident in younger generations with occupational goals distinct from those of the older generations (Naorem, 2020). Workers of today are more focused on their careers and have a clearer idea of the lifestyle they wish to lead. They are growing more conscious of their higher-level motivational needs. HRM should be more conscious of these needs and will need to create adequate plans for their employees' career growth. They should also design appropriate techniques to satisfy the higher-level needs of employees.

Training and Development

According to scholars such as Bhat (2016) and Naorem (2020), changes in the external and internal work environment of government institutions demand constant training and development. Public institutions should become more resilient and adaptable by ensuring that employees gain the necessary knowledge, skills, and competencies to adapt to changing circumstances and demands. The primary goal of providing training and development opportunities should be to make an impression that endures after the programme is over and to keep staff members informed of emerging trends (Bhat, 2016).

This concludes a brief overview of the typical challenges that HRM face. Readers should supplement this content with their own survey of the changing HRM landscape.

CONCLUSION

This chapter presented a concise scrutiny of the role of HRM in government. It is evident that changes in governance also influence HRM approaches, functions, and practices. These shifts may cause substantial challenges for line managers and HRM practitioners.

Every public institution may realize its strategic goals if its personnel are satisfied, valued, and respected. Giving staff technical and proper training will undoubtedly improve their career opportunities and lift their morale. HRM should create adequate plans for employees' career growth and design appropriate techniques to satisfy the higher-order needs of staff. This is especially true in developing contexts such as Botswana. More studies need to be undertaken to track the growth trajectory of the HRM function in this country and the continent in general.

REFERENCES

Aslam, D.H., M. Aslam, N. Ali and B.M. Habib (2013), 'Importance of Human Resource Management in the 21st Century: A Theoretical Perspective', *International Journal of Human Resource Studies*, **3**, 87–96, doi.org/10.5296/IJHRS.V3I3.6255.

Beardwell, I., L. Holden and T. Claydon (2004), *Human Resource Management: A Contemporary Approach*, London: Financial Times Prentice Hall.

Bhat, T.G. (2016), 'A Study on Challenges in Human Resource Management', *International Journal of Research and Analytical Reviews*, **3** (1), 176–186.

Daft, R.L. (2013), *Organisation Theory and Design*, 10th ed., Mason, OH: South-Western Cengage Learning.

Decenzo, D.A. and S.P. Robbins (2013), *Human Resource Management*, 11th ed., New York: Wiley.

Dlamini, P. and D.K.J. Zogli (2021), 'Challenges Facing HRM Practitioners in Achieving Organisational Effectiveness in South African State-Owned Enterprises', *International Journal of Innovation, Creativity and Change*, **15** (10), 561–571.

Government of Botswana. (1982), 'Botswana Employment Act', accessed 23 January 2023 at https://www.ilo.org/dyn/natlex/docs/WEBTEXT/842/64792/E82BWA01.htm.

Government of Botswana. (2009), *NDP10 National Development Plan*, Gaborone: Government Printers.

Hashim, M. and F. Hameed (2012), 'Human Resource Management in 21st Century: Issues & Challenges & Possible Solutions to Attain Competitiveness', *International Journal of Academic Research in Business and Social Sciences*, **2** (9), 44–52.

International Association for Human Resource Information Management (IHRIM). (2003), *HR in the 21st Century: Challenges and Opportunities*, IHRIM, accessed on 20 January 2021 at https://www.academia.edu/35396169/HR_in_the_21st_Century_Challenges_and_Opportunities_IHRIM_the_Worlds_Leading_Organisation_for_Human_Resources_Information_Technology_Professionals._International_Association_for_Human_Resource_Information_Management_IHRIM.

Modisane, K.T. (2015), 'HRD Takes Root in Botswana: From Fledging Beginnings to Positive Steps', *Human Resource Development International*, **18** (4), 429–440, doi/org/10.1080/13678868.2015.1053166.

Mondy, R. and R.M. Moe (2005), *Human Resource Management*, 9th ed. London: Prentice Hall.

Naorem, D. (2020), *Economics Discussion*, accessed 19 January 2023 at https://www.economicsdiscussion.net/human-resource-management/challenges-of-hrm-9-emerging-challenges/31627.

Nasir, S.Z. (2014), 'Emerging Challenges of HRM in the 21st Century: A Theoretical Analysis', *International Journal of Academic Research in Business and Social Sciences*, **7** (3), 216–223.

Ritter, A.F.R. (2016), 'The Impact of Technological Era in Human Resource Management', Master thesis in Management, NOVA School of Business and Economics, doi/org/10.13140/RG.2.2.25512.70400.

Schultz, C.M. (2021), 'The Future and the Role of Human Resource Management in South Africa During the Fourth Industrial Revolution', *South African Journal of Human Resource Management*, **19** (0), a1624, doi.org/10.4102/sajhrm.v19i0.1624.

Shukla, P., H.J. Wilson and D. Lavieri (2017), 'Machine Re-engineering: Robots and People Working Smarter Together', *Strategy & Leadership*, **45** (6), 50–54.

Strohmeier, S. and F. Piazza (2015), 'Artificial Intelligence Techniques in Human Resource Management—A Conceptual Exploration', *Intelligent Techniques in Engineering Management*, 149–172, doi.org/10.1007/978-3-319-17906-3_7.

Thorton, G. (2020), *Data Analytics Assessment*, Gaborone: Elementeq.

Tzafrir, S., Y. Baruch, S.L. Dolan and G.H. Harel (2004), 'The Consequences of Emerging HRM Practices for Employees Trust in Their Managers', *Personnel Review*, **33** (6), 628–647, doi.org/10.1108/00483480410561529.

Van der Westhuizen, E.J. (2005), 'Managing People in the Twenty-First Century: Integrative integrative Public Human Resource Management in Sub-Saharan Africa', *Politeia*, **24** (2), 142–160.

14. Public health governance in Africa
Gerrit van der Waldt

INTRODUCTION

Public health governance generally refers to the structures, systems, and processes through which public health policies and programmes are designed, developed, implemented, and evaluated to improve the health outcomes of the population (WHO, 2012, p. 1). This is influenced by a variety of factors, including political, social, economic, and environmental conditions. In many African countries, health systems are under-resourced and often struggle to provide adequate care to all citizens. In designing suitable health programmes, governments in Africa should consider the specific challenges facing the country, including infectious disease outbreaks, HIV/AIDS, high rates of maternal and child mortality, and the burden of non-communicable diseases such as diabetes and heart disease.

According to the World Health Organization (WHO, 2019), Africa has only 3% of the world's health workers, despite being home to 25% of the world's disease burden. The WHO also reports that the maternal mortality rate in sub-Saharan Africa is 533 deaths per 100,000 live births, compared to a global average of 211 deaths per 100,000 live births (WHO, 2023). In many African countries, public health spending is less than $100 per person per year, which is well below the WHO's recommended minimum of $86 per person per year (World Bank, 2022). The World Bank estimates that corruption in the health sector accounts for between 10% and 30% of total health spending in many African countries. According to UNAIDS (2022), in 2022, there were an estimated 36.7 million people living with HIV/AIDS globally, with the majority (68%) living in sub-Saharan Africa. These and related challenges facing health governance in Africa are complex and multifaceted. Addressing these challenges will require sustained investment in health systems, effective governance and anti-corruption measures, targeted interventions to address the burden of disease, and efforts to strengthen the health workforce. In addition, the recent COVID-19 pandemic revealed serious limitations as far as health governance on the continent is concerned. Governments had to control the spread of the virus, protecting public health while minimising economic damage, maintaining access to health care, managing public compliance with health measures, and securing and distributing vaccines. The question, however, is how citizens perceived the performance of governments in these domains. Scholars such as Kuotsai and Liou (2022) and Yaghi (2023) examined public trust during the pandemic and showed that citizens largely mistrust governments in general and public health institutions in particular because of the way the pandemic was handled. On a five-point scale, the trust in public health institutions declined from 4.44 to 2.46. There was also a decline in the overall trust in government (from 4.16 to 2.19) and in the performance of political representatives and top officials (from 3.59 to 1.67) (Yaghi, 2023).

The purpose of this chapter is to probe the current state of public health governance in Africa and to explore the typical challenges and opportunities for strengthening health governance mechanisms. It examines the nature and scope of health governance and considers the need for increased investment in health systems and the development of human capacity for the delivery of health services. The chapter also highlights the importance of private sector and civil society partnerships and collaboration in fostering health system resilience.

PUBLIC HEALTH GOVERNANCE: AN ORIENTATION

Just like other countries globally, effective public health governance in Africa is guided by a set of standardised principles, including equity, transparency, accountability, and participation (OHCHR, 2023, p. 1). Equity means that all people should have access to quality healthcare services, regardless of their social status or geographic location. Transparency and accountability require that governments be open and honest in their decision-making processes and ensure that they are held accountable for the outcomes of their policies and programmes. Participation means involving all stakeholders, including communities, civil society organisations, and healthcare providers, in the development, implementation, and evaluation of public health policies and programmes.

Public health governance in Africa covers a wide range of areas, including health policy development, health financing, health service delivery, and health information systems. Key content areas of public health governance in Africa include disease prevention and control, maternal and child health, nutrition, health promotion, and health education. Other important areas of focus include health systems strengthening, human resource development, and research and innovation. Let us briefly elaborate on each of these dimensions in the sections below.

Health Policy Development

Health policy development refers to the process of creating policies and strategies to guide decision-making and action in the healthcare sector (Sidney, 2007, p. 80). Health policies are designed to address health challenges and promote positive health outcomes for individuals and populations. According to Mousavi, Jafari and Vosoogh-Moghadam (2020) an integrated framework is required to promote health policy implementation. The typical content of such a framework should include the following:

- Health system organisation and financing: Health policies often address the organisation and financing of healthcare systems, including issues such as healthcare delivery models, payment systems, and healthcare workforce development.
- Disease prevention and control: Health policies may focus on strategies to prevent and control communicable and non-communicable diseases, such as vaccination programmes, disease surveillance, and lifestyle interventions.
- Maternal and child health: Health policies may focus on improving maternal and child health outcomes through initiatives such as prenatal care, postnatal care, and early childhood development programmes.
- Health promotion and education: Health policies may include strategies to promote healthy behaviours and provide health education to individuals and communities.
- Healthcare quality and safety: Health policies may address issues related to healthcare quality and safety, such as patient safety protocols and quality improvement initiatives.

Porter, Rutkow and McGinty (2018) argue that policy changes are necessary to address pressing public health problems. Such policy changes should cope with the complex and multifaceted nature of public health and require input from a wide range of stakeholders and a focus on evidence-based, equitable, and sustainable solutions to improve health outcomes.

Health Financing

Health financing refers to the process of mobilising and managing financial resources to pay for healthcare services (Asante, Wasike and Ataguba, 2020). It involves the collection of funds, pooling of these resources, and allocation of resources to healthcare providers and individuals. According to Wagstaff, Flores and Smitz (2018), the typical content of health financing schemes includes the following:

- Revenue generation: Health financing often involves the collection of funds through various mechanisms, such as taxes, insurance premiums, and user fees.
- Resource pooling: Health financing may involve pooling of financial resources to spread financial risk and ensure that resources are available to pay for healthcare services when needed.
- Resource allocation: Health financing often involves the allocation of resources to healthcare providers, such as hospitals and clinics, and to individuals through insurance or other mechanisms.
- Benefit package design: Health financing may involve the design of benefit packages that define which healthcare services are covered and how much individuals are required to pay for these services.
- Payment mechanisms: Health financing often involves payment mechanisms that determine how healthcare providers are reimbursed for services provided, such as fee-for-service, capitation, or pay-for-performance.

It is evident that health financing is a crucial component of healthcare systems and plays an important role in ensuring that individuals have access to needed healthcare services. Effective health financing strategies should be designed with principles such as universality, equity, efficiency, sustainability, and accountability in mind (Micah, Chen and Zlavog, 2019).

Health Service Delivery

According to Kuir-Ayius (2021), health service delivery refers to the provision of healthcare services to individuals and populations. It involves the delivery of a range of services such as primary healthcare (e.g. preventive care, health promotion, and treatment of common illnesses and conditions), specialised care (e.g. surgical and diagnostic services, mental health services, and chronic disease management), and health facilities and infrastructure, including hospitals, clinics, laboratories, and medical equipment.

Health service delivery is an essential component of a healthcare system in a country. Effective health service delivery strategies should be designed with principles such as accessibility, quality, efficiency, and equity in mind.

Health Information Systems

A further dimension of health governance is the design and utilisation of accurate and reliable health care information systems. According to Tummers et al. (2021), health information systems refer to the collection, storage, analysis, and dissemination of health-related data and information. These systems can include both paper-based and electronic systems, and they are used to support clinical decision-making, monitor healthcare quality, and improve healthcare outcomes.

According to Yusof et al. (2008), health information systems should make provision for several content areas such as:

• Electronic health records that are digital records of patients' health information, including medical history, diagnoses, medications, and test results.
• Health information exchange to allow for the sharing of health information between different healthcare providers, which can improve care coordination and reduce medical errors.
• Disease surveillance systems which track the occurrence and distribution of diseases and other health conditions, which can help identify outbreaks and inform public health interventions.
• Health registries to collect and analyse data on specific health conditions or populations, which can inform clinical research and guide healthcare delivery.
• Telemedicine systems that use technology to connect patients and healthcare providers remotely, which can improve access to healthcare services for individuals in remote or underserved areas.

It is further important that health information systems should support managerial decisions and health care analytics. As such, health information systems are critical components of healthcare systems and play an important role in supporting clinical decision-making, monitoring healthcare quality, and improving healthcare outcomes.

Disease Prevention and Control

Health governance also entails disease prevention and control. This refers to the strategies and activities aimed at reducing the incidence, prevalence, and impact of infectious and non-communicable diseases (Anderson and Mossialos, 2020). These strategies and activities can include vaccination programmes, public health education campaigns, early detection and treatment, and environmental interventions. Disease prevention and control furthermore include epidemiological surveillance, risk assessments, early detection and treatment, as well as the monitoring and evaluation of medical intervention programmes (DoH, 2015).

Maternal and Child Health

Maternal and child health refers to the health of women during pregnancy, childbirth, and the postpartum period, as well as the health of newborns, infants, children, and adolescents (Alam et al., 2015). The content areas of maternal and child health include prenatal care, child immunisation, nutrition programmes, and family planning (Kalipeni, Iwelunmor and

Grigsby-Toussaint, 2017). As such, maternal and child health programmes are critical components of public health governance.

Nutrition

According to Kimokoti and Hamer (2008), Nutritional Studies refer to research on how food impacts the human body and its healthy functioning and are considered an element of a nation's total health system. Given the importance of proper nutrition for general health and wellbeing, it is therefore a crucial part of public health governance. Moreover, nutritional education is a crucial part of health systems since it tries to encourage good eating habits and lifestyles by supplying people with resources and information. Moreover, vulnerable groups in society should be the focus of nutrition support programmes.

In the African context, food security is essential for health system resilience. Climate factors such as drought, poor agricultural infrastructure, poverty, and limited support for subsistence farming all influence food security on the continent. Food security refers to access to sufficient, safe, and nutritious food to meet the dietary requirements of the population. It is therefore essential that health governance incorporate policy and strategic interventions to address food insecurity, such as food assistance programmes and community farming (FAO, 2019). Ensuring food security requires action in multiple dimensions, including improving the governance of food systems, investments in agriculture, health education, and small-farmer empowerment (FAO, 2019, p. 1).

Health Promotion and Education

The final component of health governance in health promotion and education. Health promotion and education generally aim to improve health outcomes by promoting healthy behaviour and lifestyles and increasing knowledge and awareness of health-related issues. Health promotion and education include a range of strategies and activities, such as health education campaigns, behavioural interventions, community-based programmes, workplace wellness interventions, and health promotion policies (Raghupathi and Raghupathi, 2020).

This concludes a brief overview of the respective components of public health governance. In the next section, the focus shifts to health system resilience through collaboration and partnerships.

HEALTH SYSTEM RESILIENCE THROUGH COLLABORATION AND PARTNERSHIPS

As alluded to, public health governance refers to the policy, organisational and managerial dimensions of a health system of a country. A health system refers to the network of organisations, agencies, and individuals that work together to promote and protect the health of citizens of a country. The typical purpose of a public health system is to prevent disease, injury, and disability, and to promote the general health and well-being of a population (WHO, 2023).

Public health systems are designed to respond to public health emergencies, such as natural disasters or disease outbreaks, but also to proactively adjust capacity, systems, and processes in anticipation of future health risks. This implies resilience. Health system resilience generally refers to the ability of a healthcare system to prepare, absorb, and recover from a major health crisis or disaster, such as a pandemic or natural disaster, as well as to continuously adapt to new realities (OECD, 2023, p. 1). A resilient health system can adapt and maintain essential functions in the face of unexpected and disruptive events, ensuring that citizens continue to receive the care they need. In addition, Thomas et al. (2020, p. 5) add that resilience requires the ability to 'learn from shocks'. A shock refers to a 'sudden and extreme change which impacts on a health system' (Thomas et al., 2020, p. 5). Learning in this context also refers to analysing experiences, best practices, and cases from other countries to enhance domestic policies, strategies, and programmes.

According to Van der Merwe and Van der Waldt (2020), the COVID-19 pandemic has highlighted the importance of health system resilience, as countries with strong governance mechanisms have been better able to respond to the crisis and maintain essential health services. However, many health systems in low- and middle-income countries have been weakened by the pandemic, underscoring the need for continued investment in health governance resilience. This underscores the need to improve the capacity of health governance structures to plan, monitor, and evaluate health policies and programmes, as well as strengthening the regulatory frameworks and accountability mechanisms. Resilience in health systems requires a multi-sectoral approach that involves strengthening the capacity of health systems to anticipate, prevent, and respond to crises, as well as ensuring the continuity of essential health services (Thomas et al., 2020). It also requires a significant investment in terms of resources, health infrastructure, and capacity and competency development.

Health system resilience requires investing in building strong partnerships with key stakeholders. A resilient health system thus involves collaboration and coordination among government agencies, healthcare providers, community-based organisations, the private sector, non-governmental organisations (NGOs) and other stakeholders that work together to address a range of health issues and to ensure an effective response to emergencies.

In line with the movement towards network forms of governance, partnerships with the private sector have become increasingly important in the delivery of public health services in Africa. In the case of South Africa, for example, private-sector partnerships in healthcare are essential to strengthen the capacity of government to address the broad scope of health concerns. The South African government implemented the National Health Insurance (NHI) scheme to provide universal healthcare coverage for all citizens (DoH, 2012). The scheme involves partnerships with private sector providers, such as private hospitals and clinics, to expand healthcare access and improve the quality of care. Private health insurance companies, such as Discovery Health, also offer insurance coverage to individuals and families who can afford to pay for private healthcare (DoH, 2012). These companies may also partner with public sector entities to provide healthcare services in underserved areas. In addition, pharmaceutical companies often partner with government to develop and distribute medications for diseases such as HIV/AIDS and tuberculosis.

Apart from the private sector, also NGOs continue to play an important role in health governance in Africa. The Médecins Sans Frontières, for example, is an international humanitarian organisation that provides emergency medical assistance in crisis situations, including Ebola outbreaks, cholera epidemics, and malnutrition (MSF, 2023). A further example is PATH, a global health NGO, that works with government agencies for the delivery of health programmes by making innovative technology available. The NGO Save the Children endeavours to improve the lives of children in Africa. This NGO has been involved in a range of health initiatives, including improving access to maternal and child health services, addressing malnutrition, and responding to health emergencies (see https://www.savethechildren.org.za/).

GOVERNMENT HEALTH PROGRAMMES IN AFRICA

There are several challenges to health governance in Africa. Scholars such as Azevedo (2017) and Oleribe (2019) accentuate several challenges such as weak health systems and poor governance. Many African countries have inadequate health systems, with poor infrastructure and limited assets, insufficient healthcare workers, and limited access to essential medicines and technologies. This makes it difficult to provide high-quality and equitable healthcare services. Corruption and poor governance can lead to mismanagement of resources, lack of accountability, and a culture of impunity, which can undermine efforts to improve health outcomes. A further challenge is limited funding. Many African countries have limited financial resources for healthcare, which can limit the provision of essential services and the implementation of effective health policies and programmes.

Some African countries also struggle to service citizens in rural and remote areas. Africa is burdened with a high prevalence of infectious diseases, such as malaria, HIV/AIDS, and tuberculosis, as well as non-communicable diseases, such as diabetes and cardiovascular diseases in deep rural areas (Ogunkola et al., 2020, p. 1303). This places a further strain on the ability of the state to bring healthcare workers, medicine, and infrastructure (e.g. mobile clinics) to remote areas.

In addressing the multitude of health governance constraints, African governments have implemented key public health programmes. Some examples of these programmes in different countries are provided below.

Ethiopia

The Ethiopian government implemented the Health Extension Programme (HEP) in 2003, a primary healthcare programme which aims to improve access to essential healthcare services, particularly in rural areas (William et al., 2021) and to address the country's high burden of preventable diseases. The programme is part of the government's broader health sector reform agenda, which aims to promote universal health coverage and improve health outcomes for all Ethiopians (Assefa, Gelaw and Hill, 2019).

Health extension workers, who are trained and sent out to provide a variety of basic health services, such as health education, disease prevention and control, family planning, maternal and child health, hygiene and environmental sanitation, are primarily responsible for implementing the HEP at the community level. They are in charge of providing health services to their communities, including health education, home-based treatment, and referrals to higher levels of care as necessary. The majority of these workers are women who have finished a one-year training programme.

The HEP has been successful in expanding access to essential health services in Ethiopia, particularly in rural areas. Some of the key achievements of the programme include improved access to healthcare services and improved maternal and child health outcomes. The HEP has helped to increase access to healthcare services in rural areas, where the majority of the population lives. According to the Ethiopian Ministry of Health, the programme has expanded access to basic health services to more than 92% of the population (William et al., 2021). The HEP has contributed to significant improvements in maternal and child health outcomes in Ethiopia. For example, the maternal mortality ratio has declined from 1,250 deaths per 100,000 live births in 1990 to 412 deaths per 100,000 live births in 2016. The programme also increased the use of family planning and has created job opportunities for thousands of women who have been trained as health extension workers.

Despite these achievements, the HEP still faces challenges, including limited funding, inadequate infrastructure, and shortages of essential medicines and supplies (Assefa, Gelaw and Hill, 2019). However, the Ethiopian government remains committed to the programme and has continued to invest in its expansion and improvement over the years. The programme has generally been successful in improving health outcomes in rural areas and has been recognised as a model for other African countries (William et al., 2021).

Ghana

The Community-based Health Planning and Services (CHPS) programme is a primary healthcare programme that was launched by the Ghanaian government in 1999 to improve access to essential health services and reduce health inequities in rural and remote areas of the country (Nyonator et al., 2005, p. 25). The programme trains and deploys community health officers to provide health education, disease prevention and control services, and maternal and child health services. The programme is implemented at local government level through community health officers who are trained and deployed to provide a range of basic health services, including health education, disease prevention and control, family planning, maternal and child health, and hygiene and environmental sanitation.

The CHPS has a strong emphasis on community engagement and participation, and it works closely with traditional authorities and community leaders to ensure that health services are accessible and responsive to local needs. The programme also places a particular focus on maternal and child health, and it includes interventions to promote healthy pregnancies, safe deliveries, and newborn care (Sory, Nyonator and Tornui, 2002).

Despite its achievements, the programme still faces challenges, including limited funding, inadequate infrastructure, and shortages of essential medicines and supplies. However, it seems that the Ghanaian government remains committed to the programme and has continued to invest in its expansion and improvement over the years.

Kenya

The National Hospital Insurance Fund (NHIF) is a social health insurance scheme that was established by the Kenyan government in 2010 to provide affordable and accessible healthcare services to Kenyan citizens (Barasa et al., 2018). The programme provides access to a range of healthcare services, including inpatient and outpatient care, maternity services, and specialist care. The NHIF is mandatory for all formal sector employees and optional for the rest of the population. The NHIF is the main provider of health insurance in Kenya and is responsible for providing healthcare coverage to all formal sector employees, including civil servants, employees of private companies, and members of the armed forces (Munge et al., 2018, p. 245).

The NHIF provides a selection of health insurance plans that include maternity services, dental care, inpatient and outpatient treatment, as well as other healthcare services. These programmes are inexpensive and operate on a pay-as-you-earn basis, with monthly contributions to the fund made by both employers and employees according to their income (Munge et al., 2018). The NHIF is in charge of overseeing healthcare sector regulation in Kenya and ensuring that healthcare providers adhere to a set of quality standards in addition to providing health insurance coverage. The NHIF collaborates closely with healthcare organisations to make sure they deliver high-quality treatment and to bargain for reasonable service fees.

To date, the NHIF still faces challenges, including limited funding, fraud and corruption, and inadequate healthcare infrastructure in some parts of the country (Barasa et al., 2018). However, the Kenyan government maintains that the NHIF remains to be a suitable vehicle to address the country's health concerns.

Nigeria

The Nigerian government implemented the National Health Insurance Scheme in 2005, which aims to provide affordable healthcare coverage to all Nigerians. The programme is mandatory for all federal government employees and optional for the rest of the population. The NHIS provides access to a range of healthcare services, including primary care, specialist care, and hospitalisation (Adebiyi and Adeniji, 2021).

The NHIS offers a range of health insurance plans that provide coverage for inpatient and outpatient care, maternity services, dental care, and other healthcare services. The plans are affordable and are based on a contributory system, where individuals, employers, and the government make contributions to the fund. The programme has played a significant role in improving access to healthcare services in Nigeria, particularly for low-income earners who would otherwise be unable to afford quality healthcare services. However, the NHIS still faces challenges, including limited funding, fraud and corruption, and inadequate healthcare infrastructure in some parts of the country. In addition, many Nigerians are still not enrolled in the programme and there is a need to increase awareness about the importance of health insurance in the country (Adebiyi and Adeniji, 2021).

South Africa

South Africa's Health Plan is a comprehensive policy document that outlines the government's strategies and goals for improving the country's healthcare system. The plan was first launched in 2007 and has been updated periodically to reflect changing health priorities and challenges (Burger and Christian 2018). The overall goal of the Health Plan is to improve health outcomes for all South Africans, with a particular focus on addressing health inequities and disparities. To achieve this goal, the plan outlines a range of strategies and interventions that are designed to strengthen the healthcare system and improve the quality and accessibility of healthcare services (Pauw, 2022, p. 922).

The South African government has also implemented the Expanded Programme on Immunization (EPI), which aims to provide free vaccines to all children under the age of one (Dlamini and Maja, 2016). The EPI is designed to protect children from vaccine-preventable diseases such as measles, polio, and tuberculosis, among others DoH (2015).

These government health programmes are just a few examples of the many initiatives being implemented across Africa to improve the health outcomes of the population. Each programme is tailored to the specific needs and challenges facing the country and the population it serves. These programmes are just a few examples of the many public health programmes that have been implemented across Africa to improve the health outcomes of the population.

CONCLUSION

Health governance is critical for improving health outcomes and promoting development in Africa. While progress has been made in recent years, significant challenges remain, including weak health systems, poor governance, limited funding, a high burden of disease, and health workforce shortages. Addressing these challenges will require sustained investment in health systems, effective governance and anti-corruption measures, targeted interventions to address the burden of disease, and efforts to strengthen the health workforce. By working together to address these challenges, African governments, international agencies and other stakeholders can help to promote health and well-being for all people on the continent.

The private sector and NGOs have played an important role in health governance in Africa, often working alongside governments and other stakeholders to improve health outcomes and strengthen health systems. This collaboration increases the resilience of health systems significantly.

REFERENCES

Adebiyi, O. and F.O. Adeniji (2021), 'Factors Affecting Utilization of the National Health Insurance Scheme by Federal Civil Servants in Rivers State, Nigeria', *INQUIRY: The Journal of Health Care Organization, Provision, and Financing*, **58**, doi.org/10.1177/0046958021101762.

Alam, N., M. Hajizadeh, A. Dumont and P. Fournier (2015), 'Inequalities in Maternal Health Care Utilization in Sub-Saharan African Countries: A Multiyear and Multi-Country Analysis', *PLoS ONE*, **10** (4), e0120922, doi.org/10.1371/journal.pone.0120922.

Anderson, M. and E. Mossialos (2020), 'Time to Strengthen Capacity in Infectious Disease Control at the European Level', *International Journal of Infectious Diseases*, **99**, 263–265, doi.org/10.1016/j.ijid.2020.08.005.

Asante, A., W.S.K. Wasike and J.E. Ataguba (2020), 'Health Financing in Sub-Saharan Africa: From Analytical Frameworks to Empirical Evaluation', *Applied Health Economics and Health Policy*, **18** (6), 743–746, doi.org/10.1007/s40258-020-00618-0.

Assefa, Y., Y.A. Gelaw and P.S. Hill (2019), 'Community Health Extension Programme of Ethiopia, 2003–2018: Successes and Challenges Toward Universal Coverage for Primary Healthcare Services', *Global Health*, **15** (24), 1–11, doi.org/10.1186/s12992-019-0470-1.

Azevedo, M.J. (2017), 'The State of Health System(s) in Africa: Challenges and Opportunities', in Azevedo, M.J. (ed.), *Historical Perspectives on the State of Health and Health Systems in Africa*, Cham: Palgrave Macmillan, pp. 1–73.

Barasa, E., K. Rogo, N. Mwaura and J. Chuma (2018), 'Kenya National Hospital Insurance Fund Reforms: Implications and Lessons for Universal Health Coverage', *Health Systems & Reform*, **4** (4), 346–361, doi.org/10.1080/23288604.2018.1513267.

Burger, R. and C. Christian (2018), 'Access to Health Care in Post-Apartheid South Africa: Availability, Affordability, Acceptability', *Health Economics Policy and Law*, **15** (1), 1–13.

Department of Health (DoH). (2012), 'Some Key Messages on National Health Insurance (NHI)', Pretoria: DoH, accessed 12 March 2023 at https://www.health.gov.za/wp-content/uploads/2020/11/some-key-messages-on-nhi.pdf.

Department of Health (DoH). (2015), 'EPI Diseases Surveillance Guideline: Guidelines for Detecting, Reporting, Investigating and Responding to EPI Priority Diseases', Expanded Programme on Immunisation in South Africa (EPISA), Pretoria: DoH, accessed 12 March 2023 at https://www.nicd .ac.za/assets/files/EPI%20Surveillance%20Manual_15Dec2015.pdf.

Dlamini, N.R. and P. Maja (2016), 'The Expanded Programme on Immunisation in South Africa: A Story Yet to be Told', *South African Medical Journal*, **106** (7), 675–677, doi.org/10.7196/SAMJ.2016 .v106i7.10956.

Food and Agriculture Organization (FAO). (2019), 'Food Security and the Right to Food', FAO Regional Office for Africa, United Nations, accessed 12 March 2023 at https://www.fao.org/sustainable -development-goals/overview/fao-and-the-2030-agenda-for-sustainable-development/food-security -and-the-right-to-food/en/.

Kalipeni, E., J. Iwelunmor and D. Grigsby-Toussaint (2017), 'Maternal and Child Health in Africa for Sustainable Development Goals Beyond 2015', *Global Public Health: An International Journal for Research, Policy and Practice*, **12** (6), 643–647, doi.org/10.1080/17441692.2017.1304622.

Kimokoti, R. and D.H. Hamer (2008), 'Nutrition, Health and Aging in Sub-Saharan Africa', *Nutrition Reviews*, **66** (11), 611–623, doi.org/10.1111/j.1753-4887.2008.00113.x.

Kuir-Ayius, D. (2021), 'Sustainable Health Service Delivery', in Filho, L.W., A.M. Azul, L. Brandli, S.A. Lange and T. Wall (eds.), *Industry, Innovation and Infrastructure: Encyclopedia of the UN Sustainable Development Goals*, Cham: Springer, pp. 1–11.

Kuotsai, T.L. and A.K. Liou (2022) 'Public Value and Ethical Challenges in the COVID-19 Pandemic Response', *Public Integrity*, a16, doi.org/10.1080/10999922.2022.2147413.

Médecins Sans Frontières (MSF). (2023), 'MSF: Medical Activities', Djibouti: MSF, accessed 11 March 2023 at https://www.msf.org/.

Micah, A.E., C.S. Chen and B.S. Zlavog (2019), 'Trends and Drivers of Government Health Spending in Sub-Saharan Africa, 1995–2015', *BMJ Global Health*, **4**, e001159, doi.org/10.1136/bmjgh-2018 -001159.

Mousavi, S.M., M. Jafari and A. Vosoogh-Moghadam (2020), 'Integrated Framework to Improve Health Policy Implementation in the Way of Iran 2025 Vision: Bridging Policy to Practice Gap in Developing Countries', *Journal of Education and Health Promotion*, **9** (73), doi.org/10.4103/jehp .jehp_444_19.

Munge, K., S. Mulupi, E.W. Barasa and J. Chuma (2018), 'A Critical Analysis of Purchasing Arrangements in Kenya: the Case of the National Hospital Insurance Fund', *International Journal of Health Policy Management*, **7** (3), 244–254, doi.org/10.15171/ijhpm.2017.81.

Nyonator, F.K., J.K. Awoonor-Williams, J.F. Phillips, T.C. Jones and R.A. Miller (2005), 'The Ghana Community-Based Health Planning and Services Initiative for Scaling Up Service Delivery Innovation', *Health Policy and Planning*, **20** (1), 25–34, doi.org/10.1093/heapol/czi003.

Office of the High Commissioner Human Rights (OHCHR). (2023), 'About Good Governance: OHCHR and Good Governance', Geneva: United Nations Human Rights Office, accessed 14 March 2023 at https://www.ohchr.org/en/good-governance/about-good-governance.

Ogunkola, I.O., Y.A. Adebisi, U.F. Imo, G.O. Odey, E. Esu and D.E. Lucero-Prisno (2020), 'Rural Communities in Africa Should Not be Forgotten in Responses to COVID-19', *International Journal of Health Planning Management*, **35** (6), 1302–1305, doi.org/10.1002/hpm.3039.

Oleribe, O.O., J. Momoh, B.S.C. Uzochukwu, F. Mbofana, A. Adebiyi, T. Barbera, R. Williams and S.D. Taylor-Robinson (2019), 'Identifying Key Challenges Facing Healthcare Systems in Africa and Potential Solutions', *International Journal of General Medicine*, **12**, 395–403, doi.org/10.2147/IJGM.S223882.

Organisation for Economic Cooperation and Development (OECD). (2023), 'Health System Resilience', Paris: OECD, accessed 14 March 2023 at https://www.oecd.org/health/health-systems-resilience.htm.

Pauw, T.L. (2022), 'Catching Up with the Constitution: An Analysis of National Health Insurance in South Africa Post-Apartheid', *Development Southern Africa*, **39** (6), 921–934, doi.org/10.1080 /0376835X.2021.1945911.

Porter, K.M.P., L. Rutkow and E.E. McGinty (2018), 'The Importance of Policy Change for Addressing Public Health Problems', *Public Health Report*, **133** (1), 9S-14S, doi.org/10.1177/0033354918788880.

Raghupathi, V. and W. Raghupathi (2020), 'The Influence of Education on Health: An Empirical Assessment of OECD Countries for the Period 1995–2015', *Archives of Public Health*, **78** (20), 1–18, doi.org/10.1186/s13690-020-00402-5.

Sidney, M.S. (2007), 'Policy Formulation: Design and Tools', in Fischer, F., G.J. Miller and M.S. Sidney (eds.), *Handbook of Public Policy Analysis: Theory, Politics, and Methods*, Boca Raton, FL: CRC Press, pp. 79–88.

Sory E.K, F.K. Nyonator and J. Tornui (2002), *Community-Based Health Planning and Services (CHPS) District Cost Analysis: Technical Report*, Accra: Ghana Health Service and the PRIME II Project.

Thomas, S., A. Sagan, J. Larkin, J. Cylus, J. Figueras and M. Karanikolos (2020), 'Strengthening Health Systems Resilience: Key Concepts And Strategies', Policy Brief 36, European Observatory on Health Systems and Policies, Copenhagen: WHO Regional Office for Europe, accessed 16 March 2023 at http://www.euro.who.int/pubrequest.

Tummers, J., B. Tekinerdogan, H. Tobi, C. Catal and B. Schalk (2021), 'Obstacles and Features of Health Information Systems: A Systematic Literature Review', *Computers in Biology and Medicine*, **137**, 104785, doi.org/10.1016/j.compbiomed.2021.104785.

United Nations (UNAIDS). (2022), 'Global HIV & AIDS Statistics: Fact Sheet', accessed 14 March 2023 at https://www.unaids.org/en/resources/fact-sheet.

Van der Merwe, L. and G. van der Waldt (2020), 'City Government Resilience: Perspectives on Post-COVID-19 Recovery', *Administratio Publica*, **28** (3), 98–119.

Wagstaff, A., Flores, G. and M-F. Smitz (2018), 'Progress on Impoverishing Health Spending in 122 Countries: A Retrospective Observational Study', *Lancet Global Health*, **6**, e180–e192, doi.org/10.1016/S2214-109X(17)30486-2.

William E. Rudgard, W.E., S. Dzumbunu, R. Yates, E. Toska, H. Stöckl, M. Orkin and L. Cluver (2021). *Impacts of the Ethiopian Health Extension Programme (HEP) on Eleven Areas of Adolescent Health and Wellbeing: A Quasi-Experimental Study 2002–2013*, Acceleratehub, accessed 14 March 2023 at https://acceleratehub.org/wp-content/uploads/2021/06/210617-AH-Ethiopia-Policy-Brief.pdf.

World Bank. (2022), 'Current Health Expenditure Per Capita (Current US$) – Sub-Saharan Africa', accessed 14 March 2023 at https://data.worldbank.org/indicator/SH.XPD.CHEX.PC.CD?locations =ZG.

World Health Organization (WHO). (2012), *Governance for Health in the 21st Century*, Copenhagen: WHO, accessed 15 March 2023 at https://www.euro.who.int/__data/assets/pdf_file/0019/171334/RC62BD01-Governance-for-Health-Web.pdf.

World Health Organization (WHO). (2019), 'A Heavy Burden: The Indirect Cost of Illness in Africa', Brazzaville: WHO Regional Office for Africa, accessed 15 March 2023 at https://www.afro.who.int/sites/default/files/2019-03/Productivity%20cost%20of%20illness%202019-03-21.pdf.

World Health Organization (WHO) (2023), 'Africa Region: Maternal Health Overview', accessed 15 March 2023 at https://www.afro.who.int/health-topics/maternal-health.

Yaghi, A. (2023), 'Longitudinal Examination of Trust in Public Administration During the COVID-19 Pandemic', *Public Integrity*, a12, doi.org/10.1080/10999922.2022.2159286.

Yusof, M.M., J. Kuljis, A. Papazafeiropoulou and L.K. Stergioulas (2008), 'An Evaluation Framework for Health Information Systems: Human, Organization and Technology-Fit Factors (HOT-fit)', *International Journal of Medical Informatics*, **77** (6), 386–398, doi.org/10.1016/j.ijmedinf.2007.08.011.

15. Conflict, peacekeeping, peacebuilding and social cohesion in African governance

Eric B. Niyitunga

INTRODUCTION

Although the transatlantic slave trade and the burden of colonialism have been banished from Africa, the achievement of political independence in postcolonial African states has not resulted in an era of economic development nor peace, stability, or social order. Postcolonial African states have encountered numerous conflicts ranging from interstate to intra-state conflicts as well as civil wars. These conflicts led to the widespread destruction of lives and property and hindered economic development, which ignited deep-rooted poverty. Nhema and Tiyambe (2008) note that independence in Africa brought little respite from the ravages of war for people in many African countries. During the Cold War era in the 1960s and 1970s, Africa experienced major civil wars such as the Congo Crisis, the Nigerian Civil War, Idi Amin's butchery in Uganda, and the Ogaden War between Somalia and Ethiopia (Amoo, 1992). During the post-Cold War era from the 1990s till date, internal conflicts and terror attacks have raged in countries in North Africa all the way to the south through central Africa, and from West Africa to the Horn of Africa throughout East Africa.

At the heart of all these conflicts and wars are struggles about power and access to resources; power concentrated around the state and its structures of governance, developmental capacities, delegative practices, and distributional propensities, and resources in terms of availability, control, and access (Nhema and Tiyambe, 2008). The case in point is Burundi where the long-standing civil wars were centred on power and resource distribution. Furthermore, at the heart of the civil war in Burundi, ethnicity was used as a shield to propagate discrimination and marginalisation. One community (Hutu) was considered slaves and thus were vulnerable while the other community (Tutsi) was considered a royal community combined with the myth that Tutsis are born with seeds of leadership in their hands and are therefore entitled to power, to lead, and oppress the Hutu community. This practice was a reflection of the legacy of colonial governance which was based on divide and rule (Niyitunga, 2017a).

A person from the Hutu community was seen as a hopeless human being and was assigned to donkeywork or negligible jobs. They were also deprived of education and were prohibited from joining the national army and police. Niyitunga (2017a) compared post-independence leadership in Burundi with the apartheid leadership in South Africa. This discriminatory and oppressive style of leadership sparked numerous revolutions by the Hutus, which lead to several internal conflicts. A massacre against the Hutus took place in 1972. In 1991, a Hutu revolution movement called 'Palipehutu' launched several attacks in a bid to liberate the Hutu community from oppression. However, this movement did not last long, as the then Burundi National Defence Force overpowered it. In 1993, following the death of the first Hutu president elected democratically, the Hutu community and a few Tutsi people who had been unhappy with the oppression joined forces, which led to a civil war that lasted approximately ten years. With the help of peacekeeping missions, this civil war ended in 2002 with the establishment of a new constitution that set up the foundations for a new dawn of democratic governance in Burundi.

As was the case in Burundi, peacekeeping operations have been deployed in many African countries that had been encountering conflicts and civil wars to enable them to emerge from the conflicts and achieve ceasefire agreements between disputant parties. The missions were also tasked with efforts to persuade disputant parties to consider a peaceful mechanism in order to solve the conflicts from their root causes. The African Union Mission (AMISOM) peacekeeping troops that had been deployed to Burundi substantiated this claim as they enabled parties to consider a mediation process, which later brought them together at the negotiation table. The troops remained available during and after the mediation processes because they spearheaded the implementation of Burundi's comprehensive peace agreements which ended the long-standing civil wars. This was the result of their setting up platforms that enabled the carrying out of peacebuilding and conflict resolution initiatives that strengthened relationships between citizens and brought about social cohesion as well as democratic governance. However, there have been many relapses of conflict during the peacebuilding proceedings, which brought about insecurities that handicapped the peacebuilding processes. In 2015, Burundi experienced a coup d'état which sought to overthrow the then democratic governance, thus igniting insecurities. However, due to the establishment of a democratic governance that resulted from the peacekeeping missions, the coup d'état did not prevail, and the country was not shaken by it and remained peaceful.

This chapter aims to examine the role of peacekeeping missions in promoting conflict resolution, peacebuilding, social cohesion, and democratic governance in countries emerging from civil wars. In an effort to achieve this aim, the chapter is divided into five main sections. While the first section was an introduction, the second section explains the causes of African conflicts and highlights their effects on Africa's governance and economic development. The second section defines peacekeeping and examines its role in setting platforms that lead to peacebuilding processes. The third section explains the role of peacekeeping as well as peacebuilding in promoting social cohesion in conflict-affected states. The fourth section examines the linkages between social cohesion, governance, and peacebuilding. Lastly, the fifth section highlights lessons learnt from the Burundi case study and proffers the concluding remarks and recommendations of the chapter.

COMMON CAUSES OF CONFLICT IN AFRICA

The history of Africa as a continent is replete with conflict (Alabi, 2002, p. 41). Ajayi (2014, p. 143) opined that 'the regularity of conflicts in Africa has become one of the distinct characteristics of the continent'. In its current state, Africa is facing conflicts and wars from the north to the south, the east to the west and throughout central Africa.

Conflict is the universal experience of all life forms (Dennen, 2005). Stern and Öjendal (2010, p. 8) note that conflict is inescapable and unavoidable in society because people tend to disagree whenever they interact with one another. A constant factor regarding conflict is the fact that it is an obvious experience and/or phenomenon in social relations (Alimba, 2014, p. 180). Dennen (2005, p. 3) defines conflict as 'incompatibility of interests, goals, values, needs, expectations, and/or social cosmologies and/or ideologies'. It is a 'felt struggle between two or more independent individuals over perceived incompatible differences in beliefs, values and goals, or differences in the desire for esteem, control and connectedness' (Wilmot and Hocker, 2011, p. 11). It refers to contradictions arising from 'differences in interests, ideas, ideologies, orientation and precipitous tendencies of the people concerned' (Onwe, Nwogbaga and Nwakamma, 2015, p. 78). This means that conflict is the struggle between citizens that have antagonistic values, claims, and goals with the aim to secure scarce power or resources that require the elimination of their rivals or each other to ascertain it. Conflicts can be either violent or uncontrollable, dominant or recessive, resolvable or insolvable (Olaosebikan, 2010, p. 451).

Conflicts can be classified into two broad categories. Firstly, conflicts may be internal or intrastate involving people from the same community within the same countries fighting each other. This category of conflicts has been referred to as intercommunal conflicts. Orji (2015, p. 2) argues that 'intercommunal conflicts are those in which the participants are communal groups'. Brosché and Elfversson (2012, p. 35) note that internal conflicts are those conflicts fought between non-state groups that are organised along a shared communal identity within a particular state. Mostly, internal and intercommunal conflicts occur when political leaders are opposed by a rebellion movement that seeks to overthrow the regime or bring about political change within that regime. These conflicts are mostly armed violence that primarily occurs within the borders of a single state (David, 1997) and are mostly triggered by ethnicity. This was the case in Burundi where conflict over ethnicity resulted in ethnic conflict.

The second category is referred to as interstate or international conflicts. These conflicts occur between two or more states and might involve two additional states which leads to regional or international conflicts. Examples include the conflicts in Burundi, which later involved the Democratic Republic of the Congo (DRC) and became a Great Lakes conflict. The DRC conflicts later comprised more than ten conflicts, which resulted in it becoming one of the greatest wars ever in Africa. However, both intra-state and interstate conflicts can be internationalised. This means that the actors can involve both people from the same community and state and from neighbouring countries as well as the international community. Such internationalised conflicts are called civil wars that have all occurred in Africa.

African conflicts are caused and triggered by multiple factors. These factors include:

- divide and rule colonial policy legacy that is seen in Africa's colonial borders;
- ethnic fragmentation of African states;
- lack of able political leadership and public management;
- failure to deliver quality basic services to the people; and
- chronic poverty and corruption.

They have also resulted from a combination of the following factors:

- political and institutional factors such as weak state institutions, elite power struggles and political exclusion, a breakdown in social contract, corruption, and identity politics;
- socioeconomic factors such as inequality, exclusion, and marginalisation, and the absence or weakening of social cohesion as well as poverty; and
- resource and environmental factors such as greed and scarcity of national resources are often due to population growth that leads to environmental insecurity and unjust resource exploitation (Adinoyi and Muliru, 2015, p. 1).

Many of these African conflicts have necessitated the deployment of peacekeeping troops to resolve them and return stability, social order, and democracy. The deployment of peacekeeping operations has brought about ceasefires that resulted in mediation processes in Tanzania. This ended the ethnic conflicts in Burundi and peace has prevailed for a decade. For example, conflicts in the Great Lakes Region (Burundi, Rwanda, and Democratic Republic of Congo), conflicts in East African region and Horn of Africa. Regions such as Kenya, Uganda, Ethiopia, and Somalia were rooted in a lack of able political leadership and lack of strong public management that weakened the country. The conflict also resulted from hatred that revolved around ethnic divide, and led to ethnic fragmentations, failure to deliver quality basic services, and chronic poverty. Moreover, those conflicts were triggered by the struggle for power by the elites, political exclusion, the breakdown in social contracts, ethnic politics, poverty, inequality, marginalisation, and the presence of weakening social cohesion and suspicion among communities. For instance, Burundi is made up of three ethnic groups: 'the majority Hutu (85 percent), the minority Tutsi (14 percent), and the marginalised Twa (1 percent)' (Uvin, 1999, p. 2; Hatungimana, 2011, p. 7), this ethnic divide and the failure to manage and govern diversity became a major trigger of the conflict.

Ndikumana (2000, p. 31) notes that the rigid stratification of society along ethnic lines in Burundi was an effect of divide and rule, a colonial legacy that had not been addressed in the postcolonial era. This legacy paved the way for the Tutsi minority to be in control of the government as well as the military and the economy (Ndikumana, 2000, p. 30) while the Hutu were marginalised and excluded. Niyitunga (2017b) argued that postcolonial Burundi political leadership was a continuation of colonial governance that had been established by colonialists. This is because the colonialists established and controlled postcolonial political leadership in Burundi to advance their interests.

Based on the above, it can be noted that political leadership is the root cause while ethnicity is the triggering factor of the conflict. Niyitunga (2016) stated that during the Tutsi-controlled regimes from 1972 to 1993, and from 1995 to 1998, ethnic divisions were used to ascend to and maintain power. It is important to note, in other states, ethnicity is the source of good governance, stability, and development; however, in Burundi it became a source of internal conflict (Hatungiman, 2011, p. 5). This is so ridiculous and incomprehensible because women and men in the Hutu and Tutsi community have always intermarried. These intermarriages have always united the two communities. Furthermore, the Tutsi, Hutu, and Twa use one language to communicate and share the same culture, history, and politics. It is vital to understand that the divide-and-rule legacy brought about inequalities in service delivery.

Ndikumana (2005, p. 5) argues that inequalities regarding access to national resources and political power across ethnic groups remained at the heart of the conflict in Burundi. The rule of law has been crippled, allowing political elites to continue to engage in bloody fights to control the state, further deepening the fragility of the state. The failure of successive governments to acknowledge past state crimes has alienated large sections of the population, particularly the victims of such crimes (Nkurunziza, 2018, p. 9). Nkurunziza and Ngaruko (2008, pp. 51–59) contend that inequality in Burundi results from the behaviour of political elites, who fight to capture the state and its associated 'rents to sovereignty'. Niyitunga (2019, p. 13) illustrates that bad leadership is the root cause of the conflict in Burundi and was embedded in the constitution that had been imposed by the colonialists straight after political independence.

PEACEKEEPING AND PEACEBUILDING EFFORTS

To end the conflict in many African countries, particularly in Burundi and establish peace-building initiatives, the African Union (AU) and the international community deployed a number of peacekeeping missions. The United Nations (UN) defines peacekeeping as 'an operation involving military personnel, but without enforcement powers, established by the United Nations to help maintain or restore international peace and security in areas of conflict' (United Nations, 1996, p. 3). Peacekeeping operations are peacebuilding techniques designed to preserve peace, bring about a ceasefire and halt fighting, and assist in implementing peace agreements achieved during the mediation processes (Castellan, 2010). It is one of the strongest techniques used and adopted by the UN in its efforts to maintain international peace and security in world politics (Basu, 1993, p. 261). It has been argued that peacekeeping operations refer to 'UN-led international activity that involves the interposition of military personnel in units between conflicting groups, either to stop violence or to prevent it' (Yilmaz, 2005, p. 15).

Peacekeeping operations are established to set up conditions for a cease-fire during violent conflicts so that situations that lead to mediation, negotiation processes, peacebuilding, peace-making, and peace are established and embraced. The UN (2015) report presents peacekeeping operations as diplomatic tools to encourage peaceful settlements of conflict. Peacekeeping operations have evolved from a primarily military model of observing ceasefires and separating forces and/or fighters involved in such conflicts to lay the foundations of peacebuilding that result in sustainable peace (Castellan, 2010). Basu (1993) argued that since its inception, peacekeeping missions have used multinational forces under UN command to contain and resolve conflicts between hostile states, and between rebel movements and the national army within a single state (Basu, 1993).

Sandler (2017) groups peacekeeping operations into four categories namely (i) monitoring and observing missions, (ii) traditional peacekeeping, (iii) peacebuilding, and (iv) peace enforcement (Sandler, 2017). Sarjoon and Yusoff (2019) argue that peacekeeping operations comprise political, military, and humanitarian dimensions. Its activities and roles have been through intervention, mediation, supervision, and observations as well as assistance. Troops within peacekeeping operations have comprised military observers, civilian police monitors, and civilian support staff. They persuade disputants and opposing parties to adopt peaceful means to achieve their incompatible goals. They also assist them to help restore peace and implement any peace agreements agreed upon by the belligerents. For this reason, peace-keeping operations also assist and support peacebuilding initiatives, thus strengthening conflict prevention efforts. In some cases, such as in Burundi, peacekeeping troops provided emergency relief to civilians affected by the conflicts and restored the rule of law that led to elections that brought about democracy. They also promoted the protection of human rights, which brought about social order and security in Burundi.

There is a close linkage between peacekeeping operations and peacebuilding. It can be noted that peacekeeping operations prepare for peacebuilding activities to take place. This means that peacekeeping forces must enable the fighters to reach a mutual agreement to adopt a mediation process to solve their problem. Once a peace agreement has been achieved, peace-keeping paves the way for peacebuilding activities to take place and be conducted. However, as the Burundi case presents, peacekeeping forces at this juncture serve as observers and oversee the implementation of a peace agreement. One can say that depending on the nature of conflicts, without peacekeeping troops, peacebuilding would be hindered, thus failing to achieve sustainable peace. During peacebuilding activities, peacekeeping forces for example provide security for returning refugees and former combatants (Hansen, 2002, p. 63). They also facilitate the reintegration of former rebels into national army forces.

Boutros-Ghali (1992) defines peacebuilding as 'action to identify and support structures which will tend to strengthen and solidify peace in order to avoid a relapse into conflict'. For example, avoiding a relapse of conflict would require the existence of peacekeeping forces to strengthen and support peacekeeping activities. The UN (2000a, p. 3) defined peacebuilding as activities undertaken in post-conflict situations to reintegrate former combatants into civilian society. Peacebuilding activities also strengthen the rule of law; improve respect for human rights through the monitoring, education, and investigation of past and existing abuses; provide technical assistance for democratic development; and promote conflict resolution and reconciliation techniques (UN, 2000a, p. 3).

PRINCIPLES OF PEACEKEEPING OPERATIONS

Peacekeeping operations have been functioning on three basic principles namely consent, impartiality, and the use of force only for self-defence only (United Nations, 2008b, p. 31; Sarjoon and Yusoff, 2019). It is important to note that these principles are interrelated and mutually reinforcing. These principles play a key role in enhancing peacebuilding activities as well as creating social cohesion that enables the realisation of sustainable peace. All of these principles must be adhered to and respected by all the actors.

Consent and Trust between Parties

Peacekeeping operations can only be deployed with the consent of the main parties involved in the conflict. Niyitunga (2017b) argues that consent is closely connected to the principle of impartiality. This means that in a situation where no consent is granted, peacekeeping forces become partial, which further complicates the process of peacebuilding. However, Niyitunga (2017b) also mentioned that consent would be favourable in situations where conflict has not led to the collapse of the government. This means that consent works well in a conflict-affected state that is still a functioning government or regime. Tsagourias (2006) argued that before the deployment of peacekeeping forces, the host state must freely consent to peacekeeping operations in its territory. In the absence of consent, such deployment would constitute unlawful intervention (Tsagourias, 2006, p. 19) that desecrates the sovereignty of the state, therefore violating international law principles.

The consent of the main parties provides peacekeeping operations with the necessary autonomy to act, both politically and physically to execute its mandated tasks. In the absence of consent, peacekeeping operations run the risk of becoming part of the conflict as well as becoming involved in enforcement action. This means it will be ineffectual in its fundamental role of enabling successful peacebuilding activities that lead to sustainable peace. In the execution of their mandate, peacekeeping operations must continuously be active in ensuring that the consent of the main parties is granted, while simultaneously guaranteeing that peace processes and peacebuilding activities steadily move forward. Moreover, for these forces to bring about successful peacebuilding they must be mindful of the history, customs, and culture of the host state, and should have the capacity to assess the evolving interests and motivation of the parties (Langholtz, 2010, p. 45).

The lack of trust amongst the parties in a post-conflict environment can, at times, result in consent being unclear and untrustworthy. When consent is reluctantly granted due to external issues and because of international pressure, consent may be withdrawn in a variety of ways when a party is not completely devoted to the peace process. For instance, a party that has given its consent to the deployment of peacekeeping operations may subsequently seek to restrict the troops' freedom of action, resulting in a de facto withdrawal of consent. The annulment of consent has been one of the challenges that jeopardises rational peacekeeping operations. Without consent and parties adhering to its principles, the parameters that underpin the international community's strategy to support the peace process becomes thwarted (Langholtz, 2010, p. 46).

When there is consent in the host states, which has allowed for the deployment of peacekeeping operations, there is the propensity of achieving sustainable peace. This is because peacekeeping forces are the forerunners of peacekeeping. Peacebuilding commences when parties have granted their consent and peacekeeping forces have been deployed. The fact that the main parties have given their consent for the deployment of peacekeeping operations does not essentially infer or guarantee that there will also be consent at local levels, particularly if the main parties are internally divided or have weak command and control systems. The universality of consent becomes even less likely in unstable settings, characterised by the presence of armed groups not under the control of any of the parties, or due to the presence of other peace spoilers. To enable peacebuilding activities, the operating environment of peacekeeping operations should continuously be analysed to detect and anticipate the possibility of wavering consent. Peacekeeping personnel must have political and analytical skills, operational resources, and the will to manage situations where there is an absence or breakdown of local consent (Langholtz, 2010, p. 46).

Impartiality and Neutrality

A second principle is impartiality of peacekeeping forces. Successful peacekeeping operations that lead to peacebuilding as well as promoting the achievement of sustainable peace depend on the impartiality or neutrality of the forces while in the host territory. Niyitunga (2017b, p. 83) argued that 'impartiality means not taking sides with warring parties'. Impartiality is built on the essential idea that everyone is equal and has the right to assistance and help when they are suffering (Niyitunga, 2017b, p. 81). This means that no matter where the combatants come from or what they believe in, peacekeeping forces must regard all of them as inherently equal and entitled to the same rights (Tsagourias, 2006, p. 18). This makes impartiality very significant regarding peacebuilding in conflict-affected states.

Peacekeeping operations must discharge their mandate without favour or prejudice to any party. Moreover, impartiality is vital in preserving the consent and collaboration of the main parties during peacebuilding, but should not be confused with inactivity. Peacekeepers should be impartial in their dealings with the parties involved in the conflict. However, the need for impartiality with regard to the parties should not become justification for a lack of action in the face of behaviour that clearly hinders the peace process. Just as a good arbiter is impartial, but will reprimand breaches, peacekeeping operations should not overlook the actions of parties that disrespect the undertakings of the peace process. Nonetheless, the need to establish and maintain good rapport with the parties is paramount. Furthermore, peacekeeping forces must meticulously avoid activities that might jeopardise their impartiality (Langholtz, 2010, p. 46).

A mission should not shy away from applying the principle of impartiality for fear of misconception or reprisal; however, before acting, it is always wise to ensure that the reasons for action are well established and can be clearly communicated to all parties. If this is not done, it may undermine the trustworthiness and validity of peacekeeping, and may lead to the withdrawal of consent by one or more of the parties. This retraction can largely affect the success of peacebuilding. Mostly, conflict-affected states that experienced a relapse of conflict during peacebuilding activities are due to peacekeeping forces either not being impartial, or if force was used to compel the parties to agree and or there was withdrawal of consent along the way. However, when peacekeeping forces are required to counter such breaches, they must do so with caution bearing in mind that transparency, consensus, openness and effective communication are of the utmost importance. These measures protect the task of the forces and rationalise the nature of the mission's responses. Moreover, it will largely lessen opportunities to manipulate the perceptions against the mission, and mitigate the potential backlash from the parties and their supporters. Even the best and fairest of referees should anticipate disapproval from those affected negatively and should be in a position to clarify their actions (Langholtz, 2010, p. 47). This therefore enables the possibility of peacebuilding to lead to sustainable peace.

Non-use of Force

The principle of non-use of force only in self-defence is also linked to the principle of consent and impartiality (Niyitunga, 2017b, p. 85). The notion of self-defence means that peacekeeping forces must not engage in fighting with the parties except in excessive cases of self-defence. Yilmaz (2005, p. 16) argues that non-use of force of UN peacekeepers at times rendered peacekeeping forces ineffective, which lead to massacres and ethnic cleansing during their deployment in conflict-affected states. Niyitunga (2017b, p. 86) argues that the 'general rule for the use of force, only in self-defence, in peacekeeping operations is to protect and respect the sovereignty of the host states in which the armed UN peacekeeping troops have been deployed'. However, peacekeeping forces may use force at a tactical level, with the endorsement of the Security Council if acting in self-defence and the defence of the mandate (Langholtz, 2010, p. 47). They may also use force when there is imminent danger of the occurrence of mass killing – particularly when the parties are yet to overcome their anger, resentment, or hatred among themselves. A typical case is the intractable conflict in the DRC where peacekeeping forces have found it impossible to adhere to the use of force only in self-defence. Cox (1999, p. 27) argued that 'due to the disorder and violence in the DRC, it became evident that the United Nations Operation in the Congo (ONUC) [did] not achieve its objective as it was limited to the use of force within the confines of "personal self-defence"'. It has been argued that, in their use of force, peacekeeping forces should always be mindful of the need for an early de-escalation of violence and a return to non-violent means of persuasion (Langholtz, 2010, p. 48).

SOCIAL COHESION: AN ESSENTIAL INGREDIENT OF PEACEBUILDING

The success of peacebuilding that leads to sustainable peace depends upon social cohesion. Social cohesion is the embodiment of a sense of belonging, which translates to a common identity (Mekoa and Busari, 2018, p. 108). Social cohesion means tolerance and respect for different people and signifies mutual trust and confidence between warring parties (Mekoa and Busari, 2018, p. 108). This concept originated from sociology and has its roots in the field of political science. It gained momentum when issues such as income inequality, different political ideologies, and an increase in crime rates in society confronted world politics. It was also brought to book by raising issues such as a lack of job opportunities, the deterioration of the traditional family system, rapid migration around the world, as well as the culture of individualism versus communalism, as all these factors intensified insecurities in society. Thus, social cohesion has been used to address the abovementioned issues that destroy the ties that unite society (Mekoa and Busari, 2018, p. 108).

Social cohesion entails the process of citizens sharing a moral community, which enables them to trust each other (Larsen, 2014, p. 2). The main role of social cohesion is to promote harmony, solidarity, social order, and security in society (Larsen, 2014, p. 3). Social cohesion indicates the quality of societies since it deals with the relationships between individuals, groups, and associations. This concept highlights the importance of interdependence (Berger-Schmitt, 2000, p. 2). It fosters shared values, trust, hope, and reciprocity. Berger-Schmitt (2000, p. 3) states that there are five dimensions of social cohesion: '1) belonging; 2) participation; 3) inclusion; 4) legitimacy; and 5) recognition'. For peacebuilding activities to lead to sustainable peace they must adhere to the dimensions of social cohesion. Peacebuilding actors must blend their activities with social cohesion so that communities can be brought together, and people are enabled to own the process and have autonomy over it.

Blending social cohesion with peacebuilding activities contributes to establishing bonding ties, identity, values, as well as a necessary environment in which a culture of peace can prevail. It will also bring people together and enable them to forge their own vision for peace. This will enable them to put aside their differences and abolish issues of inequality and cultural intolerance, as well as any kind of divisions that have resulted in conflict. Blending social cohesion with peacebuilding activities will address exclusion and discrimination that exacerbate the occurrence of conflict. It will ensure that individuals pursue a common goal by using democratic processes (European Committee for Social Cohesion [ECSC], 2004, p. 3). Social cohesion is a perfect solution for solving conflicts from their root causes; however, just like the concept of good governance it is an ideal that societies should strive to achieve. Peacebuilding operations informed by a socially cohesive society will adhere to the fundamental rights of the citizens, their right to dignity and recognition, as well as their contributions to society (ECSC, 2004, p. 5). Moreover, it means that people are free to determine their own path, thus pursuing personal development (ECSC, 2004, p. 6).

It is vital to note that blending social cohesion with peacebuilding will promote adherence to the rule of law. Mulunga and Yazdanifard (2014, p. 16) argue that whenever the rule of law is adhered to and respected, people collaborate with each other, as they are driven by a similar cause and therefore tend to follow the rules, regulations and norms of society. Blending peacebuilding activities and social cohesion will foster cooperation. Cooperation is a useful force that promotes social order and security, which leads to sustainable peace and stability. It will also promote better working environments that will in turn enhance performance. It has been argued that whenever a working environment is secured, people will have sustainable livelihoods with sustainable incomes, thus leading to sustainable peace (Mulunga and Yazdanifard, 2014, p. 17). It will further improve communication between the parties, as many conflicts have occurred due to a breakdown in communication.

Improving social cohesion has become one of the cornerstones of violence prevention and peacebuilding programmes around the world. Building trust, cooperation, and a sense of shared purpose between historically divided individuals and groups in society and between society and the state, is generally desirable within itself (Corps, 2021, p. 1). Institutions such as the UNDP, the World Bank, and the OECD admit that social cohesion prevents social fragmentation and enhances the rebuilding of trust between social groups, thus becoming a cornerstone factor that leads peacebuilding efforts to success (Cox and Sisk, 2017; Sisk, 2020).

Improving horizontal and vertical cohesion reduces inequalities and is crucial in fostering sustainable peace (Brown and Zahar, 2015; King, Samii and Snilstveit, 2010). Therefore, this results in social cohesion as a focal point for peacebuilding interventions. Accordingly, scholars and practitioners often see social cohesion as an important determinant of a peaceful, democratic, and prosperous society (Cox and Sisk, 2017; Sisk, 2020). The UNDP (2009) opined that the lack of social cohesion in post-conflict peacebuilding results in increased social tension, violent crime, targeting of minorities, human rights violations, and ultimately violent conflict.

Social cohesion furthermore enforces social capital, which involves social relationships and the quality of those relationships. Berger-Schmitt (200, p. 8) claims that social order is established by bringing people together and reducing inequalities and social exclusion within society. For example, social cohesion reduces regional disparities and provides equal opportunities for women and men, different generations, different social strata, vulnerable people, and many other diverse groups in society. Social order entails adhering to rules and regulations. The lack of social order results in animosity in which society's goals no longer correspond with the legitimate means of achieving those goals (Schiefer and Noll, 2016, p. 589).

Social cohesion entails the willingness of members of society to cooperate and communicate with one another. For sustainable peace to become a reality, trust and openness are required in society. Trust enhances healthy relationships and unites people to work together with confidence and to relate to one another in a spirit of unity and oneness. Social cohesion leads to sustainable peace because it promotes resilient social relationships. Because of the mutual support and emotional connectedness of members of the community that were attained through social adhesion, it leads to trust in social institutions (Lofredo, 2020, p. 5).

In order to ensure sustainable peace, social cohesion must promote trust among the people in society. Three kinds of trust lead to maintaining peace and security in society. They include personal trust, social trust, and system trust. Among these kinds of trust, the most important one is social trust. Social trust promotes honesty, integrity, and reliability and its attributes are objectivity, consistency, openness, and fairness. However, the driving forces behind achieving social trust arise from transparency and accountability by social and government institutions, the stability of social order as well as a familiar environment. It has been argued that without social trust in the community, peacebuilding activities cease to be reliable (ACCORD, 2007, p. 16). They will lack the legitimacy of laws of the institutions and will hence lead to the collapse of the government and social institutions. This is the main reason why numerous peacebuilding activities in post-conflict reconstruction have failed – thus leading to conflict relapse (Vollhardt, Migacheva and Tropp, 2009, p. 140). Social cohesion enforces trust, which is the glue that ensures that the government functions and meets the needs of the people (Lofredo, 2020, p. 7). As such, social cohesion and peace are interdependent. There cannot

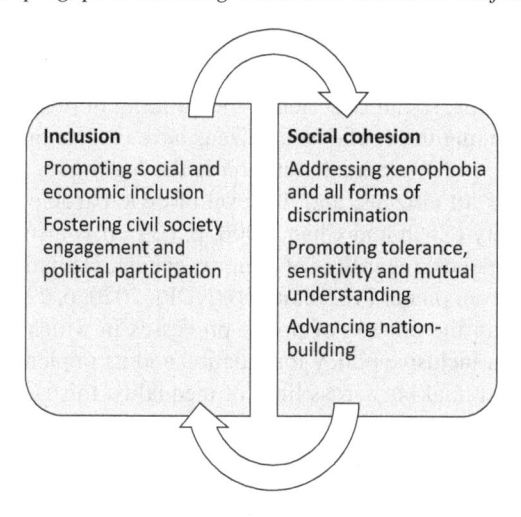

Source: Abdirahman (2017, p. 3).

Figure 15.1   Social cohesion essentials

be sustainable development without peace while, at the same time, peace is achieved through social cohesion. Atkinson (2017, p. 3) argues that for peacebuilding to lead to sustainable peace, social cohesion must be achieved to enable the sustainability of the environment, cities, and society. A socially cohesive society strives for social integration thereby setting the pace for sustainable development. Sustainable development acts as a mechanism that prevents the recurrence of conflicts. Social cohesion is the best solution for sustainable poverty reduction as it ensures inclusion at all levels (Kolev, 2017, p. 1). This is because social cohesion is about togetherness, about being united and living together harmoniously (Uzzell, Pol and Badeness, 2002, p. 1). The abovementioned facts are illustrated in Figure 15.1.

The figure illustrates the essentials of social cohesion whilst highlighting the major aspects of participation, mutual understanding, social networks, integration, and trust. It has been argued that these traits of integration cannot exist in a society without participation and nation-building (Schiefer and Noll, 2016, p. 593). Social cohesion is the driving force behind participation and integration. Nation-building is when a society with diverse origins and histories, languages, cultures, and religions come together within the boundaries of the sovereign state. Such a society is built on unified constitutional and legal dispensation, a national public education system, an integrated economy, shared symbols, and values (Schiefer and Noll, 2016, p. 593). Social cohesion promotes integration, and addresses issues such as xenophobia and discriminatory attitudes (Abdirahman, 2017, p. 3).

Promoting Social Cohesion through Peacekeeping Missions

In post-conflict reconstruction practices, social cohesion has become a vital part of the peacebuilding toolkit as argued by Brown and Zahar (2015). However, it must be understood that it is a very complex matter to consider the diversities that arise. Peacebuilding practitioners and academics argue that social cohesion can reduce inequalities (Stewart, 2010) and contribute to (re)building trust (Chan, To and Chan, 2006). It can also build bridges within (bonding) and among (bridging) communities (Ataguba and Alaba, 2012), and link state and society. In other words, social cohesion is the building of reciprocal trust between citizens and the state, including the confidence citizens have in state institutions and leadership (Chan and Chan, 2006, p. 639). Social cohesion is the legitimacy of state institutions and leadership as viewed by all citizens, and the level of civic participation as well as its level of inclusivity and quality (Chan and Chan, 2006, p. 639). It is also how the state responds to the needs of all its citizens, regardless of identity, gender, affiliation, or other characteristics (United Nations Development Programme [UNDP], 2020, p. 22). State-society relations should also be viewed in the context of policy processes in which social cohesion will be fostered with a focus on inclusive policy formulation and its implementation as well as how it relates to joint decision-making across lines of inequality, mistrust, and divisions (Brown and Zahar, 2015, p. 21).

The presence of peacekeeping forces in the host states ensures that citizens have the opportunity to build social cohesion. Building social cohesion ensures that there is good rapport between non-state institutions and society (Colletta and Cullen, 2000, p. 9). This is because non-state institutions play a decisive role in shaping the cohesiveness of society. In addition, promoting social cohesion ensures that people regardless of their class and position in society have equal access to a livelihood and employment opportunities. Social cohesion ensures fairness in the sharing, distribution, and management of resources. It ensures that goods and services are exchanged in a fair environment, and that people enjoy equal opportunities when accessing basic services of a reasonable quality regardless of their identity and location (Kamatsiko, 2021, p. 11). It provides an integrating framework that unites multiple strands of peacebuilding activities. Not only does it address horizontal inequalities, a root cause of conflict (Stewart, 2008), it also bridges top-down and bottom-up approaches to peacebuilding (Lederach, 1997). It further provides a blueprint for conflict transformation that prevents the relapse of conflicts in societies (Lederach, 2003).

THE ROLE OF GOVERNMENT IN BUILDING SOCIAL COHESION

Peacekeeping troops and peacebuilding activists must work with the government to create situations for sustainable peace and social order. Governments have the responsibility to provide and ensure the well-being of their people and, as such, provide leadership, maintain order, and provide public services, national security, economic security, social security, and economic assistance. The concept of 'government as a provider' is largely about the provision of goods and services to those who cannot provide for themselves in society (Dexter, 2003; Njozela, Shaw and Burns, 2017; Makaringe and Khobai, 2018).

Bidandi et al. (2021, p. 22) argue that the government, in this case, is considered to be a solution to collective action problems and a means by which society creates public goods that benefit everyone. However, they are also subject to recourse problems without collective obligation. In other words, government is built on the idea of protecting the people as well as providing for them. For example, it is built on protecting society from violence as well as providing public goods (knowledge, healthcare) at a level necessary to ensure a competitive economy and a well-functioning society (Koonce, 2011; Kosmatopoulos, 2011; Ataguba and Alaba, 2012; Beall, Crankshaw and Parnell, 2014).

CONCLUSION

The use of peacekeeping operations has been crucial in ending armed conflicts both inter-state and intra-state, with the goal of achieving global peace and security. The aim of peacekeeping operations is to preserve peace. These operations have been successful in achieving peace in many instances, as peacekeeping ensures social cohesion which results in local people uniting and owning the process of peacebuilding. Many of these operations have resulted in ceasefires that have led to the establishment of mediation processes, which in turn ended the conflict. Peacekeeping operations have also brought about the implementation of peace agreements that have led to democratic and political elections. Through the years, peacekeeping operations have predominantly focused on military activity, such as separating opposing forces after interstate conflicts, conducting cease-fires, as well as offering humanitarian assistance to conflict-affected citizens. Peacekeeping military forces have provided security to preserve peace, stability, and social order. They have also played a significant role in peace activities as well as state-building activities at national, regional, and international levels. In a lot of cases, the activities in which peacekeeping operations are involved have resulted in state institutions being strengthened, and the authority of states being restored as well as bringing about support for elections. As a result, the operations are also successful in reforming the security sector and strengthening the rule of law to enable the protection of people's fundamental rights. They have been successful in the training of the police forces as well as the disarmament, demobilisation, and reintegration (DDR) of former combatants. They have enhanced and promoted healthy relationships between communities in Burundi through facilitating reconciliation talks as well as assisting in the training of ordinary citizens to embrace peace. Peacekeeping operations thus became in Burundi the right hand of peacebuilding, which enabled the achievement of the peace and stability the country is currently experiencing. They have also facilitated the inclusion of marginalised groups and indigenous peoples in the government. There is a strong linkage between peacekeeping, conflict resolution, and peacebuilding. Peacekeeping operations remain the major international response for peacebuilding and peace enforcement efforts in intrastate conflicts. These operations are essential components for decreasing the number of severe armed conflicts. Peacekeeping operations promote peace after conflict, decrease the number of battle-related deaths in an ongoing conflict, and increase the likelihood of ending armed conflicts.

REFERENCES

Abdirahman, O.I.O.W. (2017), 'Integration and Social Cohesion: Key Elements for Reaping the Benefits of Migration', New York: International Organisation for Migration, accessed 21 August 2022 at https://migrationnetwork.un.org/resources/integration-and-social-cohesion-key-elements-reaping-benefits-migration.

Adinoyi, J.A., S.Y. Muliru and F.W. Gichoya (2015), 'Causes of International Conflicts and Insecurities: The Viability and Impact of Conflict Management Mechanism in International Relations', accessed 8 August 2022 at https://www.researchgate.net/publication/327861068.

African Centre for the Constructive Resolution of Disputes (ACCORD). (2007), *South Africa's Peacekeeping Role in Burundi: Challenges and Opportunities for Future Peace Missions*, Occasional Paper Series: **2** (2), Durban: ACCORD.

Ajayi, A.T. (2014), 'Methods of Conflict Resolution in African Traditional Society', *African Research Review*, **8** (2), 138–157, doi.org/10.4314/afrrev.v8i2.9.

Alabi, D.T. (2002), 'Emerging Trends and Dimensions of the Rwandan Crisis', *African Journal of International Affairs and Development*, **7** (1), 40–65, doi.org/10.4314/AJIAD.V7I1.27255.

Alimba, C.N. (2014), 'Probing the Dynamics of Communal Conflict in Northern Nigeria', *African Research Review*, **8** (1), 177–204, doi.org/10.4314/afrrev.v8i1.13.

Amoo, S.G. (1992), *The OAU and African Conflicts: Past Successes, Present Paralysis and Future Perspectives*, Institute of Conflict Analysis and Resolution, George Mason University, doi.org/10.13021/G83G71.

Ataguba, J.E.O. and O. Alaba (2012), 'Explaining Health Inequalities in South Africa: A Political Economy Perspective', *Development Southern Africa*, **29** (5), 756–764, doi.org/10.1080/0376835X.2012.730962.

Atkinson, R. (2017), 'Social Cohesion', The Wiley-Blackwell Encyclopaedia of Urban and Regional Studies, accessed 29 July 2022 at https://www.researchgate.net/publication/299975902_Social_Cohesion.

Basu, R. (1993), *The United Nations: Structures and Functions of an International Organisation*, New Delhi: Sterling.

Beall, J., O. Crankshaw and S. Parnell (2014), 'Uniting a Divided City: Governance and Social Exclusion in Johannesburg', *Canadian Journal of African Studies*, **30** (95), doi.org/10.1080/03056240308376.

Berger-Schmitt, R. (2000), *Social Cohesion as an Aspect of the Quality of Societies: Concept and Measurement*, Volume 14, Mannheim: Centre of Survey Research and Methodology, accessed 29 August 2022 at https://www.gesis.org/fileadmin/upload/dienstleistung/daten/soz_indikatoren/eusi/paper14.pdf.

Bidandi, F., N. Roman, G. Davids and F. Khaile (2021), 'The Responsibility of Government and Society Towards Social Cohesion: A Family Perspective', *Strategic Review for Southern Africa*, **43** (1), 6–33, doi.org/10.35293/srsa.v43i1.335.

Boutros-Ghali, B. (1992), 'An Agenda for Peace: Preventive Diplomacy, Peacemaking and Peacekeeping', *International Relations*, **11** (3), 201–218, doi.org/10.1177/0047117892011003.

Brosché, J. and E. Elfversson (2012), 'Communal Conflict, Civil War, and the State: Complexities, Connections and the Case of Sudan', *African Journal on Conflict Resolution*, **12** (1), 33–60.

Brown, M.J. and M.J. Zahar (2015), 'Social Cohesion as Peacebuilding in the Central African Republic and Beyond', *Journal of Peacebuilding & Development*, **10** (1), 10–24, doi.org/10.1080/15423166.2015.1008349.

Castellan, P.M. (2010), *Human rights and Peacekeeping*, Suite: Peace Operation Training Institute.

Chan, J., H.P. To and E. Chan (2006), 'Reconsidering Social Cohesion: Developing a Definition and Analytical Framework for Empirical Research', *Social Indicators Research*, **75** (2), 273–302, doi.org/10.1007/s11205-005-2118-1.

Colletta, J.N. and L.M. Cullen (2000), *The Nexus Between Violent Conflict, Social Capital and Social Cohesion: Case Studies from Cambodia and Rwanda, Social Capital Initiative*, Working Paper 23, Washington, DC: The World Bank.

Corps, M. (2021), 'Understanding the Links Between Social Cohesion and Violence Evidence from Niger', accessed 21 July 2022 at https://reliefweb.int/report/niger/understanding-links-between-social-cohesion-and-violence-evidence-niger#:~:text=Improving%20social%20cohesion%20has%20become,is%20generally%20desirable%20within%20itself.

Cox, F.D. and T.D. Sisk (eds.) (2017), *Peacebuilding in Deeply Divided Societies: Toward Social Cohesion?*, Cham: Springer.

Cox, K.E. (1999), 'Beyond Self-Defense: United Nations Peacekeeping Operations and the Use of Force', *Denver Journal of International Law and Policy*, **27**, 239–259.

David, S.R (1997), 'Internal War, Causes and Cure', *World Politics*, **49**, 552–576, doi/org/ 10.1017/S0043887100008054.

Dennen, J.M.G. (2005), *Introduction: On Conflict. The Socio-Biology of Conflict*, London: Chapman & Hall.

Dexter, P. (2003), *What Holds Us Together: Social Cohesion in South Africa*, Pretoria: HSRC Press.

Directorate General of Democracy and Political Affairs Council of Europe. (2011), 'The Interdependence of Democracy and Social Cohesion', Limassol: Council of Europe, accessed 11 November 2022 at https://www.coe.int/t/dgap/forum-democracy/Activities/Forum%20sessions/2011/Working_documents/Proceedings_en.pdf.

European Committee for Social Cohesion. (2004), 'A New Strategy for Social Cohesion', e-Council of Europe workshops, accessed 23 October 2022 at https://www.coe.int/t/dg3/socialpolicies/socialcohesiondev/source/RevisedStrategy_en.pdf.

Hansen, A.S. (2002), *From Congo to Kosovo: Civilian Police in Peace Operations*, New York: Oxford University Press.

Hatungimana, J. (2011), 'The Cause of Conflict in Burundi', Högskolan Dalarna, International Relations II, Research Paper, accessed 8 August 2022 at https://www.diva-portal.org/smash/get/diva2:519100/FULLTEXT01.pdf.

Kamatsiko, V.V. (2021), 'Vertical Social Cohesion: Linking Concept to Practice', *Peace and Conflict Studies*, **28** (1), 1–29, doi.org/10.46743/1082-7307/2021.1782.

King, E., C. Samii and B. Snilstveit (2010), 'Interventions to Promote Social Cohesion in sub-Saharan Africa', *Journal of Development Efforts*, **2**, 336–370, doi.org/10.1080/17449057.2010.504552.

Kolev, A. (2017), 'Enhancing Social Cohesion as a Means of Sustainable Poverty Eradication', accessed 12 August 2022 at https://www.un.org/development/desa/dspd/wp-content/uploads/sites/22/2017/04/Alexandre-Kolev-OECD-inputs-to-UNDESA-poverty-expert-meeting4may2017.pdf.

Koonce, K.A. (2011), 'Social Cohesion as the Goal: Can Social Cohesion be Directly Pursued?', *Peabody Journal of Education*, **86** (2), 144–154, doi.org/10.1080/0161956X.2011.561176.

Kosmatopoulos, N. (2011), 'Toward an Anthropology of "State Failure": Lebanon's Leviathan and Peace Expertise', *Social Analysis*, **55** (3), 115–142, doi.org/10.3167/sa.2011.550307.

Langholtz, H.J. (2010), *Principles and Guidelines for UN Peacekeeping Operations*, New York: Peace Operations Training Institute.

Larsen, C.A. (2014), *Social Cohesion: Definition, Measurement and Developments*, Institut for Statskundskab, Aalborg Universitet.

Lederach, J.P. (1997), *Building Peace: Sustainable Reconciliation in Divided Societies*, Washington, DC: United States Institute for Peace.

Lederach, J.P. (2003), *The Little Book of Conflict Transformation*, Intercourse, PA: Good Books.

Lofredo, M.P.P. (2020), 'Social Cohesion, Trust, and Government Action Against Pandemics', *Eubios Journal of Asian and International Bioethics*, **30** (4), 182–188.

Makaringe, S.C. and H. Khobai (2018), 'The Effect of Unemployment on Economic Growth in South Africa (1994–2016)', Working Papers 1815, Port Elizabeth: Department of Economics, Nelson Mandela University.

Mekoa, I. and D. Busari (2018), 'Social Cohesion and Its Meaning and Complexities. Indigenous Languages Media in Africa, North-West University', *Journal of Social Sciences*, **14** (1), 107–115.

Mulunga, S.N. and R. Yazdanifard (2014), 'Review of Social Inclusion, Social Cohesion and Social Capital in Modern Organisation', *Global Journal of Management and Business Research*, **14** (3), 15–20.

Ndikumana, L. (2000), 'Towards a Solution to Violence in Burundi: A Case for Political and Economic Liberalisation', *Journal of Modern African Studies*, **38** (3), 431–459, doi.org/10.1017/S0022278X00003414.

Ndikumana, L. (2005), 'Distributional Conflict, the State and Peacebuilding in Burundi', University of Massachusetts-Amherst. Economics Department Working Paper Series 49, accessed 23 August 2022 at https://core.ac.uk/download/pdf/13602815.pdf.

Niyitunga, E.B. (2016), 'African Union and the Mediated Peace in Africa: A Case of Political Unrest in Burundi', in M. Muchie, V. Gumede, S. Oloruntoba and N.A. Check (eds.), *Regenerating Africa: Bringing African Solutions to African Problems*, Pretoria: Africa Institute of South Africa, pp. 287–304.

Niyitunga, E.B. (2017a), 'Exploring the Challenges Facing African Union (AU)-led Mediation in African Peace Processes: Case Studies of Burundi, Libya, and Zimbabwe', Unpublished Thesis, submitted to the University of Johannesburg, Faculty of Humanities.

Niyitunga, E.B. (2017b), 'Critical Analysis of the Viability of the UN Peacekeeping Principles in Complex Emergencies', *Administratio Publica*, **25** (3), 76–91.

Nhema, A. and P.Z. Tiyambe (2008), *The Roots of African Conflicts: The Causes and Costs*, Addis Ababa and Oxford: OSSREA and James Currey.

Njozela, L., I. Shaw and J. Burns (2017), 'Towards Measuring Social Cohesion in South Africa: Lessons for Nation Branding Developers', *Strategic Review for Southern Africa*, **39** (1), 29–64, doi.org/10.35293/srsa.v39i1.320.

Nkurunziza, J. and F. Ngaruko (2008), *Why Has Burundi Grown So Slowly? The Political Economy of Redistribution*, Cambridge: Cambridge University Press.

Nkurunziza, J.D. (2018), 'The Origin and Persistence of State Fragility in Burundi', accessed 15 September 2022 at https://www.theigc.org/wp-content/uploads/2018/04/Burundi-report-v2.pdf.

Olaosebikan, J.A. (2010), 'Conflicts in Africa: Meaning, Causes, Impact and Solution', *International Multidisciplinary Journal*, **4**, 540–560, doi.org/10.4314/afrrev.v4i4.69251.

Onwe, S.O., D. Nwogbaga and M. Nwakamma (2015), 'Effects of Social Conflicts on the Sustainable Development of Ebonyi State. A Study of the Ezillo/Ezza Ezillo Communal Conflict (2008–2014)', *Developing Country Studies*, 78–86, accessed 21 July 2022 at https://citeseerx.ist.psu.edu/viewdoc/download?doi=10.1.1.1009.624&rep=rep1&type=pdf.

Orji, N. (2015), 'The 2015 Nigerian General Elections', *Africa Spectrum*, **50** (2), 73–85, doi.org/10.1177/000203971505000204.

The Republic of South Africa, Department of Arts and Culture. (2010), 'What Is Social Cohesion and Nation Building?', accessed 23 July 2022 at http://www.dac.gov.za/sites/default/files/WHAT%20IS%20SOCIAL%20COHESION%20AND%20NATION%20(3).pdf.

Sandler, T. (2017), 'International Peacekeeping Operations: Burden Sharing and Effectiveness', *Journal of Conflict Resolution*, **61** (9), 1875–1897, doi.org/10.1177/00220027177086.

Sarjoon, A. and M.A. Yusoff (2019), 'The United Nations Peacekeeping Operations and Challenges', *Academic Journal of Interdisciplinary Studies*, **8** (3), 202–211.

Schiefer, D. and J. van der Noll (2017), 'The Essentials of Social Cohesion: A Literature Review', *Social Indicators Research*, **132** (2), 579–603, doi.org/10.1007/s11205-016-1314-5.

Sisk, T.D. (2020), *Strengthening Social Cohesion: Conceptual Framing and Programming Implications*, New York: United Nations Development Programme.

Stern, M. and J. Öjendal (2010), 'Mapping the Security–Development Nexus: Conflict, Complexity, Cacophony, and Convergence?', *Security Dialogue*, 41 (1), 5–29, doi.org/10.1177/09670106093570.

Stewart, F. (ed.) (2008), *Horizontal Inequalities and Conflict: Understanding Group Violence in Multiethnic Societies*, London: Palgrave Macmillan.

Stewart, F. (2010), *Horizontal Inequalities as a Cause of Conflict: A Review of Crises Findings*, Washington, DC: The World Bank.

Tsagourias, N. (2006), 'Consent, Neutrality/Impartiality and the Use of Force in Peacekeeping: Their Constitutional Dimension', *Journal of Conflict and Security Law*, **11** (3), 465–482, doi.org/10.1093/jcsl/krl016.

UNDP. (2009), *Community Security and Social Cohesion: Towards a UNDP Approach*, New York: Bureau for Crisis Prevention and Recovery.

United Nations. (2000), *Brahimi Report. Report of the Panel on United Nations Peace Operations*, United Nations General Assembly Security Council, New York: United Nations.

United Nations. (2008), *United Nations Peacekeeping Operations Principles and Guidelines*, United Nations Department of Peacekeeping Operations Department of Field Support, accessed 12 October 2022 at https://www.un.org/ruleoflaw/blog/document/united-nations-peacekeeping-operations-principles-and-guidelines-the-capstone-doctrine/.

United Nations. (2015), *The Future of United Nations Peace Operations: Implementation of the Recommendations of the High-Level Independent Panel on Peace Operations*, New York: United Nations, accessed 23 October 2022 at http://www.un.org/apps/news/story.asp?NewsID=51855&&Cr=peacekeep&&Cr1=#.VfhHBRHtmkq.

United Nations Development Programme (UNDP). (2020), *Strengthening Social Cohesion, Conceptual Framing and Programming Implications*, accessed 12 June 2022 at https://www.undp.org/content/undp/en/home/librarypage/democraticgovernance/conflict-prevention/strengthening-social-cohesion--conceptual-framing-andprogrammin.html.

United Nations Security Council. (1973), 'Report of the Secretary-General on the Implementation of Security Council Resolution 340', accessed 20 June 2022 at https://www.securitycouncilreport.org/atf/cf/%7B65BFCF9B-6D27-4E9C-8CD3-CF6E4FF96FF9%7D/Chap%20VII%20S%2011052%20REV1.pdf.

United Nations. (1996), *The Blue Helmets: A Review of United Nations Peace-Keeping*, 3rd ed., New York: United Nations.

Uvin, P. (1999), 'Ethnicity and Power in Burundi and Rwanda: Different Paths to Mass Violence', *Comparative Politics*, **31** (3), 253–271, doi.org/10.2307/422339.

Uzzell, D., E. Pol and D. Badeness (2002), 'Place Identification, Social Cohesion, and Environmental Sustainability', *Environment and Behaviour*, **34** (1), 26–53, doi.org/10.1177/0013916502034001003.

Vollhardt, J.K., K. Migacheva and L.R. Tropp (2009), 'Social Cohesion and Tolerance for Group Differences', in J. Rivera (ed.), *Handbook on Building Cultures of Peace*, New York: Springer, pp. 139–152.

Wilmot, W.W. and J. Hocker (2011), *Interpersonal Conflict*, New York: McGraw-Hill.

Yilmaz, M.E. (2005), 'UN Peacekeeping in the Post-Colkd War Era', *International Journal on World Peace*, **22** (2), 13–28.

16. Fostering democratic governance in Africa: the case of SADC

Paul Kariuki

INTRODUCTION

Democratic governance is central to achieving a prosperous Africa. At the 2000 Millennium Summit, global leaders resolved to 'spare no effort to promote democracy and strengthen the rule of law, as well as respect for all internationally recognized human rights and fundamental freedoms including the right to development' (UNDP, 2020, p. 5). This implies a commitment to building open, responsive, and accountable institutions and processes that serve citizens' needs and aspirations. This commitment was further strengthened with the African Union's Charter on Democracy, Elections, and Governance (2007). Furthermore, the leaders recognized that it is upon this foundation that democratic values and standards are built and that institutions are founded according to democratic processes and norms, anchored on principles such as the rule of law, institutional accountability and responsiveness, political pluralism, an active civil society, human rights, and democratic elections. Democratic governance floundered across Africa over the past two decades as countries grappled with extensive socio-economic and political change during the transition from single-party states to multi-party democracies. The COVID-19 pandemic exacerbated the situation, further exposing the fault lines in the sociopolitical and economic architecture of most countries.

There has been much debate on whether it is possible to have a 'real' democratic society that is devoid of bad governance. According to some perspectives, Africa has a long way to go in fostering a perfect democracy. It is argued that the severed ties between Africa and the western world may make it very difficult for the continent to achieve the desired democratic structure (Mawere and Mwanaka, 2015). The one-party governance model has negatively impacted the realization of the dividends of democracy in Africa and many countries face calls for democratic governance including free and fair elections, the free flow of information, and popular participation. Internal and external pressure has been exerted to ensure accountability and for democratic governments to deliver on the promises of economic growth and prosperity they made when standing for office (National Research Council, 1992). Donors and creditors have also called for transparency and accountability. While in the past, external aid was provided to African countries regardless of the type of rule, the situation has changed, with western donors preferring to support countries with democratic rule and a good human rights record. It is in this context that former Ambassador Thomas R. Pickering, the U.S. permanent representative to the United Nations stated that 'It is not our role to decide who governs any country, but we will use our influence to encourage governments to get their people to make that decision for themselves' (US Dept of State, 1999, p. 2). The implication is that western donors will henceforth only provide aid to countries undertaking both political and economic reforms (National Research Council, 1992). Africa is gradually accommodating a sea change in political and economic systems. Speaking in his capacity as chairperson of the African Leadership Forum, former Nigerian head of state, General Obasanjo observed in April 1990:

> The changes taking place in Eastern Europe have far-reaching political implications for the Third World in general and for Africa in particular. The winds that swept away dictatorships and autocratic one-party systems and State structures, inefficient economic systems and unresponsive social institutions in Eastern Europe and fuelled a democratic rejuvenation and the observance of human rights, are not unfamiliar to Africa. The winds of change in Eastern Europe are providing considerable opportunities for the African people to intensify their just struggle for democracy. (National Academies, 1992, p. 1)

Some African countries remain under authoritarian rule, leading individual citizens and civil society movements to call for a return to true democracy. The Southern African Development Community (SADC) has embraced institutionalization of multi-party democratic governance since the 1980s and early 1990s as part of advocacy for a shift from authoritarian rule marked by one-person, one-party rule, and military juntas that characterized the region from the 1960s to the 1980s. This does not mean that there are no democratic deficits that require critical attention if democracy is expected to endure. Such deficits include the failure to transition to democracy in some of the SADC countries and the fact that those that have undergone such a transition still have a way to go. The SADC member states each have their own peculiarities. According to Matlosa (2008), a few such as Botswana and Mauritius enjoy longstanding liberal democracy while the Democratic Republic of Congo (DRC), Lesotho, Malawi, Mozambique, Namibia, South Africa, Tanzania, and Zambia have undergone a democratic transition in the recent past. In Angola, Eswatini, and Zimbabwe, democratic transition has stalled or is in a state of reversal.

Against this backdrop, this chapter examines the various types of governance and democracy practised in Africa with a focus on the SADC region in order to determine the prospects for the consolidation of democracy in Southern Africa. It also appraises democratic principles and the best way to foster democratic governance in Africa.

CONCEPTUAL FRAMEWORK

The extensive nature of concepts applicable to democracy illustrates the relatively complex nature of the theory and practice of democratic governance. Some of the key concepts in this regard are briefly defined below.

Democracy

The origins of the term democracy lie in two Greek words, 'people' (dēmos) and 'rule' (karatos). There is no universally accepted definition of democracy. However, Osaghae (1992, p. 40) notes that all definitions share the fundamental objective of 'how to govern the society in such a way that power actually belongs to all people'. Democracy involves empowering citizens to take political control. It limits the power of political leaders and ensures separation of powers between government entities. It also involves the protection of human rights and liberties. In a democratic space, the people 'rule' and control the form and functions of their government (Fleck and Hanssen, 2006, p. 117). A sound democracy is characterized by freedom of expression and competitive elections devoid of intimidation and victimization. The wishes of the people are projected by elected lawmakers saddled with the responsibility of writing and voting on laws and setting policy. Lawmakers must balance conflicting demands and obligations to maximize freedom and protect individual rights. Research points to progress in achieving true democracy around the world since the mid-1970s (Harrison and Boyd, 2018).

Democratic Governance

African countries have enjoyed democratic governance since the 1990s and most have witnessed institutional changes in this regard. For example, in South Africa, the racially based apartheid system was replaced with a non-racial democracy. African countries that were ruled by civilian and military dictatorships have gradually adopted constitutionalism and constitutional government and implemented major reforms to limit terms for successive governments. Various indices can be used to measure democratic governance in Africa (Abramowitz, 2018), including those that focus on free elections, human rights, and property rights devised by non-governmental organizations (NGOs), such as Freedom House's Freedom in the World index, the Mo Ibrahim Index of African Governance, and the Fraser Institute's Economic Freedom of the World index. The indices determine the status of states as 'free', 'partially free', or 'not free' (Abramowitz, 2018). Sub-Saharan African states such as Sudan, Cameroon, and Ethiopia were pronounced 'not free' in 2018 while Namibia, Botswana, and Ghana were pronounced 'free' (Freedom House, 2018). 'Free' implies that a country upholds the values and principles of a democratic institution such as free and fair elections with freedom of electoral participation.

Good Governance

While African countries' adoption of constitutionalism has deepened democracy and the institutionalization of constitutional government, some are still struggling to address executive shortcomings and violations of human rights. According to the World Bank's Governance Global Practice (2022, p. 1), good governance can be regarded as 'capable, efficient, open, inclusive and accountable states'. Good governance is expected to improve citizens' socioeconomic status. Without this, democracy cannot be said to have prevailed and may be difficult to consolidate (Graham, 2019). Most SADC countries have enjoyed more political rights and liberties but have yet to enjoy socioeconomic rights and justice. The authoritarian regimes that characterized many of these states prior to and following independence failed to promote good governance (Abramowitz, 2018). A lack of good governance results in joblessness, corruption, civil unrest, criminality, and social inequality as well as voter apathy and a lack of trust in government. Zambia is an example of a country that experienced unrest due to the socioeconomic challenges faced by citizens (Freedom House, 2018). Good governance promotes peace, development, and social cohesion.

Citizen Participation

The level of citizen participation in electoral activities depends on the nature of the regime (Matlosa, 2008). Citizen participation generally refers to public representation in government affairs, inclusive of voting in political elections and taking part in local decision-making (EPA,

2023). While participation in elections every five years (as occurs in most African countries) is a good sign, citizens should also be able to influence policymaking during the tenure of an elected leader. However, both political parties and citizens tend to go into hibernation as soon as the election is over, leaving the running of the country and formulation/implementation of policies in the hands of government. Citizen participation in political activities in SADC countries varies. It is relatively high in South Africa compared to countries such as Mauritius, Namibia, and Botswana, while in Lesotho, Zambia, Tanzania, and Mozambique civil society groups tend to wait to be called upon by the government to express their opinions (Matlosa, 2008). Authoritarian government stifles political participation, as witnessed in Eswatini and Zimbabwe where police brutality against citizens reaches its peak during times of elections.

Accountability

The best way to determine the level of democratization of a country is to measure the extent of accountability entrenched in governance (Fleck and Hanssen, 2006). Accountability simply refers to answerability or holding public officials responsible for their actions or inactions. The government has a responsibility to be accountable to the governed. Countries such as South Africa, Botswana, Mauritius, and Namibia generally observe this practice (Freedom House, 2018). However, one of the major challenges in some SADC countries such as Botswana is the dominance of the majority over the minority group/party as well as parliament which makes separation of powers and accountability very difficult to achieve. Despite the institutionalization of the democratic process in Mauritius, there is still a problem of accountability due to under-representation of women in positions of authority and the weakness of opposition parties which are expected to speak for the voiceless in society. In Namibia, South Africa, and Botswana, one party's dominance (i.e. the Southwest Africa People's Organisation, the African National Congress, and Botswana Democratic Party) is largely responsible for dwindling accountability (Freedom House, 2018). Civil society groups are doing a good job in confronting this challenge in South Africa but the same cannot be said of Namibia and Botswana which lack a vibrant civil society sector (Graham, 2019). While the executive dominates the legislature in Mozambique, this is not the main reason for the lack of accountability. Rather, the weak connection between the electorate and parliament has undermined it. Countries such as Malawi, Zambia, and Lesotho once used the First-Past-The-Post (FPTP) system which was inherited from the colonial era. It was designed to ensure accountability, but only rewards larger parties with broad-based support in various parts of the country (Harrison and Boyd, 2018). In 2002, Lesotho adopted a model known as the Mixed Member Proportional (MMP) system that has broadened representation in parliament and ensured political stability.

DEMOCRATIC GOVERNANCE PRAXIS IN AFRICA

African countries have undergone a democratic transformation since the early 1990s. The most notable example is South Africa's transition to non-racial democracy (Mbaku, 2020). Authoritarian regimes have gradually been replaced by rule-of-law-based governance systems characterized by constitutionalism and constitutional government, including reforms such as term limits. That is not to say that all African countries are enjoying the dividends of democracy, as some have struggled to institutionalize and deepen democratic principles and confront executive impunity, particularly that associated with the abuse of executive power and human rights violations. Countries such as Nigeria, Kenya, Ghana, and Liberia have complied with the two-term limit for the executive while other countries have attempted to subvert it by using legislatures loyal to the government to change the constitution or by eliminating the age limit for presidents (Mbaku, 2020). This is referred to as a constitutional coup and is a strategy to intimidate the opposition and prevent it from participating in elections. African presidents that have amended their countries' constitutions to overturn the two-term limit include Gnassingbé (Togo), Museveni (Uganda), Déby (Chad), Biya (Cameroon), Kagame (Rwanda), the late Nkurunziza (Burundi), and el-Sisi (Egypt) (Mbaku, 2020). A lack of strong institutions and democratic ethos enable such manipulation. As the level of democratic development improves, constitutional coups will gradually fade away. While elections should entrench and deepen democracy, countries such as Cameroon, the Republic of the Congo, and Equatorial Guinea use them to legitimize leaders' indefinite stay in power (Freedom House, 2018). According to Ideal (2021), there has been a gradual decline in democratic activities across Africa. Indeed, the number of African countries tagged as 'authoritarian' by the Global State of Democracy now outnumbers the democratic ones.

The slide into authoritarian rule in recent years undermines the remarkable improvement in democratic processes over the past three decades. In 1985, 2015, and 2020 there were 3, 22, and 18 democracies, respectively, which is indicative of a democratic relapse between 2015 and 2020. The regional distribution of countries tagged democratic shows that, except for two, they were all in Southern and West Africa, with none in Central Africa and only one each in North and East Africa. One of the major reasons is the complete democratic breakdown due to military coups in some countries. The challenges confronting the achievement of full democracy in African countries include:

(a) A lack of free and fair elections: True democracy requires free and fair elections. Violence has erupted following elections in some countries due to incumbent presidents' desire to serve a third term and intimidation of opposition parties. The military has also been deployed to stifle the opposition. International IDEA (2021) notes that South Africa, Ghana, Cabo Verde, and Senegal are the only four African countries that have a high score in representative government.

(b) The COVID-19 pandemic: The pandemic has negatively impacted the democratic process in most African countries. About 68% of African countries fall within the bottom 25% globally in terms of service delivery and welfarism. The pandemic increased social inequalities and stifled freedom of expression, with citizens prevented from openly discussing it and criticizing the government (International IDEA, 2021).

(c) Constitutional coups: These involve changes to the constitution to confer undue advantages on the incumbent government in connivance with the legislature. In its most drastic form, it could involve the unconstitutional removal of a democratically elected government through military action. According to BBC News (2022), 'African countries have experienced one coup or the other. When a country has one coup, that's often a harbinger of more coups. Coups dropped to around two a year in the two decades up to 2019. We are only three years into the current decade and while in 2020 only one coup was reported in Mali, there was a noticeably higher than average number in 2021 with six coups or attempted coups recorded. There were successful coups in Chad, Mali, Guinea and Sudan and failed military takeovers in Niger and Sudan'. In September 2021, United Nations

Secretary-General António Guterres expressed concern over the sudden reemergence of military coups and blamed this on a lack of intervention by the international community. Such coups are an affront to democracy.

(d) Ineffective legislatures: Parliament ensures civic participation and creates an enabling environment for citizens and civil society groups to operate. Many African countries have non-functional parliaments that are incapacitated by authoritarianism on the part of the executive or influence by the majority party (International IDEA, 2021).

DEMOCRATIC GOVERNANCE IN SOUTHERN AFRICA (SADC): SELECTED COUNTRY CASES

According to SADC (2022), the Southern African Development Community (SADC) is a Regional Economic Community comprising 16 member states, namely: Angola, Botswana, Comoros, Democratic Republic of Congo, Eswatini, Lesotho, Madagascar, Malawi, Mauritius, Mozambique, Namibia, Seychelles, South Africa, Tanzania, Zambia, and Zimbabwe. Established in 1992, SADC is committed to Regional Integration and poverty eradication within Southern Africa through economic development and ensuring peace and security. While most SADC countries have adopted democratic governance, some have yet to achieve institutionalized democracy (Matlosa, 2008). A number of studies (e.g. Cawthra, Du Pisani and Omari, 2007; EISA, 2008; Matlosa, 2008) have been conducted on SADC countries' successful transition from authoritarian rule toward multi-party democratic dispensations. This section examines selected cases in the region.

Angola

The 1975 constitution abolished the positions of prime minister and deputy prime minister, creating space for a one-party state headed by a president who was also the chair of the People's Movement for the Liberation of Angola (MPLA). The new constitution promulgated in 1992 created a multiparty system with an elected president as the head of state who is assisted by a prime minister and sought to protect human rights (Britannica, 2022). However, the planned transition following an election was aborted due to the extreme violence perpetrated by the main opposition party, the National Union for the Total Independence of Angola (UNITA), after the MPLA won the election. Lives were lost and property was destroyed, with livelihoods put on hold (Matlosa, 2008). While the new National Assembly included representatives of UNITA and the National Front for the Liberation of Angola (FNLA) President José Eduardo dos Santos continued to rule without democratic legitimation. Conflict continued between the armed forces of the MPLA (now the state armed forces) and UNITA, leading to the murder of the leader of UNITA, Jonas Savimbi in 2002. Guided by the 1992 constitution, from 2002 to 2010, Angola was ruled by a President, the Prime Minister, and Council of Ministers, with the governors of the 18 provinces appointed by the president. Power was concentrated in the hands of the president, with no possibility of judicial review.

Following the end of the civil war in 2002, elections were not held until 2008. The legislative elections in 2008 were the first since the 1992 general elections which led to the civil war. The MPLA secured 82% of the votes, with UNITA, the main opposition, gaining 10%. The MPLA won 191 of 220 seats in parliament. Presidential elections were planned for 2009 but could not be held due to the constitutional provision which prevents direct elections for the presidency but allows the leader of the largest party in the National Assembly to automatically become president. Legislative elections are held every five years. In 2012, the MPLA received 72% of the votes, losing 16 seats in parliament. The general election in August 2017 to elect the president and National Assembly was also won by the MPLA headed by João Lourenço by a wide margin. Further elections will be held in 2022. Thus, the new constitution of 1992 which among other things, respected human rights was instrumental in the adoption of a multiparty democratic system in Angola.

Botswana

Democratic development has been ongoing in Botswana since independence in 1966. Indeed, the country is regarded as Africa's oldest democracy due to its adoption of a multiparty system at independence. Linz and Stepan (1996, p. 15) define a consolidated democracy as 'a political regime in which democracy as a complex system of institutions, rules, and patterned incentives and disincentives has become, in a phrase, "the only game in town"'. Botswana has suffered from certain democratic weaknesses which include a relatively weak opposition, a lack of turnover in incumbents in 11 consecutive elections, and low voter participation (Lekalake, 2016). Voter apathy has been exacerbated by the lack of strong civil society groups to educate the electorate, while opposition parties are still finding it difficult to match the affluence of BDP, the main political party. Nonetheless, the country has enjoyed relative peace as well as socioeconomic and political development. It was ranked among the least corrupt African countries by Transparency International's Corruption Perceptions Index (CPI) and Freedom House classified it as 'free' since 1973 (Bentley et al., 2015; Lekalake, 2016).

Following fierce protests in 1995, Botswana was forced to hold a second reform referendum in 1997 which culminated in the creation of an Independent Electoral Commission. Citizens living in the diaspora were also allowed to vote and the voting age was reduced from 21 to 18. The 1999 elections saw the BDP winning 33 of the 40 elected seats, following a split in the Botswana National Front (BNF) in 1998. It went on to win 44 of the 57 elected seats in 2004, 45 in 2009, and 37 in 2014. Botswana has a unicameral National Assembly with 65 members. Freedom House notes that

> The BDP won 38 seats with 52.7 percent of the vote in the October 2019 elections, while the Umbrella for Democratic Change (UDC) won 15 seats with 35.9 percent of the vote, the Botswana Patriotic Front (BPF) won 3 seats with 4.4 percent of the vote, and the Alliance of Progressives (AP) won 1 seat with 5.1 percent of the vote.

The BDP has dominated the political scene since 1966 despite the country's multiparty system. This has been attributed to its long incumbency. Democracy in Botswana cannot be said to have attained its peak due to the dominance of the BDP, but it can be said to be working towards a stable and mature transition. Other parties could form a coalition that will be a formidable opposition to the BDP.

Democratic Republic of Congo

The DRC experienced much civil unrest in the past five decades due to a weak economy and interethnic conflict. Following independence in 1960, Prime Minister Lumumba was assassinated which resulted in a coup backed by the U.S. to oust President Kasavubu in 1965. The infamous Joseph-Désiré Mobutu came to power, a position he maintained until 1997. The first and second Congo wars took place between 1996 and 1997 and 1998 and 2003, respectively, preventing a transition to democracy. Mobutu's dictatorship operated as a one-party state, with most decisions taken by Mobutu who was the head of the Movement of the Revolution (MPR). He was toppled by Laurent Kabila in May 1997 who was in turn assassinated in 2001 resulting in his son Joseph Kabila being named head of state. A transition government was established in July 2003 which led to a successful constitutional referendum in 2005 and elections for the presidency, National Assembly, and provincial legislatures in 2006. The December 2018 presidential election saw opposition candidate Félix Tshisekedi taking over the presidency. A new government was formed in 2021 without input from Kabila and his supporters. Factors which negatively impacted the stability of democracy in the DRC included a deeply politicized, inadequately funded judiciary, with no officials charged with corruption during the transition (ICG, 2007). Factors such as civil unrest, poverty, a lack of access to clean water, nutrition, healthcare, and education, and women's exclusion from the democratic space all serve as impediments to democracy in DRC. Despite women's impressive participation in electoral processes, their rights were subjugated and in some cases, gender equality was not promoted. The DRC needs to continue to nurture its democratic system and ensure it is free of conflict-ridden transitions. The rights of women and the youth should also be respected.

South Africa

The apartheid system which legalized racial segregation from the late 1940s gave way to democracy in 1994 when the country held its first democratic elections and the national assembly elected Nelson Mandela, a Black South African as president (Dizikes, 2022). South Africa is one of the SADC countries that has enjoyed stable democracy for a couple of decades. However, some political analysts and critics such as Dube (2022) and Isaacs (2021) have queried its success due to uneven socioeconomic development, and high levels of crime, corruption, and unemployment among many other challenges. For instance, former South African president Jacob Zuma is charged with multiple counts of corruption. Nonetheless, South Africa has been widely accepted as practising a true democracy considering how far it has come. Liberman, a professor of Political Science and Contemporary Africa at the Massachusetts Institute of Technology (MIT) states that while

> South Africa certainly has its problems, the country looks nothing like actual failed states. Moreover, we would do well to remember where the country started almost 30 years ago. In the 28 years since apartheid ended in 1994, South Africa has developed a multiracial, pluralistic form of government that includes a multiparty parliament, independent judiciary, free press, robust civil society, and a broad social safety net. (Liberman, 2022, p. 3)

During the apartheid era, the white minority enjoyed the fruits of economic growth, while the majority black population was poor and deprived of basic services such as education, modern housing, electricity, and potable water. Since 1994, people's rights and voices have been respected and enshrined in the law and development has occurred across the divides of race, disability status, gender, and language (Liberman, 2022). The ANC has maintained power since the end of apartheid despite the multiparty system. However, other parties could come together to form a formidable opposition that could put the ANC government on its toes if not displace it from the seat of power.

A multiparty system and accountability have been identified as the major factors responsible for political stability in the SADC countries where good governance has prevailed. These factors should be considered by other African countries that have yet to embrace true democracy. A single-party system is a form of oppression as it silences the opposition and opens the door to human rights abuses.

FOSTERING DEMOCRATIC GOVERNANCE

The road to democratic governance in the form of a multi-party system in the SADC region has been a difficult one. The long period of authoritarian rule imposed a one-party system on citizens, with no room for opposing views. Omede et al. (2016) have noted that such a system limits pluralism and public participation. For instance, Malawi experienced a dictatorship under Kamudzu Banda who ruled until 1994, Lesotho experienced military infiltration in her political system between 1986 and 1993, and countries such as Mozambique, Tanzania, and Zambia had a one-party system until the early 1990s. In the pre-colonial era, there were few or no examples of authoritarian rule in Southern Africa. Omede et al. (2016, p. 36) have observed that in 'the … 1960s–1980s, except for Botswana and Mauritius who enjoyed liberal democracy [the] majority of southern African counties such as Zimbabwe, Zambia, Tanzania, Mozambique, Angola, Malawi, Lesotho and even South Africa were under the jackboots of authoritarian rule'. Most SADC countries turned to democratic governance in order to bring the dividends of democracy closer to the people. Such governance began to gain prominence in Africa in the 1990s, replacing the authoritarian one-party system that dominated the political space of most countries even after independence. A classic example was the release of Nelson Mandela after 27 years in South Africa's prisons in 1990 and the 1988 riot in Algiers. Most of the changes occurred due to the failure of leaders (be they military or civilian) to provide basic services to citizens.

Strategies to foster democratic governance in SADC countries include:

(a) Provision of essential services: Governments need to provide essential services if there is to be unity of purpose and democratic governance. The most important are housing, education, and health. There have been many protests against perceived injustice by citizens who have been denied necessary services. This was experienced in South Africa during the apartheid era. South Africa is now one of the SADC countries with a relatively stable democracy having elected presidents and members of parliament in a series of elections.

(b) Citizen participation: Citizen participation in politics is a way of influencing the government and politics. Citizens have a fundamental right to be involved in political activities as this ensures democratic governance (United Nations, 2011). In order to enhance democratic governance in the SADC region, everyone must have an equal opportunity to vote and be voted for, with no one sidelined on the basis of ethnicity, religion, sexuality, gender, class, or disability (Virendrakumar et al., 2018). In extreme instances, the party in power uses the armed forces to intimate the electorate and other political parties, thus preventing them from exercising their vote. No form of discrimination, intimidation, exclusion, or segregation can be permitted if democratic governance is to flourish.

(c) Free and fair elections: Democratic governance can only be fostered in SADC if there are free and fair electoral processes. The organization of elections in the region is dependent on the constitution and the electoral act of each country. All SADC Electoral Commissions are members of the SADC Electoral Commissions Forum. For true democracy to prevail, certain standards must be met before, during, and after elections. All citizens must be able to vote and be voted for before an election can be adjudged free and fair. The executive has a critical role to play in ensuring that democratic governance is enhanced in the SADC region.

(d) Accountability: Accountability is a way of rendering stewardship in a transparent manner. It is a central feature of good governance that ensures that citizens have control of public resources. Omede et al. (2016) posit that people's expectations on the dividends of democracy in Southern Africa are nothing to write home about. In their words: 'The governments are only good in the manipulation of the instruments of government in favour of certain classes of people. This in no small way accounted for the tension, conflict and instability being experienced in these countries. In fact, it was this scenario that had put many countries in a state of ferment because political power has been taken to mean a winner-take-all affair with respect not only to patronage and the prerogatives of office but also to the nation's wealth and resources. The concentration of power in the hands of a particular group can in that sense serve only as a source in that the resulting economic deprivation alienates the government from the majority of the people' (Omede et al., 2016, p. 78). Accountability reduces the risk of abuse of power and corruption and ensures fulfillment of citizens' basic human rights. A solid accountability architecture will foster democratic governance in SADC.

(e) Promotion of human rights: One of the best ways to foster democracy in the SADC region is the promotion of human rights. Everyone has the right to freedom of expression, the right to vote and be voted for, and the right to live a dignified life. All these rights must be respected by a democratic government. No executive abuse of power or use of military force should be allowed to intimate and infringe on human rights.

(f) Ensuring socioeconomic development: Socioeconomic development can be achieved by strengthening the economy through the provision of employment opportunities. The literature notes that a relationship exists between development and democracy. According to Ojo et al. (2014), democracy offers better prospects for development; furthermore, where citizens' developmental aspirations are met, democracy will thrive. Such a society will be free from conflict, criminality, and social vices. Thus, just as development cannot be realized without democracy, democracy cannot be sustained without development (Ake, 1996).

THE ROLE OF NON-STATE ACTORS IN FOSTERING DEMOCRATIC GOVERNANCE

The role of non-state actors in fostering democracy in the SADC region includes raising public awareness of citizens' fundamental human rights. Non-state actors include NGOs and individuals that are not funded by or affiliated directly or indirectly with the government. Civil society organizations (CSOs), the judiciary, and the legislature have a responsibility to foster democratic governance. While civil society has been poorly organized in the past, it has now become vocal in many parts of the region. Electoral bodies and the judiciary have also challenged abuse of power by the executive. Due to its absolute monarchy, Eswatini is the only country in the region that is still finding it difficult to promote participatory democracy. CSOs have filled the vacuum left by some authoritarian governments as a watchdog over the executive, judiciary, and legislature.

The roles of non-state actors can be categorized as follows:

(a) Collaboration: Non-state actors will sometimes need to partner with the executive arm of government and collaborate with international organizations in order to bring the dividends of democracy closer to citizens through socioeconomic improvement. Non-state actors such as CSOs usually have a broad geographical footprint and have extensive knowledge of local conditions and traditions. As such, these organizations are often regarded as more legitimate and trustworthy than government agencies. Collaboration thus significantly strengthens the capacity of government to address the democratic deficit in many communities.

(b) Monitoring, oversight, and criticism of bad policies and actions: The non-state actors are ideally placed to oversee and monitor programmes and projects of government. They also act as a watchdog over the executive arms of government and criticize ill-judgement and bad practices. For instance, the Zimbabwe 'neo-authoritarian one-party political system' was challenged by the Movement for Democratic Change (MDC), and other domestic and international pressure groups have queried the ruling party's actions surrounding the SADC election principles. According to Monare (2004), the 'MDC's lobbying campaign surfaced in June 2004, when Morgan Tsvangirai criticised SADC's electoral commission for 'endorsing fraudulent elections and for supporting autocratic rulers'. Tsvangirai used the Zimbabwean 2001 and Malawi's 2004 elections as examples when he said that the SADC observer team's bias "makes it possible for dictators to bludgeon their way into office using sham elections"' (Monare 2004, p. 4).

(c) Ensuring that the rule of law prevails: One of the roles of non-state actors is to ensure that democracy is respected by all irrespective of their status. Lesotho was embroiled in political conflict in September 1998, leading to military intervention by South Africa and Botswana to ensure that the rule of law prevailed. The Congress for Democracy (LCD) government lost the election, and turmoil would have resulted had it not been for this intervention by neighbouring countries. In Zambia, civil society groups and the opposition party joined forces to resist President Frederick Chiluba's attempts to amend the constitution to allow him to stand for a third term of office.

DEMOCRATIC GOVERNANCE IN AFRICA: QUO VADIS?

The COVID-19 pandemic has affected democratic activities the world over. During the pandemic, governance in most African countries including SADC virtually came to a standstill, affecting democratic activities that should have enhanced productivity. The global response to the pandemic compromised democratic processes such as decision-making. The 16 SADC members were confronted by numerous challenges ranging from rising infections to uncertain vaccination programs. As the COVID-19 pandemic gradually fades globally, there is the need for SADC to re-strategize in the areas of good governance and how to bring democracy closer to the people. Emergency laws were adopted by Botswana, Zimbabwe, and South Africa to tackle the pandemic which negatively affected accountability and transparency, undermining the fragile democracy in this region (Mathekga, 2021). For instance, South Africa invoked the Disaster Management Act, Botswana invoked the Emergency Powers Act and Zimbabwe implemented a national lockdown and legislation allowing the state to adopt new regulations to fight the virus. All these measures allowed the executive to bypass normal channels to 'assist and protect the public'. Large amounts of public funds were used to fight the pandemic with little or no transparency/accountability. South Africa experienced some lapses during emergency spending despite having a functional oversight system and the health minister stepped aside due to public outrage (Mathekga, 2021). Botswana and Zimbabwe's governments created a hostile environment that prevented journalists and other stakeholders from offering constructive criticism. For instance, Botswana approved a five-year prison term or a $10,000 fine for stakeholders accused of misleading the public on government's intentions during the pandemic.

Parliaments are expected to live up to their responsibilities by holding leaders accountable. This can only occur in a multiparty system that is not unduly sympathetic to the executive. Civil society groups may not have access to the resources required to challenge financial recklessness during the pandemic. What, then, is the way forward in the post-pandemic period?

(a) Parliament should properly scrutinize all public spending: While the government may have monopolized power, leaving little room for public participation or decision-making during the pandemic, such action must be subject to scrutiny by parliament and anyone in government found wanting should be prosecuted.

(b) Constitutional review: The constitution should be reviewed or amended to check financial recklessness by the executive in future pandemics. Such amendment should provide for accountability and oversight by parliament. The review should also limit the powers of the executive. In South Africa for instance, there is a gradual shift towards 'command council' governance which may continue after the pandemic. The constitutional amendment should also put measures in place to guide the executive. The COVID-19 pandemic is perhaps the most devastating one in recent times and without any guide or template to follow, the SADC countries resort to far-reaching measures.

(c) Proper auditing of all spending: All financial transactions during the period of the pandemic should be audited. If the executive knows its activities will be audited by the authorized organs, it might be more cautious while also offering better protection to citizens.

(d) Online engagement: Technology has made it easy to communicate online; indeed, the COVID-19 pandemic was an eye-opener in this regard. Some legislative duties can also be performed online to check the excesses of the executive before taking far reaching decisions during emergencies such as the COVID-19 pandemic.

CONCLUSION

The Southern African region has not been spared the sweeping winds of socioeconomic and political change, with most of its countries undergoing significant changes in political leadership. Political instability and conflict resulted in displacement and forced citizens to migrate to neighbouring countries. Other pressing factors include devastating flooding caused by climate change, food insecurity, and the COVID-19 pandemic, to name but a few. The chapter has examined democratic governance in Southern Africa and the status of democracy in the region, as well as the principles of liberal democracy. It shines a spotlight on the leadership situation, examining the successes and challenges as well as the role of competent public managers as agents of democratic governance.

The chapter has argued that it is imperative to foster democratic governance in the region irrespective of the changes it experiences. Political leadership must remain vigilant to ensure that democratic governance is not undermined and weakened to the extent that citizens' aspirations are not met and the gains made since independence are eroded. Political commitment to upholding the principles of liberal democracy is non-negotiable to foster democratic governance. However, safeguarding democratic institutions and processes is not the government's responsibility alone. Every citizen irrespective of their status should actively participate in the democratic governance processes in order to hold those in power accountable.

In conclusion, democratic governance in Africa and SADC in particular is very germane in bringing the dividends of democracy closer to the people. By and large, progress has been made in democratizing political activities since the 1990s. It is expected that the situation will continue to improve until a stable democratic system is attained across the SADC region.

REFERENCES

Abramowitz M.J. (2018), 'Democracy in Crisis', Freedom House. Policy Note No 4:2018, accessed 15 July 2022 at https://freedomhouse.org/report/freedom-world/2018/democracy-crisis.

African Union. (2007), 'African Charter on Democracy, Elections and Governance', Addis Ababa: African Union, accessed 27 March 2023 at https://au.int/en/treaties/african-charter-democracy-elections-and-governance.

Ake, C. (1996), *Democracy and Development in Africa*, Washington, DC: The Brookings Institution.

Bentley, T., K. Han and P. Penar (2015), 'African Democracy Update: Democratic Satisfaction Remains Elusive For Many', Afrobarometer Dispatch No. 45, accessed 27 June 2022 at http://afrobarometer.org/sites/default/files/publications/Dispatches/dispatchno45_democracy_.

Britannica (2022), 'Government and Society', accessed 18 June 2022 at https://www.britannica.com/place/Angola/Government-and-society day_africa_2015_citizen_perceptions.pdf.

Cawthra, G., A. du Pisani and A. Omari (2007), *Security and Democracy in Southern Africa*, Johannesburg: Wits University Press.

Dizikes P. (2022), 'From South Africa, a Success Story for Democracy', Massachusetts Institute of Technology (MIT), accessed 29 June 2022 at https://news.mit.edu/2022/Lieberman-south-africa-democracy-book-0519.

Dube, X. (2022), 'We're Not Going to Get Anyone Better than Ramaphosa', CapeTalk, accessed 24 February 2023 at https://www.capetalk.co.za.

EISA (Electoral Institute for Sustainable Democracy in Africa). (2008), 'Consolidating Democratic Governance in the SADC Region: Mauritius', EISA Research Report, accessed 23 February 2023 at https://www.eisa.org/pdf/RR37.pdf.

Fleck, R.K. and F.A. Hanssen (2006), 'The Origins of Democracy: A Model with Application to Ancient Greece', *The Journal of Law and Economics*, **49** (1), 115–146.

Freedom House. (2022), 'Botswana (Country Report)', accessed 23 July 2022 at https://freedomhouse.org/country/botswana/freedom-world/2020.

Graham, M. (2019), *Contemporary Africa*, London: Red Globe Press.

Harrison, K. and T. Boyd (2018), *Understanding Political Ideas and Movements*, Manchester: Manchester University Press, doi.org/10.7765/9781526137951.

Ideal. (2021), *The State of Democracy in Africa and the Middle East 2021: Resilient Democratic Aspirations and Opportunities for Consolidation*, Strömsborg: International IDEA.

International Crisis Group (ICG). (2007), 'Africa Report No. 128. Congo: Consolidating the Peace', accessed 23 June 2022 at http://www.crisisgroup.org/home/index.cfm?id=4933&l=1.

Isaacs, M.L. (2021), 'South African Politics: Parties Are Not the Problem – and Independent Candidates Are Not the Solution', Daily Maverick, accessed 24 February 2023 at https://www.dailymaverick .co.za/opinionista/2021-03-15-south-african-politics-parties-are-not-the-problem-and-independent -candidates-are-not-the-solution/.

Lekalake, R. (2016), 'Botswana's Democratic Consolidation: What Will It Take?', accessed 17 July 2022 at https://www.afrobarometer.org/wp-content/uploads/migrated/files/publications/Policy%20papers/ ab_r6_policypaperno30_democracy_in_botswana.pdf.

Lieberman E. (2022), 'The Promise of South African Democracy. Project Syndicate', accessed 27 June 2022 at https://www.project-syndicate.org/commentary/south-africa-democracy-progress-since- apartheid-by-evan-lieberman-1-2022-05.

Linz, J. and A. Stepan (1996), 'Toward Consolidated Democracies', *Journal of Democracy*, **7** (2), 14–33.

Mathekga R. (2021), 'Post-Pandemic Politics in Southern Africa', accessed 19 June 2022 at https://www .gisreportsonline.com/r/southern-africa-covid-19/.

Matlosa, K. (2008), *Consolidating Democratic Governance in the SADC Region: Transitions and Prospects for Consolidation*, Johannesburg: EISA.

Mawere, M. and T.R. Mwanaka (2015), 'Good Governance, Democracy and Sustainable Development in Africa: An Introduction', in Mawere, M. and T.R. Mwanaka (eds.), *Democracy, Good Governance and Development in Africa*, Bamenda: Langaa RPCIG, pp. vii–xiv, doi.org/10.2307/j.ctvk3gmq7.3.

Mbaku, J.M. (2020), 'Threats to Democracy in Africa: The Rise of the Constitutional Coup', Africa in Focus, accessed 12 August 2022 at https://www.brookings.edu/blog/africa-in-focus/2020/10/30/ threats-to-democracy-in-africa-the-rise-of-the-constitutional-coup/.

Monare, M. (2004), 'SADC Endorses Sham Elections', *Sunday Independent*, 6 June 2004.

National Academies. (1992), *Democratization in Africa: African Views, African Voices*, Washington, DC: National Academies Press, accessed 23 March 2023 at https://nap.nationalacademies.org/read /2041/chapter/2.

National Research Council. (1992), *Democratization in Africa: African Views, African Voices*, Washington, DC: National Academy Press.

Ojo, P.O, F. Aworawo and T.E. Ifedayo (2014), 'Governance and the Challenge of Socio-Economic Development in Nigeria Afe Babalola University', *Journal of Sustainable Development Law and Policy*, **3** (1), 132–148.

Omede, J., R. Akindola and A. Ngwube (2016), 'Democracy and Accountable Governance in the SADC Region', *African Journal of Politics and Administrative Studies*, **9** (1), 20–30.

Osaghae, E.E. (1992), 'Ethnicity and Democracy', in Ayo, F. (ed.), *Understanding Democracy*, Ibadan: Book Craft.

SADC. (2022), 'Towards a Common Future', accessed 23 June 2022 at https://www.sadc.int/about -sadc#:~:text=The%20Southern%20African%20Development%20Community,%2C%20Tanzania %2C%20Zambia%20and%20Zimbabwe.

United Nations. (2011), 'Thematic Study by the Office of the United Nations High Commissioner for Human Rights on Participation in Political and Public Life by Persons with Disabilities', The Office of the United Nations High Commissioner for Human Rights (OHCHR), accessed 9 August 2022 at https://digitallibrary.un.org/record/719452.

United States Environmental Protection Agency (EPA). (2023), 'Public Participation Guide: Introduction to Public Participation', accessed 23 February 2023 at https://www.epa.gov/international-cooperation /public-participation-guide-introduction-public-participation.

US Department of State. (1999), 'The Foreign Service: Through Ambassador Pickering's Eyes', US Dept of State, Archive, released on 20 January 2009, accessed 23 February 2023 at https://1997-2001 .state.gov/www/publications/statemag/statemag_may99/featur1b.html.

Virendrakumar, B., E. Jolley, E. Badu and E. Schmidt (2018), 'Disability Inclusive Elections in Africa: A Systematic Review of Published and Unpublished Literature', *Disability & Society*, **33** (4), 509- 538, doi.org/10.1080/09687599.2018.1431108.

World Bank. (2022), 'Governance Global Practice', accessed 12 February 2023 at https://www .worldbank.org/en/topic/governance/overview.

PART III

EMERGING TRENDS AND PERSPECTIVES ON PUBLIC MANAGEMENT

17. Public sector reform and innovation in sub-Saharan Africa: the case of Ghana

Joseph R.A. Ayee

INTRODUCTION

The public sector is critical to promoting good governance and socioeconomic development in sub-Saharan Africa (SSA) because it facilitates a capable state to deliver goods and services to citizens. This expectation has been reinforced in the 1990s onwards by the changing role of the state, the focus on good and responsive governance, effective institutions, and the move away from traditional models of public administration to public management including the New Public Management (NPM) (Robinson, 2015; World Bank, 2018). The drivers for these shifts are globalization, pluralization of service provision, and the increasingly complex, wicked, and global policy problems (Robinson, 2015). Even though these paradigmatic shifts are global in nature, their effects and impact have been mostly felt in SSA countries where contextual variables such as a weak state, corruption, policy discontinuity, and lack of meritocracy in recruitment have created implementation deficits. This means the building of a public sector which is innovative and ready to adapt to reforms that will bring lasting impact on good governance and socioeconomic development.

Against this backdrop, this chapter examines reform, innovation, and deliverology (RID) initiatives in Ghana, which followed the global paradigmatic shifts to make its public sector more effective and efficient to achieve the constitutional goal of creating a free and just society. More specifically, the chapter discusses reform delivery models and units, the role of the central government in overseeing the reform, the use of information communication technology (ICT), the role of policy think-tanks, inter- and intra-sectoral collaboration, and capacity development in the light of the managerial challenge. It concludes with the lessons learnt and some recommendations for the way forward.

To provide a better understanding of the Ghanaian case, the chapter begins with a review of the literature on the concepts of RID and their practice in SSA and the changing public sector environment with emphasis on the need for continuous process improvement, strategic adjustment, and administrative advancement.

THE CONCEPTS OF REFORM, INNOVATION, AND DELIVEROLOGY IN GOVERNANCE

At the heart of governance are the concepts of reform, innovation, and deliverology (RID) which are meant to introduce changes for improved service delivery for citizens and government business. Governance is defined as consisting of structure (the forms and standard features of the authority system), process (the rules and authenticity of decision-making), and outcomes (the quality and quantity of the performance of the government especially in public service delivery) (Jreisat, 2011, p. 424).

Reform

There has been a growing body of literature on the concept of reform since the seminal work of Caiden (1978). It includes Caiden (1988; 1991; 1999); Aucoin (1990); Miewald and Steineman (1984); Jreisat (1988); Chapman and Greenaway (1980); Guy Peters (1992); Turner and Hulme (1997); and Killian and Eklund (2008).

The burgeoning literature has resulted in a variety of definitions. In spite of this, Caiden's (1969, p. 65) definition of reform as 'the artificial inducement of administrative transformation, against resistance' stands out because it contains most of the elements of other scholars. This definition has five elements:

(i)   A moral purpose which involves the need to improve the status quo;
(ii) Artificial transformation that connotes the departure from existing arrangements and natural change processes;
(iii) Deliberate planned change which is synonymous with innovation;
(iv) Intended outcomes are improved effectiveness and efficiency in public service delivery; and
(v)   Administrative resistance that assumes opposition and thereby emphasizing its political nature rather than being technical or managerial (Caiden, 1969; Turner and Hulme, 1997). The politics of reform and the reallocation of power balance among government agencies have long been recognized by Machiavelli (1513, p. 20) with his caution that 'there is nothing more difficult and dangerous, or more doubtful of success, than an attempt to introduce a new order of things in any state'. This politics of reform has been seen as one of the major obstacles to its successful implementation in SSA (Bowornwathana and Poocharoen, 2010).

Reform has been driven mainly by four models, namely market (adoption of private sector principles and practices), participation (ownership and empowerment in the decision-making process), deregulation (removal of rules and regulations to reduce dysfunctionality), and flexible government (the belated response of hitherto functional organizations to emerging changes and problems) (Guy Peters, 2018). Even though the models have weaknesses they are still useful in understanding the drivers that have informed reform efforts.

The key strategies of reform are restructuring, participation, human resource management and development, accountability and public-private partnerships (PPPs). They have been implemented in SSA but have tended to exacerbate service delivery, accountability, inequalities, and coordination hiccups (Turner and Hulme, 1997). Notwithstanding the ineffective implementation of reform globally, there is still great interest because of its 'vitality' and the belief that it waves a magic flag that has the potential of fixing problems in the public sector (Caiden, 1988).

Innovation

Innovation emerged as one of the buzzwords in public management in the late 1970s and early 1980s, driven largely by factors including the priorities of politicians; options identification for improvement; pressure on government budgets; and rising public expectations for more accessible and flexible services (Moore and Hartley, 2008).

Innovation has defied clear-cut definition. It may, however, be defined as the application of new ideas and a new way of doing things in organizations irrespective of the form it takes (La Pierre, 1965). Some of its features include the generation or production of something new, targeted action to bring about the desired real changes, actual positive evaluation of the new change, and the determination of tangible or intangible outcomes of the new idea or product (Nazif, 2019). Some of the key requirements for innovation include transformative leadership, adequate resources, formal and informal networks, supportive culture, accessible competencies, ideas from any source, feedback, and learning, and effective organizational strategies (Albury, 2005). Some of the barriers to innovation include the multiplicity, ambiguity, and conflicting nature of some of the objectives, complex organizational arrangements that involve extensive consultation and coordination; and the large size and diversity of the mandates of the organizations (Albury, 2005; Moore and Hartley, 2008).

Deliverology

Deliverology was popularized by Michael Barber, who was the head of Prime Minister Tony Blair's Delivery Unit (DU) from 2001 to 2005. The DU was meant to help Blair deliver on the promises made by the Labour Party during the 2001 electoral campaign, which prioritized 20 public service targets including literacy for 11-year-olds, reduced road traffic congestion, and lower street crime rates (Barber, 2009). According to Barber (2009, p. 4), deliverology refers to a 'systematic process for driving progress and delivering results in government and the public sector … that requires a sharp focus on a very limited set of priorities in order to succeed'. It therefore involves the management and monitoring of the implementation of activities and maximizing successful delivery using an approach that is meant to be scientifically modified (Etheridge and Thomas, 2015).

Some of the key activities include setting up a delivery unit that consists of individuals focused on achieving impact and improving outcomes; creating a clear vision of programme success; quantifying the vision of success through performance measures and targets; closely monitoring performance against targets and taking action to address variances; and ensuring that there are consequences for good and bad performance (Barber et al., 2011; Barber, 2011).

The key advantages of deliverology are the setting up of dedicated DUs and targets and monitoring performance against them. It has been implemented in health, education, and security sectors in some countries including the United Kingdom, Canada, Australia, New Zealand, India, Pakistan, and Ethiopia with some success (Schacter, 2016; Olkaba and Tamene, 2019).

In spite of its perceived relative success, deliverology has been the subject of criticism. For instance, its effect on healthcare service delivery in England between 2001 and 2005 was seen as mixed because even though the reported performance in relation to key targets had improved, the targeting regime caused significant negative effects which were felt by both providers and recipients of healthcare. The fact that targets were met did not lead to any improvement in the overall patient experience (Bevan and Hood, 2006; Mason, 2012). Schacter (2016, p. 14) also questioned its relevance to the Canadian public service as he did not see any 'persuasive, independent evidence … that suggests that deliverology makes a significant positive difference to the quality of public management'.

The concepts of RID have both strengths and weaknesses that make them complementary benchmarks in any assessment of public service delivery and public management practices in Ghana.

THE CHANGING PUBLIC SECTOR ENVIRONMENT: THE NEED FOR CONTINUOUS PROCESS IMPROVEMENT, STRATEGIC ADJUSTMENT, AND ADMINISTRATIVE ADVANCEMENT

The diversity and complexity of the public sector have been recognized (Lane, 1993; Guy Peters, 2018). According to Lane (1993, p. 1) the 'institutions of politics, government and bureaux populate the public sector' and the public sector 'has an enormous impact on all of us ... and serves the public through a set of hierarchical structures responsible to politicians', who normatively must pursue the public interest through the delivery of value-for-money public services.

The public sector is often confused with the state, particularly in SSA. The state is seen as the public sector, which is not necessarily the case because the public sector is the institutional arm of the state which assists it in the realization of its political, extractive, regulatory, administrative, and technical capacities (Brautigam, 1996; Polidano, 2000). These five capacities are linked with the fundamental attributes of the state: geographical penetration, social regulation, resource mobilization, and efficient and credible resource allocation (Migdal, 1988; Olowu, 2011).

As the 'single most important investment instrument for the state ... which is critical for development outcomes including service delivery' (Joshi and Carter, 2015, p. 1), reform and innovation initiatives have consequences for the public sector. For instance, the World Development Report (WDR) of 1997 on 'The State in a Changing World' focuses on what role the state should play and what measures need to be taken to ensure that it becomes effective and efficient through the public sector (World Bank, 1997; Adamolekun, 2011).

Given the developments at the domestic and international levels, there is the need for continuous process improvement, strategic adjustment, and administrative advancement in the public sector. Continuous process improvement involves a review of the constitutional-legal framework, procedures, systems, standards, promoting transparency, and accountability and the introduction and sustenance of alternative modes of service delivery (Adamolekun, 2011). The strategic adjustment entails strengthening the capacity to manage core government functions such as public policymaking, coordination, regulation, and resource mobilization. The administrative advancement includes the use of ICT, capacity development for human resources, dealing with resistance, introducing citizen charters, and performance management (Pinto, 1998).

THE PRACTICE OF REFORM, INNOVATION, AND DELIVEROLOGY IN SUB-SAHARAN AFRICA

The idea of good governance has been the key driving force behind the practice of RID in SSA. This is because SSA's inability to realize its potential is attributable to 'a crisis of governance' (World Bank, 1989, p. 60). SSA has witnessed the proliferation of RID initiatives since the wind of political and economic changes blew across the continent. The changes were specifically influenced by the 'third wave' of democracy in the early 1990s including the end of apartheid in South Africa and the introduction of structural adjustment programmes (SAPs) to deal with the fiscal crises that confronted the countries. They were also shaped by international blueprints such as the Sustainable Development Goals (SDGs), conventions, charters, instruments, and the World Development Reports published since 1978 to date on several thematic areas such as agriculture, equity, public services delivery, and the state. The changes point to a results-oriented and productive public sector that spends least resources and get value for money (Economic Commission for Africa, 2003; Ayee, 2008). In the words of Radin (2000, p. 168):

> If there is a single theme that characterizes the public sector in the 1990s, it is the demand for perfor-
> mance and effectiveness. A mantra has emerged this decade, heard at all levels of government that
> calls for documentation of performance and explicit outcomes of government action.

The response of governments of SSA countries to the global changes is reflected in implementing reform and innovative initiatives whose outcomes are described as mixed or modest (Karyeija, 2012).

The Practice of Reform

Several reform initiatives have been implemented in the public sector in SSA as a result of SAPs and NPM paradigm. Some of the strategies used include 'agencification' (the creation of regulatory and executive agencies), decentralization, privatization, commercialization, downsizing, contracting out, performance contracts, and PPPs (Ayee, 2008; Economic Commission for Africa, 2010). The initiatives may be divided into three phases: 'quantitative' first-generation reforms (1980s to early 1990s), which is to 'make government lean and affordable'; 'qualitative' second-generation reforms (1990s to early 2000s) with a shift of focus from the quantity of employees to their quality; and post-Washington consensus and third-generation reforms (late 1990 to date) which include turning public service organizations into efficient, effective, and outcome-based organizations (Bangura and Larbi, 2006; Ayee, 2008).

Overall, the reform initiatives have generally achieved limited success with the public sector still bedevilled by a lack of meritocracy, corruption, low morale, and poor service delivery (Adamolekun, 2011). Some of the key lessons learnt include the need to understand the country context, garner support of stakeholders, adopt an incremental approach, and ownership of reform programmes by SSA governments (Karyeija, 2012).

The Practice of Innovation

At the political level, the key innovation is the design of more liberal constitutions by some countries including Ethiopia, Ghana, Nigeria, Uganda, Togo, and Chad, which were either under military rule or authoritarian one-party regimes and transitioned to multi-party democratic rule in the early 1990s.

The constitutions were the 'most important legal instrument in the scheme of good governance ... which gives people a sense of ownership of the political process' (Ndulu, 2001, p. 101). The position of executive president is one of the main features of the constitutions, which is a departure from the previous parliamentary split executive adopted in the post-independence era by most of the countries. The growing power of executive presidents and abuse coupled with weak checks and balances and COVID-19 abuses have led to agitations for a review of constitutions to reduce the power of the presidents (Tull and Simons, 2017; Kieh, 2018).

To redress the legacies of human rights abuses and 'scornful and sorrowed history' transitional justice mechanisms such as truth and reconciliation commission were set up in 25 African countries including South Africa, Kenya, Ghana Nigeria, Ethiopia, Togo, and Côte d'Ivoire (Gready and Robins, 2020; Fombad, 2022;). The efficacy of measures of transitional justice is dependent on each country's unique historical, socioeconomic circumstances and based on broad consultation of all segments of society with emphasis on restorative and not legal justice (Fombad, 2022).

Another innovation is the electronic revolution (e-revolution), which has two features aimed at services and relationships improvement, namely:

- e-government or digital government referring to the use of ICT in the administration of government business, public service provision, and delivery; and
- e-governance or digital governance referring to the 'electronic enablement of all the other activities of government such as management of democratic activity and ensuring fairness and transparency of decision-making in public bodies' (Bovaird, 2003, p. 38).

Digital services provided include filing of tax returns, registration for examinations and jobs, acquisition of new passports or their renewal, certificates, distance education, banking and government websites for official publications (Kariuki and Kiragu, 2011; Barasa, 2022). Countries such as South Africa, Ghana, Nigeria, Kenya, and Rwanda have implemented national ICT policies reinforced by the African Union's (2020) digital transformation of economies in SSA. National ICT authorities to act as a national data centre were set up in addition to ICT ministries in 43 of the 46 SSA countries to lead in digitalization of government and the wider economy (Kariuki and Kiragu, 2011; Barasa, 2022).

Even though the E-Government Development Index (EGDI) scores almost doubled from 0.2 in 2003 to 0.3914 in 2020, it is, however, below the world average (0.37 in 2003 and 0.6 in 2020). This seems to reinforce the uneven pace of transformation across SSA where significant differences exist between the top and bottom EGDI-performing countries (Barasa, 2022). Progress in the digital revolution has also been dogged by the poor quality of paper-based records, resistance to change, weak ICT capacity of governments, resource constraints including infrastructure and power supply, limited citizen awareness, and ineffective legislation (Kariuki and Kiragu, 2011; Barasa, 2022).

The Practice of Deliverology

According to Williams et al. (2020), SSA has the highest number of delivery units (DUs) based on a global mapping of 142 DUs adoption from 73 different countries (Table 17.1). There are five main trends in the design of DUs worldwide, which have been replicated in SSA as follows:

- The majority operate at the national level and are located in the centre of government (CoG) such as the Office of the President or Prime Minister. For example, Sierra Leone's Strategy and Policy Unit (SPU) was hosted within the President's Office to deliver the

Table 17.1   *Continents, selected countries and delivery units*

Continents/sub-continents	Number of selected countries	Number of delivery units
Sub-Saharan Africa	21	39
Latin America and Caribbean	16	29
Europe and Central Asia	12	25
East Asia and Pacific	11	19
Middle East and North Africa	6	9
South Asia	5	12
North America	2	9
Total	**73**	**142**

Source: Adapted from Mansoor (2021, p. 21).

   Presidential Agenda for Change (2007–2012) to ensure improvements in energy, transportation, health, and education (Scharff, 2012).
- The majority operate across multiple sectors rather than focusing on a single sector. For instance, Kenya's Presidential Delivery Unit (PDU) was tasked with ensuring the implementation of national priorities over five to ten years, including incrementally raising the contribution of manufacturing and agriculture to the country's GDP (Monsoor et al., 2021). Similarly, Liberia's PDU oversaw the implementation of President Sirleaf's 150-day plan including the construction of 1000 sanitation facilities (Ministry of Information, Culture, and Tourism, Liberia, 2012). However, some operate focusing on a single sector such as Ethiopia's Education Sector Delivery Unit (Olkaba and Tamene, 2019).
- Most of them are staffed exclusively by existing civil servants, although the use of external recruitment for core staffing was also common. In Sierra Leone, for instance, the SPU was set up in 2008 by President Koroma with the aim of instituting a stronger structure and greater accountability (Monsoor et al., 2021). It, however, lacked civil service representation which caused tensions and had to be addressed through the appointment of bureaucrats (ACET, 2010).
- About half received external funding for their set-up and/or functioning. Kenya's PDU was funded by the African Development Bank (AfDB) while Tanzania's President's Delivery Bureau, received funding from the World Bank and USAID (Monsoor et al., 2021).
- The use of external technical assistance is more common. For instance, the UK Foreign, Commonwealth, and Development Office (2019) provided funding for technical assistance to staff working at the Public Sector Reform Secretariat in Ghana for capacity building in monitoring and evaluation and data systems and analysis to inform decisions.

Even though some of the DUs delivered on their mandates, public service delivery in the countries in which they were set has not improved because of a lack of collaboration, coordination, mandate overlaps, conflict, and working in silos. Most of them folded up after the exit of those who set them up. (Williams et al., 2020; Monsoor et al., 2021).

PUBLIC SECTOR REFORM, INNOVATION, AND DELIVEROLOGY IN GHANA

Succeeding Ghanaian governments have been preoccupied with RID initiatives because of the belief that an effective and efficient public sector will deliver services for the realization of the country's aspiration of creating a free and just society. This notwithstanding, they have had limited impact largely because of duplication of roles and responsibilities, weak institutional coordination and collaboration, politicization, and lack of continuity in political transitions (Republic of Ghana, 2017a; Republic of Ghana, 2017b).

Reform Delivery Models and Units

The basic delivery model is the creation of a central planning unit which can be divided into the following five phases, which emphasize fragmentation and institutional discontinuity:

(i)   The Public Sector Reform Secretariat (PSRS) under the Office of the Senior Minister (OSM), which was itself under the Office of the President (OoP) (2003–2005);

(ii)   The Ministry for Public Sector Reforms (MPSR) as a central coordinating agency to champion reform interventions geared at service delivery improvement, decentralization, and agency reform (2005–2009);

(iii) The MPSR was re-designated as the PSRS with a Minister of State who was a member of Cabinet after the change of government in 2009 and placed under the OoP. This re-designation was to make the PSRS as a medium to be used by the Presidency to provide a strategic and technical back-stopping role for reforms and coordinate and oversee reform activities (2009–2017);

(iv)   The Public Sector Reform Directorate (PSRD) under the OSM to implement the National Public Sector Reform Strategy (NPSRS), 2018–2023 (2017–2020) (Essuman-Mensah, 2019); and

(v)   The PSRS under the Office of Government Machinery (OGM) with abolition of OSM (2021 to the present).

The creation of a DU in the OoP was expected to help promote coordination at the centre of Government (CoG) and remove bottlenecks to critical reforms to promote political and socioeconomic development. However, this has rarely happened as the reforms have been hampered by weak intra- and inter-sectoral collaboration and coordination, poor performance management, and duplication of roles and responsibilities (Republic of Ghana, 2017a, 2017b). The continuity of the DU to drive reforms was undermined by political transitions because of excessive politicization and polarization exhibited by the two duopolies, the New Patriotic Party (NPP) and National Democratic Congress (NDC).

Central Government's Role in Overseeing Reform

The institutional framework for overseeing the reform is fragmented and uncoordinated. Overseeing the reform is the joint responsibility of the CoG, namely the OGM, OoP, Office of the Vice President (OVP), and Cabinet and their effective management of public policy. However, guidelines for the formulation of policies and preparing a policy and legislative almanac to serve as a central reference point have not been developed while the capacity of the CoG to coordinate effectively the implementation, monitoring, and evaluation of government policies and programmes remains weak. In fact, the strengthening of national capacity to undertake policy analysis, development planning, monitoring, and evaluation has been slow (Republic of Ghana, 2017a).

There seems to be confusion over the terms OGM and OoP and their composition. The OGM, which serves the OoP, provides accountable, transparent, managerial, technical, and administrative services to the Presidency and other stakeholders for the attainment of the government's development agenda to improve living standards (Republic of Ghana, 2019). This mandate seems loaded and therefore accounts for the diversity of bodies under the OGM. The OSM used to be part of the OGM until it was abolished in the second term of the current administration of Nana Akufo-Addo.

According to the Republic of Ghana (2019a, p. 5), the following organizations resort under the Office of Government Machinery:

- Office of the President;
- Vice President Secretariat;
- Office of the Chief of Staff;
- Council of State;
- Cabinet Secretariat;
- Ghana AIDS Commission;
- Internal Audit Agency;
- National Identification Authority;
- State Interests and Governance Authority;
- Administrator General;
- Millennium Challenge Account;
- Millennium Development Authority;
- Micro-finance and Small Loan Centre (MASLOC);
- National Population Council;
- National Builders Corps;
- Public Sector Reform Secretariat;
- Scholarship Secretariat;
- Press Secretariat and Policy Coordinating Delivery Unit;
- Research Unit;
- Presidential Staffers including advisors and aides.

There are nine core functions of the OGM, which emphasize the OGM's oversight, coordination, supervisory, and centralized responsibilities. Some of its functions include formulating, implementing, coordinating, monitoring, and evaluating government policies and programmes; promoting political tolerance, stability, security, and peace in Ghana and the subregion; providing institutional capacity and an enabling environment for effective, efficient, and sustainable service delivery; and providing administrative, managerial, and other support services to the Executive (Republic of Ghana, 2019a).

Given its functions and personnel of 2,000 in the regulatory governance of the country, its capacity for planning and policy coordination at the centre remains weak (Republic of Ghana, 2017b).

The Use of ICT to Accelerate Sectoral Reform: ICT4AD Policy

The use of ICT to accelerate sectoral reform and thereby improve public services delivery was not a priority for succeeding governments until 2003 when Kufuor's NPP government developed 'The Ghana ICT for Accelerated Development [ICT4AD] Policy' (Republic of Ghana, 2003). It has a two-fold aim: (i) to 'transform Ghana into [an] information-rich knowledge-based society and economy through the development, deployment, and exploitation of ICTs within the economy and society' (Republic of Ghana, 2003, p. 2); and (ii) 'leap-frog the key stages of industrialization and transform their subsistence agriculture dominated economies into service-sector driven, high value-added information and knowledge economies that can successfully compete on the global market' (Republic of Ghana, 2003, p. 2).

The ICT4AD has 14 pillars. They include accelerated human development; promotion of ICTs in education; facilitating government administration and service delivery (e-government and e-governance); facilitating the development of the private sector; developing an export-oriented ICT products and services industry; modernization of agriculture and the development of an agro-business industry; and the deployment and spread of ICT in the community (Republic of Ghana, 2003, p. 24).

The ICT4AD led to the e-Ghana project in 2006, which merged all e-government initiatives with the intention to address the constraints in the deployment of ICT to promote good governance. The e-Ghana project supported local ICT businesses and IT-enabled services and promoted the development of e-government applications and government communications. It has three components: creating an overall enabling environment; attracting IT-enabled services; achieving greater efficiency, transparency, and accountability in selected government ministries, departments, and agencies (MDAs) (Republic of Ghana, 2006). In 2009, the National Information Technology Agency (NITA) was created as the national e-government implementation and coordination body which was followed by the setting up of the government web presence through MDAs to provide diverse services and information to citizens (Osei-Kojo, 2016).

Some of the initiatives embedded in the project include the e-justice programme, e-parliament, e-immigration, e-government procurement, and the Ghana Integrated Financial Management Information System (GIFMIS) to improve the efficiency and transparency of the government's financial management activities (Osei-Kojo, 2016). They are seen as comprising the core governance issues when it comes to building trust and confidence in government, apart from those of public service delivery and issues relating to elections (Awotwi and Owusu, 2010; Ohemeng and Ofosu-Adarkwa, 2014).

The implementation of the e-Ghana project has positively impacted the quality of public service delivery in some areas even though there is room for improvement especially when most of the e-government systems in Ghana appear to be at the interactive level which only allows citizens to access information online and complete business transactions with government by walking to a service access point. For instance, the business registration process online at the Registrar General's Department (RGD) improved but clients had to walk to its premises in Accra to make payment (Adarkwa, 2021).

The public service quality may be measured at four levels, namely efficiency, economy, service accessibility, and customer satisfaction (Osei-Kojo, 2016). At the efficiency level, one of the basic aims of the project is to make government efficient through the improvement of the quality of public service. In the area of education, some of the success stories include the introduction of the computerized school selection and placement system (CSSPS) by the Ghana Education Service (GES) in 2005 that places Junior High School (JHS) graduates into selected Senior High School (SHS) on the basis of their grades obtained which previously caused parents and guardians headaches, the checking of the results online by JHS and SHS graduates before receiving official result slip from their schools and online application and admission systems by the majority of universities in the country (Osei-Kojo, 2016; Adarkwa, 2021). Public service delivery improvements have also occurred in the Driver and Vehicle Licensing Authority (DVLA) with the introduction of the online renewal of driver's licences and change of vehicle ownership; the RGD provides a one-stop online business registration system that allows users to apply for their business registration certificate and renew it and online government documents including the budget statements and Acts of Parliament at the website of Parliament.

Economy refers to how e-government has reduced costs through reduced paperwork, delay or improved turnaround time of services and visits of clients to field offices (Osei-Kojo, 2016). The introduction of a paperless port and airport system has reduced layers, simplified the process, reduced the time needed to clear goods and avenues for corruption and increased inefficiencies and revenue mobilization in the ports. The documentation and verification processes have been reduced to '15 minutes, and the payment of import and export duty (and bank confirmation) now occurs within 10 minutes. Goods at the airport are dispatched within 1 day and in the harbour within 3 days' (Bawumia, 2021, p. 3). Similarly, passport applications are online even though the applicant has to visit the passport office for biometric data capturing, thereby eliminating middlemen. Furthermore, an applicant no longer waits for several months to receive their driver's licence but can get it in a day once all the requirements are met (Bawumia, 2021).

Service accessibility refers to the de-bureaucratization of the availability of public services through online access to citizens (Osei-Kojo, 2016). Accordingly, the *Ghana.Gov* Platform is a one-stop shop for accessing government services. All MDAs are on the Platform and have dedicated websites for service delivery. More specific progress includes the broadening of the tax net to improve domestic revenue mobilization through the designation of the Ghana Card (the national identification card) as the tax identification number (TIN) which increased the percentage of adults with TIN numbers from 4% to 86% at the end of 2020 (Bawumia, 2021), the simplification of the tax filing process through the introduction of mobile tax filing application which is available on some Apps and the application of birth certificate online (Osei-Kojo, 2016). Others include the extensive use of e-teaching and e-learning during the outbreak of COVID-19 in March 2020 to date, the introduction of e-levy with effect from May 2022 on mobile money e-transactions to broaden the tax net, and the ongoing re-registration of SIM cards by mobile phone users in the country for security reasons at the time of writing this chapter.

Customer satisfaction refers to how citizens access services using electronic means in a timely, cost-effective, and efficient manner compared with manual processes (Osei-Kojo, 2016). Of the six pillars of the NPSRS (2018–2023), pillar six has been devoted to digitized public sector services and systems aimed at facilitating the overall transformation of public service delivery through technology. The e-Transform programme includes e-Services, e-Mail, document management, e-Procurement, e-Education, e-Justice, e-Verification, e-Immigration, e-Parliament, e-Health systems, and open data platforms (Republic of Ghana, 2017a).

There is no doubt that services have improved in terms of turnaround time and reduction in manual processes. Given the progress made, Vice President Bawumia has referred to a 'new system through digital transformation', aimed at deepening the e-Ghana project by building a system that promotes transparency, accountability, improved service delivery, and enhanced domestic revenue mobilization (Bawumia, 2021).

Notwithstanding the implementation of the e-Ghana project there are problems leading to general dissatisfaction of citizens with public service delivery (Republic of Ghana, 2020). They include the digital divide; inadequate focus on e-government and e-governance; resistance to change by some service providers and citizens; inadequate ICT infrastructure; the lack of freedom of access and freedom of information; levels of general illiteracy in ICT in the areas of e-justice, e-parliament, and general participation in policy discussions; and questions over the sustainability of the Government Wide Network (GovNet) – a network consisting of MDAs – and its negative impact on all e-government applications including GIFMIS because of weak budgetary support (Osei-Kojo, 2016; Republic of Ghana, 2020; Adarkwa, 2021).

The Role of Policy Think-tanks in Reform and Innovation Programmes

Before the return to constitutional rule in 1993, Ghana had three think-tanks, namely the Institute of Statistical, Social and Economic Research (ISSER), Integrated Social Development Centre (ISODEC), and Institute for Economic Affairs (IEA) because of a 'culture of silence' created by the military rule of Jerry Rawlings' Provisional National Defence Council (PNDC) from 1981 to 1992 (Ayee, 2019). The liberal environment created by the 1992 Constitution led to the setting up of over 40 think-tanks in the country as of 2022. Their diversity is reflected in their areas of interest or activity with strong emphasis on rights- and governance-based approaches. Specifically, the areas include democratic governance, socioeconomic development, peace and security, human rights, and energy and natural resources (Table 17.2). Apart from the ISSER, which is at the University of Ghana, all the think-tanks are private, non-for-profit, and non-partisan organizations which rely heavily on development partners for funding and have fairly good human resources with about 50% of them holding PhD degrees. They, therefore, have the capacity to undertake surveys whose methodologies and findings are fairly credible but sometimes questioned by some politicians and public organizations which receive negative comments and ratings (Ohemeng, 2005). They use primary tools of engagement such as research, publications, surveys, seminars, conferences, workshops, roundtable discussions, use of the media, and advocacy, which are either attended or accessed by some politicians, members of the executive, legislature, judiciary, bureaucrats, and civil society depending on the topics and their relevance to their areas of work and interest (Ohemeng, 2005).

Based on their areas of activity and key outputs in Table 17.2, the think-tanks may be described as policy entrepreneurs, whose defining characteristics 'is their willingness to invest their resources—time, energy, reputation, and sometimes money—in the hope of a future return' (Kingdon, 1995, p. 122). They have influenced public policies and programmes either directly or indirectly through their research and advocacy activities.

The Need for Inter- and Intra-sectoral Collaboration

Even though the policy and institutional framework for reform and innovation largely exists, the proliferation of institutions has made it impossible for effective inter- and intra-sectoral collaboration (IISC). The effective performance of public sector institutions is constrained by

Table 17.2   Key think-tanks in Ghana

S/No.	Name	Year created	Areas of interest/activity	Key output(s)
1.	Institute of Statistical, Social and Economic Research, University of Ghana	1962	Conducts research in the social sciences in order to generate solutions for national development.	Its annual 'State of Ghanaian Economy' and 'Social Development Outlook' reports have been widely cited across the globe and reached policy makers. Conducts annual review of the budget statement after presentation to parliament.
2.	Integrated Social Development Centre	1987	Undertakes research and advocacy in analysis of macro-economic policy; social justice, human rights; and government accountability.	Organized national annual budget analysis and advocacy to create the space for public input into the national budgeting process at the regional level; tracks public expenditure from the national to community levels.
3.	Institute of Economic Affairs	1989	Supports research and advocacy on economic, sociopolitical and legal issues to enhance understanding of public policy.	Trained legislative research assistants in 1996 to assist the work of Parliament; organized presidential and vice-presidential debates since 2000 and 2008 to date respectively; facilitated the development of a Political Parties Code of Conduct in 2004 and a body to regulate it; provided advocacy for the enactment of the Whistleblowers and Right to Information Acts; review of the Political Parties Act and Presidential Transition Act.
4.	Centre for Policy Analysis	1993	Undertakes research and advocacy on macro-economic policies, finance, international trade, agriculture, poverty and gender of Ghana and the developing world.	Organized dissemination workshops, seminars and lectures to the business community and civil society; online publications available on website.
5.	Third World Network – Africa	1994	Undertakes research and advocacy in trade, investment, mining, environment, climate change and gender to improve the conditions of people in North-South affairs.	Established and coordinated continent-wide policy networks in trade and investment, mining and gender equity; played intermediary role at levels of both substance and process, between diverse state and non-state organizations and actors.

Table 17.2 (continued)

S/No.	Name	Year created	Areas of interest/activity	Key output(s)
6.	Africa Security Dialogue and Research	1995	Combines advocacy and dialogues on issues of defence, security, democratic consolidation; security database collation.	Publications on the security sector in some African countries; housed defence documentation centre.
7.	Centre for Democratic Development	1998	Advances democracy, good governance, and inclusive economic growth	Mobilized and organized civil society voice and activism on key national issues; built effective national and Africa-wide coalitions and networks including the Coalition of Domestic Election Observers, the Ghana Anti-Corruption Coalition, West Africa Election Observers Network and Parliamentary Monitoring Organisations; provided technical and analytic input to relevant MDAs, and Parliament for the drafting of key legislations; generated and disseminated public opinion surveys including Afrobarometer for effective advocacy and policy-making; enhanced citizens' engagement with local political authorities to demand accountability and responsiveness from duty-bearers; pioneered the Parallel Vote Tabulation methodology to independently verify presidential election results in Ghana's last four general elections.
8.	West Africa Network for Peacebuilding	1998	Builds sustainable peace to create an enabling environment for development in West Africa; founded in response to civil wars that plagued West Africa in the 1990s	Collaborative approaches to conflict prevention, and peacebuilding; establish a platform for dialogue, experience sharing and learning to complement sustainable peace and development in West Africa; entered into a partnership with ECOWAS in 2002 to implement a regional early warning and response system (ECOWARN); signed MoU with ECOWAS in 2004 to contribute to Track I response to conflicts and policy debate.
9.	Social Enterprise Development Foundation, Ghana	1998	Promotes good governance and equality of women and men.	Some initiatives on budget tracking and gender equity helped some citizens to access education and healthcare services in the poorest parts of the country.

10.	Institute of Democratic Governance	2000	Contributes to the 'establishment of a just and free society' in Ghana for the promotion of prosperity and security in West Africa.	Played technical roles in the execution of the Structural Adjustment Participatory Review Initiative and the formulation of national Poverty Reduction Strategies (2000–2009); coordinating secretariat for civil society-led initiatives to influence policies on democracy and good governance, growth and poverty reduction; since 2010 led the Civic Forum Initiative to the conduct of free, fair, and credible elections.
11.	Institute of Policy Alternatives	2001	Promotes practice-research in alternative policy analysis, development, peacebuilding, and conflict management in West Africa.	Developed methodologies to gather evidence among citizen groups, civil society organizations and members of Parliament; evaluated and facilitated the teaching and learning of evaluation through African cultural values and knowledge systems.
12.	IMANI Centre for Policy and Education	2004	Applies free market solutions in the rule of law, market growth and development, individual rights, and human security and institutional development	Shaped the national, regional and global agenda in order to close the 'citizen participation gap' in the governance through effective communication skills and the ability to work with public-spirited media and civil society.
13.	African Centre for Economic Transformation	2008	Focuses on Africa's growth and transformation in climate and agriculture; economic management and governance; gender equality; innovation and digital policy; youth employment and skills	Produced reports and provided advice and statistical information to develop, negotiate, and administer agreements between governments and petroleum and mineral companies.
14.	Africa Centre for Energy Policy	2010	Undertakes research, analysis and advocacy in the energy and extractive sector governance in Africa.	Thought leader in the energy and extractive sector; launched campaign and regional forums to demand accountability in the energy sector. Published a Manifesto before the 2016 national election to influence the campaigns of presidential candidates.
15.	Institute of Fiscal Studies	2013	Undertakes research and analysis in macroeconomic and fiscal policy management	Online publications on aspects of the Ghanaian economy including the budget, taxation, natural resources which have influenced public policy.
16.	Institute for Health Policy and Research	2013	Provides debate and ideas to build a responsive and secure health service in collaboration with local and international stakeholders.	Evaluated national health policies and monitored programmes to set agenda and promote productivity in the health sector.

Source: Compiled by the author from the websites of the think-tanks.

weak IISC and clarity in roles and functions of MDAs and duplication and overlap of functions among MDAs (Republic of Ghana, 2017b). Similarly, one of the reasons for the ineffectiveness of past public sector reforms is that

> coordination of the reforms was weak as it fell short of the following: availability of reform policies and guidelines; prioritization, target setting and sequencing; and monitoring and evaluation. Reform coordination in terms of reform alignment and harmonization was also unsatisfactory. (Republic of Ghana, 2017a, p. 3)

Consequently, for reform and innovation to succeed there is the need for an IISC that encourages consultations with agencies and stakeholders on proposed reform policies and guidelines, prioritization, target setting, implementation sequencing and monitoring and evaluation (Republic of Ghana, 2017b).

> Accordingly, IISC have been captured in some policy documents. For instance, Departments of a District Assembly shall collaborate and co-operate with non-decentralised departments, state-owned enterprises and public corporations operating in the district to ensure a co-ordinated approach to the development and management of the district, avoid duplication and ensure a more convenient and cost-effective implementation of programmes and projects. (Republic of Ghana, 2019b, p. 48)

Similarly, the NPSRS concedes that

> establishing the necessary institutional arrangements for implementation of the Strategy is a critical success factor ... because clarifying institutional responsibilities involved in reforms will significantly improve their performance, especially in the areas of policy formulation, implementation, and monitoring and evaluation and reporting and accountability relation among these institutions. (Republic of Ghana, 2017a, p. 33)

Consequently, the Strategy identifies the MDAs and metropolitan, municipal, and district assemblies (MMDAs) as the implementers and the specific groups and their tasks in a fairly elaborate manner.

Notwithstanding this realization, progress has been slow because the practice involves attitudinal and behavioural changes, internalization of reform and innovation initiatives, and resistance, which take time to change.

CAPACITY DEVELOPMENT FOR REFORM AND INNOVATION: THE MANAGERIAL CHALLENGE

The success of reform and innovation is also dependent on the availability of a strong human resource or managerial capacity to implement them given challenges such as inadequate budgetary support, human resource constraints, resistance to change, and reform fatigue. Reform and innovation are knowledge- and skills-based with changes sometimes in the legal and institutional framework, systems, processes, technology, attitudes, and behaviour which call for capacity development (CD).

The reality of managerial challenges cannot be ignored in Ghana. Accordingly, CD is required to successfully handle the initiatives. The introduction of CD entails the availability of adequate budgetary support, knowledge, skills, and willingness of staff, reprioritization of organizational goals and leadership at all levels. CD is important in development cooperation as it is a vehicle for meeting the SDGs and for long-term sustenance of the targets (Wehn, 2014). However, CD is an expensive intervention which is largely not budgeted for by governments and politicians because it is not a tangible benefit to garner votes (Ayee, 2019).

The managerial challenge in Ghana has been addressed through a number of interventions. First, a change management team consisting of local professionals is put in place to monitor and coordinate the reform and innovation strategies. Second is the use of both local and international consultants. For instance, the development of the NPSRS was done solely by local consultants from the University of Ghana, Ghana Institute of Management and Public Administration (GIMPA), a few ministries, and the private sector (Republic of Ghana, 2017a). On the other hand, the National Decentralization Policy and Strategy 2020–2024) was designed through a European Union technical assistance (TA) provided to the Inter-Ministerial Coordinating Committee on Decentralization (IMCCoD) by a combination of local consultants from some MDAs while the international consultants worked under the umbrella of ECORYS and VNG International (Republic of Ghana, 2020).

The use of international consultants to provide TA in SSA under CD has been criticized as patronizing even though the understanding is that it is a process undertaken jointly with the recipient country (Vallejo and Wehn, 2016). It is sometimes argued that the development partners (DPs) offer TA to the country using solely international consultants and not necessarily that there is no in-country capacity because they want results within the shortest possible time with the country context not taken into account. It has therefore been argued that CD is likely to be more successful if there is a healthy partnership between local and international consultants (Vallejo and Wehn, 2016).

It is instructive to note that the managerial challenge is also a leadership one that should not be ignored. Transformative leadership (TL) especially at the political and bureaucratic levels is lacking, leading to a feeling of fatalism as to how the country can realize its developmental goals (Ayee, 2019). For instance, in the political arena, there have been excessive polarization of national issues and lack of continuity in public policies and programmes as a result of political transitions, which have ended in acrimony between the two duopolies, the NPP and NDC. TL has not been exhibited to move the country away from the cycle of polarization and equalization (Ayee, 2019).

CONCLUSION

There has been great interest in the theory and practice of reform, innovation, and deliverology (RID) in public sector governance in sub-Saharan Africa (SSA). This has been reinforced by the changing public sector environment with emphasis on continuous process improvement, strategic adjustment, and administrative advancement. Like all SSA countries, Ghana has implemented RID initiatives as part of the global paradigmatic shifts to make its public sector more effective and efficient to enable it to achieve the constitutional goal of creating a free and just society. The chapter outlined reform delivery models and units, the role of the central government in overseeing reform, the use of information communication technology, the role of policy think-tanks, inter- and intra-sectoral collaboration, and capacity development in the light of the managerial challenge. It concluded with the lessons learnt and some recommendations for the way forward.

The chapter has shown that SSA countries including Ghana have implemented RID initiatives mostly through ideas and policy diffusion to improve service delivery. The public sector has spearheaded these initiatives because it has been the implementation wing of the state for development. Even though some progress has been made in the implementation of the initiatives in Ghana, there is more room for improvement given dissatisfaction by governments, citizens, and think-tanks about the quality service delivery.

Policy coordination, inter- and intra-organisational collaboration, and coordination of reforms remain key challenges in spite of efforts made at CD by DPs and succeeding Ghanaian governments. The contribution of think-tanks has, however, been enduring as most of them through their activities have contributed either directly or indirectly to reform and innovation thereby qualifying for description as 'policy entrepreneurs'.

There are a number of lessons. First, the concepts of RID are inextricably linked because their main goal is to change and improve performance especially public service delivery. Second, an effective policy and institutional framework is a prerequisite for the initiatives that cannot be ignored. Third, ineffective leadership, resistance, fatigue, and apathy can derail any good-intentioned initiative and should therefore be addressed before implementation. Fourth, effective intra- and inter-sectoral collaboration and coordination and CD, which is largely homegrown, are important for the success of the initiatives. Fifth, active think-tanks are key actors which will keep governments and bodies on their toes in service delivery, promote transparency and accountability, and demand better governance.

Given these lessons, the chapter makes some recommendations. First, RID initiatives and accompanying CD require adequate budgetary support from governments because they entail changes, new processes, systems, and infrastructure that are expensive to put in place.

Second, transformative leaders at all levels (especially political and bureaucratic levels) are required to make a difference and bring positive radical changes. It is an important choice to make as transformative leadership, that is, 'leadership that engenders widespread, demonstrable improvements in peoples' lives as evidenced in rising incomes, longer life expectancies, comprehensive social safety networks, and universal access to basic services' is regarded as critical in the realization of the SDGs and the Agenda 2063 (African Building Capacity Foundation, 2019, p. v).

Third, the policy and institutional framework needs continuous reform to make it fit for purpose. This entails proactive CD interventions and regular self-introspection by stakeholders including government, bureaucrats, and think-tanks.

Finally, implementing RID is a Herculean task which involves several stakeholders with differing interests thereby compounding their complexity. A phased strategy is therefore required to realize the goals, even if incrementally.

REFERENCES

African Center for Economic Transformation. (2010), *Functional Review of the Strategy and Policy Unit, Sierra Leone*, Freetown: African Centre for Economic Transformation (ACET).

Adamolekun, L. (2011), 'Governance Context and Reorientation of Government', in Adamolekun, L. (ed.), *Public Administration in Africa: Main Issues and Selected Country Studies*, 2nd ed., Ibadan: Evans Brothers, pp. 3–23.

Adarkwah, M. (2021), 'I'm Not Against Online Teaching, But What About Us?: ICT in Ghana Post Covid-19', *Education Information Technology*, **26**, 1665–1685, doi: 10.1007/s10639-020-10331-z.

African Capacity Building Foundation. (2019), *Africa Capacity Report 2019: Fostering Transformative Leadership for Africa's Development*, Harare: ACBF.

African Union. (2000), 'Constitutive Act of the African Union', Adopted by the Thirty-Sixth Ordinary Session of the Assembly of Heads of State and Government 11 July 2000, Lome, Togo.

African Union. (2020), *The Digital Transformation Strategy for Africa (2020–2030)*, Addis Ababa: African Union.

Albury, D. (2005), 'Fostering Innovation in Public Services', *Public Money and Management*, **25** (1), 51–56, doi: 10.1111/j.1467-9302.2005.00450.x.

Aucoin, P. (1990), 'Administrative Reform in Public Management', *Governance*, **3** (2), 115–137, doi: 10.1111/j.1468-0491.1990.tb00111.x.

Awotwi, J.E. and G. Owusu (2010), 'Ghana Community Information Centers (CiCs): E-governance Success or Mirage?' *Journal of E-Governance*, **33** (3), 157–167, doi: 10.1145/1693042.1693105.

Ayee, J. (2008), *Reforming the African Public Sector: Retrospect and Prospect*, Dakar: CODESRIA.

Ayee, J. (2019), 'Introduction: Politics, Governance and Development in Ghana', in Ayee, J. (ed.), *Politics, Governance and Development in Ghana*, London: Lexington Books, pp. xv–xxxiv.

Bangura, Y. and G. Larbi (2006), *Public Sector Reform in Developing Countries: Capacity Challenges to Improve Services*, New York: Palgrave Macmillan/UNRISD.

Barber, M. (2009), *Deliverology: A Field Guide for Education Leaders: Who Want to Ensure Significant Results*, Washington, DC: Education Delivery Institute.

Barber, M., P. Kihn, A. Moffit and McKinsey & Company. (2011), 'Deliverology: From Idea to Implementation', accessed 23 August 2022 at http://www.mckinsey.com/industries/public-sector/ourinsights/deliverology-from-idea-to-implementation.

Barasa, H. (2022), 'Digital Government in Sub-Saharan Africa: Evolving Fast, Lacking Frameworks', Africa Policy Lead, accessed 28 August 2022 at https://institute.global/policy/digital-government -sub-saharan-africa-evolving-fast-lacking-frameworks#:~:text=The%20continent's%20E-Gove rnment%20Development,2003%20and%200.6%20in%20.

Bawumia, M. (2021), 'Transforming an Economy Through Digitilization: The Ghana Story', lecture delivered at Ashesi University, Ghana by the Vice President of the Republic of Ghana. November 2, 2021.

Bevan, G. and C. Hood (2006), 'Have Targets Improved Performance in the English NHS', *British Medical Journal*, **332** (7538), 419–422, doi: 10.1136/bmj.332.7538.419.

Bovaird, T. (2003), 'E-Government and e-Governance: Organisational Implications, Options and Dilemmas', *Public Policy and Administration*, **18** (2), 37–56, doi: 10.1177/0952076703018002.

Bowornwathana, B. and O. Poocharoen (2010), 'Bureaucratic Politics and Administrative Reform: Why Politics Matters', *Public Organisation Review*, **10** (4), 303–321, doi: 10.1007/s11115-010-0129-0.

Brautigam, D. (1996), 'State Capacity and Effective Governance', in Ndulu, B. and N. van de Walle (eds.), *Agenda for Africa's Economic Renewal*, Washington, DC: Overseas Development Council, pp. 81–108.

Caiden, G. (1969), *Administrative Reform*, Chicago, IL: Aldine/Atherton.

Caiden, G. (1978), 'Administrative Reform: A Prospectus', *International Review of Administrative Sciences*, **44** (1), 106–120, doi.org/10.1177/002085237804400109.

Caiden, G. (1988), 'The Vitality of Administrative Reform', *International Review of Administrative Sciences*, **54** (3), 331–357, doi: 10.1177/002085238805400301.

Caiden, G. (1991), *Administrative Reform Comes of Age*, Berlin: W. de Gruyter.

Caiden, G. (1999), 'Administrative Reform: Proceed with Caution', *International Journal of Public Administration*, **22** (6), 815–832, doi: 10.1080/01900699908525406.

Chapman, R. and J. Greenaway (1980), *The Dynamics of Administrative Reform*, London: Croom Helm.

Economic Commission for Africa. (2003), *Public Sector Management Reforms in Africa*, Addis Ababa: Economic Commission for Africa.

Economic Commission for Africa. (2010), *Innovations and Best Practices in Public Sector Reforms in Africa*, Addis Ababa: Economic Commission for Africa.

Essuman-Mensah, D. (2019), 'A Study of the Performance of Reform Institutions: Focusing on the Evolution of Public Sector Reforms in Ghana', *Journal of International Development Cooperation*, **14** (2), 99–130, doi: 10.34225/jidc.2019.14.2.99.

Etheridge, Z. and P. Thomas (2015), *Adapting the PMDU Model. The Creation of a Delivery Unit by Haringey Council, London: A Case Study*, London: Institute for Government.

Foreign, Commonwealth, and Development Office. (2019), 'Education Beyond Aid (EBA) Business Case: Summary Sheet', accessed 12 April 2022 at https://devtracker.fcdo.gov.uk/projects/GB-GOV -1-300517/documents.

Fombad, C. (2022), 'UPDATE: Transitional Justice in Africa – The Experience with Truth Commissions', accessed 5 May 2022 at https://www.nyulawglobal.org/globalex/Africa_Truth_Commissions1. html.

Gready, P. and S. Robins (2020), 'Transitional Justice and Theories of Change: Towards Evaluation as Understanding', *International Journal of Transitional Justice*, **14** (2), 280–299, doi: 10.1093/ijtj/ ijaa008.

Guy Peters, B. (1992), 'Government Reorganisation: A Theoretical Analysis', *International Political Science Review*, **13** (2), 199–217.

Guy Peters, B. (2018), *The Politics of Bureaucracy: An Introduction to Comparative Public Administrative*, 7th edn, New York, NY: Routledge.

Jreisat, J. (1988), 'Administrative Reform in Developing Countries: A Comparative Perspective', *Public Administration and Development*, **8** (1), 85–97, doi: 10.1002/pad.4230080108.

Jreisat, J. (2011), 'Governance: Issues in Concept and Practice', in Menzel, D. and H. White (eds.), *The State of Public Administration: Issues, Challenges and Opportunities*, New York: M&E Sharpe, pp. 424–438.

Kariuki, E. and K. Kiraju (2011), 'Modernizing Public Administration Through Electronic Government', in Adamolekun, L. (ed.), *Public Administration in Africa: Main Issues and Selected Country Studies*, Ibadan: Evans Brothers, pp. 172–191.

Karyeija, G. (2012), 'Public Sector Reforms in Africa: What Lessons Have We Learnt?', *Forum for Development Studies*, **39** (1), 105–124, doi: 10.1080/08039410.2011.635378.

Kieh, G. (2018), 'The "Hegemonic Presidency" in African Politics', *African Social Science Review*, **9** (1), 36–51.

Killian, J. and N. Eklund (eds.) (2008), *Handbook of Administrative Reform: An International Perspective*, London: Routledge.

Kingdon, J. (1995), *Agendas, Alternatives and Public Policies*, New York: Longman.

Joshi, A. and B. Carter (2015), *Public Sector Institutional Reform: Topic Guide*, Birmingham: GSDRC, University of Birmingham.

La Pierre, R. (1965), *Social Change*, New York: McGraw-Hill.

Lane, J.-E. (1993), *The Public Sector: Concepts, Models and Approaches*, London: Sage.

Machiavelli, N. (1513, 2019), 'The Prince', in Skinner, Q. and R. Price (eds.), *Cambridge Texts in the History of Political Thought*, Cambridge: Cambridge University Press.

Mansoor, Z., K. Qarout, C. Anderson, L. Carano, V. Yecalo-Tecle, V. Dvorakova and M. Williams (2021), 'A Global Mapping of Delivery Approaches', DeliverEd Initiative Working Paper. July, Education Commission and Blavatnik School of Government.

Mason, S., E. Weber, J. Coster, J. Freeman and T. Locker (2012), 'Time Patients Spend in the Emergency Department: England's 4-Hour Rule – A Case of Hitting the Target But Missing the Point?' *Annals of Emergency Medicine*, **59** (5), 341–349, doi: 10.1016/j.annemergmed.2011.08.017.

Miewald, R. and M. Steineman (eds.) (1984), *Problems in Administrative Reform*, Chicago, IL: Nelson-Hall.

Migdal, S. (1988), *Strong Societies and Weak States*, Princeton, NJ: Princeton University Press.

Ministry of Education (MoE) Liberia. (2018), 'Ministry of Education: Education Delivery Unit Vacancy Announcement', accessed 18 May 2022 at https://emansion.gov.lr/doc/ECE%20S.pdf.

Moore, M. and J. Hartley (2008), 'Innovations in Governance', *Public Management Review*, **10** (1), 3–20, doi: 10.1080/14719030701763161.

Nazif, E. (2019), 'Innovation Planning', paper presented at the 14th Prof. Vladas Gronskas International Scientific Conference Kaunas: Vilnius University Kaunas Faculty, Bulgaria, 5th of December, 2019, accessed 23 June 2022 at https://www.researchgate.net/publication/342203621_Innovation _planning.

Ndulu, M. (2001), 'Constitution-Making in Africa: Assessing Both the Process and Content', *Public Administration and Development*, **21**, 101–117, doi: 10.1002/pad.163.

Ohemeng, F. (2005), 'Getting the State Right: Think Tanks and the Dissemination of New Public Management Ideas in Ghana', *Journal of Modern African Studies*, **43** (3), 443–465.

Ohemeng, F. and K. Ofosu-Adarkwa (2014), 'Overcoming the Digital Divide in Developing Countries: An Examination of Ghana's Strategies to Promote Universal Access to Information Communication Technologies (ICTs)', *Journal of Developing Societies*, **30** (3), 297–322, doi: 10.1177/0169796X14536970.

Olkaba, T. and E. Tamene (2019), 'Deliverology in Ethiopian Higher Education as a Quality Management Tool: Critical Review and the Insider's Reflection', *International Journal of Education and Literacy Studies*, **7** (4), 83–90, doi: 10.7575/aiac.ijels.v.7n.4p.83.

Olowu, D. (2011), 'Public Service Delivery', in Adamolekun, L. (ed.), *Public Administration in Africa: Main Issues and Selected Country Studies*, 2nd ed., Ibadan: Evans Brothers, pp. 192–215.

Osei-Kojo, A. (2016), 'E-government and Public Service Quality in Ghana', *Journal of Public Affairs*, **17** (3), e1620, doi: 10.1002/pa.1620.

Pinto, R. (1998), 'Innovations in the Provision of Public Goods and Services', *Public Administration and Development*, **18** (4), 387–397, doi: 10.1002/(SICI)1099-162X(1998100)18:4<387::AID-PAD30> 3.0.CO;2-0.

Polidano, C. (2000), 'Measuring Public Sector Capacity', *World Development*, **28** (5), 805–822.

Radin, B. (2000), *Beyond Machiavelli: Policy Analysis Comes of Age*, Washington, DC: George Washington University.

Republic of Ghana. (2003), *The ICT for Accelerated Development (ICT4AD) Policy*, Accra: Government of Ghana Printers.

Republic of Ghana. (2006), *Ghana: e-Ghana Project Appraisal Document*, Washington, DC: World Bank.

Republic of Ghana. (2017a), *The Coordinated Programme of Economic and Social Development Policies, 2017–2024*, Accra: Government Printer.

Republic of Ghana. (2017b), *National Public Sector Reform Strategy, 2018–2023*, Accra: Office of the Senior Minister.

Republic of Ghana. (2019a), *Medium Term Expenditure Framework (MTEF) for 2019–2022*, Office of Government Machinery, Accra: Ministry of Finance.

Republic of Ghana. (2019b), *National Decentralization Policy and Strategy (2020–2024)*, Accra: IMCCoD Secretariat.

Republic of Ghana. (2020), *Household Survey on ICT in Ghana*, Accra: National Communication Authority (NCA) and Ghana Statistical Service (GSS).

Robinson, M. (2015), *From Old Public Administration to the New Public Service Implications for Public Sector Reform in Developing Countries*, New York: UNDP Centre for Public Service Excellence.

Schacter, M. (2016), *Does Deliverology Matter?*, Ottawa: Mark Schacter Consulting.

Scharff, M. (2012), 'Delivering on a Presidential Agenda: Sierra Leone's Strategy and Policy Unit, 2010–2011', accessed 20 July 2022 at https://successfulsocieties. princeton.edu/sites/successfulsocieties/files/Sierra%20Leone%20President%20ToU_1_0_pdf.

Tull, D. and C. Simons (2017), 'The Institutionalisation of Power Revisited: Presidential Term Limits in Africa', *Africa Spectrum*, **52** (2), 79–102, doi: 10.1177/000203971705200204.

Turner, M. and D. Hulme (1997), 'Administrative Reform: The Continuing Search for Performance Improvement', in M. Turner and D. Hulme (eds.), *Governance, Administration and Development: Making the State Work*, New York: Palgrave, pp. 105–131.

Vallejo, B. and U. When (2016), 'Capacity Development Evaluation: The Challenge of the Results Agenda and Measuring Return on Investment in the Global South', *World Development*, **79**, 1–13, doi: 10.1016/j.worlddev.2015.10.044.

Wehn, U. (2014), 'Effective Knowledge and Capacity Development for Enhancing the Post-2015 Development Goals', Paper Presented at the International Development Studies Lecture Series 2014–2015, University of Amsterdam.

Williams, M.J., C. Leaver, K. Mundy, Z. Mansoor, D. Qarout, M. Asim, S. Bell and A. Bilous (2020), 'Delivery Approaches to Improving Policy Implementation: A Conceptual Framework', accessed 21 July 2022 at https://bit.ly/DeliverEdFramework.

World Bank. (1989), *Sub-Saharan Africa: From Crisis to Sustainable Growth*, Washington, DC: World Bank.

World Bank. (1997), *World Development Report 1997: The State in a Changing World*, New York: Oxford University Press.

World Bank (2018), *Improving Public Sector Performance Through Innovation and Inter-Agency Coordination*, Global Report, Washington, DC: World Bank.

18. Network and collaborative governance in Africa

Elvin Shava

INTRODUCTION

The 'Africa-is-open-for-business' theme appears to be a slogan and an economic mantra in many African countries. Zimbabwe, for instance, has been chanting this economic slogan although the economic and political environment betrays these efforts as the business has repeatedly failed to thrive (Melber and Southall, 2021). In South Africa, President Ramaphosa hosts regular business summits to attract foreign direct investment and to rejuvenate the economy. In Rwanda, President Kagame has widely publicised and encouraged investors to visit Rwanda, which he regards as a favourable destination for foreign investors as the country seeks to attain its 2050 development vision of transforming the country into a knowledge-based upper-middle-income country by 2035 (Republic of Rwanda, 2019). These examples show the extent to which African countries strive to conduct business to ensure the economic emancipation of citizens while driving national economies with a network of actors. While many challenges exist, it is evident that African countries are on a relatively steep growth trajectory to address past imbalances. Doing business in Africa is vital for economic development since it positively affects various externalities, such as wealth generation and distribution, employment opportunities, regional prosperity, exports, living standards, gross domestic product (GDP), and GDP per capita (Adu-Gyamfi, Kuada and Asongu, 2018). Network formation and collaborative governance are essential since the African continent in general falls behind other parts of the world (Tchamyou, 2018; Asongu Nwachukwu and Orim, 2018).

The purpose of this chapter is to explore network and collaborative governance on the African continent. Focus is placed on the challenges that may affect doing business in Africa in the absence of such networks. To minimise business losses and attract foreign investment, the chapter advocates for robust networks and collaborative efforts that will enable African governments to harness and coordinate the collective capabilities and strengths of multiple actors in rendering public goods and services.

NETWORK AND COLLABORATIVE GOVERNANCE: CONCEPTUAL AND CONTEXTUAL PERSPECTIVES

Despite a paradigm shift towards market-based development, improved political and economic governance, and a supportive global climate, doing business in Africa remains challenging (Asongu, Nwachukwu and Orim, 2018). This is mainly due to various factors such as poor leadership, unsuitable economic policies, and the absence of political will to drive innovative government initiatives. The literature on the ease of doing business in Africa has primarily focused on the cost of doing business (Eifert, Gelb and Ramachandran, 2008), legal challenges to doing business (Tchamyou, 2018), and determinants of doing business (Adewole and John, 2019). The golden thread running through the scholarly discourse regarding economic conditions on the continent is the need for African countries to foster partnerships, positive relationships, and collaborative initiatives with a network of actors for improving public service delivery and fostering general prosperity and well-being. Creating strategic networks and pooling resources together is critical for addressing complex issues which governments as the sole actor, simply cannot successfully deal with.

To achieve its goals, governments have become more reliant on social actors (Klijn, 2008). According to Stoker (1998, p. 18), collaborative governance refers to the means adopted by multiple stakeholders both within and external to governments to address mainly four issues. These issues are:

- joint responsibility for socioeconomic development;
- clarity regarding authority and powers with regard to service delivery;
- matter pertaining to corporate governance, both internally and collectively in networks; and
- principles and approaches to a more inclusive and collaborative form of governance.

Network and collaborative governance in essence are premised on the necessity of governments to facilitate the establishment of a coordinated system of engagement, coordination and partnership with international agencies, the private sector, non-governmental organisations, and community-based institutions. The rationale and main impetus driving such network formation is the reality that societal challenges are simply too complex, broad-based, and costly for governments alone to address. The coordinated efforts of a network of actors can significantly strengthen the capacity and capability deficits in government institutions. The success of such networks is dependent on factors such as a common socioeconomic development vision, openness and trust, mutual benefits, leadership, and resource sharing.

Collaborative governance is further emphasised in Goal 17 of the United Nations Sustainable Development Goals (UN, 2022), namely that a sustainable development agenda should be established by means of partnerships between government, the private sector, and civil society organisations. Critical success factors highlighted in this regard include collaborative partnerships, trust, inclusivity, a common development agenda, as well as civil society participation.

Theoretical Framework

Network governance theory neatly underpins network and collaborative governance. It is a multidisciplinary theory used in social sciences to explain the dynamics and relations between actors. Klijn and Koppenjan (2012) accentuate the fact that network governance theory enables scholarly inquiry into the systemic and institutional dimensions of network governance inclusive of public, corporate, and civil society players in transnational, regional, national, and local spheres. The theory is premised on the self-regulatory actions of network actors to determine how they may or may not succeed in working collectively for the achievement of common objectives. Scholars such as Lewis (2011) and Meier and O'Toole (2007) argue that network governance theory further serves as a framework to explore the interrelationships of actors. This interrelationship should be characterised by openness and transparency, resource sharing, and accountability arrangements. Klijn (2008) reasons that trust is a network's principal factor because it ensures proper planning and coordination.

A further theory to inform scholarly inquiry into network and collaborative governance is public value theory. Among the scholars who have contributed to the development of the concept of public value are Jessa and Uys (2009), Meynhardt (2009), Moore and Benington (2010) and Moore (2012). These scholars hold that public value can be divided into four categories: a) moral and ethical qualities; (b) the desire for aesthetically pleasing environments; (c) practical and purpose-driven participation by network stakeholders; and (d) sociopolitical aspirations as motivators for social justice and equity. Public value is generally guided by public purpose and public interest and considers tangible and nontangible forms of public products and services to citizens. The theory is premised on a holistic, interdisciplinary approach to human development in synchrony with broad socioeconomic objectives, such as those captured in the Africa Union's Agenda 2063 and the UN Agenda 2030.

The key components for public value production are public participation, open discourse, effective civic education, information sharing, and feedback loops (Uys and Jessa, 2017; Jessa and Uys, 2018). These components of public value are essential for investigating the dynamics associated with network formation and collaborative governance in efforts to promote economic growth, general prosperity, and the ability to render public services. Public value theory furthermore enables comprehension regarding the ways in which the public can obtain value from taxes paid through government policies, programmes, and actions.

DETERMINANTS FOR NETWORK FORMATION AND COLLABORATION

Creating networks that promote collaboration in African governments is often challenging due to either abuse of power or corrupt tendencies that collaboration may trigger. Various factors influence network formation and actor collaboration. These factors or determinants ultimately impact the extent to which African governments can promote foreign investment, establish a conducive business climate, and foster strong and collaborative relationships with network actors. Some of the most crucial determinants in this regard are outlined in the following subsections.

Corporate Governance in the Public Sector

The King I–IV reports (1994–2016) on good corporate governance outline the principles and steps that public and private institutions should take to ensure the effective and efficient management of institutions (Esser and Delport, 2018). Reports from the African Development Bank, the World Bank, the International Monetary Fund, and Transparency International all show that in Africa, adherence to these principles remains a significant challenge that impedes countries from prospering socioeconomically. The failure to implement good corporate governance principles such as sound financial management, oversight, transparency, and openness emanates from various factors. These factors include systemic corruption, poor political and administrative leadership and significant skills shortages in African public administrations. As skilled labour migrates to more prosperous economies, Africa's workforce is severely constrained by a brain drain. Furthermore, in many African countries, schooling and training programmes are misaligned with the labour market, and higher education systems are weak. In countries such as Somalia and South Sudan, education budgets are extremely limited and the focus on theory over practice is not transferable to the workplace. These impediments affect economic prosperity since economically active youth possess skills that are not relevant to drive African economies in the digital era.

Vulnerabilities to International Trends and Events

The World Bank's 2022 Africa's Pulse report reveals that international trends and events are posing significant challenges to African countries, impeding poverty alleviation and economic growth initiatives. These trends and events include tightening global financial conditions, rising food and fuel costs exacerbated by the Ukrainian crisis, climate change, and rising debt distress. The Africa's Pulse report therefore predicts a further reduction in economic growth, down to 3.3% in 2022–2023 from 4.1% in 2021.

The World Bank's 2022 Africa's Pulse report also noted that economic concerns such as rising inflation levels and the escalation in fuel and food prices internationally have increased social inequality and chronic poverty in most African countries. Income losses, especially in the informal sectors, have further widened the economic divide. Furthermore, the continent's rather sluggish recovery after the COVID-19 pandemic has accentuated the need for drastic new measures to curb socioeconomic ills such as unemployment by promoting collaborative networks with businesses, non-governmental organisations, and civil society institutions.

Infrastructure Development

Infrastructural development is one of Africa's fundamental challenges in its efforts to realise social and economic development targets. Businesses invest in countries with adequate transportation infrastructure (e.g. rail, road, ports, and airports), sufficient energy, and advanced digital telecommunication systems. The digital divide characterising the continent is exacerbated by rural and urban settings. Mitigating the digital divide and inequalities in education and health care requires African governments to invest heavily in telecommunication infrastructure (Shava and Doorgapersad, 2022). On the upside, the continent is endowed with immense natural resources and an expanding middle class which translates into purchasing power. Africa is also emerging as a significant trading partner in Asian and European markets (Adewole and John, 2019). However, low intra-African collaboration in trade is evident. This is mainly due to poor coordinated port operations, poor roads, inadequate rail capacity, political instability, and safety and security concerns.

Reliable and adequate energy generation and distribution infrastructure is a further obstacle to collaborative governance. Nigeria, for example, has a population of approximately 217 million people but only has the same power supply as Hungary, which has fewer than ten million people. This adversely affects business investment decisions. It also stifles efforts to achieve the UN Sustainable Development Goals (SDGs). In this regard, the Fiscal Monitor Report of the International Monitory Fund (IMF, 2020) shows that emerging economies will likely experience major investment needs to attain the SDGs. The IMF and observers such as Schwartz et al. (2020) therefore strongly argue for the prioritisation of investment in infrastructure development to modernise economies and support business growth on the continent. This requires the formation of collaborative agreements with the private sector by means of the establishment of public-private partnerships (PPPs). In Kenya, for example, PPPs have ensured that over 90% of the population has access to global systems for mobile communication (GSM phone connectivity) and enabled the national airline carrier to serve as major gateway to Africa (Kenya Logistics Infrastructure, 2021). A further example of the use of PPPs as collaborative governance instrument is in East and Central Africa, where the Northern Corridor is the busiest and most important transport route connecting landlocked economies such as Rwanda, Burundi, Uganda, and Eastern Democratic Republic of Congo to Kenya's Port of Mombasa via a road network, railways, inland water routes, and container terminals (Muogboh and Ojadi, 2018). Tanzania's Central Corridor was also established through a PPP and significantly enhances infrastructure development and economic growth.

Information and Communication Technologies

Although information and communication technology (ICT) systems and infrastructure is limited in Africa, this challenge became more visible during humanitarian disasters like the COVID-19 pandemic when a lack of digitalisation hindered governments' operational capacity and the distribution of humanitarian aid. Due to these difficulties, Africa has become a challenging region for the logistics industry. As argued by Adewole and John (2019), large international corporations have decreased their investments due to the nature of local conditions such as the structure of the informal economy, the absence of rail, road, and air freight capacity, and unstable political climates. These obstacles adversely affect the capacity of Africa to conduct business which has drawn calls for corporatisation and privatisation.

Corporatisation and Privatisation

African governments are generally unable to render sufficient public goods and services (Clifton et al., 2019; Voorn, Van Genugten and Van Thiel, 2020). Hence, collaborating with the private sector can be a potential remedy to address such deficiencies (Nuwagaba and Molokwane, 2020). Corporatisation typically allows governments to retain ownership of the company while allowing the company to run as efficiently as its private counterparts. The bureaucratic nature of government departments often stifles flexibility – a business requirement to be efficient (Clifton and Daz-Fuentes, 2018). Privatisation ranges from selling a minority share to all shares, at which point the firm is private (Ferry et al., 2018). As noted by Vyas-Doorgapersad and Shava (2022), privatisation is important as it allows private entities to render public services.

Some economists view privatisation of state-owned enterprises as making much business sense (Clifton, Comín and Diaz-Fuentes, 2006; Warner and Bel, 2008; Schmidt, 2014). This view is challenged by some political commentators that say such moves will weaken a more socialist, developmental governance model and simply benefit those with a capitalistic agenda (Belloc, Nicita and Sepe, 2014). In South Africa, for example, there were calls for the privatisation of Eskom, the state-owned electricity utility. These calls quickly drew harsh criticism from some political parties and civil society organisations voicing their concerns that private actors would benefit at the expense of taxpayers. Although the common argument is that the private sector is better positioned to provide the necessary infrastructure supporting socioeconomic development, some reason that corporatisation and privatisation may further trigger corrupt tendencies, especially in procurement domains (Pea-Miguel and Cuadrado-Ballesteros, 2019).

In Africa, corporatisation is an emerging phenomenon, although many governments engage in PPPs, often regarded as equivalent to corporatisation (Tavares, 2017; Brownlee, Hurl and Walby, 2018). Few studies, however, explore the political aspects driving or hampering corporatisation (Tavares and Cames, 2010; Andrews et al., 2020). Empirical research on ruling political parties, privatisation, and outsourcing of public services is thus inconclusive (Bel and Fageda, 2017; Alonso and Andrews, 2020). A study conducted by Andrews et al. (2020), for example, found no conclusive evidence of a causal relationship between political ideology and the level of corporatisation in countries. However, Häusermann et al. (2013, p. 230) argue that the provisioning of social services through corporatisation and privatisation is more politically sensitive and prone to ideological influence than other types of government services.

Managing Foreign Aid

African governments have been and are still largely dependent on foreign aid to support their socioeconomic development programmes. Many African governments receive donor and development aid from multilateral organisations such as World Bank, the International Fund for Agricultural Development, the United Nations Development Programme, the German Government Agency (GTZ), the Australian Aid Organisation (AUSAID), and various other European Union agencies. A study by Mangwanya (2022) revealed that foreign aid promotes economic growth and social development by bolstering national budgets. Foreign aid is vital for eradicating poverty and hunger, and achieving the Sustainable Development Goals (SDGs), which include providing universal primary education, eliminating poverty and need, reducing child mortality, and improving maternal health. However, in the same study, Mangwanya (2022) cautioned about the dependence syndrome attached to foreign or donor aid, which may trigger other problems such as corruption and inefficient and unproductive public administrations. In addition, Shava (2021, p. 2) states that foreign aid usually comes with conditions that may benefit or deter economic development in African countries. Foreign investors gain the influence to redirect government plans and dictate their repayment terms. Although donor and development agencies inject large sums of money into local economies the conditions often lead to significant government debt. The so-called debt trap adversely impacts taxpayers and the ability of governments to prioritise certain spending. For instance, China has gained prominence in many African countries by striking deals ranging from mining minerals such as coal, diamonds, and gold, and large infrastructure development projects. However, China's abuse of human rights and plunder of African resources are well documented in countries such as Zimbabwe and Malawi (Keenan, 2009). Also, in countries such as Kenya and Zimbabwe, where foreign assistance is dominant, Mangwanya (2022) argues that political, economic, and humanitarian woes were elevated as funds were distributed to autocratic leaders. This triggered corrupt practices, civil rights abuses, and a growing dependency culture. Therefore, foreign aid must be directed towards the economic emancipation of African citizens while foreign investors benefit from investing in transparent and accountable governments.

Regional Integration

Network and collaborative governance are critical for regional integration in Africa. Regional trade blocs are key to Africa's growth. Despite any challenges, regional integration in Africa is advancing, offering larger markets, fewer barriers, and potential economies of scale. However, for Africa to prosper there is a need to create a single African trade zone with few trade barriers. Although this may be the dream of some African leaders, championing this ideology has not been easy for Africa where approaches to economic development differ. The main regional blocs that promote regional integration in Africa consist of the Southern African Development Community (SADC), East African Community (EAC), Common Market for Eastern and Southern Africa (COMESA), and Economic Community of West African State ECOWAS (West). Since their inception these blocs have not been able to adequately address non-tariff barriers due to incompatible regulations, common external tariff clashes, and weak infrastructure. Another challenge is cross-trade bloc membership because African countries that are signatories to these organisations integrate at different speeds in the process affecting collaborative governance within a network. For example, the EAC introduced a common market in July 2010, but its impact will be gradual because many laws still need to be harmonised, and Tanzania has kept some opt-outs. Proposals for a unified trade bloc (SADC, COMESA, EAC) are advancing but may take years to realise. The EAC intends to swiftly implement a unified currency by 2012, although 2015 is a more realistic timetable given the necessity to harmonise fiscal and monetary policy. As members of the Franc Zone, the UEMOA (West) and the CEMAC (Central) already have unified currencies (linked to the euro). This strategy shows the various efforts regional blocs in Africa are undertaking to ensure smooth trade and mutually beneficial economic relations (IMF, 2016a).

GOVERNMENT AS THE CUSTODIAN OF COLLABORATIVE GOVERNANCE

The success of African economies is hinged on the state's capacity as the custodian to implement economic measures that stimulate local development while attracting investment in various economic sectors from the stakeholders. In recent decades, Africa has undergone tremendous economic liberalisation and policy implementation (Amavilah, Asongu and Andrés, 2017). The continent stands apart from other regions in doing business, which has repercussions for Agenda 2063 and the attainment of SDGs (DeGhetto, Gray and Kiggundu, 2016). A poor export sector and a huge young population are ripe for business creation and expansion. Reforms are needed to meet commercial challenges. Rising from these observations, the flourishing of global economies relies heavily on the type of leadership and government in power. For the African government to attract investment, good policies that promote trade and business must be in place.

Good leadership is commonly regarded as the epitome of conducting business in Africa; hence bureaucratic institutions must be responsive to the needs of the business sector, which is fundamental for employment creation and business opportunities. African public institutions must be governed to promote ethical business practices that help attract investment for job creation. This is critical as Africa has a bulging youthful population faced with high unemployment due to a lack of business opportunities. It is projected in the study of Asongu (2015) that by 2036, Africa's population will have doubled, making up nearly 20% of the world's population. Suppose these statistics are anything to go by. In that case, this can trigger a crucial problem for policymakers across the continent since addressing unemployment brought on by the favourable demographic change requires drastic measures to help sustain an enabling business environment. In this case, the government must ensure that policymakers are enlightened and devise strategic policies that cater to the dynamic labour environment.

Apart from creating enabling policies that promote business development, the government in Africa is expected to manage the political environment as it may scare investors and disrupt business activities. Politically unstable African countries such as Somalia, DRC, and South Sudan deter foreign investments as civil conflict and wars are not creating an enabling business environment. In this case, African leaders need to drive economic prosperity in a stable country where inflation is managed, rules of law are followed, and public situations display transparency and openness in running state affairs.

CHALLENGES OF DOING BUSINESS IN AFRICA

This section outlines some of the challenges of doing business in Africa which can be attributed to poor network and collaborative governance among African states.

Lack of Access to Business Finance

The absence of financial services in Africa has many factors (including payment systems, credit, and corporate and private insurance). These include cost, capital availability, and the lender-borrower information gap (Batuo and Kupukile, 2010). These characteristics, combined with research on surplus liquidity in African financial institutions, explain why many Africans lack access to formal financial services. Information-sharing offices or credit reporting agencies have been offered as a solution (Kusi and Opoku-Mensah, 2018) to alleviate the underlying asymmetry of information, specifically: the adverse selection on the part of lenders (ex-ante of the borrowing process) and moral hazard from borrowers (ex-post of the lending process). In addition, mobile banking has given the unbanked access to financial resources (Asongu and Odhiambo, 2017). African governments face this dilemma as conducting business has been associated with limited funding; a gap Foreign Direct Investments (FDIs) can fill in the event for a conducive economic environment.

The literature reviewed has not pointed to African countries' funding efforts, although international organisations commonly offer funding for development projects despite the condition attached. Initiating funding for business development is key for networking, although, in many African countries, local businesses find themselves without the much-needed collateral and strong business connection to secure funding. As the primary custodian of economic development, the state should be in a business to 'breathe' life into mainly struggling small businesses and supporting induvial entrepreneurs towards employment creation and income generation. As argued by Uys and Jessa (2016, p. 197), governments as key actors in networks should be flexible and responsive by adequately cooperating and collaborating with stakeholders within a partnership. This is fundamental for ensuring that any business transactions being helped between the state and private server and help enhance development in the processes catering to citizen needs for social and economic development in a transparent and accountable manner.

High Taxed and Low Cross-border Trade

Doing business in Africa is a cumbersome process due to high taxes, bureaucratic red tape, and limited cross-border trade. Business initiatives take too long to get established as they are expected to comply with various regulations and often unscrupulous practices. For example, high start-up costs necessitate registration and licensing in many African states. Literature on African entrepreneurship supports this position (Eifert, Gelb and Ramachandran, 2008; Tchamyou, 2018; Asongu, 2017). This concern extends to issues related to (i) doing business, such as the cost of business start-up procedures; (ii) contract enforcement procedures; (iii) business registration start-up procedures; (iv) time required to build a warehouse; (v) time needed to enforce a contract; (vi) time required to register a property; (vii) time needed to start a business; (viii) time to export; (ix) time to prepare and pay taxes; and (x) time to (Asongu, Nwachukwu and Orim, 2018). Improving institutional and economic governance can help start-ups and small businesses. This is because in Africa, small businesses are used as vehicles for generating employment and household income which is crucial for curbing poverty and inequalities. However, high taxes, as noted, do affect small businesses as their purchasing power is typically low, which calls for African governments to revise their tax brackets to accommodate entrepreneurs and emerging small businesses.

Shortage of Energy and Electricity

The lack of electricity in Africa is another business challenge as it limits economic activities, public services, and quality of life. This is confirmed in a study by Lukamba and Molokwane (2016, p. 72), who lamented the service delivery challenges in Sub-Saharan Africa, where electricity, sanitation, and roads are not conducive to promoting business. Africa's access to electricity lags behind the world, and regional and country variations exist. Africa's average access to electricity is 43%, compared to 87.5% globally. These figures show that insufficient electricity can increase businesses' operational costs, which must sometimes develop self-sufficient solutions to stay operational. In countries such as Zimbabwe and South Africa, where electricity outages are rife, doing business is a setback as uncontrolled power outages impede commercial operations. A study conducted by Asongu, Le Roux and Biekpe (2018) conclusively showed that Africa's energy management is insufficient to sustain economic growth. Access to energy is limited to around 5% of sub-Saharan Africa's population. The subregion's energy consumption is 17% below the global average. Africa's energy and electricity shortages are congruent with energy management and efficiency studies (Akpan and Akpan, 2012; Asongu, Le Roux and Biekpe, 2017).

Promoting greener energy and limiting fossil fuel use (mainly through subsidies) are natural measures for reducing energy and electricity shortages across the continent. It can be argued that while Africa strives to enhance economic development, various infrastructural challenges hinder the government from attracting foreign business. For instance, electricity challenges hinder business development while adversely affecting revenue flows.

Red Tape and Tough Government Regulatory Landscape

Bureaucratic red tape contributes to various inefficiencies in doing business in African states. Due to the continent's changing and challenging regulatory landscape, 62.5% of the last quartile of the World Bank's Ease of Doing Business Index (2022) is occupied by African countries. Starting a business, enforcing contracts, registering new property, obtaining regulatory permits, and protecting investors can be difficult across the continent. African countries have improved the ease of business, but more can be done to boost their global competitiveness.

A changing landscape and policies make it difficult for businesses to make long-term plans. This raises Africa's business costs. Businesses must become more strategic and proactive in their dealings with the government by being unified in disseminating their challenges, which allows policymakers to create policies that consider the needs of the private sector.

Further analysis of the literature has pointed out that by minimising red tape, the network can thrive through intersectoral and regional collaborations governed by democratic principles aimed at uplifting African countries. Classen (2017) argued that the viability of a network, in this case, will depend on how African leaders who enter into partnerships manage them, respecting the set boundaries and democratic rules to achieve sustainable development.

Effects of COVID-19

The scourge of the COVID-19 pandemic left severe scars on many developing African economies as countries struggle to procure vaccines and keep companies running owing to lockdown measures that affect production. While governments were left bleeding, COVID-19 took a toll on the administrative systems of many African states. Retrenchments in some sectors were inevitable, triggering various social and economic ills that Africa has been fighting to address. The outbreak of COVID-19 in Africa triggered several governance challenges that could have affected business investments. Managing COVID-19 funds, for instance, revealed various governance issues related to mismanagement, corruption, and diversion of funds by authorities for personal gain. In South Africa, as noted in Zindi and Shava (2022), corruption in the procurement of protective clothing for COVID-19 was recorded; in Zimbabwe, inflating prices on COVID-19 PPPs was recorded in Nigeria during the COVID-19 pandemic. In Kenya, as reported by Onsumu et al. (2021), the economy contracted due to COVID-19 and the International Monetary Fund (IMF) projected that Kenya's economic growth rate would decline by −0.1% in 2020 relative to 5.5% in 2019. Among the hardest hit sectors was the services sector. The tourism, trade, and repairs sectors were also affected as unemployment escalated during COVID-19 which triggered other governance challenges to the government as doing business was low owing to various measures taken to mitigate the spread of the virus. The ICT sector was spared as it become resilient by promoting business continuity during the COVID-19 pandemic. Other sectors such as agriculture and horticulture remain resilient in the process, making Kenya competitive in global markets.

Building a strong network and collaborative partnerships has become a challenge in Africa. Post-COVID-19 re-engagement efforts are necessary as participatory, accountable, and efficient governance are prerequisites to reigniting business in Africa. Robust leadership structure and political will are qualities for generating strong networks, which some African governments lack. Building effective collaborations is one of the determinants to drive African businesses and the economy in the case where public institutions are responsible for the needs of the citizens and stakeholders in rendering public goods and services. Auriacombe and Meyer (2020, p. 6) argue that strong leadership helps unite the public sector, business, labour, and civil society within the same network environment. The scholars' argument is hinged on the fact that solid collaborative governance in network demands that African governments address problems of common interest while advocating for their citizens to engage their government on common service delivery matters. It is clear from this discussion that network and collaborative government in Africa depend more on transparent governance structures that have good leadership with a clear political will to achieve sustainable development while African countries attain their social and economic objectives.

Market Diversification

Controversies have been put forward as to what makes African economies thrive; while several African countries such as Zimbabwe and the Democratic Republic of Congo have abundant mineral resources such as gold and diamond, the economic dividends for these countries have not been proportionally realised, which made critical thinkers develop an analytic concept called the 'resource curse'. This stems from the conflicts, civils, and gross abuse of human rights associated with such mineral wealth in Africa. Western scholars accredit African development to mineral resources such as gold, diamond, and gas, which may not be true considering other untapped resources that could be used to drive social and economic development. For instance, recently, there has been a growing scholarship on cannabis industrialisation, which some scholars view as an evolving economic accelerator that can be used to improve African business and the economy. This view is motivated by the fact that Africa has large tracts of unused land, which can be put to good use by growing cannabis for exporting. The limit to this view is that cannabis growing has been legalised in many African countries only for medicinal cannabis, which medical practitioners may recommend in isolated circumstances. Based on the evolving literature, there is a need to legalise cannabis in African governments as done in other European countries; it helps stimulate revenue that African states can emulate to empower local people in marginalised and geographically remote areas. Caution needs to be exercised as growing cannabis in some conservative African nations is taboo due to its societal effect and abuse of drugs. However, looking at these arguments, African states are positioned enough to diversify their markets and utilise agriculture to improve African economies. Advocating for Public Partnerships (PPPs) can be one way of ensuring that Africa benefits something from its mineral and agriculture. However, policies must be in place to avoid exploitation, as is happening in some African countries where Chinese companies, for instance, operate.

The Cost of Doing Business in Africa

Although tremendous economic opportunities are evident in Africa, various economic and sociopolitical risks in conducting business emerge. For instance, high taxes and low cross-border trade hinder African industry. All African fiscal regimes tax capital outflows heavily (Verhagen, 2017). Western countries limit source-of-income taxation to interest, royalties, and dividends. Economic integration and poor infrastructure have severely limited cross-border trade in Africa in recent decades (Akpan, 2014). For example, the Continental Free Trade Area (CFTA: 9, a continent-wide trade agreement signed by 44 of the 55 African Union member states in Kigali, Rwanda, in March 2018) is expected to increase cross-border trade. The importance of cross-border trade in Africa lies in its ability to bring new economic opportunities to the continent. There is a need for African countries to sign bilateral agreements that allows free movement of people and goods which is good for intercontinental trade. Mitigating trade border barriers is a step further to promoting social and economic development in Africa.

Unrefined Investment Policies

For network and collaborative governance to be a success in Africa, there is a need to revisit the business policies that may deter or enhance foreign direct investment. As noted by the International Monetary Fund (IMF, 2016b, p. 43), 'the indigenization policy and investment are intrinsically linked, and it would be desirable that authorities come up with one single harmonized law on investment'. The literature analysis has shown that African governments still have or are producing rigid economic policies that adversely impact investment and economic development. For example, Zimbabwe enacted indigenisation laws where foreign-owned companies were to cede 51% of their own, contributing to Zimbabwe's failure to be on par with its regional counterparts regarding FDI inflows. South Africa also has the Broad-Based Black Economic Empowerment Act, 53 (2003) later turned into Black Economic Empowerment (BEE), which seeks to restructure wealth to black people previously disadvantaged by apartheid. Shava (2016) argues that politicians and other individuals hijacked the BEE policies to enrich themselves by manipulating public procurement systems in local municipalities and other government entities. Arguably the enactment of investment policies in Africa is associated with underdevelopment in many economic sectors, as few economic prosperity stories recorded outweigh the initial advantages Africa should gain from collaborative governance processes. While doing business is the strategic way for Africa to move forward, gaps emerging from the literature revealed the need to revise investment policies to accommodate both local and foreign investment which is critical for generating government revenue and spearheading infrastructural development.

CONCLUSION

Africa is home to vast geographical areas rich in mineral resources that could be used to mitigate social and economic disparities. However, due to the absence of strong networks and collaborative governance, widespread underdevelopment is still experienced. This calls for renewed efforts to harness collective capacities and foreign investment to drive domestic economies. The chapter examined network and collaborative governance in Africa. To achieve this, the chapter utilised the Network Governance and Public Value Theories as they emphasise networks and collaborations African governments may establish as part of engaging foreign investors in business to achieve socioeconomic development in Africa. Numerous challenges in doing business in Africa were noted from the extensive review of documents. Among the key challenges is the presence of unrefined economic policies in some African countries that target inclusive growth in the process scaring foreign investments. Secondly, high taxes and low cross-border trade negatively impact the capacity to do business in Africa, where energy supply and electricity shortages trigger low productivity in some circumstances resulting in business closure. The effects of the COVID-19 pandemic cannot be ignored as they affect many African governments from effectively doing business with other countries. The absence of market diversification is another deterrent to economic progress in African states as various countries rely on existing mineral wealth to finance development operations without tapping into other ventures to diversify government revenue streams. The presence of red tape linked to heavy bureaucratic systems of governance in

Africa affect the networking of countries as investors might find it harder to collaborate with local African business due to heavy regulatory policies that are not flexible to allow investment. For Africa to enhance its network and collaborative governance, it is necessary to promote democratic governance structures responsive to business and stakeholder propositions regarding investments.

To realise inclusive growth through various business opportunities, African governments are recommended to implement Business Economic Enabling (BEE), advocated for by the World Bank which creates a conducive climate to attract foreign investments for stimulating local economies. Ethical governance is recommended for African governments to advance the principles of accountability and transparency while engaging foreign investors in business circles. Managing ethical institutions that comply with business rules and regulations is also key to enabling local and international businesses to thrive in an environment where political interference is minimised. To mitigate the dependency syndrome attached to foreign aid, African governments must advocate for entrepreneurship, which is key to promoting small business development, minimising unemployment, and enabling local citizens to generate household incomes. Supporting small business financing and other categories of entrepreneurs is key to advancing business in Africa for the benefit of citizens.

The chapter has contributed to an already growing body of literature on network formation and collaborative governance and how the principles of good corporate governance can be applied in African governance systems. The chapter benchmarks the determinants of doing business in Africa, provides solutions to mitigating bureaucracy and rigid investment policies, and advocates for the need to enhance innovation and creativity, which are some of the critical aspects of improving African economies. Policymakers in Africa have been enlightened on the dangers of localising their economies with policies that do not respond to the technological and economic environment. Lastly, future studies in network and collaborative governance can assess unity and coordination in networks as they are critical in every collaboration government can enter toward economic and social development.

REFERENCES

Adewole, A. and J.S. John (2019), *Logistics and Global Value Chains in Africa: The Impact on Trade and Development*, London: Palgrave Macmillan.

Adu-Gyamfi, R., J. Kuada and S. Asongu (2018), 'An Integrative Framework for Entrepreneurship Research in Africa', African Governance and Development Institute WP/18/025, accessed 7 August 2022 at https://ssrn.com/abstract=3219626.

Akpan, G.E. and U.F. Akpan (2012), 'Electricity Consumption, Carbon Emissions and Economic Growth in Nigeria', *International Journal of Energy Economics and Policy*, 2 (4), 292–306.

Akpan, U.S. (2014), 'Impact of Regional Road Infrastructure Improvement on Intra-Regional Trade in ECOWAS', *African Development Review*, 26 (S1), 64–76, doi.org/10.1111/1467-8268.12093.

Alonso, J.M. and R. Andrews (2020), 'Government-Created Nonprofit Organizations and Public Service Turnaround: Evidence from a Synthetic Control Approach', *Journal of Public Administration Research and Theory*, 31 (2), 346–362, doi.org/10.1093/jopart/muaa035.

Amavilah, V.H., S. Asongu and A. Andres (2017), 'Effects of Globalization on Peace and Stability: Implications for Governance and the Knowledge Economy of African Countries', *Technological Forecasting and Social Change*, 122 (C), 91–103, doi.org/10.1016/j.techfore.2017.04.013.

Andrews, R., L. Ferry, C. Skelcher and P. Wegorowski (2020), 'Corporatization in the Public Sector: Explaining the Growth of Local Government Companies', *Public Administration Review*, 80 (1), 482–493, doi.org/10.1111/puar.13052.

Asongu, S.A., S. le Roux and N. Biekpe (2018), 'Enhancing ICT for Environmental Sustainability in Sub-Saharan Africa', *Technological Forecasting and Social Change*, **127**, 209–216, doi.org/10.1016 /j.techfore.2017.09.022.

Asongu, S.A., J.C. Nwachukwu and S.M.I. Orim (2018), 'Mobile Phones, Institutional Quality and Entrepreneurship in Sub-Saharan Africa', *Technological Forecasting and Social Change*, **131** (C), 183–203, doi.org/10.1016/j.techfore.2017.08.007.

Asongu, S.A. and N.M. Odhiambo (2017), 'Mobile Banking Usage, Quality of Growth, Inequality and Poverty in Developing Countries', *Information Development*, **35** (2), 303–318, doi.org/10.1177 /0266666691774400.

Asongu, S.A. (2017), 'Knowledge Economy Gaps, Policy Syndromes, and Catch-Up Strategies: Fresh South Korean Lessons to Africa', *Journal of the Knowledge Economy*, **8** (1), 211–253, doi.org/10 .1007/s13132-015-0321-0.

Auriacombe, C. and N. Meyer (2020), 'Realising South Africa's National Development Plan goals: The Need for Change to a Collaborative Democracy to Facilitate Community Participation', *Centre for European Journal of Public Policy*, **14** (2), 1–13, doi.org/10.2478/cejpp-2020-0004.

Batuo, M.E. and M. Kupukile (2010), 'How Can Economic and Political Liberalization Improve Financial Development in African Countries?' *Journal of Financial Economic Policy*, **2** (1), 35–59.

Bel, G. and X. Fageda (2017), 'What Have We Learned from the Last Three Decades of Empirical Studies on Factors Driving Local Privatisation?', *Local Government Studies*, **43** (4), 503–511, doi.org /10.1080/03003930.2017.1303486.

Belloc, F., A. Nicita and S.M. Sepe (2014), 'Disentangling Liberalization and Privatization Policies: Is There a Political Trade-Off?', *Journal of Comparative Economics*, **42** (4), 1033–1051, doi.org/10 .1016/j.jce.2013.11.003.

Brownlee, J., C. Hurl and K. Walby (2018), *Corporatizing Canada: Making Business Out of Public Service*, Toronto: Between the Lines.

Classen, T. (2017), 'Integrated Public Health Action Planning Instruments– Experiences from North Rhine-Westphalia Thomas Classen', *European Journal of Public Health*, **27** (3), 280–281.

Clifton, J., F. Comín and D. Diaz-Fuentes (2006), 'Privatizing Public Enterprises in the European Union 1960–2002: Ideological, Pragmatic, Inevitable?', *Journal of European Public Policy*, **13** (5), 736-756, doi.org/10.1080/13501760600808857.

Clifton, J. and D. Díaz-Fuentes (2018), 'The State and Public Corporations', in Nolke, A. and C. May (eds.), *Handbook of the International Political Economy of the Corporation*, Cheltenham, UK and Northampton, MA, USA: Edward Elgar Publishing, pp. 106–119.

Clifton, J., M.E. Warner, R. Gradus and G. Bel (2019), 'Re-municipalization of public services: trend or hype?', *Journal of Economic Policy Reform*, **24** (3), 293–304, doi.org/10.1080/17487870.2019.1691344.

DeGhetto, K., J.R. Gray and M.N. Kiggundu (2016), 'The African Union's Agenda 2063: Aspirations, Challenges, and Opportunities for Management Research', *Africa Journal of Management*, **2** (1), 93–116, doi.org/10.1080/23322373.2015.1127090.

Eifert, B., A. Gelb and V. Ramachandran (2008), 'The Cost of Doing Business in Africa: Evidence from Enterprise Survey Data', *World Development*, **36** (9), 1531–1546, doi.org/10.1016/j.worlddev.2007.09 .007.

Esser, I.-M. and P.A. Delport (2018), 'The South African King IV Report on Corporate Governance: Is the Crown Shiny Enough?', *Company Lawyer*, **39** (11), 378–384.

Ferry, L., R. Andrews, C. Skelcher and P. Wegorowski (2018), 'New Development: Corporatization of Local Authorities in England in the Wake of Austerity 2010–2016', *Public Money & Management*, **38**, 477–480, doi.org/10.1080/09540962.2018.1486629.

Fiscal Monitor Report of the International Monitory Fund (IMF). (2020), 'Fiscal Monitor IMF Data Access to Macroeconomic and Financial Data', accessed 30 April 2022 at https://data.imf.org/.

Häusermann, S., G. Picot and D. Geering (2013), 'Rethinking Party Politics and the Welfare State: Recent Advances in the Literature', *British Journal of Political Science*, **43** (1), 221–240, doi.org/10 .1017/S0007123412000336.

IMF. (2016a), 'International Monetary Fund Zimbabwe', Article IV Consultation and the Third Review of the Staff Monitored Program', Staff Report and Statement by the Executive Director of Zimbabwe (2016) 43, Washington, DC: IMF.

IMF. (2016b), 'IMF Country Focus. East Africa Moving Toward Monetary Union', accessed 21 June 2022 at https://www.imf.org/en/News/Articles/2016/12/19/AFR191216-EAC-Monetary-Union.

IMF. (2020), *Fiscal Monitor*, Washington, DC: IMF.

Jessa, F. and F.M. Uys (2018), 'Public Value Generation: The Outcome of an Integrated Public Service System', *Administratio Publica*, **26** (1), 277–305.

Keenan, P.J. (2009). Curse or Cure? China, Africa, and the Effects of Unconditioned Wealth. *Berkeley Journal of International Law*, **27** (1), 84–126.

Kenya Logistics Infrastructure. (2021), 'Logistics Infrastructure', accessed 12 August 2022 at https://dlca.logcluster.org/display/public/DLCA/2+Kenya+Logistics+Infrastructure.

Klijn, E.H. (2008), 'Governance and Governance Networks in Europe', *Public Management Review*, **10** (4), 505–525, doi.org/10.1080/14719030802263954.

Klijn, E.H. and J.F.M. Koppenjan (2012), 'Governance Network Theory: Past, Present, and Future', *Policy and Politics*, **40** (4), 187–206, doi.org/10.1332/030557312X655431.

Kusi, B.A. and M. Opoku-Mensah (2018), 'Does Credit Information Sharing Affect Funding Cost of Banks? Evidence from African Banks', *International Journal of Finance & Economics*, **23** (1), 19–28, doi.org/10.1002/ijfe.1599.

Lewis, J. (2011), 'The Future of Network Governance: Strength in Diversity and Synthesis', *Public Administration*, **89** (4), 1221–1234, doi.org/10.1111/j.1467-9299.2010.01876.x.

Lukamba, M.T. and T. Molokwane (2016), 'An Analysis of Public Private Partnership in Emerging Economies', *Risk Governance & Control: Financial Markets & Institutions*, **6** (4), 1–12, doi.org/10.22495/rgcv6i4c2art8.

Mangwanya, M. (2022), 'Evaluating the Impacts of Foreign Aid on Low-Income Countries in Sub-Saharan Africa', *International Journal of Research in Business and Social Science*, **11** (6), 370–377, doi.org/10.20525/ijrbs.v11i6.1925.

Meier, K., J. O'Toole and J. Laurence (2007), 'Modeling Public Management', *Public Management Review*, **9** (4), 503–527, doi.org/10.1080/14719030701726630.

Melber, H. and R. Southall (2021), 'Is Zimbabwe Open for Business?', accessed 2 September 2022 at https://www.wits.ac.za/news/latest-news/opinion/2021/2021-01/is-zimbabwe-open-for-business.html.

Meynhardt, T. (2009), 'Public Value Inside: What Is Public Value Creation?', *International Journal of Public Administration*, **32** (3–4), 192–219, doi.org/10.1080/01900690902732632.

Moore, M.H. (2012), *Recognizing Public Value: Developing a Public Value Account and a Public Value Scorecard*, Cambridge, MA: Harvard University Press.

Moore, M.H. and J. Benington (2010), *Public Value: Theory and Practice*, London: Palgrave Macmillan International Higher Education.

Muogboh, O.S. and F. Ojeda (2018), 'Indigenous Logistics and Supply Chain Management Practice in Africa', in Uzo, U. and A.K. Meru (eds.), *Indigenous Management Practices in Africa: A Guide for Educators and Practitioners*, Bingley: Emerald, pp. 47–70.

Nuwagaba, I. and T. Molokwane (2022), 'A Qualitative Analysis of Public Private Partnership (PPP) Project Contracts in the Roads Sector. A Contextual Elucidation of Uganda National Roads Authority (UNRA)', *International Journal of Business Administration*, **11** (5), 44–57, doi.org/10.5430/ijba.v11n5p44.

Onsomu, E., B. Munga and V. Nyabaro (2021), 'The Impact of COVID-19 on Industries Without Smokestacks in Kenya the Case of Horticulture, ICT, and Tourism Sectors', Africa Growth Initiative (AGI) Working Paper, accessed 26 August 2022 at https://www.brookings.edu/wp-content/uploads/2021/07/21.07.27-Kenya-Covid-Update.pdf.

Peña-Miguel, N. and B. Cuadrado-Ballesteros (2019), 'Partisan and Electoral Cycles in Privatisation', *Political Studies*, **68**, 617–633, doi.org/10.1177/0032321719868648.

Republic of Rwanda. (2019), 'Voluntary National Review Report', MINECOFIN, accessed 12 August 2022 at https://www.minecofin.gov.rw/fileadmin/user_upload/Minecofin/Publications/REPORTS/National_Development_Planning_and_Research/Rwanda_Voluntary_National_Review_Report/Rwanda_VNR_Document_Final_.pdf.

Schmidt, C. (2014), 'The Diffusion of Privatization in Europe: Political Affinity or Economic Competition?', *Public Administration*, **93** (3), 615–635, doi.org/10.1111/padm.12068.

Schwartz, M.G., M.M. Fouad, M.T.S. Hansen and M.G. Verdier (eds.) (2020), *Well Spent: How Strong Infrastructure Governance Can End Waste in Public Investment*, New York: International Monetary Fund.

Shava, E. (2016), 'Black Economic Empowerment in South Africa: Challenges and Prospects', *Journal of Economics and Behavioral Studies*, **8** (6), 161–170, doi.org/10.22610/jebs.v8i6(J).1490.

Shava, E. (2021), 'Financial Sustainability of NGOs in Rural Development Programmes', *Development in Practice*, **31** (3), 393–403, doi.org/10.1080/09614524.2020.1853059.

Shava, E. and S. Vyas-Doorgapersad (2022), 'Exploring the Unintended Consequences of COVID-19 Pandemic on Achieving Smart Cities in Africa', in Osabuohien, E., G. Odularu, D. Ufua and R. Osabohien (eds.), *COVID-19 in the African Continent*, Bingley: Emerald, pp. 279–292.

South Africa (Republic), *Broad-Based Black Economic Empowerment Act 53 of 2003*, Pretoria: Government Printers.

Stoker, G. (1998), 'Governance as Theory: Five Propositions', *International Social Science Journal*, **50** (155), 17–28.

Tavares, A.F. (2017), 'Ten Years After: Revisiting the Determinants of the Adoption of Municipal Corporations for Local Service Delivery', *Local Government Studies*, **43** (5), 697–706, doi.org/10.1080/03003930.2017.1356723.

Tavares, A.F. and P.J. Camões (2010), 'New Forms of Local Governance', *Public Management Review*, **12** (5), 587–608, doi.org/10.1080/14719031003633193.

Tchamyou, V.S. (2018), 'Education, Lifelong Learning, Inequality and Financial Access: Evidence from African Countries', AGDI Working Paper WP/18/003, 1-25, African Governance and Development Institute, accessed 16 August 2023 at http://www.afridev.org/RePEc/agd/agd-wpaper/Education-Lifelong-Learning-Inequality-Financial-Access-Africa.pdf.

United Nations. (2022), 'Sustainable Development Goal 17: Strengthen the Means of Implementation and Revitalize the Global Partnership for Sustainable Development', accessed 28 July 2022 at https://www.un.org/development/desa/disabilities/envision2030-goal17.html.

Uys, F.M. and F. Jessa (2016), 'An Integrated Public Service System (IPSS) Utilising Complexity and Network Theory in the Enhancement of Public Value', *Administratio Publica*, **24** (1), 183–209.

Uys, F.M. and F. Jessa (2017), 'Network Theory: The Bricks and Mortar of Integrated Public Service Systems (IPSSs)', *Administratio Publica*, **26** (1), 277–305.

Voorn, B., M. van Genugten and S. van Thiel (2020), 'Re-interpreting Re-municipalization: Finding Equilibrium', *Journal of Economic Policy Reform*, **24** (3), 1–14, doi.org/10.1080/17487870.2019.1701455.

Verhagen, M. (2017), 'Home Insights News Tax challenges and opportunities in Africa', accessed 17 June 2022 at https://www.bakertillyberk.com/insights/news/tax-challenges-and-opportunities-in-africa/.

Vyas-Doorgapersad, S. and E. Shava (2021), 'Paradigms in Public Policy and Administration in Africa', *African Journal of Development Studies* (AJDS), **11** (4), 29–52, doi.org/10.31920/2634-3649/2021/v11n4a2.

Warner, M. and G. Bel (2008), 'Competition or Monopoly? Comparing Privatization of Local Public Services in the US and Spain', *Public Administration*, **86** (3), 723–735, doi.org/10.1111/j.1467-9299.2008.00700.x.

World Bank (2022a), 'Africa's Pulse: An Analysis of Issues Shaping Africa's Economic Future', accessed 28 April 2022 at https://www.worldbank.org/en/publication/africa-pulse.

World Bank (2022b), 'World Bank's Ease of Doing Business Index: Business Enabling Environment (BEE)', accessed 19 April 2022 at https://www.worldbank.org/en/programs/business-enabling-environment.

Zindi, B. and E. Shava (2022), 'Confronting the Monster: Exploring the Implementation of Social Protection Measures Amid COVID-19 in South Africa', in Rana, U. and J. Govender (eds.), *Exploring the Consequences of the Covid-19 Pandemic: Social, Cultural, Economic, and Psychological Insights and Perspectives*, New York: Routledge, pp. 3–19.

19. Public–private partnerships and environmental governance: the case of South Africa

Danielle Nel-Sanders

INTRODUCTION

Environmental governance is intricately linked to the broader notions of sustainable development. The primary objective of sustainable development is to ensure that positive outcomes of development are maximised and that negative consequences are minimised. Thus, environmental governance aims to manage and conserve environmental systems and to ensure socially equitable outcomes with regards to decision-making about the environment. The purpose of this chapter is to examine environmental governance reform and its manifestations. Specifically, this chapter pays attention to network and collaborative governance reform instruments to manage and govern the environment by focusing on the role and importance of public–private partnerships (PPPs). In doing so, environmental governance is firstly conceptualised followed by an analysis of the role that partnerships play in governing environmental affairs. Secondly, the chapter reveals lessons to be learned regarding the utilisation of PPPs as environmental governance instruments. Attention then shifts to current environmental governance realities in South Africa by highlighting the nature of its current energy crisis and the country's heavy reliance on so-called 'dirty' energy such as coal-fired electricity generation. This holds environmental, social, and economic risks. In response to these risks, the government has embarked on a PPP programme to procure renewable energy (RE) from independent power production service providers. Lastly, the chapter concludes with a case study on RE partnerships in South Africa accentuating best practice guidelines for developing countries in utilising PPPs to address sustainable development problems.

ENVIRONMENTAL GOVERNANCE IN PERSPECTIVE

Economic and industrial development is one of the main causes of current environmental and ecological degradation (Mori, 2013). Especially unbridled development without due consideration of its environmental impact raises serious concerns. Environmental problems and governance are not new phenomena. The earliest recorded environmental law can be traced to England with the proclamation in 1272 by King Edward I banning the burning of sea coal in London to curb smoke pollution (Benson and Jordan, 2017). After almost four decades of scholarly discourse regarding the nature and scope of environmental governance, there is still great zeal amongst theorists to comprehend the empirical, theoretical, and normative dimensions thereof (Benson and Jordan, 2017). Mngoma, Pillay and Reddy (2011, p. 6) define environmental governance as 'the process of decision-making involved in controlling and managing the environment and natural resources. It also includes the manner in which decisions are made'. According to Bennet and Satterfield (2018, p. 2), 'governance is one of the most important factors for ensuring effective environmental management and conservation actions'. Governance entails the structural and institutional functions and processes that determine who, how, and for whom decisions are made, what actions are taken, by whom, and to what effect (Bennet and Satterfield, 2018).

Nel (2014, p. 39) adds that 'good and bad governance rest upon the foundations of democratic and legitimate institutional structures and links the style of governmental interaction with society to a normative assessment of the outcomes of that interaction'. Good governance goals generally focus on 'accountability, transparency, participation, relationship management, efficiency and equity' (Edwards, 2002, p. 52). Good environmental governance is essential for sustainable development. According to Feris (2010, p. 77), 'good environmental governance should take into consideration the requirements for sustainable development'. The concept of environmental governance is a normative concept (Bennet and Satterfield, 2018), based on certain values and norms assigned by scholars, society, governments, and global actors; these norms and values are typically linked to sustainable development norms. There is an important link between environmental governance and sustainable development (Feris, 2010). Ecological problems are not a recent phenomenon. The emergence of environmental science during the 1960s started raising awareness of the impact that humans have on the environment and establishing environmental problems as a global issue (Benson and Jordan, 2017).

According to the United Nations Environment Programme (2009, p. 2), environmental governance entails the 'rules, practices, policies and institutions that shape how humans interact with the environment'. As such, environmental governance is based on how environmentally related decisions are made and whether it leads to socially sustainable outcomes.

Traditionally governments have used legislative and judicial instruments to manage the environment in a top-down manner. However, during the last two decades non-state actors have become much more directly involved in environmental governance, using innovative approaches, market forces, and network formation (Benson and Satterfield, 2017). The formulation of environmental policy was previously primarily a state-centred function. However, with the advent of the network governance paradigm, collaborative partnerships have been established that were aimed at overcoming the limitations of conventional bureaucratic, hierarchical policy-making processes (Mert and Pattberg, 2015).

Bennet and Satterfield (2018) conceptualise environmental governance based on four main objectives: effective, equitable, responsive, and robust environmental governance. These four objectives came to be known as the pillars of environmental governance. Figure 19.1 illustrates these four pillars.

The primary objective of environmental governance is conserving or improving the capacity of environmental systems to function and to produce ecosystem services through the tenacity of species, habitats, and biodiversity. Furthermore, environmental governance needs to ensure socially equitable decision-making that produces socioeconomic outcomes that are characterised by principles such as inclusivity, participation, and fairness. Equitable environmental governance should start with policies that ensure effective participation, that recognise and respect different stakeholders, especially the marginalised and vulnerable. Bennet and Satterfield (2018, p. 4) argue that 'the objective of being responsive ensures that environmental governance is adaptable both to changing environmental and social conditions and to diverse contexts'. Environmental governance should also be robust with capable and effective institutions persisting over time.

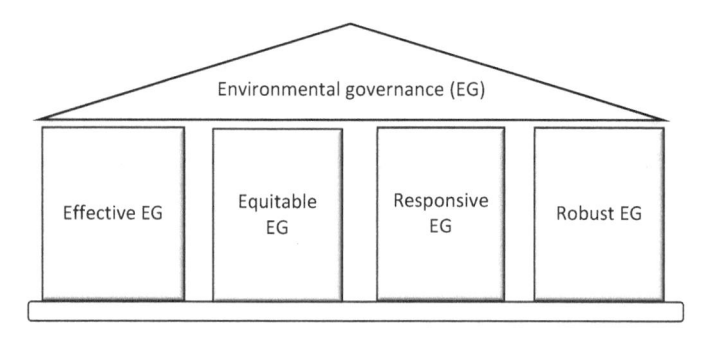

Source: Author's own based on Bennet and Satterfield (2018).

Figure 19.1   *Pillars of environmental governance*

After the publication of the United Nations' Brundtland Report (WCED, 1987), governments internationally began to share more powers and functions with nonstate actors as sustainable development emerged as a socioeconomic and political focal point. According to Benson and Jordan (2017, p. 3), 'sustainable development recognises that environmental, social, and economic issues need to be addressed holistically'. This notion was strongly underpinned by the United Nations (UN) 1992 Rio Earth Summit, encouraging governments to introduce wider-ranging and nonlegal approaches to environmental governance. The main implementing agreement of Rio, Agenda 21, outlined new roles for nonstate actors, including businesses and local communities in governing for sustainability, which have been integrated into governments' environmental decision-making processes (Benson and Jordan, 2017).

Multi-Stakeholder Partnerships (MSPs) for Sustainable Development

Environmental governance can be driven by different sectors in the economy and society. It can be driven by government in a top-down manner, or from the bottom-up by individuals, private companies, public–private partnerships, or local communities (Bennet and Satterfield, 2018). With the rapid spread of globalisation during the 1990s, sovereign nation states are becoming more and more irrelevant, being replaced by multilateral institutions and global governance organs like the World Trade Organization, the International Monetary Fund, and the World Bank (Evans, 2012). This has led to the phenomenon called the 'hollowing out of the state', with government reform characterised by more privatisation, public–private partnerships, limited public sector intervention, and other alternative service delivery mechanisms or systems (Rhodes, 1994). Thus, prior to 1990, was marked by the age of 'big government', where the state was the leader in service provision. Due to economic globalisation, reform made way for including NGOs, communities, and business in the process of governing (Evans, 2012). These government reforms adopted new governance approaches focusing on value for money, including New Public Management (NPM), market-based governance, and network and collaborative governance. This shift from 'government to governance' (Evans, 2012) marked a shift in the governance of the environmental sphere. Originally, the environment was governed by local and national organisations, now multiple actors including business, communities, and NGOs are involved in the governance of the environment (Benson and Satterfield, 2017).

Given the emergence of a new governance paradigm, MSPs originated at the 1992 Earth Summit, with Agenda 21 highlighting the need for global partnerships for sustainable development (Eweje et al., 2021). MSPs have steadily gained prominence in governance arenas. MSPs were also focal points during the 2002 Johannesburg World Summit for Sustainable Development, where they became formally known as 'Type II partnerships' (Tűrkelli, 2021a, p. 89). Typically, MSPs are partnerships between business, government, and non-profit actors to address specific economic, social, and environmental concerns (MacDonald, Clarke and Huang, 2019). MSPs are strongly enhanced by a network, meta-governance approach to governance (Beisheim et al., 2018).

Partnerships are crucial to achieving the post-2015 United Nations' Sustainable Development Goals (SDGs). The UN recognises the importance of partnerships for sustainable development by committing Goal 17 to achieve sustainable development through partnerships. The SDGs are complex, global in scope and interconnected, and are aimed at addressing wicked problems. MSPs are crucial in achieving SDGs (Eweje et al., 2021). SDG 17 refers to the global partnerships for sustainable development, which focus on financing and implementing the SDGs (Beisheim et al., 2018). As a type of partnership arrangement, MSPs are global and voluntary in nature, based on fulfilling a collective interest, focused on the pooling of specialist knowledge and resources. A further common characteristic of MSP is the fact that it aims to achieve a common sustainable development goal and serve the collective interests of partnering stakeholders (Eweje et al., 2021).

Beisheim et al. (2018) maintain that the private sector has become a key stakeholder in sustainable development issues, mainly because of its access to capital, specialised resources, geographical footprint, and capacity. This reality serves as a further catalyst to drive MSPs in the environmental governance arena. Partnering with business requires that governments move away from traditional bureaucratic forms of governance. In this regard, Okitasari, Prabowo and Santono (2020) reason that a hybrid, collaborative form of governance is more suitable to rapidly respond to emerging environmental issues. Mechanisms such as MSPs can move beyond the constraints of conventional government-based responses to global challenges (Tűrkelli, 2021b). MSPs are different to PPPs, they are voluntary and not for profit. MSPs are increasingly engaged in financing public goods for sustainable development and have gained a prominent role in the transnational policy space for development assistance (Tűrkelli, 2021a). Despite their contribution to the sustainable development space, more research is needed on MSPs, especially in terms of accountability arrangements, legitimacy, power, and influence in government policy-making processes, and their legal and technical roles (Tűrkelli, 2021a, 2021b).

Particularly during the 2000s, government-led environmental protection towards more governance-based reform continued, with governments being less and less able to deliver on the sustainable development mandate on their own (Benson and Jordan, 2017). PPPs remain to be a central feature in development interventions (Tűrkelli, 2021b).

PRIVATE SECTOR INVOLVEMENT IN ENVIRONMENTAL GOVERNANCE

PPPs are a form of networked governance and have been used since the 1980s as part of the NPM paradigm to increase efficiency and effectiveness in governments (Mert and Pattberg, 2015). Delić, Šašić and Tanović (2021, p. 56) add that the main goal of introducing PPPs was 'to improve efficiency, quality of public services and products, and legitimacy'. The PPPs label was originally conceived in the NPM era pre-1990; however, PPPs broke away from the NPM agenda a decade ago, to align more closely with the recent New Public Governance (NPG) agenda (Casady et al., 2020).

Government and public management reforms have revealed that PPPs serve as valuable instruments to promote and foster network and collaborative governance. The network and collaborative form of governance allow multiple autonomous stakeholders to partner for achieving mutual visions and goals (Evans, 2012). PPPs are also regarded as mechanisms to strengthen government capacity in delivering certain products or services. These goods and services are usually too sophisticated and complex for governments alone to successfully execute (Vinogradov, Shadrina and Kokareva, 2014). Governments typically embark on PPPs when projects are complex, politically contentious, difficult to execute, and require large financial commitments.

Mert and Pattberg (2015, p. 232) focus on the influence of networks on policy-making processes and argue that 'policy networks are polycentric governance arrangements that integrate the competing interests of actors within a horizontal structure'. Such policy partnerships serve as important instruments to deliver services at local, subnational, national, and international levels. Fenwick, Miller and McTavish (2012) accentuate the fact that a network of multiple governance actors may strongly influence policies aimed at particular sectors or economic nodes. Partnerships and co-governance mechanisms such as PPPs generally offer pragmatic solutions to complex policy issues in these sectors and nodes.

PPPs as an Instrument to Address Wicked Problems

Rittel and Webber (1973) proposed the idea of 'wicked' problems in their work on 'Dilemmas in a General Theory of Planning'. Carayannopoulos and McConnell (2018) argue that wicked problems are complex and highly uncertain in nature, while Head and Alfred (2013, p. 712) assert that they are linked to 'social pluralism (multiple interests and values of stakeholders), institutional complexity (the context of interorganisational cooperation and multilevel governance), and scientific uncertainty (fragmentation and gaps in reliable knowledge)'.

In general, governments are more equipped to implement policies and deliver services that are relatively routine and standardised in nature. They are less equipped to deal with problems non-linear, non-routine, and non-standardised (Head and Alfred, 2013). Head and Alfred (2013, p. 715) explain that 'concerns about wicked problems have also arisen in relation to dealing with disasters and crises of various kinds that throw into relief the (in-)capacities of governmental systems to prepare, coordinate, and rapidly mobilize resources'. In support, Daviter (2017, p. 574) argues that 'most if not all research on wicked problems implicitly or explicitly departs from the observation that this type of policy problem cannot be solved in a traditional governance sense'. Therefore, the New Public Governance (NPG) paradigm primarily focuses on achieving mutual goals in a collaborative manner to address wicked problems through partnerships (Velotti, Botti and Vesci, 2012). Therefore, the most prominent response to wicked problems such as climate change and sustainability has been in the form of a collaborative or networked type of governance (Daviter, 2017; Lehtonen et al., 2018). This type of governance arrangement has made PPPs ideal instruments to tackle wicked problems.

Effective cooperative networks increase the likelihood that the nature of a wicked problem and its underlying causes can be better understood, offering more diverse insights into why a situation has arisen (Head and Alfred, 2013). Collaborative partnerships are based on the principle that 'equals working together produce equity' (Velotti, Botti and Vesci, 2012, p. 350).

Particularly after the 2002 Johannesburg World Summit on Sustainable Development, PPP formations increased with more than 300 partnerships aiming at environmental concerns (Mert and Pattberg, 2015). Partnerships between governments and third-sector organisations such as community-based organisations, non-governmental organisations, and non-profit organisations increasingly play an important role in addressing capacity gaps in government (Henderson, 2002). PPPs operating in the field of sustainable development are mostly voluntary in nature but specific partnerships currently focus on achieving the SDGs (Mert and Pattberg, 2015).

The Nature and Role of PPPs

There is a lack of consensus in the body of knowledge on an exact definition of PPPs (Casady et al., 2020). This is primarily due to the fact that different variations of PPPs exist, each with unique governance requirements and objectives. Moreover, the lack of consensus in defining PPPs stems from different conceptualisations of PPPs set forth by NPM and NPG principles (Velotti, Botti and Vesci, 2012). However, in general, there is consensus that PPPs entail some form of collaboration between government and the private sector with mutual benefits for both. Furthermore, PPPs are contractual arrangements between a public and private sector party (Vinogradov, Shadrina and Kokareva, 2014). Mert and Pattberg (2015, p. 233) assert that despite the lack of a standard definition of PPPs, the following are important characteristics of such arrangements:

- Transnationality (involving cross-border interactions and non-state relations);
- Public policy objectives (as opposed to public or exclusively private goods); and
- A network structure (coordination by participating actors rather than coordination by a central hierarchy).

Irún, Monferrer and Moliner (2020, p. 268) add that a PPP implies the establishment of 'a long-term relationship between public and private partners with the shared objective of delivering and executing joint projects'. There are different types of PPPs in different sectors, some formalised in terms of government policies, and some informal collaborative arrangements. In this regard Hodge and Greve (2008, p. 5) refer to PPPs as 'a broad church of many families' and offer the following classification (Figure 19.2) of the types of PPPs based on five different families of governance arrangements.

| Institutional co-operation | Long-term infrastructure contracts | Public policy networks | Civil society/ community development | Urban renewal |

Source: Adapted from Hodge and Greve (2008, p. 4).

Figure 19.2   *Five families of PPPs as governance arrangements*

Institutional cooperation focuses on joint production and risk sharing. Long-term infrastructure contracts emphasise the tight specification of outputs in long-term legal contracts, for example the Gautrain High-speed Rail in South Africa. PPPs networks emphasise more flexible and loose stakeholder relationships. Civil society and community development emphasise social society involvement and participation. Urban renewal focuses on local economic development and urban regrowth measures (Hodge and Greve, 2008).

From these five categories or families, long-term infrastructure projects are currently the most prominent and formalised of all. Hodge and Greve (2021, p. 219) maintain that infrastructure contracts have been implemented across the globe in different sectors and argue that 'there is little doubt that we are living in an era of PPP and infrastructure governance'. Most PPP infrastructure projects usually include long-term contracts, usually for 20 years, where a private sector entity is contracted to either design, build, finance, or manage a public service, under certain legal or economic conditions (Irún, Monferrer and Moliner, 2020). Many governments have formalised policy frameworks and contractual agreements to guide these formalised PPP arrangements. Examples of these formalised PPPs include the following:

- Management or operation and maintenance (O&M) contracts: where a private company provides a service such as a utility function on behalf of the public sector.
- Affermage contracts: where a private company builds, refurbishes, and operates a service directly to the public on behalf of the government and collects a tariff for the use thereof.
- Various types of construction contracts: Build-Operate-Transfer (BOT), Build-Own-Operate (BOO), Build-Own-Operate-Transfer (BOOT), Design-Build-Finance-Operate (DBFO), Design-Construct-Manage-Finance (DCMF).
- Lease contracts: where an asset or land is leased to the private sector for refurbishment and to provide services directly to the public.
- Concession: where a private entity finances and builds, refurbishes, and operates a service directly to the public.
- Divestiture: where public assets are sold to a private company who provides services to the public and collects tariffs from the public (Delmon, 2010).

Lessons Learned for PPPs

There are many benefits of PPPs; however, there are also several challenges that should be managed. Due to the diverse nature of PPPs, the success of a PPP ultimately rests on management's capacity to develop feasible mechanisms to ensure successful projects (Nel, 2014). One goal of PPPs is to subsidise service provision. There is a question as to whether subsidisation of services via the PPP model does indeed improve service provision. There are cases where consumers complain that private service providers involved in PPPs raise the costs of products beyond reasonable prices while in some cases PPPs even drop the standards of service provision to further increase their profit margins. It therefore becomes crucial for values and ethics to form a part of PPPs to guarantee integrity and promote equity and fairness in the delivery of services. The public sector must also remain accountable and have an oversight role to ensure that service providers act ethically in their role towards providing services to consumers.

The level of investment in PPPs is limited by the amount of risk involved. Many potential investors pull out of PPPs because they learn of the high amount of risk involved in PPPs. As a result, there is a need to better manage risks within PPPs if more investors are to be lured into participating within PPPs. There needs to be further research with regard to the risks involved within PPPs and how to mitigate these risks. Research must also focus on the reasons why potential investors pull out of PPPs. Artificial intelligence which exists at the current cutting edge of technological innovations within the Fourth Industrial Revolution-based initiatives should be harnessed towards better risk management in PPPs, which might help to lure more investors.

Actors in government at times refrain from taking part in PPPs as they fear the risk of losing control over service delivery, traditionally only provided by the public sector. It may be that by using a private service provider, the government may feel removed from direct interaction with customers who form a part of their political support base. Also, there may be fear by government officials, both elected and appointed, that citizens might attribute achievements and successes made in service delivery via PPPs to private service providers and not government. These fears should be addressed since PPPPs have proven to be highly beneficial in both developed and developing countries. PPPs are especially valuable in infrastructure development such as in the construction of dams, airports, roads, and other infrastructural works.

Actors in the private sector may also refrain from becoming involved in PPPs due to the risks associated therewith. Contractual challenges with government, political interference, community dynamics, and intellectual property issues all deter potential partners to invest in PPPs. It is thus essential that these risks be minimised to make PPPs an attractive value proposition for businesses (Gawlik, 2019, p. 48).

Evaluating the successes of partnerships created in PPPs can enable more positive perceptions that allow more private-sector investment in domains traditionally dominated by the public sector (Strasser et al., 2021, p. 2). However, there is limited research that is aimed towards the monitoring and evaluation of PPPs. Monitoring and evaluation enable an organisation to determine how far it has come towards achieving set targets. Monitoring and evaluation also help in solidifying cooperation and synergy in partnerships. It also enhances integrated planning, strategic decisions, the early identification of concerns, and the proactive design of remedial actions (Poupaud et al., 2021, p. 2). The existing corpus of knowledge does reflect, however, that PPPs have the distinct advantage that partners share risks based on their ability to mitigate certain types of risk and offer innovative service delivery modalities. Monitoring and evaluation of PPPs also show that it is useful to raise capital and to inject managerial expertise and skills into the public sector (Đorđević and Rakić, 2021, p. 368). In this regard, the National Planning Commission (NPC, 2020, p. 69) views PPPs as essential to promote rapid skills development, increasing digital security, and promoting the expansion of WiFi accessibility in society.

Evaluations of the outcomes of PPPs mainly accentuate the critical success factors associated with their formation. Scholars such as Jomo et al. (2016) and Tahir (2017) highlight the following success factors:

- Transparency and trust among partnering actors.
- Sharing of business values such as respect, justice and harmony.
- The ability to perform allocated tasks and responsibilities.
- The sharing of risks and liabilities.
- The continued analysis of the existing PPP business model.
- The sharing of best practice acknowledging that the performance of PPPs is not uniform across different sectors.
- Stable socioeconomic and political conditions.

In spite of these critical success factors, insight is currently lacking regarding the roles and responsibilities of the lead partner within PPPs as well as relationship management between existing partners. The way a private partner performs a lead role within a PPP has the potential to hinder the vivacity thereof because of the possibility of policy power imbalances, minimal political oversight and controls, increased risk of irregularities, and changes in organisational values. Also, there is a need for the development of analytical frameworks that analyse performance metrics with better definitions of roles, determination of project prioritisation as well as the statistical analysis of the benefits derived from cooperation (Strasser et al., 2021, p. 14). Jomo et al. (2016, p. 22) further assert that governments need to establish the necessary support structures to develop, control and analyse PPPs.

ENVIRONMENTAL GOVERNANCE IN SOUTH AFRICA

Environmental governance is embedded in a strong legislative framework in South Africa. The Constitution of the Republic of South Africa, 1996 provides the foundations for environmental protection with Section 24 emphasising: ensuring an individual's right to an environment that will not harm his or her health or well-being (Mngoma, Pillay and Reddy, 2011). The country also has a long list of environmental management Acts, Regulations, white papers, green papers, Bills, policies, and international agreements. The National Environmental Management Act (NEMA) 107 of 1998 serves as the overarching environmental management policy framework in South Africa. The NEMA outlines the responsibility of government departments and spheres of government to successfully manage the interface between social well-being and environmental protection. The Environment Conservation Act 73 of 1989 furthermore guides particular environmental domains.

Environmental governance is cascaded across different spheres of government, with different stakeholders involved in the governance of the environment. The Department of Forestry, Fisheries, and the Environment is the lead department responsible for facilitating environmental cooperative governance across all spheres of government and providing geographically referenced environmental information for decision-making. The Department is also responsible for creating environmental awareness across society (Department of Forestry, Fisheries and the Environment n.d).

The Department of Mineral Resources and Energy also has an important role in environmental governance by ensuring sustainable development in the mining and energy sectors (Department of Minerals and Energy, n.d). In this regard Sanderink and Nasiritousi (2020) state that sustainable development goal number 7 emphasises the importance of a worldwide uptake of renewable energy (RE). Non-renewable energy has severe effects on the environment and human health. Natural reserves are also nearly depleted presenting an energy sustainability risk (Beşer and Beşer, 2021). South Africa is one of the largest greenhouse gasses (GHG) emitters in the world due to coal-fired electricity generation, ranked 14th on the world's list of top GHG emitters (Murombo, 2021). Hence it has become crucial for South Africa to diversify its energy mix. The country has been facing an electricity crisis, which has contributed to lowering economic growth rates, the discouragement of private investment, a debt deficit, and the inability of the poor to afford electricity (Baker, 2017).

National legislation furthermore emphasises the important role played by the local sphere of government in managing environmental concerns. The Local Government: Municipal

Systems Act 32 of 2000 outlines the environmental role of municipalities, requiring that their integrated development plans contribute to the realisation of municipalities' developmental mandate. The Act requires that integrated development plans must contain a spatial development framework to be compatible with national and provincial development plans (Humby, 2014).

In South Africa, PPPs are regulated by the Treasury Regulation 16 of the Public Finance Management Act 1 of 1999. Standard PPP provisions for the procurement, development, and management of PPPs, are provided by the National Treasury. PPPs are thus executed within a comprehensive regulatory framework because there is a transfer of infrastructure or an asset of public value involved.

Energy Partnerships in South Africa

Energy reform should be considered from a liberal democracy viewpoint. Reform in the energy sector in the Netherlands is a good example of this. The Netherlands reformed energy supply by unbundling the energy sector, setting up networks that function autonomously from government, declaring RE as a public and societal interest, involving the private sector and PPPs, and establishing a free energy market (Heldeweg and Sanders, 2014). Heldeweg and Sanders (2014, p. 200) argue that adding a private interest to a public context through a PPP creates better opportunities for enabling innovative and sustainable energy projects. Using PPPs as instruments for sustainable development is integral to the ecosystem services concept (Mert and Pattberg, 2015).

Governments have different stances regarding PPPs and use different approaches to PPPs and their development (Mouraviev and Kakabadse, 2016). Nel (2018, p. 33) argues that 'the power sector is one of the greatest beneficiaries of private investment through PPPs and project financing structures globally. PPPs have been recognised as hybrid governance arrangements for the provision of collective goods' (Mert and Pattberg, 2015). According to Heldeweg and Sanders (2014, p. 200), 'the hybridity of PPPs is about introducing incentives and attracting resources to an environment, which does not naturally have an appeal to them, but without them has difficulty in delivering certain goods and services, such as sustainable energy'.

Reform of South Africa's Power Sector

South Africa is currently facing an electricity crisis with dwindling coal supplies and inadequate maintenance of infrastructure and mismanagement. The state-owned electricity utility has retained its monopoly status and side-stepped global trends of power sector liberalisation in the 1980s and 1990s because the country had a cheap and abundant supply of indigenous coal and a well-developed transmission network (Baker, 2017).

In 1998 the White Paper on Energy Policy (DME, 1998) provided guidelines for the gradual liberalisation of the power sector, with gradual corporatisation and outsourcing of various functions of Eskom, anticipating the creation of a separate transmission utility and system operator, which would be owned by the state, but with a view to a possible future sale (Baker, 2017). South Africa has some of the best solar and wind resources globally (Ndlovu and Telukdarie, 2020). In 2001 a cabinet memo announced that 30% of electricity generation, including RE, would come from Independent Power Producers (IPPs), and Eskom would no longer be allowed to build a new electricity generation (Baker, 2017). However, the integration of RE only took effect in 2011 with the introduction of the Renewable Energy Independent Power Producer Programme (REIPPPP). Despite these shifts, major aspects of the 1998 White Paper were not implemented, and some are still outstanding, for instance a separate transmission utility has never been established, although between 1998 and 2003, no new generation was built. However, in 2003, due to falling reserve margins and an imminent electricity crisis, a cabinet memorandum approved that Eskom should be re-allowed to construct more power plants (Baker, 2017). The South African government set some RE targets in 2003, with the publication of a Renewable Energy Policy White Paper, for South Africa to reach 10,000 GWh of RE generation by 2013; however, for many years, very little was done to achieve this target (Eberhard, Leigland and Kolker, 2014).

In 2011, the South African government introduced a procurement programme to produce independent power production from RE, called the REIPPPP (Mosaka, Mararakanye and Bekker, 2021). The programme was developed by the Department of Energy (DOE) in collaboration with the National Treasury's PPP unit (Montmasson-Clair and Ryan, 2014). Nel (2018) argue that these IPP partnerships can be classified as 'hybrid PPPs', based on the collaboration between the private sector, government and a state-owned enterprise (SOEs) such as the electricity utility Eskom. The programme has contracted 92 RE projects since its inception, with a total of US$20.5 billion investment and 6,328 MW generation (Leigland and Eberhard, 2018). This programme is a unique approach to RE project finance and partnership development and is implemented through IPP partnerships (Nel, 2018, p. 33). The REIPPPP is aimed at developing RE using technologies such as wind, solar, biogas, and biomass energy (Leigland and Eberhard, 2018). A government led-task force of the DOE of South Africa, the IPP Unit, supported by the National Treasury of South Africa's PPP Unit, were responsible for designing and implementing a procurement process for the REIPPPP (Nel and Komendantova, 2015). The DOE as driver and coordinator of the programme, provides policy clarity and direction, which were complimented by the financial and technical support of the National Treasury (Montmasson-Clair and Ryan, 2014). Another key factor for success was having access to high-quality private advisory assistance, which was possible due to the availability of financial resources to pay for advisory and expert assistance, with funding made available from the DOE, National Treasury, and the Development Bank of Southern Africa (DBSA), bilateral donor agencies, including those representing Denmark, Germany, Spain, the UK, and the World Bank (Eberhard, Kolker and Leigland, 2014).

The Integrated Resource Plan (IRP) 2010-2030 and the 2011 ministerial determination provided a policy space for RE in South Africa in general, ensuring investors, through policy and planning, that RE would play an important role in the country's electricity mix (Montmasson-Clair and Ryan, 2014), thus opening up the policy space for the REIPPPP. In the REIPPPP a private finance model is followed where the private sector funds and owns 100% of the infrastructure and carries project risks, and the role of government is regulating the generation and distribution of RE in the country (Nel, 2018).

The private partner, and thus the IPP, the construction of the project infrastructure, which is required to generate a specific RE technology. The private partner then sells the generated RE to the central grid utility and operator – in the case of South Africa it is an SOE called Eskom and the National Treasury of South Africa provides guarantees for non-payment in the event that Eskom defaults on payment (Nel, 2018). The National Energy Regulator South Africa (NERSA) awards generation and distribution licences to IPPs for the period and MW capacity in line with the power purchase agreement (PPA) (Montmasson-Clair and Ryan, 2014).

In the REIPPPP an infrastructure facility is not transferred from the private sector to the public sector; RE is sold to Eskom and connected to the national electricity grid, thus, IPPs are also not classified under the Standardised PPP Provisions as PPPs (Nel, 2013). A regulatory review determined that the REIPPPP would not be subject to the regulations; furthermore, Eskom, which signs the power purchase agreements with private operators, is considered a state-owned enterprise rather than a government agency, and therefore its purchase of power is not subject to National Treasury's PPP regulations (Eberhard and Naude, 2014).

A competitive bidding process is followed in the REIPPPP. The programme has successfully concluded five bidding windows and is currently in the process of completing window number six (Department of Minerals and Energy, 2022). The private sector submits a bid which must meet minimum compliance requirements and evaluated on the following criteria:

- 70% of the bid is based on the price/tariff, which is evaluated based on the lowest R/kWh value proposed over the term of the agreement, whereas
- 30% is based on economic development criteria, which can include creating local jobs, manufacturing locally, black economic empowerment, local content development, and local community development (Mosaka, Mararakanye and Bekker, 2021, p. 62).

Eskom's System Operator is tasked with designing and ensuring that the grid infrastructure can equitably accommodate the RE projects to feed into the national grid, whereas Eskom's Grid Access Unit provides technical analysis on the connection of projects to the national grid and is responsible for providing IPPs with cost-estimate letters and budget quotes on connection options (Montmasson-Clair and Ryan, 2014).

The REIPPPP has been recognised worldwide as a model procurement programme for RE generation, in spite of a number of challenges, the development of the REIPP procurement programme has been an example of successful policy and regulatory learning processes (Montmasson-Clair and Ryan, 2014). The REIPPPP facilitates the achievement of three SDGs, namely: SDG 7 by producing sustainable energy, SDG 9 by contributing to resilient infrastructure development and lastly, SDG 17 by developing partnerships to contribute to sustainable development (Nel, 2018). The government has also identified Renewable Energy Development Zones (REDZs) to streamline large-scale solar photovoltaic (PV) power plants and wind development in South Africa (Mosaka, Mararakanye and Bekker, 2021). The REDZs and the REIPPPP support the implementation of South Africa's IRP (2019) and the REZs can support a just energy transition (Mandaha, 2019).

Lessons Learned from the REIPPPP

Prior to the introduction of the REIPPPP in 2011, a number of initial attempts to effectively procure power from IPPs failed, including the Pilot National Cogeneration Programme, the Medium-Term Power Purchase Programme, and the Multisite Base-load Independent Power Producer Programme (Ndlovu et al., 2020). These early programmes failed as a result of inadequate leadership, oversight, and political support. Crucial factors that ensured the success of the REIPPPP included policy and political support, institutional leadership, and political will and the active participation of all relevant stakeholders (Montmasson-Clair and Ryan, 2014). Thus, the REIPPPP was implemented against a historical background of institutional shortcomings in South Africa's energy sector, with previous efforts led by Eskom. All these efforts failed because of a lack of capacity and a lack of incentives for Eskom to weaken its monopoly on power generation (Eberhard and Naude, 2016).

The REIPPPP provides an effective procurement framework for RE development (Mosaka Mararakanye and Bekker, 2021). The REIPPPP has been acknowledged as one of the most successful programmes of its kind (Leigland and Eberhard, 2018). Private investment is stimulated if the procurement process is well designed and transparent, transactions have reasonable levels of profitability, and key risks are mitigated by government. RE costs are falling and technologies such as wind turbines are becoming competitive with alternatives (Eberhard and Naude, 2016). Some of the success was due to price outcomes that have been world-class; government was willing to assume the risk of trying new design options, rather than simply replicating international frameworks that may not necessarily have suited the country's unique requirements (Eberhard and Naude, 2016).

In spite of all the success achieved in the REIPPPP, the current South African legal environment is still not conducive to large-scale commercial deployment of RE for electricity generation (Murombo, 2021). The use of non-price factors in the economic development bidding category has generated serious criticism for several reasons; firstly, it creates non-tariff localisation barriers to trade in goods in services, some local content requirements also violate various multilateral trade agreements (Leigland and Eberhard, 2018). The programme enjoyed many early successes; however, from 2015 it experienced challenges in government blocking interventions to support the RE program, Eskom also was responsible for obstructing the programme and political opposition to the programme, all resulted in stalling the programme (Morris et al., 2020). Hence, total government support is essential for South Africa to reap the benefits of the programme and to reach its targets.

From a policy viewpoint, another shortcoming is that due to a lack of a state-guaranteed energy policy framework to ensure that investment risk is minimised and competitive decision-making is maximised (Morris et al., 2020). From a technical viewpoint, to increase RE generation it is advised that South Africa adopt a grid connection model similar to Germany and China where RE projects connect to a point closest to the plant (Ndlovu and Telukdarie, 2020). Although REIPPPPs non-trade criteria have contributed to economic development, they have in some cases applied localisation in counterproductive ways, there are still important lessons they can learn from other countries that have successfully used localisation in the past (Leigland and Eberhard, 2018).

The sixth bid window of the REIPPPP was launched in April 2022, marking renewed commitment to the REIPPPP with the President announcing a comprehensive energy response plan, amidst a time of energy crisis in South Africa, with the aim of increasing decentralised power generation and accelerating procurement of new energy capacity and doubling the scale of generation of REIPPPP (Shetty, 2022). This commitment to the REIPPPP also entails that government will take a more pragmatic approach to the local content requirements for IPP projects with the priority being fast-tracking the building of new capacity (Hall, 2022).

Continuity and predictability of RE auction programmes such as the REIPPPP is essential for the sustained success of RE projects in the country, political struggles between divergent interest groups, the failure to establish sustained continuity, and repetitive predictability, disrupted the entire bidding framework and lay waste to IPP developer foreign investment in RE projects (Morris et al., 2020). Nonetheless, the South African REIPPPP shows that competitive tenders achieve superior results to other policy instruments and offers several key lessons for policymakers in other developing countries (Eberhard and Naude, 2016).

There is a strong interest in RE projects, from international developers in Africa, and using insights from the REIPPPP could expedite the rollout of RE IPP competitive tenders in these, and other developing countries (Eberhard and Naude, 2016). The promotion of renewable technologies presents a number of benefits, including the following:

- it encourages the diversification of energy supply by reducing carbon emissions, supporting a lower carbon pathway and climate change mitigation; and
- important economic impact as electricity generated does not require fossil fuels for its operation, so fuel variations do not impact on the quantity of electricity produced, nor the performance of the energy system. (Thiam, 2012, p. 465)

Coleman and Wass (2016) developed the following guidelines for the development and negotiations of African RE independent power production engineering, procurement, and construction (EPC) contracts:

- Local market issues: local supply chains and manufacturing should be taken into consideration in terms of timing issues and aftermath suspension.
- There should be consistency in design standards in the front-end contract and technical documents.
- Interface between the operation and maintenance contract: carefully negotiated and drafted clauses are required.
- Site and access rights should be secured.
- Site and ground risk: in the IPP contract where site and ground risk is passed to the project company, sponsors and lenders may attempt to push this risk down to the EPC.
- Flow-down of risk from project documents and equivalent project relief.
- Price and payment: the period of time that the contractor holds a price should be established upfront.
- Caps on liability: a financial cap is standard practice; however, a concern is what is excluded from the cap.
- Definition of serial defects: the involvement of technical advisors is crucial to drive negotiations.
- Completion process: the commissioning process under the PPA must be fully understood to avoid gaps in liability and timing.
- Credit rating and security arrangements: negotiation should focus on details such as step-down in value of bonds and their expiry.
- Rejection and buy-down: project companies will require a buy-down clause under which the EPC is liable for the revenue that the project company will lose if the contracted capacity in the PPA is not achieved. (Coleman and Wass, 2016)

CONCLUSION

Environmental governance is essential for sustainable development. Governments adopt various measures to manage and govern the environment inclusive of partnering with multiple actors in different sectors of society. Traditional hierarchical and bureaucratic approaches to governance are no longer suitable to address wicked environmental problems. Governments simply do not have the capacity, expertise, or resources for the scope and impact of these problems. Hence, network and collaborative governance is becoming more prominent in addressing complex environmental problems. In network and collaborative governance approaches, partnerships are increasingly significant to assist government in tackling environmental concerns and in realising the post-2015 Sustainable Development Goals. As a result, public–private partnerships (PPPs) play a vital role in supporting governments in delivering goods and services in an efficient, cost-effective, and reliable manner. PPPs are increasingly utilised as a mechanism to extend governments' capacity in dealing with environmental concerns.

This chapter analysed environmental governance with particular reference to the role that various permutations of PPPs can play in strengthening capacity regarding environmental challenges. A case of the South African approach to a specific environmental problem and sustainable development goal, renewable energy (RE), is provided. It was established that the primary goal of environmental governance is to manage the environment to ensure that environmental systems have the capacity to function. Traditional environmental governance focuses on regulatory instruments to manage the environment in a top-down manner. However, non-state actors have become instrumental in contributing to environmental governance and networks have become important to overcome limitations from top-down governance. Partnerships inherently play an important role in contributing to environmental governance. For instance, multi-stakeholder partnerships have been identified by one of the SDGs as being instrumental in reaching the SDGs. Moreover, PPPs have been prominent in the past three decades in addressing service delivery, environmental, infrastructure, and sustainable development problems. Government does not have the capacity to address wicked problems by itself and therefore has been relying on PPPs to achieve results.

The chapter provided important lessons learned for developing countries facing similar challenges. These lessons include:

- Policy and political support, institutional leadership, and political and active participation of all stakeholders.
- An effective and robust procurement framework for RE development.
- Realistic price outcomes which have been world-class.
- Government should be willing to assume the risk of trying new design options.
- Non-price factors in the economic development bidding category should not prevent barriers for non-tariff localisation barriers to trade in goods and services.
- A state-guaranteed energy policy framework to ensure that investment risk is minimised and competitive decision-making is maximised.
- RE projects should connect to a point closest to the plant.
- Continuity and predictability of RE auction programmes.

Developing countries can learn lessons from South Africa's response to environmental risk in the energy sector.

REFERENCES

Baker, L. (2017), 'Post-Apartheid Electricity Policy and the Emergence of South Africa's Renewable Energy Sector', in Arent, D., C. Arndt, M. Miller, F. Tarp and O. Zinaman (eds.), *The Political Economy of Clean Energy Transitions*, Oxford: Oxford University Press, pp. 371–390, doi.org/10.1093/oso/9780198802242.001.0001.

Beisheim, M., A. Ellersiek, L. Goltermann and P. Kiamba (2018), 'Meta-Governance of Partnerships for Sustainable Development: Actors' Perspectives from Kenya', *Public Administration and Development*, 38 (3), 105–119, doi.org/10.1002/pad.1810.

Bennet, N. J. and T. Satterfield (2018), 'Environmental Governance: A Practical Framework to Guide Design, Evaluation and Analysis', *Conservation Letters: Journal of the Society for Conservation Biology*, 11 (6), 1–13, doi.org/10.1111/conl.12600.

Benson, D. and A. Jordan (2017), 'Environmental Governance', in Richardson, D., N. Castree, M.F. Goodchild, A. Kobayashi, W. Liu and R.A. Marston (eds.), *The International Encyclopedia of Geography*, Hoboken, NJ: John Wiley & Sons, pp. 1–9.

Beşer, N.Ö. and M. Beşer (2021), 'The Sustainability of Renewable Energy Consumption in South Africa', *International Journal of Contemporary Economics and Administrative Sciences*, **XI** (1), 284–296, doi.org/10.5281/zenodo.5138335.

Casady, C.B., K. Eriksson, R.E. Levitt and R.W. Scott (2020), '(Re)defining Public-Private Partnerships (PPPs) in the New Public Governance (NPG) Paradigm: An Institutional Maturity Perspective', *Public Management Review*, **22** (2), 161–183, doi.org/10.1080/14719037.2019.1577909.

Carayannopoulos, G. and A. McConnell (2018), 'Bringing Lessons from Crisis Management into the Realm of Wicked Problems', *Australian Journal of Political Science*, **53** (3), 1–17, doi.org/10.1080/10361146.2018.1450067.

Coleman, M. and D. Wass (2016), 'What Makes an EPC Bankable for an African Renewable Energy Project?', in Clean Energy Pipeline, *Clean Energy Africa Finance Guide*, London: Clean Energy Pipeline, pp. 5–68, accessed 21 July 2022 at https://cleanenergypipeline.com/.

Daviter, F. (2017), 'Coping, Taming or Solving: Alternative Approaches to the Governance of Wicked Problems', *Policy Studies*, **38** (6), 571–588, doi.org/10.1080/01442872.2017.1384543.

Delić, A., D. Šašić and M. Tanović (2021), 'Preconditions for Establishing Public Private Partnership as a Model of Effective Management of Public Affairs', *Uprava*, **12** (1), 55–69, doi.org/10.53028/1986-6127.2021.12.1.55.

Delmon, J. (2010), 'Understanding Options for Public-Private Partnerships in Infrastructure: Sorting Out the Forest from the Trees--BOT, DBFO, DCMF, Concession, Lease', Policy Research Working Paper No. 5173, Washington, DC: World Bank, accessed 12 August 2022 at https://openknowledge.worldbank.org/handle/10986/19947.

Department of Energy. (n.d.), 'Corporate Profile', Pretoria: DoE, accessed 8 August 2022 at http://www.energy.gov.za/files/au_frame.html.

Department of Forestry, Fisheries and the Environment. (n.d.), 'Service to All Government Spheres', Pretoria: DoFFE, accessed 17 August 2022 at https://www.dffe.gov.za/services/government_spheres.

Department of Mineral Resources and Energy. (2022), 'IPPPP Procurement Updates', Pretoria: DoMRE, accessed 22 September 2002 at https://www.ipp-renewables.co.za/.

Đorđević. A. and B. Rakić (2021), 'Macroeconomic Aspects of Public-Private Partnership', *Teme: Casopis za Društvene Nauke*, **45** (1), 367–382, doi:10.22190/TEME200213020D.

Eberhard, A., J. Kolker and J. Leigland (2014), *South Africa's Renewable Energy IPP Procurement Program: Success Factors and Lessons*, Washington, DC: World Bank Group, accessed 2 October 2022 at https://openknowledge.worldbank.org/handle/10986/20039.

Eberhard, A. and R. Naude (2016), *The South African Renewable Energy IPP Procurement Programme: Review, Lessons Learned & Proposals to Reduce Transaction Costs*, Cape Town: UCT Press, accessed 3 October 2022 at https://www.gsb.uct.ac.za/files/EberhardNaude_REIPPPPReview_2017_1_1.pdf.

Edwards, M. (2002), 'Public Sector Governance – Future Issues for Australia', *Australian Journal of Public Administration*, **61** (2), 51–61, doi.org/10.1111/1467-8500.00272.

Evans, J.P. (2012), *Environmental Governance*, London: Routledge.

Eweje, G., A. Sajjad, S.D. Nath and K. Kobayashi (2021), 'Multi-Stakeholder Partnerships: A Catalyst to Achieve Sustainable Development Goals', *Marketing Intelligence & Planning*, **39** (2), 186–212, doi.org/10.1108/mip-04-2020-0135.

Fenwick, J., K.J. Miller and D. McTavish (2012), 'Co-Governance or Meta-Bureaucracy? Perspectives of Local Governance 'Partnership' in England and Scotland', *The Policy Press*, **40** (3), 405–422, doi.org/10.1332/147084411X581907.

Feris, L. (2010), 'The Role of Good Environmental Governance in the Sustainable Development of South Africa', *Potchefstroom Electronic Law Journal*, **13** (1), 73–99, doi.org/10.17159/1727-3781/2010/v13i1a2629.

Gawlik. K. (2019), 'Innovations Abound: Market Leaders Navigate Challenges and Supply Demands', *ENR: Engineering News-Record*, **5** (13), 47–55.

Hall, M. (2022), 'South Africa to Allocate 5.2 GW of Renewables in Sixth REIPPPP Round', accessed 2 October 2022 at https://www.pv-magazine.com/2022/07/27/south-africa-to-allocate-5-2-gw-of-renewables-in-sixth-reipppp-round/.

Head, B. and J. Alford (2013), 'Wicked Problems: Implications for Public Policy and Management', *Administration & Society*, **47** (6), 711–739, doi.org/10.1177/00953997134816.

Heldeweg, M.A. and M. Sanders (2014), 'Towards a Design Framework for Legitimate Public Private Partnerships: A General Approach Applied to Innovative Renewable Energy Infrastructures', accessed 10 October 2022 at https://research.utwente.nl/en/publications/towards-a-design-framework -for-legitimate-public-private-partners.

Henderson, K. (2002), 'Alternative Service Delivery in Developing Countries: NGOs and Other Non-Profits in Urban Areas', *Public Organisation Review*, **2** (2002), 99–116, doi.org/10.1023/A:10160512 11179.

Hodge, G. and C. Greve (2008), 'The PPP Debate: Taking Stock of the Issues and Renewing the Research Agenda', Paper presented at International Research Society for Public Management Annual Conference, Brisbane, Australia, 26–28 March.

Hodge, G. and C. Greve (2021), 'What Can Public Administration Scholars Learn from the Economics Controversies in Public-Private Partnerships?', *Asia Pacific Journal of Public Administration*, **43** (4), 219–235, doi.org/10.1080/23276665.2021.1939744.

Humby, T. (2014), 'Localising Environmental Governance: The Le Sueur Case', *Potchefstroom Electronic Law Journal*, **17** (4), 1660–1689, doi.org/10.4314/pelj.v17i4.13.

Irún, B., D. Monferrer and M.A. Moliner (2020), 'Network Market Orientation as a Relational Governance Mechanism to Public-Private Partnerships', *Journal of Business Research*, **121** (C), 268–282, doi.org/10.1016/j.jbusres.2020.08.044.

Jomo. K.S., A. Chowdhury, K. Sharma and D. Platz (2016), 'Public-Private Partnerships and the 2030 Agenda for Sustainable Development: Fit for purpose?', DESA Working Paper, 148, New York, NY: DESA, accessed 10 October 2022 at https://www.un.org/esa/desa/papers/2016/wp148_2016.pdf.

Lehtonen, A., A. Salonen, H. Cantell and L. Riuttanen (2018), 'A Pedagogy of Interconnectedness for Encountering Climate Change as a Wicked Sustainability Problem', *Journal of Cleaner Production*, **199** (1), 860–867, doi.org/10.1016/j.jclepro.2018.07.186.

Leigland, J. and K. Eberhard (2018), 'Localisation Barriers to Trade: The Case of South Africa's Renewable Energy Independent Power Program', *Development Southern Africa*, **35** (4), 569–588, doi.org/10.1080/0376835X.2018.1487829.

MacDonald, A., A. Clarke and L. Huang (2019), 'Multi-Stakeholder Partnerships for Sustainability: Designing Decision-Making Processes for partnership capacity', *Journal of Business Ethics*, **160** (2), 409–426, doi.org/10.1007/s10551-018-3885-3.

Mandaha, D. (2019), 'Additional Renewable Energy Development Zones Proposed for Wind and Solar PV', Pretoria: CSIR Press, accessed 9 October 2022 at https://www.csir.co.za/renewable-energy -development-zones.

Mert, A. and P. Pattberg (2015), *Public-Private Partnerships and the Governance of Ecosystem Services*, Cambridge: Cambridge University Press.

Mngoma, W., P. Pillay and P.S. Reddy (2011), 'Environmental Governance at the Local Government Sphere in South Africa', *African Journal of Public Affairs*, **4** (2), 105–118.

Montmasson-Clair, G. and G. Ryan (2014), 'Lessons from South Africa's Renewable Energy Regulatory and Procurement Experience', *Journal of Economic and Financial Sciences*, **7** (4), 507–526, doi.org /10.4102/jef.v7i4.382.

Mori, A. (2013), *Environmental Governance for Sustainable Development: East Asian Perspectives*, Tokyo: United Nations University Press.

Morris, M., U.E. Hansen, G. Robbins and I. Nygaard (2020), 'Energy and Industrial Policy Failure in the South African Wind Renewable Energy Global Value Chain: The Political Economy Dynamics Driving a Stuttering Localisation Process', Policy Research on International Services and Manufacturing, University of Cape Town. PRISM Working Paper No. 2020–3, accessed 10 October 2022 at https://backend.orbit.dtu.dk/ws/portalfiles/portal/216631146/PRISM_Working_Paper_2020 _3_Mike_Morris_in.pdf.

Mosaka, T.B.M., M. Mararakanye and B. Bekker (2021), 'International Procurement Policies Influencing Renewable Energy Siting – Implications for South Africa', *Journal of Energy Southern Africa*, **32** (4), 58–68, doi.org/10.17159/2413-3051/2021/v32i4a8397.

Mouraviev, N. and N.K. Kakabadse (2016), 'Conceptualising Public-Private Partnerships: A Critical Appraisal of Approaches to Meanings and Forms', *Society and Business Review*,11 (2), 155–173, doi .org/10.1108/SBR-04-2016-0024.

Murombo, T. (2021), 'Regulatory Imperatives for Renewable Energy: South African Perspectives', *Journal of African Law*, 66 (1), 97–122, doi.org/10.1017/S0021855321000206.

National Planning Commission. (2020), *Digital Futures: South Africa's Digital Readiness for the Fourth Industrial Revolution*, Pretoria: NPC, accessed 7 October 2022 at https://www.nationalplanningcom mission.org.za/assets/Documents/DIGITAL%20FUTURES%20-%20SOUTH%20AFRICA'S%20R EADINESS%20FOR%20THE%20FOURTH%20INDUSTRIAL%20REVOLUTION.pdf.

Ndlovu, V., P. Newman and M. Sidambe (2020), 'Prioritisation and Localisation of Sustainable Development Goals (SDGs): Challenges and Opportunities for Bulawayo', *Journal of Sustainable Development*, 13, 104–118, doi.org/10.5539/jsd.v13n5p104.

Ndlovu, M. and A. Telukdarie (2020), 'An Assessment of the Factors that Influence the Successes and Failures of Independent Power Producer Projects', *International Journal of Renewable Energy Technology*, 11 (2), 186–206, doi.org/10.1504/IJRET.2020.108309.

Nel, D. (2014), 'International Best Practice in Public Private Partnerships and Risk Management', *Administratio Publica*, 22 (2), 46–67.

Nel, D. (2018), 'An Assessment of Emerging Hybrid Public-Private Partnerships in the Energy Sector in South Africa', *International Journal of Economics and Finance Studies*, 10 (1), 33–49.

Nel, D. and N. Komendantova (2015), 'Risks and Barriers in Renewable Energy Development in South Africa through Independent Power Production', *African Journal of Public Affairs*, 8 (1), 48–67.

Okitasari, M., M.H. Prabowo and H. Santono (2020), 'Multi-Stakeholder Partnerships: A Tangible Instrument to Support the Implementation of the 2030 Agenda at Local Level', *International Consortium for Social Development*, 42 (3), 61–86, doi.org/10.3998/sdi.17872073.0042.305.

Poupaud, M., N. Antoine-Moussiaux, I. Dieuzy-Labaye and M. Peyre (2021), 'An Evaluation tool to Strengthen the Collaborative Process of the Public-Private Partnership in the Veterinary Domain', *PLoS ONE*, 16 (5), 1–21, doi.org/10.1371/journal.pone.0252103.

Rittel, H. and M. Webber (1973), 'Dilemmas in a General Theory of Planning', *Policy Sciences*, 4 (1973), 155–169, doi.org/10.1007/BF01405730.

Rhodes, R.A.W. (1994), 'The Hollowing Out of the State: the Changing Nature of the Public Service in Britain', *The Political Quarterly*, 65 (2), 138–151, doi.org/10.1111/j.1467-923X.1994.tb00441.x.

Sanderink, L. and N. Nasiritousi (2020), 'How Institutional Interactions Can Strengthen Effectiveness: The Case of Multi-Stakeholder Partnerships for Renewable Energy', *Energy Policy*, 141 (2020), 1–11, doi.org/10.1016/j.enpol.2020.111447.

Shetty, S. (2022), 'South Africa to Double the Amount of Renewables in the Sixth REIPPPP Round', accessed 10 October 2022 at https://solarquarter.com/2022/07/28/south-africa-to-double-the-amount -of-renewables-in-the-sixth-reipppp-round/.

Strasser, S., C. Stauber, R. Shrivastava, P. Riley and K. O'Quin (2021), 'Collective Insights of Public-Private Partnership Impacts and Sustainability: A Qualitative Analysis', *PLoS ONE*, 16 (7), 1–18, doi .org/10.1371/journal.pone.0254495.

Tahir, M.S. (2017), 'Public Private Partnerships (PPPs): Innovations and Improvements for Future Health Care Systems in Pakistan', *Professional Medical Journal*, 24 (1), 1–9, doi.org/10.29309/ TPMJ/2017.24.01.491.

Thiam, D. and H.C. Moll (2012), 'The Constraints in Managing a Transition Towards Clean Energy Technologies in Developing Nations: Reflections on Energy Governance and Alternative Policy Options', *International Journal of Technology, Policy and Management*, 12 (2–3), 115–134, doi.org /10.1504/IJTPM.2012.046922.

Tűrkelli, G.E. (2021a), 'Multistakeholder Partnerships for Development and the Financialization of Development Assistance', *Development and Change*, 53 (1), 84–116, doi.org/10.1111/dech.12687.

Tűrkelli, G.E. (2021b), 'Transnational Multistakeholder Partnerships as Vessels to Finance Development: Navigating Accountability Waters', *Global Policy*, 12 (2), 177–189, doi.org/10.1111/1758-5899. 12889.

Velotti, L., A. Botti and M. Vesci (2012), 'Public-Private Partnerships and Network Governance: What Are the Challenges?', *Public Performance & Management Review*, 36 (2), 340–365.

Vinogradov, D., E. Shadrina and L. Kokareva (2014), 'Public Procurement Mechanisms for Public-Private Partnerships', *Journal of Public Procurement*, **14** (4), 538–566, doi.org/10.1108/JOPP-14-04-2014-B004.

World Commission on Environment and Development (WCED). (1987), *Our Common Future. UN Brundtland Report*, New York: United Nations, accessed 12 October 2022 at https://sustainabledevelopment.un.org/content/documents/5987our-common-future.pdf.

20. Managing sustainable development in African countries

Alex Nduhura, Muhiya T. Lukamba, John P. Settumba, Ivan K. Twinomuhwezi and Innocent Nuwagaba

INTRODUCTION

Sustainable development is amongst the most important international topics that are shaping the global and national governance agenda. Popularized with the ratification of the Vision 2030 agenda in 2015, today, sustainable development features prominently in national and global debates in the developed and developing world. Unlike other development concepts, sustainable development is defined with obesity. For instance, sustainable development is defined as 'a non-declining utility function or non-declining capital; non declining human welfare over time' (Hempel, 2001, p. 47). From an environmentalist perspective, sustainable development refers to

> the system does not cause harm to other systems, both in space and time; the system maintains living standards at a level that does not cause physical discomfort or social discontent to the human component; within the system life-support ecological components are maintained at levels of current conditions or better. (Hempel, 2001, p. 47)

From a systems perspective, sustainable development is viewed as 'a condition in which social systems and natural systems thrive together indefinitely' (Euston, 1995, p. 31). Sustainable development is also described as

> the system does not cause harm to other systems, both in space and time; the system maintains living standards at a level that does not cause physical discomfort or social discontent to the human component; within the system life-support ecological components are maintained at levels of current conditions or better. (Voinov and Smith, 1998, p. 112)

Meanwhile the Brundtland Commission (1987, np) defines sustainable development as 'development that meets the needs of the present without compromising the ability of future generations to meet their own needs'. The key themes that associate with the debates on sustainable development include climate and environment, with positions on reuse, remaking, and recycling.

Since 2015, many governments in Africa have commenced the journey of implementing sustainable development goals, known popularly as the United Nations Sustainable Development Goals (UNSDGs). Most recent works have indicated that while some progress has been made in working towards achieving the SDGs, a lot remains. For example, most programmes implemented to achieve a satiable world have been characterized by failure despite the colossal sums of money that have been spent in the execution of programmes aimed at not leaving anyone behind. It is important to note that programmes implemented have the potential to uplift standards of everyone, but their design, implementation, monitoring, and evaluation reside with some weaknesses; albeit some important programmes and interventions that would support the realization of sustainable development are often left out. This chapter therefore seeks to appraise existing sustainable development interventions and their assessment, and provide some additional interventions that reside with the potential to deliver sustainable development but have not been implemented. Firstly, we explore the concept and principles of sustainable development. Secondly, we probe the most popular sustainability programmes, highlighting how the programmes have been implemented, the benefits and weaknesses that have been experienced by governments across Africa in implementing the themes, programmes, and policies associated with sustainable development.

FOUNDATIONS OF SUSTAINABLE DEVELOPMENT THOUGHT AND CONCEPT

Given the multiple ways in which sustainable development is used by government private and social sector actors, there exists a considerable body of knowledge that attempts to classify different types of interventions, for instance in relation to climate, the environment, and livelihoods. Traditionally, a term for environmentalists, sustainable development is now a term that not only focuses on the first 'P' – planet – but now encompasses livelihoods that are summarized but now enhanced with wider scope of 'P's, namely; people, prosperity, and profit. The expansion of the scope of Ps for sustainable development has been the realization that it is possible to conserve the planet through mitigation, adaptation, and diversity learning interventions. In light of this perspective, studies have sought to recognize that a focus on the planet while delineating prosperity, people, and profit has been unrealistic. This is largely because the environment cannot exist with humans that are poor and exposed to poverty without an income. Indeed, there is the recognition that God created humankind not to be subdued by other creatures including climate and the environment but rather have dominion over the earth but maintaining earth in a way that God created it and handed it over to mankind. In order to create a balance between the 4Ps of sustainable development, governments across the world have designed and are implementing a range of policies and programmes.

THEMES AND APPROACHES OF SUSTAINABLE DEVELOPMENT

Existing studies confirm that public administrators pursue the journey of managing sustainable development. In this journey several themes and approaches arise. While effort is made to conceptualize themes and approaches to managing sustainability, a combined kit that dominates both policy and practice. In the proceeding section, a discussion of attempts from a public administrator's perspective is surveyed.

Local Economic Development Policies and Sustainable Development

Globally various policies have been designed to support the journey towards achieving sustainable development across governments. The objective of the policies has been largely not to leave anyone behind. Countries like South Africa, Rwanda, Kenya, Mauritius, Botswana, and Uganda designed policies supporting sustainable development, namely local economic development (LED), sustainable public procurement policy, and government decentralization policies.

LED as a policy instrument seeks to allow administrators in a given locality, province, or country to develop their own local economy. Studies by Rodríguez-Pose and Tijmstra (2005) reveal while LED has a potential to spur development, in smaller and less well-endowed localities that cannot draw on strong pre-existing institutions, an informed and involved civil society may lag behind. However, even though LED is a locally owned and implemented programme, the national and regional environment within which a locality is embedded will impact greatly its ability to create economic growth and employment. While this notion is true, some evidence points to the contrary. The view of Rodríguez-Pose et al. (2005) is consistent with earlier studies on the theory of comparative advantage that presupposes that nations must review their competencies that enable them to derive comparative advantage. Contrary to such a perspective, a study by Molavi (2005) and Portes (2020) suggests the contrary. Using the case of Dubai city, a desert island in the UAE, evidence reveals that while heritage is important, local economic development like what Dubai has witnessed can only be achieved with a visionary leadership that is able to forecast the future, develop development plans, and translate the plans into action. Additionally, governments need to design liberal trade policies and offer their citizen quality education if LED is to be achieved. It is also opined that LED is achieved by putting in place hardware, software, and 'orgware' (organizational arrangements and capacities) (Rodríguez-Pose et al., 2005). The availability of economic 'hardware' such as transport and communication networks, as well as infrastructure for the development of human capital, such as education, health, and cultural facilities, greatly facilitate the success of LED for a number of reasons. Additionally, software that is visualized in terms of data and capacity is deemed important to support the development of strategies focused to identify and develop relevant development strategies. This is important since most development strategies in Africa have largely been criticized for lacking alignment with local context. While hardware and software are required it is always largely supposed that the availability of organizational capacity or 'orgware' is vital for forming a set of requirements for LED. According to Rodríguez-Pose et al. (2005) and Tijmstra (2005), orgware seeks to nurture processes characterized by the involvement of local stakeholders, develop networks and partnerships, and co-ordinate actions at tiered layers of government, namely central, provincial, and local government. To create orgware, decentralization is viewed as a game-changer since it supports creating political and administrative structures.

Decentralization as a Vehicle for Sustainable Development

The ability of citizens to participate in making decisions on how they are governed plays an important role in improving local economic development. In Africa, decentralization has been adopted as a development policy instrument given to citizens at the grassroots to make decisions for their aspirations (Edoun, 2012). Smoke (2002) defines decentralization as an administrative policy that empowers citizens in their local community to make political, administrative, and fiscal decisions. Politically, citizens are given the power to elect and make their leaders accountable. Local administrative units are set up to serve the interests of a local community while fiscal decentralizations seek to empower citizens through their local political structures to make decisions that pertain local revenue generation and how it is spent. The idea is that central government reduces its involvement in the affairs of a local community retaining the responsibility of designing the overseeing and evaluating of policy. Decentralization as a policy has over the last decades became a popular concept in Africa but has been applied with limits. Existing studies indicate that decentralization has the potential to cause local economic development. Firstly, because, citizens know their contexts, challenges, and opportunities for development. Secondly, at the grassroots reside local solutions and innovation that fit well with the contexts of the locally governed and self-governed citizens. Additionally, it is known that local governments are where the mass of citizens reside. Adopted in the 1990s, decentralization is recognized as the major institutional framework for the phenomenal industrial growth in China and India. By implication, the adoption of decentralization can help to promote regions, provinces, districts, and cities as local economies providing markets, supply sources, enterprise, jobs, and enhanced development in the spheres of health, education, tourism, and in other sectors. Successful decentralization requires that the tripartite facets of decentralization, i.e. political, fiscal, and administrative are implemented (Smoke, 2003). Decentralization has been implemented impartially in most countries in Africa. For example, in Uganda, Tanzania, Rwanda, Burundi, and Malawi leaving out the fiscal decentralization is imperative. By retaining fiscal aspects of decentralization, most local governments have found it challenging to deliver services like street lighting, road maintenance, and agricultural extension services that are required to deliver. Notably, however, where tripartite decentralization has been delivered corruption seemingly has increased. Making full-scale decentralization work where political, administrative and fiscal aspects are implemented.

Sustainable Public Procurement

Concurrently referred to as procuring into the future, sustainable procurement refers to the practice of sourcing without negatively impacting future generations. According to Islam et al. (2017), while the agenda on sustainability has been in existence for quite some time, sustainable procurement too has existed but its popularity and link with managing sustainability has remained deficient. Yet, studies indicate that sustainable procurement practices can transform markets, save money, enhance financial viability, increase the competitiveness of eco-industries, protect natural resources, and foster job creation, which will in turn contribute to sustainable development. Therefore, it should be recognized that the state is a key actor in virtually all aspects of sustainable procurement. For instance, in the United Kingdom a sustainable public procurement law was passed and in countries such as New Zealand and Norway have also passed their own sustainable procurement policies. In sub-Saharan Africa, while governments and bureaucrats make mention of sustainable procurement few countries have in place sustainable public procurement policies. What is largely recognized is that most African governments have mainstreamed some practices into their existing public procurement and disposal of assets legal and regulatory frameworks. The participation of governments in sustainable procurement (sustainable public procurement) is guided by the view that government as the biggest buyer has a role to integrate and cause more impact in its buying decisions on matters to do with climate and the environment.

In Uganda, environmental, health, and social safeguards are now integrated in bidding documents and incorporated in the bid evaluation scores. In addition, protecting the local supplier base has been done by charging a withholding tax of 15% on foreign firms doing business in Uganda, which is 9% higher than the current Withholding Tax (WHT) of 6% charged on a Ugandan firm. The practice is now common among Southern African Development Community states like South Africa, Botswana, Namibia, and Tanzania. In addition, governments in Africa have passed policies that seek to protect the local supplier and balancing competition among the marginalized. In doing so governments have initiated, passed, and now implement policies such as Buy Uganda Build Uganda, the Broad-Based Black Economic Empowerment Programme in South Africa, and support Made in Rwanda. At regional levels for instance, at the East African Common market level, goods with EAC as their country of origin are shielded from external competition through the application of an external tariff regime that places higher taxes on goods that are produced outside the EAC bloc. In fact, to protect local enterprise, governments have further deployed technical approaches such as 'margins of preference'.

Under the application of the margin of preference and using the open international bidding methods where adverts are placed in international and local media calling suppliers to provide supplies, consultancy services, non-consultancy services, and finance works. Using the margin of preference bids from foreign suppliers are subjected to an additional 15%. At private and social sector actor levels, a range of sustainable practices has been deployed to support the realization of sustainable development. A diverse range of studies highlight sustainable procurement practices. For instance, the Hima Lafarge Group, a global cement company with operations in Uganda and other African countries, requires the bidders to have in place an environmental management policy and show evidence of execution of such policy.

In South Africa, sustainable procurement is enshrined in the nation's procurement system unlike most countries that are in the infant stages of understanding and designing policies for sustainable procurement. The Broad-Based Black Economic Empowerment (BBBEE) programme has been designed, integrated and implemented to cause societal rebalances (Department of Trade and Industry (2008), post the departure of the apartheid system that had resulted in denial of the participation of black people. The apartheid system had traditionally caused discrimination against persons of colour (collectively referred to as 'black' people in South Africa – African black, coloured, and Indian persons). To achieve economic and social equity, the people of colour, under the South African Regime guided by the BBBEE Act and subsequent regulations of 2014 and 2017, black-owned firms are given waivers on meeting requirements and preferred under preference schemes to participate in government procurement. The areas of edge in the evaluation of bids include namely, ownership, management equity with black people, employment equity for black people, skills development, preferential procurement – allocating preference to enterprises with higher BBBEE contributions, management control, enterprise development: focuses on the extent to which small, black-owned firms receive support and are helped to develop and residual factor labour-intensive production and construction methods, infrastructural support to suppliers, and other enterprises in the same area of the community, in investment in the social wage of employees investment and support to enterprises operating in rural communities. The UN's Vision 2030 (Gabay and Ilcan, 2017; Heleta and Bagus, 2021; Villavicencio Calzadilla and Mauger, 2018) slogan of 'leaving no one behind' is aligned with the objective of BBBEE as integrated in the national procurement system achieve social economic equity. In execution of the BBBEE, important lessons are derived. Front loading is common and thus deprives the social equity gains since black people are presented as owners in equity and employment but are not involved in decision-making. Secondly, BBBEE still favours formal businesses and disfavours black-owned firms that largely remain informal.

COMPARING ECONOMIC AND SOCIAL WELFARE PROGRAMMES IN SOUTH AFRICA AND UGANDA

South Africa

The rebirth of South Africa in 1994 marked a significant period in South Africa. Since then, the South African government largely led by the African National Congress (ANC) political party and other parties like the Democratic Alliance among others have sought to deliver transformational change in the lives of South Africans. To cause transformational economic and social change, a range of welfare policies and interventions have been designed and implemented. Most of the welfare policies have sought to target the black marginalized community but more importantly women and youth. The historical past shows that women in SA suffered so many challenges relating to racism, gender violence, and lack of opportunities in workplaces. The previous apartheid government created a system of discrimination between 1948 and 1994 which hampered the development and economic access of women in society. It is argued by Withmann (2012) that 'the apartheid system created discrimination at political, social, economic, and the constitutional level, and this discrimination did not simply disappear from one day to the next when South Africa became a democratic state'. The government decided to change the historical past for women to become relevant and part of development in the new dispensation. Government introduced several programmes across several years to allow women to take charge of their own development.

Currently, women in South Africa are involved in different sectors of the economy such as in the mining industries, farming, tourism, financial institutions, security industry, marketing, the academic field, and the list is quite long. In addition, to the above argument Manzini (1999) elaborates further that

> empowerment is about people taking control over their own lives; gaining the ability to do things, to set their own agendas, to change events in a way previously lacking. It also involves the radical alteration of the processes and structures which reproduces women's subordinate position as a gender.

South African women are involved in every single area where opportunities arise for them to participate and contribute. This becomes a competitive opportunity with male compatriots for the development of the country. There are several pieces of legislation in South Africa which protect women such as the Commission of Gender Equality Act 1996, Basic Conditions of Employment Act 1997, number 18491, Government Gazette, 5 December, and Employment Equity Act 1998, number 19370, Government Gazette.

Considering the implications for youth, the South African government decided to establish a National Youth Development Agency (NYDA) for any initiative to support all the youth across the country. The NYDA already implemented several programmes to support the youth, and the data shows that 8526 enterprises were established with the financial intervention of the agency. The agency provided skilled training for around 491,337 young people from different race groups benefitted from life skills training. This was a way to equip them to enter the job market with work experience. In addition, the national government decided to establish a financial aid scheme which is called the 'National Student Financial Aid Scheme' (NSFAS) to help the poor family or the middle-income class for their young children to have access to higher education. This bursary programme helps many families in South Africa to study different programmes at tertiary institutions and enter the labour market. Many young graduates in South Africa enter the labour market after graduating with the help of NSFAS. This is another strategy of the government to help cut the level of poverty in South Africa. Other interventionist welfare policy that seeks to spur economic access and prosperity has been the Broad-Based Black Economic Empowerment (BBBEE) programme that has been discussed in the previous section under sustainable public procurement.

Uganda

Located in East Africa, the government of Uganda has over the years implemented affirmative actions that have aimed at supporting women and youth. Women have been considered since they have been marginalized while youth have been included in the Uganda Women Entrepreneurship Programme (UWEP), Youth Livelihood Programme (YLP), and the Parish Development Model.

The Uganda Women Entrepreneurship Programme was initiated in 2016 to support women in accessing finances and skills to enable them to start and run their enterprises under the Ministry of Gender and Labour development. This programme is considered to be one of the most successful for women's economic empowerment. Women are organized in groups across 19 districts spread across the country and the programme has enabled women access to technical business development services. Women are given zero-interest loans and if they pay back in 12 months, they pay no interest. After 12 months, a 5% fee is charged on loans on a reduced balance. This is approximately 12/13% below the average commercial banking interest rate and below the central bank lending rate that ranges between 5% to 9% (Bank of Uganda, 2016, 2022).

Recent studies indicate that women-owned enterprises that have benefited from UWEP are better managed than those of non-beneficiaries. UWEP beneficiaries are opening up more enterprises than non-beneficiaries, UWEP beneficiaries are managing their enterprises better than non-beneficiaries, UWEP beneficiaries have better access to markets for their products than non-beneficiaries, and UWEP beneficiaries have better access to value addition innovations than non-beneficiaries (Acosta et al., 2019; Christopher, 2021; Guloba, Ssewanyana and Birabwa, 2017).

In Africa, the YLP in Uganda represents one of the ambitious youth affirmative action programmes in sub-Saharan Africa that have been designed to create enterprise, employment, and income for unemployed youth. In its execution, the YLP Programme is a fund where youth organized as individuals or in groups can apply and access loans from participating commercial banks at low interest rates. The objectives of YLP are to:

- provide youth with marketable vocational skills and tool kits for self-employment and job creation;
- provide financial support to enable the youth to establish Income-Generating Activities (IGAs);
- provide the youth with entrepreneurship and life skills as an integral part of their livelihoods; and to
- provide youth with relevant knowledge and information for attitudinal change (positive mindset change).

The project targets youth including drop-outs from schools and training institutions, youth who have not had the opportunity to attend formal education, single parent youth, youth with disability, youth living with HIV/AIDS, and youth who have completed secondary school or tertiary institutions (including university) but remain unemployed. The programme consists of three components, namely a skills development component (20%), a livelihoods component (70%), and an institutional support component (10%). Skills development has focused on the development of marketable livelihood skills that seek to generate self-employment. The areas that were targeted for skills development included fabrication, hairdressing, leather works, agro-processing, masonry, agro-processing carpentry, ICT, bakery/cooking, tailoring, videography, motor mechanics, moulding with clay among others. Secondly, livelihood support components sought to provide viable income-generating projects, namely, dairy production, high-value crops, poultry/egg production, piggery, aquaculture, animal traction, agro-forestry, post-harvest handling, value addition, trade, service sector projects. The livelihood component is justified by existing studies. For instance, Datzberger (2018) argues that while countries like Uganda have focused on providing access, equality, and quality education, it is not enough to transform citizens out of poverty advocating for new strategies. By providing skills development and livelihood support, programmes like YLP help to promote transformative development among formerly marginalized communities like the youth.

The project was implemented with national and local government. Post-evaluation studies provide interesting findings for governments. Empirical studies reveal that youth vocational skills were developed and that you largely have acquired and use skills acquired to undertake micro investments (Noah, Charles and Yiga, 2021). Previous scholars have indicated that livelihood support can help youth empowerment (Mwesigwa and Mubangizi, 2019) enabling youth to create enterprise, jobs, and employment. On the contrary, while some youth groups have benefitted, randomized study results by this chapter indicate that most youth have started enterprises but their sustainability is questionable. A review of feedback from local government leaders that are in charge of providing oversight for the programme at local government. For example, a Town Clerk in one of the districts in Western Uganda, laments:

> Youth are in transition. When they are given funds to start enterprises, they are likely to join to benefit from funds to support completion of the transition. There should be clear mapping of transition journeys of youth before they are supported. Otherwise project objectives may not be achieved. For example, I studied ICT but to benefit from YLP funds I must be ready to join a group undertaking a piggery project. Will the youth without passion in such an enterprise work and contribute effort to ensure that such a project succeeds? Misalignment, misalignment. (Town Clerk, Municipality in Western Uganda)

Another local government leader laments that

> It has been difficult for us to collect funds from the youth over the 5-year period. Partly this is because YLP was launched during elections and youth saw YLP as a political gift and not money that should be refunded to the revolving fund. (Chief Administrative Officer, District Local Government)

While previous studies on youth livelihood studies have been undertaken, the outcome of the randomized empirical investigation in this chapter indicates that politicizing livelihood programmes can support but also fail well-conceptualized programmes. This finding is consistent with works of Datzberger (2018), who recognizes that funding for affirmative action tends to increase toward political elections but shrinks or is cut off after elections. In this study we find from local leaders that we refer to leaders at the grassroots that governments will always design new programmes for every election. For instance, the YLP has been succeeded by the Emyooga and Parish Development Model, that are welfare programmes targeting the poor and launched prior to the 2021 election. By launching new programmes and perhaps reflections on failed or underperforming welfare programmes, a study by Deshpande, Tillin, and Kailash (2019) indicates that governments avoid consequences of failure that may negatively affect elections. While from a political lens, this approach can deliver, investing resources in non-impactful strategies and interventions exposes countries to achieving the sustainable vision of not leaving anyone behind. The poor benefit the most from welfare improvement programmes aimed at addressing issues such as equity, access, economic, and social justice. There is, however, a need for sober reflection on existing welfare policies in order to reform and create more programmes that can deliver sustainable impact. Lastly, YLP included the institutional support component to provide for transparency, accountability, technical, and managerial capacity.

Post-evaluation studies on the component indicate that unlike the livelihood component, while institutional support provided for the disbursement of funds and supported skills enhancement component, the capacity of the component to provide governance and empowerment of youth beneficiaries remains insufficient. Empirical findings reveal that most youths that have been advanced funds have failed to pay back while some projects that should be in existence are nonexistent. Empirical findings have revealed that several reasons exist. For instance, community development officers that are required to provide supervision of the groups lack logistical support in the form of vehicles and motorbikes and fuel to support the numerous groups benefitting from the fund. Additionally, political structures intertwined in the programme are failing fund recovery efforts from benefitting but defaulting groups of funds supposed to return monies to the revolving fund so that other youth can benefit from the fund.

DIGITAL INTERVENTIONS FOR SUSTAINABLE DEVELOPMENT

Emanating from the works of the World Bank (2016), most countries across the world, particularly in Africa are increasing their focus on digitalizing services. The notion of digitalization covers the use of digital information and communication technologies, including the interconnectivity and networking of these technologies. Digitalization differs from digitization; the latter refers to the process of making something digital. Digitalization is about the processing and networking of what has become digital data. Big data, artificial intelligence (AI), platform technologies, crypto-currencies, blockchain technology, Internet of Things (IoT), and 3D and 4D printing are some of the technologies associated with digitalization. In public administration and governance studies and practice, digitalization is viewed largely as e-Government (Van der Velden, 2018).

As a tool of sustainable development, digitalization is viewed as transformative power that posits the ability to change the way we work and live. The objective of digitalization has been to increase inclusion of citizens in service delivery but also in other aspects such as financial inclusion. In this section, we explore interventions that are being implemented by government, private and social sector institutions to increase access to information, service and resources necessary for the development of citizens no matter the geography. A range of spheres act as candidates for digitization.

According to Tsan et al. (2019), agriculture has and continues to provide opportunities for digitalization. For example, in Rwanda, farmers are able to know prevailing market prices. This helps farmers to know what prices to sell their agricultural produce. Health commodities are being delivered to patients using drone technology. In Uganda and Kenya, where mobile money is deemed to have started, micro loans have helped women in commerce access loans to shop for merchandise. In the utilities market like water and electricity, digitalization enables citizens to pay and access services remotely. Most recently, digitization of such services despite not being talked about may have saved many from contracting Covid-19 as citizens would largely transact remotely with limited physical interface.

Notably, however, it is important to recognize that the success of digitalization requires infrastructure and training for use. Governments therefore must explore strategies to reduce the cost of mobile phones. In Uganda there has been an attempt to avail citizens of free low-cost mobile phones. However, studies indicate that programmes aimed at providing citizens with completely free mobile phone access have proved to be unsustainable. Therefore, as governments explore the distribution of cheaper phones, interventions such as grant matching facilities, microloans may be explored and be more sustainable. In some cases, digitalization has been implemented in the telecommunications and banking sectors. Recent developments indicate hybridization and the seamlessly integrated ability between mobile banking and mainstream banking (Njuguna, Tsibolane and Rivett, 2022). In the education sector, the role played in supporting the sustainability education service cannot be underestimated. Traditionally, there is a digitalization-supported education service. For instance, through the use of tablets, children in early childhood learning use tablets with customized learning content to learn how to read, write, and acquire numeracy skills. During the Covid-19 pandemic, an analysis of literature on the education sector across continents including Africa, indicates that as infections and deaths due to the pandemic increased coupled with school closures, the education service reached a squawking halt. To continue learning, digitalization through virtual learning platforms supported and continues to support learning that had stopped due to the closure of schools as a means of controlling the infection and spread of Covid-19.

Currently, digitalization of education through virtual learning has now been mainstreamed in schools and higher education institutions, with preferences for both physical, virtual, and blended options for learners. By extending education, digitalization and digitization support SDG No.4, which seeks to achieve quality education. In public administration, digitalization has been applied to a range of service delivery reforms. For instance, e-tax where citizens can get to know, apply, and pay taxes online. Countries like Uganda have made it easier for application of driving permits. From application to renewal of permit a citizen spends an average of 30 minutes to one hour to get their driving permit if they have fulfilled procedures. Across the East African region, the one-stop border post initiative and implementation of ASCUDA software are enabling a reduced lead time for exporters and importers within the area. In terms of public procurement countries like Uganda are piloting government procurement (Azcarraga et al., 2022). Preliminary results indicate that bidders are able to access tender adverts with ease and low costs, reduced paper copy submission (Nabukenya, Bagenda and Muhwezi, 2022). While post-evaluation studies remain limited, it is known that reduction in the use of paper can contribute to the reduced pressure and destruction of trees that are required for precipitation.

In labour markets, digitalization has broken barriers to employment. For example, at Metaverse, jobs are advertised and employees recruited on options such as remote working giving the opportunity for Africans to work with such firms remotely while residing in Africa. Traditionally working with such firms from Africa required all sorts of stringent labour migration requirements, namely work permits, health checks (for some countries), and costs of repatriation/relocation for new employees. The costs of establishing and maintaining workstations have also traditionally been high. This includes costs associated with rented space, the provisioning of water, and utility costs such as lighting, heating, and sewerage services. By providing utilities, digitalization enables achievement of SDG No.7 Clean Water and Sanitation. Whilst useful in transforming society and industry (Renn, Beier and Schweizer, 2021), efforts and initiatives for digitalization are constrained by several limitations. Firstly, digitisation relies on access, affordability and quality of internet access. This is largely lacking in Africa. Secondly, internet availability and associated devices require electricity to power yet access to electricity remains a key challenge in Africa. While governments have sought to invest in grid solutions by signing up independent power producers (IPPs), recent research indicates that on-grid electricity solutions remain costly and unaffordable (Murenzi and Ustun, 2015), yet off-grid renewable energy solutions are increasingly scaling up access to electricity (González-García et al., 2022). In some cases, off-grid solutions have provided higher levels of access to electricity than on-grid. In fact, it is argued that the uptake of off-grid solutions such as solar has been due to lower acquisition costs (Sadik-Zada, Gatto and Blick, 2022) and customer-tailored design (González-García et al., 2022).

DELIVERING SUSTAINABLE DEVELOPMENTAL EDUCATION THROUGH PUBLIC–PRIVATE PARTNERSHIPS

World over, education is recognized as an essential tool for achieving sustainability (McKeown, 2002; UNESCO, 2014). This concurs with what Nelson Mandela once said, 'Education is the most powerful weapon which you can use to change the world'. These assertions pause the following intriguing questions: What type of education is necessary as a powerful tool to change the world? How can education as powerful weapon be delivered equitably for all, particularly in Africa to achieve sustainable development? Thus, this section aims to answer the aforesaid questions from international, regional, and national contexts and perspectives. Though the relationship between education and sustainable development is said to be complex, extant literature shows that education directly affects sustainability, owing to the fact that an educated citizenry is vital to implementing informed and sustainable development plans, which can either be enhanced or limited by the level of education attained by the nation's citizens (Deborah, Vidal and Dinis, 2021; McKeown, 2002). Besides, the provision of quality education for all (EFA) is viewed as the best equalizer in most societies owing to its distributive power through human resource capacity-building (Amuche and Kukwi, 2013; Ben-Shahar, 2015; Twinomuhwezi and Chaya, 2020). Therefore, education is deemed as indispensable for multidimensional transformation, because investing in the human mind makes all other sustainable development objectives possible (Mgaiwa and Poncian, 2016; World Bank, 2011). This assertion concurs with Deborah et al. (2021), who opine that formal education at all levels is essential to trigger a whole societal transformation for sustainable development in developing countries. In this regard, quality education not only empowers society to better understand the economy and environment in which they live and operate, but it also enhances scientific research and technological innovations for transformation and sustainable development.

Moreover, research (Brotherhood et al., 2020; Locatelli, 2018; Marginson, 2016; UNESCO, 2015) shows that public education as a common good and human right is critical for enhancing the nation's ability to develop and achieve sustainability targets; and that if collectively provided and equally shared, education contributes to improved agricultural productivity, enhanced status of women, reduced population growth rates, environmental protection, raise the standard of living for sustainability.

Furthermore, as UNESCO (2015) puts it, to achieve SDGs (1, 3, 4, and 5) of eradicating extreme poverty, providing for people's health, ensuring equitable access to quality education and gender equality, respectively, which represent the human development core of the Agenda 2030, most developing countries need to establish strong institutional capacity at various levels through educational initiatives and infrastructure development (Franks et al. 2018). Strategically, the world communities agreed upon the adoption of Education for Sustainable Development (ESD) framework as an answer to cope with sustainability issues among its three pillars of economy, society, and environment. For effectiveness and efficiency in the implementation of this global framework of ESD for 2030, UNESCO has been given the responsibility of providing guidance, standards and support for member countries to develop and expand it as a means for addressing environmental, social and economic issues in a holistic way while initiating necessary changes for sustainable development (Moratis and Melissen, 2022; UNESCO, 2015). It also provides data on the status of ESD and monitors progress on SDG4 on the extent to which global citizenship education and ESD are mainstreamed in national education policies, curricula, teacher education, and student assessment for sustainability.

In spite of UNESCO's commitment to ESD, there is still very little empirical evidence on what type and level of education are suitable/necessary as a powerful tool to manage and change Africa for sustainability, and how the desired education can be equitably delivered to all in capacity and fiscal constrained African countries for sustainable development. Thus, ESD remains a concern that needs to be explored in order to identify the right form and level of universal education required for harmoniously managing and enhancing sustainability in Africa. Essentially, ESD framework aims to facilitate learning in such a way that learners understand the world based on their own observations and develop competences to take action for sustainability (Boeve-de Pauw et al., 2015). In view of this, UNESCO (2014) recommends the need for more research and innovation on ESD initiatives and good practices, and then monitor and evaluate their effectiveness for sustainability. Likewise, having recognized that the current economic development trends are not sustainable, people around the world advocate for public awareness, education, and training as key approaches to moving society toward sustainability. Besides, the current debates on the meaning of sustainable development and whether or not it is attainable, have extended the conversation to what sustainable societies will look like and how they will function. Similarly, some stakeholders also wonder why educators have not developed education programmes for sustainability. It is from the aforesaid debates and concerns that UNESCO efforts and emphasis on education for sustainable development (ESD) emerged. As McKeown (2002) and UNESCO (2014) put it, the justification for ESD is that, when education levels are low, economies are often limited to resource extraction with low productivity. This leads to environmental depletion and pollution without socioeconomic transformation. In many countries, the current level of basic education is so low that it severely hinders social and economic development options and plans for a sustainable future. Therefore, a higher education level is necessary to create jobs and industries that are 'greener' (i.e., those having lower environmental impacts) and more sustainable. With the establishment of the sustainable development goals (SDGs) by the UN in 2015, countries worldwide agreed to a prosperous, socially inclusive, and environmentally sustainable future for all. This ambition, however, remains questionable on how and what context-specific form of education might be required, to enhance the achievement of the 17 SDGs in budget-constrained African economies. As stated in SDG17, this calls for public–private partnerships (PPPs) in the delivery of requisite educational services for sustainability.

While quality education is viewed globally as a necessary service for enhancing socioeconomic development, the resource potential for financing and providing it adequately and sustainably remains a key challenge, particularly in developing countries (Amuche and Kukwi, 2013; Luthra and Mahajan, 2013). Consequently, most budget-constrained countries have adopted public–private partnerships (PPPs) as a viable policy option for providing and financing affordable quality EFA. Moreover, the World Bank (2011) opines that in developing countries, PPPs in education (ePPPs) are justified by the demand for access to affordable schooling and the need to tap into private resources where the state cannot afford EFA. Indeed, most PPP literature emphasizes that ePPPs are a means of increasing equitable access to affordable quality EFA on a sustainable basis (Aslam et al., 2017; Fennell, 2010; Malik, 2010; Moschetti and Verger, 2020; UNESCO, 2015). PPP involves a contract arrangement between a public sector authority and a private party, in which the private party provides a public service or project on behalf of the government and assumes substantial financial, technical, and operational risks in the project. The government may provide a capital subsidy in the form of a one-time grant, so as to make it more attractive to the private investors. In some other cases, the government may support the project by providing revenue subsidies, including tax breaks, or by providing guaranteed annual revenues for a fixed period.

According to Education International (2009), ePPP models are categorized based on what kind of education service the state procures from the private sector and how it does this. The common forms of PPPs in education service delivery include: private management of public schools; education vouchers/subsidies and scholarships; contracting out the delivery of education services (purchase of educational services from private schools and firms); school infrastructure initiatives; capacity building initiatives; and education philanthropic initiatives (LaRocque, 2011; Latham, 2009; Patrinos et al., 2009). Though the contracting model seemed common (Termes et al., 2020), another popular model, referred to as build-operate-transfer (BOT), is emerging. BOT involves large infrastructure projects, where a private sector operator is granted a franchise (concession) to finance, build, and operate an educational facility. The government leases the facility for a specified period, after which it is again transferred to the respective state authority (LaRocque, 2011; Robertson and Verger, 2012). Likewise, long-term concession with private developers to construct, operate, maintain, and finance the project in exchange for rights to collect revenues related to the project like parking facilities, students' hostels, and university guesthouses ought to work better for the sustainability of educational services (EY-Parthenon, 2020). With sound and financially capable private partners, BOT is deemed a suitable PPP design for the delivery of public education services by fiscally-constrained developing countries across the globe, particularly in Africa where demand for universal education exceeds its supply by the public sectors.

Contextually, many higher education institutions are struggling to provide quality, affordable education and research while also maintaining and improving their facilities amidst tight budgets. Thus, a public–private partnership (PPP) approach may be the best option, mainly for non-core educational services such as real estate, laboratory and students' hostel facilities, and front/back-office management. These partnerships could be in the form of an operating contract/management agreement, ground lease/facility lease, availability payment or demand-risk concession. In support of this, EY-Parthenon (2020, p. 2) asserts that:

> Higher education is under pressure. Institutions are struggling to provide a quality education while keeping up with the challenges of deferred maintenance. In the face of new, overwhelming real estate operation considerations, a public-private partnership (PPP) may be an institution's best option. PPPs can provide greater flexibility and efficiency when building, financing and managing infrastructure and facilities.

This assertion indicates that some education institutions are increasingly struggling to provide highly demanded quality higher education while keeping up with the challenges of deferred maintenance against the backdrop of reductions in state funding and limited opportunities for further tuition increases in developing countries. Nevertheless, universities have continued to assume the knowledge creating (training and research) function besides the more recently so-called 'third mission' (Nabaho et al., 2022). With the expansion of higher education participation, university institutions have acquired a larger potential for contributing to societal development. Furthermore, universities undertake fundamental and applied research in sciences and humanities to improve our understanding of life (Chankseliani and McCowan, 2021). Thus, owing to the centrality of education in people's lives and its distributive effects on an economy (Ben-Shahar, 2015), PPPs in education have won much popularity and growing support as a mechanism for ensuring sustainable access to quality EFA (Fennell, 2010; UNESCO, 2015, 2016).

In developing countries, PPPs in education gained momentum in the 1980s as one of the strategic options to address the budgetary constraints and other challenges confronting their education service delivery systems (Malik, 2007; World Bank, 2009). Emerging from such reasons and concerns, most sub-Saharan African governments have adopted and incorporated PPPs into the EFA and or universal education programmes to meet the increasing demand for public education services offered in their economies (World Bank, 2013).

Prior to the United Nations' 17 SDGs agenda, the addition of universal secondary education expanded the millennium development goals (MDGs) ambition, which targeted universal primary education only. This addition was based partly on insights that, for poor countries to escape from poverty, universal primary education is not enough and therefore needs to be complemented by universal secondary education for broad segments of the population (HDR UNDP, 2018). However, as part of its broad remit, the United Nations SDGs of 2015 expanded the focus beyond primary and secondary education to include tertiary education. This was an important move as higher education was missing from the international development agenda as evidenced by previous sets of development goals – the Millennium Development Goals and Education for All. One of these goals – SDG 4 – calls for equal access to tertiary education, including university, as part of the promotion of lifelong learning opportunities for all. The above backdrop reveals that the requisite universal education for sustainability is *time-variant and context-specific* because the skills and knowledge required sustainable development seem to change with time and contexts through research and innovations. Thus, the 17 SDGs adopted by all United Nations member states in 2015 cover a broad range of issues related to socioeconomic, environmental, and technological development, and apply to all of the world's countries, and not only those normally considered to be 'developing' or 'emerging'.

Globally, PPPs in public service delivery emerged as part of neoliberal policies, which were advanced through the Structural Adjustment Programmes (SAPs) by the International Monetary Fund (IMF) and the World Bank (WB) in the late 1980s and early 1990s (Robertson and Verger, 2012). Besides, as a result of such neoliberal policies and programmes, the level of public expenditures on education declined, rather than increased (Robertson, 2007). It is presumed that under neoliberalism, PPPs allow the government to pass operational roles over to efficient private sector operators while retaining and improving its focus on core public sector responsibilities such as regulation and supervision (Olssen and Peters, 2007). In view of this, PPPs are seen as a viable alternative policy reform tool for reducing government expenditure and fiscal deficits in public service delivery through increased private sector involvement. Based on this ideology, PPPs became the IMF's and the WB's conditionality for providing aid for education service delivery to some member countries in order to build knowledge-based economies (Robertson and Verger, 2012). Being recipients of IMF/WB donor support, many African countries (like Uganda) conditionally liberalized the education sector as a way of promoting private sector participation in the delivery of quality universal education services to ensure their accessibility to all and as a strategy for building a knowledge-based economy. As Verger and Moschetti (2016) put it, PPPs in education emerged as a market-oriented solution to issues of education access and quality. Subsequently, many African countries adopted free primary universal education (UPE) to increase equitable access to basic quality EFA. Ultimately, the number of students completing free UPE increased. However, a large number of them were not able to transit to secondary education owing to poverty (MOES Policy Guidelines for PPP Schools-Uganda, 2013). This predicament, which limited many qualifying UPE students from accessing affordable secondary education, motivated the government to adopt another policy, referred to as fee-free universal secondary education (USE). Its objective was to increase and sustain equitable access to secondary school education by all through government-aided schools (MOES Report-Uganda, 2014).

The USE policy resulted in heightened demand and increasing enrolment for fee-free USE services in government-owned/aided secondary schools that exceeded their available limited supply capacity (Uganda National Development Plan, 2010). In order to achieve the objective of USE, the government realized the necessity to partner with some private secondary schools through the PPP policy to increase and sustain its delivery to all. It was owing to this education service delivery gap that the PPP in USE emerged in 2007 as a policy response. This policy was seen as a management and delivery mechanism for enhancing government capacity to provide USE and skill development (Chapman, 2009; MOES Report on USE in Uganda, 2014). Moreover, PPP policy intervention in USE delivery was perceived as a more economical and faster move since the governments would use the existing structures and human resources of private schools to meet the fast-growing rate of secondary school enrolments (ibid.). In light of this, government partnership with the private sector in the delivery and implementation of education projects is seen as an inevitable as well as the simplest way for the governments to provide subsidized and affordable universal education services to all for sustainability in developing countries in Africa.

While education is viewed as a necessary service in every country for enhancing the development of socioeconomic capabilities for its citizens and society, the resource potential for financing and providing it adequately remains limited and a key challenge, particularly in developing countries (Kukwi, 2013; Luthra and Mahajan, 2013). In response to this phenomenon, some budget-constrained countries have adopted PPPs as viable policy options for providing and financing quality education by promoting private sector involvement and participation in its delivery. Luthra and Mahajan (2013, p. 803) argue that 'poor performance of public schools combined with non-affordability of private sector schools by [the] majority of parents is another underpinning for why public-private partnership is needed'.

According to Forrer et al. (2010), the rationale for PPPs has both ideological and pragmatic perspectives: ideologically, proponents of PPPs argue that [the] private sector is superior to [the] public sector in producing and delivering more quality goods and services; and pragmatically, PPPs are viewed by governments as ways of attracting special technical expertise, funding, and innovations from [the] private sector to address complex public policy problems. This supports Akyeampong's (2009) argument that the rise and attractiveness of PPPs in education are influenced by the success stories of some non-state providers who seem to have demonstrated success in the delivery of quality education to meet their educational outcomes compared to the state agency providers. Likewise, Fennell (2010) confirms that PPPs in education are driven by the greater efficiency, superiority in ability, and corporate financing benefits of the private sector, from which the public sector can acquire more synergies in enhancing access to and the delivery of quality education. In view of this, some developing countries have pursued collaborations with the successful private sector actors to explore non-state sector such hidden potential for sustainability in financing and provision of quality education for all. In their study on PPPs in school education in India, Chaundary and Uboweja (2014) point out the rationale for education PPPs as the need to increase access to quality schooling in underserved and resource-constrained communities, because PPPs serve as innovative approaches for improving access to education Likewise, Draxler (2008) sees PPPs as complementary mechanisms, which provide enhanced expertise, synergies, resources, and responses to societal needs in times of tight and constrained public sector budgets. Similarly, the World Bank contends that in developing countries, the rationale for partnerships in the education sphere is driven by the demand for access to schooling, and the need to tap private resources where the state cannot afford EFA. Indeed, the extant literature on education PPPs puts a strong emphasis on the achievement of equitable access to EFA – which is one of the SDGs. This corroborates Malik's (2010) assertion that PPP is a means of increasing access to affordable quality education on a sustainable basis.

Finally, though the private sector has been greatly criticized for its exploitative tendencies in the delivery of school education in developing countries (Shikha Mahajan et al., 2013), some international experiences and lessons from education PPP-practicing countries (like India, Pakistan, Ghana, and Nigeria, among others) demonstrate that, by working together with the public sector through formal PPPs in education, the private sector plays a vital role in improving access to schooling while improving the quality of educational outcomes. Moreover, the central philosophy on which PPPs are anchored is that is that all organizations have strengths, but no single organization has all the strengths required to do everything alone (Rotter & Özbek, 2010). This concurs with Reim's (2009, p. 14) assertion that 'the primary objective of PPP is to deliver a better service than either the public or the private sector could do alone'. Thus, PPPs are perceived as innovative market-led policy models for improving delivery of public services cost-effectively through sharing of risks, costs, resources, and responsibilities between the public and private sectors, particularly in capacity and budgetary-constrained economies (Akyeampong, 2009; Yescombe, 2018). PPPs reinforce efficiency and synergies through attracting and crowding in private investments, capital, technology, and expertise for quick public service delivery and development of supportive infrastructure amidst budgetary challenges and pressure on traditional domestic public sources (Ismail and Haris, 2014; UNESCO, 2015; World Bank, 2011; Yescombe, 2018). Similarly, Lewis and Patrinos (2011) affirm that PPP in education not only improves the quality of education through the competition created between private and public schools in the education market but also promotes flexibility and efficiency in its delivery with an increased level of risk-sharing among partners. Therefore, for African developing countries with public sector budget constraints, PPPs in education seem to offer opportunities to attract and explore the private sector resource potential to meet a wide range of emerging educational needs for promoting increased access to and quality of education for sustainable development.

CONCLUSION

Managing sustainable development is a concern and action for public managers and governors. This chapter has identified and provided themes and approaches that public managers can utilize to make a contribution to the global sustainable development agenda. The chapter has highlighted digitalization, local economic development policies, sustainable public procurement, affirmative actions, education as the best equalizer, and PPPs in universal education for sustainability. In view of this, and owing to non-self-sufficiency in most African societies and economies, the adoption of suitable PPPs, mainly in the education sphere, remains an inevitable strategy for the achievement and management of sustainable development. While several themes have been discussed in the chapter and previous studies, this chapter recognizes that digitalization remains a key enabler for achieving sustainable development. Therefore, there is a need for public managers to view the digitalization of service not only as part of the themes but as a used medium for the delivery of services. This requires that public managers enhance their digital skills and provide propositions for avoiding citizen failure in accessing public services, whether education, taxes, or transport, among others.

REFERENCES

Acosta, M., S. van Bommel, M. van Wessel, E.L. Ampaire, L. Jassogne and P.H. Feindt (2019), 'Discursive Translations of Gender Mainstreaming Norms: The Case of Agricultural and Climate Change Policies in Uganda', *Women's Studies International Forum*, **74** (1), pp. 9–19.

Akyeampong, K. (2009), 'Public-Private Partnership in the Provision of Basic Education in Ghana: Challenges and Choices', *Compare*, **39** (2), 135–149, doi.org/10.1080/03057920902750368.

Amuche, C.I. and I.J. Kukwi (2013), 'An Assessment of Stakeholders" Perception of the Implementation of Universal Basic Education in North-Central Geo-Political Zone of Nigeria', *Journal of Education and Practice*, **4** (3), 158–167.

Azcarraga, A.A.P., T. Matsudaira, G. Montagnat-Rentier, J. Nagy and R.J. Clark (2022), 'Customs Matters: Strengthening Customs Administration in a Changing World', in *Customs Matters: Strengthening Customs Administration in a Changing World*, International Monetary Fund, accessed on 24 January 2023 at https://www.imf.org/en/Publications/Books/Issues/2022/06/15/Customs-Matters-Strengthening-Customs-Administration-in-a-Changing-World-512035.

BBBEE Commission. (2017), *Strategy of the Broad-Based Black Economic Empowerment Commission*, Centurion: BBBEE Commission.

Ben-Shahar, T.H. (2015), 'Distributive Justice in Education and Conflicting Interest: Not Remotely as Bad as You Think', *Journal of Philosophy of Education*, **49** (4), 491–509.

Boeve-de Pauw, J., N. Gericke, D. Olsson and T. Berglund (2015), 'The Effectiveness of Education for Sustainable Development', *Sustainability*, **7** (11), 15693–15717, doi.org/10.3390/su71115693.

Brundtland, G.H. (1987), *Report of the World Commission on Environment and Development: Our Common Future*, accessed 20 January 2023 at https://sustainabledevelopment.un.org/content/documents/5987our-common-future.pdf.

Chankseliani, M. and T. McCowan (2021), 'Higher Education and the Sustainable Development GOALS', *Higher Education*, **81** (1), 1–8.

Christopher, L. (2021), *Women Empowerment and Economic Prosperity in Uganda: A Case of Kabale District* (Doctoral dissertation, Kabale University).

Datzberger, S. (2018), 'Why Education Is Not Helping the Poor: Findings from Uganda', *World Development*, **110**, 124–139, doi.org/10.1016/j.worlddev.2018.05.022.

Department of Trade and Industry (2008), *Verification of Reporting on Broad Based Black Economic Empowerment in Terms of the Codes of Good Practice*, Pretoria: DTI.

Deshpande, R., L. Tillin and K.K. Kailash (2019), 'The BJP's Welfare Schemes: Did They Make a Difference in the 2019 Elections?', *Studies in Indian Politics*, **7** (2), 219–233, doi.org/10.1177/2321023019874.

Forrer, J., J.E. Kee, K.E. Newcomer and E. Boyer (2010), 'Public-Private Partnerships and the Public Accountability Question', *Public Administration Review*, **70** (3), 475–484, doi:10.1111/j.1540-6210.2010.02161.x.

Franks, M., K. Lessmann, M. Jakob, J.C. Steckel and O. Edenhofer (2018), 'Mobilizing Domestic Resources for the Agenda 2030 Via Carbon Pricing', *Nature Sustainability*, **1**, 350–357.

Gabay, C. and S. Ilcan (2017), 'Leaving No-One Behind? The Politics of Destination in the 2030 Sustainable Development Goals', *Globalizations*, **14** (3), 337–342, doi.org/10.1080/14747731.2017.1281623.

González-García, A., P. Ciller, S. Lee, R. Palacios, F. de Cuadra García and J.I. Pérez-Arriaga (2022), 'A Rising Role for Decentralized Solar Minigrids in Integrated Rural Electrification Planning? Large-Scale, Least-Cost, and Customer-Wise Design of Grid and Off-Grid Supply Systems in Uganda', *Energies*, **15** (13), 4517, doi.org/10.3390/en15134517.

Guloba, M., S. Ssewanyana and E. Birabwa (2017), *Rural Women Entrepreneurship IN Uganda: A Synthesis Report on Policies, Evidence, and Stakeholders*, Research Series 257815, Economic Policy Research Centre (EPRC), doi.org/10.22004/ag.econ.257815.

Heleta, S. and T. Bagus (2021), 'Sustainable Development Goals and Higher Education: Leaving Many Behind', *Higher Education*, **81** (1), 163–177.

Hempel, L. (2001), 'Conceptual and Analytical Challenges in Building Sustainable Communities', in Mazmanian, D.A. and M.E. Kraft (eds), *Toward Sustainable Communities: Transition and Transformations in Environmental Policy*, Cambridge: MIT Press, pp. 43–74.

Islam, M.M., A. Turki, M.W. Murad and A. Karim (2017), 'Do Sustainable Procurement Practices Improve Organisational Performance?', *Sustainability*, **9** (12), 2281–2298, doi.org/10.3390/su912 2281.

LaRocque, N. (2008), *Public-Private Partnerships in Basic Education: An International Review*, Reading: CfBT Education Trust.

LaRocque, N. (2009), *The Practice of Public-Private Partnerships*, Cambridge, MA: MIT Press.

LaRocque, N. (2011), *Non-State Providers and Public-Private Partnerships in Education for the Poor*, Manila: Asian Development Bank and UNICEF.

Latham, M. (2009), Public-Private Partnerships in Education', The Information Portal for Global Developments in Private Education, accessed 12 October 2022 at https://www.cedol.org/wp-content/uploads/2012/02/158-159-2009.pdf.

Locatelli, R. (2018), 'Education as a Public and Common Good: reframing the Governance of Education in a changing context', UNESCO Education Research and Foresight Working Papers, accessed 18 October 2022 at https://unesdoc.unesco.org/ark:/48223/pf0000261614.

Luthra, M. and S. Mahajan (2013), 'Role of Public Private Partnership in School Education in India', *Global Journal of Management and Business Studies*, **3** (7), 801–810.

Mehmood, U. (2021), 'Contribution of Renewable Energy Towards Environmental Quality: The Role of Education to Achieve Sustainable Development Goals in G11 Countries', *Renewable Energy*, **176**, 600–607, doi.org/10.1016/j.renene.2021.06.118.

Mgaiwa S.J. and J. Poncian (2016), 'Public-Private Partnership in Higher Education Provision in Tanzania: Implications for Access to and Quality of Education', *Bandung*, **3** (1), 1–21.

Molavi, A. (2005), 'Dubai rising', *The Brown Journal of World Affairs*, **12** (1), 103–110.

Moratis, L. and F. Melissen (2022), 'Bolstering Responsible Management Education Through the Sustainable Development Goals: Three Perspectives', *Management Learning*, **53** (2), 139–145, doi .org/10.1177/13505076219909.

Murenzi, J.P. and T.S. Ustun (2015), 'The Case for Microgrids in Electrifying Sub-Saharan Africa', *IREC2015 The Sixth International Renewable Energy Congress*, pp. 1–6, doi.org/10.1109/IREC.2015.7110858.

Mwesigwa, D. and B.C. Mubangizi (2019), 'Contributions of the Youth Livelihood Programme (YLP) to Youth Empowerment in Hoima District, Uganda', *International Journal of Business and Management Studies*, **11** (1), 54–73.

Nabukenya, J., B. Bagenda and M. Muhwezi (2022), 'Information Technology, Organisational Structure, Stakeholder Involvement and Supplier Order Fulfilment in Public Procurement: A Case of Selected Suppliers in Kampala–Uganda', *ORSEA Journal*, **11** (2), accessed on 12 October 2022 at https://www .journals.udsm.ac.tz/index.php/orsea/article/view/4502.

Njuguna, R., P. Tsibolane and U. Rivett (2022), 'Digitalisation of Indigenous Finance Institutions in Sub-Saharan Africa: A Critical Discourse Analysis', *International Conference on Social Implications of Computers in Developing Countries*, Cham: Springer, pp. 239–251.

Noah, S., E. Charles and A.P. Yiga (2021), 'Youth Bulge and Income Generating Activities [IGAs]: A Case of Youth Livelihood Programme [YLP] in Wakiso District, Central Uganda', *Open Journal of Social Sciences*, **9** (5), 470–487.

Nwaiwu, F. (2021), 'Digitalisation and Sustainable Energy Transitions in Africa: Assessing the Impact of Policy and Regulatory Environments on the Energy Sector in Nigeria and South Africa', *Energy, Sustainability and Society*, **11** (1), 1–16, doi/org/10.1186/s13705-021-00325-1.

Olanrewaju, B.U. and J.A. Afolabi (2022), 'Digitising Education in Nigeria: Lessons from COVID-19', *International Journal of Technology Enhanced Learning*, **14** (4), 402–419, doi.org/10.1504/ijtel.2022 .125857.

Olssen, M. and M.A. Peters (2007), 'Neoliberalism, Higher Education and the Knowledge Economy: From the Free Market to Knowledge Capitalism', *Journal of Educational Policy*, **20** (3), 313–345.

Oyewobi, L.O. and R.A. Jimoh (2022), 'Barriers to Adoption of Sustainable Procurement in the Nigerian Public Construction Sector', *Sustainability*, **14** (22), 14832, doi.org/10.3390/su142214832.

Patrinos, H.A., F. Barrera-Osorio and J. Guáqueta (2009), *The Role and Impact of Public-Private Partnerships in Education*, New York: The World Bank.

Portes, A. (2020), 'A Tale of Three Cities: The Rise of Dubai, Singapore, and Miami Compared', *Sustainability*, **12** (20), 8566, doi.org/10.3390/su12208566.

Reim, C. (2009), 'Challenges to Public Private Partnerships: The Example of the London Underground PPPs', accessed 23 October 2022 at https://www.libertas-institut.com/de/PDF/Claudia%20Reim _PPP_London_Underground_Aug-2009.pdf.

Renn, O., G. Beier and P.J. Schweizer (2021), 'The Opportunities and Risks of Digitalisation for Sustainable Development: A Systemic Perspective', *GAIA-Ecological Perspectives for Science and Society*, **30** (1), 23–28.

Robertson, S.L. and A. Verger (2012), 'Governing Education Through Public Private Partnerships', Public Private Partnerships in Education: New Actors and Modes of Governance in a Globalizing World', accessed on 23 October 2022 at https://susanleerobertson.files.wordpress.com/2012/07/2012 -robertson-verger-governing-education.pdf.

Rockart, I.F. (1982), 'The Changing Role of the Information Systems Executive: A Critical Success Factors Perspective', Sloan School of Management, MIT, accessed on 5 October 2022 at https:// dspace.mit.edu/bitstream/handle/1721.1/2010/SWP-1297-08770929-CISR-085.pdf?sequence=1.

Rodríguez-Pose, A. and S.A.R. Tijmstra (2005), 'Local Economic Development in Sub-Saharan Africa', *Environment and Planning C: Politics and Space*, **25** (4), doi.org/10.1068/c5p.

Rose, P. (2010), 'Achieving Education for All Through Public-Private Partnerships?', *Development in Practice*, **20** (4–5), 473–483.

Rotter, J. and N. Özbek (2010), 'Private-Public Partnerships–Collaborating for a Sustainable Business in Sweden', Swedish University of Agricultural Sciences, Faculty of Natural Resources and Agricultural Sciences, Department of Economics.

Sadik-Zada, E.R., A. Gatto and N. Blick (2022), 'Rural Electrification and Transition to Clean Cooking: The Case Study of Kanyegaramire and Kyamugarura Solar Mini-Grid Energy Cooperatives in the Kyenjojo District of Uganda', in Filho, W.L., D.G. Vidal, M.A.P. Dinis and R.C. Dias (eds.), *Sustainable Policies and Practices in Energy, Environment and Health Research*, Cham: Springer International, pp. 547–562.

Tsan, M., S. Totapally, M. Hailu and B.K. Addom (2019), *The Digitalisation of AFRICAN Agriculture Report 2018–2019*, CGSpace, accessed 21 September 2022 at https://cgspace.cgiar.org/handle/10568/101498.

Twinomuhwezi, I.K. and C. Herman (2020), 'Critical Success Factors for Public-Private Partnership in Universal Secondary Education: Perspectives and Policy Lessons from Uganda', *International Journal of Educational Administration and Policy Studies*, **12** (2), 133–146, doi.org/10.5897/IJEAPS2020.0656.

Van der Velden, M. (2018), 'Digitalization and the UN Sustainable Development Goals: What Role for Design', *ID&A Interaction Design & Architecture*, **2** (37), 160–174.

Villavicencio, C.P. and R. Mauger (2018), 'The UN's New Sustainable Development Agenda and Renewable Energy: The Challenge to Reach SDG7 While Achieving Energy Justice', *Journal of Energy & Natural Resources Law*, **36** (2), 233–254, doi.org/10.1080/02646811.2017.1377951.

Voinov, A. (1998), 'Paradoxes of Sustainability', *Zhurnal Obshchei Biologii*, **59**, 209–218.

Voinov, A. and C. Smith (1994), 'Dimensions of Sustainability', *1st International Symposium of Ecosystem Health & Medicine*. Ottawa, accessed 22 August 2022 at http://likbez.com/AV/PUBS/DS/Sust_Dim.html.

Yescombe, E.R. (2017), 'Public-Private Partnerships in Sub-Saharan Africa: Case Studies for Policymakers', UONGOZI Institute, Dar es Salaam: Mkuki na Nyota Publishers.

21. Towards digital governance in Africa

Adedeji Adeniran, Kunle Balogun and Ezra Ihezie

INTRODUCTION

With the pace of recent structural transformations driven by digital technologies across the world, the role of digitalization in economic and political processes has gained widespread attention (CSEA, 2022). It is obvious that, through digital technology uptake, the world economic output has received a marked boost, with a significant number of decent jobs created and a new economic sector emerging (UNCTAD, 2021). In Africa, digital technology adoption has brought about broad interconnectivity, massive digital transformation, and innovation in the public and private sectors (Manda and Backhouse, 2017). All of these have made the exchange of goods, information, and ideas become fast and cost-effective.

In an era of digital evolution, the demands and abilities of the public sector to generate, store, and use data are increasing. Digitalization has recently influenced how governments are organized as well as how public services are designed and delivered. Emerging technologies also support more government-citizen engagement and better targeting of social programmes in ways that have gained efficiency and innovation in governance. A move towards a more digitized governance is illustrated by the deployment and integration of digital technologies in the public sector, ranging from a shift from paper-based/analogue systems to digital tools for internal and external communication by governments and more recent exploration of artificial intelligence and drones in public service delivery (Butcher et al., 2021). These technological advancements raise pertinent questions about the extent to which digitalization can influence not just process but the overall ethos, culture, and efficiency within the public sector. Digitalization in governance has its perils such as confidentiality, privacy, data breaches, identity theft, cybercrime, and misinformation among others. Regulation of the digital space in a manner to maximize its potential benefit and minimize the potential risks squarely fall within the sphere of government policy and regulatory functions (Hlaka, 2022).

The discourse around data governance is emerging globally, and Africa's roles in this space are still largely undefined. The weak state of a digital governance framework can rob the continent of the many benefits of digitalization, the most part of which is socioeconomic transformation. The crisis of regulatory laws in most African countries and poor implementation of such (where available) have, for a long time, constituted a limitation to the much good that digitalization can bring to the continent. Therefore, efficiency of the public sector in supporting the design and implementation of such a digital governance framework is part of the growing functions of the state.

This chapter will explore the intersection of governance and digitalization in Africa investigating how the respective spheres of government may influence the digital space. The chapter will also probe factors driving digital adoption in African public sector management and examine its potential benefits and implementation challenges. It is argued that it is the responsibility of government to build supportive soft and hard infrastructure that will harness digitization and minimize threats emerging from technological applications. The chapter will also examine various models that national and supranational governments are implementing with regard to data governance policies and regulations and how Africa can become a key player under the new global order.

GOVERNMENT AS CONSUMER OF DIGITAL TECHNOLOGIES

As new technologies emerge, governments should consider suitable applications to support, enhance, and optimize the delivery of services to businesses and citizens. The digital technologies typically explored in public administration include but are not limited to social media, mobile telecommunication, analytics, cloud computing, and internet-based platforms. Given the growing popularity of ICT in different fields, attempts have been made globally to implement its adoption in transplanting some of the good practices in the private sector into public sector management. Africa is not an exception in this respect (Backus, 2001). This adoption is part of the revolution spurred by the New Public Management principles with emphasis on efficiency, effectiveness, economy, productivity, and transparency. The volume of data that is being generated in government operations together with the increasing access to technologies that ensure speedy collection and dissemination of management information has also made traditional paper-based tools used in the public sector almost obsolete.

THE STATE OF PUBLIC SECTOR DIGITAL ADOPTION IN AFRICA

Digital technology has revolutionized ways of life and improved service delivery methods. The widespread use of these digital technologies has led to a high degree of interconnectedness across countries, organizations, corporations, and individuals. Technology has a positive effect on society in different ways, including its effects on the transportation system, communication, education, health system, and learning process (Loubier, 2017). Also in the public sector, it has an impact on public sector administration, the delivery of public goods, and other aspects of governance. Noteworthy is the impact of digitalization on state revenue generation and efficiency. Novel approaches such as e-taxes have the potential to lower extortion loopholes in the public sector of developing economies (Okunogbe and Pouliquen, 2018).

The purpose of digital adoption in the public sector is to create governments that meet criteria such as lowering the cost of operation, ensuring quality services, strategically leveraging ICT, facilitating improved regulatory capacity, and bringing about transparency in governance (Yong, 2003). However, negative effects of digitalization abound such as privacy concerns and government loss of monopoly and control over information gatekeepers, but they are insignificant in comparison to its benefits. Additional emerging issues such as data breaches, sovereignty, localization, cross-border flows, and digital identity that raise concerns about a new role for government in the digital era (Alexandra, 2022; ADIRFC, 2021; Mishra, 2016; Couture and Toupin, 2019; Global Data Alliance, 2020; Vahisalu, 2019). Hence, policies and actions focused on promoting digital adoption and innovation are needed for inclusive development.

Africa's technological progress and constraints set the stage for digitalization in the public sector. The African continent's ICT infrastructure has grown significantly during the last two decades, notably in terms of mobile cellular subscribers, which went from fewer than three subscriptions per 100 people in 2000 to 83 per 100 inhabitants in 2022 as well as expanded broadband networks (World Bank, 2022a). In addition, Africa's demographic composition is evolving with a high youth population that are digital natives. With more people connected online, they are getting more cognizant of the government service delivery deficiencies in their economies, as well as any relative inadequacies in its availability and quality. When compared to the 1990s, African countries are becoming more digitally advanced. In 2021, 43 per cent of Africa's population were internet users, which is 42 times the percentage of the population during the 1990s (Internet World Stats, 2022). Also, the African setting is becoming more urbanizing, a development that creates a variety of demands in terms of service delivery in urban areas. Accordingly, this demographic evolution in Africa is creating new expectations for public service delivery, and these expectations require smarter and innovative ways to plan, monitor, and provide public goods to match the changing expectations.

Despite tremendous progress in digital infrastructure development, broadband penetration in Africa remains relatively low. Internet access costs are also relatively less affordable (accounting for income level) when compared to regions such as Europe, the Americas, and Asia (Connecting Africa, 2021; World Bank, 2022b). According to OECD (2021), digitalization is a necessity for better public service delivery. Therefore, the African public sector must come on board if it is to stay viable and continue to foster economic growth. However, for inclusive and sustainable development, digitalization in the public sector needs effective and comprehensive approaches that view digital technologies as a means of providing quality governance and improved service delivery, as well as fostering public-private collaborations. This will require the promotion of an inclusive information society through investment in digital literacy, digital infrastructure, and grassroots innovation (Hanna, 2016).

To appreciate the state of digital adoption in Africa's public sector, data from the E-governance Development Index (EGDI) and e-participation index based on the UN E-Governance Knowledge Base should be analyzed. The E-Government Development Index assesses the condition of digital development in the public sector of the UN Member States. The index examines the country's public sector website development trends, provision of online services, telecommunication connectivity, and human capacity. It further considers access factors such as infrastructure and educational levels to represent how a country uses information technology to improve the accessibility and inclusion of its people (UNDESA, 2022).

The regional e-government indices for Africa in 2003, 2010, and 2022 are 0.2005, 0.2632, and 0.4054 respectively. For the same period, the e-participation indices for the region are 0.0374, 0.0735, and 0.2595. Africa thus falls below the global averages for the seven consecutive surveys – trailing behind all other regions such as Europe, the Americas, Asia, and Oceania. In terms of regional e-participation, Africa also has the lowest e-participation index in the world.

Figure 21.1 shows the relative performance of Africa with respect to other regions.

A closer look at the performance of subregions reveals the weakness of Central Africa (consisting of Cameroon, Central Africa Republic, Chad, Congo, DR of the Congo, Equatorial Guinea, and Gabon) over the other four subregions including North Africa, East Africa, West Africa, and South Africa, with an average e-government index of 0.2238 and e-participation index of 0.0923. The leading subregion on average is North Africa, which consists of Algeria, Egypt, Libya, Mauritania, Morocco, and Tunisia, with an average e-government index of 0.3621 and e-participation index of 0.2149. The North African subregion is leading Africa's

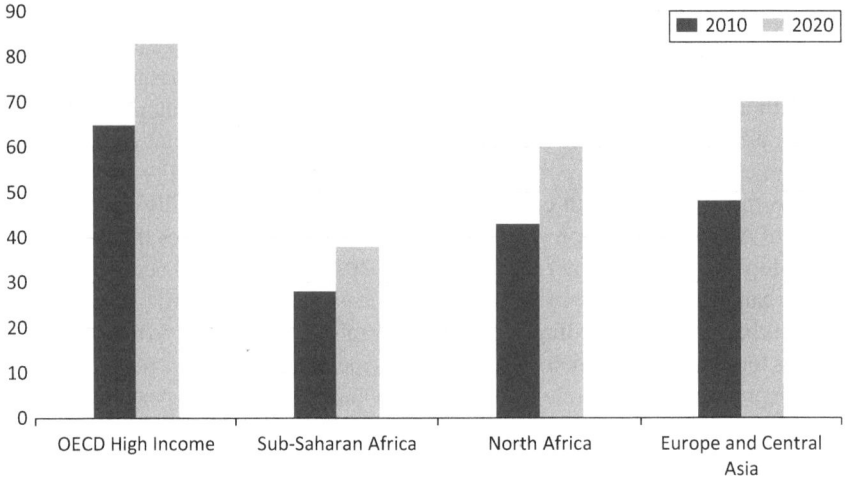

Source: UN E-Government Development Index (2022) in IMF (2022, p. 2).

Figure 21.1   State of e-governance: Africa in comparison with other regions

public sector digital adoption, particularly Tunisia, Egypt, and Morocco. For instance, digital technologies are swiftly being integrated into all government operations and procedures, while financing for ICT-related projects is also becoming significant in their national budgets. This is as a result of their governments' dedication to creating and implementing a national strategy for digital public services at the central level, investment in digital education and training, digital infrastructure development, development of national databases, and introduction of e-services (Mishrif and Selmanovic, 2010).

According to the United Nation's E-Government Development Index (2022), it is evident that Southern Africa dominated in e-government advancement during the period of 2003 to 2008. However, North Africa took over and sustained the lead till 2022. The e-participation index followed a similar trend; however, in 2022, West Africa became the regional leader. Social media plays a role in this shift, with North Africa putting in place more restrictions. Intriguingly, the most successful use of social media for citizen participation started in North Africa with the Arab Spring that began in Tunisia. This has led to more internet restrictions within the region. It is also evident that other countries in Africa have utilized internet restrictions to limit citizen participation. Examples include Uganda where the government restricted social media access to curb opposition areas of advantage. There are many sides to digitalization in Africa, but the extent to which digital access is viewed as a component of human rights will support better public sector development and transformation.

THEORY AND PRACTICE OF ICT ADOPTION: DIGITAL AMBIDEXTERITY IN GOVERNMENT

New Public Administration and more contemporary New Public Management theory and practice are largely anchored in mainstreaming private sector efficiencies into the public sector. It is argued that public institutions can benefit in this respect by becoming more responsive to societal needs, more aware of internal and external government changes, and adaptable to social, economic, and political dynamics. Digitalization can facilitate this process. However, while public administration must embrace digitalization, it has the delicate role of balancing two (sometimes competing) purposes, namely using digital tools to improve the efficiency of its existing activities and using digitalization to innovate public administration. The latter implies a redefinition of the conventional role and purposes ascribed to the public sector and the way society should be engaged (i.e. the social contract). The mechanisms and structures to balance these two goals have been described in the literature as the theory of digital ambidexterity.

Literally, ambidexterity is the human ability to use two hands equally well. The term is marked out by the idea of simultaneity, that is, the use of two things at the same time. Drawing on this dimension of meaning, March (1991) theorizes ambidexterity as the act of simultaneously pursuing both incremental and discontinuous innovation. It was Ducan (1976) who first introduced ambidexterity while incorporating the development of innovation in the organizational design of public sector management. In the public sector context, ambidexterity translates as the fight for scarce resources that have to be allocated between explorative and exploitative activities. To March (1991), public institutions need to be involved in both the continuous exploitation of existing opportunities and the exploration of new opportunities.

While developing the theory of organizational ambidexterity further to situate it within the context of the public sector's adoption of digital technology, otherwise known as digital ambidexterity, Magnusson, Paivarinta and Koutsikouri (2020) define it as the idea of balancing efficiency with innovation. In their theorizing on digital ambidexterity, efficiency, which translates as 'continuous improvements of existing services and processes', was equated with exploitation. On the other hand, exploration, which is defined as 'the acquisition and development of radically new knowledge and services', is equated with innovation (Magnusson, Paivarinta and Koutsikouri, 2020, p. 61). Public sector institutions, according to Mergel, Gong and Bertot (2018, p. 292), had been criticized for 'being poised in governance signified by a high level of bureaucracy, centralization and formal control'. To overcome these perceived deficiencies and to deliver on its core mandates, governments need to strike a delicate balance (i.e. organizational ambidexterity) between efficiency and innovation.

Various models of digital adoption in Africa have been designed to facilitate organizational ambidexterity in government (refer to the section below). However, an analysis of the adoption and utilization of these models reveals that such balance is yet to materialize. From the G2G to G2C models, it seems that African public administrations have prioritized improvement in existing activities and focused less on innovation. The traditional goals and activities of government are still largely intact and digitalization is applied to more narrow-focused managerial domains in efforts to improve efficiency. Examples in this regard are blockchain adoption in the monetary and fiscal system of governments and the use of drone technology in health service delivery. These examples illustrate progress but are still far from the end goal of making all government operations more effective and efficient.

By and large, the theory of digital ambidexterity explains the patterns of digitalization in the public sector space. This theory furthermore contributes to the understanding of how the public sector organization engages in a continuous balancing between exploiting the existing digital opportunities and exploring the new digital opportunities for its good. This understanding cannot but constrain a deep commitment on the part of the public sector management towards improving on digital governance in a way that would make it serve the organization better.

A further development as far as public administration innovation and digitalization are concerned, is closer cooperation between public and private actors. It is evident that private enterprises are increasingly recognized as valued partners in governance. In Africa, one such success story is the M-Pesa mobile phone-based innovation project in Kenya that led to higher financial inclusion and new financial products for poor and vulnerable communities. The project is an example of public-private partnership as Safaricom, Kenya's largest mobile network provider, collaborates with government agencies to offer money transfer, financing and microfinancing services to rural communities. 'M' stands for mobile, and 'Pesa' is Swahili for money. From the launch of the project in 2007, it grew to approximately 20 million M-Pesa currently. It is widely accepted as the most successful mobile phone-based financial service in the developing world (Oborn, 2022). Apart from success stories like these, most countries in Africa are still struggling with their means of deepening their financial sector due to regulatory restrictions. Governments should therefore establish a far more conducive policy and regulatory framework for public sector innovation. Public budget allocations, private sector investments, and research and development are some of the mediums through which such digital ambidexterity can be achieved.

ICT or digital adoption in the African public sector management, broadly known as e-governance, should be seen within the broader context of regional integration. Such regional integration on the continent generally aims to achieve better alignment and coordination for national, regional, and continental structural reforms and transformation in national governments. In more particular, it aims to digitize government processes and the inculcation of an organizational culture conducive to support government productivity, efficiency, and resilience.

MODELS OF NETWORKING FOR GOVERNMENT'S ICT ADOPTION IN AFRICA

New modes of governance and the adoption of a network form of government have led to cooperation and partnerships with several governance actors. Models for such networking are required to establish the architecture, values, and principles according to which governments should engage these actors. The four main digital models or forms of government networking with societal actors, known as e-governance, are Government to Government (G2G), Government to Employees (G2E), Government to Business (G2B), and Government to Citizens (G2C). Each of these, alongside its benefits and challenges, is explained below.

Government to Government (G2G)

The G2G model of ICT adoption can be regarded as the digital or electronic sharing of data and information systems between government agencies, departments, and entities. It thus simply refers to digital interaction, data sharing, and interoperability between government and its agencies. The idea of G2G is the transformation of the backend operation of government institutions. This can be vertical, if the digital tool is utilized within the same government agencies or horizontal if it transcends a line ministry to include different arms of government. G2G is also known as 'e-Administration', whereby digital technology is harnessed to improve public administration processes for better service delivery (Hafkin, 2009). Some examples of G2G ICT adoption across African countries include the following:

- The National Policy on Virtual Engagements for Federal Public Institutions, which was formulated and approved by the Nigerian federal government to formalize online meetings across government agencies or departments (ChannelsTV, 2021).
- The County Connectivity Project that is being implemented by the Kenyan ICT Authority to ensure that county government offices are connected to the internet in order to facilitate interaction through the provision of online services using telephones, emails, and teleconferencing among the County Commissioners, the Treasury Department's Civil Registration departments; the National Registry Bureau; Education Departments and the governor's office (Kamairo, 2017).
- The Integrated Financial Management Information System (IFMIS), which is in operation in Zambia to enable all levels of government to work cohesively in an efficient and effective manner thereby reducing the fragmented government processes that demote timely sharing of information (Shadrick and Tembo, 2020).
- The Woreda Net Project of the government of Ethiopia, which is a government network that provides internet connectivity such as video conferencing to federal, regional, and more than 611 woreda (local government equivalent to a district) government offices across the nation (Bezu, 2019).

The primary aim of G2G is to increase coordination, efficiency, performance, and output in government. This can be achieved through seamless interaction between various departments and parastatals, within any sphere of government (i.e. local, state, or federal) or between two governments. It allows all levels of government to work cohesively in an efficient and effective manner thereby reducing the fragmentation in government processes through timely sharing of information. It helps in the restructuring of administrative processes and the creation of greater transparency (Hafkin, 2009). However, implementation of a robust G2G in the public sector in most African countries faces potential barriers. The most immediate one is the poor telecommunication infrastructure which can exclude important public sector institutions serving in vulnerable, deep rural areas. The digitalization of government processes can exclude underserved and most vulnerable communities with limited or no access to digital networks and systems. The most important barrier, however, may be cultural in nature given the need to introduce new ways of doing things. The traditional bureaucratic ethos, hierarchical and silo mentality, as well as conventional management styles may not be conducive to supporting engagement, intergovernmental relations, partnerships, transparency, and openness. Other prominent barriers in the G2G discourse are possible trade-offs between the benefits of digitalization and issues related to national security, cybercrime, data breaches, protection of personnel privacy, and technical and resource constraints (ADIRFC, 2021).

Government to Employees (G2E)

The G2E model of government ICT adoption is simply an extension of G2G and refers to the electronic means by which government relates with its employees. It involves the government's provision of specialized services to its employees (Hafkin, 2009). The G2E is often focused on strategies or tactics that can be used to encourage the implementation of government goals and programmes, as well as human resource management, budgeting and accounting (Sikaonga and Tembo, 2020). Examples of G2E in Africa include the following:

- The Payroll Management and Establishment Control (PMEC) in Zambia, which is a decentralized system instituted by the government of Zambia to monitor and control expenditures on employees' personal emoluments (Sikaonga and Tembo, 2020).
- The regular ICT workshops organized by the Lagos State Service Commission (LGSC) of Nigeria in partnership with NITDA to enlighten and give hands-on training to the State's civil servants in order to strengthen the effectiveness of ICT towards the G2E workspace.

The G2E category of digital governance has the potential of making interactions between the government and its employees fast and efficient, thus increasing the satisfaction levels of the employees (Sikaonga and Tembo, 2020). Given the foregoing, G2E helps in facilitating increased employee morale, motivation, and productivity. Furthermore, it helps in establishing digital capabilities for the workforce and improves labour relations between the government and officials (Backus, 2001).

Despite the benefits that G2E is capable of delivering, it is often constrained by a number of challenges. One of such challenges relates to employees' low ICT literacy levels, which often stands in the way of G2E ICT uptake. It is also constrained by poor broadband connectivity that usually makes online interaction between participating groups quite difficult (Abusamhadana et al., 2021).

Government to Business (G2B)

The Government-to-Business (G2B) model is a digital domain that focuses on the interaction between government agencies and the private businesses sector via online mediated environments (Sikaonga and Tembo, 2020). It essentially involves electronic transactions with business entities and other institutions that may include non-profit organizations, large-scale businesses, and small and medium-sized enterprises (SMEs). Given the advantages that the private sector has in digital adoption, G2B helps the public sector to leverage ICT tools in learning from and interacting with business partners. Digitalization can support tax collection, ease regulation, and procurement process and transfer some of the efficiency practices in the private sector to public sector. Examples of G2B in Africa include the following:

- The Zambian government Revenue Authority (ZRA) e-Tax Online System that allows businesses, especially SMEs, to electronically register their businesses, file tax returns, and make payments.
- The South African Revenue Services (SARS) e-filing of tax, which is a coordinated effort between SARS and private business.

G2B is highly beneficial for enabling the business community to interact with the government through the adoption of e-governance tools. It eliminates red tape, as it saves time and reduces operational costs. In line with a study conducted by Ugwueze et al. (2016), one of the cardinal reasons which informed the Nigerian government's (under President Muhammadu Buhari) decision to digitalize governance was to eliminate red tape, which is considered to be one of the major causes of corruption. The G2B also creates a more transparent business environment for the government and the private businesses (Ndou, 2004). It improves on the delivery and efficiency of government by facilitating services such as licensing, procurement, permits, and revenue collection.

The success of G2B, just like that of G2E, is obviously constrained by poor broadband connectivity. Another noticeable barrier to effective ICT tools adoption in G2B is the weak ICT infrastructure (Bwalya and Healy, 2010). Most SMEs operators have low ICT literacy levels and do not have access to digital facilities. This limits the benefit of G2B to small and micro enterprises. Cyber-security threats such as interception of data, identity theft, hacking, copyright, and fraud can easily erode business managers' confidence in embracing government's ICT adoption initiative.

Government to Citizens (G2C)

The G2C model allows citizens to participate in government initiatives electronically. It involves government's engagement with citizens by providing them with details of public sector activities, increasing their input into public sector decisions and improving the quality and transparency of the public services delivered to them (Hafkin, 2009). The goal of G2C is to offer a variety of ICT services to citizens in an efficient and economical manner and to strengthen the relationship between government and citizens using technology. Among G2C services are information dissemination, providing and filing, education results, and online libraries. Examples of G2C ICT adoption in Africa include the following:

- The Rwanda Online Government Services, through which the government makes such applications as e-procurement of licenses, birth/death/marriage certificates, and tax information available and accessible to the citizens.
- The Web Portal, an online platform created by the Republic of Mauritius government as a gateway to provide Government online services like e-procurement to citizens.
- The Kenyan government's creation of a one-stop shop open data platform called Huduma Centre in Nairobi, on which the government displays an online tax returns form for citizens to fill.
- The South African Government Online website, which has, over the past year, increased the dissemination of information about travel and tourism, government notices, the dissemination of acts, bills and draft bills, and the notification of new government tenders and tender regulations.

The primary benefit of G2C is that it makes the government more accessible and citizen-focused. It enables citizens to benefit from the efficient delivery of a large range of public services. Akunyili (2010) listed this as part of the opportunities which G2C adoption of ICT tools can deliver. It also reduces labour costs by replacing or complementing face-to-face interaction between government and citizens. It widens the scope of the accessibility and availability of government services, as well as improves the quality of services. It furthermore facilitates citizen empowerment through access to information and encourages communities to participation in policy decisions and administrative processes.

G2C is largely constrained by the digital divide in the population as well as their lack of access to e-services. In addition, issues such as poor broadband connectivity, delays in providing citizens with timely feedback, cyber-security threats such as interception of data, identity theft, hacking, copyright, and fraud can easily erode citizens' confidence in embracing government's ICT adoption initiative (Ugwueze et al., 2016).

BARRIERS TO DIGITAL ADOPTION IN AFRICA

Based on the exposition of the respective models of digital interaction between government and citizen and businesses, there are emerging cross-cutting issues that are constraining effective deployment of digital technologies within the African public sector. The three key barriers are highlighted below.

- *Issue of digital divide*: The unprecedented pace of digital adoption has meant that some citizens as well as businesses are lagging and are unable to fully participate in and take advantage of the burgeoning digital economy or developing digital-government services (Munga, 2021). Africa's persistent digital divide can be explained by socioeconomic factors, with affordability of devices, digital infrastructure, and high-cost data being key inhibitors. Within many African economies, there are still considerable digital-access gaps between rural and urban areas, especially in Central Africa. Lack of digital infrastructure limits both digital-literacy acquisition and citizens' access to digital services.
- *Limited budgetary resources*: Most African governments invest 6–12 per cent of their budgetary allocations on infrastructure, which is categorized as ICT, electricity, transport networks, water, and sanitation (AFDB, 2022). Several analyses have shown a general lack of political will and a commitment to coordinate and implement digital reforms in Africa (IMF, 2006). This is exacerbated by certain governments' inadequate financial resources. Countries with low GDP prioritize poverty-alleviation programmes in their budgets sometimes due to aid dependency. The donor support in Africa has, in recent times, shifted away from infrastructure to human capital development, and this has reduced some needed investment in the digital sector. Also, budget support among donors is limited to capacity development and problem scoping. This implies that maintaining e-government programmes might be difficult because donors often only finance the initial phases.
- *Poor accountability*: Poor accountability and transparency can lead to reluctance on the part of governments to use digital technologies to improve citizen engagement in decision-making. Given that it could limit government authority, digital adoption in the public sector can be regarded as a possible danger to power. Democracy differs among African economies (Freedom House, 2022), and some nations restrict the use of technology to encourage public engagement in decision-making.

GOVERNMENT AS A REGULATORY AGENT IN THE DIGITAL VALUE CHAIN

Data Governance

Despite the rapid growth in digitalization in Africa, the structural transformation potential is not guaranteed without an economic and political environment that supports domestic entrepreneurs. Both the innovation and the benefits that are derived from digitalization have been dominated by USA and China, which control the value and supply chain around software and hardware used in the digital space. Similarly, digital space has its unique problems that could destroy both trust and connectivity that is the basis for the predicted gains through digitalization. For example, Africa lost about £3.5 billion to cybercrime in 2017 (Kshetri, 2019). As the public sector also becomes increasingly digitalized, the concerns around data protection, sovereignty, and localization also rising.

Countries are evolving different data governance frameworks to harness the benefits of digitalization while mitigating the challenges. Data governance refers to laws, institutions, and practices that guide the use, reuse, and misuse of digital data. Government has played different roles in the data governance framework across countries. The USA has a data governance system that is private sector-led and governs with limited oversight roles by government. Government is more central in the China model, with State access and control over all digital data and communication. This is often premised on the notion of national sovereignty and security. These two models suggest the importance of the political and economic system in the data governance framework.

The private sector-led or laissez-faire system is more aligned with capitalist and democratic systems of government in the USA, while the state control system is compatible with state capitalism and the communist system in China. The European Union have recently developed a more balanced system in which government is more involved in the data governance ecosystem but with emphasis on the protection of digital rights and privacy of the citizen. In the EU framework, human rights are broadened to include digital rights and privacy. The General Data Protection Regulation (GDPR) developed in 2016 exemplified the EU approach. Most African countries were stimulated into enacting their national data laws and regulations, modelling such after the GDPR. As of 2020, 29 African countries had passed data protection laws to regulate the storage, use, and transfer of their data (IBA, 2021).

Data governance extends beyond data protection and privacy, but also includes efforts at supporting the ICT sector and promoting digital inclusion among the citizens. The World Bank (2022b) identifies four domains of data governance, namely:

- Infrastructure and policies (e.g. create universal coverage of broadband networks; the establishment of technical standards; develop domestic infrastructure to exchange, store and process data).
- Laws and regulation (e.g. institute safeguards to secure and protect data from the threat of misuse such as cybercrime; ensure interoperability between government institutions, entities and agencies).
- Economic policies (e.g. establish data platforms for businesses; foster trade and data-enabled services; create taxation platforms for businesses and enhance digital trade).
- Institutions (e.g. governments should oversee, regulate, and secure data; establish security and protection agencies; foster cross-border regulation; set standards and increase data access and reuse).

These categorisations clearly illustrate the complex and multidimensional nature of digitalization in governance. It also assists in establishing a governance framework for ICT adoption.

Osakwe and Adeniran (2021) observes that African countries have prioritized national data governance framework over regional efforts. For instance, while 28 countries have a form of data protection and privacy laws, only eight countries have signed and ratified the African Union's regional protection agreement called the Malabo Convention. With a small population and economic size, most African countries are ill-equipped to effectively regulate large digital platforms. It is clear that a broader, regional approach will enable the sharing of capacity and regulatory knowledge among countries. Such a regional approach to data governance is also important in order to lock in the economic benefits of digitalization among African countries. The reality, that digitalization allows platform-based firms to run business in locations where they do not have a physical presence, has some serious implications for developing a regulatory mechanism for the effective implementation of digital taxation and online trade. In principle, the extant international taxation laws are applicable only to firms with physical presence attributable to a permanent site in a particular country.

In Africa, the growth of digital platforms calls for well-coordinated and dynamic regulation and this is more likely to be effective if enacted at the regional level. Recent evidence, however, suggests a growing recognition of the necessity for a regional approach. With initiatives like the African Continental Free Trade Area (AfCFTA), there will be more regional integration and trade. According to Wamkele Mene, Secretary General, African Continental Free Trade Area Secretariat (AfCFTA), digital trade is the next big thing in Africa. Regional data governance framework is needed to make this effective. In 2022, the AU introduced Data Policy Framework, which is a well-coordinated framework that harmonizes policies, laws, and regulations that can help drive data value creation on the continental level. However, creating regulation and laws alone does not translate into effect data governance framework. The quality of implementation is a critical component. Evidence abounds of many African countries with data protection law but have yet to enforce such laws in their domestic domains (e.g. Seychelles, Lesotho, and Madagascar). Reverting to the theory of digital ambidexterity, data governance is an area in which public sector-led innovation is critical. Most national data authorities can innovatively channel Africa's data governance pillars towards supporting local or domestic experimentation of ideas that will essentially drive their digital transformation. A potential area is laws and special financial intervention to support and promote domestic entrepreneurs. The Nigerian government creation of first digital currency is an example of regulatory innovation. Such an approach can position Africa at the frontiers of the next digital revolution. Therefore, to maximize the benefits that the rapidly developing digitalization is capable of delivering, Africa, regarded as the next frontier in the global digital space, must make coordinated efforts at the national and continental levels towards developing and strengthening digital governance framework (CSEA, 2022).

DIGITAL GOVERNANCE FOR THE NEXT FRONTIER

Globally, digitalization is entering a new and uncharted territory with the emergence of new technologies such as the internet of things (IoT), artificial intelligence, the development of smart cities, and robots, among others. It is still unclear as to the extent to which the lessons and experience from the present era will shape this and, therefore, sustain the digital transformation within the public sector. For example, technologies such as blockchain are supporting a decentralized financial system with little government coordinating role, hence, complicating the process of public sector administration. Likewise, artificial intelligence is creating a powerful decision-making tool that can either support government or weakens the conventional state functions. We briefly review the implications of these emerging technologies for public sector administration and private sector management.

Internet of Things (IoT)

Digital technologies have the potential to change how individuals, businesses, and governments connect with the rest of the world. The internet of things (IoT) system is one example of such technologies. IoT implies embedding internet tools in physical objects to improve their performance and enable exchange of information between objects. IoT solutions enable users to gain greater automation, and integration inside a system, while employing emerging technology for sensing and networking. IoT effectively makes anything 'smart', indicating it enhances every aspect of life through data collecting and analytics with artificial intelligence,

IoT in the public sector can improve citizens' participation in government activities, encourage competency in resource management, improve accuracy in information collection and service delivery, and boost internal operations efficiency. There are various examples of how IoT adoption has enhanced public service delivery in Africa. One of such is the utilization of radio frequency identification in preventing oil pilferage in Tanzania (Onyalo et al., 2015). Another is the introduction of an electronic tolling system in South Africa that helps collect tolls electronically without human intervention (Onyalo et al., 2015). There is a case of adoption of IoT smart sensors in the Kenyan system of waste management, and yet another on drug verification initiative by the Nigerian National Agency for Food and Drug Administration and Control (Onyalo et al., 2015). A key issue in IoT relates to privacy and protection of the big data that is collected. This is more critical in Africa as the digital ecosystem (hardware and software) is controlled by external players. The existing data governance framework might also be inadequate in this aspect given the scale of information collected and lack of well design cross-border flow. So far, IoT is expected to have more effect on G2B process through government regulation of private sector or in public service delivery.

Creation of Smart Cities

The concept of a 'smart city' refers to initiatives that make better use of digital and ICT-based innovation to advance citizens' wellbeing, increase the effectiveness of local government services, and create new business possibilities (OECD, 2020). Globally, the European region houses the highest percentage of smart cities, with Amsterdam, Berlin, Copenhagen, Oslo, and Paris all ranking among the top ten smartest cities, while Africa occupies the bottom position (Motion Index Report, 2022). In relation to technology spending on smart cities globally, the United States of America and Europe contributes over 50 per cent while Africa contributes less than ten per cent (Statista, 2022). Despite Africa's poor performance in developing smart cities, the region still has few smart cities. For instance, there is the Hope and King City in Ghana; Modderfontein New City and the Waterfall city in South Africa; Eko Atlantic in Nigeria; the Kigali Innovation City in Rwanda; and the Konza City in Kenya (KhumbaMuleya, 2021).

The advantages of creating smart cities are numerous because they provide scalable solutions that make use of ICT to boost productivity, reduce costs, and improve quality of life. Among them are smart metres and pipelines that track water quality and identify leaks, assist control, and monitor energy and water use (OECD, 2020). Smart cities enable citizens to use specialized mobile applications to report concerns in real time and interact directly with city services. Innovative participatory budgeting allows individuals to track and comment on how government monies are used. Platform firms like Uber, Bolt, Airbnb, and Booking.com are becoming commonplace in cities throughout the world. Smart sensors are being used to improve traffic flow, transportation efficiency, and solid waste collection routes.

Development of smart cities can improve the health outcomes of the citizenry and lower health expenses through the provision of innovative health services such as telemedicine and video consultations. The development of smart cities can be a catalyst for better public sector administration. Adopting smart cities can offer affordable options for delivering public goods, particularly for governments experiencing budget constraints. Smart cities have the potential to help SMEs access global markets and knowledge networks, establish stronger public-private partnerships, and manage public emergences (OECD, 2020).

A more immediate concern in the African context is transforming the existing cities into those of the twenty-first century. Experience with creation of special zones indicates that creating an island of effectiveness is not a sustainable development strategy. The lack of these special zones with existing economic sectors has resulted in limited effectiveness on the part of most African economies. Smart cities are built on a similar premise of an isolating place with new laws and technology that can serve as a bridge to structural transformation. Without any support policy to make existing cities better and ready for digitalization, smart cities might generate an island without effective feedback on the larger society.

Artificial Intelligence

In recent times, there has been a positive correlation between the need for digital solutions and the demand for a more efficient public service delivery. Artificial intelligence (AI), in conjunction with other digital technologies, can provide such solutions and go beyond to find deeper insights for efficient public service delivery. Generally, artificial intelligence refers to the development of machines that can perform tasks that require human intelligence. By using AI, machines can learn from experience, adjust to new inputs, and perform specific human tasks, such as pattern recognition, finding anomalies in data, image and video analysis, among others. Everyday life is now infused with the concept of AI. Thus, artificially intelligent technology is becoming more popular in many economies around the world.

The use of artificial intelligence can help government agencies to be more efficient, improve the job satisfaction of public servants, and enhance the quality of services provided. Public sector actors are using AI to facilitate welfare payments, immigration decisions, fraud detection, planning new infrastructure projects, answering citizen inquiries, monitoring and forecasting weather, adjudicating bail hearings, and triaging healthcare cases. AI is also a viable tool for controlling misinformation that is a key problem emanating from increasing digitalization. However, AI is a powerful tool and will require more nuanced understating before deployment into public administration. AI, in many ways, replicates the existing bias in data used in training them. This could have the implication of excluding vulnerable groups whose voices are excluded from the conventional statistical system. Scholars globally are developing ethics for better control of AI and responsible use in private and public sectors. The role of government will be important with laws that prevent abuses. On the other hand, it is crucial to promote aspects of AI that can support structural transformation in agricultural, health and education sectors. Balancing the benefits and potential negatives of emerging technologies is a critical way forward for the African government. This means a greater role for a more proactive data government framework and capacity development for the public sector to keep up with the pace of innovation in the digital sector and effectively regulate it.

CONCLUSION AND RECOMMENDATION: TOWARDS A SUSTAINABLE DIGITAL GOVERNANCE FRAMEWORK FOR AFRICA

Creating a successful digitalized public sector can lead to economic growth, global competitiveness, and innovation among African countries (Urutia, 2022). This chapter has examined the evolving use of digital technologies in public sector in Africa and the implications for economic development. The discussion points to an increasing digital adoption by government, albeit at a slow pace. The wide digital divide continues to limit the benefits of digitalization from underserved and vulnerable populations. This suggests that without a proactive digital inclusion drive, digitalization of the public sector can become another driver of inequality. The study also probed into the state of data governance, looking at efforts that government can enhance to support digital transformation. Again, we found higher trends in data governance. Nevertheless, efforts are still below expectations and the limited efforts are concentrated around the national framework but less supportive of regional structure that is more critical for the nascent African digital sector. Key regional initiatives such as AfCFTA can change these dynamics around more regional efforts, but coordination framework is still needed. For the public sector in Africa to undergo a digital transformation, some key factors must be recognized and prioritized. These will include, but are not limited to, the following concerns:

Digital Skill Development

Development of digital skills can act as an enabler for the adoption and use of digital technologies in the public sector operations. The public sector needs to work with different stakeholders to establish learning platforms that are outside the conventional education system aimed at capacitating all persons regardless of educational qualifications. Such partnerships with different stakeholders can help establish unconventional learning platforms that the public sector will benefit from in the future (UNDP, 2021). To harness the benefits of digital technologies, the public sector must ensure that they have the knowledge, expertise, and skills to understand digitalization. The public sector will be responsible for the regulation of digital technologies and, thus, it is critical for them to have the expertise. In order to promote digital skills within the public sector, the government may have to recruit technology experts from the private sector to provide guidance in the management of digital innovations (Ndungu, 2018). Public sector actors must provide regular training and seminars for their employees. This will enhance the quality of public service delivery. The public sector must interact regularly with businesses in the private sector so that it is aware of the latest trends in the development of technological innovations. The public sector's actors must be informed and knowledgeable about the digital space and engage closely with the private sector to understand the possibilities that the digital innovations create.

Digital Infrastructure Development

One of the biggest challenges faced by most African countries is the issue of digital infrastructural deficiency. This deficiency means few Africans have the infrastructure and this inequality heavily impacts on individuals, regions, and sectors that are ill-prepared (UNDP, 2021). Thus, a lack of readiness and inability to capture the potential of digital infrastructure may lead to increasing digital inequalities among genders, locations, income levels, and within private and public sectors. To harness the benefits of digitalization, there is a need for the public sector to work towards improving its digital infrastructure. To change the tides of inefficient public service delivery, it is crucial to provide the public sector's actors with access to reliable and affordable internet, consistent power supply, and tech-driven operational resources.

Improved Funding Allocation for Digital Technologies

Aside from the issue of digital infrastructure availability, high cost and affordability pose other challenges to digital adoption in the public sector. In Africa, most governments have given less budgetary priority to digital technologies – as a result of fiscal distress they experience. However, African governments must recognize the importance of digital technologies in the public sector operations and put in efforts to prioritize their operations. To improve funding allocation in digital technologies in the public sector, governments might consider implementing appropriate regulations such as increasing public budgetary allocation for digital technologies and promoting active involvement of private sector investors. Also, putting in place licensing incentives and assigning maintenance contracts to private sector actors are among the various measures that can improve public sector digital adoption. Government policies can further be designed to make digital public infrastructure (DPI) and increase public-private partnership arrangements.

REFERENCES

Abusamhadana, G.A.O., K.A. Bakon and N.F. Elias (2021), 'E-government in Ghana: The Benefits and Challenges', *Asia-Pacific Journal of Information Technology and Multimedia*, **10** (1), 124–140, doi .org/10.17576/apjitm-2021-1001-11.

AfDB. (2022), *African Economic Outlook*, accessed 27 November 2022 at https://www.afdb.org/en/ documents/african-economic-outlook-2022.

African Declaration on Internet Rights and Freedoms Coalition. (2021), 'Privacy and Personal Data Protection in Africa: A Rights-Based Survey of Legislation in Eight Countries', accessed 10 November 2022 at https://www.apc.org/en/pubs/privacy-and-personal-data-protection-africa -rights-based-survey-legislation-eight-countries.

Åkesson, M., S. Carsten and E.C. Ihlström (2018), 'Ambidexterity Under Digitalization: A Tale of Two Decades of New Media at a Swedish newspaper', LSE Research Online Documents on Economics 88838, London School of Economics and Political Science, LSE Library, RePEc:ehl:lserod:88838.

Akunyili, D. (2010), 'ICT and e-government in Nigeria: Opportunities and Challenges', Paper Presented at the World Congress on Information Technology Held in Amsterdam, The Netherlands, 25–27 May.

Alexandra, T. (2022). 'Antitrust Laws: What They Are, How They Work, Major Examples', *Guide to Antitrust Laws, Investopedia*, pp. 1–24, accessed 12 November 2022 at https://www.investopedia .com/terms/a/antitrust.asp.

Backus, M. (2001). 'E-governance in Developing Countries', IICD Research Brief, accessed 23 November 2022 at http://www.ftpiicd.org/files/research/briefs/brief1.

Butcher, N., M. Wilson-Strydom, M. Baijnath, D. Orlic, M. Smith, B. Neupane and J. Shawe-Taylor (2021), *Artificial Intelligence Capacity in Sub-Saharan Africa: Compendium Report*, Artificial Intelligence for Development Africa publications, accessed 12 November 2022 at https://idl-bnc -idrc.dspacedirect.org/bitstream/handle/10625/59999/27ea1089-760f-4136-b63716367161edcc.pdf ?sequence=1.

Bwalya, K.J. and M. Healy (2010), 'Harnessing e-Government Adoption in the SADC Region: a Conceptual Underpinning', *Electronic Journal of e-Government*, **8** (1), 23–32.

Centre for the Study of Economies of Africa. (2022), *Foundations for Pro-development Digital Governance Framework in Africa*, accessed 9 November 2022 at https://cseaafrica.org/foundations -for-pro-development-digital-governance-framework-in-africa/.

ChannelsTV (2021), 'FG Launches National Policy on Virtual Engagement for MDAs', accessed 16 August 2023 at https://www.channelstv.com/2021/03/30/fg-launches-national-policy-on-virtual -engagement-for-mdas/.

Connecting Africa (2021), *Sub-Saharan Africa Has World Most Expensive Data Prices*, accessed 10 November 2022 at https://www.connectingafrica.com/author.asp?section_id=761&doc_id=768680.

Couture, S. and S. Toupin (2019), 'What Does the Notion of "Sovereignty" Mean When Referring to the Digital?', *New Media and Society*, **21** (10), 2305–2322, doi.org/10.1177/14614448198659.

Ducan, R.B. (1976), 'The Ambidextrous Organisation: Designing Dual Structures for Innovation', in Kilmann, R.H., L.R. Pondy and D.P. Slevin (eds.), *The Management of Organisation Design*, New York: North Holland, pp. 167–188.

Foresight Africa. (2022), *Developing an Effective Data Governance Framework to Deliver African Digital Potentials*, accessed 10 November 2022 at https://www.brookings.edu/blog/africa-infocus /2022/03/21/developing-an-effective-data-governance-framework-to-deliver-african-digital -potentials.

Freedom House. (2022), *Global Freedom Status*, accessed 23 January 2023 at https://freedomhouse.org /explore-the-map?type=fiw&year=2022.

Global Data Alliance. (2021), 'Cross-Border Data Transfers and Data Localization', Comments to the Republic of South Africa on the proposed Data and Cloud Policy, GDA, accessed 24 January 2023 at https://globaldataalliance.org/wp-content/uploads/2021/07/05122021gdasafrdatacloud.pdf.

Hafkin, N.J. (2009), 'E-government in Africa: An Overview of Progress Made and Challenges Ahead', Paper Prepared for the UNDESA/UNPAN Workshop on Electronic/mobile Government in Africa: Building Capacity in Knowledge Management Through Partnership, Held at the United Nations Economic Commission for Africa, 17–19 February 2009.

Hanna, N.K. (2016), *A Review of World Development Report 2016: Digital Dividends*, University of the Witwatersrand, Johannesburg, accessed 23 January 2023 at https://www.wits.ac.za/linkcentre/digital -transformation-and-innovation-programme/hanna-2016---a-review-of-world-development-report -2016-digital-dividends/.

International Bar Association (IBA). (2021), *The IBA African Regional Forum Data Protection/Privacy Guide for Lawyers in Africa*, accessed 23 January 2023 at https://www.lssa.org.za/wp-content/ uploads/2021/07/Data-Protection-Privacy-Guide-Africa.pdf.

International Monetary Fund (IMF). (2006), *Africa's Infrastructure Challenges and Opportunities*, accessed 24 January 2023 at https://www.imf.org/external/np/seminars/eng/2006/rppia/pdf/estach .pdf.

International Monetary Fund (IMF). (2022), *Sub-Saharan Africa Reveals Lessons for Governance*, accessed 15 January 2023 at https://www.imf.org/en/News/Articles/2022/06/22/CF-SSA-Lessons -for-Governance.

Khumba, M. (2021), 'African Dream of Smart Cities Remains Strong', accessed 18 November 2022 at https://www.warpnews.org/human-progress/african-dream-of-smart-cities-remains-strong/#:~:text =Smart%20cities%20being%20developed%20in,R84bn%20(%C2%A35.8bn).

Kshetri, N. (2019), 'Cybercrime and Cybersecurity in Africa', *Journal of Global Information Technology Management*, **22** (2), 77–81.

Loubier, A. (2017), 'Benefits of Telecommuting for the Future of Work', *Forbes*, accessed 17 November 2022 at https://www.forbes.com/sites/andrealoubier/2017/07/20/benefits-of-telecommuting-for-the -future-of-work/.

Magnusson, J., T. Paivarinta and D. Koutsikouri (2020), 'Digital Ambidexterity in the Public Sector: Empirical Evidence of a Bias in Balancing Practices', *Transforming Government People Process and Policy*, **15** (1), 59–79, doi.org/10.1108/TG-02-2020-0028.

Manda, M.I. and J. Backhouse (2017), 'Digital Transformation for Inclusive Growth in South Africa: Challenges and Opportunities in the 4th Industrial Revolution', Paper Presented at the 3rd African Conference on Information Systems and Technology in Cape Town, South Africa.

March, J.G. (1991), 'Exploration and Exploitation in Organisational Learning', *Organisation Science*, **2** (1), 71–87.

Mergel, I., Y. Gong and J. Bertot (2018), 'Agile Government: Systematic Literature Review and Future Research', *Government Information Quarterly*, **35** (2), 291–298, doi.org/10.1016/j.giq.2018.04.003.

Mishra, N. (2016), 'Data Localization Laws in a Digital World: Data Protection or Data Protectionism?', *The Public Sphere*, NUS Centre for International Law Research Paper No. 19/05, accessed 23 November 2022 at https://ssrn.com/abstract=2848022.

Mishrif, A. and S. Selmanovic (2010), 'E-government in the Middle East and North Africa: The Role of International Organisations in the Experience of Egypt and Morocco', *International Conference on Public Administration (ICPA 6th)*, pp. 905–926.

Munga., J. (2021), 'To Close Africa's Digital Divide, Policy Must Address the Usage Gap', *Carnegie Endowment for International Peace*, accessed 24 November 2022 at https://carnegieendowment.org/2022/04/26/to-close-africa-s-digital-divide-policy-must-address-usage-gap-pub-86959.

National Information Technology Development Agency. (2021), *Adoption of Digital Technologies Imperative to Africa's Growth*, DG NITDA, accessed 23 November 2022 at https://nitda.gov.ng/adoption-of-digital-technologies-imparative-to-africas-growth-dg-nitda/.

Ndou, V. (2004), 'E-government for Developing Countries: Opportunities and Challenges', *The Electronic Journal on Information Systems in Developing Countries*, **18** (1), 1–24, doi.org/10.1002/j.1681-4835.2004.tb00117.x.

Ndung'u, N. (2018), 'New Frontiers in Africa's Potential', *Harnessing Africa's Digital Potential: New Tools for a New Age*, Foresight Africa, accessed 8 November 2022 at https://www.brookings.edu/wp-content/uploads/2018/01/foresight-2018_chapter-5_web_final1.pdf.

Oborn, E. (2022), 'Four Lessons from M-Pesa on Innovation Adoption', *IM Weekly Newsletter*, accessed 23 January 2023 at https://innovationmanagement.se/2020/06/08/four-lessons-from-m-pesa-on-innovation-adoption/.

OECD. (2016), *Digital Government Strategies for Transforming Public Services in the Welfare Area*, accessed 8 October 2022 at https://www.oecd.org/gov/digital-government/Digital-Government-Strategies-Welfare-Service.pdf.

OECD. (2020), *Smart Cities and Inclusive Growth*, accessed 11 November 2022 at https://www.oecd.org/cfe/cities/OECD_Policy_Paper_Smart_Cities_and_Inclusive_Growth.pdf.

Okunogbe, O.M. and V. Pouliquen (2018), 'Technology, Taxation, and Corruption: Evidence from the Introduction of Electronic Tax Filing', *World Bank Policy Research Working Paper*, (8452).

Onyalo, N., H. Kandie and J. Njuki (2015), 'The Internet of Things: Progress Report for Africa: A Survey', *International Journal of Computer Science and Software Engineering*, **4** (9), 230–237.

O'Reilly, C.A. and M.L. Tushman (2008), 'Ambidexterity as a Dynamic Capability: Resolving the Innovator's Dilemma', *Research in Organisational Behavior*, **28**, 185–206, doi.org/10.1016/j.riob.2008.06.002.

Osakwe, S. and A. Adeniran (2021), 'Strengthening Data Governance in Africa', Project Inception Report, Centre for the Study of the Economies of Africa, accessed 16 August 2023 at https://cseaafrica.org/wp-content/uploads/2021/08/Strengthening-Regional-Data-Governance-in-Africa-1.pdf.

Sikaonga, S and S. Tembo (2020), 'E-Government Readiness in the Civil Service: A Case of Zambian Ministries', *International Journal of Information Science*, **10** (1), 15–28, doi.org/10.5923/j.ijis.20201001.03.

Statista. (2020), *eCommerce: Africa*, accessed 10 November 2022 at https://www.statista.com/outlook/243/630/ecommerce/africa.

Statista. (2022), *Smart Cities Initiatives Spending 2018–2023*, accessed 10 November 2022 at https://www.statista.com/statistics/884092/worldwide-spending-smart-city-initiatives/.

Ugwueze, M.I., J. Onuoha and E.J. Nwagwu (2016), 'Electronic Governance and National Security in Nigeria', *Mediterranean Journal of Social Sciences*, **7** (6), 363, doi.org/10.5901/mjss.2016.v7n6p363.

UNDESA. (2022), *UN E-Government Readiness Knowledge Base*, accessed 10 November 2022 at https://publicadministration.un.org/egovkb/en-us/About/Overview/-E-Government-Development-Index.

UNDP. (2021). *Responding to the COVID-19 Pandemic: Leaving No Country Behind*, Thailand: UNDP, accessed 18 November 2022 at https://www.undp.org/sites/g/files/zskgke326/files/migration/germany/UNDP-RBAP-SDG-Responding-to-COVID-19-Pandemic-Leaving-No-Country-Behind-2021.pdf.

Urutia, B. (2022), *Advantages of Digital Immersion in International Trade*, accessed 18 November 2022 at https://bu.com.co/en/insights/noticias/advantages-digital-immersion-international-trade.

Vahisalu, R. (2019), *Digital Sovereignty: The Key to Safeguarding Africa's Booming Digital Economy*, accessed 22 November 2022 at https://www.globalvoicegroup.com/digital-sovereignty-the-key-to-safeguarding-africas-booming-digital-economy/.

Van Dyk, R. and J.P. van Belle (2019), 'Factors Influencing the Intended Adoption of Digital Transformation: A South African Case Study', *Proceedings of the Federated Conference on Computer Science and Information Systems*, **18** (10), 519–528, doi.org/10.15439/2019F166.

World Bank. (2022a), 'Sub-Saharan Africa Subscription Per 100 People', accessed on 19 November 2022 at https://data.worldbank.org/indicator/IT.CEL.SETS.P2?locations=ZG.

World Bank. (2022b), 'Sub-Saharan Africa's Fixed Broadband Subscription', accessed on 18 November 2022 at https://data.worldbank.org/indicator/IT.NET.BBND?locations=ZG.

Yong, J.S.L. (2003), *E-Government in Asia – Enabling Public Service Innovation in the 21st Century*, Singapore: Marshall Cavendish Business.

Closing remarks: public management quo vadis?

Gerrit van der Waldt

The *Handbook of Public Management in Africa* provided a comprehensive overview of the challenges and opportunities facing public managers in the African context. The chapters covered a range of topics, including public sector reforms, human resource management, service delivery, governance, and accountability. The book also explored the unique political, economic, and social factors that shape public management in Africa.

One of the key themes that emerged throughout the book is the need for context-specific approaches to public management. While there are universal principles and best practices that can be applied in any context, public managers in Africa must navigate unique challenges, such as weak institutional capacity, political instability, and limited resources. The book offers practical guidance and insights on how to address these challenges, drawing on case studies and examples from across the continent.

Another key theme is the importance of collaboration and partnership-building in public management. The book highlighted the role of civil society organizations, private sector actors, and citizens in co-creating public policies and services. It also emphasized the importance of building trust and engaging in dialogue with stakeholders to ensure effective service delivery and governance.

The handbook concluded by calling for a renewed focus on capacity-building and leadership development in public management in Africa. It argues that investing in the development of public managers is essential to achieving sustainable development goals and promoting good governance. The book offered practical recommendations for how to build the capacity of public managers, including investing in training and education, promoting knowledge-sharing and learning, and strengthening institutional capacity. It thus serves as a valuable resource for public managers, policymakers, academics, and students who are interested in understanding the unique challenges and opportunities facing public management in Africa. It offered practical guidance and insights that can help public managers navigate the complexities of modern governance and contribute to positive social, economic, and environmental outcomes.

The quest for good governance and public managerial excellence is, however, a continuous effort. The future of governance is likely to be shaped by several trends that are already underway. The knowledge production endeavours of scholars in public management should heed this challenge by pursuing an adaptive and responsive research agenda informed by emerging governance trends. One such trend is digitalization. Governments are increasingly using digital technologies to improve service delivery, enhance transparency, and increase citizen engagement. The adoption of digital technologies in government, also known as e-government or digital government, has also enabled governments to improve efficiency, reduce costs, and enhance transparency and accountability. One of the key benefits of digitalization is the ability to offer services online, enabling citizens to access government services and information anytime and anywhere. It has also enabled governments to streamline administrative processes, such as procurement and financial management, resulting in cost savings and increased efficiency. This trend is likely to continue, with governments exploring new technologies such as artificial intelligence, blockchain, and the Internet of Things.

A second trend is the decentralization and devolution of government decision-making powers and authority. There is a growing recognition that many public services can be delivered more efficiently and effectively at subnational levels. Decentralization and devolution refer to the transfer of decision-making powers and authority from a central government to lower levels of government or to non-governmental actors. Decentralization and devolution can take various forms, including political, administrative, fiscal, and legislative decentralization. Decentralization and devolution can have a number of benefits, including improved service delivery, increased citizen participation and accountability, and greater efficiency and effectiveness in decision-making. However, decentralization and devolution also pose a number of challenges, such as ensuring adequate resources and capacity at the local level, managing conflicts between central and local authorities, and maintaining national unity and cohesion.

A third trend worthy of further scholarly engagement is collaborative or network governance. Governments are increasingly working with a range of stakeholders, including civil society organizations, private sector actors, and citizens, to co-create public policies and services. This trend is likely to continue, with more emphasis on collaboration and participatory decision-making.

Environmental, social and economic sustainability is a fourth trend that deserves to be placed on the research agenda. There is a growing recognition of the need to pursue sustainable development goals, such as reducing carbon emissions and promoting social and economic equity. This trend is likely to shape governance priorities on the African continent with more emphasis on state resilience and efficiency.

To adjust to these new trends in governance, the scholarly literature of public management as a study domain should consider a number of adjustments. The first adjustment is to incorporate digital literacy in both under- and postgraduate programmes. Prospective public managers should be equipped with the necessary digital skills and literacy to manage digital technologies in government. Digital literacy includes a range of skills, such as the ability to use basic software applications, navigate the internet, understand online security and privacy, critically evaluate information found online, and use digital tools for communication, collaboration, and problem-solving. Digital literacy can also play an important role in promoting social inclusion and reducing the digital divide, as it enables individuals to access information and services that might otherwise be inaccessible.

A further possible adjustment required is more emphasis being placed on local governance. Public management should focus on building the capacity of local governments, inclusive of rural and urban contexts, to deliver services efficiently and effectively. The United Nations Sustainable Development Goals clearly emphasize the significant role that the local sphere of government can and should play in the broader socioeconomic development of states.

Programmes in public management should also foster communication, negotiation, and engagement skills of prospective public managers. Network forms of governance accentuate the need for collaboration and partnership-building across sectors and societal groupings. Prospective public managers should be skilled in building positive relationships with stakeholders to establish trust, credibility, and mutual understanding. This involves developing rapport with stakeholders, showing empathy, and engaging in dialogue to find common ground.

Public managers should also be skilled in resolving conflicts that may arise between stakeholders. Conflict resolution involves identifying the root cause of the conflict, facilitating dialogue between stakeholders, and finding mutually acceptable solutions. Finally, prospective public managers should be skilled in understanding and respecting the cultural diversity of African societies. This should involve recognizing and valuing cultural differences, adapting communication and engagement strategies to meet the needs of diverse stakeholders, and promoting inclusivity and equity.

A further possible adjustment required is the promotion of sustainability on the continent. public management text should prioritize sustainability and resilience in decision-making, policy development, and service delivery modalities. Closely related to this is the cultivation of public sector innovation and entrepreneurship. Public management should encourage innovation and experimentation in governance, leveraging new technologies and approaches to improve public services and development outcomes.

By adjusting the research agenda of public management can help public managers navigate the complexities of modern governance and contribute to positive social, economic, and environmental outcomes on the African continent.

Index